FINANCE
Environment and Decisions

FOURTH EDITION

PEYTON FOSTER RODEN, C.M.A.
North Texas State University

GEORGE A. CHRISTY
North Texas State University

1817

HARPER & ROW, PUBLISHERS, New York
Cambridge, Philadelphia, San Francisco,
London, Mexico City, São Paulo, Singapore, Sydney

This book is dedicated to our wives
Christie Lape Roden
and
Ruth Kerr Christy

Sponsoring Editor: John Greenman
Project Editor: Eleanor Castellano
Text and Cover Design: Robert Bull
Text Art: Fine Line Illustrations, Inc.
Production: Willie Lane
Compositor: Donnelley/Rocappi, Inc.
Printer and Binder: R. R. Donnelley & Sons Company

FINANCE: Environment and Decisions, Fourth Edition

Library of Congress Cataloging in Publication Data

Roden, Peyton Foster
    Finance: Environment and Decisions.

    Includes index.
    1. Finance.   2. Business Enterprises—Finance.
I. Christy, George A.   II. Title.
HG173.C58   1986   658.1′5   85–7610
ISBN 0–06–041310–7

88   9 8 7 6 5 4 3 2

Contents

Preface

Like its predecessors, this fourth edition of our book reflects three firmly held convictions of its authors. First, we believe that an understanding of financial management logically begins with a discussion of the financial system and the changing environment within which financial managers work and to which they must continually adjust. Second, an introductory course in finance should principally reflect the needs of *nonfinance* majors, who ordinarily constitute 90 percent of a class. Third, experience has taught us that a realistic account of financial management is more likely to engage the student's interest and lasting recall than an abstract and overly mathematical approach.

MAJOR CHANGES IN THIS EDITION

Along with some shifts in topic sequencing and a small reduction in the number of chapters, this carefully updated edition contains three noteworthy changes.

First, compound interest and the time value of money have become the starting points of our study. The notion of present value is, after all, the root concept of finance; in one way or another, it is the foundation of all financial principles and decisions. Given an immediate grasp of the theory, mechanics, and basic calculations by which money, time, and value are systematically linked, students begin their study of finance with the master key to the subject already in hand.

Second, a wealth of illustrative material has been added to the text. Chapters now include both extended examples that illustrate how financial problems are solved, and practice sets that enable students to test their understanding of the subject matter step by step as their reading proceeds. These instructional devices, liberally employed, should make for both faster and more solid progress by students. In addition, each chapter contains two or three special boxed items, often drawn from *The Wall Street Journal, Barron's* or *Business Week,* to demonstrate points made in the text. These add a real-world, human-interest, or historical dimension to the general principles.

Third, each chapter now begins with a short introduction that flags the main points that will be covered and ends with a summary that reviews these same key concepts.

Otherwise, the philosophy that guided the preparation of previous editions remains: to incorporate in these chapters some tangible feeling for the actual workaday world of business. Many textbooks convey the notion that financial decision making involves abstract principles or mathematical models quite removed from an individual's hopes and choices among uncertainties. It seems to us far more truthful to admit that finance is full of rough edges and befuddlements than to depict it as a well-oiled machine that permits precise decisions.

Although we have made many simplifications in order to create a more readable introductory book, we have also tried to avoid oversimplifications that might mislead students. We have not hesitated to present complicated theories (in simple language) when necessary, nor have we refrained from using elementary mathematical models where we believe they provide the briefest and clearest exposition of important theory. We have also tried to present both sides of important unresolved controversies.

The glossary at the end of the book is neither sophisticated nor comprehensive, but it should be genuinely useful to the student who is struggling to grasp the meaning of a new system of knowledge.

In short, this book is intended only to scratch the surface of finance, but to scratch it significantly.

STRUCTURAL PLAN OF THE BOOK

The structure of this book reflects the important divisions of the finance field and recognizes that most students using this text will be business administration majors. Two chapters introduce the subject. Using layman's language, Chapter 1 describes to students how a knowledge of financial principles and practices will help them, regardless of the business specialty they pursue. Chapter 2, as already noted, introduces students to the time value of money and its many applications to financial analysis and decision making.

Chapters 3 through 10 review what every businessperson should know about money, monetary policy, inflation, interest rates, security prices, credit, and financial markets and institutions. These "external factors" significantly affect most financial decisions. Unless the student grasps their nature and influences, the study of business finance becomes an academic exercise, largely devoid of real content or relevance. This is especially true of decisions concerning sources of finance and the timing of financial policy. Experience demonstrates that financial breakdowns stem at least as often from faulty forecasts of the economy and financial markets as they do from formal violations of financial rules and precepts.

Chapters 11 through 24 deal with the basic functions of financial management. We have called these the "Three A's" of business finance: (1) anticipating financial needs, (2) acquiring financial resources, and (3) allocating funds optimally within the enterprise. These chapters deal with the basic decisions that financial managers must make correctly to ensure adequate support for their colleagues in production, marketing, purchasing, engineering, and so on. They focus on financial reporting and control, where the money comes from to support business activity, the highly important process of planning and selecting capital expenditures, and the management of a company's working capital.

Three additional chapters complete our introductory view of finance. Since corporations acquire long-term funds by selling stocks and bonds, the new-issues market and investment banker's services are described in Chapter 25, "Marketing New Security Issues." The influence of international finance on business affairs increases seemingly without limit, so Chapter 26 not only deals with "Financing International Business Activity," but also describes the international financial system as well. The forecasting of business conditions is of supreme importance to all managers. Therefore, Chapter 27, "Financial Indicators for Business Timing," both describes the business cycle and introduces financial conditions as barometers for business forecasting. It also provides, at the end of the course, a useful review of the role and behavior of the financial system presented in the book's opening chapters.

END-OF-CHAPTER PROBLEMS

Continuing the highly practical innovation introduced in our third edition, Professor Roden, a pioneer holder of the Certified Management Accountant certificate, has included at the ends of our chapters a number of questions drawn from the CMA examinations of recent years. Work with these questions will strengthen the student's "feel" for the real-life financial manager's tasks and challenges.

ACKNOWLEDGMENTS

We wish to thank the many people who have played a role in our book's continuing development: students who have insisted on relevance and clarity, colleagues who have spurred us to be up-to-date and precise, and our friends in business who have given us practical illustrations of finance in action. We are sure that their efforts will greatly benefit all users—students, faculty, and business managers. We would be remiss if we failed to express our gratitude to individuals who provided us with specific suggestions for this fourth edition:

Howard R. Whitney	Reynolds Griffith
Joan M. Lamm	Wallace Davidson
Thomas V. Wright	Sharon L. Garrison
Thomas W. Lloyd	Imre Karafiath
Gary R. Bower	Robert W. Strand
Robert I. Ferguson	James L. McDonald
P. R. Chandrasekaran	Michael C. Walker
Barry R. Marks	James W. Giese

Finally, we applaud our families for their patience and encouragment. Without them, this book would not have been completed.

PEYTON FOSTER RODEN
GEORGE A. CHRISTY

ONE

INTRODUCTION

CHAPTER 1. Finance—The Subject

CHAPTER 2. Interest and Discount in Valuation

CHAPTER 3. The Theory and Behavior of Interest

Part 1 is designed to give a good introduction to finance. Chapter 1 introduces you to the areas that comprise the study of finance. The chapter is designed to give some understanding of some important terms that we shall be using throughout the book, of how diverse the area of finance is, and of where the book is headed. Chapter 2 examines what may be the most important concept in finance, the link among the time value of money, interest, and value. The concept is important because we shall use it throughout the book and because it clearly shows the relationship between future cash flows and value. Chapter 3 presents the theory and behavior of interest rates so that you may understand the way that interest rates perform over time and the influences that cause them to perform the way that they do.

CHAPTER 1
Finance-The Subject

THE ROLE OF FINANCE IN BUSINESS

FINANCE AND THE NONFINANCIAL MANAGER

Measure of Business Resources · Gauge of Business Performance · Tool of Business
Control · Source of Business Forecasts

THE LANGUAGES OF FINANCE

Finance and Economics · Finance and Accounting · Finance and Mathematics

DIVISIONS OF FINANCE

BASIC PRINCIPLES IN FINANCE

SUMMARY

Key Terms and Concepts · Questions · Problems

Welcome to the world of finance in business. The purpose of this chapter is to set out some guideposts that will give your study of this sometimes complex subject purpose and meaning. Mainly, it will provide an understanding of three ideas: (1) what financial management aims to accomplish in a business, (2) how your company's financial resources and measurements affect your career, whatever business speciality you select, and (3) what subject matter the study of finance considers and draws upon.

First, you'll take a quick look at the part money plays in running a business, the importance of adequate capital, and the help businesses receive from banks, the stock and bond markets, and other financial institutions.

Next, you'll view the extent to which financial influences shape and control your work as a business manager. The modern corporation operates through a system of objectives, budgets, reports, and controls, all of which are expressed in dollars and based on the principle of return on investment. No manager, regardless of function, escapes their impact. Beyond this, alert managers look to today's conditions in the financial system to forecast tomorrow's state of the economy.

You will also be introduced to the three main divisions of finance—money and banking, business finance, and investments—along with noting that other more specialized branches, such as international finance, real estate finance, and security analysis, are available for further study if you wish to specialize in finance. And you will be pleased to learn that what you have already mastered in your economics, accounting, and mathematics courses will make much of what you study in finance clear and easy.

This introductory chapter closes by demonstrating two sample principles of finance and showing that these notions, like everything else in the chapters to come, are, fundamentally, just common sense applied to money and its uses.

To finance something means to arrange payment for it. In civilized life many things are paid for immediately with money. Most obligations are finally settled in money. But things other than money can serve as a means of payment. A *promise* to pay, for example, can often procure the immediate use of goods or services. Indeed, IOUs and credit[1] play huge roles in financing the production, consumption, and exchange of goods. And modern business could not exist without the help of complicated financial instruments like stocks and bonds.[2] Nor could it operate for long without the help of complex financial institutions, such as banks, stock exchanges, investment bankers, and foreign exchange markets. The study of all these things, along with much more related to them, constitutes the field of finance. Finance and business are inseparably linked.

THE ROLE OF FINANCE IN BUSINESS

A business runs on money. It must have, or be able to raise, the money it needs to pay for its buildings, machinery, inventories, and other assets. It must have money to pay the wages of its employees, taxes, and other running expenses. If it sells goods or services on credit, it must have the money to finance its customers until they pay their bills. It must have enough permanently invested money, or *capital*, to buy what it needs to get started and to keep running until its cash coming in exceeds its cash going out, and it must make a profit. Seeing that all these things are done right is the basic task of financial management in a business enterprise.

What do you, the future business man or woman, need to know about finance? The answer depends partly on the career you contemplate. You may aspire to be a financial specialist—a banker, a stockbroker, or the treasurer of a business firm. For these occupations you need a varied and technical knowledge of financial rules, procedures, instruments, and markets, along with considerable background in accounting, taxes, business law, and economics. Or you may want to be an accountant, aiming at a CPA certificate[3] or at a career in business accountancy possible leading to a controller's job. In these professions a knowledge of finance is vital because at its higher levels the principles of accounting merge with those of finance. As a future accountant, you should plan to take one or more additional finance courses to prepare yourself for the day when understanding financial principles and problems will help you to handle high-level accounting tasks.

---

[1] Credit, as explained in Chapter 7, has different meanings when used in different contexts. Here it means the ability to obtain money, goods, services, or other economic resources on a promise to pay for them in the future. The promise may be oral and informal or it may take the form of a complicated legal document like a lease contract or bond indenture.

[2] For technical terms unfamiliar to you, see the Glossary.

[3] Or at a CMA (certified management accountant) certificate. For accountants whose work will be in companies rather than as outside auditors, the CMA certificate may now be preferred.

Suppose, however, that you contemplate a different kind of business career. Your interest is in sales work, production management, computer science, personnel, general or office management, or secretarial science. Do you still need a basic knowledge of finance? Yes, indeed. No matter where you work or what you do, financial events and financial problems, financial rules and financial decisions will vitally affect your work and your career.

Not only will financial considerations influence, and often dominate, what happens to your company, your duties, and even the existence of your job, but it is also true that an understanding of why and how financial forces affect your work and your company can greatly improve your performance as a salesperson, personnel officer, purchasing executive, or other business specialist. It is this broader view of your business that may well pave the way for your promotion to the top ranks of your firm. (There, of course, you will necessarily be concerned with financial matters—on a high level—dealing, as you will have to, with capital budgets, justification of major expenditures, and various kinds of financial controls for your division, department, or company.)

Whatever you do in business, you will find that financial principles, and your need to understand them, will enter significantly into four phases of your work. (1) Financial considerations will decide what resources are available to pay your salary and expenses and help you carry out your job or that of the people you supervise. (2) Financial measurements—such as how many dollars of sales you generate with each call on customers, or how the overhead expense of your department compares with the overhead for Joe's—will be applied as the basic measures of how well you are performing on the job and of what you may deserve by way of salary raises or promotion. (3) You, in turn, as you go higher in your firm or decide to run your own business, will use financial measures as the means of controlling the business functions for which you are responsible. You will do this by means of budgets, reports, cost analyses, return-on-investment studies, and other important, widely used financial tools. But your ability to use such controls effectively will depend on a sound knowledge of financial definitions, rules, principles, and calculations. (4) Finally, even as a junior executive, you will be concerned with making forecasts—forecasts of sales, of costs and expenses, of personnel requirements, and of business conditions in general. Understanding the behavior of the financial system—the best mirror of health or sickness in the economy—will help you to make sound forecasts of the future and to prepare for either opportunities or difficulties before they are upon you.

FINANCE AND THE NONFINANCIAL MANAGER

Let us look more closely at how a knowledge of finance can help the nonfinancial manager: the four ways in which an understanding of financial principles is really indispensable. (This look will also be valuable to the future financial manager because it will illustrate the challenging opportunities open to those specially trained in finance.)

Measure of Business Resources

What do the following have in common? A $100,000-a-year star sales representative? A $982.76 phone bill? An estimate that the large drill press in Division C is losing value at a rate of $800 a month? Answer: Each item has its cost or value to the business expressed in money.

Money is, in fact, the common denominator of business resources. Companies keep their accounts in money. They use money to value their assets and liabilities, measure their revenues and expenses, compute their profit or loss.

Money considerations pervade all business decisions because a business runs on money. It takes money to buy the assets a business uses—buildings, machines, raw materials, inventories. It takes money to staff and operate a business—to pay wages and salaries, rentals, utility bills, taxes, and other expenses. It takes money to extend credit to customers and to meet emergencies.

Some of that money can be obtained on credit or by short-term borrowing. Much of it, however, must come from the permanent capital of the business. To keep that capital intact, and to keep it growing in step with the needs of the business, a firm must be profitable. Expected profitability is the yardstick by which almost every undertaking or outlay proposed in a business firm is measured.

The condition of the company you work for depends heavily on the state of its finances. Businesses are in trouble if they are *undercapitalized*—that is, if they lack a sufficient investment of owners' money or of funds borrowed for long periods. Firms are in difficulty if they are *illiquid*—that is, if they lack ready cash to pay their bills. To know what is going on behind the scenes of your job, you must know enough about finance to understand the financial reasons for the decisions made in your business. Why can't Betty be given a raise? Why can't you hire a new salesman to replace Jasper who resigned? How come your advertising budget for May has been cut 20 percent? The reasons? Probably financial!

Gauge of Business Performance

A firm is in business to make a profit. Profitable operation is indispensable to business success. A lack of profit shows poor management—anything from being in the wrong line of business to an inability to make a product right, get sales, or control costs. A lack of profit also means that a business will gradually eat up its capital; often it means a company will run out of cash and go broke because it cannot pay its bills.

Profit is the normal basis of business decisions, the customary gauge of business performance. When a new plan or move is proposed in a business, the president's common question is: "How will that affect the bottom line?" The bottom line is profit.

Profit, of course, is simply a margin of revenues over costs. It can be expressed either as a total amount (which may not mean much) or as a percentage of the business resources employed to make it (which tells a great deal). Joe Blowhard may boast, "My company made a million-dollar profit last year." But if it made that profit on a $20 million investment, that was a return of only 5 percent on the capital used. Suppose, by contrast, that Busymite Corporation made a $100,000 profit on a capital

---

BOX 1-1
What Makes a Company a Top
Performer?   An important lesson you will learn in this book is that a simple kind of
                      financial analysis anyone familiar with balance sheets and income state-
ments and their meaning can perform discloses the secret of a company's success.
Take Supermarkets General Corporation, a diversified grocery chain that *Barron's*
reports has boosted sales and profits in each of the past nine years and doubled its
profits for stockholders over the past four years. Here are a couple of financially
based measurements that help explain this company's outstanding success. (1) It
generates $775 in sales per year from each square foot of floor space against an
industry average of only $410. (2) Sales per hour of labor run 15 percent ahead of
the industry average. You'd probably need access to the company's records to make
these calculations, but there's a couple of easy ones you can make from its annual
report. (a) The company brings more than a penny of each sales dollar down to
after-tax profit and (b) the company's shareholders earn 17 cents per year after taxes
on each invested dollar. You won't find another grocery chain with a performance to
match that one!

---

investment of only $500,000. That represents a 20 percent *return on investment*—a far
superior performance.

Profit also can be measured by how many cents a company keeps out of each
dollar's worth of sales it makes—called the profit margin. Together with how fast the
company turns its capital over in making sales, the profit margin determines the
firm's return on investment—the most important yardstick of business success.

As a business manager, you are almost certain to find the profit yardstick
applied to you and to the work of your section or department. After all, your company will have made an investment in you, your employees, and whatever assets it
takes to support your work. Whether that proves to be a wise investment that should
continue depends on whether it shows as much profit as that same investment might
earn applied elsewhere in the company.

Performance measurements are likely to be made for every important segment
or activity of a business. They will typically include readings on such matters as total
profit, percent earned on investment, profit margin on sales, manufacturing and
selling cost per unit, percent materials spoilage in manufacturing, machine output
per hour of operation, and units turned out per hour of labor. Each of these measurements and many others are in essence financial.

Tool of Business Control

Like a car on the highway or a football team on the playing field, a business must be
controlled. What is control? It is the process of making decisions and adjustments by
which one guides a process toward some expected result.

BOX 1-2
Using Financial Numbers to Measure
Divisional Performance   The following information illustrates one way financial managers use measurements in business planning and control: In 1984, it cost the average company $75,000 per year to keep a sales representative on the road. The sales person earned $37,000 per year in salary and bonuses and ran up $38,000 worth of annual expenses. Your question as a sales manager making use of financial analysis comes down to this: How much must each sales representative I add to my staff sell in order to cover compensation and expenses? Suppose you use the figures above and assume that compensation and expenses absorb 6 percent of each dollar of sales revenue. What annual sales must a salesman produce? Answer: $1,250,000. (Divide $75,000 by 0.06.)

The main purpose of a business is to make a profit, but to do that it must fulfill many intermediate purposes. It must have a good product, make it well, sell enough of the product, get an adequate price for it, keep its customers and suppliers happy, and have enough money on hand to pay its bills on time. All these things are stepping-stones to that good result on the bottom line, that is to say, profit.

How are business operations controlled? The principal means of control are budgets and reports. Both of these are financial in basis—that is, they are expressed in dollar terms. Budgets are sometimes referred to as "planned blueprints of intended financial results." And reports typically compare planned or budgeted results with those actually attained by a business manager, his department, or the activity for which he is responsible.

The comparison of actual results with budgeted ones enables a business management to see where, how, and why the business is attaining its goals or failing to attain them. The variation between budgeted and actual results is carefully analyzed to find the exact points at which troubles have occurred.

Example. A production manager is exceeding his budgeted cost per unit of output (90 cents) by a 3-cent margin. His budgeted labor cost is 30 cents; his "actual," 29 cents. Fine. So is his machine time cost—12 cents actual versus 12 cents budgeted. How about materials cost? Budgeted cost 48 cents, actual cost 52 cents. There is the trouble. It turns out that the materials spoilage rate is up to 10 percent from the 3 percent for which the production plan called.

Notice that the gauge slapped on operations is a money gauge. And controls throughout a company work in money terms. So many dollars or cents are allowed for this operation and that. That is how a firm's operations are kept on the path of efficiency or brought back to that path when they stray. Along with being the common denominator of resources in the business enterprise, money is also the common denominator of business plans and results.

Source of Business Forecasts

If men and women in business knew exactly what was going to happen in the weeks and months ahead, business management would be an easy task. Common sense would suffice to guide most business decisions. If, for example, your guardian angel told you prices were going up, it would be obvious that you should load up on inventory without delay. That way you would have cheaply bought inventory to sell at a juicy markup when the higher prices arrived as promised.

But most businesses operate in the face of continual uncertainty. Some uncertainties are peculiar to the firm or industry—supplier strikes, wage negotiations, the possible bankruptcy of an important customer, a breakdown of equipment at a time of peak demand. Other uncertainties affect the economy as a whole: Will a recession take place this year? How soon will it hit? How severe will it be? How much will interest rates go up? How much longer will they rise? Will the banks run out of loanable cash? These are always important questions. As a manager, you must answer them with some degree of accuracy because on the answers to those questions depend important forecasts about trends and events that will significantly affect your business: What will happen to sales? Will selling prices firm up or weaken? Will costs of borrowed money—and with them the cost of holding inventory or granting credit to customers—rise or fall? Is this a good time to think about adding more capacity, when it would take 12 months to construct a new plant?

The heads of any business must answer questions like these to make plans and arrangements to guide their business in months ahead. But even the manager of a six-member sales crew will face many of these same concerns. She must estimate how much she can expect to sell in the next quarter, whether the company must add another salesperson, what levels of travel and entertainment expense the expected sales will support, whether to tell the salespeople to stick to book prices or to offer discounts to lure business away from competitors. The answers to all these questions depend fundamentally on one thing: what kind of business conditions the manager can expect.

That is where a knowledge and understanding of finance enters the picture. The most reliable barometers we have of future business conditions are financial ones. They are provided through our interpretations of interest rates, stock prices, the condition of the banking system, ease or strain in the financial position of business firms and families, and what is happening to commodity prices, business costs, and the dollar's value at home and abroad. Business managers who can read these indicators correctly will have timely warning of changing business conditions. They will be able to alter their course and make new plans in time to avoid costly traps or to capitalize on major opportunities.

How to read these financial signs of coming business conditions is the subject of Chapter 27. First, however, you will need to learn something about interest rates, money, and the operation of the financial system and its institutions. This instruction comprises much of Chapters 2 to 10.

THE LANGUAGES OF FINANCE

Like other disciplines you have studied, finance has its own vocabulary. Much of your study of finance will consist of carefully memorizing the definitions of such things as "high-powered money," "commercial paper," and "bond indenture." Beyond its own definitions, finance also relies heavily on terms, concepts, and operations borrowed from three other disciplines. These disciplines are (1) economics, (2) accounting, and (3) mathematics. Indeed, it is no exaggeration to say that one must be familiar with the terms and ideas of these three disciplines to understand what is taught in finance. Economics, accounting, and mathematics are, in fact, the *languages of finance*. (All are subjects whose rudiments you should have studied and mastered before undertaking to study finance.) Let us examine briefly the part that your knowledge of each of these disciplines will play in helping you to learn about finance.

Finance and Economics

The basic principles of finance, and much of its vocabulary, are borrowed from economics. Economics deals with prices, costs, and the behavior of markets. So does finance. The central subject of finance—the rate of interest—is a price, the price of a loan of money or capital for a given period. Finance is concerned with many costs, especially with the cost of capital, the most important cost for any business manager to be aware of. Finally, finance gives continual attention to markets and their movement: the stock, bond, money, and foreign exchange markets are in the background of every financial decision.

To succeed as a financial manager, you must be a sound economist. You must be familiar with the laws of supply and demand, with the concepts of equilibrium price and opportunity cost, and with the roles of substitution, competition, and marginal return. A good background from your course in economic principles will help you grasp quickly many of the ideas covered in this book.

Finance and Accounting

Financial decisions are guided by a firm's balance sheet, income statement, statement of changes in financial position, and by the numerous ratios and other measures that can be developed from them. Such ratios and measures, as we have already noted, are the principal gauges of business performances and the main tools of business control. They are as important to the management of a well-run business as a compass and sextant are to a ship's officers. In both instance they are the means by which the enterprise is navigated.

For this reason accounting definitions, measurements, and ratios are the foundations of financial knowledge. You cannot understand finance or master its theories and techniques without a firm grasp of all balance-sheet and income-statement entries, how they are derived, and how they are compared through meaningful ratios. The portions of accounting most necessary for making financial calculations and judgments are summarized in Chapter 12. Unless your freshman or sophomore training in accounting was very thorough, you will find it desirable to sit down and memorize this chapter almost word for word. If you do that, most of what follows will be easy for you to understand and remember.

Finance and Mathematics

Finance deals with quantities—quantities of money, or of assets and liabilities, revenues, costs, and profits, all of which are expressed in money. Thus, like accounting, it is largely a numerical discipline. The measurements necessary to the making of financial judgments and plans are obtained by putting numbers on things.

The mathematics used in calculating the answers to financial problems can sometimes be quite complicated, but usually no more than an elementary application of arithmetic or algebra is needed. Ratios, percentages, and simple proportions provide the solutions to most financial problems.

The most challenging mathematics used in this book are the mathematics of *compound interest.* Compound interest is an unavoidable factor in financial decision making because money has what is called "time value," based on its power to earn interest; thus any investment can be justified only if it earns at least as much as the money involved could earn if it were lent out at interest. Present value, future value, and annuity (the basic compound interest calculations) are fundamental concepts in finance. They are the key to solving a wide range of financial problems. Only by understanding the operation of compound interest can you calculate the price of a bond, figure the installments needed to pay off a loan, or measure the expected return from a business investment. You will find it desirable to memorize much of Chapter 2, which deals exclusively with interest and discount in financial valuation.

DIVISIONS OF FINANCE

Like other business disciplines, finance divides into specialized areas. The study of three such areas is basic to a working knowledge of finance.

Money and banking, as the name suggests, deals with money—the "root stuff" of finance—and with the institutions that create and deal in it. Why and how does the supply of money change? How do these changes affect prices, interest rates, and business activity? What part in the economy is played by banks, the Federal Reserve System, other financial institutions? Answers to these questions, attempted in the study of money and banking, are needed before one approaches other areas of finance because the value and behavior of money vitally affect all financial decisions. Consequently, after introducing you to interest rates, we proceed with a concise but searching look at money and financial institutions.

Business finance is concerned with how the finances of a business enterprise should be managed. Most of this book focuses on business finance. As you will learn, the financial manager of a business firm has three principal tasks: (1) Assessing the company's financial needs, (2) acquiring the funds the business requires, and (3) allocating these funds in the business in the most profitable and economical way. Chapter 11 will introduce you to these all-important three As of financial management.

BOX 1-3
Wanted: A Strong Dollar or a Weak
One?   How much an American's dollar buys when it goes hunting an imported blouse,
              camera, or sports car depends on the dollar's strength in relation to the foreign
country's currency. A dollar that buys lots of Japanese yen or West German marks
puts a tiger in the American buyer's pocketbook because it makes foreign products
cost less in dollars.

But a strong dollar isn't all roses for Americans. Just as a strong dollar makes
it easy for Americans to buy foreign goods, so it makes it costly for foreigners to buy
American goods. Foreign merchandise can flood U.S. markets, and U.S. goods can
prove too expensive for foreigners to buy.

A weak dollar makes it easy for Americans to sell goods in competition with
foreigners, but it can turn Yves Saint Laurent clothes or Hondas into luxuries too
expensive for Americans to afford.

If you work for a company that sells in competition with foreign rivals, either
at home or abroad, this question of a strong or weak dollar and its effects can make
the difference between profit and loss, a job or no job. That could be another reason,
then, for learning more about finance. Chapter 26 will give you a closer look at how
the dollar's value abroad affects American business.

The third main branch of financial studies is *investments.* Investments are assets
held for the purpose of conserving capital, earning an income, or reselling at a higher
price. Traditionally, the assets dealt with in investment courses have been stocks and
bonds, but the serious price-level inflation of recent years has emphasized the investment merit of tangible things such as real estate, gold coins, and diamonds. The
three main problems treated in the study of investments are (1) selection (what to
buy), 2 timing (when to buy it), and (3) what combination of investments to buy
(what is called the portfolio problem).

Other branches of finance, more specialized in scope, include international
finance, real estate finance, security analysis, money and capital markets, and nonbank financial institutions such as savings-and-loan associations, mutual savings
banks, and several others. Each of these fields in turn may be further divided for
intensive study by the expert or professional manager.

BASIC PRINCIPLES IN FINANCE

Although finance divides and subdivides into specialized fields, you will soon see
that there are common principles that work the same way in *all* fields of finance. The
most important of these principles are interest and the time value of money (with
which Chapters 2 and 3 will give you a basic acquaintance). But two other such
principles, briefly explained, will suffice here for illustration.

The first of these principles is the *financial manager's dilemma.* It means simply that in any financial decision, profitability (how much you stand to make) is generally opposed to liquidity (how easily you can get your money back if you need to). This principle holds true whether the decision concerns an investment in corporate assets, a personal venture in securities, or what to buy for a bank's investment portfolio.

A second principle is *suitability,* or the preservation of time balance between assets and liabilities. This principle means that the assets in which money is invested should not have a longer maturity than the liabilities through which the money is raised. A vigorous paraphrase of this principle runs, "Never borrow short and lend—or invest—long." Old as this principle is, it was the most consistently violated of all financial rules during the inflationary booms of the 1960s and 1970s. In the ensuing credit crunches, most enterprises that went to the wall did so precisely because they borrowed money at short term and invested it in long-term assets that could not return to cash until after the borrowings fell due. When the credit squeeze made it impossible for the borrowers either to renew their loans or reborrow from other sources, they were forced into default and bankruptcy.

As you can see, financial principles are usually just common-sense thinking applied to money-related problems. Of course, the principles can be wrapped in complicated jargon and formidable mathematics. But this does not have to be the case, and we shall try to avoid unnecessary complication wherever possible.

SUMMARY

1. Finance is concerned with money and its uses in business—as capital and as a means of control. Whether you are a finance specialist or a business manager concerned with other duties, you will encounter finance in four main ways.

    a. Dollars are the common denominator of the resources available to a company and to each of its parts. What a company can attempt and achieve is largely governed by the strength of its financial position.

    b. Financial measurements—especially profit as a percentage return on invested capital—are the main gauge of a company's performance. In a well-run company every manager may be assigned responsibility for producing a proportionate share of the overall profit.

    c. Financial tools, notably budgets and reports expressed in dollar terms, are the principal means of controlling business operations. Along with being the common denominator of business resources, money is also the common denominator of business plans and results.

    d. Interest rates, the stock market, and the state of business balance sheets foreshadow periods of cloudiness or sunlight in the economy. Because managers must plan ahead, a close watch on trends in the financial system today can pave the way for pleasing profits tomorrow.

2. As a discipline, finance has its own vocabulary, concepts, and principles. Most of these are borrowed from three subjects you have already studied: economics, accounting, and mathematics. The mathematics of compound interest provide the basis for most calculations on which financial decisions are based.

3. As a business discipline, finance has three main areas. *Money and banking* deals with money, interest rates, financial institutions, and the behavior of the financial system. *Business finance* is concerned with how businesses assess their financial needs, acquire their funds, and allocate their financial resources in an efficient way. *Investments* look at what assets investors should hold, when to buy them, and what combination of assets to buy. Other branches of finance, more specialized in scope, are usually the domain of highly-trained professionals.

4. As an art (or, at best, applied science), finance expounds many rules and principles. Upon investigation and experience, these always come down to common sense. You have looked at two such principles in this chapter: the *financial manager's dilemma*, which teaches that profit and liquidity are normally inversely related, and *suitability*, the notion that assets and the means of financing them should have matching lives.

KEY TERMS AND CONCEPTS

Measure of business resources
Gauge of business performance
Tool of business control
Source of business forecasts

Languages of finance
Compound interest
Financial manager's dilemma
Suitability

QUESTIONS

1-1. Is money the only means of paying for things? Explain.

1-2. In what ways will a knowledge of finance help a nonfinancial manager in business?

1-3. Why is money the most useful measure of business resources?

1-4. Distinguish between a company that is "undercapitalized" and one that is "illiquid." Which, in your opinion, is worse off?

1-5. State how you as a sales manager would use financial measurements to appraise the work of your salespeople.

1-6. What are budgets? How does a budget operate to help control a business enterprise?

1-7. Why should interest rates and stock prices be useful in forecasting future business conditions?

1-8. Illustrate why and how money has "time value."

1-9. Illustrate how the manager of a manufacturing company might violate the principle of suitability.

1-10. What is a dilemma? What basic dilemmas do financial managers face?

PROBLEMS

Principles of economics and accounting are prerequisites to navigating successfully the following 26 chapters, so we recommend that you take this test in order to evaluate your readiness for this first finance course in your curriculum. The problems call for a large dose of common sense and basic knowledge of economics and finance.

1-1. If there are 2.47 new incorporations for every business failure, how many business failures are there for every 100 new incorporations?

1-2. If a firm had net working capital of $150 and current liabilities of $100, what would be its current ratio?

1-3. If a business depreciated an asset costing $30,000 with a five-year life by the sum-of-the-years'-digits method, how much depreciation would it charge in the asset's second year if the salvage value is zero.

1-4. If a preferred stock had a par value of $50 and paid a 7 percent dividend, how much would the dividend be?

1-5. A company reports $120,000 in after-tax profit. If it paid income tax at a 40 percent rate, what was its profit before tax?

1-6. In percentage terms Goofball Drug stock drops 1.5 times as fast as the overall stock market. The market index drops from 1,200 to 900. To what price should Goofball stock move from 48?

1-7. The price of eggs rises 20 percent from a dollar a dozen, then falls 20 percent from the price thus reached. Where does the price wind up?

1-8. A company sells gismos at $4.50 each. Its overhead costs amount to $150 and variable costs are $2 per unit. What profit does it make selling (a) 100 gismos? (b) 120 gismos? By what percentage does its profit rise as sales increase from 100 to 120 units?

1-9. A company's annual sales amount to four times its capital. Its profit on sales is 2.4 percent. What is its rate of profit on its capital?

1-10. A $10 sum compounds at 5.6 percent annually for three years. To what total amount has the sum accumulated at the end of three years?

CHAPTER 2

Interest and
Discount in Valuation

THE CONCEPT OF MONEY'S TIME VALUE

MATHEMATICS OF TIME VALUE
Annuity

INTEREST FACTOR TABLES
Using Interest Factor Tables · Compounding and Discounting Other Than Annually
Suggestions for Solving Problems

EXAMPLES AND PRACTICE PROBLEMS

SUMMARY
Key Terms and Concepts · Questions · Problems

BIBLIOGRAPHY

Evaluating financial alternatives requires converting amounts of money from one time period to another time period. For example, you may want to choose between putting your savings in a money-market fund or buying a common stock, each of which offers you a cash return. The choice requires restating the expected future cash flow from each choice as an equivalent single amount of money at the present time in order to allow comparisons. To compare or combine cash amounts, we must express them in the same terms—as single amounts at a common date.

The time value of money is a concept that establishes the relationship between amounts at different points in time. It is important that we understand the concept because the time value of money helps us to recognize that we prefer an immediate cash receipt to a future receipt and a future outlay of cash to an immediate outlay. The reason that money has time value is this: Money can be used to invest in interest-earning assets, so the earlier we receive money or the later we pay, the wealthier we will be because we can receive a return during the interim.

When you finish this chapter you will understand the role of the time value of money in valuation and the way that the time value of money enters into making financial choices. This chapter begins by considering the mathematical relationship between amounts at different points in time. (Equivalent amounts at different points in time may be found by using mathematical equations or interest tables.) When you finish this part of the chapter, you will be able to determine the correct mathematical equations required to solve problems dealing with the time value of money. You will also learn how to select interest tables and use them in solving financial problems. The end of the chapter provides several examples and practice problems to give you hands-on experience at calculating the value of financial assets.

THE CONCEPT OF MONEY'S TIME VALUE

To say that money has time value means that money's value depends on when it is received. Receiving a dollar immediately permits someone to use the dollar either to invest or to buy consumer goods, each of which may be worthwhile. But waiting for a dollar means that a person must wait to invest or consume.

Example. Consider a company that can sell either on a cash basis or on a trade-credit basis. If sales are made for cash, then the company immediately receives cash that it can use to invest. Or suppose that a friend can pay cash for a television set or can wait two months to pay. If she waits two months, then she can use the cash in the interim to invest in securities or to buy other consumer goods.

Waiting to receive money means that we sacrifice or give up investment opportunities and consumption, and so we incur an opportunity cost. *Opportunity cost* means the return on the best available alternative use. For example, if we invest in a security yielding 8 percent rather than in one yielding 5 percent, then the opportunity cost is the 5 percent return that we reject. Opportunity cost is central to the time value of money concept because when opportunity costs are present, someone receiving money in the future rather than immediately will want to be compensated for rejecting the opportunity to invest now in assets yielding a return. Opportunity cost is always present.

Example. State National Bank can loan you $12,800 for a Mustang with monthly payments extending over the next three years. If State National Bank could loan the money to someone else at 13 percent annually for the next three years, then the bank will charge you at least 13 percent because that is the bank's opportunity cost.

Let us examine the time value of money in a mathematical process called capitalizing. To *capitalize* means to convert an amount or amounts into a future or a present amount. There are two types of capitalizing:

- Compounding. To convert a present amount into an equivalent future amount.
- Discounting. To convert a future amount into an equivalent present amount.

Capitalizing is carried out with the help of mathematical equations. We shall begin the mathematical process of capitalizing by compounding, relating an amount of money at a single point in time to its future equivalent amount. Then, we shall examine the process of discounting, relating an amount at a future point in time to its present equivalent amount.

BOX 2-1
Simple and Compound Interest   Simple interest is the dollar cost of borrowing (or the dollar return from lending) money. This cost or return is based on three elements: the amount borrowed (the principal), the rate of interest, and the amount of time for which the principal is borrowed.

You can use an equation to find the simple dollar interest of a borrowed amount:

$$\text{Interest} = \text{principal} \times \text{rate} \times \text{time}$$
$$\text{Int} = PRT$$

Unlike simple interest, compound interest is the amount that someone pays on the original principal plus the accumulated interest. With interest compounding, the more periods for which we calculate interest, the more rapidly we see the amount of interest and the amount of interest on interest build.

Compounding annually means that there is only one period annually when the lender calculates interest. On a one-year loan, interest charges are identical whether calculated on a simple or annual compound basis. However, we must use a new interest equation—based on the simple interest equation—if there is annual compounding for more than a year or with more than one compound period within a year. Most of this chapter is devoted to explaining how to calculate compound interest for more than one year and with more than one compound period within a year.

Source: Based on *The Arithmetic of Interest Rates,* available free of charge from the Public Information Department, Federal Reserve Bank Of New York, 33 Liberty Street, New York, NY 10045.

MATHEMATICS OF TIME VALUE

A financial manager carries out compounding with an equation that relates a present amount to a future amount. The two amounts are related through the opportunity cost expressed as a rate of interest,

$$S_N = P_0 (1 + i)^N$$

where
S_N = the compound sum or future amount at time N
P_0 = present amount at time zero
i = opportunity cost expressed as an annual compound interest rate or yield
N = number of years separating the two amounts

The time value component, $(1 + i)^N$, reflects the return i sacrificed over the number of years N. The equation reflects compounding of interest because interest is received not only on the beginning amount P but also on the interest itself.

Example. Compound interest means that interest is paid on interest. An interest rate of 12 percent compounded annually means that you receive 12 percent on each year's accumulated amount. The interest and accumulated amount then provide the basis for the next year's interest payment.

If the time value component is greater than zero, then a compound sum must be greater than a present amount to reflect the opportunity cost between the two points in time. The terms *compound sum* and *present amount* are relative and correspond, respectively, to "later amount" and "earlier amount."

Example. To relate an amount in 1985 to an amount in 1995, designate the amount in 1985 the present amount P and the amount in 1995 the compound sum or future amount S.

Figure 2-1 uses a time line to show how a compound sum and a present amount are related. The figure shows that when the rate of interest is 7 percent compounded annually, $1,000 now is equivalent to $1,310.79 four years from now.

Example. Compounded at 7 percent annually, the compound sum in three years of a present $4,897.79 is $6,000 found in the following way:

$$S_N = \$4,897.79(1 + 0.07)^3 = \$6,000$$

The time value component of the compound-sum equation is in the parentheses. It indicates that a compound sum is greater than a present amount as the number of years increases that compounding occurs. Figure 2-2 illustrates this process by showing amounts to which $1,000 will grow after N years at various compound annual interest rates.

Sometimes we may want to find the present amount that is equivalent to some compound sum. That is an especially important task whenever we want to find the value of a capital (income producing) asset because its value to us is the present

FIGURE 2-1 Time line relating $1,000 now to its future value four years from now (compounded at 7 percent annually).

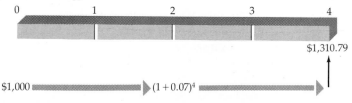

FIGURE 2-2 Relationship between compound interest, time, and compound sum.

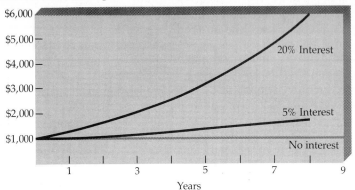

value of its future cash flows. We can use the compound-sum equation by rearranging the equation to give us a present-amount equation:

$$P_0 = \frac{S_N}{(1 + i)^N}$$

where all symbols are the same as those in the compound-sum equation. You may solve any problem involving the receipt of a single amount of money at a future point in time with either the compound-sum equation or the present-amount equation. Determine the choice by individual preference.

Example. The example above showed how $4,897.79 has a $6,000 compound sum in three years if the interest rate is 7 percent compounded annually. The present-amount equation gives the same answer by showing us that the present equivalent of $6,000 three years from now is $4,897.79 if the interest rate over the period is 7 percent compounded annually.

$$P_0 = \frac{\$6,000}{(1 + 0.07)^3} = \$4,897.79$$

The present-amount and compound-sum relationships that we have discussed so far deal with amounts at a single point in time. It is not uncommon for equal amounts to occur more than one time. For example, you may make equal monthly payments on a stereo or you may save a fixed amount of money each week. These are examples of an *annuity*, a series of equal payments or receipts over a specific number of time periods. The following discussion shows you how to use equations to determine the compound sum and present amount of an annuity.

Annuity

If someone makes equal payments into an account for a number of years, the amount in the account will increase because each payment increases the sum and

---

BOX 2-2
Some Perplexing Problems About
Discounting the Future   You may wonder about the benefit of discounting future
amounts because when the future becomes the present you
may not be the same person that you now are. By that we mean that in the future
your tastes and goals may change from what they are today so that you may regret
selling out the future for the present.

Economists are concerned about society's decision to trade future consumption
for present consumption or vice versa because the individuals who make a decision
today may not be the same ones who must live with the results of that decision in
the future. For example, if society decides today to reject investing in more plant and
equipment that would let us produce more microcomputers in the future and to
accept producing more sporting goods equipment, then the individuals who enjoy
the sporting goods today may not be the same ones who must do without the
microcomputers in the future. Joan Robinson, a British economist, has done a great
deal of thinking about such matters, and this is the way that she discusses it:

> If I discount the future, then when that future day becomes the present, I shall
> kick myself. . . . There is a choice between some jam today and more jam the day
> after tomorrow. This [social] problem cannot be resolved by any kind of calcula-
> tion based on "discounting the future" for the individuals concerned in the loss
> or gain are different. When the more mechanized . . . technique is chosen, the
> loss falls on those who would have been employed if the other choice had been
> made. The benefit from their sacrifice will come later and they may not survive to
> see it.*

> * Joan Robinson, *Economic Philosophy*, Anchor Books, Garden City, New York, Doubleday, 1962, pp.
> 85 and 125.

---

each year's amount earns interest that compounds. We can use the sum of an annuity equation to find the compound sum of an annuity under the assumption that each
payment occurs at the end of each year:

$$S_{i,N} = A \left[\frac{(1 + i)^N - 1}{i} \right]$$

where

$S_{i,N}$ = compound sum of an annuity of N equal amounts
and interest rate i compounded annually
A = annual annuity

The compound sum of an annuity is sometimes called the future value of an annuity
or the future lump sum of an annuity.

Example. Suppose that you plan to save $100 at the end of each of the next three
years in an account that pays 8 percent interest compounded annually. The sum of

FIGURE 2-3 Future value of a three-year $100 annuity compounding at 8 percent annually.

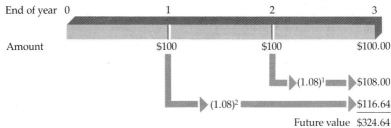

an annuity equation permits us to calculate the $324.64 compound sum of the annuity:

$$S_{i,N} = \$100 \left[\frac{(1 + 0.08)^3 - 1}{0.08} \right]$$
$$= \$324.64$$

Figure 2-3 illustrates the way that the equal $100 amounts at the end of each of the next three years sum to $324.64 if each deposit earns 8 percent compounded annually.

Practice. Calculate the compound sum of a four-year $100 annuity compounding at 7 percent annually. Answer: $443.99. Show how you find this answer and compare your mathematical solution with Figure 2-4.

You must note this important rule when deciding between using either the compound sum or the compound sum of an annuity equation: Use the compound sum of an annuity equation *only* when the amounts that you are dealing with are an annuity. If amounts are different in each period, then they are not an annuity and you must use the compound-sum equation.

FIGURE 2-4 Future value of a four-year $100 annuity compounding at 7 percent annually.

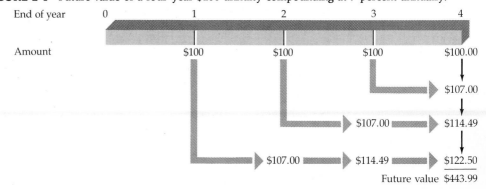

FIGURE 2-5 Present amount of a three-year $100 annuity discounted at 8 percent annually.

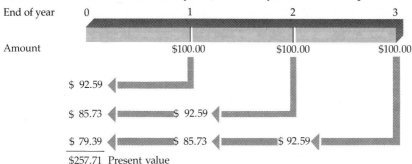

You may want to find the present value of a series of equal payments in order to evaluate a financial alternative. For example, an insurance policy may offer you for $4,000 an annual cash amount at the end of each of the next 10 years. You will want to find the present value of the equal annual cash amounts to compare with $4,000 to decide whether or not you want to buy the insurance policy. The present amount of an annuity equation helps us to find the present value of a series of equal amounts by discounting each future amount at a rate i:

$$P_{i,N} = A \left(\frac{1 - \left[\frac{1}{(1 + i)^N} \right]}{i} \right)$$

where $P_{i,N}$ is the present amount of an annuity A for N years discounted at a compound annual rate of interest i. The present amount of an annuity is sometimes called the present value or present lump sum of an annuity.

Example. The present amount of a three-year $100 annuity discounted at 8 percent compounded annually is $257.70 calculated with the present amount of an annuity equation:

$$P_{0.08,3} = \$100 \left(\frac{1 - \left[\frac{1}{(1 + 0.08)^3} \right]}{0.08} \right) = \$100 \left(\frac{1 - 0.7938}{0.08} \right)$$

$$= \$257.71$$

Figure 2-5 illustrates the relationship between the $100 annuity and its $257.71 present amount.

So far we have examined the mathematical equations used to relate amounts at different points in time. You may use these equations, or you may use tables that combine capitalizing into a single calculation. <u>These tables are called *interest factor*</u> *tables* because they combine values of N (the number of years) and i (the interest rate) into a single factor. The following discussion will show you how to use tables of interest factors to solve problems involving the time value of money.

INTEREST FACTOR TABLES

Interest factor tables combine the components of N (the number of years) and i (the interest rate) in each of the equations discussed above into a single factor that we can use to solve problems that involve amounts at different points in time. To use an interest factor table, you need to understand three basic concepts.

1. *Future Value.* Future value is the value of $1 at a future point in time. It is the amount to which $1 will grow at a specific rate of compound interest over a time period. At any positive rate of interest, this future value will always be greater than a present value. Appendix B presents compound-interest factors. Compound-interest factors are usually called future value factors.

2. *Present Value.* Present value is the value today (at time zero) of $1 from a future point in time. Appendix B-2 shows you present value interest factors. The present value factors in Appendix B-2 are reciprocals of the future value factors in Appendix B-1 because compounding and discounting single amounts (as opposed to annuities) are equivalent operations. In other words going from a present to a future value is analytically no different than going from a future to a present value.

3. *Annuity.* An annuity is a series of equal amounts. Appendices B-3 and B-4 present annuity interest factors. We can use annuity interest factors to find the future value or present value of a $1 annuity calculated with a number of payments (or receipts) capitalized at a specified interest rate.

The following discussion will consider each type of interest factor so that you will see how they are related and be able to solve problems with them.

Using Interest Factor Tables

Interest factor tables permit us to solve financial problems for future values, present values, the number of periods, or the interest rate depending on what the problem requires. Amounts on an interest factor table are comprised of combinations of i interest rate and N number of years, so that given the number of years and the interest rate we can find the associated interest factor. Also, given N and an interest-rate factor we can find the associated i, and vice versa. This relationship between the interest rate, number of years, and interest factor will help us to solve many different types of financial problems.

Table 2-1 shows the relationship between the mathematical equations examined earlier in this chapter and interest factor equivalents that we shall use to solve problems using interest factor tables located at the end of the book. You may want to refer back to Table 2-1 during the following discussion.

TABLE 2-1 Capitalizing with Mathematical Equations and Interest Factors

	Mathematical Equation	Interest Factor
Compounding Single amount	$S_N = P_0 (1 + i)^N$	$FV = PV(FVIF_{i,N})$
Annuity	$S_{i,N} = A \left[\dfrac{(1 + i)^N - 1}{i} \right]$	$FVA = A(FVIFA_{i,N})$
Discounting Single amount	$P_0 = \dfrac{S_N}{(1 + i)^N}$	$PV = FV(PVIF_{i,N})$
Annuity	$P_{i,N} = A \left[\dfrac{1 - \left[\dfrac{1}{(1 + i)^N} \right]}{i} \right]$	$PVA = A(PVIFA_{i,N})$

Present Value to Future Value. Appendix B-1 is a table of interest factors compounding amounts of money forward in time because it tells us the amount to which $1 will grow at the end of a given number of periods at the stated rate of interest. Remember that the word *present* used here does not necessarily denote *now*, but simply an earlier period at which compounding begins. You will observe in Appendix B-1 that $1 invested for 20 years (read across the row of Year 20) at 6 percent interest compounded annually (read down the column labeled 6 percent) grows to $3.207, an amount found by multiplying $1 by the 3.207 interest factor. You will note that if the $1 grows for 20 years at 2 percent, it will be $1.486 at the end of 20 years calculated in the same way.

A useful way to set up an equation to solve financial problems involving present values and future values using interest factors is

$$FV = PV(FVIF_{i,N})$$

where

$$FV = \text{future value}$$
$$PV = \text{present value}$$
$$FVIF = \text{future value interest factor from Appendix B-1}$$
$$i = \text{interest rate compounded annually}$$
$$N = \text{number of years that compounding occurs}$$

Notice that the present value to future value equation is equivalent to the compound-sum equation examined earlier in this chapter, but the present value to future value equation uses interest factors from Appendix B-1.

Future Value to Present Value. Appendix B-2 is a table of interest factors that indicates what $1 in the future is now worth after allowing for the futurity (or time lapse) of its receipt. Consequently, this table lists interest factors for discounting an amount of money backward in time. Examination of Appendix B-2 will show that $1 due to be paid or received in 20 years has a present value of $0.319 when the interest rate is 6 percent compounded annually. This answer is found by multiplying $1 by the present value interest factor at the intersection of the row for 20 years and the column for 6 percent. Notice in Appendix B-2 that if the discount rate falls to 2 percent, the present value of $1 received or paid at the end of 20 years rises to $0.673.

An equation for using interest factors to solve future value to present value problems in financial analysis is *Present Value*

$$PV = FV(PVIF_{i,N})$$

Here each variable is defined the same as in the present value to future value equation above.

Any problem involving a present value and a future value may be solved with either of the above interest factor equations because, as noted above, interest factors in Appendix B-1 are reciprocals of those in Appendix B-2.

Example. What compound annual rate of interest must $2,026 earn if you want to have $4,000 in six years? We may solve this example problem with either interest factor equation above:

1. Calculate the future value interest factor using the present value to future value equation:

$$\$4,000 = \$2,026.40 \ (FVIF_{i,6})$$
$$1.974 = FVIF_{i,6}$$

Appendix B-1 tells us that the interest rate is 12 percent.

2. Calculate the present value interest factor using the future value to present value equation.

$$\$2,026.40 = \$4,000 \ (PVIF_{i,6})$$
$$0.5066 = (PVIF_{i,6})$$

Appendix B-2 tells us that the interest rate is the same 12 percent that we found using Appendix B-1.

Future Value of an Annuity. You can solve financial problems involving the future value of an *annuity* using future value of an annuity interest factors from Appendix B-3. These interest factors give the compound sum that results from the regularly recurring investment of $1 at interest rate i and number of periods N. Each $1 of the annuity is assumed to accumulate interest from the end of each period. Refer to Appendix B-3 and you will notice that the interest factor for 20 years at 6 percent interest is 36.786. This interest factor tells us that the 20-year $1 annuity compounding at a 6 percent annual rate of interest will sum to $36.786 at the end of 20 years.

BOX 2-3
Using Calculators to Find Interest
Factors Most of you own an electronic calculator, and it is helpful in solving time value of money equations—as you no doubt already know. If your calculator has an exponent key y^x and a reciprocal key $1/x$, then you can find interest factors quickly without using the tables in Appendix B. Here's how it's done:

To find future value interest factors used in compounding, enter 1 plus the interest rate and use the exponent key. For example, to find the future value interest factor for 4.3 years (yes, you can have fractions of a year with this key) and 12 percent compound annual interest, take these steps:

	Keys	Display
1. Enter 1 plus the interest rate	1.12	1.12
2. Raise to the 4.3 power	y^x 4.3 =	1.628

If you look at Appendix B-1, you will note that this interest factor lies between the 12 percent interest factors for four and five years.

To find the present value interest factors that we use in discounting, the steps are the same as those above, but with the additional step to find the reciprocal. For example, to find the present value interest factor for six years and 10 percent annual interest, take these steps:

	Keys	Display
1. Enter 1 plus the interest rate	1.10	1.10
2. Raise to the sixth power	y^x 6 =	1.772
3. Take the reciprocal	$1/x$ =	0.564

If you look at Appendix B-2, you will note that the present value interest factor for six years and 10 percent compounding annually is within a rounding error of 0.564.

An equation for finding the future value of an annuity using interest factor tables is

$$FVA = A\,(FVIFA_{i,\,N})$$

where

$$FVA = \text{future value (sum) of the annuity}$$
$$A = \text{annuity amount}$$
$$FVIFA = \text{future value interest factor from Appendix B-2}$$
$$i = \text{compound annual rate of interest}$$
$$N = \text{number of years}$$

BOX 2-4

Approximating with Interpolation   The interest factors and years in the tables in the appendices are for whole years and interest rates. You may find that an answer to a problem requires you to find a fraction of a year or of an interest rate. When that happens, you can use linear interpolation to approximate the correct answer. The answer is approximate because we use a linear estimate when in fact the mathematical relationships are nonlinear (actually, exponential, as a look at the mathematical equations in Table 2-1 will remind you). An equation for interpolating an interest rate is

$$i = \left[\frac{(IF - IF_L)\,(i_H - i_L)}{IF_H - IF_L}\right] + i_L$$

where

$i =$ interest rate
$IF =$ interest factor that we find in the equation
$IF_L =$ lower of the bracketed interest factors
$IF_H =$ higher of the bracketed interest factors
$i_H =$ interest rate associated with the higher interest factor
$i_L =$ interest rate associated with the lower interest factor

As an example, consider how to find the interest rate associated with three years and a 1.42857 interest factor. Appendix B-1 shows that it lies between 12 and 14 percent. The equation above gives the approximate answer:

$$1 = \frac{(1.42857 - 1.405)\,(0.14 - 0.12)}{1.482 - 1.405} + 0.12$$

$$i = \frac{0.0004714}{0.077} + 0.12 = 0.12612 \quad \text{or} \quad 12.612\%$$

Example. The future value of a five-year $1 annuity compounded annually at 6 percent is $5.637 found with the future value of an annuity equation and Appendix B-3,

$$FVA = \$1(5.637) = \$5.637$$

The solution to this problem is illustrated in Figure 2-6.

Present Value of an Annuity. Appendix B-4 consists of present value of an annuity interest factors to help us solve financial problems. Refer to this table and

FIGURE 2-6 Future value of a five-year $1 annuity compounding at 6 percent annually.

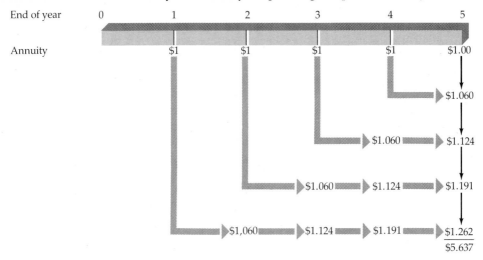

you will notice that the interest factor for 20 years at 6 percent is 11.47. This interest factor tells us that a 20-year $1 annuity discounted at 6 percent annually has a present value of $1 × 11.47 = $11.47. Given a choice between an immediate $11.47 and a 20-year $1 annuity, you would consider them equal if your opportunity cost over the period were 6 percent annually.

An equation for finding the present value of an annuity is

$$PVA = A(PVIFA_{i,N})$$

where

$$
\begin{aligned}
PVA &= \text{present value of the annuity} \\
A &= \text{annuity amount} \\
PVIFA &= \text{present value interest factor of an annuity} \\
i &= \text{compound annual rate of interest} \\
N &= \text{number of years}
\end{aligned}
$$

The present value of an annuity equation is the interest factor counterpart to the present amount of an annuity equation that we looked at earlier in this chapter.

Example. The present value of a five-year $1 annuity received at the end of each of the next five years discounted at 6 percent annually is $4.212 found with the present value of an annuity equation and Appendix B-3:

$$PVA = \$1(4.212) = \$4.212$$

FIGURE 2-7   Present value of a five-year $1 annuity discounted at 6 percent annually.

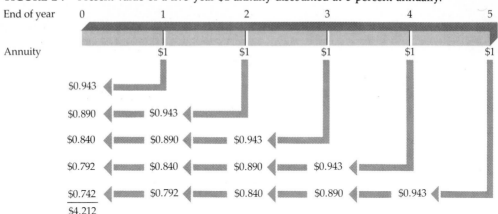

Given a choice between receiving an immediate $4.212 or a five-year $1 annuity, you would consider them equally attractive if your opportunity cost over the period were 6 percent annually. Figure 2-7 illustrates the stream of future cash in this example and its $4.212 present value.

Compounding and Discounting Other Than Annually

When compounding and discounting occur annually, the interest factor tables at the end of this book may be used directly. However, when compounding and discounting other than annually occur, then the number of years N and the interest rate i must be changed. The method to do so involves (1) multiplying N by the number of times in a year that capitalizing occurs and (2) multiplying i by the reciprocal of the number of times in a year that capitalizing occurs. If we let M be the number of times in a year that compounding or discounting occurs, then the adjustments are the following:

$$\text{Adjustment to } N: \quad N \times M$$
$$\text{Adjustment to } i: \quad i \times \frac{1}{M}$$

When a bank computes daily interest, the value of M is set at 365 because that is the number of times in a year that compounding occurs, and N becomes 365 and i becomes $i/365$.

Example. An account at a local savings-and-loan association pays depositors 8 percent annual interest compounded semiannually. To calculate the future value of an amount left on deposit for 10 years requires adjusting N and i to reflect compounding twice a year:

$$\text{Adjustment to } N: \quad 10 \times 2 = 20$$
$$\text{Adjustment to } i: \quad 0.08 \times \tfrac{1}{2} = 0.04$$

You will solve a problem with these conditions by using interest factors for 0.04 and 20 years.

Once you adjust the number of periods and the interest rate to reflect other than annual compounding or discounting, any problem is solved using the interest factor equations and the interest factor tables.

Example. How much will there be in an account in 10 years if $10,000 is initially placed on deposit and the interest rate is 8 percent annually compounded semiannually? This example requires us to adjust the number of years and the interest rate that we will use in the future value equation. The number of years becomes $10 \times 2 = 20$ and the interest rate becomes $0.08 \times \tfrac{1}{2} = 0.04$. The future value interest factor uses an i of 4 percent and an N of 20 from Appendix B-1:

$$FV = \$10,000(2.191) = \$21,190 \quad \text{\small 21, 910}$$
$$\text{\small 2.191}$$

Future Value Formula (other than annual comp.)

When an annuity is compounded or discounted other than annually, an adjustment in addition to those above must be made: We must adjust the annuity itself to reflect its payment or receipt at times other than annually.[1] For an annuity, the adjustments are

$$\text{Adjustment to } N: \quad N \times M$$
$$\text{Adjustment to } i: \quad i \times \frac{1}{M}$$
$$\text{Adjustment to } A: \quad A \times \frac{1}{M}$$

Example. How much must each quarterly deposit be to an account for five years at 12 percent annual interest compounded quarterly in order to accumulate $20,000? The items in the problem must be adjusted as follows:

$$\text{Adjustment to } N: \quad 5 \times 4 = 20$$
$$\text{Adjustment to } i: \quad 0.12 \times \tfrac{1}{4} = 0.03$$
$$\text{Adjustment to } A: \quad A \times \tfrac{1}{4} = \frac{A}{4}$$

---

[1] If withdrawals or payments are made at times other than on capitalizing dates, the equations become cumbersome and tedious. You may want to see the discussion in *Business Analyst Guidebook*, Texas Instruments Incorporated, 1982, pp. 9–45 through 9–52. We have kept things fairly simple in this chapter by assuming that payments and withdrawals occur simultaneously with capitalizing dates.

Then, we use the future value of an annuity equation to solve the problem:

$$\$20{,}000 = \frac{A}{4} \; (\text{FVIFA}_{0.03,20})$$

$$\$20{,}000 = \frac{A}{4} \; (26.87)$$

$$\$744.32 = \frac{A}{4}$$

The quarterly deposits are $744.32.

Example. Suppose that you invest $2,538 in a security that pays you $1,000 annually for three years in equal semiannual payments. What interest rate or rate of return does the security pay?

First, notice that the security in fact is going to pay you twice a year for three years, so you will receive six payments of $500 each. Here are the adjustments needed to solve the problem:

Adjustment to N: $3 \times 2 = 6$

Adjustment to i: $i \times \tfrac{1}{2} = \dfrac{i}{2}$

Adjustment to A: $\$1{,}000 \times \tfrac{1}{2} = \$500$

Use the present value of an annuity equation to solve the problem:

$$\$2{,}538 = \$500 \; (\text{PVIFA}_{i/2,6})$$

$$\frac{\$2{,}538}{\$500} = \text{PVIFA}_{i/2,6}$$

$$5.076 = \text{PVIFA}_{i/2,6}$$

Now, from Appendix B-4 you will notice that the interest rate associated with a 5.076 interest factor and an N of 6 is 5 percent. However, this interest rate is associated with $i/2$. So, to find i we solve the following equation:

$$\frac{i}{2} = 0.05$$

$$i = 2 \times 0.05 = 0.10 \text{ or } 10\%$$

The security pays 10 percent annual interest compounded semiannually.

We shall use the present value of an annuity equation adjusted for semiannual payment when we examine the value of a corporate bond because bonds pay interest twice a year. Corporate bonds are a topic we examine later in this chapter.

Suggestions for Solving Problems

Essentially a solution calls for converting an amount of money at one point in time to its equivalent amount at another point in time. The time value of money must be considered because there is an opportunity cost over the intervening time period. Plotting each problem on a time line can help you analyze problems. To do this, simply draw a horizontal line and scale it to show different points of time, as in Figure 2-1. Next, at the appropriate points in time, plot the amounts given in the problem. Then ask yourself, What amounts and what points in time must amounts plotted be made equivalent? Graphic analysis should suggest the correct solution to your problem.

Before beginning to solve an annuity problem, find a benchmark. This benchmark will be an answer using a zero interest rate and is found intuitively without using the interest factors at the end of the book. Then, compare your answer with your benchmark to see if your answer makes sense.

Example. How much must each of five equal, annual deposits be in order to accumulate $10,000 if each deposit earns 6 percent interest compounded annually? The benchmark with a zero interest rate is

$$\frac{\$10,000}{5} = \$2,000 \text{ annually}$$

Our answer must be less than $2,000 annually because interest is earned on each deposit.

Practice. Solve the problem immediately above using the future value of an annuity equation and Appendix B-3. Answer: $1,773.99. Now explain how you would know by using the benchmark that the present value of an annuity equation and interest factors from Appendix B-4 would give you the wrong answer. (Notice that your answer then would be an incorrect $2,374.17.)

Figure 2-8 diagrams a method to help you solve capitalization problems—both discounting and compounding. First, ask yourself if this problem is one involving a single payment of money. If the answer is yes, then you may use either the present value or future value equation and its appropriate appendix. However, if you decide that you are dealing with a series of equal payments, then which equation and appendix you use are important because interest factors in Appendix B-3 are not reciprocals of those in Appendix B-4. Ask yourself when dealing with an annuity if you are accumulating a future amount: Does the series of equal periodic payments begin at zero (or some small amount) and accumulate to a larger amount in the future? If the answer is yes, then the problem is one involving the future value of an annuity requiring Appendix B-3. If the answer is no, then you are dealing with a problem involving the present value of an annuity requiring the present value of an annuity equation and Appendix B-4.

Someone said (we believe that it was John McEnroe) that the right kind of practice makes perfect. With that maxim in mind, let us turn our attention to some

FIGURE 2-8 Flowchart of logic for solving compound interest problems.

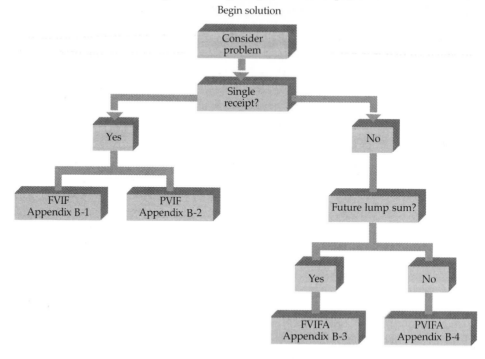

examples and practice problems. We guarantee that time spent working through the following section will pay large dividends in the remainder of this course.

EXAMPLES AND PRACTICE PROBLEMS

Example. An acquaintance in your finance class is certain to receive $50,000 ten years from now. She wishes to sell you this future amount. What price can you afford to pay if your opportunity cost is expected to remain at 7 percent annually over the next 10 years? The solution in steps follows:

1. Draw and label a time line depicting the problem.
2. Ask yourself if you are dealing with an annuity. No, the problem involves a single amount.
3. Define your known and unknown. You know the $50,000 must be future value because it is a single amount, later in time than your unknown—the value of the present amount. This unknown can only be present value because it is earlier in time than your known.
4. Connect your unknown to your known with the appropriate interest factor:

$$PV = FV(PVIF_{0.07,\,10})$$
$$PV = \$50,000(0.508)$$
$$PV = \$25,400$$

The calculation tells us that $50,000 received in 10 years is the equivalent to $25,400 today if today's amount can be invested to yield 7 percent compounded annually.

Not all problems involve using a single equation. And the flow of cash may be irregular so that it is not an annuity. In such cases you must break the problem into several miniproblems, perhaps involving more than one appendix.

Example. What is the present value of an annuity of $3,000 per year for 6 years on a 9 percent basis (that is, discounted at 9 percent) if the first payment is to be received 15 years from now (that is, at the end of 15 years)?

Solution: The problem involves an annuity, and we are asked about the present value; in that case the present value of an annuity equation must be used. The present value of a $3,000 annuity discounted at zero interest is $3,000 \times 6 = $18,000 so our annuity must have a present value less than this benchmark:

$$PVA = A\,(PVIFA_{0.09,\,6})$$
$$PVA = \$3,000(4.486)$$
$$PVA = \$13,458$$

Thus, $13,458 is the present value of a six-year $3,000 annuity if purchased one year before the first annuity payment. The first payment is 15 years from now, and Figure 2-9 shows us that the annuity has been discounted to the beginning of

FIGURE 2-9 Present value of a six-year $3,000 annuity with the first receipt in 15 years discounted at 9 percent annually.

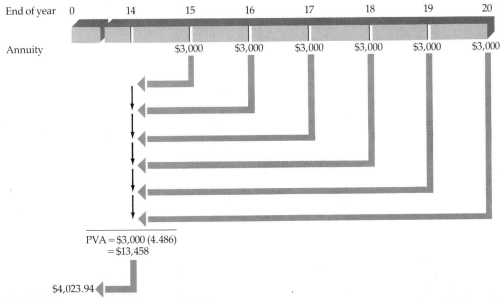

End of year   0   14   15   16   17   18   19   20

Annuity $3,000 $3,000 $3,000 $3,000 $3,000 $3,000

PVA = $3,000 (4.486)
    = $13,458

$4,023.94

year 15, which is the end of year 14. Next, the problem is to determine the present value of $13,458 discounted at 9 percent. This solution involves converting a future value to its present value 14 years earlier at a 9 percent discount rate. Therefore, turn to Appendix B-2 for factors for converting future value to present value. The interest factor suggests that for each $1, you need to pay only 29.9 cents now. The present value of the amount today is $13,458 $\times$ 0.299 = $4,023.92.

The solution in a single equation is

$$PV = A(PVIFA_{0.09,\,6})\,(PVIF_{0.09,\,14}) = \$3,000(4.486)(0.299)$$
$$PV = \$3,000(1.34131) = \$4,023.92$$

Practice. Before continuing to the next problem make sure that you can explain why the present value of the $3,000 annuity is discounted using $N = 14$ rather than $N = 15$.

Practice. A corporation seeks a loan of $80,000 at 6 percent annual interest for 15 years. The corporation must make equal annual payments for principal and interest. (Payments of interest and principal are called *debt service*.) The lender is unwilling to complete the loan on the basis of equal payments over the entire period because it wants to reduce the loan more rapidly in the early years. The lender agrees to make the loan, provided that payments be $15,000 in each of the first five years. The remaining payments are to be equal in amount. What will be the amount of these payments?

Solution: $3,059.34. Show the steps involved and verify that the present value of the second annuity must be discounted for five years. Compare your answer with Figure 2-10.

Practice. Suppose that in the previous practice a bank agrees to lend the corporation $80,000 for 15 years at 6 percent interest with equal annual debt service payments. Calculate the amount of each payment. Answer: $8,237.23. Show how this answer is calculated.

Example. John Bears Fitztipton III establishes a $600,000 cash account for marketing research at a private university. The professor managing the account wants to make equal annual withdrawals at the end of each year for four years. The account pays 10 percent interest compounded annually. How much must each equal withdrawal be in order to have no cash remaining at the end of the fourth year? The answer calls for using the present value of an annuity equation because the account is not accumulating to some large, future amount. A benchmark answer is found by dividing the beginning amount by the number of equal withdrawals.

$$\text{Benchmark} = \frac{\$600,000}{4} = \$150,000$$

FIGURE 2-10 Payments to pay off (amortize) an $80,000 bank loan at 6 percent interest compounded annually.

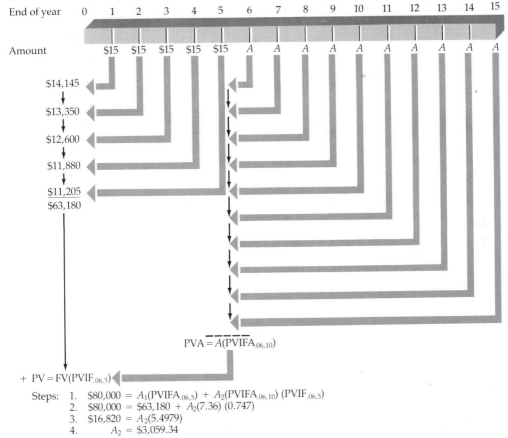

Steps:
1. $\$80,000 = A_1(\text{PVIFA}_{.06,5}) + A_2(\text{PVIFA}_{.06,10})\,(\text{PVIF}_{.06,5})$
2. $\$80,000 = \$63,180 + A_2(7.36)\,(0.747)$
3. $\$16,820 = A_2(5.4979)$
4. $A_2 = \$3,059.34$

Our answer must be *greater* than $150,000 because the account is earning 10 percent interest compounded annually. The answer is $189,274 using the present value of an annuity equation and Appendix B-4:

$$\$600,000 = A(3.170)$$

$$\frac{\$600,000}{3.170} = A$$

$$\$189,274 = A$$

We mentioned earlier in this chapter that corporate bonds typically pay interest twice a year so that an investor calculates the bond's value by discounting the semiannual interest payment and principal to the present at a rate reflecting semiannual compounding. *Principal* is the face value of the bond, and the company selling the bond returns the principal to the bondholder at maturity. The dollar amount of annual interest that a bond pays is stated as a *coupon rate,* the interest as a percent of face value. Thus, a 12 percent coupon $1,000 face value bond pays 0.12 × $1,000 = $120 interest each year in two $60 payments.

The following example will show that bond valuation is an application of the annuity equation adjusted for semiannual compounding. Notice that we must adjust all discount items for semiannual compounding.

Example. Brisbane Corporation has a $1,000 face value bond outstanding that matures (that is, will be repaid) in six years. The bond has a 7 percent coupon. The value of the bond capitalized at 10 percent is $867.21 found in the following way. First, we note that the bond pays $35 twice a year for six years so that it makes 12 payments:

$$\text{Adjustment to } N: \quad 6 \times 2 = 12$$
$$\text{Adjustment to } i: \quad 0.10 \times \tfrac{1}{2} = 0.05$$
$$\text{Adjustment to } A: \quad (0.07 \times \$1,000) \times \tfrac{1}{2} = \$35$$

Now, we use Appendix B-2 for the principal and B-4 for the interest payments to find the present value:

$$PV = \$35(PVIFA_{.05,12}) + \$1,000(PVIF_{.05,12})$$
$$= \$35(8.863) + \$1,000(0.557) = \$867.21$$

Practice. Suppose that someone investing in the Brisbane Corporation's bond in the example above capitalizes the interest and principal at 8 percent rather than the previous 10 percent. Should the present value be greater or less than the $867.21 that we found above? Answer: It should be greater. Verify this answer by solving for the present value ($953.48).

You probably noticed that each annuity problem that we have examined so far in this part of the chapter uses the present value of an annuity equation rather than the future value because most financial problems use present value analysis. Now let us examine a future value problem. You will notice how you are analytically moving from a present value to a future value.

Practice. Janus Corporation has outstanding a $600,000 bond issue that must be paid off in 12 years. The company's financial manager wants to set aside equal amounts of cash each year to provide for paying off the issue. A query to a money-market fund discloses that an account there will earn 8 percent compound annual interest. How much must each deposit be if the interest rate remains constant over the 12-year period? Answer: $31,617. Show the steps needed to get this answer.

The time value of money is a cornerstone of business finance because it plays a crucial role in valuation, and valuation helps us to allocate a company's cash among investments. The next chapter applies the concepts and calculations that you have learned in this chapter to the area of interest-rate theory so that you will understand how interest rates are determined in our economy and the role that they play in influencing economic behavior.

SUMMARY

1. The time value of money relates amounts at different times by expressing the rate of return sacrificed by waiting to receive a future amount. Waiting to receive money means that the individual incurs an opportunity cost, which is the return on the best available alternative use of money.

2. There are two types of capitalizing: Discounting is capitalizing a future value to find its equivalent present value and compounding is capitalizing a present value to find its equivalent future value.

3. Mathematical equations are available for measuring equivalent present and future values. Look at Table 2-1 as you read the rest of this summary and answer the questions and problems that follow.

4. An annuity is the receipt or payment of a fixed amount of money for a number of years.

5. Interest tables contain interest factors for solving time value of money problems. An interest factor is a number that combines the number of years N and a capitalization or interest rate i. The interest factor equations are summarized in Table 2-1.

6. Discounting and compounding other than annually require that adjustments be made before you use the interest factors at the end of this book. If M is the number of times in a year that capitalizing occurs, the required adjustments are

$$\text{Adjustment to } N: \quad N \times M$$

$$\text{Adjustment to } i: \quad i \times \frac{1}{M}$$

$$\text{Adjustment to } A: \quad A \times \frac{1}{M}$$

7. The following hints can help you solve problems involving the time value of money:

    a. You will have one equation and only one unknown for which to solve.

    b. When solving an annuity-type problem, establish a benchmark by assuming a zero interest or capitalization rate.

    c. When in doubt about which annuity equation to use, you should use the present value of an annuity equation and Appendix B-4 because almost all annuity time value of money problems in finance require this equation and this table.

8. Investors determine the value of a bond by finding the present value of the future cash receipts capitalized at a required rate of return reflecting their opportunity cost. A bond pays interest semiannually, so it is necessary to adjust the annual interest payment, the number of periods, and the annual required rate of return to reflect semiannual compounding.

9. The time value of money is a cornerstone of financial management because the value of a capital asset is the present value of the asset's future cash flows.

KEY TERMS AND CONCEPTS

Opportunity cost   Compound interest
Capitalizing   Present value
Discounting   Interest factor
Compounding   Semiannual compounding
Benchmark solution   Future value

QUESTIONS

2-1. The concept of the time value of money reflects an opportunity cost incurred by an investor or lender. Define the term *opportunity cost* and give an example of how it influences the time value of money.

2-2. Examine the equations in Table 2-1 and explain why the same problem can be solved with the tables in Appendices B-1 and B-2 but not with Appendices B-3 and B-4.

2-3. Place the appropriate abbreviation(s) for an equation in the space provided with each explanation. Use these abbreviations: FV, PV, FVA, and PVA.
  a. _____ Future value.
  b. _____ Capitalizing.
  c. _____ Present value.
  d. _____ Discounting.
  e. _____ Compounding.
  f. _____ Annuity.
  g. _____ Equal annual payments.
  h. _____ Accumulating a future amount for a vacation.
  i. _____ Used to calculate interest rate on a bank loan.
  j. _____ When in doubt, use this equation for an annuity problem.
  k. _____ The same problem may be solved with either of these.
  l. _____ Bond valuation (two answers).

2-4. Mr. Smith makes two equal investments at the same time for the same maturity (five years) offering the same annual interest rate. One investment compounds annually and the other semiannually. Will each accumulate to the same future amount? Why or why not?

2-5. A benchmark solution can help solve an annuity problem. Explain the term *benchmark solution* and describe how you would use one in measuring the annual dollar contributions to an account in order to accumulate a future value.

2-6. CMA Examination (modified). Which of the following equations expresses the relationship between a present and future sum of money where FV is the value of the ending amount, i is the interest rate, P is the principal, and N is the number of years:
  a. $FV = (1 + i)(1 + P)$ **d.** $FV = (1 + i)(1 + P)$
  b. $FV = P(1 + i)^N$ **e.** $FV = (1 + P)(1 + i)^N$
  c. $FV = (1 + P)(1 + P)$ **f.** $P = FV(1 + i)^N$

2-7. Interest factor equations and tables can be used for other than annual compounding.

Explain what must be done to the number of years N, the annual interest rate i, and the annuity A under each of these conditions:
a. Interest compounded daily.
b. Interest compounded quarterly.
c. Interest compounded semiannually.

2-8. The chapter says that the time value of money is a cornerstone of valuation. Explain how the time value of money is used to value a capital (income producing) asset and use as a specific example the valuation of a corporate bond.

PROBLEMS

See Table 2-1 for a summary of the important equations in this chapter.

2-1. A friend has $600 to invest in an account that pays 12 percent annually. If the money is left on deposit for six years, how much will be in the account?
a. Solve this problem using the mathematical equation.
b. Solve this problem using the interest factor equation.

2-2. Grand National Bank and Trust offers two types of savings accounts: one pays 10 percent interest compounded annually and the other pays 10 percent compounded quarterly.
a. In which account would you prefer to invest your money?
b. Support your answer by showing the future value of a $500 account left on deposit for five years compounding annually and quarterly.

2-3. Show which of the following you would prefer. In your calculations assume a 12 percent annual compound-interest rate.
a. $1,000 immediately or $2,600 eight years from now.
b. $2,600 eight years from now or $9,400 in 20 years.
c. $20,000 immediately or a six-year annuity that pays $3,000 at the end of each of the next three years and $10,000 at the end of each of the following three years.
d. $43,428 six years from now or a six-year annuity that pays $3,000 at the end of each of the next three years and $10,000 at the end of each of the following three years.
e. $1,000 immediately to compound annually for four years or to compound quarterly for four years.

2-4. A company sets aside a $60,000 account to replace a deteriorating scrap compacter. The company's president tells you $8,000 must be withdrawn at the end of each year during the scrap compacter's 10-year life to replace the part of the machine deteriorated. No cash must be remaining in the account at the end of the 10 years. How much compound annual interest must be earned on the account to permit $8,000 to be withdrawn at the end of each of the next 10 years?

2-5. Philpot Realty invests $12,000 in rental property expecting the price to appreciate 8 percent annually. Given that the price does appreciate at 8 percent annually, calculate the expected price of the property at the end of three years and at the end of six years.

2-6. This letter was published in *Life Magazine*, August, 1959:

> Sir:
> The Indian who sold Manhattan for $24 was a sharp salesman. If he had put his $24 away at 6 percent compounded semiannually, it would now be $9.5 billion and he could buy most of the now improved land back.
>
> S. Branch Walker
> Stamford, Connecticut

If the original $24 (or $17.16 billion at the end of 1969) continued to compound at 6 percent semiannually, how much would the Indian have at the end of 1979? At the end of 1989?

2-7. What compound annual rate of return is required for an amount to increase by 90 percent in three years? Show your calculations.

2-8. How long will it take the gross national product to double in amount if GNP increases by 8 percent compounded annually? Show your calculations.

2-9. To what value will $10,000 grow if invested at 5 percent for 25 years?

2-10. The retirement plan for the Hodges Corporation calls for a semiannual contribution by the company of $2,000. If the cash earns 8 percent per year compounded semiannually, how much would a person accumulate after 10 years?

2-11. How many semiannual compounding periods would be required for $1,000 to grow to $2,653 at an annual growth rate of 10 percent per annum?

2-12. The Jackson Investment Company promises an annual return of $2,000 a year for 10 years on an initial investment of $13,400. What is the approximate yield on the investment?

2-13. Wanda Fried has a 10-year loan at 8 percent for $20,000.
   a. How much should the annual equal payment be?
   b. How much total interest will be paid over the life of the loan?

2-14. A business is allowed to purchase a piece of machinery with payments deferred until the end of the third year. From the end of year 3 through the end of year 10 (eight years), it must pay $3,000 per year. At a 10 percent discount rate, what is the present value (at time zero) of the annuity payments? Sketch a figure like Figure 2-7 to illustrate the cash flows.

2-15. Calculate the value of a 12 percent coupon bond that matures in five years under the following conditions. The bond has a $1,000 face value and the company pays interest semiannually to the bondholder.
   a. Your opportunity cost and the discount rate that you apply to the future cash flows is 10 percent.
   b. Your opportunity cost and the rate of return that you apply to the future cash flows is 8 percent.

BIBLIOGRAPHY

Cissell, Robert, Helen Cissell, and David C. Flashpohler, *Mathematics Of Finance*, 5th ed., Boston, Houghton-Mifflin, 1978.

Clayton, Gary E., and Christopher B. Spivey, *The Time Value Of Money*, Philadelphia, W. B. Saunders, 1978.

Greynolds, Elbert B., Jr., Julius S. Aronofsky, and Robert J. Frame, *Financial Analysis Using Calculators: Time Value Of Money*, New York, McGraw-Hill, 1979.

CHAPTER 3
The Theory and Behavior of Interest

This chapter begins by explaining why interest is, and can be, paid. The key concepts here are *productivity* and *time preference*. Be sure you understand their meaning.

Next we consider interest rates as prices—the prices of money loans. Like other prices, interest rates are set by market forces of supply and demand. The *loanable funds theory* shows how these forces operate.

Then we address interest-rate changes. *Cyclical* changes, extending over two- to five-year periods are products of the business cycle, of regularly recurring expansions and recessions. Interest rates rise as prosperity increases the demand for loans; fall, as loan demand shrinks in recessions. *Secular* trends continue over several business cycles and carry interest rates to permanently higher or lower levels. These very long-term moves reflect changes in the general cost of living, along with lenders' tendency to raise or lower their charges to reflect the buying power of the money in which they expect to be repaid.

How investors react to interest-rate changes occupies the chapter's following section. Having read Chapter 2, you should readily understand that the longer an investment's time to maturity, the more sensitive its price will be to a rise or fall in interest rates. You will also see why investors try to buy short-term securities when they expect rates to rise; long-term securities when they expect rates to fall.

Interest-rate structures comprise the next topic: Here we examine *term structure*, interest rates plotted against their time to maturity, and the *quality structure*, which links interest-rate levels to risk. You also will see why these structures change with changing business conditions and how their changes can be used to predict the economy's changes of direction.

A short discussion of two methods of forecasting interest rates concludes the chapter.

When you borrow money from a bank or other lender, you are expected to pay interest. When you deposit money in a savings account or buy a bond, you expect to be paid interest. All of us are long accustomed to money interest—namely, a payment for the use of borrowed funds. This payment is typically expressed as an annual rate—a ratio of the premium paid for use of the money to the principal amount borrowed. Interest, in everyday language, is simply the cost of a loan. In a mathematical sense interest is the discount rate that equates a loan's repayment (that is, its debt service) to the cash borrowed. In the language of Chapter 2, interest is the capitalization rate relating the present value of a loan's cash flows to each other.

THEORIES OF INTEREST

Not surprisingly, interest is a subject that has stirred many questions over the centuries. Why is interest paid? Why can it be paid? Is it right to charge interest? What determines the level of interest rates? Why do interest rates change through time? Why do interest rates vary from one kind of loan to another? At various times each of these questions has proved both difficult to answer and controversial. We shall answer most of them in the following discussion. Let us begin by examining why interest is and can be paid.

Why Interest Is (and Can Be) Paid

The reasons why interest is, and can be, paid can be summarized in two expressions: (1) productivity and (2) time preference. In economic writings these two concepts sometimes have other names. Productivity, for example, is also referred to as *opportunity to invest*. Time preference is often referred to as *impatience to spend*, although sometimes the term *thrift* or *abstinence* is used.

Productivity means that borrowed money gives a business person the chance to make enough money while using the loan (a) to repay the principal borrowed, (b) to pay a fee to the lender, and (c) to have some profit left over. This is what business people expect will happen when they borrow money to buy inventory to sell in their stores, or when they borrow to buy machinery or raw materials to make finished goods for resale. The productivity of money used in business provides both the business person's incentive to borrow and his wherewithal to pay interest to the lender.

Time preference means that people generally prefer to have money now rather than in the future. Interest is, therefore, the rate—or add-on—at which future money is traded for present money. If someone is agreeable to trading $1 today for $1.08 that is sure of repayment a year from now, then the interest rate is 8 percent per year, and he is receiving 8 cents as a reward for being thrifty.

Productivity is important mainly in business loans. But time preference affects all loans and is the basis for consumer borrowing. Consumers typically finance their purchases by borrowing in order to enjoy the goods sooner.

Example. Your recently married ex-roommate could save $15 per month for 30 months to buy a $450 washing machine, but she can hardly be blamed for preferring to buy the washer now "on time" to replace the old machine while she repays perhaps $18 per month (counting interest) for 30 months.

DETERMINING INTEREST-RATE LEVELS: SUPPLY AND DEMAND

An interest rate is a price—namely, the price of a loan of money. As with other prices, interest rates are set by the interacting forces of supply and demand. The supplies and demands that decide interest rates are supplies of, and demands for, money loans. Indeed, one of the leading theories of interest rates is known as the loanable funds doctrine.

Supplies of money for lending are furnished by various classes of savers. Individuals, business firms, and governmental bodies all save various amounts of money for different purposes. However, only individuals are net savers—that is, as a class, they save more than they borrow. Of course, most savings are actually loaned to their final borrowers through financial institutions, which are the so-called intermediaries (like banks, savings-and-loan associations, insurance companies, and so on) to which individuals commit their money for safekeeping plus interest. But the supply of loanable funds is also augmented by the money-creating activities of the banking system, as Chapter 5 will describe in detail. If the Federal Reserve System supplies new reserves to the commercial banks, the banks can make new loans equal to several times the dollar amount of the new reserves. The process, as you will see, creates new demand deposits (checkbook money) equal to the amount of the new loans. So the two sources of the supply of loans are (1) people's savings and (2) the money-and-credit-creating activities of the banking system.

What about the demand for loans as a factor in interest-rate determination? Individuals, business firms, and governmental bodies borrow large amounts of money. Individuals borrow to pay for houses, automobiles, appliances, travel ex-

FIGURE 3-1 Loanable-funds theory of interest.

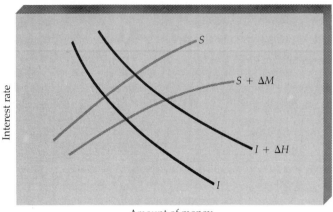

Amount of money

penses, education, and to meet various emergencies. Companies borrow to finance new buildings and equipment, to carry inventories, and to finance credit to customers. Governmental bodies borrow to meet deficits and to finance permanent improvements such as roads, schools, and sewer lines. All these demands constitute what might be called the *spending* demand for loans. But besides wanting to spend, people also borrow money to hold in reserve, against the proverbial rainy day or to take advantage of expected bargains. This type of demand for money loans is usually described as the *holding* demand. Thus, the total loan demand that affects interest rates is simply the sum of the economy's spending and holding demands.

Figure 3-1 portrays the theoretical operation of the loan market. First, look at the supply curves for loans, which slope upward to the right, showing that the supply of money available for loans rises as interest rates rise. Economists would call this supply "interest-elastic." We begin with the curve S, which shows (for each level of interest measured on the vertical axis at left) what volume of money savings will be offered in the loan market. But in addition to savings, loanable funds can also be created by pumping up the supply of currency and bank deposits. We label this added source of money ΔM and add it to the money available from savings. This gives the curve $S + \Delta M$, which represents the total supply of loanable funds. Since added money will bring down the interest rate, this new curve clearly belongs below the curve S.

Now consider the demand curves for loans. The basic demand curve I (for investing) shows the volume of loans people will demand at each level of interest for the purposes we already have broadly described as spending. But we have seen that, besides borrowing money to spend, people also borrow money to hold. This holding demand for loans is shown as an addition, ΔH, to the demand curve I. This gives you the total demand curve for loans, $I + \Delta H$. Since the additional holding demand for money will clearly raise interest rates, the curve $I + \Delta H$ is added above the demand curve.

BOX 3-1
"Old Bankers Never Die . . .   they just lose interest." That's the way a popular saying goes. But it's not really true. Few bankers, young or old, have ever lost much interest—or are likely to, if you think about it. That's because bankers are middlemen. They're not operating, to any extent at least, with their own money. The money they lend out they get from their depositors. So long as they make the "spread" between the rate they pay for money and the interest they charge their borrowers, they couldn't care less whether interest rates are high or low. And, to make sure they keep spreads in the right adjustment, bankers have increasingly restricted their loans to the floating-rate variety, under which the rate the customer pays automatically rises and falls with the banker's cost of funds.

This analysis gives reasons for the rise and fall of interest rates that agree with our common experience. Rates rise if people borrow more money to finance business or consumption needs or if people hold on to money more tightly in order to stay liquid. Rates also rise if people save less (spend a higher fraction of their incomes), or if a shortage of reserves keeps the banks from creating as much money as they did before. Conversely, interest rates fall if the economy's rate of investment declines, or if people are spending to reduce the size of their cash balances. Interest rates also fall if people's savings increase or if the banking system creates more money for lending. In short, interest is simply the price of a loan of money.

As with other prices, interest rates change across time. In fact, interest rates are among the most changeable of all prices. What accounts for these changes? Although both supply and demand forces are readily identifiable, two fundamental influences largely shape the behavior of interest rates. These influences are the business cycle and price-level changes—that is, inflation and deflation. Now let us look at each influence in some detail.

WHY INTEREST RATES CHANGE

Interest rates change for two reasons: changes in the demand for and supply of loanable funds over the business cycle and changes in expected inflation. We now examine each of these causes.

The Business Cycle and Interest

American business as a whole has long alternated between periods of expansion and contraction—that is, between prosperity and recession. This more-or-less regular movement upward and downward is called the business cycle. (It takes about four years for the average business cycle to complete a full swing from peak to valley and back to the peak again.)

Business cycles are a major influence on interest rates. Interest rates rise in times of prosperity and boom. They fall in times of recession and slack demand. It is not unusual for short-term interest rates, which are more volatile (changeable) than long-term rates, to double and triple between the bottom of a recession and the peak of the next boom. Although bond and mortgage interest rates do not swing this widely, rises of 50 percent and declines of 30 percent or more have not been uncommon.

What accounts for these cyclical swings in interest rates? Although supplies of money available for lending are considerably altered by changes in business conditions, the major factor pushing interest rates up or down over the business cycle is the *demand* for loans. As business activity increases, all kinds of borrowers flock to the loan market. Companies borrow to finance larger inventories, to carry more receivables, to expand their factories, and to buy more machinery. Consumers, expecting good times ahead, borrow to finance new houses, automobiles, appliances, and vacations. State and local governments borrow to finance the construction of schools, highways, streets, and housing projects. Thus, the demand for loans mushrooms.

As people's incomes rise and companies make larger profits, the supply of loanable money also increases. However, the supply of loanable money does not increase in nearly the same proportion that the demand for it does. Moreover, most business expansions soon become inflationary, and the Federal Reserve begins cutting back on the availability of bank reserves and bank credit. This also serves to brake the increase in loanable funds. Consequently, the demand for loans outraces the supply. Because of this, interest rates behave just as any other price does when demand increases relative to supply—they rise, thus pricing some bidders out of the market.

When business activity decreases, just the opposite happens. Consumers, business people, and state and local governments (though not usually the federal government) now become pessimistic and cut back on their borrowing. During a recession, though, the demand for loans falls much faster than the supply does. People still save money, and the Federal Reserve aggressively expands bank reserves to restart the stalled economy. Soon, then, the amount of money looking for interest-paying outlets is more than the demand for loans. Savers and investors with money begin bidding against each other for the available supply of bonds, bills, and other debt securities. Banks, savings-and-loan associations, and other savings institutions find that, to attract deposits, they don't have to pay as much interest as before. Thus, interest rates drop. Until business expansion starts up again, interest rates usually remain quite low compared to their levels in the preceding prosperity.

Obviously, a recession is a good time for those who are farsighted to borrow against what they think their needs will be for the next boom period. Conversely, if you fail to anticipate your money needs and thus postpone your borrowing until the top of the next business boom, then you will be in some trouble. You will certainly have to pay a much higher interest rate in order to borrow. And if bond or money markets become very tight or if your bank becomes hard-pressed for funds, then you may not be able to borrow at *any* interest rate. Thus, a knowledge of how interest rates behave across the business cycle is indispensable to the financial manager or to the successful head of any company, large or small.

Expected Inflation and Interest Rates

The other dominant influence on interest rates is inflation. *Inflation* is a decline in the purchasing power of money measured by an increase in the average price level. You must realize that what is fundamentally loaned and borrowed is not just money, it is purchasing power—the ability to buy goods and services or to command economic resources. For this reason people who loan or borrow money need to look carefully into their transactions to see what is happening to the purchasing power that is lent and repaid. If they do so, they quickly perceive that there are two kinds of interest rates:

1. *Money* (or *nominal*) *rates,* which are ratios of dollars repaid to dollars borrowed.
2. *Real* (or *deflated*) *rates,* which are ratios of buying power borrowed and repaid.

One who fails to distinguish between these two kinds of interest is a victim of *money illusion.*

What effect will inflation have on interest rates? Consider the answer to this question from a lender's perspective. If inflation is expected, a lender will want to receive more cash than it lends not only to be compensated for being thrifty, but also to preserve the purchasing power of the dollars loaned. In other words the lender will increase the money interest rate to reflect anticipated inflation. Irving Fisher, an economist who wrote a great deal about inflation, developed an equation that relates the money rate of interest to the real rate. The Fisher Equation is

$$(1 + i_M) = (1 + i_R)(1 + \Delta P)$$

where

$$i_M = \text{money rate of interest}$$
$$i_R = \text{real rate of interest}$$
$$\Delta P = \text{expected change in the price level (inflation)}$$

We can rearrange the terms in the equation to emphasize the money interest rate:

$$i_M = i_R + \Delta P + (i_R \times \Delta P)$$

The Fisher Equation tells us that the nominal or money rate of interest is equal to the real or deflated interest rate plus an adjustment for expected inflation.

Example. You are going to lend $300 to a friend for one year. If you want a 9 percent real return and you expect inflation to be 8 percent, the interest rate that you charge must be 17.72 percent, calculated with the Fisher Equation:

$$i_M = 0.09 + 0.08 + (0.09 \times 0.08) = 0.1772 \quad \text{or} \quad 17.72\%$$

Practice. Calculate the money rate of interest that you will charge on a loan if you want a 6 percent real return and you expect inflation to be 8 percent. Answer: 14.48 percent. Now, show how you found this answer.

Rearranging the Fisher Equation again gives us the real rate of interest related to the money rate and expected inflation:

$$i_R = \frac{(i_M - \Delta P)}{(1 + \Delta P)}$$

Practice. What real interest rate will a lender receive (and borrower pay) if an amount is loaned at a 12 percent money rate and inflation is 7 percent? Answer: 4.67 percent. Make sure that you know how this answer is found before you continue to the next section.

The Fisher Equation is useful in explaining the way that interest rates perform in our economy. In fact, there is every indication that interest rates adjust to expected changes in the price level with little delay. As a matter of fact, one of the most dependable relations among economic statistics is the close correlation over the past century between the trend of the general price level and the long-term direction of interest rates.

FIGURE 3-2 Secular movement of bond yields and consumer prices in the United States, 1865–1983.

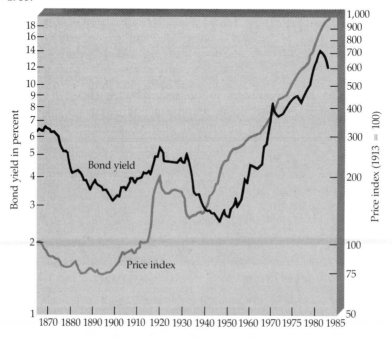

Figure 3-2 depicts the joint movement of bond yields (long-term interest rates) and the price level since 1865. From 1865 to 1896, prices declined secularly—or in very long-term, cycle-to-cycle movements. Bond yields, despite ups and downs over several business cycles, also trended lower until they reached about $3\frac{1}{2}$ percent in 1899. Then, at the turn of the century, as prices turned up, so also did interest rates, with bond yields reaching a peak of about 6 percent in 1920. After World War I prices turned downward and did not begin rising strongly again until 1946. In this interim bond yields fell to their lowest level in history—less than $2\frac{1}{2}$ per cent in 1946. Inflation and rising prices have continued since World War II, and they began to accelerate in the late 1960s. During this same period, bond yields have risen almost continuously, reaching levels above 9 percent in 1974–1975, 13 percent in 1980, and 15 percent in 1981.

This record suggests that, after a while at least, lenders demand compensation for being repaid in the depreciated money. It also demonstrates the folly of inflating the money supply in an effort to keep interest rates low because in the long run this maneuver actually runs the interest rates up. At first, additional money may supply banks and others with further loanable funds, and, for a while, lenders may cut their interest rates. But, as the new money gets into circulation, it leads to full employment, or at least to wage-push tactics by labor unions and to rising expenditures by business people. Prices start increasing faster than before. Lenders then increase their interest charges in order to avoid losses from repayment in debased money.[1]

Long experience suggests that lenders basically demand a real 3 percent return on the *buying power* they lend. If the price level were always steady, then interest rates would fluctuate around a 3 percent average. But since price levels are generally expected to rise, lenders seek compensation for their resulting loss of purchasing power. They seek it by adding an extra charge—equal to the expected inflation rate—on to their basic 3 percent requirement. This behavior, which affects long-term interest rates more noticeably than it affects short-term ones, is called the rule of "3 percent plus."

What this rule says, in effect, is that *real rates* of interest tend to stay around 3 percent. The money rate fluctuates above this level, and possibly below it, depending on the expected rate of inflation or deflation. The higher the expected rate of inflation, the higher—on the average—interest rates will be.

LONG-TERM VERSUS SHORT-TERM RATES

We have already noted that short-term interest rates swing much more widely than long-term rates. The contrast is often great. In the 1980–1982 period, which included two recessions and a business recovery, three-month commercial-paper rates (one

[1] In fact, the run up in interest rates may begin as soon as savers and investors see the Federal Reserve stepping up the growth of the money supply. The rational expectations hypothesis, a recent economic theory, contends that this is exactly what happens once experience teaches people what to expect when the Fed prints money. Knowing what is ahead, lenders respond in a way suggested by the Fisher Equation: They step up their charges at once to compensate for the loss of buying power they see coming on their loans.

BOX 3-2

Best of Both Worlds?   Bond holders suffer when the cost of living accelerates and
their interest receipts stay fixed because their ability to buy
goods and services declines along with the purchasing power of their fixed return. Is
there any way out of this trap? For the holders of $25 million worth of Sunshine
Mining bonds issued in April 1980, maybe yes. These bonds pay $8\frac{1}{2}$ percent annual
interest, which should be adequate if inflation subsides. But if it doesn't, bondhold-
ers have another protection: When the bonds mature in 1995, holders have their
choice of either getting back the $1,000 they paid for the bonds or 50 ounces of silver
(the company's principal product). So if a runaway cost of living pushes the price of
silver above $20 an ounce, inflation protection comes into action for these two-way-
protected investors. Best of both worlds? Maybe so.

---

measure of short-term interest) went as low as 8 percent and as high as 18 percent.
The corresponding long-term rate—the yield on highest-grade corporate bonds—
swung only between $10\frac{1}{2}$ and $15\frac{1}{2}$ percent.

Short-Term Rates Have Greater Volatility

Why are short-term rates so much more volatile than long-term rates? There are at
least four reasons.

1. **Inventory financing**   Much short-term borrowing is done to finance inventories,
which are the widest-swinging investments that companies make.
2. **Federal Reserve actions**   Federal Reserve open-market operations to control the
money supply take place in the money market, actions causing short-term rates to
swing widely when Federal Reserve objectives change.
3. **Participant indifference**   Lenders and borrowers are less concerned about what
rates they will receive and pay on a loan for a few months than they would be if the
loan were for 20 or 30 years. Much short-term lending is really just a way of putting
one's money on ice at whatever interest rate available while waiting for a better
opportunity to make a long-term investment.
4. **Expectations**   Financial theory suggests that long-term rates are an average of expected short-term rates, and an average is more stable than the numbers are that
compose it. This last point demands further explanation.

The Role of Expectations

The expectation theory of interest rates states that long-term rates are an average of
expected short-term rates.

Example. Suppose that you have some money to invest and you expect the following
interest rates to prevail during each of the next four years: 4 percent the first year, 8
percent the second year, 12 percent the third year, and 8 percent in the fourth year.

TABLE 3-1 Expected Short-Term Rates and Long-Term Yields

Time Period 1		Time Period 2	
Year	Expected Rate (%)	Year	Expected Rate (%)
1	4	2	8
2	8	3	12
3	12	4	8
4	8	5	6
Average	8	Average	$8\frac{1}{2}$

What would be the average rate? The first two columns of Table 3-1 show the answer, 8 percent. Now suppose that you will make a single investment that runs for the entire four years. What would be the logical required return? Eight percent. At that rate you would be indifferent whether to make one four-year loan or four one-year loans of equal risk.

Practice. Now suppose that the first year ends. A fifth year comes into view. The one-year rate expected for this fifth year is 6 percent. How much will this percentage change the interest rate on a four-year loan one year from now? Answer: $8\frac{1}{2}$ percent. The two right-hand columns of Table 3-1 show how this answer is found.

How much have the rates on one-year and four-year loans changed between year 1 and year 2 ? Table 3-1 shows us that one-year rates have doubled from 4 to 8 percent. By contrast, four-year rates have risen from 8 to $8\frac{1}{2}$ percent—an increase of $(.085 - .08)/.08 - 1 = 6.25$ percent. This illustration emphasizes why interest rates on long-term securities are less volatile than rates on three- or six-month commercial paper: Bond prices and yields reflect not only the interest rates of the month or year at hand, but also the average interest rate expected for many years to come.

Practice. Suppose that expected annual interest rates are as follows:

Year	Rate
1	12%
2	14%
3	12%
4	10%

Calculate the yield on a four-year loan of equal risk. Answer: 12 percent. Make sure that you know how this answer is found before continuing to the next section.

The role of expectations is important in explaining not only the volatility of interest rates but also the relation between short- and long-term rates. This relation is called the yield curve, which we discuss below.

Interest-Rate Risks for Investors

We must note one other reason for the greater stability of long-term interest rates. This reason has to do with the effects of interest-rate changes on the prices of debt securities having different life spans. If the time to maturity is very short, then even a large change in interest rates will not affect the price of a security very much. On the other hand, if the time to maturity is very long, then even a small change in interest rates will affect a security's price quite drastically.

First, let us consider the impact of a two-percentage point interest-rate increase on a security that will pay $1,000 one year from now, a one-year note (*note* means IOU). The price will decline by $17.47 calculated with the present value equation from Chapter 2,

Present value before change:
$$\$1,000/(1 + 0.06)^1 \qquad\qquad \$943.39$$
Less present value after change:
$$\$1,000/(1 + 0.08)^1 \qquad\qquad \underline{925.92}$$
$$\$\ 17.47$$

By contrast, consider what happens to a $1,000 face value 10-year maturity bond that has a 6 percent coupon yield. When interest rates on bonds with similar risk rise to 8 percent, its price declines by $136.30 calculated in the following way:

Present value before change:
$$PV = \$30(14.877) + \$1,000(0.554) \qquad \$1,000.00$$
Present value after change:
$$PV = \$30(13.590) + \$1,000(0.456) \qquad \underline{863.70}$$
$$\$\ 136.30$$

Practice. Why did the bond calculations above use $30 and 20 periods rather than $60 and 10 periods? If you cannot answer this question, then turn back to page 38 and review the material there.

It takes only minor changes in interest levels to produce large changes in the price of long-term debt obligations. However, *very short-term* debt obligations can take very large changes in interest rates with relatively little effect on their prices. Short-term interest rates swing more widely than long-term rates because it takes much larger changes in interest rates to affect short-term security prices—that is, to stimulate or deter short-term lending and borrowing. On the other hand, relatively slight changes in long-term interest rates will decisively influence both long-term security prices and the incentives of long-term borrowers and lenders.

We should also note that the greater interest-rate sensitivity of long-term debt securities is important to investors. An investor's risk is much greater with a 20-year bond than it is with a one-year note. *Risk* is the likelihood that an actual return or amount will differ from its expected value. The risk here is called interest-rate risk because the actual value of a capital (income producing) asset may differ from what the investor expects as interest rates change. On a one-year note the price effect of

BOX 3-3
A Technical Note About Interest-Rate
Risk   This chapter discusses interest-rate risk and the way that it differs according to the maturity of the capital asset that we are considering—the greater the maturity, the greater will be the interest-rate risk. Financial experts quantify interest-rate risk in two ways, one way with interest elasticity and the other with duration. We shall consider each of these.

Interest Elasticity. Interest elasticity quantifies the change in the present value of an asset relative to a proportional change in the interest rate. We measure interest elasticity by the percentage change (not percentage point change) in the present value of the asset (or liability, if appropriate) divided by the percentage change (not percentage point change) in the interest rate. The result is the approximate percentage change in the present value that occurs with a one percent change in the interest rate.

For example, the interest elasticity of the one-year note at 6 percent interest on page 54 is 0.0185/0.333 = 0.05556 so that for every one percent change in the interest rate the present value of the note changes in the opposite direction by approximately 0.05556 percent. The interest elasticity of the 10-year, 6 percent coupon bond is 0.1363/0.333 = 0.4089.

Duration. Duration is a number expressed in units of time that ranks the interest sensitivity of capital assets: It is the average deferred time of the cash flows. We calculate duration by weighting a cash-flow's present value by the time period in which it occurs, beginning with one for the first cash flow and increasing to N for the final one, then dividing this weighted present value by the market value of the capital asset.* As the duration of an asset increases, its interest elasticity and interest-rate risk will increase. If a capital asset returns only one cash flow or single amount (like the note on page 54) then duration is the same as maturity. For a capital asset with more than one cash flow (like the 10-year, 6 percent coupon bond on page 54) duration is less than maturity.

Financial managers use interest elasticity and duration to help estimate the impact of interest-rate changes on their investments and financial sources.

* The equation for duration is

$$D = \sum_{t=1}^{n} \frac{C_t T/(1 + i)^t}{M}$$

where

C_t = each period t's cash flow
T = number of the specific period
i = interest rate
M = market value of the capital asset

A readable and informative source on this topic is G. J. Santoni, "Interest Rate Risk and the Stock Prices of Financial Institutions," Federal Reserve Bank Of St. Louis *Review*, August/September 1984, pp. 12–20.

an interest-rate rise is minimal because the investor will receive the principal in a year and will then be able to invest at the new, higher interest rate. On a 10-year bond the effect is great because the investor must incur the opportunity cost of losing the higher interest for 10 years.

Of course, the opposite is true, too. If interest rates fall, then an investor will make a large capital gain as the price of the 10-year bond rises, but only a small capital gain on the price increase of the one-year note.

The preceding discussion points out an important principle for anyone making financial decisions: If you expect interest rates to rise, then you can play safe by selling your long-term securities and investing the money in very short-dated ones. On the other hand, if you expect interest rates to fall, then you should buy the longest-term securities available, because in that way you would maximize your capital gains. Professional investors make these shifts promptly whenever they expect interest rates to change direction.

INTEREST-RATE STRUCTURES

Up to this point, we have treated interest rates largely in the abstract. We have discussed long-term rates and short-term rates, conveniently overlooking the fact that there are interest rates of almost every conceivable maturity, as well as interest rates on loans to many different kinds (and calibers) of borrowers. Now we can turn to the real world and deal with the larger constellation of interest rates that actually exists. To classify actual interest rates most conveniently, we must look at the interest-rate structures. *Structure* means rates ordered according to some organizing principle such as time, place, or risk. Four important and illuminating structures are: (1) term, or time-to-maturity structure, (2) risk, or quality structure, (3) geographical structure, and (4) taxability structure.

Term Structure

A *term structure*, Figure 3-3, depicts interest rates as a function of time to maturity. To hold other factors the same (or "to maintain *ceteris paribus*," as economists say), all securities shown in a term structure must be of the same quality. Most term-structure studies use U.S. Treasury securities. Time to maturity is plotted along the horizontal axis. The vertical axis portrays interest rates (security yields).

Normally, in the past generation at least, the term structure (sometimes called the yield-to-maturity curve) has sloped upward from left to right, as does the curve depicting the December 1983 term structure in Figure 3-3. This is because, as we have already noted, if interest rates should rise, then long-dated securities would incur the largest loss in market price. So, as a premium for greater risk,[2] holders of

---

[2] Strictly speaking, *uncertainty* is the proper term here. Risk, accurately used, denotes a situation in which the various possible outcomes follow a known probability distribution. The probabilities of the different possible results of an investment are never known and can rarely be accurately estimated. However, the term *risk* is generally applied to the hazards of investment, and to avoid confusion, the authors defer to customary usage.

FIGURE 3-3   Term structure of interest rates on Treasury securities (different dates).

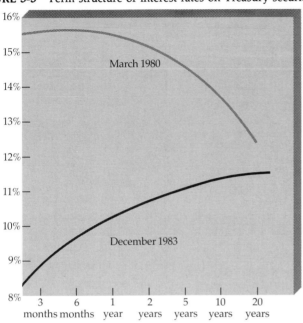

more distant maturities demand higher rates of interest than holders of short-term paper do. This is in agreement with the *liquidity-preference theory* of interest rates: Individuals prefer liquidity to illiquidity. A gracefully upsloping yield curve is typical of times when business activity is normal, as in late 1983.

On the other hand, the yield curve for March 1980 (Figure 3-3) is inverted—that is, short-term rates are actually higher than long-term rates. Why? This is because an interlude of boom and inflation had reached its peak, and three conditions were present: (1) money was tight, (2) all interest rates were very high, and (3) a fall in all interest rates was expected soon. Under these conditions short-term rates were above long-term ones for two reasons. First, borrowers preferred to bridge the period of high long-term rates with short-term loans, and they were willing to pay very high rates for short-term money. In other words, it is better to pay 15 percent at short term for a year and then sell bonds at 10 percent than to be saddled with 12 percent for 10 years.[3] Second, lenders had analogous incentives. Lending money at long term, they salted it away at a good return for many years. They could also expect large capital gains if interest rates fell and bond prices rose. Lending at short term, they might get a high rate for a brief time, but then when interest rates fell and

---

[3] When bond yields are very high, buyers typically insist that new issues be made noncallable for at least 10 years. This restricts an issuer's freedom to refinance debt at lower cost if interest rates subsequently decline. We discuss callable bonds along with quality ratings in Chapter 18.

TABLE 3-2   Quality Structure of Corporate-Bond Yields, Two Recent Dates

Bond-Quality Rating	Yield to Maturity (%)	
	January 1973	December 1974
High-grade	7.15	8.89
Medium-grade	7.90	10.55
Spread: medium-grade minus high-grade	0.75	1.66

SOURCE: *Adapted from* Federal Reserve Bulletins.

they were repaid, they would have to relend at a much lower rate. Under these circumstances, only very high rates would persuade lenders to lend at short term.

Quality Structure

Quality structure means bonds arrayed or ordered in terms of their estimated reliability. Quality structure reflects *default risk,* indicating that an actual return from a bond may differ from the expected return because the issuer may default, that is, fail to pay interest and principal. As you might expect, bond yields always rank in inverse order to their quality. Highest-grade bonds yield least, lowest-grade, most. This ranking conforms with the fact that, wherever possible, investors charge a risk premium in terms of extra interest when a risk is ascertainable.

However, the size of the risk premium on different bond qualities varies widely, depending on how much confidence investors have in economic and credit conditions. Sometimes, a so-called bad bond looks almost as good as a good one. This is likely to be true in boom times, when all companies look prosperous and when people are little concerned about a depression. This explains the very small gap between medium- and high-grade bond yields in January 1973, a time of headlong boom. With only 0.75 percentage points of difference between high- and medium-grade bonds, it is evident that investors were not much worried about quality risks.

Now look at the yield spread for December 1974 in Table 3-2. The yield gap between high- and medium-grade bonds has more than doubled. Why? The Franklin National Bank and other business failures during the preceding spring and summer had shaken investors to their boot-tops. Suddenly they realized that there really was a difference between "gilt-edge" bonds and speculative ones. Money then "rushed for cover": investors dumped doubtful bonds or refused to buy them. The prices of these bonds fell and their yields rose momentously. High-grade bonds were virtually unaffected by the spreading fears because these bonds represented companies with sound financial structures that were earning their interest requirements by comfortably wide margins.[4]

---

[4] All bond yields had risen since January 1973 because of inflation and tight money, but high-grade yields had risen only 1.74 percentage points, as against 2.65 points for medium-grade yields.

Geographical Structure

The *geographical structure* of interest rates in the United States reveals the following rule: interest rates rise from Northeast to Southwest—that is, moving from Maine to Southern California. This is in part because the older (northeastern) regions generate, on the average, a larger volume of savings than they can utilize. The Sunbelt of the southern and western regions, which is growing more rapidly, generates an excess demand for capital. The magnet of rising interest rates gives money an incentive to move across country—from where it is in surplus to where it is lacking.

Taxability Structure

The *taxability structure* views interest rates on different securities in light of the extent to which returns are subject to federal income tax. The main division here is between tax-exempt (state and municipal) bonds and all other bonds, which are referred to as taxables. Quality for quality, tax-exempt securities almost always carry lower yields than taxables because we need a higher yield on a taxable security to get the same after-tax return as we could get from a tax-exempt security.[5]

PATTERNS OF INTEREST-RATE CHANGES

Like other economic time series, interest rates have three well-defined patterns. The first—the short-period variation—is unimportant, due to small shifts of the daily balance of supply and demand in the loan market. The other two—cyclical and secular movements—are extremely important to business managers.

Cyclical Movement

On the whole, interest rates move in concert with the cycle of general business activity. They rise as business expands, and they fall as it contracts. All interest rates, long and short, typically reach their peak for the cycle at about the top of a business boom, when money is very tight and many people are trying to borrow it. They reach their bottom at approximately the low point of the recession. At that point, loans of the boom period have largely been paid off, hardly anyone is borrowing money to expand inventories or plant, and idle money is accumulating and "looking for some place to go."

Secular Movement

Much less recognized by most business people (preoccupied, as they must be, with what is going to happen tomorrow or next week) is the secular, or cycle-to-cycle, movement of interest rates. Such long-term trends, which carry the general level of interest rates significantly higher or lower over a series of business cycles, have already been noted and are depicted in Figure 3-2. Since secular movements in interest rates invariably seem to last for two decades or longer, it is worthwhile to examine what causes them.

[5] Calculations for taxable versus tax-exempt returns on bonds are found in Chapter 18.

We have already noted that secular trends are closely correlated with price-level shifts—that is, with changes in the purchasing power of money. This association, however, does not prove that inflation and deflation are always, or necessarily, the causes of these long swings in interest rates. Some economists think that inflation and rising interest rates (or deflation and falling ones) are not so much cause and effect as products of a common cause. Not surprisingly, the common cause is usually a combination of productivity and time preference. Consider the following analysis.

Interest rates fell during the 1920s and 1930s at least partly because of a growing lack of productive outlets for capital and savings. Population increases were slow, few revolutionary new inventions appeared, and world trade was disorganized in the backwash of World War I. By contrast, the persistent rise in interest rates from 1946 to about 1970 was spurred by a sharp rise in productivity; snowballing demands for capital arose from rapid population growth, the spread of television, computers and other innovations, a strong revival of world trade, and a massive rebuilding of cities and factories destroyed by World War II. Since 1970 time preference has largely dominated the further rise of interest rates. A "now" generation has increasingly demanded the "good life" immediately and without the waiting required in the past. Consumers, governments, and businesses all have insisted on spending more than they were willing to save. To satisfy these demands, the banking system has created ever-growing volumes of credit. The resulting inflation of money supply has permitted spending to rise, even when goods and services could not be created to match it, and prices have climbed faster and faster. To protect their buying power, savers and lenders have required steadily increasing rates of interest.

FORECASTING INTEREST-RATE MOVEMENTS

Interest rates are a cost to borrowers, a source of income to savers, and a regulator of debt-security prices. Thus, their shifts are important, eagerly watched, and widely forecast. How are interest rates forecast? In the short run there are two main methods.

Sources and Uses of Funds

Loanable-funds theory indicates that interest rates are set by the interaction of supplies of, and demands for, money loans. Thus, one way to forecast interest rates is simply to tabulate and total all the supplies of, and demands for, money loans in prospect for the year ahead. Supplies of money are called sources, demands are called uses, and the result is a table like Table 3-3, which shows expected sources and uses of funds for 1984.

Of course, total sources must always equal total uses. How, then, can such a table predict the level of interest rates? The answer is that the finished table does not predict rates. Rather, the prediction is made in getting the table to balance. In drawing up such a table, you begin by listing all the different sources and uses you foresee for the coming year. Then you total them. If projected sources (supplies) are bigger than projected uses (demands), you can expect interest rates to fall from their present level. If uses exceed sources, then you can expect rates to rise. How much

TABLE 3–3   Expected Sources and Uses of Funds by Economic Sectors, United States, 1984

Item	Billions of Dollars
Sources	
Thrift institutions (savings-and-loan associations, mutual-savings banks, etc.)	104.0
Insurance companies and pension funds	128.8
Investment companies	36.0
Commercial banks	144.6
Other financial institutions	20.4
Business corporations	11.5
State and local governments	7.7
Foreigners	18.1
Individuals and others	72.3
Total funds supplied	543.4
Uses	
Mortgages	83.1
Corporate and foreign bonds	24.6
Short-term business loans	64.6
Other short-term loans	70.5
U.S. government debt	256.7
State and local government debt	43.9
Total funds demanded	543.4

SOURCE: Salomon Brothers.

TABLE 3–4   Assumed Worksheet for Deriving Table 3-2 and 1984 Interest-Rate Forecast

Item	Billions of Dollars	
Sources (expected before adjustment)		
Thrift institutions	104.0	~~100.0~~
Insurance companies and pension funds	128.8	~~126.5~~
Investment companies	36.0	~~35.0~~
Commercial banks	144.6	~~135.6~~
Other financial institutions	20.4	~~11.0~~
Business corporations	11.5	~~11.8~~
State and local governments	7.7	~~7.5~~
Foreigners	18.1	~~16.7~~
Individuals and others	72.3	~~66.0~~
Total funds foreseen	543.4	~~520.1~~
Uses (expected before adjustment)		
Mortgages	83.1	~~90.0~~
Corporate and foreign bonds	24.6	~~25.5~~
Short-term business loans	64.6	~~67.0~~
Other short-term loans	70.5	~~75.0~~
U.S. government debt	256.7	~~256.7~~
State and local government debt	43.9	~~45.0~~
Total funds sought	543.4	~~560.0~~
Excess of uses over sources	0	~~39.9~~

BOX 3-4

"When Henry Speaks . . .   Wall Street listens." They're talking about Dr. Henry
                                    Kaufman, partner in the New York brokerage firm of Sa-
lomon Brothers and undoubtedly the nation's most listened to interest-rate prophet.
Dr. Kaufman isn't always right, but he boasts an impressive track record. His announcement in August, 1982, that he had changed his mind—that interest rates
would go down instead of up—touched off 1982–1983's 60 percent surge in stock
prices. His forecast in January 1984, that interest rates were headed up helped tumble the stock market to its biggest loss in two years. Then, in July 1984, he forecast
that interest rates would continue their rise, dragging down bond prices with them.
But interest rates failed to rise in 1984, prompting one observer of Kaufman forecasts to comment:

> . . . His continuous ability to influence securities is a bit of a puzzle. For it's true
> that he's never in doubt. But it's equally true that he's not always right. Indeed, it
> speaks well for his even-handedness that in recent years, he's been wrong about
> the direction of interest rates as often as he's been right.

As this chapter and the previous one have shown, interest rates are important
in many ways to many people—as costs to companies and consumers and, when you
invert them, as the prices of bonds and other debt securities. So the public's always
looking for "word from the horse's mouth" on what interest rates are going to do.
Dr. Kaufman may not neigh or whinny, but when he talks, stocks and bonds get
chills or fever.

Source: Based in part on Alan Abelson, "Up and Down Wall Street," *Barron's,* October 29, 1984,
p. 47, and on a note in *The Wall Street Journal,* December 13, 1984, p. 31.

---

will rates rise or fall? It depends on how hard sources or uses—whichever is bigger—
have to be squeezed to make one fit the other. You do this by reducing individual
items in your list to smaller size. Table 3-4 suggests how Table 3-2 might have been
trimmed to make these items fit.

A rule of thumb to follow in using such a table to forecast interest rates is to
concentrate on the amounts supplied by foreigners and individuals and others. The
greater these amounts must be, the higher interest rates must be in order to attract
their savings.

Obviously, the trimming and fitting are a matter of judgment. The fact that an
interest-rate forecast is supported by an impressive-looking table of figures does not
keep it from being anything but "quantified guesswork." This is what most forecasts
actually are.

Real Rate and Add-On

Some observers of historical interest trends (especially those who subscribe to the
Fisher Equation) are convinced that real rates of interest do not change very much.

The real rate on bonds, for example, in recent years has remained around 3 percent. The rest of the *money rate* of interest consists of an add-on for expected change in the price level. (Note that we are discussing *expected* price-level change, not the change that actually takes place.) Thus, in the early 1960s, when price increases were expected to (and actually did) average only about $1\frac{1}{4}$ percent per year, high-grade corporate bond yields remained around $4\frac{1}{4}$ percent. In 1969–1970, when price increases leaped to $5\frac{1}{2}$ percent per year, high-grade corporate yields rose to $8\frac{1}{2}$ percent. In both instances the yield was about 3 percent plus the expected rate of increase in prices. In 1974–1975, and again in 1979–1980, amid double-digit inflation, high-grade corporate bond yields failed to reflect fully the arithmetic of "3 percent plus," apparently because bond buyers believed that the ongoing surge in the price level was temporary. By contrast, in 1983–1984 bond yields overshot the "3 percent plus" level because investors feared that the decline in inflation would not last; so the inflation premiums they demanded ran as much as 7 or 8 percentage points over the ongoing inflation rate to reflect the *expected* inflation rate.

Long and Short Rates: Cyclical Divergence

In forecasting interest-rate structures, of course, you must remember that short-term interest rates fluctuate a great deal more than long-term rates do. Whether short rates are above or below long rates, and by how much, depends on the kind of business activity you predict. We have seen that, in an inflationary boom, short rates may well be higher than long rates. In recessions, they may be far below long rates. The best answer to where short rates are going in the year ahead seems to lie in answering this sequence of questions: (1) How much will long rates move up or down next year? (2) What level are short rates starting from as of now? (3) How strongly can business be expected to improve or decline? (4) How much can price inflation be expected to accelerate or slow down? The more the answers to these questions suggest a vigorous economy, the more you are entitled to lift your forecast of short rates.

SUMMARY

1. People will pay interest because money loans can be used to make money (*productivity*) and because present money commands a premium over future money (*time preference*).

2. Interest rates are the prices of money loans. Like other prices, they are set by supply and demand. The *loanable-funds* theory shows that money supplies come from savings plus new money created in the banking system; the demand is for money to spend and for money to hold for future use.

3. Interest rates change across time in two major ways. Rates rise *cyclically* with business expansions and fall cyclically during recessions. The basic force is the alternating rise and fall in loan demand. Rates rise *secularly* with long-term inflation of the general price level, decline secularly if the cost of living experiences a prolonged decline. The effort of lenders to maintain the buying power of their money is the key factor here, with interest rates tending toward a level equal to *3 percent plus* the rate of change in prices.

4. Interest-rate changes also affect investment values. How greatly they affect them depends on the time span of the investments. Short-term investments are little affected by fluctuating interest rates. By contrast, a one or two percentage-point rise in rates may shrink the price of a long-term bond dramatically, while an equivalent decline in rates may cause its price to soar. (These effects are explained by the compound-interest calculations studied in Chapter 2.) When investors expect rates to rise, they sell bonds and buy short-dated securities; an expected fall in interest prompts them to reverse these moves.

5. Two interest-rate structures are of major importance. The *term structure,* which plots interest rates against their time to maturity, has great value in forecasting business conditions. Short-term rates below long-term ones signal prosperity ahead. When short-term rates exceed longer ones, prospects are for recession. The *quality structure,* which plots rates against default risk of the underlying loans, is also sensitive to business conditions. As recession fears increase, investors raise the premiums they charge for making risky loans instead of safe ones.

6. Interest rate forecasts proceed by two main methods. One is to add up prospective supplies of, and demands for, loanable funds, then figure what change in interest rates is required to bring the totals into equality. The other is to add the expected inflation rate to a "real" rate of 3 percent.

KEY TERMS AND CONCEPTS

Productivity	Term structure of interest rates
Time preference	Default risk
Money (nominal) rate of interest	Cyclical movement
Deflated (real) rate of interest	Secular movement
Fisher Equation	Sources and uses of funds
Rule of "3 percent plus"	Real rate and add-on
Interest-rate risk	

QUESTIONS

3-1. Why *can* a business borrower pay interest? Why *will* a consumer?

3-2. Do loanable funds come only from savings? Is money borrowed only to spend? Explain.

3-3. Why is it correct to say that the demand for funds, rather than the supply, dominates cyclical swings in interest rates?

3-4. Why do alert businessmen not wait until business is booming to arrange for their borrowing?

3-5. Distinguish between real and monetary rates of interest. Which would you prefer to have guaranteed if you were a lender? A borrower? Always?

3-6. Explain the rule of "3 percent plus." Does it always work? Why might it not work?

3-7. Explain what is going on in the economy when the term structure of interest rates is (1) sloping steeply upward and (2) sloping downward?

3-8. Which of these swings more widely over the business cycle: long-term interest rates or short-term rates? Are price changes on long- and short-term debt securities of similar size? Why or why not?

3-9. What is meant by the secular trend of interest rates? Why is it important to lenders? To borrowers?

3-10. Name and briefly describe the two main methods of interest-rate forecasting.

PROBLEMS

3-1. If a lender collects $7\frac{1}{2}$ percent interest, pays income tax at a 40 percent rate, and experiences a 3 percent rise in his cost of living, what is his real rate of return?

3-2. Suppose you are a lender paying income tax at 50 percent. You want a real return of 3 percent after income tax, and prices are rising 8 percent per year. What nominal rate must you charge?

3-3. In 1983 U.S. Treasury bonds yielded an average return of about 11.4 percent. According to the rule of "3 percent plus," what average rate of price inflation did investors in these bonds seem to expect in the future?

3-4. If the interest rate on a one-year loan is 6 percent and on a two-year loan is 7 percent, what rate would lenders and borrower appear to expect during the second year?

3-5. Suppose you hold a very long-maturity bond that pays you 4 percent per year on a par value of $1,000 (the price you paid for it). If the yield to maturity on that bond rises to 8 percent, how much do you lose? Treat the bond as a perpetuity, as discussed in Chapter 2.

3-6. Imagine that you hold a three-month Treasury bill bought at a 4 percent *annual* rate of discount from its $1,000 maturity price. If the rate of discount suddenly rises to 8 percent, how much do you lose?

3-7. From your answers to problems 5 and 6, calculate the percentage losses suffered from the doubling of interest rates on the bond and bill. Is there a lesson here for what investors should do when they expect interest rates to rise?

TWO

MONEY
AND
THE ECONOMY

Part 2 examines the role of money in our society—what it is, what it does, how it is created, and the role that it plays in determining economic behavior. Chapter 4 addresses what may be an obvious issue by explaining what money is and does. This chapter shows in a theoretical and practical setting the way that money affects individual and aggregate economic behavior. Chapter 5 presents a description of the way money is created and loaned by commercial banks lending their excess reserves. The discussion will indicate the potential power that our Federal Reserve System has on our economic behavior because the Federal Reserve can cause large changes in the money supply by changing the amount of excess reserves in the banking system. Chapter 6 examines the way that monetary and fiscal policies are implemented to control economic activity. This chapter will show you that the potential power that the Federal Reserve System has for controlling economic activity is often implemented in concert with fiscal policy in the hope of maintaining income, output, and employment at a high noninflationary level.

CHAPTER 4

What Money Is and Does

Money is whatever is generally accepted in exchange for goods and services or in payment of debts. By general agreement, money consists of currency plus deposits in financial institutions on which depositors may write checks.

First, you are introduced in turn to money's four functions as (1) a medium of exchange, (2) standard of value, (3) store of value, and (4) a way to measure debt. Connected with these four functions are several other key concepts important to your further study of finance: near-money, liquidity, credit, and velocity. It will pay you to study each of these notions carefully and to memorize their definitions before reading on.

Knowledge of what money is will prepare you to understand later sections describing what money does. Centerpiece of your study will be the Equation of

Exchange, which you will meet in two versions. First, you will examine the Fisher version, which states that money has two dimensions—quantity and velocity. Multiplied together, they produce the national income expressed in current dollars, itself the product of the nation's output of goods and services times the price level. A recognition of these relations paves your way for a realistic insight into inflation and its consequences.

The second form in which you will meet the Equation of Exchange consists of its Cambridge, or Cash Balances, version. Here you will examine what economists call people's demand for money, actually their desire to hold money instead of some interest-bearing asset. You will look at people's three main motives for holding cash and at how they regulate spending by comparing their actual cash balances with their desired cash balances. This concept is important to understanding how monetary policy influences the economy and business.

DEFINITION OF MONEY

Since finance deals largely with money, a definition of this central item sets the cornerstone of our study. A thing can be defined according to what it is, what it does, or what it consists of, and money is no exception. As we shall see, money serves several functions in economic life. But one function in particular marks the essential attribute of money—that of serving as a *general medium of exchange. Money* is thus defined as anything that is generally acceptable in payment for goods and services, or in discharge of debts.

General acceptability, not being made of a particular stuff, is the essential characteristic of money. However, the stuff that money consists of may play an indispensable role in limiting its supply and thus preserving its value. Some authorities believe that modern money was doomed from the day that paper currency began replacing gold and silver coin, simply because it is too easy for an unscrupulous government to print paper money in any quantity it desires.

In the past many things have served their turns as money—decorative shells, beads, stone axes, metal bars; bronze, gold, and silver coins; and engraved notes of banks and governments. Today, by widespread agreement, the U.S. money supply consists of four components: (1) coin, (2) currency (non-interest-bearing notes of the Treasury and the 12 Federal Reserve Banks), (3) checkable deposits in commercial banks and other financial institutions that are immediately transferable from one

TABLE 4-1 U.S. Money Stock, February 1984

Item	Billions of Dollars
Federal Reserve notes, Treasury currency and coin	148.3
Demand deposits in commercial banks	237.9
Other deposits subject to check writing	130.9
Traveler's checks outstanding	4.7
Total	521.8

BOX 4-1
The U.S. Treasury
Helps Redeem Damaged Bills   Have you ever wondered if you can salvage your dollar bills if they should be damaged? Well, you can. About 25 employees in the U.S. Treasury's Office of Currency Standards spend all day at their desks trying to piece together money that has been burned, buried, torn, chewed, or otherwise mutilated. Using such low-tech tools as magnifying glasses, pins, and adhesive tape, the currency examiners painstakingly reconstruct bills from confetti-sized bits of ash. "They arrive with 20–20 vision," Melvin Gabourel, the office's assistant chief says, "and leave with 40–40."

If a currency examiner manages to put together more than half a bill, the Treasury will redeem it for the owner. If that much can't be reconstructed, the department will replace the money only if it is certain that the rest of the bill has been destroyed.

About 75 percent of all money claimed is redeemed. In 1982 the office handled 32,000 cases and redeemed nearly $13 million.

Source: Based on Laurie McGinely, "If a Fool and His Money Are Parted, These Folks May Be Able to Help," *The Wall Street Journal*, May 31, 1984, p. 27.

---

person to another by means of checks, and (4) traveler's checks not yet presented for payment. (Some experts would also include time deposits in commercial banks as a fifth component because they are so quickly and dependably converted into cash.) Table 4-1 shows that as of February 1984, the nation's total money supply, as customarily measured, was approximately $521.8 billion.[1]

Why Money?

Why did money come into use? The answer is convenience. The use of money enriches economic life by broadening the scope of exchange, production, and consumption. Money is generalized purchasing power. It is a common denominator of

---

[1] The $130.9 billion of Other Deposits Subject to Check Writing in Table 4-1 consisted of Negotiable Order Withdrawal (NOW) accounts at thrift institutions (mostly savings-and-loan associations), credit union shared draft accounts, demand deposits in mutual-savings banks, and Automatic Transfer Service (savings) accounts that switch money to a depositor's checking account if it is needed to cover checks. Recent years have produced great debate over what the best measure of money supply is. Almost certainly, there is no single best measure for all purposes. Consequently, to get a number of readings on money supply, economists have defined various measures with serialized names, such as M_1 (coin, currency, demand deposits at commercial banks, traveler's checks, and the other "checkable" deposits named just above). M_2 adds to M_1 such things as savings deposits and money-market deposit accounts. M_3 includes everything in M_2 plus specific types of investments, such as large certificates of deposit ($500,000 and up) issued by commercial banks and transferable by endorsement. Many studies of the effect of changes in money supply on economic activities revolve around statistical tests in which economic changes are correlated with (or regressed on) a money supply that is defined in various ways. The goal is to find which kind of the various measures of money supply is most closely linked—in its ups and downs—with fluctuations in economic activity.

buying power and economic choice. It broadens the scope of exchange by eliminating the need for a "double coincidence of wants," necessary in barter. (If A makes fishhooks and B grows yams, no barter is possible—except through an appropriate third party—unless B wants fishhooks at the same time A desires yams.) It amplifies the range of goods and services people can produce by making possible a wider specialization and division of labor. Wider markets and greater time devoted to production become possible when one can sell his labor or output for money instead of seeking out barter trades with those who have what he needs. Finally, money adds flexibility to economic consumption. It enables each consumer to distribute his spending as he wishes: he can pick the kinds and amounts of goods he personally desires, and he also can save part of his money income, thus exercising the option of transferring some of his consumption to a future when he may enjoy it more.

Real Flows Versus Money Flows

All economic activity can be represented as two matching flows. These flows take place on two levels, as shown in Figure 4-1. The upper level consists of the economy's real flows—the flow of labor, materials, and machine services into products and the final flow of goods and services from producers to consumers. These flows account for the satisfaction of wants and needs, or utilities, that are the end purpose of economic effort. Below them is the lower level, consisting of money flows. These flows involve the innumerable payments of currency or checks that assist the production, exchange, and consumption of the real wealth moving above. Figure 4-1 indicates that almost every economic transaction involves a double movement. One part is the movement of goods from seller to buyer. The other is the movement of money from buyer to seller. Thus, it is easy to think of money as a fluidizer of economic life—that is, flows of money are a kind of river on which goods and services pass quickly and without friction through their various stages of production to their final destination in consumption and human satisfaction.

Given the complex structure and intricate functioning of modern economic

FIGURE 4-1 Economic flows.

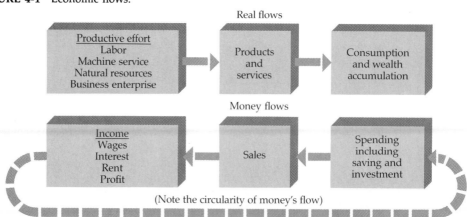

life, money's role as a common denominator of buying power and economic choice is indispensable. Without money we would find it hopelessly cumbersome to hire labor, buy machines, raise capital, pay interest, make savings, keep accounts, reckon costs, compare spending alternatives, and perform innumerable other behind-the-scenes functions that make possible the mass production, mass marketing, and mass consumption that support today's high living standards.

These considerations should warn people how important it is to maintain the value and acceptability of their currency. If runaway inflation ever causes the individual workers, farmers, merchants, and other producers to refuse to accept dollars for their output, then families would have to barter—and probably battle—for the fast-shrinking supplies of food, clothing, medicine, and other vital goods. The American way of life would swiftly sink into poverty, violent barbarism, and chaos.

Yet, although money is indispensable, it is still only a facilitating agent. It cannot logically be an end in itself because, in the final analysis, money is only good for what it will buy. A million dollars in cash on a desert island would be less valuable to the castaway than a single glass of water. Another trillion dollars added to the U.S. money supply—with no increase in the volume of goods and services—would only bring on a disastrous inflation of prices. Thus, while money is an indispensable vehicle for financing, exchanging, distributing, or saving wealth, it is not wealth itself. Money, in short, is a necessary but not a sufficient condition for prosperous economic life.[2]

MONEY'S FOUR FUNCTIONS

Money is usually viewed as serving four purposes.[3] It functions as (1) a general medium of exchange, (2) a standard of value (or price), (3) a store of value, and (4) a measure of debt. How reliably money serves these purposes determines how effectively it contributes to economic life and whether or not a society is free from money-related problems.

A Medium of Exchange
We have seen that money as a medium of exchange makes possible many of the complex efficiencies of modern economic life. The varied services of money depend,

---

[2] A necessary condition must be present before an effect will take place. A sufficient condition ensures that an effect will take place. Oxygen is a necessary condition for fire but not a sufficient one, since its presence does not produce fire if combustible materials and enough heat are not present.

[3] Usually, but not always. Some economists restrict the name money to precious metal coin that has intrinsic value equal to its face value. To these writers, paper currency and bank deposits are not money but mere credit instruments, i.e., promises to pay that have no value apart from their general acceptability in discharge of debts. Thus the principal medium of exchange today consists of credit instruments, not of money. *True* money has served two purposes: (1) it has functioned as a medium of exchange where credit instruments were not practicable or acceptable; (2) it has served as a metallic base for paper money to limit the amount of such paper that governments or central banks can issue. See R. G. Hawtrey, *Currency and Credit*, New York, Arno Press, 1978 (a reprint of his 1919 work) and Ashby Bladen, *How to Cope with Developing Financial Crisis*, New York, McGraw-Hill, 1979.

however, on its having purchasing power. It must have an acceptability in exchange for goods and services that is based ultimately on people's confidence that when they get around to spending it, it will also be acceptable in exchange for the goods and services *they* want to buy. In other words money must have what economists call *value in exchange*, since money—usually consisting of just a piece of paper—has no *value in use*. We shall see, a few paragraphs from now, that money's value ordinarily depends on one property: relative scarcity.

A Standard of Value

In modern societies most values are prices, or values expressed in money. Money provides a convenient unit for comparing values—regardless of an item's size or kind—and for reducing values to a common denominator. Money is thus the common yardstick by which people keep their accounts, determine their incomes and profits, prepare their budgets, and regulate and apportion their spending, savings, and investments. In serving this function as well, money contributes to superior accuracy, flexibility, and efficiency in economic life.

Since money is the yardstick by which economic choices are measured, it is important that this yardstick be as fixed and unchanging as possible. When the value of money—its buying power—fluctuates too rapidly, or moves up or down too far, financial planning becomes extremely difficult, and poor decisions and mistaken economic policies are likely to result. Suppose that a businessman pays $1,000 for a machine that brings him $1,500 in sales. If there are no other costs, he may count—and pay taxes on—$500 in profit. But, if over the machine's life, the dollar's buying power is cut in half, the businessman has actually incurred a loss (if he has not doubled his prices). It will cost him $2,000 to replace the machine, and his real loss, or the loss measured in purchasing power, is $500 in depreciated money, plus the income tax he was obliged to pay. You can see that money-value comparisons and accountings hold true only so long as money's buying power remains relatively stable. To continue thinking in terms of dollars when the value of the dollar itself is changing is a common and often costly mistake, one that an American economist has labeled the *money illusion*.[4]

A Store of Value

Receivers or holders of money can choose between spending their purchasing power (immediate enjoyment) or saving it (deferred enjoyment). Saving money assumes various forms, but the most common involve holding either money itself (currency or demand deposits) or money substitutes (savings deposits, E-bonds, Treasury bills, and so forth), which pay interest on the money borrowed and repay—or permit withdrawal of—fixed dollar sums. Both forms of saving have their advantages and disadvantages. Keeping our savings in cash assures us of instantly available spending power, but we collect no interest. Money substitutes pay interest, but have various disadvantages—delay or inconvenience in getting cash, fluctuation in market price prior to maturity, and (if the issuer of the money substitute should have difficulty) freezing, or even loss, of principal and interest.

---

[4] See Irving Fisher, *The Money Illusion*, New York, Adelphi Co., 1928.

With either form of saving—holding a money substitute or holding money itself—the store of value depends for its effectiveness on a stable price level. In recent years money and money substitutes have performed very poorly as stores of value because of persistent price inflation. Based on the rise in consumer prices, today's dollar will buy less than one-sixth as much as 1939's dollar.

A Measure of Debt

Debts arise when people receive goods or services or borrow economic resources (including money) on promises to pay (or repay) in the future. Debts are ordinarily expressed in money, giving rise to money's fourth and final function—its function as a measure of debt. Debts measured in money range from short-term obligations such as accounts payable, six-month promissory notes, and U.S. Treasury bills to very long-dated IOUs such as bonds and mortgages. Their common characteristic is that the principal owed and the interest, if interest is formally payable, are denominated in dollars.[5]

Money's efficiency as a measure of debt, like its efficiency as a store of value, suffers from price-level changes that alter money's purchasing power. If other factors are constant, good financial strategy calls for borrowing to the limit of your ability when prices are expected to rise, for then you can pay off your debts in cheaper dollars. Lenders, of course, need additional compensation for loss of purchasing power when price inflation takes place. Over the past generation, lenders have steadily increased their interest charges, and this has helped offset the cheaper dollars in which they are being repaid. However, a dollar whose value fluctuates is much less fair and reliable for business purposes than a dollar whose buying power remains stable. With a stable dollar, business firms, lenders, and debtors need only concern themselves with the value of goods bought or sold; with a fluctuating dollar, one must try to outguess the acrobatics of money value as well. This is not easy to do, and a changing dollar always leads to windfall gains and severe losses that are unintended or involuntary parts of business transactions. In short, unstable money is a hindrance to orderly economic life.

THE VALUE OF MONEY

What has been said above suggests that money today has value only for what it will buy. Indeed, the common definition of the value of money is, simply, its purchasing power. But what does purchasing power depend on? In answering this question, we need to note that the present age has broken sharply with the past on what it will accept as money. This break accounts for many of today's money problems.

---

[5] Some IOUs are not formally interest-bearing. Investors in these get their interest by paying less than face (maturity) value for them, or by discounting them. An investor, for example, would be getting interest at a rate of approximately 8 percent per year by buying a U.S. Treasury bill (which matures at $10,000 in three months) at a price of $9,800;

$$\text{Annual percentage rate} = \left(\frac{\$10,000 - \$9,800}{\$9,800}\right) \times \left(\frac{12 \text{ months}}{3 \text{ months}}\right) = 0.082 \quad \text{or} \quad 8.2\%$$

In former times money consisted of objects that had intrinsic value—notably, gold and silver coins. This gave money a double assurance of purchasing power because its value depended not only on its stated worth as money but also on its precious metal content. It is true that late in the seventeenth century, paper money began to appear. But until about 50 years ago, paper money in most countries was redeemable in gold or silver coin. Often it was simply a warehouse receipt for precious metal coin or bullion on deposit at the national treasury or central bank. So governments in those days did not dare, as a rule, to overissue paper money. If too much paper money was issued, people became suspicious that the government was polluting, or debasing, the money supply. So they would take their paper dollars, pounds, or francs to the banks and redeem them in gold or silver coin. This threat to clean out the nation's supply of precious metal ordinarily sufficed to keep the government honest in issuing paper money, since the government's debts and the country's bill for imports had to be paid in gold or silver coin. Inflation was thus much less a threat than it has become in recent times.

When paper money alone is used, as it is today, money's value is regulated only by its scarcity. Once people become used to accepting irredeemable paper money, it works well enough as long as its supply is conscientiously controlled by the monetary authority. (Have *you* ever thought to worry about what is actually behind the dollars you spend?) As a later section of this chapter will indicate, if the supply of paper money were allowed to expand exactly as fast as the nation's output of goods and services grew, then the value of money would remain constant.[6] There would be no rise in the general price level, and therefore no need to scramble to take advantage of it or to protect oneself against it. All over the world, however, governments have found that expanding the money supply is a seemingly easy way to pay for expenditures without arousing voter resentment through increased taxes, and (so they long thought) without running up interest rates by competing with other borrowers for people's savings. A great deal of government spending is therefore financed by expanding the money supply, usually by having the central bank create deposit or checkbook money for the government. When the government spends its new deposits, they become part of the public's money supply. Soon more money is chasing the same amount of goods, and a new cycle of rising prices has started.

Inflation is often called America's number-one economic problem. As Figure 4-2 shows, the post-World War II inflation has differed from all others in the nation's history. Eras of price inflation have always accompanied our major wars, from the Revolutionary War onward, because the government has always issued large volumes of new paper money to finance its wars. But until World War II, each wartime inflation was followed by a period of price deflation. Money then regained its lost value and lenders of money recouped what they had temporarily lost through

---

[6] This statement assumes, as you will soon see, that the income velocity of money holds steady. If the velocity of money rises, then an offsetting reduction in the growth of money supply will be required to hold the price level steady. The mechanics of this relation are explained in the section on the Equation of Exchange in this chapter.

FIGURE 4-2   Price inflation in the United States, 1820–1990 (1913 = 100).

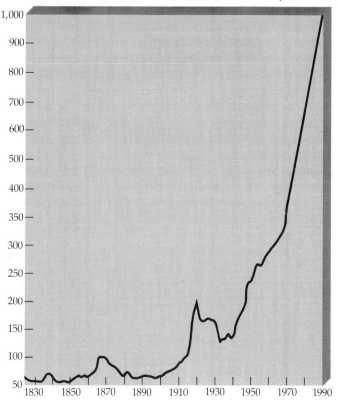

rising prices. These postwar price declines were caused largely by the public's un-willingness to accept paper money, which had depreciated relative to gold and silver coins. People who had been foolish or unlucky enough to accept quantities of paper currency found themselves saddled with money of inferior purchasing power. Paper money thus became unpopular. So the government gradually got rid of it, or at least did not let the supply increase.[7] But the gold standard, which gave citizens the right to demand gold in exchange for paper dollars, was abandoned by our government in 1933. After World War II, therefore, there was no gold coin in circulation—thus, nothing to make paper money look bad by comparison—and there was no limit on the government's ability to keep on issuing paper money to pay for war, welfare, aid to education, and other public services. Thus, while the value-of-money curve on

[7] It took 14 years, after the Civil War ended in 1865, before the paper dollar got back to full equality with the gold dollar. At one time during the war, a gold dollar was worth three paper ones. (However, customs duties and interest on the federal debt remained payable in gold throughout the war.) When the war ended, the Treasury quit issuing paper money and retired paper notes whenever it ran surpluses. By 1879, paper dollars were again redeemable in gold. The lapse from the gold standard during World War I was brief and scarcely noticeable, but in 1919 the Federal Reserve contracted the supply of "checkbook money" so sharply that a major depression followed in 1920.

BOX 4-2

Jake's Billions   His first name's Jake, and he's a highly respected retired German professor at our university. But as a young man growing up in post-World
War I Germany, Jake lived through the Great Inflation of 1922–1924, when, as the
saying went, it took "a wheelbarrow full of paper money to buy a loaf of bread."

Jake's the only authentic billionaire the authors have ever known. In fact, he
was a multibillionaire. He told us that one week in August—we forget whether he
said 1923 or 1924—his wages for a week's work in a grocery store came to 33 billion
paper marks (the German monetary unit at the time). If he had smoked, that would
have bought him an expensive cigar.

The Great Inflation of the 1920s in Germany ruined the thrifty German middle
class, already impoverished by the huge losses of World War I. Their bitterness and
desperation paved the way a few years later for the rise to power of . . . guess who?
Adolph Hitler.

Even though governments often seem unaware of it, inflation can prove disastrous to a nation's health. Ask the Germans who watched it bring Adolph Hitler to
power.

Figure 4-2 fell back after previous wars, you can see that it has risen steadily since
World War II.

NEAR-MONEY

Only money can act as a general medium of exchange, but its store-of-value function is shared by many other kinds of assets. Recall that most of a person's stored
wealth is represented not by currency and demand deposits, but by stocks, bonds,
notes, savings accounts, real estate, and perhaps an owner-operated business. Some
of these assets may take considerable time to sell—the house or business, for example—and some, such as stocks and bonds, have values that change unpredictably.
But others are either quickly redeemable in cash at the owner's demand—savings
accounts and E-bonds, for example—or ordinarily marketable at a reasonably certain price not less than the owner originally paid. In this second class one would find
U.S. Treasury bills and negotiable time certificates of deposit in commercial banks,
popularly known as CDs. These quickly cashable dollar claims are called *near-money*
because they are the closest thing to cash that can still earn interest. It is important
to remember, of course, that while near-monies are assets to their holders, they are
liabilities (debts) to their issuers.

Liquidity

The key to whether or not an asset is near-money is whether it is convertible into
cash—quickly convertible, and with little chance of loss. This quality of assets is
called *liquidity*. We also speak of a person, business, or bank being liquid when they
have on hand, or can readily raise, enough cash to meet their maturing obligations.

Behind liquidity, however, must stand some apparatus to ensure easy encashment of these near-money claims. Deposit-type financial intermediaries—savings-and-loan associations, mutual-savings banks, savings departments of commercial banks, and credit unions, for example—all maintain cash reserves normally equal to a certain percentage of their deposit liabilities. This percentage of cash will be set by the institutions' managers, or required by regulatory agencies, on the basis of experience. Fundamentally, this percentage reflects two principles: (1) that only a small percentage of depositors is likely to cash its claims at any one time and (2) that over any substantial period, deposits of cash will exceed withdrawals as the institution grows.

Short-term marketable securities like Treasury bills and CDs have three circumstances favoring their easy encashment. First, the underlying promise to pay is very reliable, which gives them wide acceptability as investments. Second, their time to maturity is relatively short—one year or less—so their market value can never diverge far from their face or maturity value.

Example. If the prevailing discount on Treasury bills is 8 percent, a $10,000 bill with one year to maturity will sell for approximately $9,259.26 and a three-month bill will sell for about $9,803.92.

Third, they have an active resale market with almost assured demand. So—like savings accounts, savings-and-loan share accounts, E-bonds, and the cash value of one's life insurance policy—Treasury bills, CDs, and other high-grade, short-term marketable claims have high liquidity. In the short run, at least, they make dependable stores of value.

The Money-to-Assets Ratio

Usually, this practice of putting one's purchasing power on ice in near-money form works smoothly and dependably. Ordinarily, only a small number of the nation's holders of near-money will demand cash (or have their near-money mature) on any single day. This permits an enormous volume of near-money claims to be piled on a much smaller supply of actual money. How large this ratio of near-money to money is can be seen in Table 4-2.

We can formulate a ratio M/A (money-to-assets) or A/M (assets-to-money) to measure the economy's potential liquidity. A look at such a ratio should quickly abolish the illusion that everyone in the economy could get cash at once. If all near-money claims were simultaneously presented for cashing or offered for sale, then their prices would fall close to zero, since enough money would be available to redeem or to buy only a small fraction of them. Thus, a claim that the economy as a whole is liquid depends on the assumption that only a small fraction of near-money claims will be offered for cash at any one time.[8]

---

[8] This assumption is based on the law of large numbers, and is the principle on which fractional reserve banking is based. The law of large numbers states that as populations grow numerically larger, their probability distributions become increasingly stable and predictable.

TABLE 4-2   Money and Near-Money: Comparative Amounts, February 1984[a]

Item	Billions of Dollars
Money supply[b]	521.8
Near-monies	
Deposit-type	
In commercial banks	
Savings deposits	129.9
Money-market deposit accounts	238.3
Small-denomination time deposits	355.3
Large-denomination time deposits	229.1
Savings-and-loan share accounts	645.0
Mutual-savings bank deposits	171.6
Credit union accounts	77.2
Money-market securities	
U.S. Treasury bills	350.2
Commercial and finance-company paper	190.7
Bankers' acceptance	74.4
Money-market fund shares	183.8
Total near-money	2,645.5

[a] This list of near-monies is far from exhaustive.
[b] For composition of the money stock on this date, see Table 4-1.
SOURCE: *Selected from various tables in* Federal Reserve Bulletin, *April 1984. Not seasonally adjusted.*

The ratio of money to near-money (and to other assets in which people store their purchasing power) plays an important part in regulating economic activity, for it measures the degree of ease or strain with which people can convert their stored purchasing power back into readily spendable money balances.

When strain develops in the ratio of near-money to money, its first symptom is a rise in interest rates. If an increasing proportion of near-money holders decide they need or would prefer to hold cash, sellers of bills, paper, and other promissory notes used to raise money will try to attract new holders by offering higher rates of interest. Similarly, deposit-type intermediaries will increase their interest rates to arrest withdrawals and attract new holders.

As we shall see, rising interest rates and tight money do not go on forever. At some point the shortage of money and cost of borrowing money will become severe enough to slow down the boom in economic activity that has caused the rising demand for cash. This slowdown, typically accompanied by rising unemployment and some fall in output, will restore a better balance between money supply and the total amount of spending that people wish to engage in. At this point interest rates will fall because reduced economic activity will once more create surplus money—that is, money looking for interest-bearing near-money investments.

The momentary significance of the money-to-assets ratio depends, in fact, on whether there are more money holders looking for assets than asset holders looking for money. So long as money holders are actively storing their buying power in near-monies, even a low ratio of money to assets may not bring immediate strain. Conversely, if asset holders are actively dumping assets to raise money, a much higher money-to-assets ratio may still be accompanied by acute strain. Thus the economy's feeling of liquidity, and the trend of interest rates, depend not only on the M/A ratio but on whether people are currently moving from money into assets, or vice versa.

CREDIT AND VELOCITY

What has been said concerning liquidity and near-money suffices to illustrate two further notions—credit and velocity. Credit, of course, has different meanings, such as being worthy of trust with other people's money or having the ability to obtain a loan when necessary. But the tangible evidence of credit is simply a loan of money, so when we speak of credit outstanding, we mean the volume of loans made and still unrepaid.

Credit arises when someone who has ready purchasing power lends it to a borrower in exchange for an IOU, typically an interest-bearing promise to pay. Over the term of the loan—the time period in which the credit is outstanding—the borrower uses the money and the lender holds the borrower's promise to pay. Or, if the promise is transferable, then the lender may sell it to some third party and, in effect, get money back ahead of time, possibly to lend again.

The important points to recognize about credit are the following: (1) A lender who extends credit must give up his purchasing power and accept a paper promise of payment. (2) A very large part of the economy's claims to wealth are tied up in such promises to pay, or credit instruments. (3) Since credit claims are not spending power, but have to be converted into spending power under various uncertainties, their prices are less certain than—to put it quaintly—the price of cash. (4) The freedom with which credit is granted varies widely, depending on economic conditions, on people's confidence in the future and in would-be borrowers, and on the potential lenders' own need for cash. (5) Finally, the ease or tightness of credit obviously affects the spending ability of all who must borrow in order to spend, and is thus an important force regulating the economy's activity.

The notion of *velocity*, which simply means the turnover rate of money, is also illustrated in the preceding discussion. Consider the following sequence. McTavish deposits $10,000 in a savings-and-loan association. The savings-and-loan lends the $10,000 to Earnest, who is buying a house. Earnest pays the $10,000 to Clawhammer, who built the house. The same $10,000 has turned over three times, twice in credit transactions and once in payment of a debt. As you can see, credit and velocity are often linked. The first two transactions described above led to the creation of credit claims.

As we shall see in the next section, rising velocity—which means that the money supply is working harder—is a symptom of strain in the credit system. So too, of course, is a rise in interest rates. The two symptoms normally occur together.

THE EQUATION OF EXCHANGE

We are now prepared to ask how, in principle, does money function in the economy? Let us look next at two simple models, or conceptual representations, of how it operates.

We begin by defining four symbols. Let

$$M = \text{money supply}$$
$$V = \text{velocity, or the turnover rate of money}$$
$$P = \text{the average price level}$$
$$O = \text{the economy's real output of goods and services}$$

Then we can write the simple equation

$$MV = PO \qquad\qquad (4\text{-}1)$$

to show that money supply times velocity equals output times price level. As you can see, the equation is actually a truism—it simply says that the total outlays spenders make equal total receipts obtained by sellers for their goods and services.

This equation, a modification of Irving Fisher's well-known Equation of Exchange (the same Irving Fisher discussed in Chapter 3 in reference to the link between inflation and interest rates) brings home some important truths about money and the economy. We shall examine them in the following sections.

Money's Two Dimensions

How much economic activity money can support depends, as Equation 4-1 shows, both on how much money there is (M) and on how fast that money turns over (V). Thus, money is sometimes said to have two dimensions: supply and velocity. An old saying (coming, we believe, from sixteenth-century England) asserts that "A nimble shilling can do the work of a lazy crown."[9] In other words, a small amount of money turning over rapidly can serve an economy as effectively as a large amount of money turning over slowly.

How quickly money turns over depends on many factors. Some of them are: (1) the current and prospective level of people's incomes, (2) the strength of their incentives to spend (including expected inflation), (3) the availability of credit, (4) the ease of cashing near-money, (5) the existing supply of money (since that will partly determine how hard the money supply needs to be worked), and (6) development and efficiency of the payments mechanism (speed of check clearing and so on). Clearly, much depends on people's optimism about the future and what they expect prices to do. It is wise to try to buy quickly to beat rising prices and to postpone spending if prices are expected to fall. Institutional arrangements are also important. If well-developed financial markets, trustworthy banks, and highly liquid nonbank

---

[9] The crown, no longer minted or circulating, was a five-shilling piece. A shilling was a British quarter.

TABLE 4-3 Income Velocity of Money in the United States, Selected Years, 1945–1984

(1) Year	(2) Money Supply (billions of dollars)	(3) National Income (current dollars[a])	(3) ÷ (2) = (4) Income Velocity
1945	94.1	181.2	1.92
1950	110.2	241.9	2.20
1955	130.6	330.2	2.53
1960	141.0	415.5	2.95
1965	163.4	620.6	3.80
1970	209.4	800.5	3.82
1975	295.2	1,215.0	4.12
1979	364.3	1,835.4	5.04
1984[b]	545.5	2,965.0	5.44

[a] *Current dollars* mean dollars unadjusted for changes in purchasing power (that is, for inflation).
[b] Estimated.
SOURCES: *Derived from various issues of* Federal Reserve Bulletin, *Historical Statistics of the United States.*

financial intermediaries encourage people to lend money with little fear of loss or illiquidity, then velocity will be much higher. Table 4-3 shows how one measure of velocity in the United States has risen since the end of World War II, an interval of remarkable development in our financial institutions.

Velocity can be defined in two ways. If we ask how often a dollar (of demand deposits or currency) turns over physically, then we speak of *transactions velocity, V_t.* If we ask how often a dollar turns over in creating income for someone, or in generating gross national product, we speak of *income velocity, V_y.* The velocity in Equation 4-1 is income velocity since the economy's output, O, times its average price level, P, equals its income. Transactions velocity can only be guessed at. Statisticians can measure demand deposit turnover through debits (reductions) to checking accounts, but there is no way to measure currency turnover. It seems likely that in recent years the total volume of money payments has run 20 times or more the level of the gross national product, or output of the economy.

Which sort of velocity we use depends on what our purpose is. Ordinarily, transactions velocity is probably a rather steady multiple of income velocity.[10] How many transactions it takes to produce a dollar's worth of income depends on how long a chain of processors and middlemen stands between first producer and final consumer. If 20 stages separate the farmer who raises the calf from the grocer who finally sells the consumer a dollar's worth of hamburger, then it may take $10 to $12 worth of transactions to produce the final $1 of income.

---

[10] This would seem to hold true unless bank debits were swollen by stock market or other financial speculation, or unless currency payments rose abnormally as a result of income tax evasion, narcotics traffic payments, or other illicit transactions.

BOX 4-3
Interest Rates and Velocity—The Bobbsey
Twins   Chapter 3 traced the link between interest rates and inflation (remember the
                Fisher equation), a long-verified historical tendency. But interest-rate changes
over the decades also coincide with something you study in this chapter—the velocity of money. As interest rates rise, money turns over faster; as rates fall, money's
turnover slows down.

Why interest rates and velocity coincide isn't really difficult to figure out. To
use economists' jargon (we hope you remember it from your introductory economics class) the opportunity cost of lending rises as interest rates do. In plain English, if
interest rates are 1 percent—as some were at the end of World War II—investors
and others just let their money lie dormant in checking accounts. If rates jump to 10
percent, alert savers will go to extremes to lend and invest their cash. That's most of
the story behind the high rise in velocity shown on Table 4-3. As interest rates have
grown juicier, people have activated their idle cash balances by squeezing down
their holdings of cash and lending the difference out at interest. Money has been
lent, spent, and lent again at a faster and faster pace. Year by year, each dollar has
chalked up more mileage because the higher the mileage, the more interest it has
earned.

If we are interested in transactions velocity, then we must rewrite Equation 4-1 to
read

$$MV_t = PT \qquad\qquad (4\text{-}1A)$$

where V_t replaces V, and T (a measure of total transactions) replaces O. For the rest
of this book, however, we shall use Equation 4-1, in which V stands for V_y, income
velocity.

Effects of Spending

Although Equation 4-1 is a truism, it is nevertheless informative. Since each side is
broken down into two factors, these can explain how particular changes take place.
What, for example, accounts for a rise in spending? Is it an addition to money
supply, which monetary authorities can largely control? Or is it a rise in velocity,
which is much harder to restrain? What result does the rise in spending produce?
Does it increase output, which is good, or the price level, which is ordinarily bad?
Equation 4-1 illustrates the meaning of *analysis,* or the breaking down of something
into its components, for further study.

Let us look at MV, or total spending. We see that a rise in spending can result
from various combinations of change in both money supply and velocity. For example, money supply may increase while velocity remains constant. Or with no increase in M, a step-up in V may still increase total spending. Both M and V can rise,
or a fall in V can cancel a rise in M. Equation 4-1 suggests that money-supply
managers must take careful note of changes in both M and V if they hope to

regulate the public's spending successfully. The goal of monetary management, as we shall see, is to provide just enough spending power to keep the economy fully employed at constant prices. Monetary managers, however, can only regulate, within limits, the supply of money; they have little influence over its velocity. Therefore, they must basically guess the velocity factor and then provide the money supply they think will permit maximum employment without inflation. Often they are wrong. In general, velocity has been rising since the end of World War II. Table 4-3 shows that in 1984 the average dollar turned over (as income to someone) nearly $5\frac{1}{2}$ times, whereas it turned over 1.9 times in 1945.

What effects will a rise in MV, or total spending, produce? Equation 4-1 tells us that this must raise either output, O, or price level, P, or both. Traditional theory states that the precise effect depends on whether or not the economy is fully employed. That is, if substantial reserves of unemployed labor and excess plant capacity exist, then added spending will theoretically put these unemployed resources to work and add to output (and real income) without much effect on prices. If the labor force and plant are already fully employed, then prices will increase much more than output will. Even before full employment is reached, bottlenecks—shortages of key skills or particular kinds of plant capacity or materials—have often precipitated a price rise. Similarly, in boom years like 1979, probably all productive grades of labor were employed, even though joblessness ran high among the poorly trained or poorly motivated. In both cases, skills in demand were in short supply and provided a bargaining lever for higher wage rates at the same time that less employable categories showed high unemployment.

Different effects theoretically take place if spending falls, as it may when the Federal Reserve inaugurates a tight money policy to slow down inflation. Since wages and many prices are difficult to cut,[11] the main impact of a slowdown in spending is typically on O instead of P; output and employment usually fall while prices continue to rise—a condition called "stagflation," a blending of stagnation and inflation.

Of course, if presidents and monetary authorities had the courage to risk voter disapproval and allowed unemployment to increase for a while, the price rise—according to traditional theory—would ultimately slow down. It would slow down because unemployed workers and plants would keep wages and prices down by competing for scarce jobs and sales. But since 1945 the nation has been increasingly unwilling to endure prolonged spells of unemployment. In that year Congress

---

[11] It has been economic dogma since the 1950s that wages and most administered prices are *inflexible in a downward direction*. How true this is is open to debate. That they have shown little downward flexibility since World War II cannot be denied. However, since 1945, no one has seriously expected money-supply managers to tighten money to an extent that would force wages and prices down (as tight money usually succeeded in doing in earlier decades). So the notion of downward inflexibility may simply reflect the general expectation that money-supply managers will lack the courage to force them down, and thus there may be no *inherent* resistance to decline. Certainly, the numerous wage give-backs agreed to by labor unions during 1982–1983 to save members' jobs demonstrated that wage cuts often will be accepted when the alternative is clearly unemployment.

TABLE 4-4 Buying Power of the Dollar, Selected Years, 1939–1984

Year	Consumer Price Index	Dollar's Buying Power in 1939 Cents
1939	100	100
1945	129	78
1950	172	58
1955	194	52
1960	213	47
1965	226	44
1970	279	36
1975	388	26
1979	517	19
1984	742	13

SOURCE: Derived from various issues of Federal Reserve Bulletin.

passed the Employment Act, making maximum employment, economic growth, and purchasing power stability national objectives. Maximum employment has been a more politically profitable objective to pursue than purchasing-power stability. Thus, inflation has been a chronic worry. Table 4-4 shows the price level's steady rise and the dollar's steady decline in purchasing power since 1939.

THE NATURE OF INFLATION

To most people the term *inflation* means a rise in the general price level. But this usage confuses effect with cause. Inflating a football means blowing it up. The rigidity of the blown-up pigskin is the effect of the inflation, not the inflation itself. A similar distinction applies to a rising price level. The rise in prices is the consequence of too fast an increase in the supply of money. Inflation takes place when the money supply is blown up at a faster rate than the economy's supply of goods and services is increasing.[12]

This distinction is important. To solve a problem, we must define its cause correctly. Otherwise, we are almost certain to apply the wrong remedy.

So far, this has happened in dealing with the soaring cost of living. It has become fashionable to blame "big business," "greedy labor unions," or "OPEC profiteers"; and politicians propose to control inflation by means of wage and price guidelines, windfall profits taxes, and more government regulation. The facts are (1) that none of these whipping boys is fundamentally responsible for the rising price

---

[12] Webster's *Third New International Dictionary* (1971) confirms the foregoing statements. It defines inflation as *"An increase in the volume of money and credit relative to available goods* resulting in a substantial and continuing rise in the price level" (italics added).

BOX 4-4

"Old Copper Nose"   That's the irreverent way sixteenth century Britishers referred to King Henry the Eighth, as they cast a rueful look at his image on a silver coin of the day. While the much-married monarch had no lack of wives, he was chronically short of money for his court, military, and other expenses. So he did what financially squeezed kings and governments have done since ancient times—he began debasing the coinage. On silver coins, you usually debase with copper. Hence old Henry's disrespectful nickname "Old Copper Nose."

Naturally, time brings progress. Nowadays we've replaced silver coins with paper money. So governments need no longer trouble themselves to melt down pure silver coins and remint them with a generous dose of copper. Today, they can just add zeros to the denomination of the bonds they sell and bills they print.

What blessings modern technology heaps upon us!

level and (2) that none of the proposed remedies has any chance of working so long as spending power rises faster than the supply of goods and services.

The cause of inflation is not economic, but political. As one observer has commented, inflation is caused by too many politicians chasing too few votes. It gets started because the government, to keep things prosperous, pumps more money and credit into the economy than can be absorbed at constant prices. For a while, this monetary stimulus may seem to work if its first effect is to increase O in the equation $MV = PO$. But since O cannot rise enough to match the increase in M (V remaining approximately constant), a rise must take place in P. When P has risen enough to absorb all the effect of the new money and credit, the stimulative effect of inflation is exhausted. Then, to maintain output at the new level of prices and to avoid economic slowdown and unemployment, the government has to increase M some more. Soon the cycle becomes automatic and self-reinforcing. That is why the price level has risen faster in each five-year period since the middle 1960s.[13]

[13] Fundamentally, what must be controlled is not the growth of money but the growth of debt. Unless the nation's sum total of borrowing—governmental, business, and individual—is held to approximately the same rate of increase as output, prices are bound to rise, because too many dollars will wind up chasing too few goods. Why is this so? Because, directly or indirectly, the growth of debt *forces* a corresponding growth in the money supply. As Chapter 5 explains, lending by commercial banks increases the money supply directly because new demand deposits are created in favor of the borrowers. But any rapid increase in borrowing and indebtedness generates pressure to increase the money supply. This is true because unless money is kept abundant, debts become hard to pay off or to pay interest on. When money gets tight, businesses or families with large debts must reduce spending to accumulate funds to pay their debts. But the resulting fall in spending threatens the economy with recession and unemployment. Knowing that recessions are unpopular, governments and monetary authorities then act to increase the money supply. This relieves the money shortage, banishes the recession threat, and keeps the politicians in office. But two other things also have happened. (1) The increase in debt has forced an increase in the money supply. (2) If debt has increased faster than the supply of goods and services, the increase in money will have pushed prices up.

People's rational expectations[14] eventually compound inflation's effect on the price level. The public learns by experience that the faster money supply is increased, the further and faster prices rise. Consequently, they begin trying to "beat inflation to the punch" by buying things now instead of later, by borrowing money to buy goods before they go higher, and by putting their savings into real estate, gold, and diamonds (which do not create jobs and output) rather than into stocks and bonds (which finance new machines and factories). More and more, additions to the money supply act to push up prices rather than to increase output and living standards.

THE CAMBRIDGE EQUATION

If we divide both sides of Equation 4-1 by V, we get

$$M = \frac{PO}{V}$$

If we define $k = 1/V$, the equation then reads

$$M = kPO \qquad\qquad (4\text{-}2)$$

This is known as the *Cambridge Equation* because it was developed by economists at Cambridge University in England. Alternatively, it is called the Cash Balances Equation. Although based on the same identities as the Equation of Exchange, the Cambridge Equation advances our knowledge of monetary behavior by emphasizing what is called people's *demand* for money to *hold*, not to spend.

The Significance of k

Since PO is the national income, k tells what fraction of national income M, the money supply, represents. This focuses our attention on a pivotal consideration: how large is the money supply in relation to people's incomes? Or in different terms, how big are people's cash balances in relation to their incomes?

Let us begin by observing that at any given moment someone must hold each dollar in existence. The total of all such money ownership equals people's total money balances, and the sum of individual balances equals the total money supply. But why do people hold money? Why not near-money or goods? Given any actual or

---

[14] The "rational expectations" hypothesis is a theory of economic behavior dedicated to explaining, among other things, why inflation, as a government policy, works less and less well as time goes on. The principle is simply that people get harder to fool the more times you trick them. Consequently, policies like inflation, which are based on deception, become less and less effective because people increasingly foresee their final effects. Not only are people no longer fooled, but in acting to protect themselves against the adverse results of the policies, they destroy whatever short-run benefits the policies might have had. If, for example, people spend all the new money created by inflation to buy land as a hedge, the new money will do nothing to improve output, employment, or living standards.

expected price level, the demand for money to hold is limited by an individual's choice between holding money and holding other kinds of assets—many of which pay interest (for example, debt securities and savings deposits) or may go up in price (for example, stock and real estate). Therefore, beyond a certain point, people do prefer to hold near-money or goods, but up to a certain point they feel more comfortable holding money. The reasons why they want to hold a certain amount of money constitute what economists call their demand for money. This demand is very closely linked to k in the Cambridge Equation.

Cash-Holding Motives

The English economist John Maynard Keynes described three reasons why people want to hold cash.

1. **Transactions motive** To keep enough cash on hand to bridge the intervals between expected payments and anticipated receipts of cash. For example, you are paid $400 every two weeks and, let us suppose, must spend all you make. Then you must stretch each $400 paycheck to last for two weeks. If you begin each biweekly period with $400 and end up with nothing, your average cash balance will be very close to $200. This is your *transactions balance.*
2. **Precautionary motive** To keep money on hand for emergencies, and to prevent a linkage of disasters. Failure to meet an unanticipated expense, no matter how small, causes creditors to lose confidence in your ability to pay. Their pressing for immediate payment may force you into bankruptcy. You may have $500 in reserve to cover doctor bills, car repairs, traffic fines, and so on. This is your *precautionary balance.*
3. **Speculative motive** To keep cash on hand to take advantage of opportunities. You are still holding in cash the $10,000 you inherited last year from your late Aunt Minerva because you have your eye on two choice city lots, which you expect to fall in price during the next several months. This is your *speculative balance.*

All businesses and individuals maintain total cash positions that are really a sum of these three basic balances. The sum of each person's transactions, precautionary, and speculative demands for cash constitutes that person's total demand for money.

k_a Versus k_d

The significance of k in people's monetary behavior now becomes apparent. If we add together everyone's demand for money, we get $k_d(PO)$. The term k_d then stands for that fraction of people's total income that they *desire* to hold in the form of money (currency and demand deposits). But this desired fraction may differ from the *actual* fraction, which we can designate k_a. If so, then we can expect people to alter their spending behavior in order to align k_a with k_d—that is, to adjust their actual cash holdings to the level desired.

Suppose, for example, that people in general find their actual money balances larger than they think they need so that $k_a > k_d$. They then feel wealthy and are willing to spend their surplus money. Total spending will rise. If, however, their actual balances are less than desired ($k_a < k_d$), they will reduce their spending in order to rebuild their cash holdings. Because it focuses attention on these motives for spending or not spending, the Cash Balances Equation is probably more useful than the Equation of Exchange as a device for explaining monetary behavior and policy.

How Monetary Policy Works

Monetary policy works essentially by making people feel richer or poorer. By changing the money supply, it alters people's margins of *spendable funds.* People compare their actual money balances with the balances that they want to hold. This provides the psychological leverage through which money supply changes induce changes in the public's spending behavior.

Actually, as we shall see in Chapter 6, monetary policy works mostly through the banks and affects spending by changing the amount of loanable funds. But since a great deal of important spending relies on borrowed money—notably, spending on consumer durables, housing, industrial and commercial construction, and factory plant and equipment—the availability of bank loans strongly influences the economy's final demand for goods and services.

SUMMARY

1. Conventionally, money is defined as anything generally accepted in exchange for goods and services or in settlement of debts. Today, most economists view it as consisting of currency plus checking deposits in financial institutions.

2. Money serves four functions in the economy: (1) a medium of exchange, (2) standard of value, (3) store of value, and (4) a measure of debt. Money has two dimensions: quantity (or amount) and velocity (or rate of turnover). The velocity of money can be measured either as *transactions* velocity (how many times a year a dollar turns over physically) or *income* velocity (how often it turns over to produce income for someone). Income velocity is simply the national income divided by the money supply.

3. Closely linked to money is a host of money substitutes, or near-monies. These are interest-bearing IOUs or deposits of various kinds that substitute for money as a store of value. However, they cannot be used directly as means of payment. Most near-monies are *credit* instruments, promises to pay fixed sums of money on demand or at a given date.

4. Money's role in the economy is illustrated by the two versions of the Equation of Exchange. The Fisher version runs

$$MV = PO$$

where M is the money supply, V is income velocity, P is an index of the general price level, and O a measure of the economy's physical output. Obviously, P times O equals the national income, while M times V is the economy's total spending on newly produced output. You can explain inflation by simply noting that if M times V goes up too fast, and O cannot keep pace, P is bound to rise.

5. The second version of the Equation of Exchange consists of the Cambridge, or Cash Balances, form. This one runs

$$M = kPO$$

A little algebraic manipulation will show that k is mathematically nothing more than the reciprocal of V. But economically speaking, it is the proportion money supply constitutes of the national income, PO. Monetary policy works essentially through k by making money either plentiful or scarce relative to people's demand for it. Using the Cambridge Equation, we can consider how the economy responds to changes in the relation between k_d (people's desired relation of money to their incomes) and k_a (the actual relation between people's money and their incomes).

6. When economists speak of demand for money, they are not talking about the demand for money to spend. (That's probably infinite.) They are referring to the demand for money to hold as opposed to holding some interest-bearing asset. On this basis people have three main motives for holding money: *Transactions motive* (money to bridge the gap between receipts and payments), *precautionary motive* (money for meeting emergencies), and *speculative motive* (money to take advantage of opportunities). The sum of demands arising from these three motives constitutes the demand for money, whether we are looking at an individual or the economy as a whole.

KEY TERMS AND CONCEPTS

Money	Value of money
Real flows versus money flows	Near-money
Medium of exchange	Liquidity
Standard of value	Money-to-assets ratio
Store of value	Credit
Measure of debt	Cambridge Equation
Equation of Exchange	Cash-holding motives
Velocity	

QUESTIONS

4-1. Would less money necessarily mean less wealth and lower living standards? Why or why not?

4-2. The narrow definition of money supply, M_1, refers to
  a. all currency and coins outstanding.
  b. all demand deposits.
  c. demand deposits plus time deposits at commercial banks.
  d. all government bonds outstanding.
  e. all currency, coins, and checkable deposits.
  Explain your choice.

4-3. What problems arise in connection with money's service as a store of value? Is money the only store of value? Explain.

4-4. What is the value of money? How is it decided?

4-5. On what does the liquidity of a savings-and-loan deposit depend? On what does the liquidity of a Treasury bill depend?

4-6. Distinguish between money and credit. Which is there more of in the U.S. economy? Why?

4-7. Would you expect the velocity of money to rise or fall during a business boom? Why?

4-8. Distinguish between the income velocity and the transactions velocity of money. Which is higher? Why?

4-9. Will increased money supply result in increased output or in higher prices? Discuss this question with reference to the Equation of Exchange.

4-10. Distinguish inflation from a rise in prices. What difficulty does confusion of the two notions create?

4-11. Explain, by referring to the Cambridge Equation, how monetary policy works.

4-12. What do economists mean by the demand for money? Why isn't this demand infinitely large?

4-13. Discuss how the three cash-holding motives might guide a store owner in deciding how much cash to keep in her company's bank account.

4-14. Which one of the following items is considered to be a component of the money supply?
 a. Personal consumption expenditures.
 b. Demand deposits in commercial banks.
 c. New issues of common stock by corporations.
 d. U.S. Treasury bonds.
 e. Federal government expenditures.
 Explain your choice.

PROBLEMS

4-1. If the discount rate on a three-month Treasury bill ($10,000 maturity value) jumped from 4 to 6 percent, approximately how much would its price decline? What would be the percentage drop? Does your answer point to any desirable quality in near-money?

4-2. Calculate the assets-to-money ratio shown in Table 4-2.

4-3. The growth in real GNP is measured after adjustments of current dollar GNP for
 a. the rate of inflation.
 b. personal income taxes.
 c. social security payments.
 d. foreign exchange rates.
 e. none of the above.
 Explain your choice.

4-4. If the national income is $2.5 trillion and the money supply is $565 billion, what is the income velocity of money?

4-5. If the money supply remained constant while the national income (in current dollars) rose 50 percent, by what percentage would the income velocity of money have increased?

4-6. If the national income remained unchanged while the money supply rose 25 percent, what percentage change would have taken place in income velocity?

4-7. If the nation's output of goods and services remained constant while money supply increased 20 percent and income velocity fell 30 percent, what would happen to the price level?

4-8. According to Table 4-3, what percentage increase took place in the income velocity of the U.S. money supply between 1945 and 1984?

4-9. Looking at Table 4-3, calculate the value of k in the Cambridge Equation as it would apply to 1984.

4-10. If the income velocity of money is rising at a steady rate of 4 percent per year and the economy's output of goods and services is growing by 3 percent per year, at what rate, approximately, should the Federal Reserve System be increasing the money supply? (Assume the goal is price stability.)

4-11. Consider Table 4-4. If the dollar's buying power shrinks from 1984 on at a rate of 5 percent per year, what percentage of the buying power of 1939's dollar will be left by the year 2000?

CHAPTER 5
How Money Is Created

As we understand it today, money originates in a monetization or debt or in a substitution of promises—the promise of a bank is exchanged for that of some less acceptable promisor. If the bank providing the promise is a central bank, the money thereby created is high-powered money capable of generating several times its own amount of low-powered or checkbook money, the familiar demand deposits. Commercial banks create checkbook money, but only against reserves provided them by our central bank, the Federal Reserve System.

This chapter describes the money-creating process in detail, following its ramifications through a series of steps called multiple-deposit expansion. Table 5-2 traces this process and deserves your close attention. How changes in money supply may originate through changes in the Federal Reserve System's balance sheet, the various equations telling how much the money supply rises or falls as changes occur in Federal Reserve asset holdings, and how the division of high-powered money between currency and member-bank reserves affects the money supply, all, call for your thorough understanding. The distinction between demand deposits and time and savings deposits and how shifts in the public's preference for one or other can affect money supplies are other important concepts.

Discounts and advances also alter money supplies by adding temporarily to commercial-bank reserves. Make sure you can describe the process.

In addition, you will examine methods of gauging ease or tightness in the nation's banking system. Concepts such as free reserves, borrowed reserves, and net free-reserve position are important. And, above all, memorize the Bank-Reserve Equation.

The chapter closes with a look at gold's single, but nonetheless vital, role in today's money system.

Two statements describe the creation of modern money. They are:

1. Money originates in a *monetization of debt*. To monetize means "to make money out of."
2. Money originates in a *substitution of promises*. Most money today is the promise of a *bank* to pay. What, precisely, will be paid is rather vague, but this does not ordinarily affect money's acceptability—at least as a medium of exchange.

The creation of money is mainly the task of the nation's commercial banks. True, other financial institutions offer interest-bearing accounts against which checks or similar written orders-to-pay may be drawn. Savings-and-loan associations provide negotiable order of withdrawal accounts, mutual-savings banks maintain demand deposits, and credit unions supply share draft accounts, all of which comprise checkbook money. But the great bulk of people's checking balances still resides in commercial banks, and this chapter will study creation of the nation's money primarily from the viewpoint of the banking system.

HIGH- AND LOW-POWERED MONEY

Most U.S. money is a liability of the nation's banks. The bulk of our currency is a liability of the Federal Reserve Banks; our central banking system. Federal Reserve notes of $1, $2, $5, $10, and $20 and higher denominations are issued by the 12 regional banks of the Federal Reserve System. The notes declare on their face that they are "legal tender for all debts public and private," and on their back, "In God we trust." Quite clearly we can only trust God if we do not trust the Federal Reserve because these notes are not redeemable in any better kind of money and are backed only by U.S. government bonds in the Federal Reserve Banks' vaults.[1]

Demand deposits (which, as checkbook money, are the real workhorse of the U.S. money system) are liabilities of the nation's commercial banks. However, the commercial banks' ability to create these liabilities is limited to a multiple of *their* deposits in the Federal Reserve Banks. These deposits, called member-bank reserves, are—like currency—a liability of the Federal Reserve System. In fact, cur-

---

[1] As of December 1983, the total U.S. money stock included only about $13.8 billion in Treasury currency and coin. By comparison, bank-liability money comprised $169.7 billion in Federal Reserve notes, $241.6 billion in demand deposits at commercial banks, and $128.4 billion in other checkable deposits.

rency and member-bank reserves are exchangeable on a dollar-for-dollar basis by the commercial banks at their district Federal Reserve Banks. When the member banks need more till money, or vault cash, they simply draw on their reserve account at their Federal Reserve Bank, which sends them the currency and reduces their reserve account by the number of dollars shipped.

Thus the volume of Federal Reserve liabilities regulates the size of the nation's money supply. A dollar's worth of Federal Reserve liabilities may take the form of either (1) $1 worth of currency in circulation or (2) $1 worth of member-bank reserves. And because each dollar's worth of member-bank reserves can back up approximately $7 worth of deposit money (as you will soon see), these reserves and the currency (which is exchangeable for them) are often referred to as *high-powered money*. Demand deposits, by contrast, are *low-powered money*.

The Monetary Base

High-powered money is often referred to as the nation's *monetary base*, since, in principle, all of it can become the foundation of multiple-deposit expansion. For purposes of regulating the economy, a number of economists and central bankers[2] believe that Federal Reserve policy should focus on controlling the monetary base rather than on control of the $M1$ money supply or interest rates. This target, they contend, would provide the Reserve Board with greater leverage over credit conditions by controlling reserve funds directly rather than by trying to adjust them to some desired level of money supply and often missing the target.

In recent years the money supply has run about 2.7 times the monetary base. Since the ratio has held relatively stable, the question of which element the Federal Reserve should regulate may be less than urgent.

HOW THE FEDERAL RESERVE CREATES HIGH-POWERED MONEY

Since both components of high-powered money—currency and member-bank reserves—are Federal Reserve liabilities, they must originate in transactions that produce Federal Reserve assets. Look at Table 5-1, a simplified consolidated balance sheet of the Federal Reserve system. Notice particularly two items listed under assets: government securities and discounts. When the Federal Reserve buys U.S. government securities or discounts eligible paper (bank loans to quality customers to finance production and distribution of merchandise), it acquires an asset. Offsetting this asset will be a liability. If the Federal Reserve discounts Treasury bills for a member bank, it will directly credit the member bank's reserve account. If the Federal Reserve buys a government security from an individual, it pays with a check. The seller deposits the check in a commercial bank, receiving a deposit credit to his

---

[2] Notably, and for the longest time, economists and officials of the Federal Reserve Bank of St. Louis believe this. The Federal Reserve Bank of St. Louis is one of the nation's 12 Federal Reserve Banks, each of which is entitled to voice its own opinion on the policies and methods of guiding monetary policy and the economy.

TABLE 5-1 Consolidated Balance Sheet of the Federal Reserve System (simplified),[a]
End of February 1984

Item	Billions of Dollars
Assets	
U.S. government and agency securities	149.4
Gold	11.1
Discounts and advances	1.0
Other assets[b]	24.7
Total assets	186.2
Liabilities	
Federal Reserve notes outstanding	152.4
Reserves of banks and other depository institutions	20.3
Other liabilities[b]	10.5
Total liabilities	183.2
Capital	**3.0**
Total liabilities and capital	186.2

[a] More detailed presentations of these and related data are given in Table 8-1.
[b] Other assets and liabilities consist mostly of debits and credits arising out of check clearings
between Federal Reserve Banks in different districts. The process, not important to understanding money supply, is explained under "Float" in Chapter 6.
SOURCE: Federal Reserve Bulletin, March 1984.

account or, perhaps, receiving currency. The commercial bank then sends the check to the Federal Reserve receiving either credit to *its* reserve account, or currency.

This is the core of the creation of high-powered money: The Reserve banks monetize debt when they buy securities to hold as assets and pay for these assets with liabilities of their own creation, which serve the nation as money. In effect, the Reserve banks merely substitute their credit (a Federal Reserve IOU) for the Treasury's credit (a Treasury IOU).

T-accounts, or miniature balance sheets, illustrate how various Federal Reserve transactions affect the nation's supply of high-powered money, or currency and member-bank reserves. Bookkeeping entries at commercial banks and the Federal Reserve accomplish the credit-monetization process.

Example. Consider the following transactions involving commercial banks. Only the first affects the volume of high-powered money, the second shifts high-powered money from one form to another, and the third transaction does not affect it.

a The Federal Reserve Buys $10,000 in U.S. Government Securities

+ U.S. Government Securities $10,000	+ Member-Bank Reserves $10,000

BOX 5-1
"You Can Lead a Horse to Water
But . . .   you can't make him drink." So said Mariner S. Eccles, Federal Reserve Board
Chairman in the late 1930s. Ex-Utah banker Eccles was referring to the Fed's
less than absolute control over the money supply. That was during the Great Depression when both the Fed and the Roosevelt Administration were trying to pep up
the economy by putting more dollars into circulation. The problem was the Fed
could inject reserves into the banking system, but it couldn't get them to "multiple"
into checkbook money. Depression had killed the demand for loans, and sky-high
bond prices had scared the banks out of making investments. So bankers just chose
to sit on idle reserves.

In history, this Fed misadventure goes by the impressive name of the liquidity
trap. You can learn all about it by taking a course in U.S. economic history. For now,
just remember the main point it illustrates: The Federal Reserve can only control the
asset side of its own balance sheet. It can't control the liability side completely
because the public decides how much currency it wants in its pockets, and currency
draw-downs displace member-bank reserves dollar for dollar, as this chapter explains.

b The Member Banks Withdraw $10,000 in Currency to Meet the Public's Demand for Hand-to-Hand Money

	− Member-Bank Reserves $10,000 + Currency in Circulation $10,000

c The United States Sells $10,000 in Gold to France, but the Federal Reserve Simultaneously Buys $10,000 in Government Securities

− Gold Certificate Reserve $10,000 + U.S. Government Securities $10,000	Member-Bank Reserves (no change)

MULTIPLE-DEPOSIT EXPANSION

We have said that each dollar of member-bank reserves can support approximately
$7 of *demand deposits*, or low-powered money. It is now time to explain why this is
so.

The U.S. commercial banking system—and, indeed, every banking system in the world—is a *fractional-reserve* banking system. This means that both the legal reserves (in the form of member-bank reserves) that commercial banks are required to keep and the vault cash backing their deposit liabilities are only a small fraction of those liabilities. In 1984 the Federal Reserve required all member banks to maintain a *reserve ratio* that increased from 7 percent on the first $2 million of demand deposits to $16\frac{1}{4}$ percent on deposits above $400 million. Overall, required reserves averaged about 14 percent of the banks' demand deposits.

How High-Powered Money Expands: An Example

Let us assume that the Federal Reserve buys a $1,000 Treasury bond from an individual. The Federal Reserve takes the bond and gives the seller a check for $1,000 drawn on itself. The Federal Reserve's accounts read:

Assets		Liabilities	
Government securities	$1,000	Checks payable	$1,000

The seller of the bond deposits this check in a commercial bank, Bank Number One, and receives credit in a demand deposit account. The account of Bank Number One reads:

Assets		Liabilities	
Due from Federal Reserve	$1,000	Demand deposits	$1,000

Bank Number One now sends the check to the Federal Reserve Bank, which cancels the check and credits Bank Number One's reserve account $1,000. The Federal Reserve's accounts now read:

Assets		Liabilities	
Government securities	$1,000	Member-bank reserves	$1,000

The accounts of Bank Number One now read:

Assets		Liabilities	
Reserves with Federal Reserve	$1,000	Demand deposits	$1,000

Let us now examine the reserve position of Bank Number One. To legally back its $1,000 of demand deposits, it needs reserves of $142.86, or one-seventh of $1,000. The other $857.14 of its $1,000 reserve credit constitutes excess, or nonrequired, reserves. The bank is free to lend or invest these excess reserves for profit, and it *will* lend or invest them, given suitable opportunities, since banks are profit-motivated institutions. Bank Number One's total reserves consist of required reserves and excess reserves.

Total reserves:	$1,000.00
Less required reserves:	
Demand deposits × reserve ratio	
($1,000 × $\frac{1}{7}$)	142.86
Excess reserves	$ 857.14

Assume that Bank Number One lends the entire $857.14 to Needy. In so doing it has acquired an asset, Needy's note (IOU) for $857.14. It also has created a new liability, the demand deposit of $857.14 in Needy's checking account. Recall the two statements about money creation at the opening of this chapter. Low-powered money has just originated here in a monetization of debt. The bank has made demand deposit money out of Needy's debt, his personal note. Also, the new money has originated in a substitution of promises. The bank has substituted its promise, a demand deposit, for Needy's promise, his IOU.[3] This transaction illustrates the basic nature of the banking process—the bank creates and issues claims against itself (a demand deposit in this case) and uses this claim to acquire and hold income-producing assets (in this case Needy's IOU, which will produce interest income for the bank).

You may wonder why, with only a one-seventh reserve requirement, the bank does not lend seven times its $857.14 in excess reserves. The bank cannot prudently lend more than its excess reserves because borrowers typically use their loans to pay bills. When a borrower writes a check, chances are that the payee will deposit the check in a different bank than the one on which the check is written. In this event Bank Number One will lose its $857.14 reserve to the other bank when the check is cleared through the Federal Reserve. Therefore, an individual bank cannot lend more than its excess reserves—or invest more either, since the seller of the investment as well will probably use a different bank.

At the moment Bank Number One makes its loan, its accounts will look like this:

Assets		Liabilities	
Reserves with		Demand deposits	$1,857.14
Federal Reserve	$1,000.00		
Loans outstanding	857.14		
Total	$1,857.14		

[3] The bank, a recognized and widely trusted public institution, has substituted its promise (demand deposit) for the promise (personal IOU) of the less widely trusted individual, Needy. In the same way, the Federal Reserve converts government securities (large-denomination, interest-bearing promises of the Treasury) into currency in convenient denominations or into book entries that serve as backing for member-bank deposit money.

Now suppose Needy writes a check for $857.14 to his creditor, Dunmore, who banks with Bank Number Two. Dunmore endorses Needy's check and deposits it in Bank Number Two, which increases Dunmore's account by $857.14 and forwards Needy's check on Bank Number One to the Federal Reserve. The Federal Reserve shifts $857.14 from Bank Number One's reserve account to the reserve account of Bank Number Two. It then sends Needy's check back to Bank Number One, which reduces Needy's deposit account by $857.14 and also subtracts from its reserve account the $857.14 it has just lost to Bank Number Two. At this point, Bank Number One's accounts will read:

Assets		Liabilities	
Reserves with		Demand deposits	$1,000.00
Federal Reserve	$142.86		
Loans outstanding	857.14		
Total	$1,000.00		

Bank Number Two's accounts will read:

Assets		Liabilities	
Reserves with		Demand deposits	$857.14
Federal Reserve	$857.14		

With deposits of $857.14 Bank Number Two will have required reserves of $122.45 and excess reserves of $734.69. The latter it is free to lend or invest.

This is the process that repeats itself as member-bank lending (and investing), followed by check clearings, moves a gradually diminishing body of excess reserves through a large number of banks, creating demand deposits in its wake. Table 5-2 traces this process through the first 17 banks. You will note the regularity with which the figures in most of the columns change. Note also that excess reserves, loans or investments made, and additional deposits created, are always the same for each bank in the series. Note that the cumulative total (for all banks) of loans and investments is always less, by the original $1,000 of new money, than the total of deposits. Finally, notice in the last column that each additional bank in the series absorbs another chunk of the original $1,000 of new reserves, leaving a continually smaller volume of excess reserves still circulating to create new deposit money.

The Limits of Expansion

The bottom row of Table 5-2 shows the limits toward which the multiple expansion of deposits works. As the first five columns indicate, after migrating through a very large number of banks, the steadily dwindling excess reserves fall to zero so that no new loans or investments can be made and no new deposits created. At that point, however, the last three columns would approach arithmetically predictable limits:

1. Total reserves required by the expansion of demand deposits would approach $1,000—that is, all reserves would finally be absorbed by the multiplication of checkbook money.
2. Total deposits supported by the reserves would approach $7,000.
3. Total loans and investments growing out of the multiple-deposit expansion process would approach $6,000.

EQUATIONS OF MONEY EXPANSION

We are now equipped to develop some basic relations among money-supply variables. We begin by defining the following symbols:

M = total money supply
C = supply of currency
D = supply of demand deposits
R = supply of reserve funds (Federal Reserve liabilities—corresponding to the assets it holds—which are capable of adding to *either* member-bank reserves *or* currency)
r = ratio of required reserves to demand deposits (reserve requirements, or the reserve fraction)

Let us now calculate the limits of money-supply expansion for any given volume of reserve funds, R, assuming a reserve ratio equal to r. Since total money supply is the sum of currency plus demand deposits, we have

$$M = C + D \qquad (5\text{-}1)$$

What volume of money will reserves equal to R create? First, since currency absorbs reserve funds on a dollar-for-dollar basis, the volume of reserve funds available to create demand deposits will be equal not to R but to $R - C$. If multiple-deposit expansion based on these funds is carried to the limit, then the volume of demand deposits will be

$$D = \frac{R - C}{r} \qquad (5\text{-}2)$$

and, substituting this value for D into Equation 5-1, we finally obtain

$$M = C + \frac{R - C}{r} \qquad (5\text{-}3)$$

Example. Let us work through an example that uses the equation. Assume, first, that the reserve fraction against demand deposits is 14 percent. Assume, second, that the monetary system has no excess reserves. At this point, the Federal Reserve buys *an*

TABLE 5-2 Multiple-Deposit Expansion (assuming a one-seventh—14.286 percent—reserve requirement)

	This Bank					All Banks		
Bank No.	Deposit Recd.	Reserve Required	Excess Reserves	Loans or Investments Made	Additional Deposits Created	Total Deposits	Total Loans and Investments	Total Reserves Absorbed
1	$1,000.00	$142.86	$857.14	$857.14	$857.15	$1,857.14	$ 857.14	$ 265.31
2	857.14	122.45	734.69	734.69	734.69	2,591.83	1,591.83	370.27
3	734.69	104.96	629.73	629.73	629.73	3,221.56	2,221.56	460.23
4	629.73	89.96	539.77	539.77	539.77	3,761.33	2,761.22	537.34
5	539.77	77.11	462.66	462.66	462.66	4,223.99	3,223.99	603.44
6	462.66	66.10	396.56	396.56	396.56	4,620.55	3,620.55	660.09
7	396.56	56.65	339.91	339.91	339.91	4,960.46	3,960.46	708.65
8	339.91	48.56	291.35	291.35	291.35	5,251.81	4,251.81	750.27
9	291.35	41.62	249.73	249.73	249.73	5,501.54	4,501.54	785.95
10	249.73	35.68	214.05	214.05	214.05	5,715.59	4,715.59	816.53
11	214.05	30.58	183.47	183.47	183.47	5,899.06	4,899.06	842.74
12	183.47	26.21	157.26	157.26	157.26	6,056.32	5,056.32	865.21
13	157.26	22.47	134.79	134.79	134.79	6,191.11	5,191.11	884.48
14	134.79	19.27	115.52	115.52	115.52	6,306.63	5,306.63	900.98
15	115.52	16.50	99.02	99.02	99.02	6,405.65	5,405.65	915.12
16	99.02	14.14	84.88	84.88	84.88	6,490.53	5,490.53	927.24
17	84.88	12.12	72.76	72.76	72.76	6,563.29	5,563.29	937.63
Limit	0.00	0.00	0.00	0.00	0.00	7,000.00	6,000.00	1,000.00

additional $1 million in Treasury securities. Simultaneously, the public's demand for currency rises by $300,000. By how much can total money supply expand? Equation 5-3 makes the calculation easy. Since we are calculating *additions* to money supply, we preface the numerator symbols in Equation 5-3 with Δ, meaning "change in." We write

$$\Delta M = \Delta C + \frac{\Delta R - \Delta C}{r}$$

Substituting, we obtain

$$\Delta M = \$300,000 + \frac{\$1,000,000 - \$300,000}{.14}$$

$$= \$300,000 + \frac{\$700,000}{.14}$$

$$= \$5,300,000$$

As you can see, the public's decision to convert some of the newly added reserve funds into currency constitutes a leakage from the multiple-expansion process. If there had been no rise in the demand for currency in the above example, then the entire expansion could have occurred in checkbook money, and the money supply could have risen by $1,000,000/.14, or $7,142,857.

Practice. The Federal Reserve buys $10,000 of U.S. Treasury securities. What is the potential maximum expansion of the money supply if the reserve requirement ratio is 20 percent and the public's demand for cash rises by $800? Answer: $46,800. Verify this answer by showing the calculation with Equation 5-3.

Time and Savings Deposits

Commercial banks also receive time and savings deposits, which we encountered in the discussion of near-money in Chapter 4. *Time deposits*, when issued in denominations of $100,000 or more, are usually represented by certificates of deposit (CDs), which are not withdrawable until a definite date but are negotiable, or salable to another party. Savings deposits are the familiar passbook accounts, which pay interest at fixed dates.

Time and savings deposits are subject to much lower reserve requirements—typically, 3 to 6 percent—than demand deposits are. Consequently, when people shift their funds from demand to time or savings deposits, the banks gain lending power. Suppose the Last National's reserve requirements are 17 percent for demand and 5 percent for savings deposits. If Moe writes a $1,000 check for deposit in her savings account, then the bank at once increases its lending power by $120, which is the difference between the $170 reserve required against Moe's demand deposit and the $50 reserve needed against his savings deposit.

BOX 5-2
Will the Real Money Supply Please Stand
Up?   One slick alibi available to experts who predict the economy's future trends from
what happens to money supply is that there are always several money supplies to
choose from—and likely one whose behavior fits a particular prophet's prophecy. In
mid-1984, for example, along with $M1$, you had $M2$, which added things like savings accounts and small time deposits to $M1$, and $M3$, which added things like large
denomination CDs to $M2$. Then, the M family had added another member with the
unharmonious name of L. (We assume that L stood for something connected with
liquidity.) Anyhow, L added things like Treasury bills, bankers acceptances, commercial paper, and U.S. savings bonds to $M3$.

Of course, the general character of the M family seems clear. The higher an
M's number, the less liquid, that is, the farther from cash, it supposedly is. A few
years ago, the M's used to go up to $M4$ and $M5$, and $M1$ was given a split person-
ality that divided it into $M1A$ and $M1B$. Our spies assured us that privately some of
the Federal Reserve's bushy brains had identified family members as far up in count
as $M16$. At the time, that left us pondering this question: Would $M17$ have included
the salvage value of the Washington Monument?

A large flow of checkbook money into savings accounts and CDs expands the
banks' ability to make new loans and investments. The gain in lending power may
be large enough to offset the additional interest cost the banks incur (since they must
pay interest on time and savings deposits). Conversely, a shift of depositor claims
out of time and savings deposits back into demand deposits reduces bank lending
power by increasing the percentage of reserves that must be held against total deposits. An example will show how shifts in savings and checking deposits affect
bank lending powers.

Example. The Last National Bank has $1 million in savings deposits and $1 million
in checking deposits. With 5 and 17 percent reserve requirements, respectively, the
bank's reserve needs would be $50,000 plus $170,000, or $220,000 in total—an effec-
tive overall reserve fraction of 11 percent. The bank could maintain a theoretical
maximum of $1,780,000 in loans and investments, the amount of its excess reserves.

If its savings deposits shifted to demand deposits, reserve requirements would
rise to $340,000, or 17 percent. Then the maximum of loans and investments for the
bank would fall to $2 million minus $340,000, or $1,660,000. For the banking sys-
tem, if all banks were at the limit of their reserve ratios with no excess reserves, a
shift by the public from savings to demand deposits would force a multiple contraction of loans and investments throughout the banking system.

FACTORS AFFECTING MONEY SUPPLY:
RESERVE POSITION OF THE BANKS

The bulk of the country's working money supply consists of demand deposits. However, as we have seen, demand deposits can only be erected on a base of reserve funds supplied to commercial banks by the Federal Reserve. Thus the reserve position of commercial banks is the pivot of the monetary system.[4]

Measuring Ease or Tightness

The principal measure of ease or tightness in the system is how the member banks stand with respect to the reserves legally required for the volume of demand deposits they are carrying. If a bank's total reserves exceed its required reserves, it has excess reserves and is then in a position to make additional loans or investments. If its total reserves fall short of required reserves, it has a reserve deficiency and is obliged to curtail its credit-granting activities, sell investments, and refuse to make new loans or to renew old ones.

Seldom will member banks collectively have a reserve deficiency. Some banks will have excess reserves because they have not lent or invested to the maximum limit. Their excess reserves may be borrowed by reserve-deficient banks through the *federal funds market,* in which excess reserves are lent daily at interest among the nation's banks. Other banks may cover reserve deficiencies by borrowing at the Federal Reserve discount window, as you will see below.

If reserve deficiency is a widespread phenomenon among individual banks, the resulting pressure on reserves may produce multiple-deposit contraction as banks collectively reduce their loans and investments. That is, if banks generally are short of reserves and are reluctant to borrow on discounts at the Federal Reserve, they usually try to obtain reserves by liquidating investments—especially Treasury securities and municipal bonds. The purchaser of these securities writes a check that, in clearing, gives the seller bank additional reserves equal to the price of the securities sold. However, the purchaser's bank loses reserves in the same amount. Thus the pressure of reserve shortage spreads throughout the banking system.

This pressure in the system will not subside until the banks as a group reduce their loans and investments by a multiple of the reserve deficiency. Suppose, for example, that a certain group of banks has a reserve deficiency of $100 million. If the average reserve requirement of these banks is one-seventh of their deposits, they will remain "under pressure" (in other words, dependent on federal funds purchases or on discounts from the Federal Reserve) until their loans and investments fall by $700 million. Thus ease or tightness in the credit situation—and in interest-rate levels—is closely linked to the reserve position of the commercial banks.

[4] Only about half of all U.S. banks in 1984 belonged to the Federal Reserve System. Some reserves must be deposited by nonbank financial institutions against any accounts they hold which are subject to check writing. This applies to NOW (negotiable order of withdrawal) accounts, offered by savings-and-loan associations, demand deposits and NOW accounts maintained by mutual-savings banks, and share-draft accounts held by credit unions. Thus changes in reserve requirements are felt throughout the financial system; no money-creating institution is exempt from their effects, although the predominant ease or strain will be on the commercial banks.

Free Reserves

For the banking system as a whole, the most significant indicator of bank credit availability is the free-reserve position of the member banks. *Free reserves* are the difference between excess reserves and borrowed reserves in the banking system. If excess reserves exceed borrowed reserves, the member banks have *net free reserves.* If borrowed reserves exceed excess reserves, the banks have *net borrowed reserves.*

As indicated above, member banks collectively usually have excess reserves. Otherwise, they would be violating reserve requirements. However, it makes a difference whether excess reserves are owned or borrowed. To see why, let us consider the significance of an item we have already noticed in the Federal Reserve System balance sheet (Table 5-1)—discounts and advances.

Discounts and Advances

One of the facilities the Federal Reserve offers its member banks is the privilege of obtaining temporary additional-reserves to tide them over an interval of reserve deficiency. The vehicle for providing these temporary reserves is a discount or advance by a Reserve bank to its member bank.[5]

Suppose, for example, that the Last National Bank of Muleshoe has a $12\frac{1}{2}$ percent reserve requirement, $9 million in demand deposits, and only $1 million in its reserve account at the Federal Reserve. Actual reserves fall $125,000 short of the $1,125,000 ($9,000,000 times .125) reserve requirement. The Last National's management, however, has reason to believe the reserve deficiency is only temporary—that is, in the next few days the bank will gain enough reserves from other banks (through new deposits and check clearings) to restore balance between the bank's owned reserves and its deposits. Therefore, the bank takes government securities or other eligible paper to the Federal Reserve and pledges them as security for a short-term loan of reserves. Depending on the arrangement, this temporary accommodation is called either a discount or an advance, but for our purpose the distinction is not important. What *is* important is the fact that such borrowed reserves are only an emergency accommodation. Federal Reserve regulations prohibit banks from relying for prolonged intervals on reserves borrowed at the discount window.

Bank's Free-Reserve Position

We are now prepared to see why the free-reserve position of the member banks is such an important indicator of ease or tightness in the monetary system. Net borrowed reserves leave the member banks in an uncomfortable position; they prefer using new reserves to pay their way out of debt to the Federal Reserve rather than making new loans or investments. By contrast, net free reserves indicate unencumbered lending and investing power in the banks. For these reasons the free-reserve position of the member banks is perhaps the most closely watched of all Federal Reserve System statistics.

[5] The Federal Reserve may refuse discounts to a member bank that abuses the privilege. Funds obtained through discounts are not supposed to be re-lent or invested for profit at a higher rate than the discount rate of interest that the Federal Reserve charges the borrowing member bank.

BOX 5-3

Shaw On Gold   Testy George Bernard Shaw, playwright, critic, political activist, and all-around man of affairs, is a more familiar figure in your English courses than in your economics or business studies. Yet the versatile and articulate Englishman in the 1920s wrote a solid, sensible, and highly readable book on economic principles still well worth perusing. The title, forward-looking in its day, was *The Intelligent Woman's Guide to Socialism and Capitalism.*

Shaw was a socialist, but his leftward-leaning set of social values didn't blind him to realities. When it came to money, his oft-quoted advice was to stick to a gold standard if you wanted your savings to be worth much down the road. Here's how he summed up his hard-hitting chapter on "Money."

> . . . the most important thing about money is to maintain its stability, so that [it] will buy as much a year hence or ten years hence or fifty years hence as today, and no more. With paper money this stability has to be maintained by the Government. With a gold currency it tends to maintain itself even when the natural supply of gold is increased by discoveries of new deposits, because of the curious fact that the demand for gold in the world is practically infinite. You have to choose (as a voter) between trusting to the natural stability of gold and the natural stability of the honesty and intelligence of the members of the Government. And with due respect for these gentlemen, I advise you, as long as the Capitalist system lasts, to vote for gold.

Source: Bernard Shaw, *The Intelligent Woman's Guide to Socialism and Capitalism,* New York, Brentano's Publishers, 1928, p. 263.

The Bank-Reserve Equation

How reserve funds are supplied to, and absorbed by, the monetary system is explained by the *Bank-Reserve Equation.* As you will easily see, this equation is actually just a special-purpose rearrangement of the Federal Reserve System balance sheet. It runs:

Sources of reserve funds (gold, government securities held by Federal Reserve Banks, discounts and other loans by the Federal Reserve to member banks, plus Treasury currency)

minus	Factors absorbing reserve funds (chiefly, currency in circulation)
give	Total member-bank reserves
less	Required reserves
give	Excess reserves
less	Borrowed reserves
give	Net free (or net borrowed) reserves

ROLE OF GOLD

Along with government securities, the Federal Reserve's gold-certificate reserve is a major factor in supplying member banks with reserve funds. The certificates are mostly warehouse receipts for gold stored in Fort Knox and elsewhere by the U.S.

government. However, the gold certificates do not circulate as money, and neither U.S. citizens nor foreigners may redeem dollars for gold.

Until the 1960s federal laws imposed gold-reserve requirements for both member-bank reserve deposits and Federal Reserve currency. The purpose of these requirements was to limit expansion of the nation's money supply and thus prevent inflation. However, when this restraint collided with the federal government's desire to print more money—even if it might lead to runaway prices—the restriction was removed. Gold-backing requirements for member-bank reserves were eliminated by Congress in 1964 and for Federal Reserve notes in 1967.

Until 1971 foreign governments and central banks could exchange unwanted dollars for gold from the U.S. Treasury at the rate of $35 an ounce. After 1957, billions of U.S. dollars moved into foreign hands as Americans spent, invested, or gave away more dollars abroad than foreigners spent or invested here. Foreigners became reluctant to hold all the dollars they received and increasingly redeemed them for gold. By 1970 more than half the gold owned by the United States at the end of World War II had flowed abroad.

As gold flowed out, the Federal Reserve's gold-certificate reserve declined. How did the Federal Reserve replace the lost gold? It did so by buying more government securities. This prevented gold losses from reducing member-bank reserves (or currency) and forcing a multiple contraction of the nation's money supply. The T-account (c) on page 98 shows you how.

Although replaceable on the Federal Reserve's books, the gold loss threatened national security. Many materials vital to the country's defense must be imported from overseas. Only the possession of enough gold—the unquestioned international buying power—guarantees access to these strategic resources. So when the U.S. gold reserve fell below $10 billion, in 1971, President Nixon suspended the right of foreign official holders to exchange their dollars for gold.

Today, gold plays a single but vital part in the nation's monetary system. Since only gold has unquestionable, ultimate acceptability in international payments, the U.S. gold stock represents the final reserve buying power—or borrowing ability[6]—of the nation.

SUMMARY

1. Money originates in a substitution of promises, wherein a bank monetizes (makes money of) the debt of some less widely accepted promisor. Central banks, such as our Federal Reserve System, create high-powered money, usually by taking in government securities as assets and paying for them with a newly created liability: either currency or member-bank reserves.

2. Commercial banks, working through the multiple-deposit expansion process, can expand each $1 of newly added member-bank reserves into approximately $7 worth of demand deposit or checkbook money. They do so by using their excess

---

[6] In 1974, for example, Italy—which was otherwise bankrupt—obtained a $2 billion loan from West Germany by pledging its gold reserve as security for repayment.

reserves to make loans or investments. The sum of demand deposits plus currency in circulation, as you recall from Chapter 4, comprises the nation's working money supply. And since member-bank reserves and currency are exchangeable dollar for dollar, their sum is known as the monetary base—the total of high-powered money available to support money-supply expansion.

3. Time and savings deposits have lower reserve requirements than do demand deposits. As the public shifts its holdings from the latter to the former, additional reserves automatically become available to feed the growth of checkbook money. A shift out of time and savings deposits back to demand deposits would tighten the reserve position of the commercial banks.

4. The Federal Reserve supplies temporary reserves to the commercial banks by means of short-term loans called discounts and advances. Their creation is reflected in temporary additions to the money supply.

5. Ease or tightness in the banking system depends greatly on whether the commercial banks have *net free reserves* (excess reserves exceeding borrowed reserves) or *net borrowed reserves* (which put them in debt to the Federal Reserve Banks). Which position the banks arrive at can be traced through the Bank-Reserve Equation.

6. Gold no longer plays a part in our domestic monetary system, but it still constitutes the nation's last-ditch reserve of international buying power in the event of war or some other serious emergency.

KEY TERMS AND CONCEPTS

Monetization of debt	Monetary base
Substitution of promises	Expansion limit
High- and low-powered money	Time deposits
Multiple-deposit expansion	Free reserves
Demand deposits	Bank-Reserve Equation
Reserve ratio	Role of gold

QUESTIONS

5-1. Why does currency in circulation count as high-powered money?

5-2. Name the two largest assets and the two largest liabilities of the Federal Reserve Banks.

5-3. What are the components of the public's money supply?

5-4. What does the term *fractional-reserve system* mean? What does it imply for a central bank's ability to regulate money supply?

5-5. What would happen to the money supply (assuming it was expanded to its legal limit) if the public suddenly decided to draw down into circulation a great deal more currency than the commercial banks had on hand?

5-6. You have recently received a $50 check from another individual. Which of the following statements is not true?
   a. If you cash the check, the money supply will be unchanged.
   b. If you deposit $25 in your bank savings account and $25 in checking, the money supply will decrease by $25.
   c. If you deposit the check in your checking account, the money supply will be unchanged.

d. If you deposit the check in your bank savings account, the money supply will decrease by $50.

e. If you cash the check, the money supply will be increased by $50.

Explain your choice.

5-7. Does the banking system's lending capacity increase, diminish, or stay the same when the public shifts large sums from checking accounts into time or savings accounts? Explain why.

5-8. What does it mean to say that commercial banks have "net borrowed reserved?"

5-9. Write out the Bank-Reserve Equation.

5-10. Explain why a reserve deficiency in the banking system puts upward pressure on interest rates.

5-11. Briefly discuss the present role of gold in the U.S. monetary system.

5-12. A key to controlling the money supply in the United States is the monetary authority's control over

a. federal government expenditures.

b. personal savings.

c. business investment expenditures.

d. U.S. government gold stocks.

e. member-bank reserves.

Explain your choice.

PROBLEMS

5-1. If the reserve requirement in a bank system were 20 percent, and the central bank added $1 million to member-bank reserves, what total volume of new demand deposits would be created as the new reserves traveled through the first five banks?

5-2. If, as a result of the reserves added in problem 1, demand deposits in all banks eventually increased to $5 million, by how much would loans and investments have increased?

5-3. Using T-accounts, show what happens to member-bank reserves on each of the following transactions:

a. Federal Reserve buys $500 million in government securities.

b. Bank redeems $5 million in discounts at Federal Reserve.

c. Banks deposit $500 million in currency at Federal Reserve.

5-4. Using a reserve requirement of 20 percent, compute the ultimate theoretical effect that each transaction in problem 5-3 has on the volume of member-bank demand deposits.

5-5. If, in a system with a reserve requirement of 10 percent, the central bank buys $20 million in government securities from commercial banks, to what limits may each of the following theoretically expand?

a. demand deposits

b. bank loans and investments

c. excess reserves

5-6. Given a reserve requirement of 12 percent, what increase in total money supply would be possible if the central bank purchased $25 million in government securities and, simultaneously, the demand for currency in circulation rose $17 million?

5-7. The banks have $31.4 billion in total reserves, $30.7 billion in required reserves, and $0.5 billion in borrowed reserves. What is their free-reserve position?

5-8. If sources of reserve funds total $72 billion, currency in circulation is $50 billion, required reserves are $21 billion, and Federal Reserve discounts and advances to the banks are $2.5 billion, then what would be the amount of net free or borrowed reserves?

5-9. Required reserves are 14 percent against demand deposits and 4 percent against time deposits. How much will the Last National Bank's lending power theoretically fall if customers shift $20 million from time deposits to demand deposits?

CHAPTER 6

Monetary
and Fiscal Policy

Begin your study of this chapter by memorizing the definitions of monetary and fiscal policy. Make sure you can explain the objectives of monetary policy and the conflicts that occur among them.

Next, get well acquainted with the Federal Reserve System: its managing Board of Governors, its structure of 12 district banks, and the tools with which it operates. These comprise three general tools that affect the overall supply of money and credit, without attempting to govern particular end-uses of borrowed funds: (1) the regulation of reserve requirements for depository institutions, (2) discount rate changes, and (3) open-market operations. Selective tools aim at controlling particular uses of credit. Only one such tool is currently in operation: the regulation of margin trading in the nation's securities markets.

After this comes a review of the three main channels through which monetary policy exerts its influence: (1) the availability of money and credit, (2) the cost of funds, and (3) capital-value effects (important for you to memorize). Then follows a theoretical discussion of a large unsettled question: What main principle should guide the nation's monetary policymakers? Mostly, this section discusses the opposing claims and merits of monetarism versus discretionary management of the money supply. It provides background for the ways of measuring ease or strain in the banking system, comparing such measures as interest-rate levels, deposit velocity, and the free-reserve position of the nation's banks.

Fiscal policy, familiar to you from your economics courses, is reviewed briefly and contrasted with monetary policy. The chapter closes with a short look at how monetary and fiscal policy may work effectively together, given the strengths and weaknesses peculiar to each of them.

There are two devices by which modern free-world societies try to steer economic affairs instead of leaving them entirely to chance, free-market, or automatic forces.

1. *Monetary policy* is the central bank's effort to regulate the economy by managing the supply, cost, and availability of money and credit.
2. *Fiscal policy* is the government's effort to control the economy through taxation, spending, and management of the public debt.

This chapter deals principally with monetary policy and with its principal manager—the Federal Reserve System.[1] It deals more briefly with fiscal policy, as it affects the business person.

OBJECTIVES OF MONETARY POLICY

Five main objectives are usually ascribed to monetary policy. The first three apply equally to fiscal policy. The last two are the primary domain of monetary policy. The five main objectives are: maximum employment, a stable price level, maximum sustainable economic growth, balance in international payments, and maximum freedom of economic choice. Let us briefly describe each goal.

1. **Maximum employment** This objective, encompassed in the Employment Act of 1946, is difficult to define precisely. Statistically, does it mean 4, 5, or 6 percent of the labor force unemployed? Disagreement is largely over how much unemployment is (1) inevitable—when people are between jobs or are being too choosy about taking jobs or (2) necessary—to discipline the excessive wage demands that result from "overfull" employment.

---

[1] The authors acknowledge their debt in this chapter to William Tennyson, treasurer of the French American Banking Corporation, New York City. We borrowed many insights and expressions from his concise and distinctively phrased memorandum of December 23, 1970, written to acquaint his bank's Paris directors with the background of Federal Reserve policies and operations.

2. **A stable price level**   Since inflation and deflation redistribute wealth and affect purchasing power, this objective seeks to keep the general price level steady. Overall price stability would still allow individual prices to move up and down as supply and demand changed for particular goods and services. But again a statistical problem emerges: which of several price indices to stabilize? Should it be the Consumer Price Index? the GNP Deflator? or some other?

3. **Maximum-sustainable economic growth**   This goal emphasizes the desirability of a rising standard of living and an expanding economy that can create jobs for an increasing population and minimize racial and other social frictions that arise from unemployment. The world *sustainable* is important, for experience shows that efforts to make the economy grow too fast breed inflation, dislocations, and eventual recessions.

4. **Long-term balance in international payments**   Foreign trade, investment, lending, direct aid, military expenditures, and so on lead either to our owing foreign countries a net balance due or to their owing us a net balance due. Ordinarily, we must settle the claims we owe to foreign nations either by persuading them to accept dollars or by paying them in acceptable foreign monies (or possibly in gold). But foreign creditors, such as the oil-exporting Arab countries, may someday refuse to accept more dollars, and the United States could exhaust its reserves of foreign currencies and gold. This outcome would leave our country internationally bankrupt. Thus, in the long run the United States must balance its international income and outgo.

5. **Preserving maximum economic freedom**   U.S. monetary policy has long aimed at having the central bank create the right *total* amount of money and credit, but letting the market allocate this amount according to the strength of different demands. In this way the rationing of financial resources by government is avoided, and maximum scope is given to individual initiative.

CONFLICTS AMONG OBJECTIVES

Clearly, these objectives are a mixed bag. They are not all compatible, and three notable conflicts have arisen.

Maximum employment versus price stability is one significant conflict. These goals have been at odds since World War II. When money supply has grown fast enough to hold unemployment below 5 percent, the price level has accelerated its rise. When money supply has been restrained enough to slow down inflation, unemployment has increased. In 1971–1973 President Nixon tried using price controls to hold down inflation while pumping up the money supply to boost employment. But, of course, prices went on rising in spite of controls. The root cause for this is that if excess money is relied on to keep employment full, then inflation seems bound to continue, regardless of how the government tries to check it.

Balance of payments versus full employment and growth is a second conflict. The standard remedy for international payments exceeding receipts is to (1) cut money supply to reduce imports and (2) raise interest rates to attract foreign funds. However, doing so will enfeeble domestic demand and possibly start a recession. Since our politicians seem to worry more about the next election at home than the dollar's fate abroad, those in power have chosen to continue running deficits. Also, every time a recession strikes, the Federal Reserve and Treasury try to inflate the country back to prosperity with cheap money and runaway budgets. This new flood of dollars weakens the U.S. balance of payments.

Maximum employment versus growth is a third conflict. If full employment is impossible without inflation, a further conflict arises between full employment and rapid economic growth. Frequent interludes of monetary restraint needed to prevent runaway prices will then slow the pace of economic expansion. This leads to what has been called a stop-and-go economy.

THE FEDERAL RESERVE

Monetary policy in the United States is decided and carried out by the Board of Governors of the Federal Reserve System, the nation's central bank. The Board is composed of seven members appointed for 14-year terms by the President and confirmed by the Senate. Its outstanding feature is its legal independence of both the executive and legislative branches of government in day-to-day operations. Only one member's term expires every two years, and so it would take a President almost two full terms in office to appoint a majority. Furthermore, the Federal Reserve System has its own source of income in its huge portfolio of government securities. Thus, it finds no need to ask Congress for money to carry on its operations. The Board is free to follow its collective conscience, though generally it cooperates with the political administration in power. Like the Supreme Court, it tends in the long run to read the election returns.

Founded in 1913 as a system of 12 district banks, each serving a particular region with its own local problems, the Federal Reserve has long since become a unified system implementing nationwide policies. But although they have outgrown local autonomy, the district banks and their branches still play important administrative roles locally and serve as listening posts for national policy making and policy changes.

TOOLS OF MONETARY MANAGEMENT

To implement monetary policy, the Federal Reserve relies on a kit of assorted tools. Broadly, these are classed as *general* and *selective* tools. General tools aim at creating or maintaining some given *total amount* of money (or credit) and letting the market mechanism allocate it according to supplies and demands originating in the economy's various sectors. Selective tools are aimed at regulating *particular uses* of money or credit.

The three general instruments of control used by the Federal Reserve are (1) member-bank reserve requirements, (2) discount rate changes, and (3) open-market operations. These instruments operate directly on the reserve position of the member banks and constitute the fulcrum for the leverage that Federal Reserve actions can exert on our fractional-reserve money system. Let us examine each of them in turn.

Reserve Requirements

The most powerful of the Federal Reserve's general controls over money available for lending by the banks is the reserve requirement against member-bank deposits. Small changes in member-bank reserve requirements can permit huge changes in money supply, a process discussed in Chapter 5. The word *permit* in the previous sentence deserves emphasis. The money-supply expansion will not take place unless it is generated by loan demand, by investments made by commercial banks on *their* initiative, or by a combination of the two.

It should be stressed that reserve requirements exist only to limit member banks' money-creating and credit-granting activities. Required reserves play no part in bank safety or solvency, since these reserves cannot be paid out or drawn down. To meet withdrawals, banks must rely on their reserves of vault cash and short-term marketable securities, called *secondary reserves*, plus a properly spaced flow of loan maturities. Since required reserves are only a regulatory device, the Federal Reserve has found it convenient to reduce them occasionally in recent years—when there has been a strong need to expand money and credit. In March 1984 the reserve requirement for all member banks was a ratio that started at 7 percent on the first $2 million of demand deposits and increased to $16\frac{1}{4}$ percent on everything over $400 million.

Discount Rate Changes

The Federal Reserve's second general tool of money control is the discount rate on short-term loans to banks to cover temporary deficits in their reserve requirements. By raising the discount rate charged on these loans, the Federal Reserve can raise the cost for the banks to run deficits. By lowering the rate, it can reduce the cost. In this way the Federal Reserve can either discourage banks from making loans and investments that force them into debt to the Federal Reserve, or—alternatively—encourage such indebtedness and, with it, credit expansion. Discounts are used at the member banks' initiative, but the Federal Reserve decides their cost.

Banks temporarily needing reserves may borrow the excess reserves of other banks on an overnight basis. The rate on these borrowings is called the *Federal-funds* rate. When this rate is lower than the discount rate, banks have little incentive to borrow from the Federal Reserve. Conversely, as interest rates at which banks can borrow from one another rise above the discount rate, their incentive to borrow from the Federal Reserve increases. It increases still more as yields rise on Treasury bills and other reserve assets. This is so because it is cheaper for a bank to raise needed funds by borrowing money from the Federal Reserve at, for example, 7 percent than to sell a Treasury bill yielding 8 percent. As profit-seeking enterprises, banks always try to relieve their reserve deficiencies in the cheapest way possible.

The Federal Reserve System—or "the Fed," as it is commonly referred to—considers discounting to be a privilege of member banks, rather than a right. However, banks whose need for funds is clearly of a seasonal nature can obtain discounts almost automatically.

Open-Market Operations

Reserve requirements are seldom changed. Discount rates are changed infrequently. The board's real power is felt in the money market. The Federal Reserve sells securities to absorb member-bank reserves and buys them to supply reserves. A policy directive is drafted and voted on by the Open Market Committee (composed of the Board of Governors and five Reserve Bank presidents). The manager of the Open Market Account (a vice-president of the New York Federal Reserve Bank) then translates this directive into day-to-day decisions to buy and sell specific quantities of securities in the market.

It might seem that speculators could make big money in the government securities market by buying when the Federal Reserve buys and selling when it sells, since the market will move the way the Federal Reserve intends. However, in conducting open-market operations, the Federal Reserve covers its tracks quite well.

Example. To buy a net of $500 million in securities, it might engage in $5\frac{1}{2}$ billion worth of transactions, of which $2\frac{1}{2}$ billion might be sales transactions. Also, there are a number of dealers in the government securities market, and by using different dealers for different trades, the Federal Reserve effectively conceals its ultimate intentions concerning the market's direction.

The New York securities market is a well-lubricated and instantly responsive channel through which the Board's policy finds its way into the economy. Besides the impact on member-bank reserves, open-market purchases and sales also bring about prompt and carefully graduated changes in the cost and availability of borrowable money.

Because of their ability to make relatively fine adjustments in bank reserves, open-market operations are the most flexible, versatile, and continuously used of all monetary tools. Unlike discounts, this tool is used at the Federal Reserve's initiative.

Moral Suasion

Moral suasion is often mentioned among the general tools of Federal Reserve control. It simply means that the Federal Reserve lets the commercial banks know that it wants them to behave a certain way. *Suasion* means persuasion, and it ranges from innocuous statements for publicity (to which the banks pay no attention) to ferocious browbeating that terrorizes bankers and brings hasty compliance. Member banks depend on the Federal Reserve's good will for discounts and other accommodations, and they recognize that the Federal Reserve can use its other tools to achieve its objectives if banks do not cooperate voluntarily. So, if seriously intended, moral suasion is another version of the iron fist in the velvet glove.

In the past the Federal Reserve has employed a still wider list of general tools. Ceilings on the interest rates commercial banks could pay for time or savings deposits proved useful in slowing the flow of deposits into the banks in times of boom and inflation. On occasion, too, the Reserve Board imposed special reserve requirements on the amounts large banks borrowed from their foreign branches.[2] These controls have seen reduced use in recent years, and the Federal Reserve's legal power to apply them was reduced by the Monetary Control Act of 1980, but an emergency or dangerous revival of inflation could bring about their revival.

SELECTIVE TOOLS

The general tools of Federal Reserve action affect monetary totals (or aggregates), leaving the market mechanism to allocate the credit available. Their effect can be likened to that of a shotgun. At times, however, credit restraint is needed in particular sectors. On these occasions the Federal Reserve has resorted to selective credit controls. Their action can be compared to a sniper's rifle.

During World War II and the Korean War, Congress authorized the Federal Reserve to place special controls on purchases of housing and appliances—goods subject to wartime shortage and panic buying. These anti-inflationary regulations set minimum down payments and maximum payment periods, thus damping demand by making credit harder to acquire. Such controls expired long ago, but a new crisis could possibly revive them.

Stock Market Margins

The only selective tool currently in the Federal Reserve's arsenal is the power to prescribe margins—or minimum down payments—for the purchase of securities, particularly common stocks. The theory of this power, vested in the board since 1934, is the ability to kill speculation without killing prosperity. Margin requirements strongly regulate the flow of credit into the stock market. The Federal Reserve appears to watch both the use of credit to buy stocks and the market level itself. When speculation seems to be getting the upper hand, the Federal Reserve increases margin requirements to 70, 80, and even 100 percent. High margins usually coincide with bull-market peaks, business booms, and accelerating price inflation. When business drifts into recession and stock prices deflate, margins are lowered again, typically to 50 percent.

CHANNELS OF INFLUENCE

Aside from the theoretical effect on people's cash balances,[3] how does monetary policy alter economic activity? Amid considerable debate, there is broad agreement that its effects are felt through three main channels of influence.

---

[2] Technically, these amounts were *Eurodollars,* a term defined and discussed in Chapter 26. The special reserve requirements raised the cost of Eurodollar borrowings to the banks since they paid interest on the total dollars borrowed but could only lend the dollars left after reserve requirements were met.

[3] See the subsection "How Monetary Policy Works" in Chapter 4.

BOX 6-1

The "Fed-Watching" Game   Fed watching is more than a sport. For bankers, bond traders, stock speculators, and corporate treasurers, it's a serious endeavor. Knowing where interest rates are headed is the key to making profits or avoiding losses in many lines of business, and Federal Reserve policies can offer timely clues to developing trends in money costs and security prices. Fed watching began in 1975 when the Federal Reserve and Congress agreed that the Federal Reserve must publish annual targets for monetary growth.

What constitute the Fed watchers' favorite guides? Though they change from time to time, there are some perennial favorites: Interest-rate changes, the reserve position of the banks, changes in money supply, and the monetary base have their staunch advocates.

On an hour-to-hour basis, however, what holds most Fed watchers' attention is the rate on *federal funds*, excess reserves that banks lend to each other on an overnight basis. Banks that need reserves to maintain required-reserve positions, make unexpected payments, or provide sudden large loans often borrow Fed funds from other banks instead of selling off investments or wearing out their welcome at the Federal Reserve's discount window.

What is lent, though, are excess reserves, and the supply of excess reserves available is largely at the Fed's control. It can wipe out excess reserves by selling Treasury bills in the open market or add to excess reserves by buying bills. Where the Federal funds rate moves therefore reflects the direction in which the central bank is moving the supply of reserves and, by inference, interest rates. A big jump in the Fed funds rate or a persistent move by the rate in one direction is the typical forerunner of a corresponding trend in interest rates generally.

1. **Availability**   When bank reserves are too small to accommodate the full demand for loans, banks must ration funds. They become more selective in accommodating potential borrowers, reduce loan sizes, and lend for briefer periods. The resulting general shortage of money imposes similar restrictions on nonbank lenders, who find funds harder to acquire. Conversely, plentiful reserves make the banks more willing to lend and less selective. Idle money is then also deposited with nonbank intermediaries, thus increasing the availability of funds there. This channel of influence acts basically on the supply of lendable funds.

2. **Cost**   When tight reserves create a shortage of money, lenders raise interest rates. This increase in the cost of funds helps reduce borrower demands by pricing marginal borrowers out of the market. But large excess reserves have the opposite effect of lowering interest rates and making borrowing attractive to those who would not have borrowed before. This channel acts primarily on the demand for lendable funds.

3. **Capital-value effects**   Rising interest rates reduce the market price of bonds and mortgages held by banks, insurance companies, and other lenders. Ordinarily, these

institutions sell off such investments when they can lend the proceeds at a better return, but they are less anxious to do this when their investments must be sold at a loss. Thus rising interest rates are said to "lock" lenders into their portfolios. Conversely, a fall in interest rates, which raises capital values, makes investment portfolios liquid again and enlarges the supply of funds available for loan. This channel of influence, like the first, affects the supply of loanable funds.

As money tightens, the capital-value effect is strengthened by the forced selling of debt securities. As we have seen, individuals and companies also use debt securities as stores of value. When tight money makes it difficult for them to obtain loans and brings a slowdown in their own cash inflows, these groups sell their investments to raise cash. Such selling increases the supply of debt securities, pushing their prices down and their yields up.

TECHNICAL GUIDES TO MONETARY POLICY

It is unlikely that people will ever agree on the objectives of monetary policy. But even if they should, they would still disagree on how to implement these objectives. Disagreement has centered on two issues. (1) Should money supply be increased at a fixed, noninflationary rate? Or should the Fed have discretion to regulate money supplies according to economic conditions? (2) What statistical measures should the Fed rely on in making its decisions?

Monetarism Versus Discretionary Management

Monetarists are advocates of a fixed rate of money-supply expansion. They argue that discretionary management has had such a bad record and proved so error-prone that it is best replaced by expanding money supply at a steady rate of perhaps $3\frac{1}{2}$ percent per year, come what may. They point out that the output of goods and services has grown at about that rate over the past century, so that a $3\frac{1}{2}$ percent increase in money should be both adequate and noninflationary. They argue further that a fixed $3\frac{1}{2}$ percent annual increase in the money supply would discourage inflationary booms and excessive wage and price demands because money to sustain them would not be created. Thus, recessions and unemployment—which, since World War II, have resulted primarily from efforts to stop inflation—would be less likely. Tendencies toward recession or slowed growth would be offset by the continuing steady growth of money supply at a predictable rate.

Discretionists counter this by arguing that a fixed rate of money expansion ignores changes in velocity,[4] which have upset the economy in the past even when the money supply was not changing rapidly. Since people's desire to hold or spend money depends on other factors besides the amount of available money, central banks must take continual note of the changing *demand* for money and alter the

---

[4] Table 4-1 shows that, over the past generation, the income velocity of money in the United States has more than doubled.

supply accordingly. The same amount of money might be inflationary under one set of conditions and start a recession under another. Therefore, discretion and judgment must be applied to monetary decisions as to other economic questions.

A few comments on this debate seem appropriate. (1) Discretionary monetary policy has had a poor record, but there is no guarantee that the fixed-rate "automatic pilot" would be better. (2) Fixed-rate advocates have had their own debate over (a) what rate to fix and (b) how to measure money. (3) Even if a fixed rate worked, people would not continue to accept it if it led to high unemployment. Monetary policy today is the creature of politics, and if voters are complaining, politicians change a policy (however right it may be) just to please them. Discretionary policy gives the central bank leeway to take action, whereas a fixed rate of expansion would suggest to voters that the central bank was indifferent to their hardship. (4) Those who fear inflation are likely to be fixed-rate advocates. Those who want full employment, even at the price of inflation, prefer discretion. This suggests that fixed-rate monetary policy offers, at the least, a greater promise of price stability. Certainly, over the past generation, discretionary management has proved to be an engine of price inflation.

Guides to Monetary Decisions

Given discretionary management, what statistical measures should be the central bank use as a guide to tell it how and when to act? What should central bankers watch? Should they watch interest rates? the total mount of money (currency plus demand deposits) in existence? the rate of increase in demand deposits plus currency? demand deposits plus currency plus time deposits? the total amount of bank credit outstanding? the total amount of all credit outstanding? the total volume of bank reserves? reserves available to support private deposits (known as RPDs[5])? the readily lendable reserves of commercial banks? the nonborrowed reserves of the banks? the monetary base (high-powered money)? some estimate of "general liquidity" for the whole economy? Each of these measures has its advocates and critics.

Over the past decade the Reserve Board has set targets for both interest-rate levels and money-supply growth. However, it has given priority to controlling interest rates, and its interest-rate target has usually proved to be less than borrowers were willing to pay. Excess demands for loans have developed, and to hold interest rates down, the Fed has had to create more reserves and permit greater money-supply growth than would satisfy its money-supply target. The end result has been accelerating price inflation.

Many experts argue that money supply, the monetary base, or total credit growth are the proper measures to regulate and that interest rates should be left free to seek whatever levels a reasonable supply of credit dictates. Critics have likened the Fed's policy to efforts to control the weather by rigging the thermometer reading. In retrospect, it does seem clear that the Fed has paid too much attention to interest rates and too little to the so-called monetary aggregates.

---

[5] Officially known as "reserves available to support private nonbank deposits—defined specifically as total member-bank reserves less those required to support government and interbank deposits."

TABLE 6-1   Combined Balance Sheet of the Reserve Banks (October 31, 1984)

Item	Billions of Dollars
Assets	
Gold certificates	11.1
Depository-institution borrowings	5.0
U.S. government and agency securities	156.7
Cash items in process of collection	7.0
Other assets[a]	17.6
Total assets	197.4
Liabilities	
Federal Reserve notes	161.0
Deposits	
Reserves of depository institutions	19.7
U.S. Treasury	3.8
Foreign	0.3
Other	0.3
Deferred-availability cash items	6.4
Other liabilities	2.3
Total liabilities	193.8
Capital	
Paid-in capital	1.6
Retained profits	1.5
Other capital	.5
Total Capital	3.6
Total Liabilities and Capital	197.4

[a] Includes foreign currency holdings, special drawing rights on the International Monetary Fund, and bank premises.
SOURCE: Federal Reserve Bulletin, *January 1984.*

CONDITION OF THE BANKING SYSTEM

To make sound financial decisions, a manager must know whether money is easy or tight, the direction in which interest rates are moving, and whether financial markets are headed for ease or strain. The point of departure for these judgments is a correct reading of the condition of the country's banking system. Assessment begins with consideration of the Federal Reserve System's balance sheet, a simplified version of which is presented in Table 6-1. Most of the items are probably clear to you, but two call for explanation.

Float

"Cash items in process of collection" consist of checks written on banks in one Federal Reserve district, credited to the reserve accounts of banks in another Federal Reserve district, but not yet deducted from the reserve account of the payor bank. To offset this reserve increase, a liability—"deferred-availability cash items"—is entered for the same amount as each in-process-of-collection check. "Deferred-availability cash items" is a very brief entry, however. It stays on the books only for the time normally required for the check to clear the payor's district Federal Reserve bank. Then the check is subtracted from the payor's bank's reserves. But weather, slow mail service, clerical mixups, and other causes always delay a fraction of collectible checks beyond their deferment periods. Thus "cash items in process of collection" typically exceeds "deferred-availability cash items" by a billion dollars or more, meaning that the same reserves are being counted twice—at two different Federal Reserve banks. This unintentional and rather unpredictable increase in member-bank reserves is called *float*. It can be troublesome to Federal Reserve officials trying to "fine-tune" the money supply.

Measuring Ease or Strain

The Reserve System balance sheet shows the aggregate size of central-bank resources backing the nation's money system. But it reveals little about the degree of ease or strain in that system—that is, how abundant or scarce money is in relation to the demand for money, how intensively the money supply is being worked, and how much pressure banks are experiencing in trying to meet loan demand and still maintain their required reserves. Among generally accepted measures of the monetary system's condition are (1) interest rates, (2) deposit velocity, and (3) free-reserve position of the nation's banks. Figures relating to each of these indicators are published monthly in the *Federal Reserve Bulletin* and are widely followed and interpreted as barometers and forecasts of business conditions.

The *trend*, as well as the level, of these indicators is watched by company managers, bankers, economists, and others. What happened in any given week to interest rates, velocity, or free reserves may not be significant. Short-run changes in these figures often reflect the Federal Reserve's miscalculations of the consequences of its money-supply moves. They may also stem from temporary influences, such as even-keel policy to facilitate a Treasury borrowing. But persistent changes that predominate in one direction for several weeks almost always indicate one of two possibilities: either the Federal Reserve has embarked on a policy of ease or of tightness or the economy is moving so strongly that the Federal Reserve cannot immediately oppose the underlying trend.

FISCAL POLICY

Fiscal policy is concerned with government spending, the way it is financed, and the extent to which it seeks to stimulate or restrain the economy. GNP, the economy's total spending, is

$$C + I + G$$

where,

C = consumption spending
I = kinds of real (as distinguished from monetary) investment
G = government spending

BOX 6-2
Our Modern Day Goliath: The "Off-
Budget" Deficit   The official deficit and national debt figures, alas, are far from reveal-
ing the whole truth about what big-hearted Uncle Sam spends, bor-
rows, or lends in a typical year. What it comes down to is the unsavory fact that
government finance has a front door (the Treasury) and a back door. . . . Well, read
on.

The budgets of some federal agencies are just left out of the Treasury's budget:
the Postal Service, the Pension Benefit Guarantee Corporation, the Federal Financing
Bank, the Rural Electrification and Telephone Revolving Fund, the Synthetic Fuels
Corporation, and the Strategic Petroleum Reserve. Congress has arbitrarily classified
their borrowings, which in mid-1983 had reached an estimated $100 billion per year,
as off-budget borrowing so that it doesn't show up in the official red ink figures.

The government's inflationary impact on the credit markets expands further
with these and other guaranteed loans, which divert money from ordinary businesses and consumers to politically favored classes of borrowers.

Finally, Uncle Sam dons his business-suit disguise to tap the credit markets for
still more billions through such government-sponsored enterprises as the Federal
Home Loan Bank, the Federal National Mortgage Association, the Farm Credit Administration, and the Student Loan Marketing Association. These organizations, now
nominally private, are still regulated and backed by the federal government.

One estimate, made in mid-1983, found that over the preceding 10 years federal off-budget borrowings had totaled $486 billion, coming as an addition to the
Treasury's on-record debt increase of $494 billion over the same period.

Using the GNP format, you can think of fiscal policy as *G*, but it also has side effects
on *C* and *I*.

Fiscal policy affects the economy through three channels: (1) government
spending, (2) taxation, and (3) debt management. What government spending and
taxation are seems obvious enough. Debt management is the way the Treasury's
debt, either new or accumulated, is financed.

Revenues, mostly taxes, minus expenditures equals a deficit if negative, a surplus if positive. Deficits stimulate the economy, because the government is putting
more dollars back into people's hands than it is taking out of them. A surplus
restrains the economy because the government is taking more dollars away from
people through taxes than it is adding through spending.

In theory, the Treasury should run a deficit in periods of high unemployment
and low inflation, and a surplus in periods of overfull employment and high inflation. History teaches that politicians prefer stimulating to restraining—particularly in
election years—so fiscal policy has consisted almost entirely of deficits.[6]

---

[6] The U.S. Treasury ran deficits in 23 of the 24 years from 1961 through 1984.

Monetary and Fiscal Policy Contrasted

The role of monetary policy is permissive. That is, although central banks can create high-powered (and to some extent low-powered) money, they cannot force people to use it, and they cannot assure that the money will be spent in ways that create demand and jobs.

By contrast, fiscal policy directly adds to or subtracts from the economy's steam of spending. We can see this and other important points by considering the equation

$$GNP = C + I + G$$

Presumably what the government takes in taxes, it takes away from either C or I. To the extent that G is financed with taxes, it may simply replace C or I. Only to the extent G is financed either with (1) newly created money or (2) borrowed money that would otherwise not be spent on C or I can G be considered an economic stimulant.[7] If there is a surplus, then presumably more dollars are taken away from C and I than are replaced through G.

Combining Monetary and Fiscal Policy

Ideally, monetary and fiscal policy should work together, reinforcing or complementing each other. In practice, however, each has proven to be a one-edged tool. Monetary restraint has been effective in choking off booms, but monetary ease has proven a feeble stimulant during recessions. (Typically, the excess money created during recessions has lain almost dormant until the next inflationary boom.)

Fiscal stimulation has been not only effective but also inviting to apply, since politicians always like to spend money, even when the federal deficit soars. Fiscal restraint, however, has proved all but impossible to apply (however effective it might really be), because government spending creates vested interests, which politicians are hesitant to offend (by cutting off expenditures). So, in the main, fiscal policy is relied on to fight recessions, and monetary policy to do the "dirty work" of killing off inflationary booms.

Frequently, monetary policy is prostituted to help fiscal policy. Politicians in the federal government often want to spend more money but are afraid to raise taxes. So the Federal Reserve quietly "prints" the required money. It does so by adding enough to reserves so that the banking system can buy enough Treasury bonds to cover the deficit. But the banks' bond purchases create new demand deposits, and this addition to the money supply remains in circulation to drive up the price level.

---

[7] Some studies suggest that government spending financed by taxes or bonds simply crowds out an equivalent amount of private spending. See, for example, R. W. Hafer, "The Role of Fiscal Policy in the St. Louis Equation," Federal Reserve Bank of St. Louis *Review*, January 1982, pp. 17–22.

MONETARY POLICY: FINAL ASSESSMENT

In theory, monetary policy is an application of the equation of exchange, $MV = PO$. M (total money supply) is controlled by the central bank by regulating the quantity of commercial-bank reserves and currency (high-powered money) to just the right amount. This in turn keeps O (output) continually at the full-employment level without raising P (price level). Like most ideal models of economic or financial behavior, this one breaks down in practice. Its shortcomings are both technical, related to the process itself, and moral, related to the wills of the people who manage it.

SUMMARY

1. Monetary policy is a central-bank's effort to regulate a nation's economy by managing the supply, cost, and availability of money and credit. Although its five main objectives are clear-cut, some notable conflicts appear among them, especially between maximum employment and a stable price level.

2. In the United States monetary policy is carried out by the Federal Reserve, a system of 12 district banks directed by a seven-man Board of Governors in Washington, D.C. The "Fed" regulates money and credit with two kinds of tools. General tools aim only at controlling the total supply of money and credit; they include (1) reserve requirements for deposit-type financial institutions, (2) discount rate changes, and (3) purchases and sales of government securities in the open market. Selective tools, such as stock market margin requirements, attempt to control particular uses of credit.

3. Monetary policy affects economic activity through three main channels: (1) availability of money and credit, (2) the cost of borrowed funds, and (3) the effect of interest-rate changes on capital values. A major dispute hinges on the proper guide for monetary policy, with both monetarism and discretionary management having their strong advocates. Ease or strain in the nation's banking system is gauged by a variety of measures, including interest-rate levels, the turnover rate of demand deposits, and the free-reserve position of the banks.

4. Fiscal policy is the government's effort to control the economy through taxation, spending, and management of the public debt. Deficits stimulate economic activity, though they lead to price inflation if the Federal Reserve creates new money to finance them. Surpluses would probably restrain the economy, but they have rarely occurred since World War II.

5. Both monetary and fiscal policies have notable strengths and weaknesses. Fiscal policy stimulates effectively by putting money in its beneficiaries' pockets; the vested interests that develop in government spending, however, make it difficult to cut back. Monetary policy works uncertainly as a stimulant; "easy money" may prove a slow cure for a recession. However, tight money and high interest rates can always halt an inflationary boom. The result has been that the government has relied

principally on deficits to cure recessions, while a tight monetary policy has done the "dirty work" of restraining an overexuberant economy.

KEY TERMS AND CONCEPTS

Monetary policy

Fiscal policy

Objectives of monetary policy

Tools of monetary policy

Stock market margins

Availability effect

Cost effect

Capital-value effect

Discretionary monetary policy

Monetarism

Float

QUESTIONS

6-1. Which pairs of monetary policy objectives appear incompatible? Why, in each instance?

6-2. One important objective of fiscal policy is full employment. Another is price stability. There is considerable evidence that the simultaneous achievement of these two objectives may be difficult or impossible in the U.S. economy. This "tradeoff" between unemployment and price stability is due, in part, to

a. the tendency for wage inflation to accelerate as the economy approaches full employment.

b. the tendency for wage inflation to slow as the economy approaches full employment.

c. the positive, direct association between the unemployment rate and the inflation rate.

d. the decrease over time in the natural rate of unemployment.

e. the positive, direct association between the money supply and the unemployment rate.

Explain your choice.

6-3. Tight money shrinks capital values, thereby slowing down business activity. How does this occur?

6-4. "In a fractional-reserve system, the reserve position of the member banks is the fulcrum of monetary policy." Explain.

6-5. Open-market operations serve as the "workhorse" of monetary policy. Explain.

6-6. Name three selective tools of credit control that the Federal Reserve has used. What has been the purpose of each?

6-7. In inflationary times considerable attention in the communications media is focused upon the issue of balancing the federal budget. In this context balancing the federal budget means

a. equating federal receipts with federal expenditures.

b. equating commercial-bank reserves with commercial-bank stocks of gold.

c. equating exports and imports of goods and services.

d. equating federal expenditures with the total money supply.

e. equating total personal income with GNP.

6-8. Resolved: That money supply should be put on the "automatic pilot" and left there. Make your case for or against this proposition.

6-9. What statistical measure should guide monetary policy decisions: interest-rate levels? money supply? the monetary base? something else? Defend your choice.

6-10. How does "float" arise in the banking system?

6-11. How is ease or strain in the nation's credit structure measured? Which barometers are most closely watched?

6-12. Can the Federal Reserve really create too much money when the economy is in a recession? Explain.

6-13. Assume there is unemployment. If the money supply were increased, the most likely impact would be
  a. an increase in interest rates and investment as well as the price level.
  b. a rise in interest rates, a decrease in investment, and an increase in the price level.
  c. a rise in interest rates, an increase in investment, and a constant or falling price level.
  d. a fall in interest rates, an increase in investment, and an increase in the price level.
  e. an increase in interest rates and investment and a fall in the price level.
  Explain your choice.

6-14. CMA Examination (modified). Suppose that the Federal Reserve has instituted a new monetary policy by lowering reserve ratios on demand deposits, reducing the discount rate, and greatly increasing its purchases of government securities. As economic advisor to the President of a large corporation manufacturing consumer durables, you are asked to analyze this new policy with respect to the following list of questions. In presenting your analysis, assume that the economy is currently experiencing a balance of payments surplus, present inflation is running at 6 percent per year, the national unemployment rate is 5.5 percent, the local unemployment rate 2.7 percent, and your corporation is a major employer in the local labor market.
  a. Present a step-by-step description of the process by which this policy will affect domestic sales of your product.
  b. Is this new policy likely to have an effect on your exports? Explain.
  c. Your company is considering a new bond offering. What will be the immediate impact of this policy on interest rates?
  d. How might this new monetary policy affect your upcoming local labor negotiations?

THREE

FINANCIAL MARKETS AND INSTITUTIONS

Recall from your reading in Chapter 1 that one of the major areas of finance (along with business finance and investments) is the area of financial markets and institutions. This part of the book examines financial markets and institutions in detail so that you will become familiar with how they operate and the role they play in our economic lives. Chapter 7 looks at the types of financial markets that exist in the United States, the securities that trade in these markets, and the way that a manager uses information from the markets to plan financial activity. Chapter 8 does for financial institutions what Chapter 7 does for financial markets: It looks at the types of institutions in the United States and the ways that they are related and used by managers. An important task of Chapter 8 is to impress upon you the ways that financial institutions are becoming more alike as a result of deregulation of the banking system. Chapter 9 returns our attention to financial markets by discussing the money, bond, and mortgage markets. Chapter 10 concludes our analysis of the financial markets by addressing the markets for common and preferred stocks. Chapters 9 and 10 give you insight into the way that these markets operate and provide a network of information to the astute investor and business manager.

CHAPTER 7
Credit, Securities, and Financial Markets

This chapter offers an extended description of three key concepts: (1) credit, which can mean either a loan of money, goods, or other resources, or, alternatively, the quality in a borrower that enables him to get the loan; (2) securities, which are paper claims to future payments, fixed or contingent in amount; and (3) financial markets, facilities wherein money and securities are exchanged, one for the other.

Begin by mastering the five Cs of credit: character, capacity, collateral, capital, and conditions. This will give you clear insight into future sections of the chapter that classify credit in different ways and point out how it serves to facilitate production and consumption in the economy. Note especially the unique role played by bank credit.

Your introduction to securities will point out that these may be either marketable or nonmarketable; long term, short term, or somewhere in between; and of high, medium, or low grade. Security yields not only move inversely with security prices but serve also as a system of signals and incentives for borrowers and lenders, security issuers and security investors.

Your studies in economics should have familiarized you with markets. Financial markets, however, may present features you have not encountered before. The five tasks they perform in the economy are important. Next, you will have a preliminary look at the different kinds of financial markets and the leading kinds of securities traded in each one. The money—or short-term securities—market will first occupy your attention. Then you will receive a birds-eye view of the long-term, or capital, markets, dwelling particularly on the *primary*, or new-issues, markets for U.S. government bonds, state and local government bonds, and in a very brief view, the market for mortgages.

CREDIT: THE FIVE Cs

Few words in the finance vocabulary are more versatile than *credit*. It can mean (1) a loan of money, (2) the right to draw a loan of money, (3) a quality in borrowers that enables them to get a loan of money, or (4) the state of feeling in the financial community that makes loans easy or hard to get. In Latin, *credit* means "he trusts" or "believes." Clearly, some feeling of trust must lie at the root of credit, no matter which of the above definitions we use.

Whether we are considering the state of credit in the economy or the credit-worthiness of individual borrowers, the "five Cs" of credit are a useful checklist to remember. They are (1) character, (2) capacity, (3) collateral, (4) capital, and (5) conditions. Let us examine their relevance.

Character in a borrower is clearly important to his credit-worthiness. Is the borrower honest, sincere, a man of his word? Does he seriously intend to repay his debts? Is he a sober, hard-working, self-denying person who attends to business and puts first things first? Is he, in a word, responsible? This is the first thing any lender needs to know about a prospective borrower.

Capacity answers the question of whether a borrower is likely to prove capable of repaying a loan. Is he an efficient businessman? Does he have his affairs in good shape, keep neat books, have a firm grip on his business, maintain close control, and make correct decisions? Above all, is his business profitable? Does he generate the cash income that will enable him to repay the loan? However good a borrower's character or intentions, if he is a slipshod or unprofitable manager, his likelihood of repaying a loan is seriously diminished.

Collateral means the assets that a borrower pledges to secure his loan. Not all loans are secured. Some borrowers are so obviously strong that no assurance of repayment beyond their bare word is necessary. But as borrowers sink in the scale of credit-worthiness, collateral becomes increasingly important as a guarantee of re-payment. Thus, for weaker or less well-known borrowers, the amount, quality, and ready salability of the collateral they can pledge becomes crucial. For marginal bor-rowers the ability to offer acceptable collateral is often the key to obtaining credit.

Capital refers to the borrower's own stake, or equity, in his enterprise. Such equity is needed (unless collateral is very large in relation to the loan) as a cushion to protect the lender from loss. A business borrower is always asked: "How much of your own money have you committed to this proposition?" A borrowing consumer will be asked: "How large a down payment are you prepared to make?" The logic of this requirement should be clear. If the buyer of a $60,000 house must put up $10,000 of her own money before borrowing the other $50,000, the lender is pro-tected in two ways. First, the price of the house must fall to $50,000 before the collateral is worth less than the loan. Second, since the borrower has already made a substantial commitment of her own funds, she is less likely to consider defaulting on her loan. Lenders often refer to capital as the "borrower's equity." It is the real foundation and justification for borrowing power because a borrower must always provide her lender with some "margin of safety."

Conditions involve the state of business. They answer such questions as: "What are prospects that loans in general will be repaid without difficulty? Are sales and profits strong? Are people's jobs secure? Are their incomes rising? Are past borrow-ers meeting their repayment schedules?" If the answers to these questions are yes, then credit conditions are good. Loan availability will be high and qualifications for borrowers will be moderate. But if the answers are no, then credit conditions are poor. Loan availability will be low and borrower qualifications will be more strict.

KINDS OF CREDIT

The kinds of credit can be classified according to their (1) user, (2) time span, and (3) quality. Each class contains many divisions and subdivisions, but all types of credit are strongly related. Both borrowers and lenders often have considerable ability to compare the merits of different types of loans and to move from one to another as advantage dictates. These powers of mobility and substitution on both the supply and demand sides of a many-segmented credit market link the various segments together. Thus cost, terms, and availability often show a common trend throughout the entire credit structure. This is particularly true when money is very easy or very tight throughout the economy.

Credit by User

Users of credit fall into three broad categories: businesses, consumers, and govern-ments. Short-term credit to business is advanced by manufacturers, wholesalers, or other suppliers of merchandise ("trade" or "open-book" credit)[1] and by commercial banks, commercial credit companies, factors, and buyers of commercial paper. Inter-

---

[1] Trade credit and its costs are discussed in detail in Chapter 24.

BOX 7-1
"Credit" and Its Progeny   Words can be the parent of ideas as well as their reflection. Down through history, few words have parented a bigger brood of related notions in many languages than the Latin word *credit*, third person singular, present tense, active voice, indicative mood of the verb *credo*, meaning "I believe" or "I trust."

How many words in English can you think of that derive from this stem? Well, for a start consider the following list: credible, creditable, credence, credential, creed, credulous, credulity. To say nothing of the numerous family of compound words that includes such everyday terms as creditworthy, credit card, credit rating, and credit line.

All of which should alert us to the indispensable part that belief and trust play in the lives of civilized peoples, flourishing as they do through a division of labor, the exchanging of goods and services, lending and borrowing to create capital, and a wide reliance on the promises and good faith of others. In a complex, specialized economic society like our own, almost no one is self-sufficient, and a general breakdown of promises would mean anarchy and disaster. A breakdown in credit thus has a far deeper meaning than the mere fact that large numbers of loans are not repaid. It signifies the failure of the very glue by which a prosperous, civilized society is held together: The belief and trust implied in the word *credit* and its multifarious offspring.

---

mediate-term credit reaches business firms through term lending by commercial banks, equipment credit (ordinarily supplied by equipment manufacturers), and the purchasers of three- to seven-year notes that corporations may sell in the open market. Long-term credit is provided to businesses by bond buyers, by insurance companies that buy the long-term IOUs (privately placed notes) of corporations, and sometimes by mortgage lenders.

Consumer credit is of four main types: (1) residential-housing credit, or the familiar home mortgage; (2) installment credit, used largely to finance purchases of automobiles, appliances, and furniture, but increasingly for such other purposes as education, vacation travel, and so on; (3) mercantile credit, familiar as department-store and bank-credit-card charge accounts; and (4) consumer small loans, made for a variety of purposes by many agencies, ranging from banks and "legal-rate" consumer-finance companies to loan sharks and the Mafia.

Credit also is extended to governments at all levels. Credit to the federal government is largely embodied in the direct obligations of the United States (such as the Treasury debt) and in the obligations of a growing array of federal agencies, such as the Government National Mortgage Association, Federal Land Banks, and Tennessee Valley Authority. A large volume of credit also reaches the 50 states and their numerous subdivisions—cities, counties, school districts, sanitary districts, port authorities, and the like. Most longer-term credit to governmental bodies is supplied

through purchases of their securities. Banks are large buyers of these. Shorter-t_
credit is supplied to larger governmental bodies through open-market sales of short-
dated securities. Very small governmental bodies—too small to sell frequent issues
of short-term, open-market IOUs to investors—are largely reliant on bank loans for
temporary funds.

Credit by Time Span

The second important classification of credit is according to the length of time for
which it is extended. It is customary to distinguish (1) short-term credit, running one
year or less; (2) intermediate-term credit, running from 1 to 10 years; and (3) long-
term credit.

The chief concern of those extending *short-term credit* is that the borrower have
the cash in sight to repay the loan, since the period is too short to permit repayment
out of the borrower's earnings. That is, a borrower at 8 percent would have to repay
108 percent of the loan in a year's time, and paying all of this amount solely out of
profits would require profits of 108 percent—a phenomenal achievement. Consequently, short-term credit is typically made available only where the borrower satisfies one of three conditions: (1) He has enough income assured over and beyond
expenses to meet the repayment obligation. An example would be a $1,000 personal
loan for one year to an executive whose secure job clearly paid him a sufficient
margin over his family living expenses to enable him to retire the loan in the year
ahead. (2) The transaction for which the loan is made is self-liquidating and will
itself provide the means of repayment. For instance, a toy store operator may borrow
seasonally to lay in a merchandise inventory for its peak business at Christmastime.
Sale, at a profit, of the merchandise in which the loan is invested will enable it to pay
back the money. (3) The borrower is in position to provide repayment funds by
liquidating an excess of current assets over current liabilities.

Short-term loans may call for either lump-sum or installment repayments.
They may be made on either a secured or unsecured basis, depending on the lender's assessment of the risks. Short-term loans may be evidenced by private IOUs, as
bank borrowings ordinarily are, or by marketable securities, as loans to the U.S.
Treasury or federal agencies typically are.

Intermediate-term credit includes such items as commercial-bank term loans,
equipment financing (extended, for example, by a manufacturer of dental equipment
to a dentist-purchaser), and the 1 to 10 year notes that are obligations of the U.S.
Treasury. The borrower's principal requirement for obtaining intermediate-term
credit is income or earnings in the case of a business borrower. This is because
intermediate-term credit is usually extended for the purchase of long-lived assets,
such as machinery. Term and equipment loans are usually repaid in regular installments over the life of the loan.

Long-term credit is evidenced by bonds, mortgages, and privately placed corporate notes (IOUs). Since long-term credit is almost always used to finance permanent
asset requirements, eligibility depends almost totally on a borrower's profits. Over
the loan's life the borrower must appear to be able to generate sufficient earnings
from the assets the loan finances (1) to pay periodic interest at the contracted rate

and (2) to repay the loan at maturity. As with intermediate-term loans, long-term loans are usually paid off at intervals over their lifetimes.

Two final points should be emphasized about credit for different time periods. (1) Within prudent limits, both lenders and borrowers enjoy considerable freedom in substituting one length of loan for another. We have seen, in the previous chapter, that at times when *all* interest rates seem abnormally high, borrowers will seek to bridge the high-interest period by substituting short-term loans for long-term. Similarly, when all interest rates appear abnormally low, lenders often substitute short-term lending for the long-term loans ordinarily made. (2) Business and governments have much greater access to intermediate- and long-term credit than do private persons. Most individuals find long-term loans available only to buy a house, and intermediate-term credit available only for purchases of consumer durables—autos, appliances, furniture, or house repairs—and then typically only for two- or three-year periods.

Credit by Quality

Quality of credit usually means the strength of the borrower's promise to repay, and various systems of rating borrowers have been developed. For example, Standard & Poor's Corporation and Moody's Investor's Service rate corporate and municipal borrowers on their bonds, and Dun & Bradstreet rate business enterprises. Table 7-1 describes the rating process of Standard & Poor's Corporation.

Access to credit is strongly affected by credit ratings. When you borrow, ratings not only determine whether you will get credit but also decide how large a premium you will have to pay above some risk-free rate of interest, whether your loan will have to be secured, how long you can borrow for, and how much you can borrow.

CREDIT'S TASK IN THE ECONOMY

Credit adds much to the power and flexibility of economic life. It makes possible new cycles of production and consumption, distribution and exchange, by doing two things: (1) activating idle money, and by so doing (2) activating idle resources—people, machines, and materials. It also makes possible the accumulation of capital, which is the foundation of most of our business and personal wealth.

When people fail to spend their incomes promptly, their demand is lost to the nation's marketplace. The result *could be* unemployed workers and idle plant capacity. But this does not ordinarily happen. Why? Because nonspenders (savers) typically deposit their savings in banks or other credit institutions where credit-worthy borrowers may obtain them to spend against promises of future repayment at interest. Thus, the savings of the nation are made available for building new plant and equipment for industry, new schools and highways for governments, new houses and automobiles for consumers. This added demand, called *capital formation,* is made possible by credit transactions. Capital formation plays a key part in maintaining total demand and thereby maintaining the economy's output and employment.

TABLE 7-1   The Rating Process

Types of Long-Term Obligations Rated

Standard & Poor's rates practically all public corporate bond and preferred stock issues of $10 million and over, with or without a request from the issuer. There are some exceptions to this policy and in some instances publication rights rest with the issuer. The exceptions are as follows:

S&P at the present time will not rate corporate long-term debt obligations of:

(1) Organizations with less than a five-year operating history unless there are special circumstances

(2) Certificates of deposit of banks

Also, at the present time, S&P will rate only upon request obligations of the following types of organizations, with the issuer having publication rights to the rating:

(1) Private placements
(2) Non-U.S. domiciled entities
(3) Banks and bank-holding companies
(4) Brokerage firms

(5) Mortgage-related financings such as mortgage-backed bonds and pass-through certificates of banks and thrift institutions

(6) Any other type of organization which S&P does not have a long history of rating

Finally, S&P will rate the following only upon the request of the issuer, and S&P retains the right to publish such a rating unless the issue is a private placement:

(1) Industrial revenue or pollution control bonds (regardless of size)

(2) "Best efforts" financings

The fee charged for S&P's corporate long-term rating services is paid either by the issuer or underwriter of the securities rated. This fee is based in large part on the time and effort expended in the determination of the rating. Generally, the fees range from $5,000 to $30,000 for domestic issues, and from $10,000 to $40,000 for initial international ratings.

Types of Short-Term Obligations Rated

S&P will rate short-term obligations (having an original maturity of no more than 365 days) only upon request. All publication rights to the initial rating rest with the issuer. However, once published, S&P reserves the right to publish a change in its rating.

S&P charges an initial and subsequent annual fee to issuers whose short-term obligations are rated. The fees are based on the time and effort expended in establishing and reviewing such ratings and generally range from $7,500 to $15,000.

SOURCE: *Standard & Poor's Corporation*, Credit Overview, *1982, p. 7.*

SPECIAL ROLE OF BANK CREDIT

Banks not only "mediate" credit (shift existing money from savers to borrowers) but, as we saw in Chapter 5, banks can also create money if either new customer deposits or securities purchases by the central bank provide the banks with excess reserves. The banks will then have an incentive to extend more credit to business people, governments, and consumers, either by making loans to them or by buying their securities. (Money creation—or deposit expansion—is simply the fallout of this *credit-creation* process.)

Will this credit-creation process be inflationary? It depends on whether resources are available to carry out the new projects that borrowers contemplate, or whether capital and labor must be bid away from other projects. If some industries are in recession and are freeing their economic resources, then the borrowers can utilize these. But if the economy is fully employed, the new money will only bid up the price level, a point emphasized in the Equation of Exchange in Chapter 4.

If inflation develops, the central bank should take steps to reduce the money supply so as to maintain stable prices. It could do this by increasing reserve requirements in such a way as to force the commercial banks to curtail their credit extensions. But often neither the central banks nor the politically minded governments behind them have the courage to do this. So the bank-money mechanism of credit creation—aided and abetted by the reserves "fed" to it by the central bank—has accounted for most of the world's inflationary ills.

Misuse of Credit

Loans and interest are repaid mainly because firms create economic value above the amount of the loan. In addition, borrowers must do nothing to strain their positions in ways that would weaken their repayment capabilities. But we must stress that credit, extended or used unwisely, can endanger economic stability and lead to undesired cycles of boom and bust.

In the real world, credit is often misused. Some credit is obtained through fraud or for fraudulent purposes, and such borrowers do not intend to repay. But much more credit is misused because of borrowers' and lenders' errors of judgment.

Suppose that a business boom is on and the widget business is booming. Ima Promoter decides to consolidate Shaki-Widgets Corporation and Bustable Widgets Company into Giganticus, Inc. The Overboard National Bank lends Giganticus enough money to acquire the two companies' stocks, which are selling at 10 times their price of two years before. A great euphoria sweeps the country when the deal is made, and all stock prices look reasonable. But then the boom ends. A flood of widget imports from Bulgravia destroys the price structure and profits of the widget industry. Giganticus, Inc., is unable to repay its loan to Overboard National, and the bank fails, ruining many of its own depositors[2] and starting a financial panic. This is, in fact, the way all serious depressions in the past have started.

SECURITIES

Securities are documentary titles to wealth. The genus, or family, of securities includes both equity and debt instruments. Equity securities, such as shares of stock, are evidence of ownership interest in private enterprises or property. Debt securities are IOUs that borrowers give lenders as evidence of a loan and of their promise to repay. They are the embodiments of credit transactions. We will study both kinds of

[2] Federal Deposit Insurance Corporation protection runs only to $100,000 per account. Large depositors are thus unprotected against bank failures. Their only protection is to remove their money from a shaky bank before it folds.

securities in more detail in later chapters, but for the remainder of this chapter we shall be mainly concerned with debt securities and their characteristics.

Marketable Versus Nonmarketable

An IOU to the bank for a $1,000 auto loan is a security, but it is not a *marketable* security. No organized secondary market exists for the promises to pay of little-known private persons. By contrast, a bank's own promise to pay, for example, $1 million with 8 percent interest on June 30 (a negotiable time certificate of deposit) *is* a marketable security, because a number of security dealers make a market in this kind of IOU by continually offering to buy them at a certain price (the bid) and resell them at a slightly higher price (the offer). The most marketable of all securities are those issued by the U.S. Treasury. Next come those issued by the largest corporations, including banks.

For many purposes investors prefer marketable securities because they can be disposed of if the holder needs to sell them. Furthermore, their continual quotation in the marketplace gives them a more or less definite value—as property or as collateral for getting a loan. Finally, since their greater liquidity means less risk for the holder, the issuers of marketable securities can usually obtain their loans at lower rates of interest than can issuers of nonmarketable IOUs.

Time to Maturity

The most significant classification of securities is by time to maturity, paralleling our earlier division of credit transactions into short-term, intermediate-term, and long-term. Among Treasury securities, bills are short term, notes intermediate term, and bonds long term. Both Treasury bills and the commercial paper issued by large, well-known corporations are simple, non-interest-bearing IOUs that pay a face amount at maturity. The purchaser receives interest by buying them at a discount in step with the prevailing discount rate for high-grade, short-term securities. Notes of the Treasury and of many corporations are really short-term bonds, maturing in from 1 to 10 years. They bear semiannual interest coupons (bearer form) or pay interest semiannually by check (registered form). The principal amount—usually some multiple of $1,000—is paid at maturity on surrender of the note itself. Bonds, which run more than 10 years (and often as long as 40 years), have much the same appearance as notes, and they pay interest the same way.

Prices and Their Consequences

We have seen in Chapters 2 and 3 that market values of debt securities move opposite to interest rates, and that quality-rating spreads among securities fluctuate according to the state of confidence prevailing in the economy. For these reasons debt-security markets are closely watched by managers seeking a clue to the future moves of business. Rapidly rising yields not only bring falling security prices but also forecast the advent of tight money and a squeeze on companies and other borrowers. Falling yields suggest that money is becoming easier and more readily available. High or rapidly rising yields are typical of a boom that is becoming unsustainable, while low or falling yields are typical of a recession that is beginning to bottom out.

Security yields are basically a system of signals and incentives for lenders and borrowers of money. But security markets attract speculators as well as investors. Therefore, over short periods of time, the direction that market yields are taking may not have much significance. However, *sustained* moves that keep the same direction for many months and change prices by appreciable percentages are significant indicators of both the state of money and the state of business.

THE FINANCIAL MARKETS

A market is a set of facilities that make it possible to exchange money for goods, or goods for money, on a regular basis. Securities are the goods exchanged in financial markets. In making these exchanges possible, the financial markets play a central part in business and economic life.

Functions of Financial Markets
The financial markets discharge five major functions: (1) shifting credit from suppliers to users, (2) liquefying securities, (3) pricing securities, (4) foreshadowing the future, and (5) allocating funds and economic resources. Let us consider each function briefly.

Shifting Credit
The first task of the financial markets is to gather and mobilize—from thousands of individuals and separate financial institutions—a large part of the vast sums of money needed each day for the short- and longer-term requirements of business, governmental bodies, and consumers. Banks, other financial institutions, governments, and large business firms must have a dependable, central market where they can (1) bid for money in wholesale amounts when they need it or (2) sell money for various periods when they have an oversupply of it. The money and capital markets, which will be examined later in this chapter, meet these needs by permitting people with excess money to exchange it for securities and by enabling people who need money to raise it by selling securities. This exchanging of money for new-issue securities is the central task of the *primary*, or new-issues, securities markets. As we shall see, there is both a primary money and a primary capital market to accomplish these exchanges for short- and long-period money transfers, respectively.

Liquefying Security Holdings
A second function of financial markets is to liquefy security holdings. Essential to security buying is the holders' confidence that, if they want to sell their securities, they can do so readily. Thus security buyers demand marketability, and sometimes liquidity, for their holdings. Supplying these properties is the task of the other main division of the money and capital markets—the *secondary*, or resale, markets. It is mainly because of investors' confidence that their security holdings are readily mar-

BOX 7-2

We Live by Paper   How much money does a person have? How much is it worth? If you count cash, you typically reach only a tiny fraction of the total wealth claimed by the average well-to-do American. And for a high percentage of fortunate Americans, the biggest part of their wealth is lodged in securities.

Webster defines a security as "any evidence of a debt or ownership of property, especially a bond or a stock certificate." The word "security" comes to us from the Latin *securitas,* meaning freedom from care. What is it about the securities bought and sold in Wall Street that links them to this freedom-from-care notion inherent in the root word *securitas?*

Much of the freedom-from-care link comes from the fact that securities permit the separation of ownership or other claims from the physical possession, management, or responsibility for tangible properties or business operations. A bond holder, for example, collects periodic interest and expects repayment of the principal at maturity, but the bond holder need not exert himself beyond banking checks so long as promised payments are received. A stockholder is part owner of the corporation whose stock he holds, but aside from the right to vote for directors and on certain matters of corporate governance, a stockholder, like the bond holder, is a passive participant in money making.

Don't conclude, however, that securities offer their owners anything approaching security in the sense of safety. All securities are subject to risks. What we usually consider risk-free securities, U.S. Treasury issues, are acutely sensitive to loss from rising interest rates and from inflation. The prices of stocks in the biggest and strongest corporations can go to smash in a stock market debacle like that of 1929, even though their earning power remains largely unimpaired. And stock prices are forever changing—usually they're down when you want to sell and up when you want to buy.

ketable in secondary markets, at somewhat predictable prices, that they are willing to buy new issues and thus provide a continuing flow of funds to the economic system.

Pricing

A third major function—pricing—is shared by both primary and secondary markets. Interest rates, as you know, determine the price of debt securities, and interest rates are set by the supply of, and demand for, money for various time periods. It is in the money and capital markets that these supplies and demands converge. That is, the inflow of money into financial markets must always suffice to buy the total volume of new and old securities sold. Interest rates and security prices are simply the result of this process. Of course, the relative prices of different securities may shift considerably from day to day. For example, old issues may go up because few are offered, new issues may fall because the supply is large, and stocks may be up, bonds down, and bills steady. The different patterns of price and yield movements in these markets are multitudinous, but each has a logical explanation rooted in supply-demand factors.

Foreshadowing the Future

The fourth and most elusive function of financial markets is foreshadowing the future. How is this done? It is handled largely through price movements and particularly the trend of prices. Nothing else is as important to most people as money, and foreseen events typically cast long shadows before them as people race to make profits or avoid losses on what they expect will happen. Their action reflects the speculative demand for money that we saw in Chapter 4. Thus, in large degree, the economic future is often readable *today* in the money and capital markets. For example, if people expect profits to slide, then the stock market falls. If people think money will become scarcer and interest rates will rise, then they will race to dump bonds (and avoid capital losses) and acquire bills or cash instead. Because financial markets faithfully mirror people's expectations about the future, they are important barometers of business confidence and business forecasting. All top business professionals and financial executives follow the ups and downs of financial markets meticulously, interpreting every twist or turn in hope of getting a handle on how business will move in weeks or months ahead.

Allocating Resources

The markets' fifth and final task is to allocate economic resources. Ostensibly, of course, the financial markets allocate money. Parties supplying funds compare the merits of different bids for them. These parties weigh yield, safety, growth, resalability, and other qualities that the bidders offer in their securities. Having judged these merits, money suppliers buy some securities and reject others. Long- and short-term funds flow to the successful bidders (including companies, governmental bodies, and financial institutions) and are denied to those groups whose securities are not so attractive.

Behind the allocation of money, something much more fundamental also takes place. Successful bidders use their funds to acquire labor, machinery, raw materials, and other factors of production. By expanding their money resources, they will have enlarged their control of real economic resources. In this way the money and capital markets guide the economy's all-important allocation of its productive powers.

Financial Markets Classified

Financial markets can be classified in several significant ways. There is the *primary* (new-issues) market versus the *secondary* (resale) market. There are *debt* versus *equity* markets. There are *central* financial markets (such as those of New York or London) versus *local* ones (such as Buffalo). There are markets made by *dealers* (who buy and sell for their own account and risk) and markets operated by *brokers* (who merely act as their customers' agents and do not take title to the securities they buy or sell). And finally, there is the *money market* (for short-term securities, or loans) versus the *capital market* (which deals in long-term loans, equity shares, and the securities evidencing them).

THE MONEY MARKET

The money market is important for three main reasons. First, it is the basic influence on the nation's structure of short-term interest rates. Second, it is the focal point—indeed, the injection point—of Federal Reserve monetary and credit policy. Third, its tone and moves have powerful repercussions on the capital market, on the business community's thinking, and on economic activity in general.

The money market is the central market, or set of facilities, where large amounts of money are lent and borrowed for periods of less than one year. It is the central wholesale market for short-term debt securities or for the temporary investment of large amounts of short-term funds. It has two key characteristics: (1) The loans (and thus the financial instruments) in which it deals are relatively risk-free. (2) Lender-borrower relations are largely impersonal. The money market comprises several major sectors. Table 7-2 lists the characteristics of several securities traded in the money market, and you should refer to this table in the following discussion.

Treasuries

The market for short-term Treasury securities is the largest, broadest, and most important money-market sector. Traded here are Treasury *bills*, or IOUs sold at a discount from face (maturity) value, and Treasury bonds and notes within a year or less of maturity. This market has five major participants: (1) The Treasury is, of course, the borrower. (2) Nonfinancial corporations lend short-term surplus funds in this market. (3) Commercial banks buy and sell short-term Treasuries as secondary reserve instruments. (4) The Federal Reserve buys and sells short-term Treasuries to increase or diminish the reserves of member banks. (5) Dealers, both banks and nonbank houses, maintain a market in short-dated Treasuries by buying and selling for their own account.

Closely linked to the Treasury section of the money market is the market in short-term federal agency obligations. This includes the bills and notes of the Federal Land Banks, the Bank for Co-Operatives, the Federal Home Loan Bank, the Federal National Mortgage Association, the Government National Mortgage Association, and the Federal Intermediate Credit Banks. While the debt of most of these agencies is not guaranteed by the Treasury, no one expects Congress to let their obligations default. Consequently, these securities enjoy almost as high an investment standing and almost as low a yield as Treasury securities of the same maturity. The markets, however, have fewer active participants, and choice of maturities is more restricted than in Treasuries. Notice that Treasury and agency paper are sold on a *discounted basis:* A purchaser buys them at a discount from face value and the issuer redeems them at face value.

Commercial Paper

The commercial-paper market—the second-largest branch of the money market—averaged during 1984 more than $200 billion in outstanding obligations. Commercial paper consists of non-interest-bearing IOUs through which well-known corporations raise short-term funds. Like Treasury bills, they are marketed at a discount. Yields on commercial paper are higher than on Treasury obligations of equal matur-

TABLE 7-2 Characteristics of Money Market Instruments

Type	Obligation	Secondary Market	Maturities
Treasury bills	U.S. government obligations	Excellent secondary market	3 month 6 month 1 year
U.S. agency paper	Obligations of U.S. agencies established by Congressional acts	Good secondary market	30 days to 1 year
Prime commercial paper	Promissory notes of issuing companies (industrial & financial)	No secondary market	30–270 days
Certificates of deposit	Obligation of bank accepting the deposit	Good secondary market	1–12 months and occasionally up to 18 months
Bankers acceptances	Obligation of bank against which draft is drawn and which "accepts" draft	Good secondary market	30–180 days 90 days is most common primary market maturity
Federal funds	Obligation of the bank borrowing funds	No secondary market	Usually overnight

ity. Issuers typically alter the spread between commercial paper and Treasury bills to attract or repel money. The chief markets for commercial paper are banks outside of money centers (who hold it as part of their secondary reserves) and corporate treasurers, who use it as an interest-earning investment for temporarily surplus funds.

Other Segments

Other major money-market segments include negotiable CDs, bankers' acceptances, and federal funds.

Negotiable CDs are issued by commercial banks in large denominations and transferable form primarily to attract corporate-deposit balances in competition with Treasury bills and commercial paper. Notice on Table 7-2 that CDs are sold on a *yield basis:* A purchaser of a CD in the primary market pays face value and receives principal and interest at maturity.

TABLE 7-2 (Continued)

Denomination	Volume	Quotation Basis
$10,000–$1,000,000	$245 billions outstanding end of 1981. $357 billions at end of 1984	Discounted. Interest based on actual days in 360-day year
$1,000–$100,000	$126.3 billions outstanding at end of 1980. $154 billions at end of 1984	Discounted or interest bearing. Interest based on 30-day month or 360-day year
$5,000–$5 million $100,000 basic trading unit	$165.5 billions outstanding at end of 1981. $228 billions in October, 1984.	Discounted or occasionally interest bearing. Based on actual days in 360-day year
$100,000 and up; $500,000 minimum trading unit; $5,000,000 most common trading unit	$94.6 billions outstanding in May 1980. $263.2 billions in October 1984	Yield basis: interest paid on actual days in 360-day year, interest & principal paid at maturity
Issued in odd denominations; traded in $100,000 lots	$69.2 billions outstanding at end of 1981. $77.9 billions in September 1984	Discounted. Interest based on 360-day year
Negotiated among participants, generally $1 million	$72.4 billions outstanding in April, 1980. $63.5 billions in November 1984	Par basis. Interest paid based on 360-day year. Interest & principal paid at maturity

SOURCES: T-Bill Futures: Opportunities In Interest Rates, *International Monetary Market of the Chicago Mercantile Exchange, pp. 20–21*; Handbook Of Securities Of The United States Government and Federal Agencies, *First Boston Corporation, 1982*; Federal Reserve Bulletin, *January 1985*.

Bankers' acceptances begin as business firms' promises to pay. They are usually issued to finance imports and exports in foreign trade. They are termed *accepted* when a bank guarantees their payment at maturity. This market is growing rapidly—acceptance credit outstanding in 1984 averaged about $78 billion. For tax reasons the market is dominated by foreign investors.

The *Federal-funds market* is a market in one-day loans of Federal Reserve member banks' excess reserves to other members having reserve deficiencies. The rate on Federal funds may run a percentage point or more above the discount rate if reserve deficiencies are widespread and acute.[3] If free reserves are very large, it may fall

---

[3] Banks often would prefer paying a little more to borrow "Fed funds," because requests for discounts invite questions from the Fed about why the bank is borrowing. The answers would be embarrassing if the bank is borrowing to re-lend to speculators, to hoarders of scarce commodities, or to others whose activities run contrary to the Federal Reserve's wishes.

TABLE 7-3 Characteristics of Capital Market Instruments

Type	Secondary Market and Quality	Maturities
U.S. Treasury and Agency issues U.S. Treasury Notes and Bonds	Excellent to good. Highest quality	1 year to 30 years
U.S. agency Federal Home Loan Mortgage Corporation	Average, extremely high quality	Up to 30 years Up to 30 years
Government National Mortgage Association	Average; extremely high quality	1 year to 25 years
Tennessee Valley Authority	Average; very high quality	3 to 25 years
Corporate issues Notes and bonds	Good; quality varies	1 to 50 years
Preferred stock	Average to below average; quality varies	Usually no maturity
Common stock	Average to above average; quality varies	No maturity
State and local government Notes and bonds	Average to good; very high to low quality	1 to 50 years

SOURCE: Federal Reserve Bulletin, *March 1984.*

below the discount rate. Daily volume in this market typically runs many billion dollars. Fed funds are sold on a par basis: A purchasing (borrowing) bank acquires the total amount and pays interest and principal at maturity.

THE CAPITAL MARKET

The capital market includes all agencies concerned with the issuance and trading of long-term securities. These include (1) investment bankers (the "midwives" for new issues of stocks and bonds) and (2) brokers, dealers, and stock exchanges (the key

TABLE 7-3 (Continued)

Denominations	Volume	Interest and Tax Status
$1,000 minimum	$475 billion in marketable securities outstanding end of 1981. $735 billion in January 1984	Semiannual interest; federal: taxable; state: exempt
$100,000 minimum	$2.5 billions outstanding end of 1980. $6.7 billion in January 1984	Semiannual interest; federal and state taxable
$25,000 minimum	$2.8 billion outstanding end of 1980. $2.17 billion in January 1984	Semiannual interest; federal and state taxable
$1,000 minimum	$11.2 billion outstanding end of 1980. $15 billion in January 1984	Semiannual interest; federal: taxable; state: exempt
$1,000 minimum	$47.3 billion publicly offered in 1983. $3.2 billion in December 1983	Semiannual interest; federal and state taxable
Any size	$7.2 billion offered in 1983. $253 million in December 1983	Quarterly dividend; federal and state taxable
Any size	$44.3 billion offered in 1983. $3.4 billion in December 1983	Dividends when declared; federal and state taxable
$5,000 minimum	$80 billion offered in 1983, $8.6 billion in December 1983	Semiannual interest; federal: exempt; state: possibly exempt

cogs in the secondary markets for bonds and stocks.[4] Table 7-3 lists the characteristics of securities traded in the capital market. Refer to this table during the following discussion.

Primary Capital Markets

The primary capital markets consist of four major segments. These deal with (1) corporate securities, (2) federal government obligations, (3) state and local govern-

[4] The secondary capital market is discussed in Chapters 9 and 10.

ment securities, and (4) mortgages.[5] Primary-capital-market transactions are for one of two purposes: (1) sale of net new securities, which adds to the issuer's capital funds, and (2) the refunding (refinancing) of outstanding securities about to mature. Prices and yields at which securities can be sold in primary capital markets are closely aligned with prices and yields on similar obligations traded in secondary capital markets. In general, new issues carry slightly lower prices and higher yields to promote prompt sales.

The primary market for corporate securities is described in detail in Chapter 25. Since a knowledge of its organization and mechanics is unnecessary at this point, we move on to consider other capital-market sectors.

Primary Government Market

The capital markets include the market for intermediate- and long-term securities of the federal government. The Treasury issues two classes of longer-term securities. Notes have maturities of 1 to 10 years and, like bonds, carry semiannual interest coupons. Bonds run (at issue time) 10 years or longer, though some are callable (or subject to being retired or paid off before maturity at a fixed cash price) any time within 5 years of maturity.

The Treasury issues bonds for two purposes—to finance new federal debt and to refund (roll over) maturing debt issues. An issue of Treasury securities involves three essential steps: (1) an announcement by the Treasury of the issue and its terms, (2) action by the Federal Reserve as the Treasury's agent in accepting orders and payments, and (3) implicit underwriting of the issue both by the Federal Reserve and by the large government security dealers, who are tacitly committed to taking the unsold residue of any issue. During the period immediately preceding a Treasury issue, the Federal Reserve pursues an even-keel policy. It attempts to stabilize bond prices and yields so the capital market will absorb the government issue. The even-keel policy means that Federal Reserve efforts to slow down inflation must be temporarily halted when the Treasury is floating a new issue.

New Treasury borrowings present some interesting contrasts with refundings. New borrowings have a greater impact than refundings do on the capital market— that is, they take more money out, shifting it from the capital market to the Treasury. Refundings generally lead to no net loss of funds, because holders merely swap maturing issues for new bonds. However, refundings of maturing securities may shift funds from the capital market to the money market. This is because maturing bonds, having become short term, are often held by money-market investors who will not exchange them for new long-term issues. To avoid this problem, the Treasury has introduced *advance refundings,* under which holders of bonds maturing in, for example, two years are encouraged to swap them *now* for new seven-year securities.

---

[5] Every financial market transaction—in either primary or secondary markets—involves the exchange of money for securities, or near-money. So it really doesn't matter whether we think of these markets as markets for money loans of various duration, or, alternatively, as markets for various kinds of securities evidencing these loans. It makes no difference, for example, whether we think of the money market as the market for short-term funds (loans) or for short-dated debt securities.

BOX 7-3
The Tax-Exempt Edge of Municipal
Bonds   Tax-exempt bonds may offer an economic advantage to investors on an after-tax basis because their interest is exempt from federal taxation (although usually not from state income taxation). And the advantage rises with the investor's tax bracket.

The table below shows the taxable yields equivalent to tax-exempt yeilds for investors in various marginal tax brackets. Aside from the left-hand column, the other columns contain equivalent taxable yields (Y_{TE}) found by multiplying the taxable yield (Y_T) by one minus the investor's marginal tax bracket (T):

$$Y_{TE} = Y_T - TY_T = Y_T(1 - T)$$

For example, an investor in the 40 percent marginal tax bracket could receive a 9 percent yield on a tax exempt, and that would be the same as a 15 percent return on a corporate bond of equal risk:

$$Y_{TE} = 0.15(1 - 0.60) = 0.09 \quad \text{or} \quad 9 \text{ percent}$$

Notice that these values are shown below.

Tax-Exempt Yield	Investor Marginal Tax Bracket				
	25%	33%	**40%**	44%	50%
7	9.33	10.45	11.67	12.50	14.00
8	10.67	11.94	13.33	14.29	16.00
9	12.00	13.43	**15.00**	16.07	18.00
10	13.33	14.93	16.67	17.86	20.00
11	14.67	16.42	18.33	19.64	22.00
12	16.00	17.91	20.00	21.43	24.00
13	17.33	19.40	21.67	23.21	26.00

State and Local Government Bonds

State and local government bonds, also known as municipals or tax-exempts, fall into two important classes. (1) General obligation bonds are supported by the full taxing authority of a governmental unit. (2) Revenue bonds are supported only by revenues collected from services provided by some public authority not having taxing power—for example, municipally owned electric systems or toll-road authorities.

The primary market for these issues has several distinct characteristics. The volume of issues is more sensitive to interest rates than that of corporate bonds. Many states and municipalities have laws setting ceilings on the interest rates they can pay to borrow money. When market rates exceed these ceilings, the borrower is priced out of the market. Second, governmental bodies usually wholesale their is-

---

BOX 7-4

Are Municipal Bonds Risky?   Ask the holders of WPPSS bonds, and they'll tell you
that they are. The 1983 default by Washington Public
Power Supply System on two series of bonds reminds us that municipal bonds have
a great deal of default risk that we must consider before we invest in them. WPPSS
(sometimes called Whoops) issued $2.25 billion of the tax exempts to finance Proj-
ects 4 and 5 nuclear generating plants. When the default announcement was made
on July 25, 1983, Project 4 and 5 bonds fell as low as $120 per $1,000 face value
bond. By the following Thursday, bids for the bonds had climbed to the $160 range.
The rebound was attributable to the hope that WPPSS would meet its financial
obligation or that the U.S. government would bail out the company, perhaps through
a loan guarantee program.

Problems with Projects 4 and 5 damaged the company's ability to service other
bonds. The power system insisted that it would not file for bankruptcy for fear of
entangling in lengthy court proceedings the $6.1 billion in bonds that it sold to
finance three other projects. A public corporation such as WPPSS cannot be forced
into bankruptcy.

Source: Based on articles in *The Wall Street Journal, Barron's,* and *Business Week.*

---

sues to underwriters on a competitive-bid basis. Sales to final investors proceed less
rapidly than with corporate bonds. It may take underwriters two or three weeks to
dispose completely of an issue once it is taken onto their shelves. Finally, municipals
have a rather definitely segmented market. Fully taxable corporations are large buyers of short-dated municipals, primarily for the tax-exempt interest. Commercial
banks are large buyers of both short and intermediate maturities, and casualty companies and trustees also buy intermediate maturities. Wealthy individuals buy most
long maturities, especially when the outlook for common stocks is poor.

Mortgage Market

The primary market for mortgages is entirely a negotiated market, although rates on
similar kinds of loans are kept in alignment by force of competition. However,
geographical differentials are quite pronounced.

The chief mortgage lenders are savings-and-loan associations, life-insurance
companies, mutual-savings banks, and commercial banks. Most life-insurance-com-
pany loans are placed through mortgage bankers. These local specialists make mortgage loans and sell the loans to insurance companies but continue to earn fees by
servicing the loans (collecting principal and interest, insurance premiums, and es-
crow tax payments).

Mortgages are the largest single segment of the capital markets and typically
absorb at least one-third of the net annual flow of savings in the United States. They
may be resold to three government-backed institutions that function as secondary

markets—the Federal National Mortgage Association (now privately owned), the Government National Mortgage Association, and the Federal Home Loan Mortgage Corporation. The task of these institutions is to buy mortgages when they are in oversupply and when mortgage prices fall. This is done (1) to keep mortgage yields from rising excessively and (2) to provide mortgage lenders with new funds. When investors' demand for mortgages overtakes the supply again, these agencies then make a profit by selling mortgages out of their inventory on a rising market.

SUMMARY

1. The term *credit* can refer either to a loan of money or to the qualities, personal or otherwise, that enable a borrower to obtain a loan. Central to credit-worthiness are the traditional "five Cs" of credit: character, capacity, collateral, capital, and conditions.

2. Credit can be classified in three main ways: by user (business, consumer, or governmental), by time span (short, intermediate, or long term), or by quality (evidenced for large borrowers by the credit ratings they receive from independent agencies). Borrower identity, loan duration, and credit ratings may powerfully affect the interest rate paid.

3. By activating otherwise idle money, credit makes possible cycles of production and consumption the economy would not otherwise undertake. The most crucial role is played by bank credit because bank lending or investment adds to the nation's money supply. Excess credit creation, however, can lead to inflation and a runaway cost of living.

4. Securities are documentary titles to streams of income, either fixed (as in the case of bonds, Treasury bills, or other IOUs) or contingent (as in the case of common stocks). Securities may be marketable or nonmarketable; short, intermediate, or long term; and of high, low, or medium grade. Their yields and prices are inversely related and serve as a system of signals and incentives for suppliers and users of funds.

5. Financial markets are simply markets where securities are exchanged. In primary markets issuers sell new securities to raise new funds or to roll over (refund) old, maturing securities. Secondary markets are resale markets for securities that have had at least one owner. Investors may purchase securities in either kind of market. Financial markets perform five functions: (1) shifting funds from suppliers to users, (2) making people's securities-holdings liquid, (3) pricing securities, (4) foreshadowing the future, and (5) allocating funds, and with funds, economic resources.

6. The money market is the nation's central market for raising short-term funds through sale of short-term securities. Its leading "merchandise" includes U.S. Treasury bills, commercial paper, and the large CDs sold by commercial banks. The capital markets exchange long-term and equity funds for securities of equivalent maturity. Traded therein are bonds, mortgages, and the common and preferred stocks of business corporations.

KEY TERMS AND CONCEPTS

Definitions of credit
Five Cs of credit
Credit's task
Credit creation
Credit mediation
Securities
Financial-market functions

Foreshadowing the future
Primary market
Secondary market
Money market
Federal funds
Capital market

QUESTIONS

7-1. Discuss the relations between "conditions" and credit-worthiness.

7-2. Why should eligibility for a short-term loan depend on a borrower's *liquidity?* For a long-term loan, on the borrower's *profitability?*

7-3. Why is bank credit the most important kind of credit under a fractional-reserve money system?

7-4. Discuss the conditions under which credit creation is, and is not, inflationary. (Hint: recall the Equation of Exchange.)

7-5. Name the five Cs of credit. Explain briefly how each affects credit-worthiness.

7-6. Why are ups and downs of the securities markets so closely watched by experienced businessmen?

7-7. Name and briefly describe the five major functions of financial markets.

7-8. Explain how prices in the securities markets can be said to foreshadow the future.

7-9. How do changing stock market prices guide resource allocations in the economy?

7-10. Why are prices in primary and secondary markets closely aligned?

PROBLEM

7-1. Your mother is considering investing in some securities in order to receive as high a return as she can without incurring an excessive amount of risk. Two opportunities are available to her: She may invest in a City of New York municipal bond that pays 9 percent interest annually or in a U.S. Treasury bond that pays 12 percent annually.
   a. If she is in the 30 percent marginal tax bracket, which bond will she prefer based only on after-tax yield? (Hint: use the equation in Box 7-3.)
   b. Suppose she expects income tax rates to decline in the future. How would that expectation affect her choice?
   c. Does the secondary market and quality information about each type of issue in Table 7-3 influence the advice that you give her? Explain your answer.

CHAPTER 8
Financial Intermediaries and Their Role

There is much to learn in this chapter, starting with the fact that all types of financial institutions are now busily diversifying into new fields of endeavor. Master at the outset the difference between banks, which create money through their lending, and nonbank intermediaries, which merely bridge the gap between savers and borrowers.

Careful study of a typical bank's balance sheet will prove rewarding. You should remember what percentage of the whole each kind of asset or liability represents. This will give you a good appreciation of a bank's financial leverage and help you understand the use banks make of particular assets and liabilities. Do not leave the section on bank earnings until you can explain why a bank can earn 15 percent on capital by making ¾ percent on total assets. The recent increases in bank's lending risks, especially the meaning and hazards of liability management, also deserve close attention.

The chapter views nonbank financial intermediaries largely through a discussion of savings-and-loan associations. Familiarize yourself with their financial structure and with the two highly important concepts this section introduces: the distinction between *illiquidity* and *insolvency*, and the notion of *disintermediation*. The five ways in which the S&Ls may meet the disintermediation threat should be clear to you.

Thumbnail sketches of other deposit-type intermediaries will follow. Except for the section on mutual-savings banks—of great importance in some parts of the country—treatment of these amounts to little more than extended definitions for you to remember.

A brief look at insurance companies should familiarize you with the two main types: life insurors and fire and casualty companies. Be sure you understand why and how each type plays its part as a financial intermediary.

A condensed treatment of other savings institutions—pension funds, investment companies, and personal trusts—will close this somewhat detailed chapter.

When company managers look for credit or other financing, they typically invoke the service of financial intermediaries. These are institutions, often highly specialized, that serve the economy by linking particular classes of suppliers and users of funds. Some, such as banks and savings-and-loan associations, receive deposits from savers and lend the proceeds to borrowers. Others, such as *investment bankers*, may merely assist corporations and others to raise funds directly by selling securities in the primary capital markets described in the preceding chapter.

ONGOING CHANGES AND THEIR IMPACT

Although financial institutions continue to be known and regulated under their traditional names, the differences between them have begun to blend and blur. Two trends are responsible for this flux. First, mergers and acquisitions reaching across longstanding lines of separation are creating composite types of institutions with operations in two or more of the traditional fields of finance. Second, savings-and-loan associations, mutual-savings banks, and credit unions have gained the right to offer demand deposits, so the money-creating power is no longer the sole prerogative of commercial banks.

Let us view each process in more detail.

Diversification and Mergers

Changes in earning power and value for different kinds of assets held by financial intermediaries bring continual changes in the public's distribution of savings. The

---

BOX 8-1

Nonbank Banks   This chapter has emphasized how nonbank financial institutions are entering banking. A move by Dreyfus Corporation illustrates the procedure. Dreyfus, an investment fund management company, set up a nonbank bank by buying the Lincoln State Bank of New Jersey in December 1983, then selling off the bank's commercial loan portfolio. The sale of the loans removed Dreyfus from Federal Reserve control, because the Bank Holding Company Act defines a bank as an institution that *both* takes deposits *and* makes commercial (business) loans. Dreyfus has been steadily increasing its presence in consumer lending, first offering cut-rate consumer loans and more recently making mortgage loans. The bank now offers a line of credit based on a customer's home equity. Dreyfus has always been consumer-oriented, so it suited the company to dispose of Lincoln State Bank's commercial loans. And Dreyfus does no underwriting so it maintains the spirit of the Glass-Steagall Act, which separates banks and brokers.

The nonbank concept has its limits, but if Dreyfus' experiment proves successful, the proliferation of similar nonbanks could make Congress reluctant to stop the process. The amount of loans initiated thus far by the nonbank bank represents only a small sliver of business for them. But says one observer: "I remember when money funds were a small sliver. These things start very small. But if they're right, they grow."

Source: Based on reports in *Business Week* and *The Wall Street Journal,* various dates.

---

hugh outflows of savings from savings-and-loan accounts as interest rates rose sharply during the later 1960s and the 1970s illustrate the hazards that a nondiversified intermediary may face.

To insulate themselves from the misfortunes connected with a single kind of financial business, financial institutions—like nonfinancial corporations—are diversifying and/or merging. These moves broaden the base of their business and lessen their sensitivity to changes in particular lines of finance. Investment bankers have merged with brokers, life-insurance companies have acquired mutual funds, and savings-and-loan associations and mutual-savings banks are striving to become more like commercial banks. Almost every kind of financial intermediary seems headed toward becoming a department store of finance—a one-stop center where clients can satisfy all their financial needs, be they interest-bearing savings, stock-market investment, life insurance, mortgage financing, or credit-card charge accounts.

Financial institutions usually diversify by becoming *holding companies*—corporations that acquire other firms by buying up their stock. By acquiring enterprises in other lines of financial business, the holding companies can then offer multiple-line financial services under the control of a single management. While this arrangement may serve the public's convenience, it also opens the door to major abuses and dangers. A similar merger trend in the late 1920s contributed heavily to the financial ruin that followed 1929. A holding company may be tempted to lend the money of a sound subsidiary to another subsidiary that is in trouble, and wind up with both of them going broke.

Intermediation Versus Money Creation

You saw in Chapter 4 how banks create demand deposit money by lending and investing their excess reserves. To the extent that other financial institutions offer demand deposits, they now share in this money-creating power. However, most savings accounts offered by nonbank intermediaries only permit the lending of currency or demand deposits that are transferred to them by the public.

Example. Suppose that Hannah W. Campbell has a $1,000 checking account at the Whattatown State Bank, as shown in Figure 8-1. She decides to take advantage of the high interest offered by the Friendly Savings and Loan Association. Campbell makes a deposit at the savings and loan by writing a check on her account at the Whattatown State Bank. For simplicity, assume that Friendly Savings and Loan keeps its checking account at the same bank as Campbell. What happens? As we see in step 2 of Figure 8-1, the savings-and-loan enters $1,000 in Campbell's passbook (share) and sends the check to the bank. The bank switches $1,000 from Campbell's demand deposit to the association's. No new money has been created, but near-money *has* been created. Campbell's $1,000 passbook entry—to her an asset, to the association a liability—is erected on the $1,000 money base.

Now visualize the Friendly Savings and Loan lending the $1,000 to Thomas M. Kelly to finance part of a house purchase. The association will trade its $1,000 demand deposit for Kelly's mortgage note, and the bank will transfer the $1,000 to his account. These transactions are illustrated in step 3. Now another financial claim—the mortgage—has been created, but still no new money. When Kelly uses the $1,000 deposit to pay the builder, Kane Construction Company, there is still in existence only the same $1,000 in demand deposits. This final transaction is shown in step 4.

If you total the changes in demand deposits (DD) in steps 2 through 4, then they would all cancel out. The banking system is left with the same amount of reserves and deposits. What has changed? The volume of financial claims—of credit or near-money—has changed. Two financial claims and a real asset (the house) have come into being through the savings-and-loan association's intermediating—its activation of idle money balances. The velocity of money has increased.

Figure 8-1 emphasizes the chief role of nonbank intermediaries—they accelerate the lending and re-lending of otherwise idle money balances, thus giving the nation's money supply better mileage to the dollar. Their chief inducement for activating money is, as we have seen, the offer of interest to those who lend money to them. To the extent these institutions hold demand deposits, they may be treated as banks, although the range of loans they are permitted to make is generally more restricted.

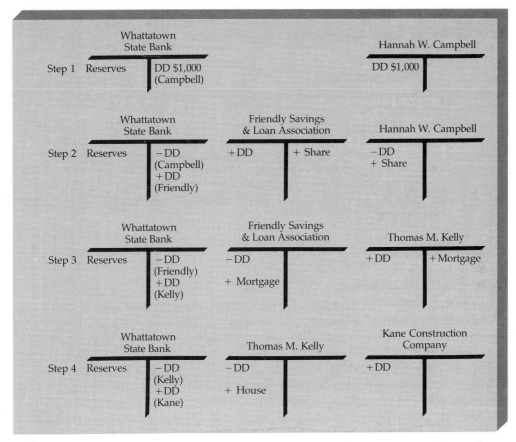

FIGURE 8-1 Commercial bank and nonbank intermediaries.

COMMERCIAL BANKS: GENERAL OBSERVATIONS

For four reasons, commercial banks are the nation's most important financial institutions. (1) They hold most of the nation's money supply. (2) They lend money on a vast scale. (3) They are the only lenders that typically create money when they lend. (4) They play a central part in implementing or thwarting monetary policy.

Some facts about commercial banks are quickly revealed when you look at the items making up their balance sheet. Table 8-1 is a representative balance sheet that displays, in typical proportions, the main kinds of assets and liabilities a bank holds. Three observations about this balance sheet seem noteworthy.

1. Banks hold relatively little cash, only about 2 percent in their vaults and tills. How do they stay liquid? It cannot be through the 5 percent of assets that banks generally maintain in required reserves,[1] because these are kept on deposit at their

---

[1] The 5 percent figure used here is less than 14 percent of the bank's total deposits because the reserves shown in Table 8-1 are reserves held against *both* demand and time deposits.

TABLE 8-1   Balance Sheet of a Typical Commercial Bank, Percent Distribution of
Major Assets and Liabilities

Item	Percent of Total
Assets	
Cash	2
Reserves at Federal Reserve	5
Secondary reserves	12
Loans	60
Investments	21
Total	100
Liabilities	
Demand deposits	35
Time and savings deposits	50
Other liabilities	8
Capital accounts	7
Total	100

reserve banks. Banks therefore rely for liquidity partly on their *secondary reserves*—
ordinarily about 12 percent of assets—which consist chiefly of short-term, readily
marketable securities. Other sources of liquidity, not shown on the balance sheet,
include the privilege of borrowing at the Federal Reserve discount window, borrowings from other banks, and the ability to raise cash by selling certificates of deposit
in $100,000-plus denominations,[2] or by having their bank holding companies sell
commercial paper in the open market.

2. The largest single class of assets is loans. This is because loans are the most
profitable way a bank can use its money. Loans (business loans, mortgages, and
personal loans) yield banks a higher interest return than do investments. Investments, which consist mainly of marketable securities, have lower yields than loans
but possess the advantage of being more marketable. Thus investments are more
liquid and serve as an emergency source of cash. If a bank sells securities to raise
cash, it will first sell its secondary reserves. However, a bank's higher-yielding,
longer-term investments—ordinarily Treasury and municipal bonds—can also be
sold for cash, though sometimes at large losses if interest rates have risen substantially since the banks bought the bonds. Loans, of course, have a definite maturity
and are less liquid than investments. A bank tries to keep its loan portfolio reasonably liquid by (a) making a prudent percentage of its loans for short periods only
(typically one year or less) and (b) spacing its loan maturities evenly to assure a
steady return of cash.

3. Banks have great financial leverage. *Financial leverage* is the use of debt. For
the typical bank, *all* capital accounts amount to only about $1 for each $13 raised

[2] These large-denomination CDs have usually been exempt from the interest-rate ceilings imposed
on CDs of less than $100,000. Thus banks selling big CD's to raise money to meet lending or other
commitments are free to bid whatever rate they must to attract funds.

BOX 8-2

Whence Our Word *Bank*?   It comes from the Italian world *banco*, which originally meant a money-changer's bench. Yes, the Western world's first bankers were money changers—people who bought, sold, and above all knew the value of the great variety of gold and silver coins circulating in the turbulent days "when knighthood was in flower" and people met to buy and sell their goods at the great medieval fairs.

Originally a mere exchanger of money, the men at the money benches eventually began to offer other services. A famous one was the *bill of exchange,* an order on a money changer in a distant city or country to pay the bearer of the bill a given sum of money. Such bills were safer to carry than coin in that dangerous era of robber barons and widespread banditry.

Eventually, too, "bankers" began to offer safekeeping services, thus accepting deposits. They and their closely related professionals, the goldsmiths, soon stumbled onto a profitable principle that became the root of modern-day fractional-reserve banking: They found that since only a small fraction of depositors ever asked for their money at one time, it was safe to lend out most of the coin they received, keeping back a small percentage as a reserve. Meanwhile, the receipts they issued to depositors began themselves to circulate as money, ancestors of our present-day paper currency. By the late seventeenth century, all of these ingredients of present-day banking had fallen into place and were developing vigorously.

The major banks today are giant, many-pronged institutions. Yet Chase Manhattan and the Bank of America are really no more than the distant decendants of the wooden bench at which medieval money changers bought and sold the coin of Lombard, Provence, and other long-forgotten principalities.

through customer deposits and orther short-term liabilities. Thus a drop of only about 7 percent in the value of the bank's assets would wipe out its capital and begin eating into depositor's funds. Since a bank also has a fiduciary, or good faith, obligation to its depositors, it must take particular care not to risk their funds through imprudent loans or investments. Its obligation to depositors should always take precedence over its obligation to borrowers—a principle that has long served to distinguish good bankers from bad ones. Since as much as half of a bank's liabilities *may* consist of deposits withdrawable on demand, any rumor that a bank is in trouble can quickly produce a ruinous run by fearful depositors, and this can close the bank.[3] A bank must shut its doors if it is unable to pay depositors on demand or

---

[3] Federal Deposit Insurance has not ended the chance of bank runs. The $100,000 per account insurance limit leaves large deposits still exposed to loss. If General Electric's treasurer hears that a bank in which his company has deposited $10 million is in trouble, he has a duty to his stockholders to withdraw the deposit at once. Thus bank runs involving *large* depositors are still a potential danger.

to honor, at once, any checks drawn on their accounts. Thus, a bank can fail for lack of cash to meet withdrawals, even though its total assets still exceed its total liabilities.[4]

Bank Management: An Overview

Banking clearly illustrates the financial manager's dilemma that we discussed in Chapter 1 because banks borrow at short term and lend at long term. Banks are run for profit and owned by private stockholders, yet important fiduciary obligations should prevent the banker from wheeling and dealing as the ordinary business manager is free to do. A bank's pursuit of profit is thus greatly restrained by the need to preserve the assured liquidity that will maintain the bank above suspicion and keep it from failing.

The central principle of bank management is that the bank should at all times preserve a proper time symmetry between its assets and liabilities.

A bank's liabilities must be paid when due or the bank must close its doors. Thus the character of a bank's liabilities governs the assortment of assets it can safely acquire. This principle does not entirely rule out what has come to be called "liability management"—that is, a bank can obtain new flexibility for asset acquisitions by intentionally altering the amount and kind of liabilities it will hold. Banks may, for example, expand their term-lending capacity by special attempts to procure more time deposits. But it is nevertheless true that the distribution of assets a bank can prudently hold depends on the nature of its liabilities.

For example, a bank whose deposits are mostly those of individual householders on salaries has an inherently stable liability structure. It needs only small secondary reserves and can probably afford to make a substantial percentage of term and real estate loans. On the other hand, a bank whose deposits, both demand and time, depend on the continuing prosperity and patronage of a few very large corporations must maintain very large liquidity reserves and lend for much shorter average periods. This is so because if the bank loses one big account, or if one large company decides to withdraw the bulk of its money in order to buy another company, both the cash position and the reserve position of the bank will be badly strained.

Of particular importance in bank management is the proper balancing of a bank's assets—whether loans or investments—between long- and short-term categories. The more volatile a bank's money sources, the more urgent it is for the bank to maintain liquidity. The eternal temptation and frequent ruin of bankers has been to lend money for very lengthy periods, making their banks too illiquid to withstand unexpected outflows of money.

---

[4] This is a main difference between banks and nonbank financial intermediaries. A bank fails if it is illiquid—if it lacks cash to pay off claims. Nonbank financial intermediaries fail only if insolvent—if total liabilities exceed total assets. A bank failing from illiquidity may, of course, be reorganized and reopened. But confidence in the former management will have vanished, and the bank will almost certainly have to install a new set of officers and directors. Losses, if any, will fall first on stockholders.

BANK LIABILITIES

Banks obtain funds for loan, investment, or liquidity and required reserves largely by trading liabilities of their own creation for depositor (or other) cash.

Demand Deposits

Demand deposits are claims against a bank, payable in cash, and immediately upon demand, either to a named claimant (the depositor) or to his order (given by check). A bank creates two kinds of deposits.

A *primary* deposit arises when someone deposits cash or a check on another bank for credit to his account. The receiving bank thereby gains reserves. Under a fractional-reserve system, the bank will hold only a fraction of these funds in reserve and lend the excess.

When it lends the excess, the bank creates a second kind of deposit, a *derivative deposit*. It is through this creation of derivative deposits that a bank is said to be a money-creating institution.

Although theoretically a bank can lend its excess reserves, a point we discussed in Chapter 4, in practice no bank could afford to lend its last dollar of excess reserves. It would be likely to keep some margin of excess reserves on hand at the Federal Reserve in case the daily check-clearing balance went against it for a while—that is, in case it had to pay out more of its reserves to banks presenting checks on it than it gained in reserves from banks on which *it* had presented checks. In addition, a bank needs to keep some cash on hand—an alternative to excess reserves—to meet cash claims by its depositors.

Banks operate on the premise that only a small fraction of demand deposits will be withdrawn in cash or by check on any given day. Therefore, margins of excess reserves and vault cash are typically small—only 3 or 4 percent of total assets, at most. As a result, any protracted drain on cash or reserves must be met by selling secondary-reserve assets or through emergency borrowings from the Federal Reserve or other banks.

Time Deposits

In contrast to demand deposits, time deposits represent depositor funds on which a bank has the right to withhold repayment for various periods. Time deposits fall into two main classes: (1) savings accounts (passbook savings) and (2) fixed-period time deposits (typically evidenced by certificates of deposit, or CDs).

Savings deposits ordinarily can be made in any amount. Although passbooks always contain a warning that the bank may require 30 or 60 days notice of withdrawals, banks typically repay savings on demand. However, a depositor forfeits the interest payable at fixed intervals if she withdraws between interest dates, ordinarily the last day of each quarter. Interest rates on passbook savings are lower than those paid on savings-and-loan share accounts, deposits in mutual-savings banks, or by U.S. savings bonds.

Time deposits have a definite maturity date, and ordinarily banks will repay

---

BOX 8-3

Jumbo CDs Are Riskier than You Think   Corporate financial managers used to think of CDs in the same way they did savings accounts—insured amounts that are there no matter what happens to the bank. But unlike certificates for under $100,000 that banks sell to individuals, jumbo CDs—negotiable CDs issued in amounts of $100,000 or more—aren't fully insured by the FDIC. In the past this lack of insurance posed no problem because federal regulators routinely merged troubled banks with healthier ones, thereby protecting even large depositors who weren't insured.

Now, however, managers are considering negotiable CDs to be risky because the bank may default on all or a part of their payment. CDs are risky because bank regulators seem to have become less willing to bail out a troubled bank by merging it with another, successful one. The result is that holders of jumbo CDs may lose all or part of their investment, just as a bond holder of an industrial corporation might. The collapse in 1982 of Oklahoma City's Penn Square Bank was the first to be closed in this way and led nervous institutional and corporate financial managers to take another look at bank certificates of deposit. In July of 1982 the government ordered the closing of Penn Square Bank. As a result, owners of about $190 million of jumbo CDs lost part of their money.

Losers included large New York City banks, a Chicago bank that almost went bankrupt in 1984, and several savings-and-loans that had invested in the CDs. Another loser was the bank's auditor, Peat, Marwick, Mitchell & Company. The FDIC in 1984 sued the auditor for more than $130 million, charging that the accounting firm didn't conduct a proper audit and that several of its partners compromised the firm's independence by accepting more than $1 million of loans, directly and indirectly, from Penn Square.

---

the sums involved prior to maturity only after assessing a penalty. Maturities may run from one month to five years, and CDs have been issued in denominations ranging from $25 to $1 million. Small-denomination CDs are typically nonnegotiable and nonmarketable. That is, they are not transferable to another person and have no resale market. Large denominations of $100,000 or more are negotiable (they can be transferred to another party by endorsement) and they have an active secondary, or resale, market, as a look at Table 7-2 reminds you. In fact, yields on the CDs of large, well-known banks are often quoted in the financial sections of newspapers. Interest rates on CDs of all sizes usually rise with their time to maturity, and large-denomination CDs have yields that exceed the yield of Treasury bills and compare favorably with those of commercial paper.

As with demand deposits, the Federal Reserve Act as amended requires banks to maintain reserves against time deposits, but time-deposit reserve requirements are much lower, ranging between 1 and 6 percent during 1984. Consequently, banks can re-lend a much higher fraction of funds raised through time deposits. However, banks must pay interest on time deposits at rates competitive with those prevailing on money-market investments of similar maturity; this cost narrows, and at times destroys, their advantage over demand deposits as a source of loanable funds.[5]

The distinction between time and demand deposits has been blurred by the Depository Institutions Deregulation and Monetary Control Act of 1980, which permits all depository institutions to offer interest-bearing checking accounts, such as the NOW (negotiable orders of withdrawal) acccounts available at banks, and the money-market deposit accounts, which offer still higher interest rates along with limited check-writing privileges.

Bank Capital

Equity, or ownership money, typically supplies about 7 percent of the funds for a bank. It consists of (1) common stock; (2) paid-in capital in excess of par, which is money paid in by stockholders in excess of par, or stated, value of their stock; and (3) retained earnings, which are the profits the bank keeps for expansion instead of paying them out in dividends to stockholders. A bank's equity serves chiefly as a cushion for absorbing possible large losses. Recall that banks are expected to maintain capital resources equal to about 7 percent of deposits and other short-term liabilities. Clearly, if a bank's business is growing, it must either sell more stock from time to time or retain a large part of its profits. Since most banks prefer to grow as much as possible through retained earnings—in order to avoid diluting the control enjoyed by existing stockholders—they ordinarily pay out no more than 50 percent of their profits in dividends.

Large banks and bank holding companies usually borrow part of their capital through long-term IOUs, as nonfinancial corporations have long done. Long-term IOUs issued by banks are called *capital notes* and closely resemble corporate bonds. Money raised through capital notes is not risk money as equity is, but it is subordinate to deposits in priority of claim and does not usually have to be paid back for 10 to 25 years from date of borrowing. So, like equity, it helps provide a cushion to protect depositors.

BANK ASSETS

A bank's liabilities show how it *raises* the money it has. The bank's assets show how it *uses* its money either (1) to make money or (2) to provide reserves. Aside from its banking premises, furniture, and equipment, a bank's assets fall into three main classes: (1) cash reserves, (2) loans, and (3) investments. Since these assets and the logic of their proper proportions were discussed earlier in this chapter, we will limit this discussion to only a few additional significant details about each class.

[5] This is particularly true when bankers make a wrong guess that interest rates will fall and so use short-term CDs to raise money for longer-term loans at fixed rates. They may lose heavily as their cost of money continues to soar while rates on money already loaned remain fixed. However, more and more bank lending is being done on a floating-rate basis, under which the rate a borrower pays automatically rises or falls with the bank's cost of funds.

Cash Reserves

Banks try to minimize cash reserves because such reserves earn nothing. Banks seek to lend or invest excess reserves and get by with as little vault cash as possible.

Loans

Banks lend money to business firms, to consumers, and to governmental bodies. Further details of bank credit to business will be discussed in Chapters 18 and 19, but two broad classes are important to note here.

Commercial loans are for relatively short periods, typically one year or less, and are made chiefly to finance short-term bulges in a company's inventories or accounts receivable, or to serve as interim financing for fixed-asset purchases until permanent financing can be arranged. In theory, two observations usually are true of such loans. (1) They finance self-liquidating transactions—that is, short-term business transactions whose successful outcome will automatically supply funds to repay the loan with interest. (2) The bank funds to make the loans are provided by demand deposits and so should not be loaned for long periods.

Term loans, which have greatly increased in recent years, are made for longer periods, usually from three to eight years. However, the money returns to the bank sooner, because loans are repaid in a series of quarterly or annual installments. Funds for term loans are theoretically provided from longer-term sources, notably time deposits.

Banks make consumer loans for almost every purpose, from meeting doctor bills to financing purchases of automobiles and appliances, but they tend to confine such lending to individuals who are high-grade credit risks. Real estate lending by banks is usually moderate in amount, selective as to risk, and ordinarily for a smaller percentage of appraised value than that for which savings-and-loan associations or life-insurance companies lend.

Investments

Bank investments, as we have seen, fall into two classes. Short-term investments constitute a bank's secondary reserves. Most of them are also highly marketable. Favorite investments for secondary-reserve purposes include U.S. Treasury bills, commercial paper, negotiable CDs of other banks, and banker's acceptances. Secondary-reserve investments seek liquidity first, then whatever degree of interest return is attainable. A bank's medium- and longer-term investments are made primarily for income, and they consist almost entirely of U.S. Treasury notes and bonds and tax-exempt municipal bonds. However, the bonds of smaller municipalities are quite illiquid.[6]

Banks make most of their long-term investments in recession periods when loan demand is abnormally small and the Federal Reserve is practically showering

---

[6] On such bonds, the underlying promise to pay interest and principal may be sound, but the bonds, because of the small size of the issue, lack an organized or ready resale market.

BOX 8-4

Banking's Historic Failing   A long-dead deputy governor (director) of the Bank of
England once observed: "Banking is a relatively simple
trade. It requires only that the banker be able to distinguish between a bill of
exchange and a bill of mortgage." (A *bill of exchange* was a short-term promise to
pay, and a *bill of mortgage* was a long-term promise to pay, usually given by a
purchaser of land to the lender.) This has been a necessary principle of sound
banking from Adam Smith's time to the present day.

It seems as though banking's historic failure has been to forget this distinction
between short-term and long-term borrowing and lending. You see all the world's
great monetary panics have stemmed in some degree from bank's abandonment of
their exclusive role as short-term lenders and their excursion into long-term lending,
securities underwriting, equity investment, and the like. Sooner or later, something
has happened to "freeze" the banks' money in long-term, illiquid obligations where
it couldn't be freed to pay off depositors when they wanted their money back.

Banks' ventures into other businesses present another hazard. If something
goes wrong with one of a bank's sidelines, there is the ever-present temptation to
use the bank's cash to bail out the ailing venture. In the past, at least, that temptation's been overpowering for too many bankers.

Banks (and insurance companies) control great masses of other people's money
on a relatively small amount of equity or owner's funds. That can easily tempt their
managers to gamble on a "heads we win, tails our depositors lose" basis.

Maybe letting banks diversify isn't such a smart idea after all. Both history and
psychology would seem to sound some definite warnings.

them with reserves to fight the business slowdown. Short-term yields are likely to be
quite low at such times. So, to improve their interest returns, the banks "reach out"
for longer-dated debt securities.

BANK EARNINGS

Most of a bank's earnings consist of interest received from loans and investments,
although revenues from trust and collection services, foreign exchange operations,
and similar sources sometimes contribute importantly. A bank's two biggest costs
are (1) the interest it must pay for money received through time and savings deposits
and (2) operating expenses such as employee wages and salaries. After deducting
costs, a bank typically earns only $\frac{5}{8}$ to 1 percent on its total assets. How, then, can a
bank make money? The answer is financial leverage.

Since a bank employs about $13 in depositors' funds for each dollar of owner-
ship capital, its overall return on assets provides a much larger return on equity—

from 9 to 14 percent on the figures just quoted.[7] Moreover, in comparison with most other businesses, bank earnings tend to be quite stable despite the ups and downs of business.

It is often assumed that banks make the most money when interest rates are very high, but this is not necessarily so. Generally, profits are highest when business is good but not booming. In booms, money becomes tight for everyone, including banks. Banks then may have to pay almost as much to attract money as they can legally (or at least ethically) earn by lending it. The two factors that most affect bank earnings are (1) volume of loans and (2) the spread, or difference, between what banks must pay for money and what they can earn by lending or investing it.[8]

Sometimes bank earnings rise during business slowdowns, despite some fall in loan demand, because the banks' cost of money falls much more rapidly than do bank-interest charges (which are administered prices and so do not respond rapidly to market forces). Then, too, a recession, bringing easier money and generally lower interest rates, boosts bond prices, so that banks sometimes realize substantial gains on their investment portfolios.

BANKS' RECENT ROLE

Over the past two decades, banks have played a riskier role in extending credit both at home and abroad. At home, small or weak companies have been increasingly unable to obtain long-term financing in the bond market, and this has enlarged their reliance on bank lending. In their zeal to increase profit, bankers have made a growing percentage of questionable loans. A considerable amount of purportedly short-term lending has, in fact, been disguised long-term lending (the borrowers could not possibly repay within the usual one-year limit, and the banks have been obliged to renew the loans over several years). These developments have substantially reduced banks' liquidity and increased their vulnerability to cyclical business downturns, such as the one of 1981–1982, which caused heavy losses to banks that had made imprudent loans to overextended companies in such boom-and-bust industries as oil, real estate, steel, and trucking.

Bank liquidity also has been undermined by what bankers call *liability management*.[9] This means that when banks run short of funds to lend their customers, the banks no longer say no or sell off Treasury bills to raise money. Instead, they increase their IOUs. They sell large-denomination CDs at whatever rate they must offer to attract funds. If, as often happens, a bank is borrowing money for a shorter

---

[7] You can relate a bank's return on equity (ROE) to its return on assets (ROA) with the equation (ROE = ROA $(D/E + 1)$), where D is debt and E is equity. Let ROA = $\frac{3}{4}$%, D = $95, and E = $5. Then ROE = $\frac{3}{4}$%($95/$5 + 1) = $\frac{3}{4}$%(19 + 1) = 15%. Financial leverage is discussed in Chapter 14.

[8] The best measure of this spread is ordinarily the gap between the banks' prime lending rate and the interest banks must pay on CDs.

[9] Actually, the idea is very old. A similar approach to banking during the 1920s brought one-third of the nation's banks to failure by 1933.

period than it is lending it, then a further rise in interest rates can plunge the bank into heavy loss and impair its credit-worthiness.

Finally, a number of the country's largest banks have made huge, ill-advised loans to bankrupt foreign governments, especially in Latin America. As of January 1, 1984, Citicorp had $4.6 billion in loans outstanding to Brazil, BankAmerica had $1.5 billion to Mexico, Manufacturer's Hanover had $1.3 billion to Argentina, and Chase Manhattan had $1.2 billion to Venezuela. In 1984, the regulatory agencies were still allowing these banks to make new loans that enabled their borrowers to pay interest on the old ones. But it seemed likely that eventually the banks would be required to write off much of this international dole as uncollectible. Whether bank stockholders or American taxpayers would foot the final bill for this indiscretion on the part of bank managers (who by then will be safely retired on fat pensions) remains to be seen.[10]

BANK REGULATION

Banks are regulated by many state and federal government agencies. Such regulation has two main purposes: (1) to control the nation's supply of money and credit and (2) to keep bankers honest and banks solvent. Banks in the United States are inspected regularly. Presumably, their loans and lending policies are reviewed, their investments are scrutinized, their cash is counted, and a full report is rendered by the examiner team to both bank managements and heads of the regulatory agency.

Improved bank-examination practices, better banker education, deposit insurance, and the "thinning out" of inferior bank managements by thousands of bank failures during the Great Depression reduced the number of bank failures to a trickle during the 1940s and 1950s. Since the late 1960s, however, bank failures have been rising in both number and size. This rise has reflected, in part at least, a lack of regulatory vigilance. In spite of their deteriorating safety record, the banks have made aggressive efforts to have regulatory laws relaxed to permit them to branch out into other fields of business, both financial and nonfinancial. Many banks, and practically all large ones, have reorganized into bank holding companies, which then own the bank as well as other enterprises. Regulatory laws have been relaxed on many fronts to permit this diversification.

SAVINGS-AND-LOAN ASSOCIATIONS

These are the best-known nonbank financial intermediaries. Originally organized to make mortgage loans to their own members, they have increasingly emphasized

---

[10] The excuse for shifting the cost to the taxpayers would be that the failure of large, important banks would risk collapsing the entire financial system. Actually, the public could wind up paying in three different ways: directly, if tax revenues were used to bail out the banks; in higher interest costs on the public debt, if the government borrowed the money; and in an increased cost of living, if the Federal Reserve System "printed" the money.

their role as savings institutions catering to small investors. In early 1984, only the interest rates paid on passbook savings and negotiable order of withdrawal (NOW) accounts remained subject to regulatory ceilings. Like commercial banks, the associations offered money-market certificates and CDs of assorted sizes and maturities at rates competitive with those paid by other depository institutions. The growing volume of NOW accounts, which allow customers to write checks on interest-bearing deposits, was subject to reserve requirements under Federal Reserve rules and formed a part of the nation's M_1 money supply.

Savings-and-loan associations may have either state or federal incorporation charters. They may be either *mutual institutions,* owned and controlled by their depositor-shareholders, or business corporations owned by stockholders, as commercial banks are. One who places money in a savings-and-loan account is technically not a depositor. A depositor has the legal status of a creditor. The savings-and-loan depositor is not a creditor but rather an owner of shares in the association. When he withdraws money, he is technically not withdrawing a deposit. Instead, the association "repurchases" his shares.

Over the past three decades, savings-and-loan associations have almost always been both able and willing to pay off their shareholders on demand. This has given savings share accounts their present near-money status. Since share accounts typically pay higher interest rates than do savings accounts in commercial banks, the public has shown an increasing preference for savings-and-loan shares over savings deposits. However, unlike banks, savings associations in most states have no legal obligation to provide withdrawals if they lack the cash. Instead, they can simply file shareholders' "repurchase requests" in a waiting list and pay them off when money becomes available.

The foregoing point involves an interesting and basic distinction in financial terminology—the distinction between *insolvency* and *illiquidity.* A business or financial institution is insolvent if its liabilities exceed its assets—that is, if it owes creditors a sum greater than its properties would bring when sold, taking due time and care. If it simply lacks the cash to pay off creditors whose claims have come due but still has total assets worth more than its total liabilities, then the institution is merely illiquid. This distinction is important with respect to federal insurance of savings-and-loan share accounts.

Share accounts in federally insured associations are usually insured to $100,000 by the Federal Savings and Loan Insurance Corporation (FSLIC). Technically, this insurance only protects the shareholder against association insolvency. In this respect, FSLIC insurance differs from that of the Federal Deposit Insurance Corporation (FDIC), which is legally triggered whenever a bank is merely illiquid. However, the savings-and-loan industry has a powerful lobby and millions of depositor-voters. So to date, FSLIC-insurance accounts have been paid off whenever an association is illiquid and an immediate merger with a sound neighboring association has not proven practicable.

Borrowing Short and Lending Long

A longstanding weakness of savings-and-loan associations is that they violate a major—perhaps *the* major—rule of sound financial management, the principle of suitability, because they borrow short and lend long. That is, they obtain money on the understanding (implicit, not legally binding) that the shareholder can withdraw it on demand. Yet they re-lend that money for very long periods in using it to make mortgage loans. This leads to a serious imbalance between their assets and liabilities. Their liabilities are—or so the public has been persuaded—demand liabilities. Yet their assets are largely frozen in mortgage loans for very long periods. Only three sources of funds are regularly available to meet withdrawal demands from shareholders: (1) inflows of money from new "deposits," (2) monthly interest and principal payments from mortgage debtors, and (3) the association's own liquidity reserves.

Somewhat easing the precarious financial imbalance of the associations is their ability to borrow from the Federal Home Loan Bank (FHLB) system, which functions as a kind of Federal Reserve for savings-and-loan associations. This federal agency often raises funds to re-lend to the associations by selling its own securities (IOUs) in the open market.

Savings-and-loan associations have followed aggressive lending policies, preferring to be "loaned to limit" at practically all times. In the years when interest rates remained relatively stable, these tactics caused no problems. But the rapid rise in interest rates after 1965 subjected them to a new hazard, which won the formidable name of disintermediation.

Disintermediation

Disintermediation occurs when people withdraw their money from deposit-type financial intermediaries in order to buy higher-yielding marketable securities.

Example. If associations are paying $5\frac{1}{4}$ percent and U.S. Government Treasury notes are yielding $9\frac{1}{2}$ percent, then, by switching funds, the small saver can make $42.50 more per year on each $1,000 invested. In 1966, 1969, and 1974, large numbers of savings-and-loan shareholders made just this kind of switch. The resulting disintermediation could have broken the associations. Even in the years 1979–1982, when the associations could offer high-yielding money-market certificates to hold their savings, liquidity and profit problems proved severe.

The reason that liquidity and profit problems proved severe should be clear. When yields on marketable securities rise, savings-and-loan associations cannot afford to make competitive increases in the interest rates they pay their shareholders. Most of their loans date from past years when interest rates were lower, and their average interest earning on mortgages responds only slowly to the rise in rates at which new loans are being made. To cover operating costs, associations require at least $1\frac{1}{2}$ percentage points of difference between the average rate earned on their mortgage loans and the rate they pay on savings share accounts. For savings-and-loan associations to offer share-account rates at levels competitive with Treasury bills, commercial paper, and corporate bonds in high-interest periods would entail ruinous losses. In 1981, for example, the associations were almost fatally squeezed— they were paying an average interest rate of about 10.7 percent for funds against an average yield on assets of only 10.64 percent. In both 1981 and 1982, the savings-

and-loan industry ran losses in excess of $4 billion, equal in each year to more than 15 percent of the associations' total net worth.

To counter disintermediation, the savings-and-loan associations have five defenses.

1. They are permitted to expand tremendously their borrowings from the Federal Home Loan Bank System. At times, as much as 15 percent of the total liabilities of the nation's associations were to the FHLB.
2. By offering higher interest rates for time deposits, the associations are raising an increasingly proportion of their funds from savings certificates, which lose interest if cashed before maturity.[11] This enables the associations to hold their funds for longer periods, even if market rates of interest are rising.
3. The government confines Treasury bills, U.S. agency notes, and sometimes the Treasury's own two-to-ten-year notes to relatively large denominations—$10,000 or more—thus making them too expensive for the average savings-and-loans depositor to buy.[12]
4. The associations have promoted the use of adjustable-rate mortgages on which the rates paid by borrowers rise and fall at least partly in step with the general level of interest rates. In early 1984, about two-thirds of all new mortgage loans made by the industry were of the adjustable-rate variety.
5. Federal law now permits the associations to invest up to 20 percent of their assets in consumer loans, commercial paper, and corporate debt securities, all of which offer greater liquidity than their traditional mortgage loans.

The asset-liability structure of the savings-and-loan industry is shown in Table 8-2, the combined balance sheet of all savings-and-loan associations. Its dominant features are those discussed earlier in this chapter—relatively small liquidity reserves (cash and U.S. government securities), very large holdings of mortgages (conventional, Veterans Administration, and Federal Housing Administration loans), huge liabilities in the form of share accounts (savings balances), and substantial liabilities to the FHLB and other "emergency" lenders.

MUTUAL-SAVINGS BANKS

Similar in structure and function to savings-and-loan associations are the mutual-savings banks, found in 17 of the 50 states. A mere three states—New York, Massa-

---

[11] In 1966, passbook accounts comprised 88.3 percent of all savings at insured U.S. savings-and-loan associations; certificates and special accounts, only 11.7 percent. By the end of 1982, passbook savings had shrunk to 14.6 percent of the total, with certificates and special accounts amounting to 85.4 percent, some six-sevenths of total association "deposits."

[12] Formerly, this condemned the small saver to accepting an inferior return while subsidizing the residential housing market. Since 1973, however, the growth of money-market funds has offered savers with as little as $500 to invest the chance to share in the high interest rates paid by large CDs and commercial paper during tight-money periods. Money-market funds pool the savings of their investors to buy high-yielding, large-denomination money-market securities and pass the interest through to their fund holders, retaining, typically, one percentage point of interest as a management fee. During the high-interest interludes of the early 1980s, money-market funds were paying their holders as much as 15 to 16 percent interest.

TABLE 8-2 Condensed Statement of Condition of All Savings-and-Loan Associations as of December 31, 1982

Item	Millions of Dollars	Percent of Total[a]
Assets		
Cash and U.S. government securities	70,179	9.9
Mortgage loans and mortgage-backed securities	545,264	77.2
Other loans	20,544	2.9
Federal home loan bank stock	5,900	0.8
Real estate owned	3,600	0.5
All other assets	60,558	8.6
Total assets	706,045	100.0
Liabilities and Reserves		
Saving deposits		
Earning regular rate or less	95,912	13.6
Earning more than regular rate	470,277	66.6
FHLB advances and other borrowed money	97,979	13.8
All other liabilities	15,720	2.2
Net worth	26,157	3.7
Total liabilities and net worth	706,045	100.0

[a] Percentages may not add to totals, because of rounding.
SOURCE: Savings and Loan Sourcebook, *1983.*

chusetts, and Connecticut—account for three-fourths of their numbers and four-fifths of their assets. Historically, mutual-savings banks have emphasized their role as savings institutions, and they compiled an enviable safety record during the Great Depression. Though technically *mutual* institutions run by vote of their depositors, mutual-savings banks are actually controlled by self-perpetuating boards of trustees, typically well-to-do people interested in promoting the welfare of small savers.

More than half of the typical mutual-savings bank's funds are raised through certificates of deposit maturing in three months or longer. About 45 percent of its liabilities consist of legal-debt deposits, payable on 30 to 60 days' notice, although in practice on demand. Great stability of deposits has precluded the need for large liquidity reserves, and so less than 2 percent of assets are typically held in cash. About 60 percent of total assets consists of real estate mortgages. Another 25 percent consists of corporate bonds, primarily issues with distant maturities and substantial yields. Up to 5 percent of their assets may be invested in business loans to borrowers within a 75-mile radius. Interest rates on deposits are generally competitive with those paid by savings-and-loan associations, and NOW accounts are available to depositors. Like the S&Ls, mutual-savings banks have been subject to severe disintermediation in times of very high interest rates.

OTHER DEPOSIT-TYPE INTERMEDIARIES

Credit unions are mutual-thrift institutions serving the members of some common-interest group such as a church or lodge or the employees of a business firm. Chartered by either state or federal government, they provide both a savings outlet and low-cost loans to members. Loans made are typically to finance purchases of automobiles, household appliances, vacations, and so forth and to keep members out of the clutches of loan sharks.

Practically all a credit union's liabilities consist of savings shares, which are not legally deposits. (These may include share-draft accounts, which are interest-bearing checking accounts.) Earnings after expenses are ordinarily paid out in dividends to shareholders, typically at annual intervals. Loans to members, including a limited proportion of mortgage loans, make up more than 80 percent of assets. To assist liquidity, most remaining assets are held in cash and government securities.

Credit unions have enjoyed popularity and rapid growth since World War II, and have paid higher rates to savers than savings-and-loan associations or mutual-savings banks. But since most of their loans are made to people with a common occupational or geographical tie, their operation is less diversified and considerably riskier.

Other kinds of intermediaries engaged in consumer or real estate lending sometimes accept (and even advertise for) small-saver accounts, but their collective role in the economy is not important. Often offering above-average rates of interest, they are seldom subject to effective regulation and are best avoided by all but the most knowledgeable savers.

INSURANCE COMPANIES

The nation's huge insurance industry, although primarily a provider of protective services to policy holders, is also a major financial intermediary. Funds provided by premium payments are invested in a wide range of securities and debt-type obligations, thereby furnishing financing to many sectors of the economy.

Life-insurance companies have the largest total assets of any financial institutions except for commercial banks and savings-and-loan associations. Life-insurance companies raise funds by selling policies on which the insureds pay fixed-amount premiums over a series of months or years. Except for term insurance, which is protection alone, all life-insurance contracts involve a combination of protection and savings elements. Policies with savings features range from ordinary life to limited-pay life insurance and endowment policies on which cash values and insurance reserves (the savings element) build up quite rapidly.

Chartered by the 50 states, life-insurance firms are of two kinds: (1) mutual companies, which are largest and which hold about 60 percent of life insurance in force and (2) stockholder-owned companies, which are more numerous but smaller. Since the Great Depression, regulation of the industry appears to have been satisfactory. Now that failures are infrequent, life insurance has proved to be a secure form of dollar saving, but inflation has rapidly reduced the buying power value of this savings element.

Life-insurance companies can lend out practically all of their funds since, for two reasons, their liquidity needs are small. (1) Reliable mortality tables enable them

---

BOX 8-5

They Don't Sell Just Life Insurance   The giant life-insurance companies take your money in premium payments and, after using part of it to meet the year's claims and expenses, invest the balance in bonds, mortgages, stocks, and other financial instruments that help power our private-enterprise business economy. Banks typically provide short-term credit to the nation's companies and consumers, but life-insurance companies supply them with an important part of their long-term capital.

Life companies sell another important product to large numbers of Americans: annuities (discussed in Chapter 2). Typically, people buy annuities to guarantee themselves retirement income. In 1984, for example, a woman 65 years old could buy a lifetime income of $7.10 a month for $1,000.

Just as life insurance is a safeguard against living too short a time, so annuities protect you against the chance of living too long. And there's one thing you can count on. Your friendly life-insurance agent is always happy to sell you either at the drop of a check.

---

to predict with great accuracy what volume of death benefits will have to be paid out in any coming year. (2) A continuous inflow of contractual premium payments keeps them well supplied with cash. Thus, most of their assets (investments) consist of long-term corporate bonds and real estate mortgages—which are the highest-yielding classes of debt securities—and small but increasing amounts of common stock. Stock investments have developed as a result of growing policy holder dissatisfaction over savings losses resulting from inflation. To meet rising demands for inflation-resistant forms of insurance savings, companies have begun offering variable annuities and, to a limited extent, "variable life insurance," wherein benefits and cash values are backed by common-stock investments.[13]

Fire and casualty insurance companies are also important financial intermediaries. They are not savings institutions, but in the course of insuring property against damage, they collect premiums in advance and invest the proceeds for periods of up to three years, almost entirely in fixed-income securities such as bonds and notes.

OTHER SAVINGS INSTITUTIONS

A few other kinds of savings institutions that handle large volumes of funds and play important parts in the financial system should be mentioned.

---

[13] In recent years many life-insurance companies have also acquired or started mutual-fund investment company subsidiaries. If prospects express worry about inflation eating up their savings, then the insurance agent can suggest that they buy term life insurance and invest the difference in the mutual fund.

Pension funds are built up through employer and employee contributions to provide employees of business firms and government bodies with retirement income. Since continuous cash inflows more than meet liquidity needs, these funds are almost entirely invested in stocks and bonds.

Investment companies sell stock to the public and purchase securities of other corporations with the proceeds. The investment company stockholder owns a small slice of a diversified security portfolio that is professionally managed. The investment company may aim at safety, long-term capital growth, successful speculation, income, or some combination of these objectives, and it may concentrate its investment in bonds, conservative stocks, or fast-fluctuating stocks, as is appropriate.

Investment companies are of two kinds. *Open-end companies,* or mutual funds, stand continually ready to sell new shares or repurchase old ones on the basis of the current value of the fund's own securities portfolio. Funds ordinarily sell new shares at the prevailing net-asset value of existing shares plus a 4 to 10 percent "load," or sales fee. They redeem shares at asset value. *Closed-end investment companies* have a fixed amount of stock outstanding, which is bought and sold on the same basis as other marketable stocks—namely, whatever people think the company is worth. Prices per share are related—but seldom conform precisely—to what a proportionate slice of the underlying security portfolio should sell for.

Most important among investment companies are the giant *money-market funds,* which pool investors' funds to buy large-denomination bank CDs, commercial paper, Treasury bills, and other high-grade, short-term investments, and pass most of the interest received through to their shareholders, who typically enjoy the privilege of writing checks against their fund shares. In early 1984, the money-market funds held total assets of more than $170 billion.

Personal trusts relieve individuals of responsibility for managing their funds and are administered by bank trust departments to meet the needs of individual beneficiaries. Testamentary trusts are often set up under a will to care for (and invest) the funds left to a decedent's heirs.

SUMMARY

1. Historically, banks have been distinct from other financial intermediaries because they alone have created money through their lending and investing activities; other institutions have merely shifted money from savers to borrowers. This distinction is disappearing as other depository institutions begin offering checking account services and, to that extent, fall under Federal Reserve regulation. At the same time, diversification by all types of financial institutions has commenced to blur traditional lines of separation. Nonetheless, financial intermediaries retain individual characteristics.

2. Banks, the nation's most important financial intermediaries, are highly leveraged, as a glance at their balance sheets will show. Since a 7 or 8 percent shrinkage in total assets will plunge a typical bank into insolvency, banks must carefully limit their lending risks. A bank must also maintain enough liquid reserves to meet demand obligations at any time, and "time" obligations as they mature. Otherwise, it must close its doors.

3. A bank's largest assets are its loans—business, consumer, real estate, government. Banks invest chiefly in federal government and tax-exempt bonds, and in *secondary-reserve* instruments—short-term, interest-bearing securities—that they can sell at need to meet cash withdrawals or reserve requirements. Their principal liabilities consist of demand and time deposits made by customers. Capital accounts for the typical bank comprise 7 percent or less of its balance sheet's right side.

4. Savings-and-loan associations are the country's most numerous nonbank depository institutions. Because their assets average a longer maturity than their liabilities, they have been seriously subject to *disintermediation*. Unlike banks, however, they are not bankrupt if merely illiquid; failure requires insolvency. From being real estate lenders only, the S&Ls have diversified into other (and generally shorter-term) kinds of lending and through NOW accounts share in the economy's money-creating function. Mutual-savings banks, important in three states, closely resemble the savings associations.

5. Insurance companies are important links between the public and long-term financial markets because they invest their capital and loss reserves in securities, chiefly bonds. Life-insurance firms and fire and casualty companies form the industry's two main divisions. Other important intermediaries include pension funds, investment companies (notably the giant money-market funds), and personal trusts, each with its specialized function of linking suppliers and users of the nation's savings.

KEY TERMS AND CONCEPTS

Secondary reserves	**Term loans**
Derivative deposits	**Liability management**
Time deposits	**Insolvency**
Capital notes	**Illiquidity**
Commercial loans	**Disintermediation**

QUESTIONS

8-1. What liquidity needs does a bank have? How does a bank provide for liquidity?

8-2. How much leverage does the typical commercial bank have? Illustrate.

8-3. Explain how the composition of a bank's liabilities restricts the assets it is free to acquire.

8-4. Distinguish between primary and derivative demand deposits at a commercial bank.

8-5. What sources can a bank tap when it is short of reserve funds? How does it decide among the sources available?

8-6. Why do bank investments often prove unprofitable over a two- or three-year period? How might banks avert such investment losses?

8-7. "Banks make their biggest earnings when interest rates are highest." True or false? Explain your answer.

8-8. Compare the liquidity needs of a savings-and-loan association with those of a life-insurance company. Which are greater? Why?

8-9. What central rule of sound financial structure do savings-and-loan associations violate? Name the trouble to which this violation leads in high-interest periods. In what ways do the associations preserve their liquidity at such times?

8-10. Does a savings-and-loan association *create* money like a commercial bank? What property of money does an S&L affect?

8-11. Distinguish between open-end and closed-end investment companies.

8-12. Do you see any dangers in the "department store of finance" idea? What sort of dangers?

8-13. A savings and loan keeps its account at the same bank you do. You write a $100 check opening an account at the S&L to take advantage of a free fifth of bourbon they are offering to new depositors. Which statement below is correct after this transaction?

    a. Bank reserves have increased $100; total demand deposits have expanded $100; and interest rates have fallen.

    b. Reserves show no change; total demand deposits increase $100; the velocity of money has increased; and interest rates are higher.

    c. Reserves and total demand deposits show no change; the velocity of money has increased; and interest rates have fallen.

    d. Reserves and total demand deposits show no change; the velocity of money has increased; and interest rates are higher.

    e. Reserves and total demand deposits show no change; you have increased your financial liquidity; and interest rates have not changed.

Explain your choice.

PROBLEMS

8-1. A bank earns $\frac{3}{4}$ percent on total assets. Capital is 5 percent of total assets. What rate does the bank earn on capital? Ignore income taxes in your calculation.

8-2. A bank earns $\frac{5}{8}$ percent on total assets. Capital is 6 percent of total assets, and one-third of capital consists of 8 percent debentures. Ignoring taxes, what rate does the bank earn on its common equity?

8-3. A bank must hold 12 percent reserves against demand deposits, 4 percent reserves against time deposits. If a large customer shifts $1 million from her checking account to a negotiable CD, how much additional lending capacity does the bank have?

CHAPTER 9
The Money, Bond, and Mortgage Markets

This brief and relatively easy chapter will introduce you to the three principal markets in which debt securities are traded from old to new owners, viewed from the standpoint of a corporate treasurer.

In studying the money market, make sure you understand the criteria a treasurer should bear in mind when choosing among the short-term instruments catalogued in Table 9-1. Pay careful attention to the main strengths and weaknesses of each instrument. A brief concluding section emphasizes the role of commercial paper as an alternative to bank loans for large, strong corporations.

The section on the bond market should provide you with answers to several questions: Why is timing so important for a corporation contemplating a bond issue? (Cost, availability, and indenture terms give you the answer here.) How do correct interest-rate forecasts help a bond issuer? How are the desirability of bond financing and effective timing of bond sales affected by the secular yield trends studied in Chapter 3? What technicalities enter into a company's designing of a bond issue? And will there always be a bond market?

In your quick look at the mortgage market, understand why other users of long-term funds can outbid mortgage seekers and how this gives the housing industry a contracyclical pattern of activity. This will make clear why Fannie Mae, Ginnie Mae, and Freddie Mac form a growing family of mortgage-market godparents.

THE MONEY MARKET

This short addendum on the money market is intended to answer four questions. (1) How does the corporate treasurer use the money market? (2) What is the chief problem in dealing with it? (3) What outstanding properties of money-market instruments fit them for particular uses? (4) How should money-market investments be decided?

Liquid Storage of Funds

Corporations accumulate temporary funds for dividend payments, tax installments, and other purposes. Reduced working-capital requirements pile up idle cash in slack periods. Such sums today are capable of earning substantial interest returns over short periods, provided they can be invested with safety and liquidity. These properties are provided in varying degrees of money-market instruments.[1] While the money market is not the only place corporate treasurers can turn for short-term investments, it is ordinarily their safest and most familiar recourse.[2]

Selection rather than timing is the treasurer's main problem in making money-market investments. We have seen that short-dated, high-grade debt securities typically provide high yields in boom periods, low yields in recessions: rising yields when business is expanding, falling yields as the economy contracts. But the availability of corporate funds for short-term investment typically moves counter to the juiciness of yields. Business organizations have the most surplus money to lend at interest during times of slack business—at recession bottoms when yields are low. When yields are invitingly high, as they are during booms, corporate needs to finance peak levels of inventories and receivables are typically large: companies are much more likely to be borrowers in the money market—sellers of commercial paper—than lenders to it.

The Treasurer's Problem

Since the timing of money-market investment is decided almost automatically by timing of corporate cash flows, the main problem facing the treasurer is not when to invest but *what to invest in?* In large degree the decision comes down to the classic financial dilemma: yield versus liquidity.

Money-market instruments differ with respect to (1) ease of resale, (2) how closely maturities can be tailored, or at least selected, to meet an investor's need, (3) yield, and (4) to some degree safety. The extent to which a tradeoff between yield and liquidity is necessary depends on predictability of the lender's need for cash.

If a treasurer needs cash back to meet a dividend date or tax payment, and is sure no intervening need will arise, then he is free to pick the highest-yielding instrument among those of the right maturity. If, however, the treasurer is merely

---

[1] Introduced by name and generally described in Chapter 7.
[2] Small corporations may invest in small-denomination CDs at commercial banks (under $100,000 and nonnegotiable), in savings-and-loan shares, or small-loan company certificates.

BOX 9-1

A Trap for the Unwary A financial manager seeking temporary storage for a company's surplus money should emphasize safety first and interest return second. Of course, most short-term investments are reasonably safe, so trouble from overly venturesome choices surfaces only rarely. But when it does, it can rise with a vengeance.

One trap a good many corporate treasurers fell into during 1980–1981 was buying the CDs of Mexican banks. Banks south of the border were paying fantastic interest rates, 25 or 30 percent annually, to attract investors. The trouble for Americans was that to earn this fat interest, they had to sell their dollars for Mexican pesos, then invest the pesos. The rub was that too few of these venturesome treasurers looked into the problem of what could happen to the dollar value of the peso.

Suddenly, the oil boom that supported Mexico's unstable economy collapsed. And down with it came the peso. In a series of devastating currency devaluations, pesos that went into CDs worth a nickle in American money came out worth less than a penny. The lesson: If you face a loss of 80 percent or more of your principal, 25 or 30 percent interest doesn't count for much.

This episode carries a larger warning for all investors: Risk and return are closely related so that the way to get higher returns is to take on additional risk. Remember, people rarely give money away. They don't pay 25 or 30 percent interest out of the goodness of their hearts. Invariably, it's because their finances are unsound, and because really smart lenders shun them, so they play for sucker money by offering ultra-high interest rates.

So when you see that kind of interest offered, ask yourself a simple question: Why should Flub-Dubb, Inc., pay 30 percent when Rock-of-Gibraltar Corporation can get all the money it wants at 10 percent?

"storing money at interest" against *unpredictable* needs, then questions of marketability and liquidity arise. The investor can get a better yield by buying a longer-dated instrument. This may cause him no embarrassment or loss if the instrument is highly marketable, as U.S. Treasury bills typically are. He might get a better yield on bills maturing five or six months hence than on one- or two-month bills, and if he had to sell them after a month or so, he might come out no worse on his interest return for the period. But if he bought five- or six-month commercial paper (which ordinarily has no resale market), he might suffer an actual loss getting someone to take it off his hands a month or two later.

Choice of Instruments

A look back at Table 7-2 will remind you of the characteristics of leading money-market instruments. It deserves your careful study, and there is little we need add to its catalogue of facts.

Issuing Commercial Paper

For the medium- or large-size company, commercial paper is a possible source of short-term cash. If the company's credit standing is high enough (and how high is high enough depends on credit conditions and on how many scares lenders have recently had), it can sell commercial paper. The yield on commercial paper is typically less than the prime loan rate at the banks, and the sale of paper involves no compensating balance requirement, so borrowers enjoy the use of all the funds they pay for. The main disadvantages of commercial paper are (1) that it includes none of the advisory services a good bank can provide and (2) that lender-borrower relations are impersonal—that is, there is no "loyalty" required or expected on the part of lenders. Lenders can be expected not to renew their loans when the paper matures if better lending opportunities occur elsewhere. As Chapter 24 will discuss, commercial paper is usually backed with standby credit lines at commercial banks, so that if the paper cannot be renewed, cash to pay it off is assured.

THE BOND MARKET

Whereas business organizations use the money market both for storage and borrowing of funds, most of them use the bond market only to borrow. Since bond sales always involve intermediate- or long-term borrowings, timing is a crucial factor in a decision to sell bonds.[3] Thus an understanding of price trends and yield movements is of key importance to the businessman involved in bond issues or refundings.

Bond-Yield Fluctuations

Chapter 3 dealt with interest-rate fluctuations in general. Like other interest rates, bond yields rise in booms, fall in recessions—they display a *cyclical* pattern of movement. This means that firms can sell bonds at a smaller interest burden in times of recession, while bonds floated during booms typically carry much higher interest burdens. This behavior of bond-interest costs injects a basic difficulty into the timing of bond financing. Firms are most likely to need long-term debt (and other financing) during booms and least likely to need it in recessions. Thus the basic movement of bond yields makes bond money most expensive when it is needed and least expensive when it is not.

Availability, as well as cost, of bond money moves contrary to needs. In a deep recession, few bond issues are coming to market and the calendar of offerings is clear and uncluttered. But at the peak of a boom, it may be "standing room only" in the new-issues market. In fact, so many companies may be lining up to sell debt issues that there isn't room for all of them. In this case, only companies with the

---

[3] Some people would say the crucial question is whether to sell stock (common or preferred) or bonds in the first place, and this is undeniably important. But given the decision to finance with debt, the problem then becomes one of timing. If it is not a good time to sell bonds—too many issuers, or much lower rates expected soon—a strong company can always substitute short-term borrowings temporarily while awaiting a better opportunity in the bond market. (Of course, the judgment that waiting will pay off must be right.)

biggest names and best credit ratings are able to sell bonds—there aren't enough bond buyers to take care of the rest.

Example. Companies may go to their investment advisors with proposals to market $25–$30 million worth of new bonds, only to be told, "There isn't room on the calendar, because a $360 million Telephone issue, several large power companies, and a couple of mammoth industrial concerns (like GE and Texaco) have preempted all the debt funds in sight for the next two months." In such cases, smaller, less well-known issuers must usually postpone their bond sales and seek temporary, substitute financing (bank loans or possible commercial-paper sales), cancel their projects for lack of finance, or seek a merger partner.

Not only cost and availability, but *terms of indentures* also are geared to the business cycle. In recessions, money is cheap, abundant, and looking for bonds to be invested in. Savers and investors are glad to find bonds that will pay them a halfway decent interest rate, and they are not inclined to debate an issuer's reasonable requirements regarding call period, call premiums, sinking funds, and other provisions of the indenture. By contrast, in boom times, a "buyer's market" for bonds exists. More issues are looking for buyers than the market can accommodate. Buyers can pick and choose and bargain with issuers for the most advantageous terms. Since yields are temporarily much above the average expected over the next few years, bond buyers almost invariably demand *call protection*—an indenture provision prohibiting the company from redeeming the bonds for 5 to 10 years. This, of course, ensures that the buyers will continue to collect their contracted high rate of interest for this period, even though "market" bond yields fall drastically. If a company refuses to make its issue "noncallable," then it may have to pay an extra one-half or three-quarters percentage point of coupon interest. And in tight bond markets, other indenture provisions—working-capital requirements, dividend restrictions, limitations on other debt financing, and so on—are likely to be tighter simply because investors are in the driver's seat.

Bond-Market Strategy: Its Rewards

These considerations suggest that one key to effective bond financing by corporation managers is proper foresight—a willingness and ability to look far enough ahead to foresee the need for debt capital and thereby avoid both high yields and traffic jams in the bond market. Foresight to time bond-market forays advantageously comes primarily from a sound understanding of interest-rate history, recurring business-cycle patterns, and conditions in one's own industry. It also calls for correctly forecasting both when a company will need debt capital and what the future movement of interest rates will be. Since 1966, companies have shown a growing desire to forecast both future bond-market conditions and their own needs. This has been a major factor preventing a deep or prolonged decline in bond yields during recent recessions. During the 1970–1971 and 1974–1975 recessions, the Federal Reserve was pumping up the money supply at a frightful rate and business leaders guessed that faster inflation and new peaks in interest rates lay ahead. So, even though business was sluggish, major companies continued to sell new bonds in record amounts.

Secular Yield Trends

Chapter 3 discussed the secular (or supercyclical) trend in interest rates: persistent moves upward or downward lasting through several business cycles and carrying yields far above or below their starting level. Such trends, of course, affect suppliers and users of long-term funds more drastically than they do money-market participants. Bonds are issued and held for longer intervals; decisions to issue or purchase them must be lived with for decades rather than months or years. Subsequent changes in yields may produce immense fluctuations in bond prices. Subsequent changes in the buying power of money may also vastly alter both the real burden to bond issuers and the real return to bond holders.

Only the main implications of secular swings in bond yields can be mentioned here, but you should see at once the advantage of being on the right side of these prolonged moves—namely, issuing bonds early when yields are trending up (and money is falling in value) and buying bonds early (as an investor) when a fall in yields (and rise in money's value) is under way. For example, corporations that sold large volumes of long-dated bonds before 1965 at yields of $4\frac{1}{2}$ percent or less have ridden through the 1970s practically free. The average rise in prices of about 7 percent per year has far exceeded the interest rate on these borrowings, effectively reducing the real rate of interest to less than zero. Beyond this, the deductibility of interest for income tax purposes has cut the nominal rate of interest almost in half, measured in after-tax dollars.[4] By contrast, some companies failed to anticipate the secular movement of yields and postponed their heavy bond borrowing until after 1968. Such companies have had to float bonds at 7 to 15 percent near what may turn out to be the top of a long cycle of rising bond yields. If it is, and if bond yields fall and inflation changes into deflation, then the real burden of bonded debt contracted (1) at high interest rates and (2) in cheap money will rise painfully, since it will have to be paid back in an era of low interest rates in "dear" money. Many a company might not survive the experience.

Since 1952 inflation has exerted a growing influence on interest rates. Since 1965 this influence has become prompter and more visible. Why are 1952 and 1965 pivotal years? The year 1952 is important because it was the first full year in a decade that the Federal Reserve was able to use open-market operations to absorb bank reserves. In 1951, the Treasury and the Federal Reserve reached an accord, relieving the Federal Reserve of the responsibility it had assumed in 1942—that of supporting the price of government securities near par. With this accord, monetary policy was set free to influence the economy, and open-market operations became a full-fledged tool of monetary policy. In 1965 came the beginning of the great wave of

---

[4] As Equation 20-1 in Chapter 20 will point out, the cost of debt expressed in after-tax dollars is k_d = $Y_m(1 - T)$, where k_d stands for the after-tax cost of debt, Y_m for the yield of the debt to maturity expressed in current dollars, and T is the corporation's tax rate. With a 50 percent income tax rate, 50 percent of any amount deductible before taxes will be saved by a corporate taxpayer.

inflation that has gripped our economy throughout recent years. Inflation, rather than any shifts in underlying savings and investments, has accounted for nearly all the increase in interest rates since 1965.

Bond yields reached a twentieth-century peak in 1981, then fell in the ensuing recession but failed to reach the lows made in the previous recession of 1980. By early 1984, they were rising again, in step with a renewed climb in the economy.

What will happen if inflation and bond yields keep on rising to new high levels? The bond market may disappear, with long-term debt capital becoming unobtainable. If it becomes evident to long-term creditors that they will continue to be robbed by higher and higher inflation rates, then savers may refuse to make long-term loans at any rate of interest. Then in the United States, as in many European countries today, business people will be able to obtain only short-term loans, which lenders can refuse to renew—or can up the interest rate on—if they find inflation accelerating. Since this would cluster all of a company's debt maturities within the few months or years immediately ahead, the business picture would become increasingly unstable, and susceptible to panic and collapse. At intervals through the 1970s, many large companies (notably the weaker electric utilities) were only able to sell short-term bonds, with maturities of 5 to 10 years. Lenders did not trust these shaky borrowers for more than a few years. However, the politicians and central bankers who have masterminded our economy have shown little concern over this growing deterioration of our long-term debt market, and for all their fine words and empty rhetoric, they do not really seem the least bit anxious to curtail inflation. So there is a valid question to raise here: Will there always be a bond market?[5]

Bond-Market Technicalities

The foregoing account of how a manager should look at the bond market gives only a simplified, high-spot impression. If you were contemplating an issue of bonds, many problems not yet mentioned would confront you. You would have to decide not only your timing but a host of other questions as well. Should you put a low coupon on your bond and sell it at a discount, a high coupon and sell it at a premium, or a current coupon and sell it at par? Sometimes the market favors one, sometimes another. To what extent should you trade a longer noncallable period for a lower-interest coupon? Should your bonds have a sinking fund, be convertible into common stock, or have an indenture permitting management greater freedom at the cost of a higher yield? What maturity should the bonds have? Should the company lock in its use of the borrowed funds for 20 to 40 years? Or should it sell 5- or 10-year bonds, gambling that yields will drop, and permit the bonds to be refunded at a lower interest rate? There also is registration with the SEC to consider. As you can see, the actual design and selling of a bond issue is a complicated proceeding.

Alert financial managers follow bond prices on a daily basis, watching for

---

[5] Another possibility would be a universal resort to "indexed" lending—loans on which interest (and perhaps principal) would rise with the general price level. The variable, or adjustable, rate mortgages, which constituted about two-thirds of all residential home-buyer loans in early 1984, are illustrative of a trend that could extend to business and government borrowing as well.

BOX 9-2

A Hot Item that Never Caught Fire   They're called "floating-rate notes." Actually, they're bonds that pay a changing interest rate from one period to the next, depending on how interest rates in general change. For example, Citicorp issued floating-rate notes in 1984 that pay semiannual interest at a rate one percentage point above recent rates on U.S. Treasury bills. They operate similarly to adjustable-rate mortgages that have interest rates that change with some market rate like the Treasury bill yield.

Since these corporate notes pay a current-market rate, their price is always stable around the $1,000 par. You'd think they'd be popular with safe and sane investors who dislike seeing the value of their bonds go up and down like a yo-yo.

Well, just the opposite's happened. Since the prices of these bonds have little reason to fluctuate, most investors have shunned them. Hot-shot bond traders *want* bonds that fluctuate so they can rack up capital gains. Other investors can get the benefits of current interest rates and price stability through a series of investments in Treasury bills, commercial paper, or negotiable CDs, or by buying shares in a money-market fund. Many home buyers feel the same way because they don't want an adjustable-rate mortgage that may push their mortgage payments up to an intolerable level.

So, despite what looked like a good idea, floating-rate notes and mortgages have not become the popular financial items that many experts thought they would. A few corporations have issued floating-rate notes, usually in high-rate periods, to take advantage of an expected fall in interest rates later on. As for most investors, they've just yawned and bought something else. Mortgagees like to issue adjustable-rate mortgages because they make a homeowner-borrower assume the risk of higher interest rates. But homeowner-borrowers seem still to prefer fixed-rate mortgages with fixed payments.

important trends to begin, continue, or be reversed. At all times, they stay aware of the state of the bond market, of how easy or difficult it would be for their companies to sell new bonds, and of what yields, maturities, and other terms would be required. Most successful, high-level business people, regardless of their specialty, watch the bond market as an indicator of business conditions. Table 9-1 will show you briefly how to read the bond quotations in the financial section of your daily newspaper. The quotations in Table 9-1 illustrate the reporting of corporate bond prices. These are prices of bonds traded on the New York Stock Exchange on Friday, March 23, 1984. Columns from left to right identify successively the bond, its approximate yield at the current price, the number of bonds (volume) traded during the day, the highest, lowest, and closing price of the bond, and its net change of price from the previous trading day. For example, the first bond shown is the Illinois Bell Telephone Company bond paying $7\frac{5}{8}$ percent ($76.25 annually per $1,000 bond) and maturing in the year 2006. On its present price, well below its $1,000 par value, it

TABLE 9-1 Reading Corporate Bond Prices

Bonds	Current Yield	Volume	High	Low	Close	Net Change
Ill Bell $7\frac{5}{8}$ 06	13.	17	$58\frac{3}{4}$	$58\frac{3}{4}$	$58\frac{3}{4}$	$+\frac{7}{8}$
Infrst $7\frac{3}{4}$ 05	cv	120	$73\frac{1}{2}$	$72\frac{1}{2}$	$72\frac{1}{2}$	-1
Int Hvr 9s04	15.	66	$58\frac{3}{4}$	$57\frac{1}{2}$	$58\frac{3}{4}$	—
Int Hvr 18s02	17.	146	$105\frac{5}{8}$	$104\frac{1}{2}$	105	$-\frac{5}{8}$
JCP $9\frac{5}{8}$ 06	14.	41	70	69	70	$+1$

SOURCE: The Wall Street Journal, *Monday, March 26, 1984, p. 37.*

yields a new purchaser 13 percent. Seventeen of these bonds changed hands on March 23, and the price was $58\frac{3}{4}$ percent of par ($587.50 per bond) all day. (Bond prices are always quoted in percentages and eighths of their $1,000 par value.) Quotations from the other bonds are interpreted similarly. These bonds, reading downward, are InterFirst Corporation $7\frac{3}{4}$ percent bonds, due in 2005; International Harvester 9 percent series bonds, due in 2004; International Harvester 18 percent series bonds, due in 2002; and J. C. Penny $9\frac{5}{8}$ percent bonds, due in 2006. Note the designation "cv," which shows that the InterFirst bonds are convertible into the bank's common stock.

THE MORTGAGE MARKET

The chief fact of life surrounding the mortgage market is its residual, contracyclical position. It is residual because long-term loan money flows strongly into mortgages only after the demands of stronger bidders—corporations, the Treasury, and federal agencies (through which the government does its "back door" financing)—are satisfied. These strong bidders are not handicapped by artificial ceilings on the interest rates they can pay. Hence, in times of tight money, they pay what the market requires to get funds and so "suck" money away from mortgages. Then, when recession comes and corporations, particularly, are no longer selling bonds aggressively, more money becomes available for mortgages. This gives rise to the contracyclical pattern of money availability—plentiful money for mortgage financing in recessions, less in booms.[6]

Like bond yields, mortgage interest rates rise and fall with the business cycle and with interest rates generally, but their moves tend to be "stickier" and more restrained. Mortgage rates are administered rates, set by lending institutions and changed rather infrequently, in contrast to bond yields, which reflect daily bond trades in the open market. Mortgages compete with corporate bonds for investment by several kinds of financial institutions, notably life insurers. The spread between

---

[6] This fact has tended to make the housing industry a so-called automatic stabilizer of business since World War II.

mortgage and bond yields largely regulates the flow of life-insurance money between the two investments. When bond yields skyrocket, as they have in recent
booms, life-insurance companies desert the residential-mortgage market to invest in
higher-yielding bonds.[7] Commercial and industrial mortgages fare less poorly because here the lender may demand "a piece of the action," in the form of some
sweetener or automatic inflation hedge. Thus an apartment builder may obtain a
mortgage loan at, for example, 10 percent interest plus 1 percent of gross receipts. If
inflation continues and rentals rise, the lender will automatically share in the apartment's increased income.

Since individual home ownership has long been a goal of government policy,
Washington has tried in various ways to support and fortify the residential mortgage
market. The Federal National Mortgage Association (formerly a government institution, but now in private hands, known as Fannie Mae) has exercized strong borrowing power as a government-sponsored agency, has raised large sums in the bond and
money markets when housing loans were tight, and has used the cash to buy mortgages from insurance companies, savings-and-loan associations, and other lenders.
These lenders then recycled the cash into new mortgages. This operation has been
very profitable because Fannie Mae buys mortgages when yields are high and prices
are cheap and later sells many of them when yields are low and prices are high
again.

Two newer and federally owned institutions now share this task with Fannie
Mae: the Government National Mortgage Association (Ginnie Mae) and the Federal
Home Loan Mortgage Corporation (Freddie Mac), both started in 1970. Ginnie
Mae's chief contribution is to assist mortgage lenders in setting up large pools of
government-insured or government-guaranteed mortgages and selling *participation
certificates* in them to medium- and large-sized investors. These PCs, which range in
denomination from $25,000 up, entitle each holder to a pro rata share of the interest
and principal payments from the underlying pool of mortgages. The interest and
principal are fully guaranteed by the government, and yields on the PCs are about
equal to those available on high-grade bonds. Ginnie Mae PCs enjoy an active
secondary (resale) market. This marks a step toward turning home mortgages into
marketable securities. Freddie Mac performs a similar service for conventional mortgages.

SUMMARY

1. Corporate treasurers use the money market for liquid storage (at interest) of
short-term funds and also to raise short-term funds by selling commercial paper if
their companies are strong enough to qualify.

2. In choosing among the several money-market investments available, a trea-

---

[7] A rule of thumb is that to compensate mortgage lenders for the added bother of servicing the
mortgage—monthly collections and accounting for the loan—they need about 150 "basis points"
(equal to $1\frac{1}{2}$ percentage points) more on a mortgage than they can get on a high-grade corporate
bond.

surer should consider (1) how closely its maturity fits its need for money, (2) whether it needs easy resalability, (3) and what tradeoff between yield and safety it desires. For short-term corporate financing, commercial paper is typically cheaper than a bank loan. On the other hand, its use includes none of the valuable services a bank loan often carries with it.

3. Since bond yields rise and fall with the business cycle, timing is of great importance to a bond issuer. Typically, a recession is the best time for a corporation to sell bonds because yields are low, money is readily available, and indenture terms are least restrictive. The key to timing bond issues advantageously lies in understanding both the cyclical and secular movements of interest rates and in correctly gauging where rates currently stand with respect to both kinds of movements. An ability to judge what bond yields will be one, two, or five years in the future can provide the corporate treasurer with a priceless crystal ball. Technical questions involved in designing a bond issue—discount or premium pricing, call provisions, convertibility, maturity, and the like—are usually decided jointly by corporate officers and their investment banker.

4. Mortgage offerors have problems in tight capital markets because corporations and the government find it easy to outbid them for funds. This means that mortgages can be sold in the largest amounts and at the lowest interest costs in recession periods when corporations, in particular, are selling few bonds. Consequently, home-building follows a largely countercyclical pattern, reviving strongly in recessions and shrinking back during business booms. To aid housing, the federal government has established institutions with exotic nicknames, such as Fannie Mae, Ginnie Mae, and Freddie Mac to help market home mortgages, largely by packaging them into participation certificates that offer investors many features akin to those found in bonds.

KEY TERMS AND CONCEPTS

Liquid-funds storage	Residual position of mortgage
Bond-market timing	market
Secular yield trend	Ginnie Mae "PCs"
Interest-rate risk	Money-market certificates

QUESTIONS

9-1. Why is selection, rather than timing, the corporate treasurer's chief problem in making money-market investments? How does this involve the classic financial dilemma, yield versus liquidity?

9-2. Discuss the merits and shortcomings of commercial paper as a *source* of short-term funds.

9-3. What money-market instrument would best suit the needs of a corporate treasurer who is accumulating funds to meet a large dividend payment due exactly on June 10?

9-4. Distinguish between cyclical and secular fluctuations in bond yields and describe the characteristic pattern of both fluctuations.

9-5. How do cost, availability, and indenture provisions of bond flotations typically change over the business cycle?

9-6. Does inflation make bond financing cheaper and easier for corporations? Discuss.

9-7. What features of a bond issue must the issuer design to fit the market? Where can one get advice on best design?

9-8. Why does the availability of funds for residential mortgages appear to move contracyclically?

9-9. Why do commercial and industrial mortgages fare better in times of tight money than residential mortgages?

9-10. Explain how Fannie Mac, Ginnie Mae, and Freddie Mac assist the home mortgage market.

CHAPTER 10
The Stock Market

A good grasp of this chapter can prove doubly rewarding; it should serve in both your business career and your personal investment endeavors.

First, identify clearly the leading investor groups active in the stock market and the differences between the listed (exchange) and over-the-counter markets, differences that hinge principally on the trading procedures used. Then be sure you can distinguish between—and explain what causes—the four main kinds of movement in stock prices: secular, primary, secondary, and day to day.

Turning to the prices themselves, the discussion answers several key questions. Why can stock prices be said to *discount* the future? How do *discounted* and *undiscounted* news differ in their effects on the stock market? What is the *efficient market hypothesis*? Why do stock quotations reflect the operation of marginal pricing? Very important among the concepts presented in this chapter are margin trading and short selling. Make certain you can explain exactly what happens when a stock trader sells short. (Remember, there is a buyer on the other end, and that buyer must receive the purchased shares.)

Looking at long-term changes in the general level of stock prices, you should recognize the importance of investors' expectations concerning economic growth and stability, the presence or absence of inflation, and the effects of tight or easy money, rising or falling interest rates. For stock price changes over shorter periods, a knowledge of how different classes of stock traders operate will be especially helpful; be sure, too, that you can define major-swing, short-term, and special-situation trading. Also of great importance is the difference between the valuation approach and technical analysis.

Finally, a recognition that the stock market moves in anticipation of business profits, and not in step with them, will serve as useful background when you reach this book's all-important final chapter which highlights stock prices as "leading indicators" of business conditions.

By the *stock market* we mean the market for common and preferred stocks, which are equity interests (ownership rights) in incorporated companies. This market comprises the whole apparatus dedicated to helping people buy, sell, price, select, and finance the securities in which they invest or trade. It embodies brokers, dealers, investment bankers, security analysts, portfolio managers, professional investment advisers, banks and other financial institutions, the organized stock exchanges, the over-the-counter securities market, state securities commissions, and the Securities and Exchange Commission in Washington, D.C.

CUSTOMERS OF THE STOCK MARKET

Customers of the stock market include both individuals and institutions. Individuals hold an estimated three-fourths of the total dollar volume of stocks, and institutions hold the other one-fourth. However, the proportion of stocks held by institutions has risen year by year, and the proportion held by individuals is slowly falling, as pension funds, investment companies, and other institutional investors have progressively bid a rather static supply of shares away from individual holders.[1]

Institutions trade in the stock market at a faster pace than individuals; in recent years, institutional buying and selling have accounted for more than half the total share turnover on the New York Stock Exchange. These trends in institutional ownership and activity have largely been accounted for by two factors: (1) the growth to enormous size of pension funds, which invest much of their money in common

---

[1] The rather static supply of shares since World War II has reflected corporations' strong preference for bond financing. As Chapters 18 and 20 will point out, the tax deductibility of interest has typically held the cost of debt financing below the cost of equity (on which earnings accrue only after income tax has been paid). Then, too, to give their shares a growth stock image, most companies prefer to increase their equity through retained earnings rather than by selling new shares of stock.

stocks, and (2) the tendency of institutions to trade for quick profits instead of holding stocks passively for long-pull investment gains.

Major institutions active in the stock market include the following:

1. Investment companies, notably the mutual funds. A mutual fund operates by selling its own shares to investors, then investing the receipts in a wide variety of corporate stocks. "Professional" portfolio management and greater diversification than a small investor could achieve alone have been the mutual funds' chief selling points.
2. Bank-administered trust funds.
3. Pension, profit-sharing, religious, charitable, and college and university endowment funds.
4. Fire and casualty—and to an increasing extent, life—insurance companies.

OVER-THE-COUNTER AND LISTED MARKETS

Stock trading facilities are furnished both by the organized stock exchanges—the New York, American, Midwest, Pacific, and others—and also by the over-the-counter markets. The latter are a loosely organized nationwide network of many thousands of security dealers and dealer houses that make markets (by quoting bids and offers) on perhaps 50,000 different stocks. In recent years, there has been considerable talk about merging both types of markets into one central market by means of modern communications devices.

In general, the stocks of large, well-known companies are listed (admitted to trading) on the nation's major stock exchanges. Stocks of secondary companies—always including some bright and younger firms—are typically traded over the counter (actually over the telephone). Let us look more closely at trading processes in the two markets.

The Over-the-Counter Market

The key person in the over-the-counter market is the middleman called a dealer. A *dealer* is one who makes a market in something by buying and selling it for his own account and risk. A securities dealer makes a market in one or more stocks by standing ready to buy at one price (called the bid) and to sell at another—and slightly higher—price (called the offer). The difference between bid and offer is termed the spread. This constitutes the dealer's expected gross profit on any transaction. Customers use the over-the-counter market by buying stock from a dealer, who maintains an inventory of shares for sale, or by selling their stock to a dealer when they want to dispose of it. The dealer makes his market by trying to keep his bid and offer, and the spread between them, at prices where the amounts of stock he buys and sells are roughly equal through time. If he starts buying more stock than he sells, he responds by dropping both his bid and offer. This discourages customers from selling him so much stock and encourages them to buy more stock from him.

If he finds he is selling out his inventory, then he raises his bid and offer prices to restore balance.

Dealers' bids and offers are published in newspapers, stock-quotation sheets, and elsewhere, but published spreads must be interpreted merely as general indications of prices at which business can be done.[2] The prices quoted by various dealers are kept in rough alignment by forces of competition. Trading is by a process of private negotiation. Usually one party is a private investor and the other is a dealer, although dealer can—and often does—trade with dealer. Dealers may charge their customers a commission, adding it to the offer price or subtracting it from the bid, or they may quote a net price that includes the equivalent (or more) of a commission.

The Listed Market

Almost any stock can trade over the counter, but to be eligible for trading on an organized exchange, a stock must first be listed. This means that the issuing company must apply for trading privileges and meet specific requirements set by the exchange. Companies list their stocks to obtain more active markets and enhance their prestige.

The listed market relies on a process known as auction trading. The key person here is the *broker*, who serves merely as a customer's agent to buy and sell stock. Unlike dealers, brokers do not take title to the stock they handle. The firms that brokers work for are members of one or more stock exchanges.

When you give your broker an order to buy or sell stock, he sends your order to the trading floor of the exchange. Trading in the stock is conducted by an exchange member called a specialist. A *specialist's function* is to make a market in one or more stocks. He or she does this mainly by acting as a broker for people who want to do business at prices above or below the present market.

Example. Suppose General Electric Company is trading around $50 a share. People who want to buy at prices under 50 leave their buy orders (bids) with the specialist; people who want to sell at prices above 50 leave their sell orders (offers) with him. Bids are ranked from highest to lowest and used to fill sell orders in that sequence. Offers are ranked from lowest to highest and used to fill buy orders in that sequence.

The specialist's book thus reflects the structure of bids and offers making up the market. Today, the book is simply a computerized memory file of orders left with the specialist to be filled when, as, and if possible at different prices. Many customer orders are filled by brokers communicating with the specialist's computer without intervention on the specialist's part. A specialist may buy and sell for his account, subject to rules that prohibit him from competing unfairly with orders left by customers.

---

[2] Technically, most over-the-counter quotations are bids to buy, and offers to sell, 100 shares at the stated prices. Larger or smaller transactions are subject to further negotiation.

The Auction Process

We can illustrate the auction process with the following example. Suppose you give an order to buy 100 shares (a round lot) of General Electric at the market. This means at the best price immediately available. An employee of the brokerage company you trade with queries the computer. "Quote offer on GE." The computer responds by quoting the lowest price at which GE is offered on the specialist's book. Suppose that is $50\frac{1}{4}$. Unless you have indicated some limit to the price you will pay, your brokerage firm will simply accept 100 shares of GE at $50\frac{1}{4}$.

Orders involving 500 or more shares are handled on the exchange floor by a process of personal negotiation between the specialist and an exchange member representing the buyer's or seller's brokerage firm. But the same process is followed. Stock is bought by taking it at offered prices from the specialist's book, it is sold against bids entered on his book, although the specialist also may buy or sell for his personal account. On very large orders, he may take time to contact outside parties whose help may be needed to supply or take stock in the quantity required. Odd lots of stock, less than 100-share amounts, trade at a price based on the next round-lot transaction to occur after the odd-lot order is received on the trading floor. On substantial amounts of stock, New York and American Stock Exchange commissions run around 1 percent of the value of stock bought or sold. (Both buyer and seller pay a commission.)

REGULATION OF STOCK TRADING

Several agencies, governmental and otherwise, supervise and regulate the stock markets, largely in hope of preventing—or at least punishing—fraud and manipulation. Each organized exchange has its own machinery, including a board of governors and various committees, to police the business ethics of its members. These officials try to make sure that trading is fair and that customers are dealt with honestly. The National Association of Security Dealers (NASD), organized under the Maloney Act of 1938, aims at similar surveillance of the over-the-counter market. In addition, there are federal and state laws regulating securities transactions. These will be discussed in Chapter 25.

STOCK MARKET BEHAVIOR

How you describe the movement of the stock market depends on the time period you have in mind. Four general kinds of movements in stock prices have long been noted: (1) secular, (2) primary, or cyclical, (3) secondary, or technical, and (4) day to day.

Secular Movement

Secular, or very long-term, movement appears to have been raising stock prices an average of about $2\frac{1}{2}$ percent per year since about 1870. This average rise, however,

BOX 10-1

The Folklore of Wall Street   Like other sectors of life, Wall Street has developed its share of proverbs and maxims. A short collection of them, some taken from a 1931 book by Humphrey Neill, appears below. We don't guarantee a single one.

A bull can make money in Wall Street, a bear can make money in Wall Street, but a hog never can.

Many "healthy reaction" has proved fatal.

Never mind telling me *what* stock to buy; tell me *when* to buy it.

Aimless switching gathers no profits—except for your broker.

One profit in cash is worth two on paper.

No tree grows to the sky.

Trend goes with the volume.

When to buy is easier to tell than when to sell.

The only sure tip from a broker is a margin call.

An investor is a disappointed speculator.

Negative expectations yield negative results. Positive expectations yield negative results.

A portfolio that goes down 50 percent and comes back 50 percent is still down 25 percent.

To err is human. To hedge divine.

The stock doesn't know you own it.

All growth is temporary.

Growth will bail you out—if you live long enough.

Source: Neill, Humphrey B. Tape Reading and Market Tactics, B.C. Forbes Publishing Co., New York, 1931.

has applied only to broad, representative groups of stocks, not to individual issues. It also has been dependable only over very long intervals of time—spans of three to four decades, equal roughly to the working lifetime of a college graduate. Stocks have risen historically at this rate because the earnings and dividends of the nation's major stockholder-owned companies have also tended to move upward over time at about $2\frac{1}{2}$ percent. In addition to the $2\frac{1}{2}$ percent growth, stocks over most of the past century have paid dividends averaging about 5 percent on current price. This has given long-term stockholders a total return over the years of around $7\frac{1}{2}$ percent.

Primary Movement

Primary, or cyclical, movement of stock prices reflects investors' expectations of business conditions six months or so ahead. Typically, this trend is geared to anticipated swings of the business cycle and accompanying changes in corporate profits and dividend payments. Usually—but not always—the stock market moves in advance of, or leads, the business cycle. Market breaks in 1966 and 1977, for example, were false alarms—they were not followed by the expected recessions. The lead of stock prices over changes in business also varies widely from one market cycle to the next.

Since World War II, *bull markets*—cyclical rises in stock market averages—typically have lasted two to three years. *Bear markets*—cyclical declines in the prices of most stocks—have lasted for an average of about one year. Thus, the stock market spends the bulk of its time rising. However, when it falls, it falls much faster than it rises. It should be emphasized that these statements about bull and bear markets apply only to broad averages of stock prices, which reflect the behavior of a majority of stocks. Almost always, some issues are able to buck the trend—to rise when the general market is falling and to fall when it is rising.

Secondary Movement

Secondary, or technical, movement consists of irregular rises and declines extending over several weeks' time. If we visualize the primary trend up or down as a straight line, then the secondary movement appears as a wavy line, swinging first above and then below the main trend line. This secondary movement seems largely based on trader and investor emotion, on people's tendency to "overbuy" or "oversell" stocks. That is, a prolonged move by stocks makes their prices overly responsive to unexpected news and overly vulnerable to profit taking by traders who have had the market move their way. So-called weak buyers or sellers tend to come into the market only after a rise or fall has lasted some time. These people are the market's chronic money losers, lacking the judgment to trade profitably. When the market becomes cluttered with these unfortunate amateurs, it is said to be "technically weak." A market is technically strong after most such traders have been washed out by a "healthy reaction," or downturn, in prices.

Day-to-Day Movement

Day-to-day movement in stock prices depends on small, random changes in the daily pressures of supply and demand. It is relatively unimportant and is best ignored by all but the most trigger-happy short-term traders. The newspapers often account for a few points rise or fall in the market averages by citing attention-getting events in the day's news: earnings reports by major companies, promises or threats of legislation by members of Congress, pronouncements by the Federal Reserve or industry spokesmen, release of business statistics by government bureaus, and the like.

Examples of these four kinds of market movements are illustrated in Figure 10-1.

Discounting the News

The reason why a single day's news seldom has an enduring effect on the market is that most so-called news has been discounted in advance by the stock prices already prevailing. It comes about in this way.

The future is not altogether a closed book. Some traders in the market often have advance knowledge of coming events or make accurate assessments of their probability. To the extent that future developments can be foreseen, they are always

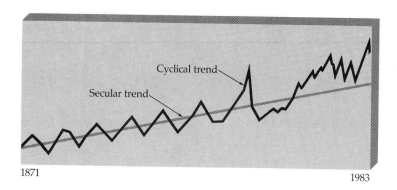

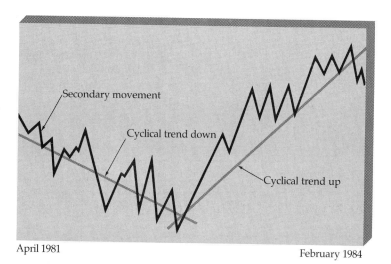

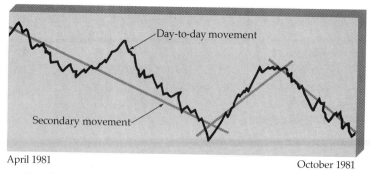

FIGURE 10-1   Four kinds of market movement: secular, cyclical, secondary, and day-to-day.

acted upon *immediately* by alert traders, who alter their bids or offers accordingly. In addition, "insiders" in the companies or government bureaus where news first breaks can often profit illegally by buying or selling before the news is made public. The result is that prices have often changed in anticipation of news before the news itself is widely known.

Marketwise, therefore, there are two kinds of news: discounted and undiscounted. *Discounted news* may affect the market weeks or months in advance of its public announcement. By contrast, *undiscounted news* takes the market by surprise. This distinction provides an important yardstick for assessing the market's reaction to news announcements. Discounted news, when finally made public, is (in traditional market metaphor) water over the dam—knowledgeable traders have long since acted on it. Thus its influence is pretty certain to be temporary. On the other hand, if announced news is of a kind that no one could have known about in advance or predicted, then its effect may be more lasting. For this reason, the most important question for a trader or market analyst to ask when news breaks is: Could this news already have been discounted?

The stock market's ability to discount most news is highlighted in what is called efficient market hypothesis (theory): Security prices quickly reflect all publicly held information so that investors cannot make money on news and events already known. The notion that the stock market is efficient is popular with finance professors (who apparently lose money trying to trade it), but most stockbrokers and security analysts reject it (probably as "dangerous to the health" of their profession).[3]

TWO PRINCIPLES OF MARKET PRICING

Stock exchanges merely provide a marketplace where anyone, acting through a qualified broker, can offer money for stocks or stocks for money. Nor does the exchange set stock prices or control them in any way. Stock prices, like most other prices in an enterprise economy, are set by the forces of *supply and demand*. They are also an instance of what economists term *marginal pricing*. A correct understanding of these principles is so important that we now discuss them at some length.

Supply and Demand

Whatever the background forces at work (boom, bust, Federal Reserve, taxes, profits, mergers, foreign buying, war scare, and whatnot), the immediate determinants of stock prices are always supply and demand. Only through stocks bid for or offered at definite prices in the market can so-called ultimate factors affect the pricing process. Thus if some new influence in the market is noted, your first question should always be: How will this affect supply and demand? Will it cause buyers to offer, or

---

[3] Some experts point to a weak form of the efficient market hypothesis, the *random walk* theory of stock prices, which holds that successive price changes in individual stocks are statistically independent—in other words, that the past action of a stock's price is of no value in predicting its future performance. The theory takes its name by analogy from the aimless staggerings of a blind-drunk sot.

sellers to accept, lower prices? If so, the market will move down. Or is it likely to persuade sellers to demand, and buyers to pay, higher prices? In this event, the market can be expected to move up.

Marginal Pricing

Securities markets differ from commodity (goods and services) markets in that *total supply* is relatively fixed. Companies issue new stock only at infrequent intervals. Meanwhile, of course, somebody has to hold all the shares currently outstanding. This means that one way to look at the present price of any stock is to recognize that this is the price to which the stock must fall to get someone to hold that last share in existence. This holder of the final share is called the marginal holder, and the principle involved is termed marginal pricing.

Figure 10-2 illustrates the marginal-pricing principle. The rather horizontal curve is really a demand curve laid on its side, but a special kind of demand curve. It is based on the supposition that successive shares of the stock could be auctioned off according to how much buyers would pay for them if the buyers thought each share was the last share available. The curve shows that while someone would pay as much as $120 per share for the first share of General Gismo Corporation, the price per share would fall as more shares became available. Since 3 million shares are on the market, and it takes a price of $60 to get the three-millionth share held, General Gismo trades at exactly $60 a share.

Usually, most shares of stock issued by a company are simply held by investors and do not trade at all. But to the extent that any part of the total supply is offered for sale, the price must fall until a buyer is found. Similarly, if anyone wants to buy the stock, he must continue raising his bid until a price is reached that will pry stock loose from some present holder.

This means two things. First, stock prices are set by the small or marginal portion of the issue that actively trades. Second, if markets are "thin" (buyers and

FIGURE 10-2   Supply-demand pricing of common stock, General Gismo Corporation.

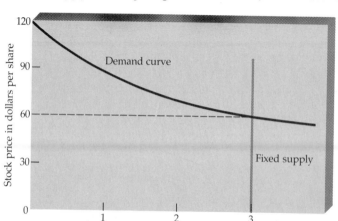

Numbers of shares available, in millions

sellers few and far between), wide swings in prices may take place. If, for example, few buyers are bidding for a stock and a substantial amount of it is offered for sale, the price is likely to fall a long way before enough buyers can be found to absorb the dumped supply. Such stocks and their markets are called "volatile." In contrast, broad, active markets are manned by numerous buyers and sellers. Here price changes usually occur in small fractions, and large bids or offers may be absorbed by the market without noticeable price variations.

MARGIN TRADING AND SHORT SELLING

Two other factors affecting the demand for stocks are margin trading and short selling. These are usually the tools of traders rather than of investors.

Margin trading is simply the privilege of borrowing a percentage of the purchase price when you buy stock. Literally, *margin* refers to the money you must put up out of your own pocket—what you borrow is termed your debit balance or broker's loan. Margin requirements on original purchases of stock are regulated by the Federal Reserve Board. If the margin requirement is 70 percent, then you would have to put up $7,000 in cash to buy $10,000 worth of stock.

By controlling margin requirements, the Federal Reserve regulates the flow of credit into the stock market and thus helps prevent speculative excesses from developing. If you borrow money from a broker to buy stock, you must pay interest on the loan. Sometimes interest charges on margin accounts rise very high, and this has a tendency to cool off speculation in the market.

Besides the initial margin requirements imposed by Federal Reserve regulations, your broker also requires you to preserve a *maintenance margin* in your account, the *difference* between the value of the stock in your account and the amount of your broker's loan. Typically, maintenance margin requirements run to at least 25 percent of the value of stock held in a margin account.

Technically, *short selling* is any sale of a security that is consummated with the delivery of a borrowed certificate. Speculative short selling involves selling securities one does not own, in the hope of profiting on a future fall in price. Actually, the procedure simply reverses the usual one of buying low and selling high by selling high first and then buying back low. Since the original sale is completed with a borrowed certificate, the short seller owes dividends on the borrowed stock as they come due. There is no time limit on how long a seller can remain short. Sometimes so much stock in a particular issue is sold short that the stock can no longer be borrowed. Then, if the lenders demand their stock back, the short sellers have to "buy in" the short shares at whatever prices holders of the stock demand. This predicament is called a "squeeze." It is a main reason why stocks of smaller companies with only a few hundred thousand shares outstanding should not be shorted—squeezes are too easy to engineer in such stocks.

The foregoing are some, though far from all, of the influences that affect the daily course of stock prices as reported in the financial section of daily newspapers. Table 10-1 presents a small sample of daily stock market quotations.

TABLE 10-1   Sample of Daily Stock Market Quotations

High	Low	Stock	Dividend	Yield Percent
$61\frac{3}{4}$	$41\frac{3}{8}$	Gn Dyn	1	2.2
$80\frac{1}{2}$	56	GMot	3.20e	5.0
$9\frac{3}{4}$	$7\frac{1}{8}$	GPU	—	—
$51\frac{1}{2}$	$40\frac{7}{8}$	Gillette	2.44	5.1
$40\frac{3}{8}$	$38\frac{3}{4}$	GtLkIn	.80a	2.2
46	$38\frac{3}{4}$	Greyh	pf4.75	12

The specimen quotations in Table 10-1 illustrate the reporting of stock-market prices. These are prices of stocks traded on the New York Stock Exchange during April 3, 1984. Columns from left to right successively identify the highest and lowest price each stock has reached over the preceding 52 weeks, the name of the stock, its annual dividend rate, its price-earnings ratio, the number of 100-share unit (round-lot) sales of the stock made during the day, its highest, lowest, and closing price for the day, and its net change in price from the previous day. Stock prices are reported in dollars and eighths of dollars. The first stock shown, General Dynamics, sold as high as $61.75 and as low as $41.375 over the past year. The dividend established for this stock is $1 per year, the stock yields 2.2 percent on its dividend, and sells for nine times its most recently reported 12 months' earnings. On April 3, 103,200 shares of the stock changed hands. The high, low, and closing prices were, respectively, $46.25, $45.625, and $45.625; and the stock closed down $37\frac{1}{2}$ cents from its closing price of the previous day. Reports on the other stocks are similarly interpreted. These stocks, reading downward, are General Motors, General Public Utilities, Gillette, Great Lakes International, and Greyhound $4.75 per year preferred. Dividends shown are annual rates except for General Motors (where e indicates the amount paid in the past 12 months) and Great Lakes International (where a shows that one or more extra dividends also are paid). The designation d beside the low price for Greyhound preferred informs you that $38\frac{1}{2}$ is a new low price for the past 12 months. The z accompanying the sales of Greyhound preferred indicates that the day's trading volume was 520 shares, not 520 lots of 100 shares.

PATTERNS OF STOCK PRICES THROUGH TIME

Historically, the stock market's course has been marked by wide swings in prices, in earnings and dividends per average share, and in the multiples of earnings and dividends investors have been willing to pay. Examples of this volatile behavior appear in Table 10-2.

Notice the general pattern of variation between market peaks and bottoms over the years. The largest source of variation seems to be the change in price-earnings ratios—the multiples of earnings investors are willing to pay, given their expectations for business profits in the next year or so. Because price-earnings ratios

TABLE 10-1   (Continued)

P/E Ratio	Sales 100s	High	Low	Close	Net Change
9	1032	$46\frac{1}{4}$	$45\frac{5}{8}$	$45\frac{5}{8}$	$-\frac{3}{8}$
5	7420	$64\frac{3}{8}$	63	$63\frac{3}{4}$	$-\frac{1}{8}$
7	898	$8\frac{1}{4}$	$8\frac{1}{4}$	$8\frac{1}{8}$	$-\frac{1}{8}$
10	345	$47\frac{5}{8}$	$47\frac{3}{8}$	$47\frac{5}{8}$	—
11	32	37	$36\frac{1}{2}$	$36\frac{3}{4}$	$-\frac{3}{8}$
—	z520	$38\frac{3}{4}$	$d38\frac{1}{2}$	$38\frac{1}{2}$	$-1\frac{1}{2}$

shrink with pessimism, stock prices can fall—as they did in 1977 and again in 1979—even when earnings and dividends are rising. In most bear (down) markets, dividend yields also rise because prices fall faster than dividends, which most companies try to maintain. Conversely, in bull (up) markets the price rise outstrips the gain in either earnings or dividends, so that price-earnings ratios increase and yields fall.[4]

[4] You may be curious about the high price-earnings ratio (16.70) prevailing at the end of 1932, the nation's worst depression year. This was due almost entirely to the fact that corporate earnings had all but vanished, so that very low stock prices still resulted in a substantial price-earnings multiple. Analogous influences explain the even higher price-earnings ratio for 1945 (at the end of World War II, when earnings were temporarily depressed by post-war reconversion of the nation's industry), and the high ratio for 1983's second quarter (when earnings reported for the preceding 12 months were still depressed by a recent recession).

TABLE 10-2   Standard & Poor's 400 Industrial Common Stocks Selected Statistics, 1928–1983

Year	Price Dec. 31	Earnings per Share	Dividends per Share	Price-Earnings Ratio	Yield	Market Peak (P) or Bottom (B)
1928	20.85	1.20	.73	17.38	3.50	P
1932	5.18	.31	.39	16.70	7.53	B
1945	16.72	.65	.61	25.72	3.65	P
1948	15.06	2.34	.91	6.44	6.04	B
1965	98.47	5.58	2.89	17.65	2.89	P
1966	85.24	5.77	2.98	14.77	3.50	B
1972	131.87	6.83	3.22	19.31	2.44	P
1974[a]	71.01	10.18	3.71	6.98	5.22	B
1976	119.46	10.68	4.25	11.10	3.56	P
1978	107.21	13.12	5.35	8.17	4.99	B
1980	154.45	16.13	6.55	9.58	4.24	P
1982	122.42[b]	15.18	7.18	8.06	4.67	B
1983	189.98[b]	12.98	7.20	14.63	3.79	P(?)

[a]End of third quarter.
[b]End of second quarter. The second-quarter price in 1983 was the bull market peak at time of writing. It may or may not prove to have been the final high.
SOURCE: *Standard & Poor's Corporation*, Statistics, various years.

BOX 10-2
Have We Found the Ultimate Stock
Market Predictor?   Want to play the market with 16 out of 17 odds of coming up a
                        winner? Then forget about reading Standard & Poor's *Industry Sur-*
vey and Value Line's *Investment Survey.* Instead, just relax and watch pro football.
Because it's the Super Bowl Stock Market Predictor for you.
    Here's how it works. If a National Football Conference team (or a former NFL
team now in the American Conference) wins, the market will go up for the year. If
one of the 10 original AFL teams wins, the market will go down.
    In the 17 Super Bowls played from 1967 through 1983, this barometer worked
every year but one. The sole exception came in 1970 when Kansas City (an original
AFL team) won, and the Standard & Poor's 500 Stock Index (a measure of market
performance) went up one-tenth of one percent.
    Would that flubs by the authors' brokers were always by such small margins.

        The chief factor affecting the general level of stock prices in any decade seems
to be investors' expectations concerning economic growth and stability.[5] If investors
are confident that business expansions will be well sustained and relatively noninflationary, and that recessions will be brief and mild, then stock prices are likely to rise
strongly from one market cycle to the next, as they did throughout the 1950s (the
years of "Eisenhower stability"). On the other hand, investors may lack confidence—they may foresee weak booms, inflation that will devour companies' real
earning power and require tight-money restraint, and long, deep recessions that
could slide into major depressions. In this case, stocks will probably recede in price,
or at least advance very little, from bull market to bull market. This was the general
pattern of stock-price movement during the years of accelerating inflation,
1966–1980. Greater hope that inflation would taper off in the wake of 1981–1982's
recession pushed stock prices to new highs by substantial margins during
1983–1984. Whether a new long-term advance by the market was under way or
whether, as before, stocks would drop as inflation and interest rates surged upward
again, remained in doubt.

Short-Period Price Changes in Stocks

Predicting short-term price movements is very difficult. If it were easy, few people
would need to work for a living, least of all stockbrokers. The market's shorter
swings depend heavily on the kinds of participants who dominate the trading, for
different sorts of operators have very different goals, strategies, and methods.

---

[5] At times, too, as you would logically expect, interest rates have played an important role in
governing stock prices. After all, stocks are in competition with bonds, mortgages, and other
interest-bearing securities (and at times even with Treasury bills and commercial paper). They can
hardly be attractive to rational investors unless their *total return* (dividend yield plus expected
growth in the dividend payment or stock price) exceeds the interest rate available on fixed-income
investments.

In general, those who buy and sell stocks can be classified either as investors or speculators. Investors are people who buy stocks to hold a long time and who aim at gradual capital growth with dividends while they wait. Speculators, on the other hand, aim to buy low and sell high over relatively short periods of time (or sell high and buy back low, if they operate as short sellers). As a class, speculators include the following:

1. Major-swing traders, who try to buy in recessions (when stocks are cheap) and sell in booms (when their prices are high).
2. Short-term traders, whose holding periods may run anywhere from a day to more than six months (the dividing line for long-term capital gains).
3. Dealers and stock-exchange specialists.
4. Special-situation traders, who trade in "turn-around" companies (an earnings reversal is expected), acquisition candidates, companies about to announce new inventions, stock splits, and other bullish news.

STOCK SELECTION AND TIMING

Both speculators and investors in the stock market face two main problems: what to buy and when to buy it—problems of selection and timing, respectively. Of the two, timing seems clearly the more crucial and difficult. Correct timing is closely associated with two factors: (1) price level and (2) group action. At or below some bargain price, the stock of any solvent company becomes a worthwhile purchase. On the other hand even a stock like IBM selling more than 30 times earnings can be dangerously overpriced.[6] Investors must always bear in mind that the strongest-looking companies can suffer misfortunes that reduce their earnings and take the bloom (meaning high price-earnings ratio) off their stock.[7] However, the fact that a stock is selling at a bargain price does not mean people will immediately recognize its true worth and drive the price back up to where it belongs. Undervalued stocks often "lie on the bottom" a long time before the market awakens to their merit. A trader interested in a quick move must be satisfied not only that a stock is soundly priced but also that the market is becoming conscious of its attractiveness so that it will move upward fairly soon. One evidence of a coming move in a stock is increasing interest by traders and/or investors in the industry group (oils, electronics, food chains, and so on) to which the stock belongs.

Investors use several methods to select stocks and to time their purchases and sales. Prominent among these are (1) the valuation approach and (2) technical analysis.

---

[6] RCA sold at 100 times earnings in 1929. People who bought this popular "growth" stock at this inflated level waited nearly 35 years to break even on price alone.

[7] Consider, for example, the case of Polaroid Corp. Through 1970 earnings per share on this famous growth stock had risen steadily for many years. In 1973 it sold as high as $143 per share on the strength of large anticipated profits from the company's new X-L 100 camera. But immediate returns from the new camera proved disappointing, and amid general market weakness the stock in 1974 plunged as low as $14\frac{1}{8}$. Buyers at 1973's highest price had "paper" (and in some instances, actual) losses of 90 percent of their investment.

TABLE 10-3   Exxon Corporation Figures

Year	Average Price	Earnings per Share	Average Price-Earnings Ratio	Dividends per Share	Average Yield (%)
1978	24	$3.10	8	$1.65	6.9
1979	28	4.87	6	1.95	7.0
1980	35	6.49	5	2.70	7.7
1981	35	6.44	5	3.00	8.6
1982	29	4.82	6	3.00	10.3

Fundamental Analysis

Fundamental Analysis is essentially an appraisal process. It relies on quantitative standards of value derived from historical experience. One looks back on a stock's previous record to see what average yield and price-earnings ratio[8] it has sold at, what its earning power has been in good and bad years, and what growth its earnings and dividends have had in the past decade or so. From these data an intrinsic value is computed. *Intrinsic value* is subjective or personal value. Typically, this is its normal, or average-year, earnings at the present time times its average price-earnings ratio of the past 5 or 10 years. If the stock is selling below this intrinsic value (say as much as 20 percent), it should be bought. If it is selling above its intrinsic value, it should be sold and the funds switched to an undervalued issue.

Consider, for example, Exxon Corporation late in 1982 (see Table 10-3).

At prices as low as 25, the stock was statistically cheap. It was selling only 5 times the depressed earnings of the current year, compared with 12 times or more for stocks in the popular market averages. The company enjoyed the strongest financial ratings,[9] earnings and dividends per share had increased in six of the preceding seven years, and both earnings and prices of the depressed oil stocks were poised for a rebound. During the next year, 1983, Exxon's earnings per share rose to $5.74, the dividend was increased to $3.30, and the stock sold at prices as high as $40.

An alternative way to determine an intrinsic value is to find the present value of the stock's expected dividend and selling price. We shall examine this method in Chapter 17.

[8] Price-earnings ratios are perhaps the common-stock investor's most widely used valuation device. As the term implies, the ratio is simply the proportion of a stock's price to its annual earnings. If General Motors earns $10 per share and sells at $60 per share, the price-earnings ratios is 6. Price-earnings ratios may be calculated in various ways; the price may be the price of the moment, an average price for the current year, or some other; similarly, the earnings may be those of the most recently reported 12 months, the average earnings of the past three or four years, or the average earnings expected over, say, the next five years. Great care must be used in comparing or evaluating stocks by means of price-earnings ratios, however, because, as common sense should suggest, a stock's price typically reflects more than the earnings of the present year alone. A stock whose earnings per share are expected to increase rapidly in years ahead may have a very high price-earnings ratio and still be a much greater bargain than one that has a very low price-earnings ratio but a prospect of stagnation or even decline in its earning power.

[9] The nation's two most widely consulted stock-rating agencies have continually given Exxon stock top ranking for safety. The company's bonds have had the highest rating, triple-A, from both major bond-rating agencies.

BOX 10-3

Selecting Stocks Based on Litigation   There are many different approaches to fundamental analysis, and one of the most unique is that of Calvert Crary, a litigation analyst with Bear, Stearns & Company. It is an investment banking and investment research firm that publishes monthly *Bear Stearns Litigation Review*, a 15- to 20-page update of developments in important lawsuits. Crary is the editor.

In selecting which lawsuits to follow, Crary has two criteria. First, the stock of the companies involved must be widely held. "You might be able to find a stock that's going to go up ten times or down ten times depending upon the outcome," he notes, "except that it's only held by three people. Who cares?" Second, he looks at the dollar size of the suit; the larger it is, of course, the larger its potential impact on the company's stock price.

However, Crary has found that the facts don't always determine how a suit will be resolved—such subjective factors as which judge is presiding, where a case is being tried, and how persuasive the oral arguments are can be just as influential.

Here is how Crary saw the outcome of four cases and how they actually turned out:

1. Patent infringement (involving 10 patents) brought by Polaroid Corporation against Eastman Kodak. Crary's position is that Polaroid has a better argument and will win on one film patent and two camera patents. But he thinks that Kodak has the upper hand on the remaining seven. No decision had been reached in the case at the beginning of 1985.

2. Toxic-shock syndrome suits against Proctor & Gamble Co., charging that the company knew its Rely tampon caused the disease. Crary thinks it unlikely that the number of cases against P&G will rise significantly. In any case, he suspects that the cost of the settlements could rise considerably without having investment significance. The cases fell into place as described with no investment significance.

3. Plywood antitrust action against Georgia-Pacific Corporation, Weyerhaeuser Company, and Willamette Industries. The lower court determined that the 3 companies conspired with 16 others to charge *phantom freight*, calculating freight charges that were higher than actual weight. The damages could exceed $1 billion, but the case is before the U.S. Supreme Court, and Crary is convinced the verdict will be set aside. The case was settled for an insubstantial amount before the U.S. Supreme Court had a chance to rule.

4. Copyright suit against Sony Corporation brought by Walt Disney Productions and MCA. "Home copying on videotape is not exempt from the copyright laws," acknowledges Crary. Yet he believes that the Supreme Court will hold that the manufacturers are not liable for infringement and that it will reverse the imposition of harsh relief that was ordered by the lower court. In fact, the Supreme Court ruled that the manufacturers were not liable for infringement and, as predicted, reversed the imposition of the harsh remedies that had been ordered.

Source: Based in part on Anise Wallace, "The Letter of the Law," *Institutional Investor*, January 1983, pp. 59–60. You may obtain information about subscriptions to *Litigation Review* by contacting Calvert D. Crary, Bear, Stearns & Company, 55 Water Street, New York 10041.

Technical Analysis

Advocates of technical analysis reject the notion that economic data have power to predict stock prices. They contend that such fundamental developments as sales, earnings, and dividends are typically discounted in price changes well before they are published by the financial press or reporting services. And since, as statisticians have long noted, no other statistical series runs dependably ahead of the stock market, technicians argue that only the market itself is able to predict the market. Technical approaches therefore rely on data generated by the market's own behavior. They include a number of charting methods and doctrines that may be applied either to the overall market or to the behavior patterns and statistics of particular stocks. Since the technical market doctrines are part of the Wall Street tradition, they deserve some illustration. Four such doctrines are briefly reviewed below.

1. **Support and resistance points** Stocks show strength by overcoming resistance (prices that have stopped previous rises) or by holding support (prices that have arrested earlier declines). Symptoms of weakness are just the opposite—that is, failure to overcome resistance or a penetration of support levels.

2. **Price-volume relation** "Trend goes with the volume" is a market adage. If volume of trading rises (in the market or in a particular stock) as the price rises, then strength is indicated and an upward trend will follow. A rise accompanied by dwindling volume will not hold.

3. **Short interest** A large short interest (stock sold short and not yet bought back, or *covered*) is considered bullish. If prices fall, the shorts must buy back their borrowed stock in order to take profits, and this will cushion the decline. If prices rise, the shorts will be panicked into covering, which will force prices still higher.

4. **Contrary opinion** A near-unanimous opinion about the market is usually wrong. Do the opposite of what everybody recommends.

THE MARKET'S ROLE IN THE ECONOMY

Whole volumes have been written on the stock market without beginning to exhaust the subject, so we can only scratch the surface in these few pages. But in closing we should say something about the market's broad usefulness and potential hazards in the economy as a whole.

There seems little question but that over the decades the stock market performs two great services. It is (1) a barometer of economic conditions and (2) a guide for allocating economic resources among different industries and companies. The gradual rise of major market averages mirrors the country's economic progress. The market's ups and downs give convenient warnings of coming recessions and recoveries, and sometimes—as when speculation becomes excessive—stock prices serve as a thermometer of fever in the economic body. The greater profitability and growth over time of certain industries is advertised by the superior performance of their stocks, and this makes it easier for companies in sectors of rising demand to obtain resources for expansion. It is easier for a "growth" company, or a consistently profitable one, to raise money by selling new stocks or bonds than for a company with only a drab record to show.

On the other hand, the stock market's structure and machinery undoubtedly lend themselves to gambling and even to occasional speculative excess. Keynes wrote:

> Speculators may do no harm as bubbles on a steady stream of enterprise. But the position is serious when enterprise becomes the bubble on a whirlpool of speculation. When the capital development of a country becomes a by-product of the activities of a casino, the job is likely to be ill-done.[10]

The greatest fear, of course, is that someday the market will blow up into another balloon of speculation like 1929 and then collapse, ruining hundreds of thousands of people, destroying billions of dollars' worth of collateral values, wiping out pension funds, trust funds, and people's savings, and plunging the country into deep depression. Some people say this could not happen again because there are laws on the books to prevent it, but one should also remember that unpopular laws can be ignored or repealed, and that this would probably happen if the nation ever got well launched on another speculative joyride.

All in all, the stock market is like other human institutions. The mechanical system it represents is morally neutral. Whether the institution works for good or evil depends, in the final analysis, on the morality and good sense of the people operating it. A right-thinking, right-doing citizenry needs few laws to keep its lives straight, while all the laws in history cannot keep a shortsighted or undisciplined culture from destroying itself.

SUMMARY

1. The secondary stock market serves both individuals and a varied list of financial institutions as a means of investment or speculation. Its main divisions consist of the organized exchanges, the listed market, where trading proceeds by the auction process, and the unlisted or over-the-counter market, in which investors buy from or sell to dealers.

2. Stock prices show four kinds of movement: secular (a very long-term rise, roughly in keeping with the nation's economic growth), primary (following the ups and downs of the business cycle), secondary (largely based on swings in trader's emotions), and day to day (which is usually unimportant). The dominant factors in stock price changes are (1) supply and demand and (2) marginal pricing.

3. Because traders must guess future conditions correctly to make profits, stock-price moves typically discount the future. The efficient market hypothesis suggests that all information about stocks and their companies is quickly reflected in

---

[10] John Maynard Keynes, *The General Theory of Employment, Interest, and Money* (New York: Harcourt, Brace, 1936), p. 151. Anyone wishing to understand the role and occasional dominance of speculation in the stock market should read the whole of Chapter 12, from which this quotation is taken.

stock prices. Margin trading and short selling (the latter based on the delivery of borrowed shares to the buyer) play important roles in the market's speculative swings.

4. Long-term changes in stock prices reflect changes in the economy, especially in investors' confidence—or lack of it—in future growth and stability. Inflation, for which investors must adjust stock prices, and interest rates, with which the prospective returns from stocks must compete, are also of basic importance. The market's two- to four-year swings, as noted, anticipate changes in the business cycle, with major-swing, short-term, and special-situation traders all endeavoring to profit in their particular ways. Some investors buy stocks on their appraised values (the fundamental approach). Others believe the market forecasts its own future movement and so make use of technical analysis.

KEY TERMS AND CONCEPTS

Listed market	Margin
Over-the-counter market	Short sale
Auction market	Selection and timing
Negotiated market	Fundamental analysis
Odd-lot	Technical analysis
Discounted news	

QUESTIONS

10-1. Distinguish between auction and negotiated markets. Does this parallel the difference between the stock exchange and the over-the-counter markets? Explain.

10-2. Name and describe the four main kinds of common-stock price movements.

10-3. Why is it said that the market usually discounts news? Why do discounted and undiscounted news have different effects?

10-4. Name and describe the two main principles of stock market pricing.

10-5. Explain the meaning of the term *efficient market*. What implications do you see in the efficient market hypothesis?

10-6. What is margin? In what ways is margin trading regulated?

10-7. What is a short sale? How does a short seller obtain stock to deliver to the buyer?

10-8. Study carefully the data on Exxon Corporation (see Table 10-3). Why should this stock have been a highly attractive investment late in 1982?

10-9. How do traders differ from investors?

10-10. Distinguish between the fundamental approach and technical analysis in their approach to stock market selection and timing.

10-11. If the "short interest" in Goofball Drug Company stock is large, is that a reason for or against a trader's buying the stock? Explain your answer fully.

10-12. What guidance could you, as a financial or other corporation manager, expect to get from watching the stock market carefully?

PROBLEMS

10-1. McCoon buys 100 shares of Amalgamated Petrochemicals at 50 on a 60 percent margin. The stock rises to 70. Disregarding commissions and interest on his broker's loan, what percent profit does he make on his investment?

10-2. Chutney buys 100 shares of Diston Tools, Inc. at 40 on a 50 percent margin. The stock drops to 32 and Chutney sells out. What percentage of his capital has he lost?

10-3. Suppose that you sold 100 shares of Feeblegauss Electric short at 60 and covered the short sale at 40. What percent did you make on the transaction. (Ignore margin requirements.)

10-4. A speculator sold 100 shares of Great Eastern Computing short at 50. The stock went to 70. What percent of her capital did she lose? (Ignore margin requirements.)

FOUR

FINANCIAL MANAGEMENT AND MEASUREMENT

Part 3 concentrated on the way a financial manager uses information from outside the company to make decisions. Now, we begin our study of the way a financial manager uses information about the company, itself, to make investment and financial decisions—decisions that affect the company's stock price. In this part we examine the specific tasks of a financial manager, how a financial manager uses financial reports to measure a company's operating and financial health, and how he plans and controls a company's performance.

CHAPTER 11
The Three A's of Financial Management

Every business, however small, has a financial manager. Someone must make the key decisions concerning money. It may be a vice-president, treasurer, or controller, or the harassed proprietor or partner who wears three other managerial hats. Or it may even be (heaven help the business!) one of the clerks or other subordinates. But, whoever it is, the financial manager is always there because *the function* is always there. Someone must handle the "three A's" of financial management.

Why three A's? Because, reduced to its essential elements, financial management involves three inescapable tasks—and each begins with the letter *A*. The financial manager must:

1. Anticipate financial needs
2. Acquire debt and equity
3. Allocate cash in the business

If a financial manager handles each of these tasks well, the firm is on the road to good financial health.

THE CHANGING ROLE OF FINANCIAL MANAGEMENT

Before looking at the three A's of financial management in detail, let us view financial management in perspective and appraise its place in the business scheme.

Figure 11-1 shows where financial management fits within a typical corporate organizational structure. It reflects a basic distinction between some activities that are line and some that are staff. A *line activity* is one that concerns itself directly with the company's output. A *staff activity* is one that supports or services the line organization.

Example. Your university has both faculty and staff positions. Faculty positions are line activity because faculty concern themselves directly with the school's output, educated graduates. Secretarial and administrative positions are staff activity because they support and service the faculty.

Line activities on Figure 11-1 are manufacturing and marketing because these two activities deal directly with the company's output. Finance is a staff activity because it supports and services the two other activities.

Treasurer and controller report to the company's chief financial officer, its vice-president for finance. Although related because they report to a company's chief

FIGURE 11-1   Finance activity within a company.

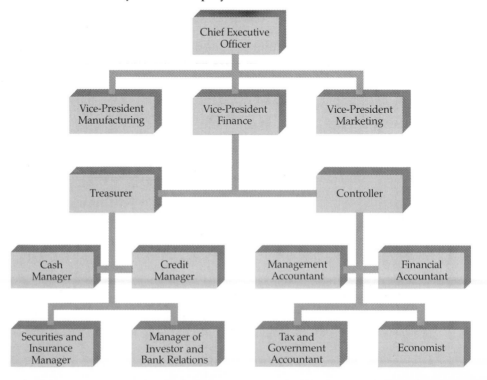

financial officer, these two functions perform different tasks within a company. The treasurer function concerns itself with identifying the best sources of finance (debt and equity) to use in the company and with timing the acquisition of money and credit. In this way, the treasurer function is largely external. On the other hand, the controller function concerns itself primarily with selecting appropriate assets to use in the company's operations, measuring and presenting results in such a way that they are meaningful and useful to management and to investors, filing necessary reports with the Internal Revenue Service and government agencies, and measuring and interpreting economic events. The controller function is largely internal.

Effective management of financial matters is indispensable to every firm. Without it, assets and capital soon leak away. But good financial management alone cannot guarantee that a business will succeed. It cannot make up for a decision to enter the wrong industry. It cannot atone for poor management of sales, costs, or personnel. Financial management is thus a necessary condition for business success but not a sufficient one.

Records kept through the years by Dun & Bradstreet highlight the importance of effective financial management. These records show that financial failure is always present at the corporate death. Financial mismanagement ranks just below lack of experience as a principal explanation for the thousands of business failures that occur each year. Unwise extensions of credit, improper inventory policies, and excessive investment in fixed assets also are immediate causes of failure that are at least partly financial in character. What the records do not reveal, however, is the way that the role of financial management itself has changed in recent years.

Two generations ago, business students ordinarily took a dry course called Corporation Finance. More often than not, it described 57 or so varieties of stocks and bonds, and revealed which kinds big corporations should issue when they needed long-term capital (which, in those days—the 1930s—was rarely).

Today, business students study Financial Management—the dynamic, evolving art of making day-to-day financial decisions in a business of any size. The old conception of finance as treasurership has broadened to include the new, equally meaningful conception of controllership. The treasurer is an officer who keeps track of money and raises it when necessary from the banks or through security issues. The controller's duties extend to the planning, analysis, and improvement of every phase of a company's operations that is capable of being measured with a financial yardstick. The manager's growing role reflects an aggressive new doctrine: profits don't just happen—they must be planned in advance. Profits are the result of more than hard work, and more even than foresight. They are the product of ambition and determination in the people who manage a business—a determination that, far from having to react passively to its environment, the successful firm can reach out and, in many ways, bend the environment to its own will.

The treasurer's job has also grown bigger and more challenging. Thirty years ago, aside from infrequent episodes of external financing, the treasurer was regarded as a passive custodian of company cash. Today, the treasurer is still a custodian, but no longer passive. With the big rise in interest rates since 1951, he has become responsible for investing the company's short-term surplus cash in order to bring maximum interest return. In an era of stop-and-go monetary policy, recurring credit

BOX 11-1

Importance of Maximizing Stock Price   This book emphasizes the importance of maximizing stock price as a financial objective, but we should ask ourselves if it plays the dominant role in managing a corporation. It probably doesn't. A financial objective is only one among a number of corporate objectives and, as such, is not necessarily dominant in any specific decision. Even when the financial objective is subordinated to other corporate objectives, however, management should measure both the cost of a decision and its effect on the value of the corporate common shares.

Other parties with a stake in the corporation—employees, customers, suppliers, bankers, and management itself—are hardly likely to be preoccupied with stockholder interests. But those who criticize the goal of stock price maximization are forgetting that stockholders are not only beneficiaries of a corporation's financial success but also referees who determine management's financial power. Failure to please stockholders means that management may find itself looking for employment elsewhere.

crunches, and inflation-battered stock markets, the treasurer stays on the jump, keeping in close touch with bankers, brokers, stockholders—and everyone else in the business of lending or investing money. Most of all, treasurers are the watchdog's of their company's financial environment. It is their responsibility to give timely warning of tighter, more costly money; to pick the cheapest and most reasonable lenders; and to devise new tactics for raising money when it is needed.

Financial managers undertake treasurer and controller functions with the objective of maximizing the company's common-stock price. No longer do they want merely to maximize profit, but to maximize the way that profit is measured in the financial market. The main idea behind maximizing the company's stock price is to give the company's owners the greatest cash return that they can get from their investment in the company so that they can spend or invest at their highest level.

ANTICIPATING FINANCIAL NEEDS

The first A of financial management is Anticipate. How does a financial manager anticipate a company's financial needs?—by forecasting expected events and noting their financial implications. Every event that leads immediately or later to cash entering or leaving the company should be forecast.

Anticipating cash requires that a financial manager forecast cash flows, the inflow and outflow of cash. A cash budget prepared by Elaine Luferac, owner of a toy store at the mall, shows us how a cash budget helps us to anticipate a company's financial needs. Suppose that Ms. Luferac anticipates the following cash flows for October:

1. She estimates her total sales for the month at $13,000 based on sales for the past three years. She forecasts cash sales at $11,200 and credit sales at $1,800.
2. She has receivables of $2,200 on the books at the end of September. Experience tells her she will collect about $1,800 of these accounts during October.
3. She expects a refund of $100 from Moe Jenkins Company for a damaged shipment she returned last month.
4. She will take a salary of $1,600 for the month. Her shop assistant's salary will be $1,100.
5. Her utility bills will run about as follows: gas, $150; electricity, $100; and water, $30.
6. She will order $30,000 worth of merchandise (mostly for Christmas). She expects to pay $9,000 of the total cost in cash during October to take advantage of prompt payment discounts.
7. She has accounts payable of $19,000. She expects to pay $17,000 of these during October.
8. A new display case, installed last month, must be paid for. The bill is $1,000.
9. The insurance on her plate glass window and the fire insurance on her premises is due. That will be another $500.
10. The washroom plumbing needs fixing. Allow $100 for that.

Ms. Luferac's bank balance in late September was $18,164. She writes each item down as she thinks of it. That way, important events are less likely to be overlooked. She tries to think of anything else that might be important, and then simply summarizes the events in a list of cash inflows and outflows, as follows:

Cash Inflows		Cash Outflows	
Cash sales	$11,200	Salaries	$ 2,700
Collections	1,800	Utilities	280
Refund	100	Payments for	
Total	$13,100	merchandise	26,000
		Display case	1,000
		Insurance premiums	500
		Plumbing repairs	100
		Total	$30,580

This shows Ms. Luferac that her cash outflow in October will exceed her cash inflow by more than $17,000. It looks as if she will have less than $1,000 left in the bank at the end of the month.

Luferac (spell it backwards) will make similar forecasts of her cash flows each month. She will compare her expected cash position with her desired cash balance to see whether she needs to borrow money. If she has a surplus of cash, then she must decide what to do with it until she needs it in the business.

Of course, this rudimentary cash forecast is the kind that the proprietor of a very small business can easily figure out in a few minutes of careful thinking. If the proprietor is able to think of all the receipts and expenditures, then this simple cash-flow summary is quite adequate as a basis for anticipating financial needs.

Anticipation in the Large Company

In a large company, a financial forecast expands into an impressive array of documents. It would include the following items.

A *cash budget*, which is essentially the cash-flow statement given above and covers several months in the same detail as Luferac's October forecast.

A *pro forma income statement* summarizes sales, other income, costs, taxes, and net income for the period.

A *pro forma balance sheet* shows how assets, liabilities, and net worth will look at the end of the forecast period.

A *statement of changes in financial position* shows where the funds to operate the business will come from and how they will be absorbed during the period.

In a large company, the cash budget itself is based on a series of other forecasts—a sales budget, collections budget, wages-and-salary budget, purchases budget, and capital budget. The capital budget includes expenditures for fixed assets. We shall examine in detail how a manager prepares a cash budget in chapter 23.

Considering Lags and Growth

Often, items that are bought or sold in one period result in cash flows in another. Luferac's cash budget illustrates this. Her display case was installed in September, but she pays for it in October. She seems to pay for most of her inventory of toys about 30 days after it is delivered. On the other hand, some of her sales are credit sales. She does not collect the cash on these sales until a month or so later. The financial needs of an enterprise are strongly shaped by lags such as these.

Lags between flows of assets and flows of cash are particularly crucial when a company is just getting started. Almost any business faces a period of several months—or even years—before cumulative cash inflows equal cumulative cash outflows. This is especially true of a new company that sells on credit and ties up a large part of its starting capital in customer receivables. Unless the owners painstakingly forecast their cash needs and make sure that cash will be available, then even a highly profitable new business may fail for lack of cash with which to pay its bills. Forecasts, too, should always include an extra margin of reserve cash for meeting unexpected expenses, delays in receipts, sales declines, and so on.

Growth presents another problem. As a successful company expands its sales volume, it must sooner or later add more plant, equipment, and facilities, and carry more inventory and receivables. These needs for long-term financing must be carefully anticipated. Sometimes a company can satisfy its expanding capital needs from internal sources: from retaining earnings rather than paying dividends. But if internal flows are relied on for expansion capital, then management must carefully avoid distributing too much of the profit in dividends or payments to partners. If external financing—stocks and bonds—must be relied on, then plans for selling these securities must be made well ahead of time. Chapter 15 presents a method to forecast a company's needs for debt and new common stock.

BOX 11-2
**Lever Brothers Financial Manager Works
with All Managers**   A company's financial manager is not a No man, but rather an
important part of a management team that concerns itself with
maximizing the company's profit and stock price. Consider the role of the financial
manager at Lever Brothers Company. Joseph Barra, one of the company's financial
managers, is responsible for in-house seminars to keep marketing, production, and
personnel managers informed about activities affecting their areas by discussing
events that are important to each specific group of listeners.

For example, a group of marketing managers will hear a discussion that concentrates on the way that present and future events are affecting the marketing
function. Sales managers are usually concerned about two important areas of their
job, getting new accounts and increasing volume. Barra points out that with this
group he talks about cost of a sale and how a present sale might affect future sales.
"In other words," he says, "If you feature a special offer one month, you may be
adversely affecting more profitable volume the following month or two." When he
turns his attention to a discussion of volume with marketing managers, Mr. Barra
concentrates on the way that volume affects overhead costs and the volatility of
company profit.

An important task of a financial manager is to let all managers know that they
are in fact financial managers who must be able to interpret and use financial information in their day-to-day decisions as well as in their long-term planning. "The
various management disciplines need not be altered," says Barra, "But all managers
are at least made aware of the financial implications of their proposals."

Source: Based on Joseph A. Barra, "Marketing the Financial Facts Of Life," *Management Accounting,* March, 1983, pp. 29–32.

Interlocking Forecasts

The previous section suggests that in a well-run company of any size, financial
requirements are not forecast merely for the next few months. Financial managers
must make the most detailed forecast of financial requirements for the months
immediately ahead. But they also need to forecast, in a more general way, financial
needs a year from now, two years hence, five years in the future.

Well-armed financial managers always have within easy reach a comprehensive set of *interlocking forecasts* of their company's financial needs, tied to the long-
term profit and growth plan decided on by top management. Detailed forecasts over
the next three months or the next year prepare financial managers for the months
ahead—when cash will be short or abundant, when they will need to borrow cash, or
when they will have cash to invest on a short-term basis. More general forecasts
over the next 1 to 5, or even 10, years will warn the manager of the time when (1) the
company must sell new issues of stocks or bonds or (2) the cash flows will become
large enough to begin or increase dividends to owners.

2. ACQUIRING FINANCIAL RESOURCES

Acquiring the financial resources is obtaining the debt and equity that a company needs. It involves keeping in touch with providers of debt and equity, making timely requests, and supporting requests with convincing facts and figures. Financial managers often call the acquisition the *financial decision* because it deals with the credit or right side of a company's statement of financial position (balance sheet).

When to Acquire Debt and Equity

A financial manager should acquire debt and equity before the company's need for them becomes embarrassing. Needy borrowers usually get rough treatment. The mere fact they have waited so long before approaching the investor is itself evidence of poor management. On the other hand, a timely request for a loan or a new sale of common stocks supported by a detailed forecast of operations and financial needs, indicates that management has a firm grip on the business and invites an investor's confidence and favor.

Advance notice of financial needs also eases investors' problems and makes them more receptive. It is usually easier for them to commit themselves to lending or investing two months from now than to provide the money on 10 minutes' notice. Also, advance checking of sources of finance may prevent a later cash crisis. If the regular lender cannot assure funds, then there is still time to try elsewhere.

Where to Acquire Debt and Equity

Where a financial manager goes to raise debt and equity depends on how long the company needs it and on the basis on which it can be raised. At the outset, therefore, we must ask two questions: (1) Do we need long- or short-term financing? (2) How strong is our position as borrowers?

Access to sources of finance and the terms on which it can be obtained depend on the size and strength of a company. For a small, weak company, suppliers' credit may be the only source of short-term finance available. Unless the company's credit standing is first-class, bank loans will have to be secured by pledges of receivables, inventories, or securities. Long-term finance is a special problem for the small company, especially if the company is growing rapidly. For most smaller companies, the only reliable source of long-term finance for growth is retained earnings. This means that partners or stockholders must reconcile themselves to a Spartan existence until the company has attained substantial size.

In choosing a lender, the financial manager should consider three questions: (1) How do the interest charges compare with those of other lenders? (2) How stable and reliable will the lender be in meeting future needs? (3) Is the lender capable of giving valuable advice along with the loan?

How to Acquire Debt and Equity

Trade creditors are impressed by records of prompt payment and by settlement of accounts on the dates promised. Bankers like evidence of orderly, efficient management and financial awareness. Managers impress bankers when they support their loan requests with recent balance sheets and income statements (certified by a public accountant), and careful, detailed projections of cash flow over the period of the requested loan. Many investment advisors like an aura of youth and vigor in management and an impressive record of earnings growth. These are features they can dramatize to an investing public that is hungry for glamour stocks and growth companies. If the company is retaining profits instead of paying them out, it is important that stockholders understand this, so that the maximum sustainable market price of the stock can be attained. Stockholders should be kept aware of the company's progress and dividends to come.

You must remember that financial institutions are managed by people and that many benefits are obtained by favor as well as merit. Thus a financial manager should maintain close, friendly relations with a banker, and perhaps use the bank's other services—its trust department, personal loans, safety deposit vault, and so forth. The manager might also take newcomers and employees to the bank to discuss opening accounts. It is worthwhile to find out what services the bank can offer if they are not already known. Finally, the financial manager might try to get acquainted with other suppliers of corporate finance and let them know what plans are being made for building the company. In short, the financial manager must become known and respected in financial circles *before* the company needs help.

ALLOCATING CASH IN THE COMPANY

The third A of financial management is Allocate. Allocating cash in a company means investing in the best balance of assets. Assets are balanced by weighing their profitability against their financial liquidity. Profitability means the power of an asset to produce a stream of cash flows greater than the cash required to acquire the asset. Financial liquidity means closeness to money. (We shall look at these ingredients of cash allocation in Chapters 12 to 15.) Financial managers often call the allocation decision the *investment decision* because it deals with the way the company's debt and equity are invested in assets.

A financial manager must steer a prudent course between too much cash and too little cash. Squeezing cash to the last dollar may boost profitability, but doing so runs the risk that the company will lack the cash needed to meet unexpected emergencies or opportunities. An abundance of cash will keep the business liquid (and thus safe), but profitability will fall because highly liquid assets yield a low return.

The Marginal Principle

Allocating cash in a company concerns itself with the debit or asset side of the balance sheet. Investing in each asset helps a firm operate more smoothly and efficiently. But in adding to each sort of asset, a point is reached where additions become less and less profitable, especially if some other kind of asset needs the investment more urgently. Here, then, is the problem of allocation.

In allocating the total available cash, financial managers should not overemphasize one sort of asset and slight another. For instance, they must guard against

BOX 11-3

A Financial Manager's Job Has Many
Dimensions   Today the job of a financial manager has become important in many
                     areas of business. Finance people aid in strategic planning, mergers, and
operations. James A. Hodges, Jr., the chief financial officer at Sargent-Welch Scientific Company, has helped his company's personnel department revise life and medical insurance plans. He found the policy that offered the most coverage while minimizing the company's cash outflow for premiums. As a result, he says, the company
was able to control cash outflows while adding dental insurance coverage.

Sargent-Welch also needed Mr. Hodges's knowledge of financial markets in
1982 after it sold its Inter-Collegiate Press division for $9.7 million. The company
had previously put cash in bank certificates of deposit, but now the company is
investing the money in securities such as floating-rate preferred stock, municipal
securities, and Eurodollar securities.

Lawrence F. Nein, president of a maker of scientific implements asked Mr.
Hodges to work with operating managers to reduce inventories, which can cut costs
and increase income. "Every dollar of inventory you can turn into cash, you can stick
in the bank and earn a . . . good rate," Mr. Nein explained.

The record suggests that financial managers get a greater percentage of their
compensation from performance-related bonuses than do other top employees, according to a study by Hewitt Associates, a Chicago consulting firm. Short-term
rewards such as bonuses can add between 40 and 50 percent to a financial officer's
compensation, and long-term rewards such as stock options can add another 35 to 40
percent.

Source: Based on Heywood Klein, "Financial Officers Often in Demand as Companies Seek Cost-
Cutters," *The Wall Street Journal,* November 22, 1982, p. 25.

sinking so much cash in a building that the company cannot pay its bills on time.
They should not invest so heavily in machinery that the company cannot afford to
offer customers the credit terms important to making sales. They must not become
so loaded with inventories that the company cannot find cash to replace worn-out
delivery trucks.

How can financial managers preserve a proper balance among various assets?
They can do so by using the *marginal principle:* A financial manager chooses first
assets offering the greatest return and least risk followed by assets yielding margin-
ally (or incrementally) less return and more risk. Following the marginal principle
helps a financial manager make decisions that maximize the company's stock price.
We shall use the marginal principle extensively when we discuss capital budgeting
in Part 6 of this book and working-capital management in Part 7.

Ratio Analysis

Financial ratios offer guideposts for implementing the marginal principle when
choosing between various kinds of assets. The ratios compare different items on the

balance sheet and income statement with each other. Each ratio is designed to tell a financial manager something specific about how effectively a particular asset is contributing to the company's performance.

Collectively, the ratios measure four factors:

1. **Activity**   (How fast do inventories, receivables, or circulating capital turn over?)
2. **Profitability**   (What is the percent return on total assets, fixed assets, and owners' investment?)
3. **Liquidity**   (What part of total assets consists of cash or quickly cashable assets?)
4. **Leverage**   (What part of current, fixed, or total assets is financed with borrowed funds rather than with owner investment?)

As a financial manager, if you know what ratios are correct for your line of business, then you can appraise investment in each kind of asset from the standpoint of its activity, profitability, liquidity, and leverage. You can then see whether a commitment in a particular asset is too small for safety, about right, or too large for liquidity. We shall examine the usefulness of ratios and other financial measures in Chapters 13 and 14.

Ratios, of course, have their limitations. They are a screening device, not a final answer to how a business should use its cash. One or more ratios may be badly out of line with the average of an industry, but special circumstances in a company (such as different sales categories or a different class of customers) may more than justify the deviation. In the final analysis, ratios, like other management tools, are subject to the judgment and discretion of the manager applying them.

Equalizing Cost of Capital and Return

Finally, you should note—and only note at this point—an important principle that summarizes the conceptual foundation of business financial policy: A company should carry its business activities to the point where its marginal (or last chunk of) return just equals the risk-adjusted cost of its marginal (or last added) increment of capital. By doing so, a company accomplishes two important objectives: (1) correctly deciding what its total amount of investments (or volume of assets) should be and (2) maximizing the price of its common stock. Roughly, at least, a financial manager accomplishes these objectives when he keeps a company's key ratios and financial measures at the top of its industry.

SUMMARY

1. Financial management is a staff function within a company's organizational structure. The objective of financial management is to make investment and financial decisions that will maximize the company's stock price.

2. Stock price maximization is implemented with the three As of financial management. The three A's (and associated financial management terms and rules) are

Three A's	Financial Management Task	Rule
Anticipate financial needs	Forecasting	Forecast cash flows
Acquire debt and equity	Financial decision	Keep in touch with sources of debt and equity
Allocate cash	Investment decision	Apply key ratios to the company and use the marginal principle

3. If you keep in mind the three As and their corresponding rules, then you may be surprised at the ease with which you can comprehend and master the detailed presentation of financial management that follows this chapter.

KEY TERMS AND CONCEPTS

Objective of financial management   Investment and financial decision
Treasurer and controller   Financial forecast
The three A's   Profitability and liquidity
Financial management's new look   Marginal principle
Cash budget   Key ratios

QUESTIONS

11-1. Someone has said, "The objective of financial management is to maximize the price of the company's common stock." Do you agree? Explain your answer.

11-2. Why does every business need a financial manager?

11-3. Discuss the expanded roles of the controller and treasurer in modern financial management.

11-4. Describe how a small-business person can anticipate financial needs.

11-5. What documents constitute the complete financial forecast of a large company?

11-6. Would the rapid growth of a business impose special financial problems?

11-7. Describe the three A's of financial management and tell which is the investment decision and which is the financial decision. Which one do you believe to be more important? Explain your answer.

11-8. Explain the nature and operation of interlocking forecasts.

11-9. What principles and rules should the financial manager follow in acquiring financial resources from outside lenders?

11-10. What does proper allocation of funds in a business mean? How can financial managers help assure themselves that they are properly allocating funds?

11-11. What four properties of a business do key ratios measure? Define them.

11-12. How could a firm hold 50 percent of its assets in the form of machinery and only 2 percent in cash yet still abide by the marginal principle?

CHAPTER 12
Financial Statements and
What They Indicate

Investors, creditors, and financial managers use financial statements to help them make decisions about a company. These statements consist of a statement of financial position (balance sheet), an income statement, a statement of reconciliation of retained earnings, and a statement of changes in financial position. This chapter introduces each of these statements, explains their relationship to each other, and discusses their usefulness in financial decision making.

The first part of the chapter discusses the statement of financial position. After reading this section you will recognize the difference between a company's assets and liabilities and understand the way that assets and liabilities affect shareholders' equity. The next part examines the income statement. You will learn that the income statement measures the change in a company's retained earnings account and reflects the difference between the revenues and expenses over a period of time. After completing this part of the chapter, we shall study a company's reconciliation of retained earnings statement. You will learn that this statement shows the dollar changes in the company's retained earnings for a specified period of time. We conclude our study of financial statements with the statement of changes in financial position to show how financial analysts construct and use the statement in their decisions. When you finish this discussion you will know how to construct a simple statement and to use it in your own assessment of a company's financial condition.

HOW FINANCIAL STATEMENTS RELATE TO EACH OTHER

The three most important documents in a company's financial report are

1. A statement of financial position, which is usually called a balance sheet.
2. An income statement, which is often called a profit and loss or P and L statement.
3. A statement of changes in financial position, which is often called a sources and uses or a funds statement.

Figure 12-1 portrays the relationship between these three statements. A company begins an operating period with a collection of assets and generates earnings over a period of time. Earnings are measured on the company's income statement. They provide more assets to the company so that ending balance-sheet amounts differ from beginning amounts. A company also undertakes investment and financial activities that do not show up on its income statement. These activities are measured on the company's statement of changes in financial position. Ending balance-sheet amounts differ from beginning amounts as a result of these investment and financial activities.

FIGURE 12-1   How financial statements relate to one another.

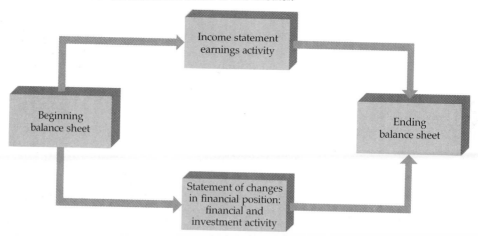

The following discussion begins our analysis of a company's financial reports with the balance sheet in order to familiarize you with its terminology and construction. After looking at a balance sheet, we will turn our attention to the income statement and the statement of changes in financial position.

STATEMENT OF FINANCIAL POSITION

To understand a statement of financial position you must remember that a corporation is legally an artificial person separate and distinct from the real people or financial institutions that own it. A corporation in turn is legally separate from the property that it owns. Properties owned by the corporation (or by any company) are assets. And although the company itself owns all of the assets, various outsiders have claims against the total value of these assets. Claims of creditors to whom the company owes money or other assets are liabilities. These claims have priority over the residual or remainder claims of the owners. Residual claims are net worth or equity.

Statement Layout

Table 12-1 is a layout of a sample statement of financial position for the hypothetical Harper Distributing Company. It is typical of the type used by a medium-size company, neither the simplest that could be issued nor the most complicated.

The balance sheet is a financial photograph of a company at an instant in time, typically the close of a business day. The statement is divided into two parts—one part is assets and the other is claims against assets. The assets column (Table 12-1) lists all of the property owned by a company, including its own claims against other companies yet to be collected. The claims against the company's assets (Table 12-1) are divided into liabilities and net worth. The liabilities column lists all debts that the company owes, and these are the creditors' claims against the assets. Net worth for a corporation is usually called shareholders' equity, and it measures the owners' claims against the assets. Net worth is the residual claim on assets because it is the amount remaining after substracting the creditors' claims. The fundamental accounting equation shows the way that net worth is a residual claim:

$$\text{Assets} = \text{liabilities} + \text{net worth}$$

Subtracting liabilities from each side of the equation and rearranging terms show us that net worth is the residual remaining after the claim of the company's creditors:

$$\text{Net worth} = \text{assets} - \text{liabilities}$$

Assets

An asset is a future benefit because it has the potential to provide a company and its owners with future cash flow. Resources recognized as assets are those for which a

TABLE 12-1   Harper Distributing Company, Statement of Financial Position as of December 31 (000 omitted)

Assets	19x0		19x1	
Current assets				
Cash	$ 1,325		$ 1,547	
Receivables (net of bad debts)	10,447		10,047	
Inventory	3,236		3,599	
Prepaid expenses	244		245	
Total current assets		$15,252		$15,438
Fixed assets				
Land and buildings	$ 1,771		$ 2,044	
Machinery and equipment	1,241		1,460	
	$ 3,012		$ 3,504	
Less accumulated depreciation	1,056		1,248	
Total fixed assets		1,956		2,256
Other assets-investments		252		289
Total assets		$17,460		$17,983
Liabilities and Equity				
Current liabilities				
Accounts payable	$2,479		$2,386	
Notes payable	7,280		7,360	
Loans payable	204		571	
Accrued wages and taxes	1,229		1,200	
Total current liabilities		$11,192		$11,517
Noncurrent Liabilities				
Loans (net of current portion)	$ 215		$ 213	
Mortgage	5		5	
		220		218
Total liabilities		$11,412		$11,735
Net worth				
Preferred stock (60,000 shares authorized and 10,000 shares outstanding; $20 par value)	$ 200		$ 200	
Common shareholders' equity				
Common stock (1,000,000 shares authorized and 400,000 shares outstanding; $1 par value)	$ 400		$ 400	
Paid-in capital in excess of par	$ 200		$ 200	
Retained earnings	$5,248		$5,448	
		6,048		6,248
Total liabilities and equity		17,460		17,983

company has acquired rights to their future use as a result of a past transaction or exchange and for which the value of the future benefits can be measured with some precision and accuracy. Management assigns a dollar amount to each asset and asks an accountant to prepare financial statements based on either their acquisition cost (called historical value) or market value, whichever is lower.

Acquisition cost is all cash outlays or debt required to put the asset into usable condition. Transportation expenses, installation, handling charges, and any other necessary amounts in connection with the asset up to the time that the company places it in service are a part of acquisition cost.

Example. Acquisition cost of an asset might be calculated in the following way:

Invoice price of equipment		$12,000
Less 2 percent cash discount		240
Net price		$11,760
Add other costs		
Transportation	$300	
Installation	700	
		1,000
Total cost of equipment		$12,760

A company may acquire assets in ways other than by paying cash or incurring a liability. For example, a lawyer may donate her services to the company or the company may acquire another company by issuing its own common stock. In these cases the accountant measures cost by the market value of the services or of the asset the company receives.

Current Assets. The first group on the asset part of the balance sheet is current assets. It includes cash and those other assets which, in the normal course of business, will be turned into cash within the coming year. Cash consists of currency and coin in the till (petty cash) and money on deposit at the bank.

Accounts receivable are the amount not yet collected from customers to whom merchandise was shipped prior to payment. The total amount due from customers in 19x1 shown on Harper Distributing's statement of financial position is $10,907,000. However, management has determined that some customers fail to pay their bills, so the total amount of receivables is reduced by a provision for bad debts. The statement of financial position in Table 12-1 shows the amount of accounts receivable less the estimated provision for bad debts:

Accounts receivable	$10,907,000
Less provision for bad debts	860,000
Net accounts receivable 19x1	$10,047,000

Three components make up a company's inventory—raw materials, partly finished goods in process of being assembled, and finished goods ready to be shipped to customers. The accountant values inventory at the *lower* of its historical value or current replacement cost (called market value), giving a conservative amount for financial reporting purposes. Accountants use current replacement cost only if the company will realize an amount less than historical value when it sells the merchandise.

Three items within a company's current assets make up the cash cycle. The *cash cycle* is the flow of cash from the cash account to inventory as the company buys or constructs merchandise and makes it ready to sell, then from inventory to accounts receivable as the company sells merchandise on credit, and then from accounts receivable back to cash as the company collects payment. The amount of cash returning after the cycle is larger than that which began the cycle by the amount of profit less bad debts.

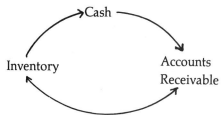

The next item in Harper Distributing Company's current assets is prepaid expenses. *Prepaid expenses* are the unexpired portion of costs paid in advance so the company will receive benefits in the future. An accountant sometimes places a deferred charge on a company's statement of financial position. A *deferred charge*, like a prepaid expense, is the unexpired portion of costs paid in advance, but a deferred charge has benefits that are expected to extend over a period longer than that of a prepaid expense.

A prepaid expense and a deferred charge have three characteristics in common:

1. The company has already paid cash but will receive part of the benefit in the future.
2. The company's accountant enters an asset on the company's statement of financial position to reflect the value paid but not yet received.
3. The accountant allocates the remaining cost embodied in the asset to future years in which the company receives benefits. The future allocation reduces assets and net worth (net worth is reduced as the expired portion of the asset is expensed on the company's income statement).

Noncurrent Assets. All items not being used up or consumed within one year are called noncurrent assets. A part of noncurrent assets are fixed assets on Table 12-1. Fixed assets include land, buildings, machinery, equipment, furniture, trucks, autos, and other durable items. These items (1) are used to manufacture, warehouse, or transport products and (2) are not intended for resale.

The generally approved method of valuing fixed assets is cost minus depreciation accumulated to date of the balance sheet. Depreciation, in the economic sense, represents decline in the useful value of a fixed asset. The loss of value is due to wear and tear from use, obsolescence, or action of the elements. In the accounting sense, depreciation means matching a fixed-asset's cost with the revenue produced over the asset's useful life.

Our sample statement of financial position shows an amount for accumulated depreciation that is a total for buildings, machinery, and office furniture. Land is not subject to depreciation, and its statement value remains unchanged from year to year.

The next amount, total fixed assets, is the value for statement purposes of the company's investment in fixed assets. It consists of the historical cost of the various kinds of fixed assets reduced by the depreciation accumulated to date. For Harper Distributing Company on December 31, 19x1, total fixed assets are $2,256,000:

Land and buildings	$2,044,000
Machinery and equipment	1,460,000
Gross fixed assets	$3,504,000
Less accumulated depreciation	1,248,000
Total fixed assets	$2,256,000

Total fixed assets on a statement of financial position that an accountant prepares for financial reporting purposes are not intended to reflect either current replacement cost or replacement cost in the future. Likewise, accumulated depreciation does not correspond with the depreciation rate at which value or usefulness actually declines. Depreciation is merely a way to distribute the original cost (called historical value) over the asset's useful life. For the sake of clarity and consistency, depreciation (the using up of fixed assets) is recorded as though the dollar's value remains fixed. (If inflation raises the cost of fixed-asset replacement, then management should recognize that some profits will be needed to replace fixed assets.)

The term *depreciation* applies to allocating the cash outlay of man-made non-monetary assets. Two other related terms occur in financial accounting: depletion and amortization. Depletion recognizes the using up of some natural resource—a deposit of oil, coal, clay, gravel, and the like. In a similar sense amortization accounts for the loss of value in a patent, leasehold, franchise, or some other intangible right owned by a company.

The section of the balance sheet labeled "Investments" includes primarily the investments in securities of corporations where the purpose of the investment is long-term.

Example. Harper Distributing might buy shares of a supplier's common stock to help assure itself of continued availability of raw materials. Or the company might buy the shares of a corporation in another line of business to permit Harper Distributing to diversify its operations.

When one corporation (called the parent) owns more than 50 percent of the voting stock of another corporation (called the subsidiary), management usually prepares a consolidated statement in which specific assets and liabilities are consoli-

---

BOX 12-1

Careless Financial Manager + Careless

Bank = $50,000 Loan   Some financial managers are not careful in preparing the financial statements they submit when they apply for a bank loan. And some banks are not careful in examining the financial information. Consider as an example the case of a California small business that submitted with a loan application a specimen financial statement that it had received from an accounting firm: The accounting firm gave the specimen statements to the company's owner, and the company subsequently became the accounting firm's client.

Months later the company's owner called a partner of the CPA firm to complain that the financial statements made no sense. Her company's name was missing, replaced by a string of Xs, and the numbers were wrong.

"We hadn't done a financial statement for her," the CPA says. She had looked at the specimen he had given her earlier. And she had given it to her bank—a big one—on applying for a $50,000 loan. Even though the specimen was unclear about the company's business (it says the "company is a California corporation engaged in the promotion and sale of xxxxx") and the results didn't conform with the company's earlier years' results, the company got the loan.

Source: Based on a report in *The Wall Street Journal,* November 14, 1983, p. 29.

---

dated or combined. An accountant eliminates the account "Investment In Subsidiaries" when preparing consolidated statements. Notice the Harper Distributing's statement of financial position shows an account "Investment In Subsidiaries." This account tells us that the balance sheet is not a consolidated statement.

Liabilities

The liability section of a statement of financial position shows the debt claims against a company's assets—their amounts and, roughly, the priority of their claims in the event that the company becomes bankrupt and liquidates it assets for cash. Along with the company's net worth, liabilities are the *sources* of finance that a company has used in the past (that is, up to the statement date) to acquire assets.

The liabilities part of a statement of financial position first presents current liabilities. _Current liabilities_ are all debts that fall due within the coming year. *Accounts payable* are amounts the company owes its suppliers and other business creditors. Most of these represent purchases of goods for which the company has 30, 60, or 90 days to pay. *Notes payable* are amounts owed banks and other lenders and evidenced by written promissory notes. *Accrued expenses* include a variety of amounts owed but unpaid on the date of the balance sheet—salaries and wages of employees, interest on borrowed money, pensions, attorney fees, and the like. *Federal income tax payable* is usually stated separately from other accrued items. Finally, total current liabilities are the total of items listed in this classification.

Long-term liabilities, the next part of a company's liabilities on its statement of financial position, are all debts on which the principal falls due more than one year after the statement date. Our sample statement of financial position in Table 12-1 lists only two long-term liabilities, bank loans and a mortgage loan. A mortgage loan is a loan that has real property—land or buildings—pledged to assure repayment.

Shareholder's Equity

Shareholder's equity comprises the total of ownership claims on a corporation's assets. It is often called by its other name, net worth. For legal, accounting, and financial purposes shareholders' equity can be separated in various ways. Two headings usually appear within a corporation's shareholders' equity account: (1) Preferred stock and (2) Common shareholders' equity. A corporation issues stock certificates to its preferred and common shareholders.

Preferred stock is a limited kind of ownership, entitled to dividend payments at a fixed rate before the company can pay dividends on common shares. It also is paid off before the common shareholders' claim if the corporation is liquidated. Harper Distributing Company had outstanding on each of the statement dates 10,000 shares of preferred stock with $20 per share par value. *Par value* means a stated value for legal purposes. Many states require that common and preferred stock have a par value. *Cumulative* means that the company must pay any preferred stock dividends missed (called dividends in arrear) before its directors can declare a common-stock dividend.

Common shareholders' equity includes three items: common stock, paid-in capital in excess of par, and retained earnings. Common shareholders' equity for Harper Distributing Company on December 31, 19x0 is,

Common stock	$ 400,000
Paid-in capital in excess of par	200,000
Retained earnings	5,448,000
	$6,048,000

Managers often call the first two components of shareholders' equity *external* because these accounts increase as a result of selling new common stock. Managers often call retained earnings *internal equity* because this account increases as a result of the internal operations of the company. Retained earnings are the profit from past periods plowed back into the company instead of paid out as dividends to the company's preferred and common shareholders.

Changes in a company's retained earnings result primarily from events that affect the company's income statement. A profitable company will have an increase in retained earnings (if it does not distribute all of its earnings to its shareholders) and an unprofitable company will have a decrease in its retained earnings. The following part of this chapter will familiarize you with a company's income statement and some of the difficulties of measuring the amounts that comprise it.

AN INCOME STATEMENT

An income statement summarizes a company's operating results for a period, typically one year. It matches amounts received from sales and services with all expenses that a company incurs. The difference between receipts and expenses is the company's net profit (or loss) for the period. A statement of financial position is like a photograph because it shows a specific point in time. An income statement is like a moving picture because it shows what has happened over a period of time.

Years ago the length of time covered by an income statement varied a great deal among companies. Income statements were prepared at the end of an activity such as after a military campaign or ocean voyage. Earnings activities of most companies today are not so easily separated into distinct projects because income-generating activity is carried on continually.

Example. A company acquires and uses a building in manufacturing products for a period of 40 years or more. It purchases delivery equipment to use in transporting merchandise to customers for five, six, or more years.

If we postponed preparing an income statement until all earnings activities were completed, the report might never be prepared and would probably be too late to help statement users evaluate performance and make decisions. Companies, therefore, usually use an accounting period with a uniform time period to help investors and creditors in their comparisons among companies.

An accounting period of one year underlies the principal financial statements distributed to owners and potential investors. Most companies prepare their annual reports using the calendar year as the accounting period. A large number of companies, however, use a fiscal (business) year. By using a fiscal year, management attempts to report performance at a time when earnings activities have been substantially concluded. The ending date of a fiscal year varies from one company to another.

Example. Sears uses a fiscal year ending on January 31, which comes after completion of the Christmas shopping season. Electronic Data Systems uses a fiscal year ending June 30, a time when demand for its facilities has slacked off for a period.

In order to provide even more timely information, most publicly held corporations also report earnings data for interim periods within the regular annual accounting period. These interim reports generally cover three-month periods, or quarters. The Securities and Exchange Commission requires that companies under its jurisdiction and meeting specific criteria issue quarterly statements.

Recognizing and Measuring Revenue

A company's revenue is what it receives from selling its output. To most companies this means sales revenue, but to many, like a bank or savings and loan, it may mean interest income or service fees. Revenue increases a company's net worth (through the income statement) and assets.

Example. The local bank charges you interest for your car loan. Interest is revenue to the bank and shows up as a plus item on its income statement. As a result, net worth increases. The statement of financial position stays in balance because assets increase by the amount of the revenue.

The way that revenue affects the statement of financial position through a company's income statement can be pictured in the following way:

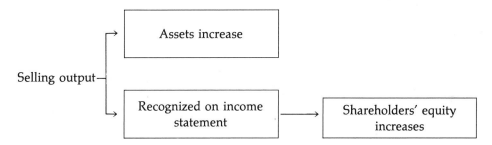

When the company sells output, the assets increase by the amount of revenue received and the accountant records the same amount on the income statement. The increase in the income statement increases the shareholders' equity item on the statement of financial position so that this statement remains in balance, and the system follows the fundamental accounting equation—assets equal liabilities plus shareholders' equity.

Recognizing and Measuring Expenses

Expenses are used-up assets. The amount of the expense is the portion of the asset that is used up in producing revenue. Assets are stored costs that are carried forward to future periods and then expensed on the company's income statement as they are used up:

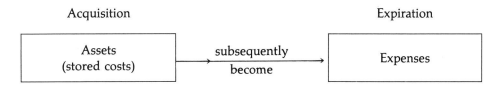

Expenses are usually measured by a portion of the historical value of assets because assets are carried on the company's statement of financial position at historical cost.

Expenses are an estimate of the assets used up in producing revenue. When assets are used up an expense reduces the amount of revenue on the income statement, and an amount equal to the expense reduces the assets on the company's statement of financial position. Assets and claims against assets remain equal (or stay in balance) because the reduction on the income statement reduces net worth or shareholders' equity on the statement of financial position.

Statement Layout

An income statement contains some or all of the following categories depending on the nature of the income during the period:

1. Income from continuing operations.
2. Income, gains, and losses from discontinued operations.
3. Adjustments for changes in accounting principles, and
4. Extraordinary gains and losses.

Most income statements include only the first section, and the other sections are added if necessary. The following discussion concentrates on income from continuing operations for Harper Distributing in Table 12-2.

The first item in Table 12-2 is net sales. It represents the revenue recognized by the company from its customers for goods or services sold. Net means that allowance has been made for goods returned and discounts taken by customers for prompt payment.

Cost of goods sold and operating expenses, the first subtractions made in determining profit, include four components. (1) Cost of goods sold covers cash payments made or liabilities incurred in the operating period for raw materials, direct labor, and factory overhead items such as supervision, rent, electricity, supplies, maintenance, and repairs. (2) Depreciation is the allowance made each year for loss of value in long-lived assets (plant, equipment, and machinery) used in production. With minor exceptions, depreciation on the income statement will equal the change in the accumulated depreciation shown on the balance sheet over the ac-

---

TABLE 12-2 Harper Distributing Company, Income Statement for the 12-Months Ending December 31, 19x1 (000 omitted)

Net sales		$26,473
Less cost of goods		21,299
Gross profit		$ 5,174
Less operating expenses		
Depreciation	$ 192	
General and administrative	1,299	
Selling and shipping	2,680	
Bad debt expense	115	
		4,286
Net operating profit		$ 888
Less interest expense		321
Earnings before provision for taxes		$ 567
Less provision for taxes		284
Earnings after taxes		$ 283

BOX 12-2

Rhymes From Heinz   Reading this chapter may give you the impression that a company's annual report must be a dry, half-dead statistical fact book. That's not necessarily the case. In the H. J. Heinz Company 1982 annual report, a Canadian forklift operator rhapsodizes about the changes that have occurred in a neighborhood park over his lifetime; an Australian salesclerk ponders her destiny; and a Puerto Rican plant superintendent laments the cruel life of working the sugarcane fields " 'til death knocks on your door." They are just 3 of 10 poems written by Heinz employees, each accompanied by a full-page illustration, that are sprinkled through the Pittsburgh-based company's latest report.

Every year Heinz focuses on some aspect of the lives of its 42,000 employees. "We did it to achieve maximum relationship," explains company spokesman Thomas McIntosh. "And we'd like to be seen as a very human institution that places value on individual achievement and individual diversity." When staffers were asked to submit poems, McIntosh admits, he wasn't sure he'd get even one entry. Actually, he got 750, including a California grandmother's ode to Elvis Presley and 196-line defense of tennis pro John McEnroe. He also got plenty of the more predictable type, as "Oh Heinz, I love your beans and ketchup." McIntosh submitted the entries to the International Poetry Forum, whose judges narrowed the field down to 20. Several hundred letters have come in praising the report, he reveals, "double to three times normal."

Source: Mary Rowland, "Gimmicks, 1983," *Institutional Investor,* March 1983, p. 72.

---

counting period that these financial reports cover. (3) General and administrative expenses along with selling and shipping expenses comprise sales representatives' salaries and commissions, advertising, promotion, travel, and entertainment outlays (selling expenses) and executive salaries, office payroll, and office expenses (administrative expenses). (4) Bad debt expense is the estimated amount of sales that will not be paid. Net operating profit is computed by subtracting cost of sales and operating expenses from net sales. Harper Distributing Company's net operating profit is $888,000 for the 12 months ending December 31, 19x1.

Interest expense is the sum paid to suppliers of debt capital (in this case, the bank and mortgage holders) for the use of their money. It is sometimes referred to as a fixed financial charge, since it must be paid whether the company is making money or not. Other fixed financial charges, not owed by Harper Distributing Company, include payments that a company is required to make to retain use of leased or rented property.

Tax laws treat interest as a cost of doing business, so interest is deductible from total income in arriving at the earnings before provision for federal income tax entry. Provision for federal income tax is the last item subtracted in arriving at net profit or earnings for the year.

Net profit or earnings after taxes represents what a company has left after meeting all costs of a year's operations. It is the amount available to pay dividends on the preferred and common stock and to use in the business. Earnings after taxes for Harper Distributing are $283,000 for the 12 months ending December 31, 19x1.

You need to be aware of three points of caution with respect to earnings after taxes. First, the net earnings of any single year are a much less reliable indicator of a company's earning power than is its earnings trend over several years. A single year may be one of business boom or recession, and hence unrepresentative so that the trend as well as the level of earnings is important. Second, the amount of earnings after taxes may differ drastically from distributable income, especially when current replacement costs are rising rapidly. *Distributable income* is the amount of earnings after taxes that the company can use to distribute as dividends without impairing its operating capacity. (We shall examine distributable income in Chapter 19.)

Finally, the earnings after taxes that an income statement shows are affected by a company's accounting practices. Different ways of calculating depreciation, of charging for cost of goods sold, or of showing costs or receipts not typical of the company's operations—all these can result in very different final profit figures.

RECONCILIATION OF RETAINED EARNINGS

Beginning and ending balances in retained earnings must be reconciled or explained in the financial statements. The reconciliation can appear either in a separate statement or as the lower section in a combined statement of income and retained earnings. In most cases, net income and dividends are the only reconciling items. Occasionally an adjustment or correction of prior years' income statements appears as an addition to or a subtraction from the beginning balance in retained earnings.

An accumulated retained earnings statement summarizes the change in retained earnings from the figure shown on the previous year's statement of financial position. As the statement for Harper Distributing Company in Table 12-3 illustrates, the structure is simple and straightforward:

Previous retained earnings + net income for year past − dividends paid
= new balance of retained earnings

In this illustration and in most situations, the change in retained earnings is explained by profit for the year less dividends.

STATEMENT OF CHANGES IN FINANCIAL POSITION

A statement of changes in financial position shows why and how either cash or net working capital has increased or decreased from one balance sheet date to another. Net working capital is current assets financed from long-term debt or equity sources, and we measure it by the difference between current assets and current liabilities.

TABLE 12-3 Harper Distributing Company, Statement of Accumulated Retained Earnings
(December 31, 19x1)

Beginning retained earnings		$5,248,000
Add earnings after taxes for 19x1		283,000
Total		$5,531,000
Less dividends:		
Preferred stock (10,000 shares × $2)	$20,000	
Common stock (400,000 shares × $0.1575)	63,000	83,000
Ending Retained Earnings		$5,448,000

Unlike current assets financed from current liabilities, net working capital does not disappear when current liabilities are paid off. It is an important amount because it represents the volume of current assets that will dependably stay with a company.

Example. Stetson, Inc., has had large profits during each of the preceding three years, but the company has had difficulty paying its bills. The problem results from a lack of cash, a problem that can be anticipated and analyzed with a statement of changes in financial position on a cash basis.

The experience of Stetson, Inc., is not unusual. Many companies, particularly those growing rapidly, may discover that their ability to pay current liabilities from their current assets is deteriorating despite an excellent earnings record. The statement of changes in financial position provides useful information to assess changes in a company's liquidity by reporting on the flows of funds into and out of the business during a period. (Recall that liquidity is a financial term meaning nearness to money.)

The role of net working capital as a pool that rises and falls with the flow of company activity is illustrated in Figure 12-2. Operations, acquiring long-term finance (debt and equity), and selling long-term assets increase a company's net working capital. Paying dividends, redeeming (paying off) long-term debts and buying back common stock, and acquiring long-term assets decrease a company's net working capital.

Cash Flows and Net Working Capital

The statement of changes in financial position reports on the flows of funds into and out of a business during a period. Funds can be viewed as cash, in which case a statement of changes in financial position is a statement of cash receipts and disbursements. The term *funds*, however, is a general one having different meanings. Consider the following two questions, which a company's management might ask itself:

1. Do we have sufficient funds to acquire new equipment immediately?
2. Will we have sufficient funds to acquire new equipment within the next six months?

In answering the first question, management is likely to consider the amount of cash on hand and in its bank account. It would also consider if the equipment could be acquired on account from one of its regular suppliers. In answering the second question, management would consider if the company had marketable securities or other assets that could be sold for cash during the next six months. Time is an important factor in determining the way that we define funds. When the time horizon is short, the meaning of funds is more restrictive than when the time horizon is longer.

Statements of changes in financial position of most publicly held corporations define funds to be net working capital because many experts believe that this broader definition provides more useful information to investors and other users of financial statements than the more restrictive cash definition.

Constructing a Statement

Constructing a statement of changes in financial position calls for scrutiny of both the most recent balance sheet and last year's balance sheet, the income statement, the statement of retained earnings, and sometimes other sources. By examining these documents, we can determine where working capital came from or was lost during the year. Briefly, the following items are classified sources and uses of net working capital. Notice that each is a change occurring in the noncurrent section of the balance sheet.

Sources	*Uses*
1. Net profit for the year	1. Net loss for year
2. Depreciation or other noncash expenses	2. Dividend payments
3. Sale of noncurrent assets	3. Purchase of noncurrent assets
4. New equity or long-term debt financing	4. Retirement or repurchase of stock or long-term debt

FIGURE 12-2   Net working capital as a pool reflecting transactions.

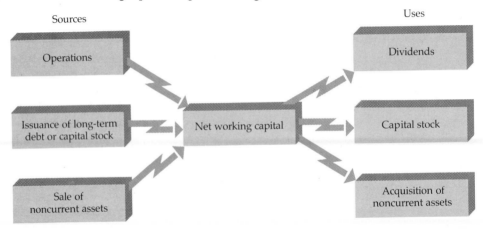

Changes in net working capital are explained by changes in balance-sheet items other than current assets and current liabilities. Sources are increases in long-term liabilities (or equity) and decreases in noncurrent assets. Uses are increases in noncurrent assets, reduction of long-term liabilities, and dividends or net losses (both of which reduce equity).

To construct a statement of financial position on a net working-capital basis, you need to follow these steps:

1. Ignore all items in the current asset and current liability components of a balance sheet.
2. Calculate the dollar changes in each of the noncurrent items on a balance sheet
   a. An increase in an asset and a decrease in a liability or equity account is a *use* of net working capital.
   b. An increase in a liability or equity account and a decrease in an asset is a *source* of net working capital.

   Use: ↑ Asset, ↓ Liability or Equity

   Source: ↓ Asset, ↑ Liability or Equity

3. The difference in long-term uses and sources is the change in net working capital.
   a. If long-term sources are greater than long-term uses, then net working capital must rise.
   b. If long-term uses are greater than long-term sources, then net working capital must fall.

The process of constructing the statement begins by blocking off the short-term items on two statements of financial position. Table 12-4 shows this blocking for Harper Distributing Company's balance sheet from Table 12-1. Then, we decide if an item is a source or a use of net working capital by using the rule above:

Sources		*Uses*	
(Decrease in asset, increase in liability and equity)		(Increase in asset, decrease in liability and equity)	
Change in depreciation	$192,000	Land and buildings	$273,000
Change in retained earnings	200,000	Machinery and equipment	219,000
		Investments	37,000
		Loans	2,000
Totals	$392,000		$531,000

Practice. Before continuing, make sure that you know where we got the $192,000 change in depreciation expense above and why we classified it a source. (Hint: Examine Table 12-2.)

TABLE 12-4 Harper Distributing Company, Statement of Financial Position as of December 31 (000 omitted)

Assets	19x0		19x1	
Current Assets				
Cash	$ 1,325		$ 1,547	
Receivables (net of bad debts)	10,447		10,047	
Inventory	3,236		3,599	
Prepaid expenses	244		245	
Total current assets		$15,252		$15,438
Fixed assets				
Land and buildings	$ 1,771		$ 2,044	
Machinery and equipment	1,241		1,460	
	$ 3,012		$ 3,504	
Less accumulated depreciation	1,056		1,248	
Total fixed assets		1,956		2,256
Other assets-investments		252		289
Total assets		$17,460		$17,983
Liabilities and equity				
Current liabilities				
Accounts payable	$ 2,479		$ 2,386	
Notes payable	7,280		7,360	
Loans payable	204		571	
Accrued wages and taxes	1,229		1,200	
Total current liabilities		$11,192		$11,517
Noncurrent Liabilities				
Loans (net of current portion)	$ 215		$ 213	
Mortgage	5		5	
		220		218
Total liabilities		$11,412		$11,735
Net worth				
Preferred stock (60,000 shares authorized and 10,000 shares outstanding; $20 par value)	$ 200		$ 200	
Common shareholders' equity				
Capital Stock (1,000,000 shares authorized and 400,000 shares outstanding; $1 par value)	$ 400		$ 400	
Paid-in capital in excess of par	$ 200		$ 200	
Retained earnings	$5,248		$5,448	
		6,048		6,248
Total liabilities and equity		17,460		17,983

Use only these long-term items.

Use only these long-term items.

Our calculations show that long-term uses increased by $531,000 and long-term sources increased by $392,000. Net working capital declined by the difference:

Long-term uses	$531,000
Less long-term sources	392,000
Decline in net working capital	$139,000

The fact that our calculations are correct is verified by calculating the amount of net working capital on each statement date and directly measuring the change. The statement in Table 12-4 shows the amounts of each item,

	19x0	19x1
Current assets	$15,252,000	$15,438,000
Less current liabilities	11,192,000	11,517,000
Net working capital	$ 4,060,000	$ 3,921,000

Change in net working capital: $4,060,000 − $3,921,000 = $139,000 decrease.

Statement Layout

The accountant prepares a statement of changes in financial position for financial reporting purposes so that various activities are distinguished from each other. The presentation usually shows these activities:

1. Operations (earnings activities)
2. Financial activities
3. Investment activities
4. Dividends

The amount of working capital provided (or used) by operations is typically shown in the statement by beginning with the amount of net income for the period and adjusting net income for expenses not using working capital and revenues not providing working capital. This procedure leads some people to the mistaken conclusion that an item such as depreciation is a source of net working capital when in fact it is not: We are adding back depreciation because it was previously subtracted from revenues, but it did not reduce net working capital. Changes in net working capital as a result of financial activities include issuing and redeeming common or preferred stock or long-term bonds.

The sources and uses of working capital from investing activities include the purchase and sale of land, buildings, equipment, and other noncurrent assets. The declaration of dividends (income distribution) is a use of working capital.

These activities are presented in Table 12-5 for Harper Distributing Company. Notice that although the decrease in net working capital is the same $139,000 calculated above, the amounts measuring it are different. The difference occurs because the table shows the two items that affect retained earnings rather than the change in retained earnings alone. In other words, rather than list the change in retained earnings as a $200,000 source, Table 12-5 shows earnings after taxes to be a $283,000 source and dividends declared to be an $83,000 use.

TABLE 12-5 Statement of Changes in Financial Position for the 12-Month Period Ending December 31, 19x1

Sources of net working capital		
Working capital provided from operations		
Earnings after taxes	$283,000	
Add back expenses not using working		
capital—depreciation	192,000	
		$475,000
Uses of net working capital		
Dividends declared and paid	$ 83,000	
Loan repayment	2,000	
Investment in land and buildings	273,000	
Acquisition of machinery and equipment	219,000	
		614,000
Decrease in net working capital		$139,000

The accountant must supplement a statement of changes in financial position like that in Table 12-5 with a summary of the change in each working capital component. The summary may be a part of the statement, itself, or presented in a footnote.

The statement of changes in financial position for Electronic Data Systems Corporation is presented in Table 12-6. Notice that it is much more detailed than our Harper Distributing Company example and that a footnote presents the summary of changes in each working capital component.

Practice. Before continuing to the next section be sure that you can explain why an issuance of common stock is classified a source and additions to purchased software a use on the statement in Table 12-6.

How the Statement Is Used

Creditors and investors use a statement of changes in financial position to determine the company's financial liquidity and to discover transactions that affect the company's assets and equity but not its income statement.

Liquidity. An important element not reported on the balance sheet and income statement is how the operations of a period affect the company's liquidity. It is tempting to assume that increased earnings mean increased cash or other liquid assets, but that is not necessarily the case. Liquidity may decrease because a new plant may have been acquired and other similar events could have occurred. On the other hand, increased liquidity can accompany reduced earnings if cash is allowed to accumulate rather than being used to replace plant and equipment.

When you use information from the statement of changes in financial position in assessing changes in financial liquidity, you must keep in mind that funds are usually defined to be net working capital. If near-term liquidity is more important than intermediate- or long-term liquidity, then you should define funds to be cash.

Assets and Equities. In addition to providing information about changes in liquidity during a period, the statement of changes in financial position also indicates the major transactions causing changes in the structure of a company's assets and

TABLE 12-6 Electronic Data Systems Corporation, Consolidated Statements of Changes in Financial Position
[for the years ended June 30, 1982, 1981, and 1980 (in thousands)]

	1982	1981	1980
Financial resources provided by			
Operations			
Net income	$46,967	$37,816	$28,890
Charges (credits) to income not involving working capital in the current period:			
Depreciation and amortization	15,629	10,259	6,460
Equity in earnings of unconsolidated subsidiary	(4,739)	(4,110)	(3,835)
Other	449	130	394
Working capital provided from operations	58,306	44,095	31,909
Increase in notes payable	17,083	4,954	7,371
Noncurrent deferred revenue	11,621	—	—
Proceeds from sale of land held for investment	858	3,359	3,636
Increase in retained earnings due to acquisition	2,672	—	—
Issuance of common stock (including Treasury shares)	10,860	4,853	7,588
Decrease in noncurrent notes receivable	934	2,179	589
	102,334	59,440	51,093
Financial resources used for			
Additions to land held for investment and development	3,202	11,152	13,210
Additions to property and equipment	28,772	16,496	9,075
Additions to cost in excess of net assets of acquired companies	—	—	3,773
Additions to purchased software	14,628	4,317	3,925
Dividends declared	16,957	15,728	10,365
Purchase of Treasury stock	680	10,562	515
Decrease in notes payable	2,258	2,265	3,975
Increase (decrease) in noncurrent notes receivable and other investments	(2,991)	318	6,011
Increase in bonds and notes	21,030	—	—
	84,536	60,838	50,849

TABLE 12-6 (Continued)
Increase (decrease) in working capital
(Note 1)

Note 1: Changes in Components of Working Capital (in thousands)

	1982	1981	1980
Increase (decrease) in current assets			
Cash and marketable securities	$ 9,516	$ 3,144	$(16,159)
Accounts receivable	12,787	20,053	13,275
Other current assets	1,319	5,398	4,353
	23,622	28,595	1,469
Increase (decrease) in current liabilities			
Accounts payable and accrued liabilities	(3,473)	19,894	(1,524)
Current deferred revenue	3,328	(57)	(771)
Income taxes	8,069	10,071	3,646
Current portion of notes payable	(2,100)	85	3,222
Dividends payable	—	—	(3,348)
	5,824	29,993	1,225
Increase (decrease) in working capital	$17,798	$(1,398)	$ 244

equity. For example, a statement of financial position reports acquisitions and sales of noncurrent assets such as buildings and trucks. In addition, the statement discloses issues and redemptions of long-term debt and common stock. These types of transactions are difficult or impossible to see by looking at an income statement or balance sheet.

Example. Changes in total fixed assets in Table 12-1 could be attributable to depreciation charges, to acquisition of new buildings and equipment, to disposition of old buildings and equipment, or to a combination of these. The statement of changes in financial position will help an analyst explain the changes in fixed assets.

FINANCIAL STATEMENTS: FURTHER FEATURES

We should examine a few additional features of financial statements before we analyze in Chapter 13 what the amounts on the statements mean to an investor. The additional features are footnotes, reliability, and usefulness.

Footnotes

Financial reports of many companies contain this statement: "The accompanying footnotes are an integral part of the financial statements." Although footnotes are usually printed in small, hard-to-read type, they call for careful reading. Financial statements are after all condensed summaries, and important explanatory matter not readily abbreviated must be, and often is, presented in footnotes. In addition, unfavorable or embarrassing items that a management is required to disclose but wishes to play down are often buried in footnotes. Thus, corporate outsiders—investors, bankers, or suppliers—neglect footnotes at peril. The bottom part of Table 12-6 shows important financial information stated in a footnote.

Reliability

In recent years many companies have played a game that might be called "get the earnings up." The object of the game is to show large profits (whether earned or not) in order to raise the price of the common stock. A high or rising stock price will (1) make a company's stock more valuable to use in buying other companies, (2) enhance the value of stock-purchase options held by the company's executives, and (3) enable the company to finance itself more cheaply by bringing in more money for each new share sold. Consequently, much imagination, to put it charitably, has gone into the preparation of financial reports. The investing public—and even bankers—have become increasingly skeptical of so-called generally accepted accounting principles that seem to stretch like rubber when the aim is to produce higher reported earnings. One difficulty is that the accounting profession, itself, cannot agree on what accounting principles ought to be.

Example. Accounting principles are outlined in various numbered opinions of the Accounting Principles Board of the American Institute of Certified Public Accountants and of its successor, the Financial Accounting Standards Board. Regulations and directives of the Securities and Exchange Commission also exercise considerable influence on the accounting practices of publicly owned companies.

Accountants rightly argue that no single way of reckoning profits, assets, liabilities, revenues, costs, and so on would fit every company in every situation. Therefore, some flexibility in interpreting each company's position and performance is needed. But variations in accounting practice have gone far beyond this degree of necessity. Accounting firms often appear to have been intimidated by the corporate managers that hire them. Management says, in effect, to its CPAs, "Show it our way or we'll fire you and hire some other CPA firm that will show what we want." Instead of presenting a united front in support of sound practice, the accounting profession has apparently permitted itself to be divided and conquered by some of its less scrupulous clients.

To improve the reliability of reporting, financial statements usually include a 5- or 10-year historical summary of financial information. Amounts listed in the summary often include net sales revenue, income taxes, net income, earnings per share, dividends per share, working capital, total assets, long-term debt, and stockholders' equity. To enhance comparability of the data, restatements of previously reported amounts may be required.

Usefulness

The usefulness and reliability of financial reports is different for those inside the corporation and those outside. The outsider—unless it is a bank, some other powerful lender, or a government regulator—can rarely demand a company's full financial story. It must be content with the condensed summary of financial history and position reflected in the audited reports made public. An outsider can rarely look behind the published figures to see how they were derived.

Some critics have complained that the information disclosed is too aggregated, or condensed, to be of much help to readers in assessing operating performance and financial position. The presentation of earnings data by segments or lines of business is one response to this criticism. Another response is in the expanded use of notes to the financial statements, providing further elaboration on items in the body of the statements.

A company insider, being one of the company's managers, directors, or controlling stockholders, need not—indeed, should not and must not—rest with the bare financial summary. She must go behind the figures and look at the subsidiary accounts, at how important transactions were entered on the books, and at the host of adjustments made in the books themselves in the process of preparing the financial statements. In addition, she must segment costs into fixed and variable, and classify expenses as cash and noncash. Only with these adjustments is the ground laid for effective decision making.

As we shall see in the next chapter, the highly detailed financial reports available to a company's management aid that management in three main activities: analysis, planning, and control. (1) Financial analysis reveals both the extent of a company's financial resources and the ability with which management is using them. Specifically, financial analysis discloses where a company stands with respect to profitability, liquidity, leverage, and the efficient use of its assets. (2) Financial reports provide the framework within which business planning takes place. All plans call for resources (inputs) and results (outputs). These must be financed and measured with money. Typically, corporate plans are embodied in budgets for which dollars serve as a common denominator of resources applied and results expected. (3) Financial reports are the key to the effective control of a company. Managers compare results stated in money terms with budgeted (intended) performance, and note deviations and exceptions. This review paves the way for rewarding good performance and penalizing poor performance, for corrective action, and for subsequent stages of planning.

SUMMARY

1. An income statement measures a company's earnings for a specific period, and a statement of changes in financial position shows for the same period the investment and financing activities not appearing on the income statement. Each statement shows how a company's ending and beginning balance sheets differ.

2. A statement of financial position lists for a specific date a company's assets and the debt and equity claims against assets. Assets may be either monetary or nonmonetary items, but each is assigned a dollar value. The statement layout calls for assets to be classified either current assets or noncurrent assets.

3. Liabilities are the debt claims against a company's assets. The statement layout calls for liabilities to be classified either current or noncurrent liabilities.

4. Shareholders' equity (SHE) or net worth (NW) is the total of ownership claims on a company's assets. It is measured by the difference between total assets (TA) and total liabilities (TL):

$$NW = SHE = TA - TL$$

Shareholders' equity consists of preferred and common stock:

a. Preferred stock is a limited ownership entitled to dividends at a fixed rate before dividends are paid on common shares.

b. Common shareholders' equity is the residual claim of owners. It consists of external equity that reflects new shares sold and internal equity that reflects the retention of earnings from profitable operations.

5. A company's income statement shows the way that revenues and expenses have affected the company's shareholders' equity. Revenue increases assets and shareholders' equity and expenses decrease assets and shareholders' equity.

6. Beginning and ending balances in the retained earnings account must be reconciled or explained. An accumulated retained earnings statement reconciles these balances.

7. A statement of changes in financial position may be constructed using either a cash or a net working capital definition of funds. Defining funds as cash is useful for short-term analysis of liquidity and as net working capital for long-term analysis. Most statements are constructed on a net working-capital basis.

8. Changes in net working capital are explained by changes in balance-sheet items other than current assets or current liabilities. A source is an increase in long-term liabilities or equity and a decrease in long-term assets. A use is a decrease in a long-term liability or equity and an increase in a long-term asset.

9. Anyone using financial statements must consider footnotes in order to assess accurately the reliability and usefulness of the statements.

KEY TERMS AND CONCEPTS

Assets	Cumulative preferred stock
Current assets	Stock
Prepaid expense	Internal and external equity
Deferred cost	Net working capital
Depreciation	Funds
Liability	Liquidity

QUESTIONS

12-1. A company's ending and beginning balance sheets are related with each other by two additional statements. Name and briefly describe these two statements.

12-2. Assets and liabilities can be classified as current and noncurrent. Explain how current assets differ from noncurrent assets.

12-3. Managers are often interested in a specific section of current assets called the *cash cycle*. Explain what this term means and illustrate a cash cycle.

12-4. CMA Examination (modified): Working-capital policy raises questions that relate both to a company's profitability and liquidity. Which one of the following statements would most accurately describe financial relationships if it were aggressively pursuing high profits?

    a. The company would probably have a high ratio of current assets to total assets and high ratio of long-term debt to total debt.

    b. The company would probably have a low ratio of current assets to total assets and a low ratio of current liabilities to total debt.

    c. It would probably have a low ratio of fixed assets to total assets and a low ratio of current liabilities to total debt.

    d. The company would probably have a high ratio of fixed assets to total assets and a high ratio of current liabilities to total debt.

    e. None of the above responses accurately describes the financial relationships of a company aggressively pursuing high profits.

    Explain your choice by using T-accounts representing a statement of financial position.

12-5. Preferred stock and common shareholders' equity comprise an important part of a company's claims against assets. Explain what each of these financial claims is and note which one (or ones) is an external source.

12-6. Someone has said that an income statement details changes in the retained earnings component of a balance sheet. Do you agree with this observation? Explain your answer.

12-7. One of your friends studying with you for the test comments, "An increase in any asset or a decrease in any claim is a use of net working capital. A decrease in any asset or an increase in any claim is a source of funds." Do you agree? Explain your answer.

12-8. "Funds" is a word that can be defined in two different ways. Define funds each way and explain the role that the time horizon plays in determining which definition is appropriate for constructing a statement of changes in financial position.

12-9. A statement of changes in financial position on a net working-capital basis is compiled by emphasizing changes in the long-term components of a statement of financial position (balance sheet). Explain how this procedure is undertaken and calculate the impact on net working capital for a company with $127,000 long-term sources and $96,000 long-term uses of finance.

12-10. Examine the statement of changes in financial position for EDS in Table 12-6. Explain how in 1980 net working capital can increase and cash decrease over the same period. Which measure—cash or net working capital—most accurately reflects liquidity? Explain your choice.

PROBLEMS

12-1. The statement of financial position for Thacker Company is presented below. Fill in the amounts needed to complete the statement.

Thacker Company
Statement of Financial Position
December 31, 19x6

Assets		*Liabilities and Stockholders' Equity*	
Current assets		Current Liabilities	
Cash	$ 250,000	Accounts payable	$ 620,000
Accounts receivable		Notes payable to banks	130,000
(less allowance for		Accrued wages	—
doubtful accounts of		Taxes payable	100,000
$20,000)	1,320,000	Total Current Liabilities	$1,250,000
Inventory	1,410,000	Long-term debt	—
Total Current Assets	—	Stockholders' equity	
Land	—	Preferred stock	1,000,000
Plant and equipment		Common stock ($1 par,	
($3,100,000 less accumulated		750,000 shares authorized,	
depreciation)	2,110,000	700,000 outstanding)	—
Total Assets	$5,390,000	Retained earnings	—
		Total common stock-	
		holders' equity	3,140,000
		Total Liabilities and	
		Equity	—

12-2. The items listed below are mixed up from a company's income statement and statement of financial position. Unsort the items and construct the two statements.

Total claims on assets	$2,000,000
Gross plant and equipment	$1,800,000
Depreciation expense	$100,000
Federal income tax	$80,000
Cost of goods sold	$2,555,000
Cash	$50,000
Common stock	$600,000
Administrative and marketing expense	$90,000
Accounts payable	$60,000
Accumulated depreciation	$500,000
Marketable securities	$150,000
Interest expense	$70,000
Gross profit	$445,000
Receivables	$200,000
Other payables	$110,000
Retained earnings	$400,000
Inventory	$300,000
Other income	$15,000
Accumulated taxes payable	$130,000
Sales	$3,000,000
Long-term liabilities	$700,000
Net plant and equipment	$1,300,000
Earnings after taxes	$120,000

12-3. Septem Company concluded 19x8 with $1,746,000 in retained earnings. Its earnings before taxes in 19x9 were $760,000. The company paid 40 percent of its earnings to the IRS for corporate taxes. During 19x9 Septem Company declared and paid $70,000 in dividends. Construct an accumulated retained earnings statement for 19x9.

12-4. Jill Luciano is examining her company's statement of changes in financial position. It shows the following entries:

Long-term sources $626,400
Long-term uses $718,200

a. What happened to net working capital over the period? Show your calculations.
b. Briefly explain how a statement of changes in financial position is prepared and what its usefulness is.

12-5. Menego Toys, Inc., has two balance sheets that look like these (in millions of dollars):

	January 1, 19x7	January 1, 19x8
Assets		
Cash	$ 7	$ 5
Accounts receivable	4	9
Inventory	3	7
Fixed assets	10	13
(Reserve for depreciation)	(2)	(4)
Claims		
Accounts payable	3	8
Taxes payable	1	4
Bonds	8	12
Shareholders' equity	10	6

a. How much was net working capital on each of the two dates?
b. Compile a statement of changes in financial position.

12-6. Gayla Wright, assistant controller for Feldspar Supplies, is asked by her superior to prepare a funds statement for 19x2. She is given the comparative balance sheets below.
a. Show a completed statement of changes in financial position (net working capital basis) for 19x2 and discuss the financial implications. (Note: Earnings after taxes were $60,000 in 19x2 and the company paid a $40,000 dividend.)
b. Does the change in net working capital tell Gayla the same thing that the company's change in cash tells her? Support your answer by referring to the change in the cash account.

Feldspar Supplies
Statement of Financial Position
(As of December 31)

	19x1	19x2
Assets		
Current Assets		
Cash	$ 50,000	$ 40,000
Marketable securities	40,000	30,000
Accounts receivable (net)	100,000	120,000
Inventory	150,000	180,000
Prepaid expenses	10,000	0
Total current assets	$350,000	$370,000
Investments	20,000	40,000
Plant and equipment	400,000	450,000
Less: Accumulated depreciation	80,000	100,000
Net plant and equipment	320,000	350,000
Total assets	$690,000	$760,000
Liabilities and Stockholders' Equity		
Current Liabilities		
Accounts payable	80,000	100,000
Notes payable	10,000	0
Accrued expenses	20,000	10,000
Total current liabilities	$110,000	$110,000
Long-term liabilities		
Bonds payable, 19x3	200,000	170,000
Total liabilities	$310,000	$280,000
Stockholders' equity		
Preferred stock, $100 par value	90,000	90,000
Common stock, $1 par value	60,000	60,000
Capital paid in excess of par	160,000	230,000
Retained earnings	80,000	100,000
Total stockholders' equity	$380,000	$480,000
Total liabilities and stockholders' equity	$690,000	$760,000

CHAPTER 13
Profitability and Turnover

FINANCIAL ANALYSIS
Uses · Sources

PROFIT AND RISK
Opportunity Cost · Reward for Risk Taking · Returns and Market Equilibrium

MEASURES OF PROFIT
Gross Operating Profit · Net Operating Profit · Earnings Before and After Taxes ·
Return on Assets · Return on Common Shareholders' Equity

ACTIVITY RATIOS
Accounts-Receivable Activity · Inventory Activity · Total Asset Activity

COMBINING PROFITABILITY AND ACTIVITY

NOTE ON MEASURING PROFIT WHEN COSTS AND PRICE LEVEL CHANGE

SUMMARY
Key Terms and Concepts · Questions · Problems

Analyzing a company's financial performance and setting standards against which the performance can be measured are important to financial managers, investors, and creditors. Managers need to analyze performance in order to carry out successfully the investment and financial decisions that will maximize the wealth of the shareholders. Investors need to measure and analyze financial statements in order to estimate the future cash flows from owning the company's stock and to evaluate the company's risk. Creditors want to assess the likelihood that the company will have sufficient cash flow to pay interest and repay principal of the amount borrowed.

All analysis begins with two important financial statements: the income statement and the statement of financial position (balance sheet). We shall use each of these statements in the following analysis of profitability, activity, liquidity, and leverage. These terms will be examined more precisely later, but they tell us specific information about a company's performance. *Profit* measures tell us how large the return is that a company is making for its owners. *Activity* measures indicate how effectively a company is using its assets. *Liquidity* measures suggest the company's ability to pay its short-term bills, pay interest, and repay the principal amount of borrowed money. *Leverage* measures indicate the company's ability to meet its long-term and short-term debt and describe how rapidly earnings change in relation to changes in sales. This chapter describes how financial managers, investors, or creditors (we call them analysts) use financial statements to measure profitability and activity because these two items combine to generate a company's total return on assets. Chapter 14 continues the analysis of performance by measuring a company's liquidity and leverage, grouped together because they deal with the company's ability to meet its short-term and long-term financial obligations.

When you finish this chapter, you will be able to understand how a financial manager uses ratios in trend analysis and in comparative analysis to gauge a company's business performance. In addition, you will become familiar with sources of industry and corporate financial data helpful for use in financial analysis. Calculation and interpretation of measures of profit are important, and much of this chapter is designed to help you construct and interpret such measures as gross operating profit, net operating profit, return on assets, earnings before and after taxes, return on equity, and several per-share measures. We shall calculate and interpret activity measures such as receivables turnover, inventory turnover, and total asset turnover after we examine the profit measures. The chapter concludes with an analysis of the Du Pont system of operating analysis that combines a company's net operating profit ratio and total asset turnover into a single measure of performance, the return on total assets.

Profit means the amount remaining after subtracting from operating revenue all costs associated with operating and financing the company for a specific time period. Profit is measured as a dollar amount or as a rate (or ratio) when the dollar profit is divided by another amount such as the dollars invested. We will want to calculate ratios in order to remove the influence of size on the level of profit so that we can get a better understanding of how profitable a company is.

Example. Two companies make $150,000 profit each during a period time. An investor would consider the companies equally desirable without further information. But suppose that one company had $500,000 in total assets and the other had $2 million. The company with the smaller amount of assets is more profitable because its profits divided by its total assets is greater than the same ratio for the company with more assets. Management of the more profitable company is doing a better job for the owners because it is generating more profit per invested dollar.

Before we begin the analysis of profit and activity with which this chapter is concerned, let us first briefly examine the uses and sources of financial information available to investors, creditors, and financial managers.

FINANCIAL ANALYSIS

Financial managers, creditors, and investors examine a company's business performance using dollar amounts from an income statement, a balance sheet, or both. (In addition they often use a statement of changes in financial position that we shall examine in Chapter 23.)

Uses

For a financial measure to have a meaning, we must interpret it against some standard. There are two main ways to interpret a measure.

Trend Analysis. The first way is trend analysis, seeing how a measure behaves across time. An analyst can plot the movement of a financial measure over time in order to see the direction that the measure is taking. In this way the analyst gets some idea of whether the measure is improving or deteriorating.

Comparative Analysis. The second way to analyze a financial measure is comparative analysis. Here, a financial analyst observes how the ratio is performing at a single point in time and compares it with other companies in the industry or with some other generally accepted industry standard. Comparative analysis usually proceeds on the assumption that an industry average is a yardstick of performance for companies in that industry. Consequently, analysts expect companies to achieve at a minimum the industry norm or average. If a company's measure persistently differs adversely from an industry standard, the company's common-stock price may fall and creditors may increase the interest rate charged on corporate borrowing.

Sources

Where does an analyst find information for a company and its industry? Four convenient sources are *Dun's Review and Modern Industry* published by Dun and Bradstreet, *Annual Statement Studies* published by Robert Morris Associates, the *Almanac of Ratios* published by Prentice Hall, and Standard and Poor's *Industry Surveys* published by McGraw-Hill. In addition, a company or individual may subscribe to investment advisory services such as *Value Line Investment Survey* and to the Compustat data tapes of Standard and Poor's. Compustat data tapes present financial information in machine-readable form for approximately 4,000 corporations. An additional source of information for the canny manager is the annual financial reports of the competition. Some companies own stock in their competitors so that management can receive financial statements and send representatives to the annual shareholder's meeting. Finally, a financial analyst may obtain Forms 10K and 10Q from the Securities and Exchange Commission (SEC). These forms contain annual and quarterly financial information of corporations registered with the Securities and Exchange Commission.

PROFIT AND RISK

Before looking at profit measures, we need to recall that accountants and economists define *profit* in different ways. For the accountant profit is synonymous with owners' earnings: it is found by subtracting operating and financial costs from the total revenue accruing during the operating period.

An economist views profit differently. To the economist profit is a differential return, a special reward for risk bearing or for being cleverer or more enterprising than competitors.[1] Very often, too, as the economist will point out, in the case of small, owner-operated businesses, much of what an owner may call profit is actually an unrecognized salary for work as manager. This last point introduces the concept of opportunity cost.

Opportunity Cost

Profit must include recognition of *opportunity cost*, return rejected on alternative uses of assets. For example, two investment opportunities of equal risk may be available, yielding different returns as below:

Investment	Return
A	10 percent
B	8 percent

The opportunity cost of investing in investment A is the rejected 8 percent return on investment B. Alternatively, the opportunity cost of investing in investment B is the rejected 10 percent return on investment A. The two investments should offer the same return because they have the same risk, so that we would say that their returns are in equilibrium when they are the same. *Equilibrium* means that there is no tendency for the prices and returns to change.

Reward for Risk Taking

This concept of opportunity cost is fruitful because it reminds us that accounting profit lumps together two different sorts of returns. First, there is a basic return on the owners' money, equal to the rate they could earn by investing in very low-risk instruments such as U.S. Treasury bills. If the owners do not earn *at least* that much, they would do better to shut down their business and become investors in Treasury bills. Second, there is true economic profit—reward for risk bearing, or what is much the same thing, a reward for superior ability to take, manage, or outguess the risks. For these reasons we can write a rate of profit as consisting of a risk-free rate of return plus a risk premium,

$$RJ = RF + RP$$

where

RJ = rate of profit on investment J
RF = risk-free rate of return (best taken as the yield on U.S. Treasury bills)
RP = risk premium for the particular investment

[1] For true risk to exist, the probabilities of the various outcomes—making it big, losing a little, losing it all—would have to be known. Risk refers to a situation in which the probability distribution of outcomes can be calculated, as in a spin of a roulette wheel. Otherwise, the matter adds up to uncertainty, which is another name for ignorance. Economists and financial analysts often quantify risk with the standard deviation of expected returns—the greater the standard deviation is, the greater they assume the risk will be.

Rearranging terms in the equation yields an investment's risk premium,

$$RP = RJ - RF$$

Risk is the likelihood that an actual return will differ from its expected amount, although we usually think of risk as the likelihood of incurring a financial loss. Financial managers measure the risk premium in a portfolio context, which means that they look at the way that the variation in an investment's expected return fits with the other investments that the company has. Many books point out that there is a difference between an investment's total risk and portfolio risk: Total risk is the risk of an investment considered in isolation; whereas portfolio (or systematic) risk is the risk of an investment considered in a portfolio. We will not go further into the distinction here, but you may want to take an advanced course in finance in order to understand the meaning and usefulness of the difference.

A financial manager can calculate the rate of return that the company is generating and subtract the yield on a U.S. Treasury bill to obtain the company's risk premium. We examined this procedure above.

Figure 13-1 portrays the systematic relation between risk and return suggested by the equation. The intercept, RF of the risk function, is the rate of return available at the minimum expected risk. As the expected risk increases, the financial manager should insist on receiving a greater return on invested capital to compensate the company's investors for accepting a greater risk. The positive, or increasing, relation between risk and return is signified by the upward slope of the market line, the line that shows how returns relate to risk in the financial market.

Returns and Market Equilibrium

Buying and selling assets changes their market prices and returns. Prices and returns will change until equilibrium is reached. Equilibrium is a condition in which there is no tendency for market prices to change because all returns, adjusted for their

FIGURE 13-1   Relation between risk and expected return.

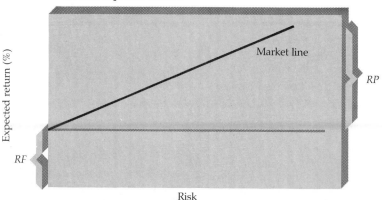

expected risks, have become equally attractive. In the preceding analysis of opportunity cost, individuals buying investment A to take advantage of its 10 percent return might drive its price upward and reduce its return or yield. Selling investment B (or not demanding it) might cause its price to fall and its return or yield to rise. Equilibrium would be reached when the two returns, adjusted for risk, were equal. If investors judged investment A to require one percentage point more compensation for risk than investment B needed, A would wind up yielding $9\frac{1}{2}$ percent; B, $8\frac{1}{2}$ percent.[2] Equilibrium on Figure 13-1 would show each investment lying exactly on the market line so that each is priced to reflect its risk.[3]

MEASURES OF PROFIT

Financial analysts want to measure a company's profit to help them determine the cash flow shareholders can expect to receive from owning the company's common stock. A financial manager will want to maximize the company's profit and minimize risk in order to maximize stock price.

Financial analysts begin measuring a company's profit with its financial statements. Table 12-1 presented two statements of financial position (balance sheets) showing two years of performance for the Harper Distributing Company, a hypothetical toy manufacturer. The company's income statement for the year 19x1 was presented in Table 12-2. We shall use these statements for the calculations that follow.

Gross Operating Profit

A company's gross operating profit tells a financial manager the revenues remaining to replace assets used up in producing goods and services, to pay remaining operating costs, and to make interest payments. When gross operating profit is divided by operating revenue (sales for Harper Distributing Company), the resulting ratio is called the gross operating profit ratio, which tells an analyst the gross operating profit per dollar of operating revenue.

We measure Harper Distributing Company's gross operating profit and gross operating profit ratio using information from the company's income statement.

---

[2] Return (or yield) and price move inversely. That is why the returns from investments change as their prices change. Suppose, in the example above, that A required an investment of $100 and paid $10 per year, while B required $100 of investment and paid $8 per year. However, A is riskier and investors want one percentage point more return on A than on B. At what prices will equilibrium be reached? A will go to $105.26, where the $10 per year payment will provide a yield of $9\frac{1}{2}$ percent ($10/$105.26 equals $9\frac{1}{2}$ percent.) B will drop to $94.12, where its $8 per year payment will provide an $8\frac{1}{2}$ percent return. ($8/$94.12 equals $8\frac{1}{2}$ percent.) At these prices, the yield on A will exceed the return on B by exactly one percentage point—precisely the risk premium investors require.

[3] Advanced textbooks will tell you that an investment's total risk is measured by the standard deviation of its expected returns, and its systematic risk by its covariance of returns with a portfolio. Covariance introduces the correlation between the investment's expected returns and those of the portfolio, so it is quite possible to have a measure of systematic risk that is much less than the investment's total risk. Research shows that return is closely related to systematic risk rather than to total risk.

	Amount	Percent of Sales (rounded)
Sales	$26,473,000	100.0
Less cost of goods sold	21,299,000	80.5
Gross profit	$ 5,174,000	19.5

$$\text{Gross operating profit ratio} = \frac{\$5,174,000}{\$26,473,000} = 0.195 \quad \text{or} \quad 19.5\% \text{ of sales}$$

The gross operating profit ratio tell us the percentage that selling prices and operating revenue can fall before gross operating profit disappears. Harper Distributing's prices and with them operating revenue can decline by 19.5 percent—units sold remaining constant—before gross operating profit disappears.[4] The gross operating profit ratio suggests the vulnerability of a company to competition because a small gross operating profit ratio means that price competition may quickly eliminate gross operating profit.

Net Operating Profit

Net operating profit (often called net operating income) is the amount of profit that a company has from operations after deducting all operating costs from operating revenue. The costs to be deducted from gross operating profit are administrative and selling costs and depreciation expense. Depreciation expense is the estimated reduction in the value of a long-term or fixed asset to reflect a decline in its productive ability: We deduct in our calculation of net operating profit an estimated amount, called depreciation expense, that reflects a decline in the company's ability to produce future goods and services. When a financial manager divides net operating profit by operating revenue, the resulting ratio is called the net operating profit ratio. We calculate Harper Distributing's net operating profit and net operating profit ratio with amounts from the company's income statement.

	Amount	Percent of Sales (rounded)
Gross profit	$5,174,000	19.5
Less other operating expenses	4,286,000	16.2
Net operating profit	$ 888,000	3.3

$$\text{Net operating profit ratio} = \frac{\$888,000}{\$26,473,000} = 0.033 \quad \text{or} \quad 3.3\%$$

Like a gross operating profit ratio, the net operating profit ratio tells a financial manager about the impact of price decreases on profit, but the net operating profit

---

[4] The concern with changes in quantity is because changes in the quantity produced affect a company's variable costs. We shall examine this relationship in detail in Chapter 15.

ratio concentrates on the percentage price decline that endangers the company's ability to meet all operating expenses and not just cost of goods sold. In this example, if prices and sales revenue fall by 3.3 percent (Harper's net operating profit ratio), then the company would have only enough operating revenue to meet its cost of goods, to pay its selling and administrative expenses, and to allow for depreciation on its fixed assets. Net operating profit would be zero. A price decline greater than 3.3 percent would mean that Harper Distributing could not meet its operating expenses out of operating revenue.

Practice. Suppose that the toy industry's average net operating profit ratio is 5.8 percent. Interpret this ratio and briefly state whether or not Harper's ratio is better or worse than its industry average.

Earnings Before and After Taxes

A company usually uses debt to finance its assets, so it is necessary to subtract interest expense from net operating profit to arrive at a company's earnings reflecting the profit available to pay taxes, distribute to owners, and to reinvest in the company. A company's earnings reflect management's investment and financial decisions because we calculate earnings after measuring operating profit (which reflects investment decisions) and interest expense (which reflects financial decisions).

A company's earnings may be calculated either before or after taxes. After-tax earnings are a more useful measure to the company's owners because after-tax earnings can be distributed to preferred stockholders and common shareholders or reinvested in the company. An analyst calculates a profit (or earnings) margin ratio by dividing earnings before or after taxes by operating revenue. The calculated ratio measures the amount of earnings per dollar of operating revenue. The before-tax profit margin ratio is more useful than the after-tax ratio to a financial manager because the before-tax ratio measures the percent that selling prices and operating revenue can fall before earnings before *and* after taxes disappear. After-tax earnings disappear along with before-tax earnings because if before-tax earnings are zero then the company pays no taxes and after-tax earnings are zero, too.

We calculate the earnings measures for Harper Distributing Company using amounts from the 19x1 income statement:

	Amount	Percent of Sales (rounded)
Net operating profit	$888,000	3.3
Less interest expense	321,000	1.2
Earnings before taxes	$567,000	2.1
less taxes (15%)	284,000	1.1
Earnings after taxes	$283,000	1.0

Harper Distributing has $567,000 to pay taxes, to distribute to preferred stockholders and common shareholders, and to reinvest in the company. It is earning

---

BOX 13-1
Maximizing Profit to Maximize Stock
Price: The Case of Lee Data
Corporation   A financial manager wants to measure profit in order to determine how good a job he and other managers are doing relative to other companies in the same line of business. When profit is maximized, it usually follows that shareholders' wealth increases because the company's stock price rises, too.

An example of the link between profit and stock price is Lee Data Corporation. Lee Data is in a rapid-growth industry, designing, manufacturing, and marketing multifunction interactive terminal systems that are IBM compatible. Sales for the industry were about $750 million in 1982 and will probably be about $1 billion in 1986. IBM is the industry leader with 50 to 60 percent of the market share. Lee Data ranks about fifth largest in the industry.

How has Lee Data fared in the IBM-dominated market? Company per share profits were 14 cents in 1982, 95 cents in 1983, and $1.25 in 1984. For the first two years, the company's stock price went up along with its earnings. In 1982 and 1983, the company's stock price rose from $3.50 per share to $19 per share in November, 1983. The increase in earnings and in expected earnings showed up as an increase in shareholders' wealth through the increased stock price. However, in 1984 (November) the stock price fell to about $8 per share, probably as a result of the increased market dominance by IBM. Lee Data's 1984 experience (profit up, stock price down) reminds us that stock price is not determined by actual earnings, but by investors' expectations of future earnings and risk.

Source: *The Wall Street Journal*, November 11, 1982, p. 31, November 3, 1983, p. 54, and Standard & Poor's *Over the Counter Stock Report*.

$0.021 \times \$1 = 2.1$ cents before taxes per dollar of sales. The profit margin ratio before taxes tells us that if prices and operating revenue decline by 2.1 percent there will be no earnings either before or after taxes.

Practice. Suppose that the toy industry's before-tax profit margin ratio is 7.9 percent. Interpret this ratio and comment on how Harper Distributing's ratio compares with the industry average.

Profit measures calculated so far have used amounts from only the income statement. As a result, the measures reflect investment and financial decisions over the same time period. Now, we are going to examine ratios that combine amounts from an income statement and a balance sheet. Unlike an income statement that shows activity over an elapsed period of time (usually one quarter or one year), a balance sheet shows a company's assets, liabilities, and shareholder's equity on a specific date. We must be careful when we calculate ratios using amounts from each of the two statements because the amount from the statement of financial position may not be typical of its level throughout the period covered by the income statement.

BOX 13-2
A Misconception About Profit Rates   Results of a questionnaire conducted in 1983 suggest how wrong the public is in its estimate of profit. According to Opinion Research Corporation in Princeton, New Jersey, the public's estimate of the average manufacturer's after-tax profit margin ratio is 37 percent. The actual 1982 ratio was 3.8 percent.

Source: The Wall Street Journal, November 11, 1983, p. 1.

Example. A toy manufacturer would show its lowest inventory level around Christmas because it will sell its output to dealers during November and December. A financial analyst using the January 1 inventory level with a full year's profit measure to calculate a ratio would make a mistake because the January 1 inventory level is not typical of its annual level.

Here is the rule that we must follow whenever we combine amounts from each of the two statements: The balance-sheet amount used in the ratio must be an average calculated over the same period as that covered by the income statement. If we are calculating a ratio using a three-month measure from the income statement, then we must use a three-month average from the balance sheet.

Practice. A financial manager for a company wants to calculate ratios for the third quarter of 19x7. Should she use amounts from the August 19x7 balance sheet? What amounts should she use? Answer: She should not use the August 19x7 amounts but an average of the amounts over the three-month third quarter of 19x7 if these amounts are available.

Return on Assets

A widely used measure of profitability is return on assets (sometimes called earning power) because it indicates how much net operating profit a company is making per dollar of total assets without considering the way the assets are financed. It does not consider the way that assets are financed because (1) net operating profit is not affected by the amount of interest a company pays (interest reflects the use of debt) and (2) the company's use of debt in the financial structure is not considered. Return on assets is the ratio of net operating profit divided by the average amount of total assets. Harper Distributing Company's return on assets is 10 percent calculated in the following way:

$$\text{Return on assets} = \frac{\$888,000}{(\$17,460,000 + \$17,983,000)/2}$$

$$= 0.05 \quad \text{or} \quad 5\%$$

Harper Distributing Company is earning $0.05 \times \$1 = 5$ cents net operating profit per dollar of average total assets. Notice that the calculation uses the average of total assets over the same 12-month period covered by the income statement in order to minimize the likelihood of using an unrepresentative amount from the balance sheet.

Return on Common Shareholders' Equity

A company's common shareholders want to know how effectively management is using the shareholders' original investment and retained earnings to make profit for them. The return on common shareholders' equity is such a measure because it tells analysts how much a company is earning on capital contributed by common shareholders after all expenses, including interest and preferred stock dividends, have been met. We calculate the ratio by dividing a company's earnings available to common shareholders by common shareholders' equity. Return on common shareholders' equity is sometimes referred to as *return on book value* because shareholders' equity used in the ratio is measured in book values rather than market values: Common shareholders' equity is the book value of total assets less total liabilities and preferred stock.

Return on common shareholders' equity in 19x1 for the Harper Distributing Company is earnings available to common shareholders divided by average common shareholders' equity on the balance sheet. A look back at Harper Distributing's accumulated retained earnings statement on page 241 tells us that the company paid a $20,000 preferred stock dividend. We must subtract this amount from the company's earnings after taxes to find earnings available to common shareholders:

Earnings after taxes	$283,000
Less preferred stock dividend	20,000
Earnings available to common shareholders	$263,000

We use the $263,000 amount to calculate the company's return on common equity because this is the amount of earnings that can be distributed to the company's common shareholders. The amount in the denominator of the ratio is the average amount of common shareholders' equity,

$$\text{Return on common shareholders' equity} = \frac{\$263,000}{(\$5,848,000 + 6,048,000)/2}$$
$$= 0.044 \quad \text{or} \quad 4.4\%$$

Practice. Suppose that Harper Distributing had a 6.3 percent and 6.8 percent return on common shareholders' equity in each of the two previous years. Comment on this year's return.

Earnings per Share of Common Stock. A useful way to look at earnings is to calculate a company's earnings per share of common stock. It is a measure useful to analysts because many sources of financial information report amounts on a per-share basis and calculating a specific company's results on a per-share basis makes comparison easy. A financial analyst usually measures earnings per share of common stock by dividing earnings available to common shareholders by the number of common shares outstanding. Measured in this way, the result is called *basic earnings per share*. There are other ways to measure earnings per share of common stock, but we shall examine only this one because of its widespread use.[5] The number of shares outstanding over a statement period might change because the company may issue new shares or buy back already issued shares.[6] As a result, calculating basic earnings per share requires an analyst to use a weighted average of the number of shares outstanding. The weights are the proportion of the period that a number of shares are outstanding.

Example. The Kennedy Corporation has 7,000 shares of common stock outstanding for the first three months of 19x8. On April 1 it issues 2,000 new shares. The company's basic earnings per share for 19x8 are the year's earnings available to common shareholders divided by the 8,500 weighted average number of common shares outstanding,

(1) Time	(2) Proportion of Year	(3) Shares	(2) × (3) = (4) Product
3 months	0.25	7,000	1,750
9 months	0.75	9,000	6,750
12 months	1.00		8,500

Harper Distributing Company's statement of financial position shows the same number of common shares outstanding at the end of 19x0 and end of 19x1, so we can conclude that shares were neither sold nor repurchased during 19x1. Consequently, no weighted average need be calculated when we calculate basic earnings per share. Harper's basic earnings per share of common stock are $0.6573 calculated as follows:

$$\text{Basic earnings per share} = \frac{\$263,000}{400,000 \text{ shares}}$$

$$= \$0.6573$$

[5] A company may calculate and report earnings per share of common stock in two ways other than basic earnings per share. *Primary earnings per share* are per-share earnings available to common shareholders after both earnings and the number of shares outstanding are adjusted for common-stock equivalents, securities that can be converted into shares of common stock. Primary earnings per share are reported only when the resulting calculated decline in earnings per share of common stock is 3 percent or more from its amount calculated without considering common-stock equivalent securities. *Fully diluted earnings per share* are earnings available to common shareholders after considering *all* common-stock equivalents whether or not they are dilutive.

[6] The number of shares outstanding also changes when a company declares a stock split or pays a stock dividend, events that we shall examine in Chapter 19. It is unnecessary as a result of these events to calculate a weighted average of the number of shares outstanding because the same shareholders have a claim on the company's earnings, and the company's assets and return on equity are unchanged.

BOX 13-3
How a Texas Bank Manufactured

Profit   When you look at a company's profit picture you should always be skeptical because generally accepted accounting principles permit profit to be calculated and recognized in any of several different ways. Consider the example of Mercantile Texas Corporation, a Dallas-based bank holding company. In 1983 it successfully manufactured profit through an ingenious ploy: It sold $90 million in credit and receivables to Southwest Bancshares, Incorporated, a Houston banking concern that subsequently agreed to merge with Mercantile Texas. The sale helped prop up the company's sagging earnings, generating a $7.2 million pre-tax gain (14 cents a share after taxes). In effect, therefore, Mercantile Texas sold its credit-card operations to itself and made a profit.

"In all honesty, I've never seen a bank try to slide one by like this," said Lawrence W. Cohn, a Dean Witter Reynolds Incorporated securities analyst who reads dozens of bank earnings reports each quarter. He believes the transaction could cost Mercantile shareholders money in the end because the bank must eventually pay taxes on the profit from the sale.

Source: Based on Daniel Hertzbert, "Texas Bank and Its Merger Partner Reach an Unusual Agreement," *The Wall Street Journal,* January 24, 1984, p. 32.

Investors are often interested in a stock's price-earnings ratio because it suggests the way that the market is valuing the company's earnings. A price-earnings ratio (often called a price-earnings multiple) is calculated by dividing a share's price by basic earnings per share. If Harper Distributing's common stock is trading for $8.25 per share, then its price-earnings ratio is slightly over 12, calculated as follows:

$$\text{Price-earnings ratio} = \frac{\$8.25}{\$0.6573}$$

$$= 12.55$$

Dividends per Share of Common Stock. Investors are often interested in the amount of dividends per share of common stock that a company pays because such a figure tells them how many shares they must own in order to receive a desired total dividend. The calculation of dividends per share of common stock requires dividing the company's common-stock dividend by the weighted average number of shares outstanding. Harper Distributing's common stock paid a 15.75 cents per share dividend in 19x1, calculated as follows:

$$\frac{\$63,000}{400,000} = \$0.1575$$

ACTIVITY RATIOS

Activity ratios indicate whether the level of assets used by a company is too small or too large by measuring the number of times total operating revenues can be divided by the level of assets. *Activity* means the number of times that a company's sales exceed the dollar amount of an asset.

Example. A record dealer may stock for an entire month 100 Toto albums with a wholesale value of $236. If Toto album sales in the month are $346, then sales have exceeded the inventory of albums by $346/$236 = 1.46 times. The record store manager can get an idea of whether the store's inventory of Toto albums is too large or too small by examining the activity for other stores and for the industry.

It is easy to remember how to calculate activity ratios because they always have operating revenue (or sales) in the numerator.

Accounts-Receivable Activity

The activity in accounts receivable is measured by the accounts-receivable turnover, the ratio of credit sales divided by the average amount of net accounts receivable (net of bad debts). We use credit sales rather than total sales because credit sales result in accounts receivable, but cash sales do not. If there are any cash sales, then they must be deducted from total sales to find credit sales. If we assume that all of Harper Distributing Company's sales are on credit, then its accounts-receivable turnover is 2.58 times, calculated as follows:

$$\text{Accounts receivable turnover} = \frac{\$26,473,000}{(\$10,447,000 + \$10,047,000)/2}$$

$$= 2.58$$

This ratio tells Harper's financial manager that 19x1 credit sales were 2.58 times greater than the 19x1 average amount of accounts receivable.

A ratio related to the accounts-receivable turnover is the *average collection period* (ACP), sometimes called number of days' sales in accounts receivable. Since Harper Distributing is turning over its accounts receivable 2.58 times in a year, it takes on the average 360 days/2.58 = 140 days to collect its receivables. (It is conventional to use a 360-day year in the calculation.) If Harper Distributing made no more sales, it would take 140 days for the last sale to be collected and become cash. An alternative way to calculate the average collection period is to divide the average amount of net accounts receivable by daily credit sales. For Harper Distributing this method results in the same 140 days:

$$\text{Average collection period} = \frac{(\$10,447,000 + \$10,047,000)/2}{(\$26,473,000/360)}$$

$$= 140 \text{ days}$$

The average collection period is a useful measure to a financial manager because it can be compared with the company's credit terms to tell him the effectiveness of the company's credit and collection policy. A long average collection period relative to the credit terms granted to customers suggests that a company's credit and collection policy is poorly handled—credit is granted to customers who cannot pay their bills or the collection department is not vigorous in enforcing the payment period. A short average collection period relative to the industry average and credit terms means that customers are paying their bills early. Credit and collection policy are discussed in detail in Chapter 23.[7]

Inventory Activity

Most companies have inventory because they want to have merchandise to sell when demand increases or when there are delays in receiving delivery of ordered items. Having an inventory on hand means that the company will not miss sales due to a shortage of merchandise. Inventory activity is measured by the *inventory turnover ratio,* which has operating revenue (or sales) in the numerator and average inventory in the denominator. A financial manager can measure operating revenues for this ratio in either of two ways, with the choice determined by the way that industry inventory turnover is measured: Operating revenue may be in terms of selling price or in terms of cost of goods sold. Some sources of financial data present inventory turnover using one measure, and other sources use the other measure. We need to be aware of the difference and make certain that we measure a company's inventory turnover in the same way that the source we use for comparison measures it.

Harper Distributing Company's inventory turnover is 7.75 using annual sales and 6.23 times using cost of goods sold:

$$\text{Inventory Turnover} = \frac{\$26,473,000}{(\$3,236,000 + \$3,599,000)/2}$$

$$= 7.75 \text{ times}$$

or

$$\text{Inventory Turnover} = \frac{\$21,299,000}{(\$3,236,000 + \$3,599,000)/2}$$

$$= 6.23 \text{ times}$$

A look back at Harper's income statement in Table 12-2 will show you that the difference between sales and cost of goods sold is the company's $5,174,000 gross profit. This information tells us that using sales in the numerator of the inventory turnover ratio includes the company's gross profit margin so that the ratio measures not only inventory turnover but also the company's ability to generate profit. Some

[7] An important way for a financial manager to assess credit and collection policy is to age accounts receivable, which determines the amount of receivables that are past due. Aging accounts receivable is discussed in Chapter 23.

analysts believe that mixing inventory turnover and profit in this way is improper because it combines two separate decision areas: inventory management and pricing. They suggest that inventory turnover measured with cost of goods sold is a better measure because it uses sales measured at cost and inventory measured at cost.

The inventory turnover ratio suggests whether or not a company has too much or too little inventory. A low turnover ratio suggests that inventory may be too large so that the company may have obsolete items and may be incurring excessive inventory carrying costs such as storage fees and insurance. A high turnover ratio suggests that inventory may be too small so that the company may be losing sales because it cannot supply merchandise whenever customers want it. Management should compare a suspicious-looking turnover ratio with industry norms in order to determine if the ratio is out of line and whether or not management should take corrective action.

Total Asset Activity

A financial manager can measure the company's total asset activity by determining its total asset turnover. As with other activity measures, total asset turnover suggests whether or not the company has too few or too many assets. Total asset activity is measured by operating revenue divided by the average dollar amount of total assets. For Harper Distributing the ratio is 0.90 times:

$$\text{Total asset turnover} = \frac{\$26,473,000}{(\$17,460,000 + \$17,983,000)/2}$$

$$= 1.49$$

Harper's sales were 1.49 or 149 percent of its average total assets for the year 19x1. Management determines whether or not this is too high or too low by examining industry data.

COMBINING PROFITABILITY AND ACTIVITY

A financial manager can combine a company's net operating profit ratio and total asset turnover to find the company's operating return on assets or earning power. Finding return on assets in this way is useful because it emphasizes that return is comprised of profit and turnover and suggests that a way to diagnose a low return on assets is to examine the components of profit and turnover.

We can find a company's return on assets by multiplying its operating profit ratio or margin by its asset turnover:

Return on assets = Net operating profit ratio × total asset turnover

Example. A company's operating profit ratio is 3 percent and it turns its assets over four times annually. The return on assets is

Return on assets = 0.03 × 4 = 0.12   or   12%

Combinations of net operating profit ratio and turnover vary widely among different industries. For example, a retail grocery chain will have a low net operating profit ratio and a high turnover, and an oil refiner will have a much higher net operating profit ratio but lower turnover. Table 13-1 shows for five companies the way that operating margin and total asset turnover combine to yield a return on assets. Notice the widely varying margins and the turnovers reflecting each company's ability to earn a profit on its sales and to turnover its assets rapidly or slowly.

We find the return on assets for Harper Distributing by using the net operating profit ratio and total asset turnover:

$$\text{ROA} = \frac{\$888,000}{\$26,473,000} \times \frac{\$26,473,000}{(\$17,460,000 + \$17,983,000)/2}$$

$$= 0.0335 \times 1.49 = 0.0499 \quad \text{or} \quad 5\%$$

Sometimes a financial manager modifies the return on assets in order to find the company's return on investment. This measure lets us see how the company is performing when both operating and financial characteristics are considered. The return on investment is measured by the ratio of earnings after taxes divided by total assets. Notice that it is affected by the way assets are financed—that is, by how much debt and equity are used—because it uses profit after deducting interest expense.

Decomposing a company's return on assets into its net operating profit ratio and turnover and then analyzing each one's components is the *Du Pont system of operating analysis* because that company's managers developed and refined it in the 1950s and 1960s. The way that we can subdivide net operating profit ratio and asset turnover into components is illustrated in Figure 13-2.

The figure shows that return on assets results from interaction between income statement amounts and amounts from a balance sheet: income statement information comprises the left side of Figure 13-2 and balance sheet information, the right side. The Du Pont system provides the financial manager a framework for asking meaningful questions about a company's operating performance. First, consider questions raised from a turnover level that is too low: Are insufficient sales being generated for the volume of assets? If so, should the company consider advertising more to increase the sales volume? Or, is the company's asset investment too large for the sales volume that can fairly be expected? If so, is the company carrying too large an investment in fixed assets, in current assets, or in both?

Similarly, too low a net operating margin can raise significant questions: Is sales volume too low to absorb fixed costs adequately? Is the spread between prices and costs too low? Are we getting an insufficient price for our products? Or, is it costing too much to manufacture our product?

The list of meaningful questions suggested by the Du Pont method of operating analysis demands that managers explore many aspects of a company's operations. Industry-average ratios and the trend of the company's return on assets, net operating profit ratio, and total asset turnover for the past several years should offer management likely answers to questions surrounding the company's profitability.

TABLE 13-1 Companies with Differing Margins, Turnovers, and Returns on Assets (1982)

(1) Company	(2) *Operating Margin* (Net Operating Profit + Depreciation)/ Sales (%)	(3) *Turnover* Sales/ Total Assets	(2) × (3) = (4) *Return on Assets* (New Operating Profit + Depreciation)/ Assets (%)
Philip Morris	16.0	1.29	20.60
Boeing	6.4	1.46	9.34
Colgate-Palmolive	8.9	2.05	18.25
DeBeers	64.1	0.04	2.56
Digital Equipment	19.0	0.98	18.62

SOURCE: Value Line Investment Survey *Summer and Fall, 1983.*

FIGURE 13-2 Du Pont system of operating analysis.

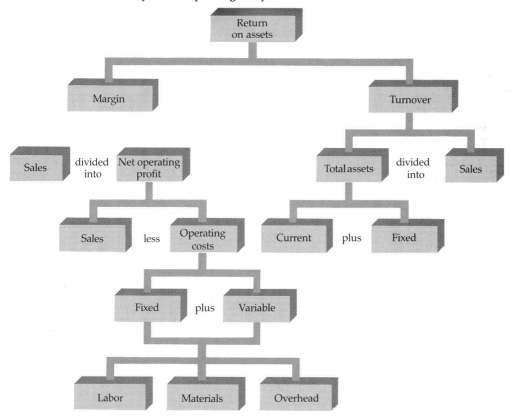

Table 13-2 presents a summary of the profit and activity measures discussed in this chapter. It is probably no surprise that there are 15 of them. In spite of the fact that the number is great, the measures are important because they give a financial analyst a picture of how the company is performing. The measures in this chapter are usually supplemented with measures of liquidity and leverage to give a more complete picture of a company's performance. We shall examine liquidity and leverage in Chapter 14.

NOTE ON MEASURING PROFIT WHEN COSTS AND PRICE LEVEL CHANGE

A company's profit depends on the difference between revenues and costs, each of which is usually changing. In addition, an investor usually wants to measure profit in such a way that investment can be tracked over time in dollars with constant or equal purchasing power because that gives a measure of the investor's ability to consume. The first of these issues—the fact that profit results from the difference between revenues and costs—suggests that calculations should be made using current costs (sometimes called replacement values) rather than historical costs on the company's financial statements. Current costs are difficult for an investor to obtain because he does not have access to the company's invoices and to other internal

BOX 13-4
Profit Measures of Selected
Companies   The fact that inflation and changing current costs affect profit means that companies may not fare as well as historical statements suggest. Here is the way that 1983 earnings of some companies fared ranked in order of their historical profit. (All amounts are in millions.)

Company	Historical Profit (Loss)	Current Cost Profit (Loss)
IBM	$5,485	$5,131
Exxon	$4,978	$1,632
General Motors	$3,730	$3,414
ITT	$ 675	$ 209
SmithKline Beckman	$ 486	$ 442
Time	$ 143	$ 125
Coors	$ 89	$ 53
Apple Computer	$ 77	$ 76
Zenith	$ 46	$ 41
Cessna Aircraft	($ 19)	($ 22)

Source: Business Week, April 30, 1984.

TABLE 13-2 Summary of Profit and Activity Measures

Name	Measure	Meaning
Profit		
Gross operating profit	Sales − cost of goods sold	Measures profit of operations considering only cost of goods sold
Gross operating profit ratio	(Sales − cost of goods sold)/sales	
Net operating profit	Sales − all operating expenses	Measures profit after considering all operating costs
Net operating profit ratio	Net operating profit/sales	
Before-tax earnings	Net operating profit − interest expense	Measures profit after considering operating and financial expenses
Before-tax profit margin ratio	(Net operating profit − interest expense)/sales	
After-tax earnings	Before-tax earnings − taxes	Measures profit after operating and financial expenses and taxes
After-tax earnings ratio	(Before-tax earnings − taxes)/sales	
Return on assets (earning power)	Net operating profit/total assets	Indicates net operating profit per dollar of total assets without considering the way that assets are financed
Return on common shareholders' equity	(After-tax earnings − preferred stock dividend)/average common shareholders' equity	Suggests how effectively management is using common shareholders' original investment and retained earnings to make profit
Activity Ratios		
Accounts receivable turnover	Credit sales/average accounts receivables	Tells whether or not accounts receivable are too large or too small, the effectiveness of credit policy, and the vigor of collections
Average Collection Period	Average accounts receivable/daily sales	
Inventory turnover	Sales/inventory or cost of goods sold/inventory	Tells whether or not inventory is too large or too small
Total asset turnover	Sales/total assets	Tells whether or not total assets are too large or too small
Combining Profit and Acitivity		
Du Pont system of operating analysis	ROA = Net operating profit ratio × total asset turnover	Decomposes total return on assets into income statement and balance-sheet components

information about the company's costs. A company's managers have this information and must make calculations based on current costs.

The second issue mentioned above—the fact that an investor wants to measure profit in such a way that he can see how his ability to consume performs over time—suggests that calculated amounts from different periods should be measured in dollars with the same purchasing power. *Inflation* is an increase in the general or average price level so that money's purchasing power declines. Restating amounts in dollars with constant purchasing power permits performance comparisons that show how an investors' purchasing power is being maintained.

We leave the study of the way to adjust financial statements for inflation and changing current costs for your advanced courses in accounting and finance.

SUMMARY

1. Financial managers, creditors, and investors (called financial analysts) examine the trend of financial measures and the way that measures compare with those of other companies to judge how good a job a company's management is performing.

2. Gross operating profit is operating revenue (or sales) less a company's cost of goods sold. The gross operating profit ratio is gross operating profit divided by operating revenue. It tells an analyst the percentage that operating revenue can fall before gross operating profit disappears.

3. Net operating profit (often called net operating income) is the amount of profit from operations remaining after deducting all operating costs from operating revenue. The net operating profit ratio is net operating profit divided by operating revenue. It tells an analyst the percentage that operating revenue can fall before eliminating the company's net operating profit.

4. A company's earnings tell analysts the amount of profit available to use for paying taxes, distributing to owners, and reinvesting. The before-tax profit margin ratio is calculated by dividing a company's before-tax earnings by operating revenue. This ratio tells analysts the percentage that operating revenue can fall before earnings before and after taxes disappear.

5. Return on assets is the ratio of net operating profit divided by the average of total assets. It tells analysts the amount of net operating profit per dollar of total assets without considering how assets are financed.

6. Return on common shareholders' equity uses earnings available to common shareholders divided by the number of shares outstanding to tell analysts how profitably the company is using shareholders' original investment and retained earnings. Earnings per share of common stock are earnings available to common shareholders divided by the average number of common shares outstanding. A stock's price-earnings ratio (or multiple) tells analysts how much investors buying the stock in the financial markets are paying for a dollar of earnings. Dividends per share of common stock are the company's dividends divided by the average number of shares outstanding.

7. Activity ratios tell analysts whether the level of assets used by a company is

BOX 13-5

The Little Things in Life Cost More   Raymond F. Devoe, Jr., constructed his own trivia index to show how his (and perhaps our) cost of living has changed. The trivia index suggests why many of us believe that inflation continues even though the government statistics say that it's been stopped. The period that he used to compare his index with inflation was 1979–1982.

One of the most spectacular drops ever in the rate of inflation occurred between the years 1980 and 1982: From May 1979 to May 1980, the Consumer Price Index (CPI) shot up 14.4 percent and, the next year, rose again by 9.8 percent. But from May 1981 to May 1982, the CPI was up 6.5 percent, less than half the 1979–80 advance. Yet, in a 1982 New York Times/CBS Poll, 70 percent of the respondents claimed they saw no evidence of such a decline. In the sample, 34 percent thought the inflation rate was higher than a year earlier, 36 percent judged the rate about the same, and only 27 percent believed that it was lower. Presumably, 3 percent evidently couldn't make up their minds.

PRICE CHANGES OF SPECIFIC ITEMS

Item	1974	1979	July, 1982	1979–1982 Change (%)
Time and *Newsweek*	$0.50	$1.25	$1.50	+20
The Wall Street Journal	0.50	0.75	1.25	+33
McDonald's Quarter Pounder (with cheese)	0.79	1.35	1.69	+25
Baskin-Robbins ice cream cone (one scoop)	0.30	0.60	0.85	+42
Stein of beer at singles bar	0.50	1.25	1.50	+20
New York subway	0.30	0.50	0.75	+50
Razor haircut	4.00	6.00	8.00	+33
Woman's wash and set	6.00	8.75	11.00	+26
Bounced check charge	3.00	5.00	6.00	+20
First-class postage stamp	0.08	0.15	0.20	+33
Obscene greeting card	0.60	1.00	1.25	+25
Spearmint gum	0.10	0.30	0.35	+17
Dog license	6.10	8.10	8.50	+05
American Express fee	15.00	25.00	35.00	+40
Panhandler's request	0.10	0.25	1.00	+300
Sunday church donation[a]	1X	2X	3X	+50

[a] Devoe's modesty—or guilt—prevents his disclosing how much he contributes each week.

Here's the way that Devoe summarizes the index above:

The index's latest theme can be summed up in the term "piranha syndrome," named for the voracious South American fish. Traveling in packs of hundreds, these six- to eight-inch creatures rarely bite off a portion more than the size of a fingertip. Frequently, the victim is not aware of the initial bite—the teeth are that sharp. Yet they can reduce a cow to the memory of a moo in less than an hour. In like fashion, the price increases in little-ticket items are rarely felt, yet collectively they can act like piranhas on a paycheck.

Source: Based on an article appearing in *Barron's*, August 2, 1982, p. 26.

too small or too large. All activity ratios have operating revenue (or some variation) in the numerator.

8. Accounts-receivable turnover is credit sales divided by the average of net accounts receivable. The average collection period is 360 days divided by the accounts-receivable turnover or the average of net accounts receivable divided by daily sales. An analyst compares the average collection period with the industry average and the company's credit terms to measure the effectiveness of the company's credit policy and vigor of its collection practice.

9. Inventory turnover may be calculated using either operating revenue or cost of goods sold in the numerator divided by the average level of inventory.

10. Total asset activity is measured by the ratio of operating revenue divided by the average amount of total assets.

11. A financial manager can analyze a company's return on assets (or earning power) by decomposing it into the net operating profit ratio (from the income statement) and total asset turnover (from the balance sheet). Decomposing return on assets in this way is the Du Pont system of operating analysis and permits management to ask meaningful questions about the company's operations.

12. An analyst should consider the way that changing current costs affect a company's profitability. In addition, investors want to measure profit in dollars with constant purchasing power in order to see how their ability to consume out of profit performs over time.

KEY TERMS AND CONCEPTS

Trend and comparative analysis	**Price-earnings ratio**
Gross operating profit	**Activity**
Net operating profit	**Accounts-receivable turnover**
Operating margin	**Inventory turnover**
Earnings	**Du Pont system**

QUESTIONS

13-1. The chapter presents a discussion of the two ways that we may examine financial statement measures to see if a company is performing poorly or well: comparative and trend analysis. Discuss each of these ways.

13-2. Here are the ratios for a company and its industry average. Explain what each of the ratios tells you about the company and comment on whether or not the ratio is better or worse than the industry average. (First, calculate the company's return on assets.)

	Company	*Industry*
a. Gross Operating Profit Ratio	16%	13%
b. Net Operating Profit Ratio	12%	11%
c. Total Asset Turnover	1.1	1.0
d. Return on Assets	—	11%
e. Return on Common Shareholders' Equity	18%	15%

13-3. An income statement presents a company's performance over a specific time period, and balance sheet presents its assets, liabilities, and shareholders' equity at a specific time. Do you see any problem associated with calculating a ratio with an income and a balance-sheet amount? Explain your answer and briefly describe how you will calculate ratios that use income statement and balance sheet amounts.

13-4. Marianna Tomasco is calculating her company's return on common shareholder's equity for March, a month in which the company doubled the number of shares outstanding. Explain which of the following choices is the best method for determining the company's common shareholders' equity for use in the ratio:

a. Use the March 1 amount.

b. Use the March 31 amount.

c. Use the total of the January 1 and December 31 amounts divided by 2.

d. Use the total of the March 1 and March 31 amounts divided by 2.

13-5. "I don't get it," Steve Smith commented on his dad's company, "The company had a much higher net operating profit than its competition, but the competition made a much higher return on assets." Explain how these results could occur and comment on whether his dad's company has too many or too few sales.

13-6. A local grocery chain points out in the local newspaper that its net operating profit ratio is only 6 percent. Is the grocery unprofitable? Explain your answer and comment on the need to use a ratio to improve our evaluation of profit.

13-7. The chapter points out that earnings after taxes are a meaningful amount, but that the before-tax profit margin ratio is more useful than the after-tax profit margin ratio. Explain why that is so.

13-8. Explain how we should calculate a company's basic earnings per share of common stock when the company sells new stock during the period of time covered by the income statement.

13-9. Some analysts point out that the return on assets does not reflect the way that assets are financed, but that the after-tax profit margin ratio does. Do you agree? Explain your answer.

13-10. Can a company have an inventory turnover that is too large or too small? Explain your answer.

13-11. Nickel Publishing has sales of $760,000 in 19x3. Of this amount, $60,000 were cash sales. Accounts receivable in 19x3 averaged $35,000. Calculate the company's average collection period (using a 360-day year) and comment on the company's performance if the industry average collection period is 26 days.

13-12. Which of the following measures would best disclose effective management of an asset by a company relative to other companies in the same industry?

a. A high number of days' sales uncollected relative to the industry average.

b. A high turnover of accounts receivable relative to the industry average.

c. A high number of days' sales in inventory relative to the industry average.

d. A low turnover of total assets relative to the industry average.

Explain your choice.

13-13. How does the Du Pont system of operating analysis combine an income statement and balance sheet to help management ask meaningful questions about the company's performance?

13-14. Ratio analysis often is employed to gain insight into the financial character of a company because the calculation of ratios can often lead to a better understanding of a company's financial position and performance. We can calculate and use a specific ratio or a number of selected ratios to measure or evaluate a specific financial or operating characteristic of a company.

a. Identify and explain what financial characteristic of a company would be measured by an analysis in which the following two ratios were calculated:

(1) Accounts-receivable turnover

(2) Inventory turnover

Do these ratios provide adequate information to evaluate this characteristic or are additional data needed?

b. Identify and explain what specific characteristics regarding a company's operations would be measured by an analysis in which the following four ratios were calculated:

(1) Gross operating profit ratio

(2) Net operating profit ratio

(3) Before-tax profit margin ratio

(4) Return on assets

Do these ratios provide adequate information to an analyst to evaluate a characteristic, or are additional data needed?

PROBLEMS

13-1. For the first eight months of 19x5 the Fina Company has 600,000 shares of common stock outstanding. On September 1, the company issued 50,000 new shares. The company's statement of financial position shows that the company had the following amounts in its common shareholders equity at the close of 19x5:

Common Stock (650,000 shares, $1 par value)	$ 650,000
Paid in Capital in excess of Par	1,250,000
Retained Earnings	3,000,000
	$4,900,000

The company's earnings available to common shareholders for 19x5 were $900,000 and the price-earnings ratio on the company's common stock at the end of 19x5 is six.

a. Calculate the weighted average number of shares outstanding in 19x5.

b. Calculate basic earnings per share of common stock and the stock's market value per share.

13-2. Roxby Company has earnings after federal and state income taxes of $182,000. It has a capital structure as follows:

Shares	Type	Annual Dividend Per Share
40,000	Preferred	$4
40,000	Common	$1

a. Calculate total dividends paid to preferred stockholders.

b. Calculate earnings available to common shareholders and basic earnings per share of common stock.

13-3. Collegmaster Distributors, Inc., has a 6 percent after-tax profit margin ratio and is in the 40 percent tax bracket. By what percent can prices and operating revenue fall to eliminate profit *after* taxes?

13-4. McDonald Sheetrocking has $100,000 credit sales and $20,000 average accounts receivable. Sales increase during the next operating period by 10 percent and average accounts receivable by 20 percent.

    a. Calculate the receivables turnover and average collection period before and after the increase.

    b. What is the level of receivables before and after the sales increase?

    c. Write a memo to the executive vice-president suggesting what you as the financial manager see to be the implications of the changes that have occurred.

13-5. The following comparative quarterly income statements reflect operations of the Camco Exploration Company:

	For The Three Months Ended March 31	
	19x5	*19x6*
Net sales	$17,303,000	$14,969,000
Costs and expenses		
Cost of sales	10,429,000	9,102,000
Selling, general, and administrative	4,590,000	3,650,000
Interest	281,000	224,000
	$15,300,000	$12,976,000
Income before income taxes	$ 2,003,000	$ 1,993,000
Provision for income taxes	728,000	987,000
Net income	$ 1,275,000	$ 1,006,000

    Camco's total assets average $57 million and $63 million in each of the respective quarters. Calculate and interpret for Camco in the first quarter of 19x6,

    a. Gross operating profit ratio

    b. Net operating profit ratio

    c. Return on assets

    d. Before-tax profit margin ratio

13-6. Selected information from the accounting records of the Coda Company are

Cost of Goods Sold for 19x8	$1,200,000
Inventories at December 31, 19x7	$ 350,000
Inventories at December 31, 19x8	$ 310,000

    a. Assuming a business year consisting of 360 days, what was the inventory turnover in 19x8 based on cost of goods sold?

    b. Coda Company has a 20 percent gross operating profit ratio. Calculate Coda Company's operating revenue and inventory turnover in 19x8 based on operating revenue.

    c. Do you have enough information to comment on the size of Coda's inventory? If not, explain what additional information you need.

13-7. The Scriblerus Company has a return on assets (earning power) of 12 percent. It has $2 million in sales and turns its assets over three times a year.

    a. What is Scriblerus Company's net operating profit ratio?

    b. What are its total assets?

    c. What are its earnings after taxes if the company pays $16,000 interest expense, has a 28-day average collection period, and pays 40 percent of its taxable earnings in taxes?

d. Which part of the Du Pont system refers to the income statement and which part to the balance sheet?

13-8. CMA Examination (modified). Herken Company is a closely held corporation with a capital structure composed entirely of common stock and retained earnings. The stockholders have an agreement with the company that states the company will purchase the stock of a shareholder should a shareholder want to sell his or her holdings in the company. The agreement states that the stock would be purchased at a price equal to the stock's previous year-end book value per share.

Early in October 19x8 Mrs. John Vader, a widow of one of Herken's major stockholders, expressed an interest in selling her stock in accordance with the buy-back/pricing arrangement. Mrs. Vader owns 600,000 shares of the 3 million shares of Herken Company common stock.

The board of directors has concluded that the company must replace the capital used to repurchase the shares. The board has assurances that it would be able to finance the acquisition of stock by borrowing the necessary cash on 10-year notes through private placement at an annual interest rate of 10 percent.

The board and Mrs. Vader agreed that the exchange will take place on January 1, 19x9. The book value per share of common stock is projected to be $50 on December 31, 19x8.

The financial manager of Herken Company had prepared a forecast and pro forma statements for the 19x9 year. An excerpt of the forecasted earnings statement for the year ended December 31, 19x9 is presented below. Herken used a 40 percent income tax rate in the forecasted statement. The pro forma statements do *not* reflect the repurchase of Mrs. Vader's shares or the new issue of debt required to pay for the shares.

Pro-Forma Statement
(in thousands)

Income before income taxes	$50,000
Less: income taxes (40%)	20,000
Net income	$30,000
Shares outstanding	3,000
Earnings per share (30,000 ÷ 3,000)	$ 10.00
Dividends per share	$ 0

a. Revise the excerpt from Herken Company's forecasted earnings statement for the year ended December 31, 19x9, to reflect the long-term debt financing to be used to purchase Mrs. Vader's common stock. Assume the 40 percent tax rate will still be applicable.

b. Explain the impact the long-term debt financing would have on Herken Company's earnings per share and return on stockholders' equity using the forecasted data for 19x9.

CHAPTER 14
Liquidity and Leverage

This chapter continues our analysis of financial statements begun with Chapter 13. That chapter examined the meaning and measurement of company profitability and activity. This chapter concentrates on financial liquidity and leverage.

Financial managers, creditors, and investors (called analysts) must be concerned about the company's liquidity and its leverage. *Liquidity* is the ability of an asset to be cashed, and it determines a company's ability to pay its bills as they become due. The first part of the chapter considers three measures of a company's liquidity so that you will be able to calculate these measures and determine their meaning. Most of the chapter deals with leverage. *Leverage* is the power to change or influence. In financial management leverage is the power of changes in company output or activity to change profit. Leverage results from management's decision to use fixed costs either in operations or in financing assets. We shall examine two types of leverage: operating and financial leverage. Operating leverage is examined using a company's income statement to show the way that changes in company output act to change a company's net operating profit. After reading this material you will be able to measure operating leverage and to understand the role it plays in increasing a company's business risk. We shall examine financial leverage after we complete our examination of operating leverage. The discussion begins by examining four measures of financial leverage. The discussion then considers financial leverage using a company's income statement to show how changes in a company's net operating profit act to change its earnings after taxes. When you finish this part of the chapter, you will know how to measure financial leverage and to recognize the role it plays in increasing a company's financial risk. The chapter concludes with a brief discussion designed to show you how operating and financial leverage combine to increase the total risk of a company.

MEASURES OF FINANCIAL LIQUIDITY

Static measures of financial liquidity—current ratio, quick ratio, and net working capital—are static because we measure them at a single point in time and do not consider the changing quality of each item over the business cycle. A financial manager can calculate these measures using a statement of financial position alone or an income statement and balance sheet together. You will note below, however, that when you calculate a ratio that requires combining an income statement amount with an amount from a balance sheet you must average the amount from the balance sheet.

Current Ratio

The current ratio is the most widely used measure of company liquidity. It indicates the extent to which the claims of short-term creditors—a company's most pressing claims—can be met by assets that are due to become cash within one year or less.

To calculate a company's current ratio, take the ratio between the company's current assets and current liabilities. For Harper Distributing Company (see Table 12-1 on page 230) the current ratio on December 31, 19x1, is

$$\text{Current ratio} = \frac{\text{current assets}}{\text{current liabilities}}$$

$$= \frac{\$15,438,000}{\$11,517,000} = 1.34$$

This ratio tells analysts that Harper Distributing is covering its current liabilities 1.34 times with its current assets and that long-term assets need not be liquidated to meet current liabilities. Analysts should compare this ratio with that of other companies in its industry and should examine the ratio's trend for the past several years in order to evaluate its strength and direction.

Net Working Capital

Net working capital represents the volume of current assets financed from long-term sources—the part of a company's current assets that will stay with it for more than one year. Management will use the company's current assets financed by current liabilities to pay current liabilities within the year, when the current liabilities are paid. These current liabilities may or may not be replaced with other current liabilities. Current assets financed from long-term debt and equity need not be used to repay a current liability. Net working capital is therefore a measure of the company's immunity from financial pressure because net working capital need not be used to pay short-term liabilities. Net working capital is available to meet unexpected cash needs or to make investments in long-term assets.

For Harper Distributing Company (see Table 12-1) $11,517,000 of its $15,438,000 in current assets on December 31, 19x1, are financed from short-term sources (that is, current liabilities are $11,517,000). The remaining $3,921,000 are financed from long-term debt and equity sources and comprise the company's net working capital. We measure net working capital by subtracting current liabilities from current assets. Because the amounts come from the balance sheet alone, for Harper Distributing we calculate net working capital on December 31, 19x1, without averaging:

$$\text{Net working capital} = \text{current assets} - \text{current liabilities}$$
$$= \$15,438,000 - \$11,517,000 = \$3,921,000$$

This measure tells analysts that $3,921,000 of Harper Distributing's current assets are financed from long-term debt and equity and, therefore, are not needed to repay current liabilities.

Quick Ratio

A company's current ratio tells an analyst the company's ability to pay current liabilities without liquidating long-term assets. However, inventory is considered in current assets so that the current ratio may be misleading because inventory is often converted into cash (that is, liquidated) only with some sales effort. The quick ratio, sometimes called *acid test ratio*, removes inventory from current assets to indicate how liquid a company would be if operations were to halt abruptly—for example, should a fire destroy all of the company's production facilities. For Harper Distributing the quick ratio on December 31, 19x1, is calculated as follows:

$$\text{Quick Ratio} = \frac{\text{current assets} - \text{inventory}}{\text{current liabilities}}$$
$$= \frac{\$15,438,000 - \$3,599,000}{\$11,517,000} = 1.028$$

Figure 14-1 illustrates current and quick ratios for U.S. nonfinancial corporations. Harper Distributing Company's 1.34 current ratio suggests that it is about as liquid as the average nonfinancial corporation. Its 1.028 quick ratio is greater than the average and confirms our interpretation of the current ratio: The company should be able to meet its current liabilities from its current assets.

Liquidity exists only when a company has cash available to pay bills at the precise instant payment is required. If a company could always raise cash at the exact instant needed to pay its bills, any level of liquidity would be ample. The ability to raise cash changes over the business cycle, so an analyst must consider the stage of the business cycle in interpreting a liquidity measure. The following discussion examines the way that interpretation of a liquidity measure is affected by the stage of the business cycle.

Interpreting Liquidity Measures over the Business Cycle

A satisfactory level for a liquidity ratio changes with the business cycle: A liquidity measure that seems ample and safe in prosperity or mild recession may prove strained, even precarious, in a financial depression.

Why does a company's satisfactory liquidity vary over the business cycle? It does so primarily for three reasons. First, a company's liquidity is affected by the amount of credit available to it, and the availability of credit varies over the business cycle. During early stages of business recovery, banks have large reserves and are anxious to make loans. A company may rely on short-term bank loans to finance plant and equipment, thereby pulling down its current ratio, and because the bank has sufficient reserves, the company can obtain cash by renewing the short-term loan. Therefore, although the current ratio is low, the company is more liquid than the current ratio implies. However, later in a business cycle, when banks find themselves short of reserves due to a restrictive monetary policy, a company may be unable to renew its short-term loan. Many companies may find themselves in this situation at the same time so that a large volume of financing may then be forced into other markets as borrowers search for credit: Companies sell bonds, liquidate assets, or even merge with others that can provide them with cash. We must examine a company's liquidity measure within the context of credit availability in order to interpret accurately the company's liquidity.

Second, liquidity measures are affected by the changing market value of assets.

FIGURE 14-1   Nonfinancial corporate current and quick ratios.
(*SOURCE: Statistical Abstract of The United States,* 1984)

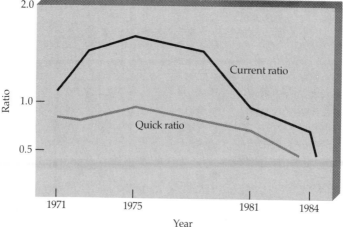

The market value of assets changes over the business cycle as interest rates rise and fall. The influence of changing interest rates on the value of assets means that assets are subject to *interest rate risk*, the likelihood that an actual return from the asset will differ from the expected return because interest rates rise and fall. Securities (such as U.S. Treasury bills, notes, commercial paper, corporate bonds, and municipal bonds) in which companies and financial institutions invest their cash are especially sensitive to changes in interest rates. As interest rates rise during a boom, the market value of securities held by investors declines below the price paid in times of low interest rates. Some security holders become locked into their existing portfolio because the threat of realizing large capital losses makes them unwilling (and perhaps unable) to liquidate these securities in order to get cash. Other assets become harder to sell or to borrow money on because interest rates are high and rising. In short, all assets become less marketable during such times, so any liquidity measure examined without considering the marketability of assets is likely to be misinterpreted.

Finally, liquidity is related to the credit-worthiness of a company, and credit-worthiness varies over the business cycle. During an economic boom, earnings are high and cash is available so that companies can readily pay their debts. Accounts receivable in a company's current assets are financially sound. But when the business cycle begins to turn down, companies find it increasingly difficult to meet their current obligations and resort to putting off payments as long as possible, running past the date payment is due. Hence, the interpretation of a liquidity measure varies over the business cycle because soundness of the accounts-receivable component in current assets varies.

LEVERAGE

Leverage is the power of changes in output (activity) to change profit more than proportionally or percentage-wise. For example, if a company's output increases by 8 percent, then leverage may cause its profit to rise by 12 percent. Leverage results from two specific management decisions, one involving the investment decision and the other involving the financial decision. There are two types of leverage and each is associated with each decision.

Operating leverage is the power of changes in output to change net operating profit more than proportionally. Operating leverage results from fixed operating costs such as advertising costs, utilities, salaries, and depreciation expense. A *fixed operating cost* is a cost that does not change as output changes.

Financial leverage is the power of changes in net operating profit to change earnings after taxes more than proportionally. Financial leverage results from interest expense.

The following discussion addresses each of these types of leverage so that you will be able to understand the role of each type, to calculate a number for its measure, and to understand how they relate to each other.

BOX 14-1
How Contribution Margin Changed "No"
into "Yes"   This chapter concentrates on the difference between fixed and variable costs in decision making. Here's an example of how a small-business manager used the difference in a decision.

A big company, whose business a small motorcycle parts company had vainly tried for years to get, finally caved in to the extent of offering a proposition. The big customer would buy $5,000 worth of motorcycle tires (a big order), but it wanted a 15 percent discount from the usual wholesale price.

The numbers from financial analysis helped management evaluate the proposal: The supplier's gross margin on sales was 33 percent and cost of goods sold 67 percent. Other expenses were 28 percent of sales. Before-tax profit margin was 5 percent. On that basis the order should be turned down because the 15 percent discount from the usual wholesale price would result in a 10 percent before-tax loss.

How did contribution margin affect the decision? The supplier's operating costs were 0.67 + 0.28 = 0.95 or 95 percent of sales, but 80 percent of sales were variable. With this information, management decided to accept the order because the contribution margin ratio suggested that the supplier would have $0.20 of every sales dollar to contribute toward fixed costs,

Sales	100%
Less Variable Costs	80%
Contribution Margin	20%

Actually, though, the final decision would hinge on answers to four further questions.

1. Is the company operating below capacity so that overtime and overhead costs won't increase?
2. Is the merchandise readily available?
3. If the company sells tires at 85 cents on the dollar, will that cut out 100-cents-on-the-dollar sales to other customers?
4. Will a heavy discount to this customer imperil sales to other customers so that they will expect the same?

Financial analysis, you see, won't give you a completely final answer. But it will get you about 90 percent of the way down the track.

OPERATING LEVERAGE

Operating leverage occurs because a company must make fixed operating payments. It is this fact that gives a change in output the power to change net operating profit more than proportionally. If a company has no fixed operating costs, then it makes no fixed operating payments and any change in output will change net operating profit by the same percent.

Operating leverage suggests a company's business risk because operating leverage indicates the variability in the company's net operating profit. *Business risk* is the likelihood that a company's actual net operating profit will differ from its expected amount. Operating leverage directly affects differences between expected and actual net operating profit amounts: A company with little or no operating leverage will have small changes in net operating profit as output changes when compared with a company having a great deal of operating leverage. In this way the more operating leverage a company has, the greater its business risk will be.

Even though operating leverage results from a company's fixed operating costs, we will use variable costs to measure operating leverage. *Variable costs* are costs that change as the level of output changes: As output rises and falls, variable costs rise and fall at the same rate so that a 10 percent decline in output is associated with a 10 percent decline in variable costs. Most raw material and hourly labor expense are variable costs. We use variable costs in measuring operating leverage by calculating a contribution margin. The following discussion will familiarize you with the contribution margin, then we shall return to our discussion of operating leverage.

Contribution Margin. The distinction between variable and fixed costs is shown in a company's contribution margin. *Contribution margin* is the amount of sales revenue that remains to pay (contribute toward) fixed costs and net operating profit after paying variable operating costs.

Contribution margin is measured either using total amounts or unit amounts. Using totals, the contribution margin is sales revenue less total variable costs:

$$\text{Contribution margin} = \text{sales revenue} - \text{total variable costs}$$

A financial manager measures unit contribution by using price per item sold and variable cost per item produced. The unit contribution margin is price less variable cost per unit:

$$\text{Unit contribution margin} = \text{price} - \text{variable cost per unit}$$

A financial manager uses variable and fixed costs calculated by the company's cost accountant to arrange a contribution margin statement. Table 14-1 presents a unit contribution statement for Harper Distributing Company. The contribution margins (at 2 million units sold) are found using information from the unit contribution statement,

Selling price	$12.00	Total revenues	
Less variable costs	9.00	(2,000,000 × $12)	$24,000,000
		Less total variable costs	
		(2,000,000 × $9)	18,000,000
Unit contribution			
margin	$3.00	Contribution margin	$6,000,000

TABLE 14-1 Harper Distributing Company, Unit Contribution Statement for the Year Ended December 31, 19x1

Selling price		$12.00
Less variable costs per unit		
Raw materials	$4.50	
Direct labor	2.30	
Manufacturing overhead	1.25	
Selling expenses	0.80	
		9.00
Unit contribution margin		$3.00
Period fixed costs		
Depreciation	$ 192,000	
Selling	3,006,249	
General and administrative	3,420,000	
Total	$6,618,249	

Practice. Before leaving this section, calculate the contribution margin for a company with $6.5 million sales revenue; $2.6 million variable costs; $2.3 million fixed costs. Answer: $3.9 million. Show how this answer is calculated and interpret the answer.

Measuring Operating Leverage

An analyst uses the contribution margin to measure a company's operating leverage at a specific level of output. The measure of operating leverage is called the *degree of operating leverage,* and it measures the percent change in net operating profit associated with a 1 percent change in output. Specifically, the degree of operating leverage at a specific output level (noted by x) is measured by dividing the contribution margin by the amount of net operating profit:[1]

$$\text{Degree of operating leverage}_x = \frac{\text{contribution margin}_x}{\text{net operating profit}_x}$$

Recall that net operating profit is measured by sales revenue less total operating costs, both fixed and variable. Consequently, the greater the amount of fixed costs,

---

[1] The degree of operating leverage (DOL) can be derived from a slightly more complicated-looking equation that uses the unit contribution, output, and total fixed costs:

$$\text{DOL}_x = \frac{Q(P-V)}{Q(P-V) - FC} = \frac{TR - TVC}{(TR - TVC) - FC}$$

where

$$Q = \text{volume of output}$$
$$P = \text{price per unit}$$
$$V = \text{variable cost per unit}$$
$$FC = \text{total fixed costs}$$
$$TR = \text{total revenue}$$
$$TVC = \text{total variable costs}$$

Notice that the numerator is in fact the contribution margin and the denominator is the contribution margin less total fixed operating costs or net operating profit. The equation in the text tells us the same thing, but is less intimidating.

the less will be net operating profit, and the greater will be the degree of operating leverage. In this way fixed costs directly determine the degree of operating leverage even though fixed costs do not appear in the equation.

Example. Two companies have the same contribution margin, but fixed costs are different. The resulting degrees of operating leverage differ so that the company with larger fixed costs has a larger degree of operating leverage:

	A	B
Contribution margin	$100,000	$100,000
Less fixed costs	80,000	40,000
Net operating profit	$ 20,000	$ 60,000
Degree of operating leverage		

$$A \quad \frac{\$100,000}{\$20,000} = 5$$

$$B \quad \frac{\$100,000}{\$60,000} = 1.67$$

Practice. Calculate the degree of operating leverage for Harper Distributing at 2.4 million units of output. (Use the information on Table 14-1 to calculate the contribution margin and net operating income.) Answer: 12.38. Show how you found this answer before continuing.

Using the Degree of Operating Leverage. An analyst uses the degree of operating leverage to forecast the expected level of net operating profit. If output is expected to change, then the expected percent change in net operating profit can be found by multiplying the percent change in output by the degree of operating leverage. In an equation, the way that a degree of operating leverage (DOL) tells us the expected change in net operating profit is

$$\%\Delta \text{ net operating profit} = \%\Delta \text{ output} \times \text{DOL}$$

where the symbol $\%\Delta$ is percent change.

Example. Harper Distributing Company's marketing department may forecast a 5 percent decline in sales during 19x2. This information and Harper Distributing's 12.38 degree of operating leverage mean that net operating profit will decline by an expected 61.9 percent calculated as follows:

Percent change in net operating profit $= 12.38 \times -0.05 = -0.619$ or -61.9%

This information tells Harper Distributing's financial manager that there may be 61.9 percent less operating profit to pay interest expense next year because interest expense is the next item to be deducted from net operating profit.

Three characteristics of degree of operating leverage are important to keep in mind.

1. You can get a negative as well as a positive degree of operating leverage, depending on the amount of your net operating profit. The degree of operating leverage is negative when calculated at an output level with a negative net operating profit and positive when calculated at an activity level with a positive net operating profit.

2. Calculating an accurate degree of operating leverage using sales revenue rather than a physical measure of output depends on inventory and prices remaining constant so that changes in sales are directly associated with changes in production costs. If inventory or price change, then net operating profit changes in a way different from that expected using the degree of operating leverage equation. For example, if total revenue rises as a result of selling off inventory, production will not change and net operating income will rise more than the calculated degree of operating leverage suggests.

3. The degree of operating leverage changes according to how close the output level is to a net operating profit of zero. The closer activity is to the break-even level (that is, where net operating profit is zero), the greater will be the degree of operating level. For example, at the exact point where the net operating profit is zero, the degree of operating leverage measure has zero in the denominator, and the degree of operating leverage will be infinite (or not defined).

The three characteristics above suggest that the degree of operating leverage is influenced by the level of net operating profit. The following discussion will show how a company's net operating profit is affected by its volume of output and its fixed costs.

Operating Break-Even Analysis

The relationship between fixed and variable operating costs and a company's net operating profit is illustrated by break-even analysis. *Break-even analysis* (often called cost-volume-profit analysis) calculates the sales volume that a company needs to just cover its sum of fixed and variable costs. We can calculate the operating break-even level of output in either unit sales or dollars.[2]

Break-Even in Units. We can find the number of units needed to break even in the following way. Total revenue (TR) is equal to the average price (P) of each item that a company sells multiplied by the quantity (Q) that it sells. A company's total operating costs (TC) are the sum of its fixed costs (FC) and its variable cost per unit (V) multiplied by its quantity produced and sold (Q). If we use these relationships and find Q, then we will have an equation for finding the break-even quantity of sales and output, the level of activity at which net operating profit is zero:

---

[2] An additional method to measure the degree of operating leverage is

$$ DOL_x = \frac{1}{1 - (BE/Q)} $$

where BE is the break-even level in units and Q is the output level in units or dollars. Because a company with no fixed costs has a zero break-even point, this equation quickly shows that its degree of operating leverage is one at all levels of output except zero.

$$TR - TC = 0$$
$$TR = TC$$
$$P \times Q = FC + (V \times Q)$$
$$(P \times Q) - (V \times Q) = FC$$
$$Q(P - V) = FC$$
$$Q = \frac{FC}{(P - V)}$$

The quantity break-even equation tells us that the break-even amount of units produced and sold is found by dividing the company's fixed operating costs by its unit contribution margin.

Example. The unit break-even level of output (activity) for Harper Distributing Company is 2,206,083 units calculated with the information on Table 14-1:

$$Q = \frac{\$6,618,249}{(\$12 - \$9)} = 2,206,083 \text{ units}$$

Now we know that if Harper Distributing produces and sells this many units, then it will have a zero net operating profit.

Break-Even in Dollars. To find the operating break-even point in dollars, we use the fixed costs and the contribution margin ratio, calculated by dividing unit contribution by average price or the contribution margin by total revenue—you will get the same ratio with either measure.

$$\text{Contribution margin ratio} = \frac{P - V}{P}$$

or

$$= \frac{TR - TVC}{TR}$$

The contribution margin ratio tells us the percent of each sales dollar that remains to contribute toward fixed costs and net operating profit.

Practice. Calculate the contribution margin ratio for Harper Distributing at 10,000 units of output from the information on Table 14-1 using units and totals. Answer: 25 percent.

The dollar break-even level of output Q_D for Harper Distributing is $26,472,996 found with the dollar break-even equation,

$$Q_D = \frac{\$6,618,249}{0.25} = \$26,472,996$$

Figure 14-2 shows the break-even variables for Harper Distributing. Both parts of the figure indicate the same thing, but the presentations differ. The break-even point is 2,206,083 units, and when output declines to zero units, net operating profit is a

−$6,618,249—the amount of fixed costs. As output rises above the break-even point the amount of profit increases. Some people like the presentation format on the bottom part of Figure 14-2 because it emphasizes the way that net operating profit changes with volume.

Operating leverage and break-even analysis address the relationship between a company's output and net operating profit. Therefore, it examines only the part of an income statement from sales through net operating profit. Financial leverage continues the analysis of leverage by examining the influence of interest expense on a company's earnings before and after taxes. Our study of financial leverage begins by discussing the impact of financial leverage on earnings, then presents ways that financial leverage is measured on a company's balance sheet.

FINANCIAL LEVERAGE

Financial leverage is the power of changes in net operating profit to change earnings after taxes more than proportionally (percentage-wise). Shareholders and financial

FIGURE 14-2 Break-even analysis for Harper Distributing Company.

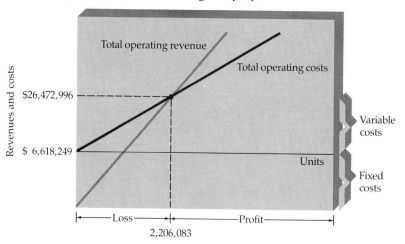

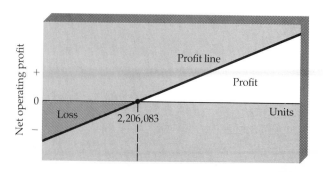

BOX 14-2
The Break-Even Point for Major League
Baseball Teams   Financial managers of major league baseball teams calculate the attendance break-even level as a part of their planning procedure. The figure below shows a break-even chart for two teams and the American League average in 1978. The break-even attendance amounts for the 1978 season were,

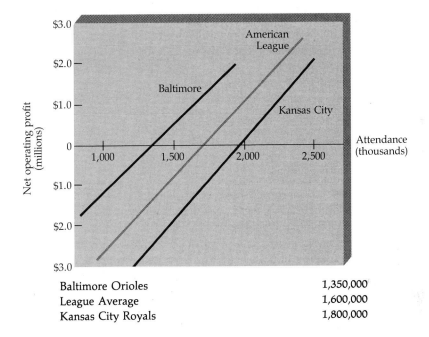

Baltimore Orioles	1,350,000
League Average	1,600,000
Kansas City Royals	1,800,000

Baltimore needed fewer paying fans to break-even on operations than did Kansas City because the Orioles had a much more lucrative broadcasting contract than the Royals. Notice, too, that the Royals had the largest amount of fixed operating costs, a point illustrated by its having the largest negative intercept at the net operating income axis. The slope of the Oriole's net operating income line is slightly less than that of the others, suggesting that the Orioles had the lowest contribution margin ratio and the least degree of operating leverage. Other revenues lower the Oriole's break-even attendance level and help all major league teams, but they are particularly large for the Orioles. Examples of these other revenues are radio and television contracts and outside endorsements such as Fenway Franks sold in Boston and Yankee Dogs at Yankee Stadium.

Source: Based on Michael E. Herman, *The Economics Of Major League Baseball,* Midcontinent Perspectives, Session 8, June 26, 1980, Midwest Research Institute, Kansas City, Missouri, pp. 16–17.

managers are concerned about the amount and stability of earnings after taxes because earnings after taxes determine the size of dividend that the company pays and
the amount of internal equity that will be reinvested in profitable assets. In addition,
a financial manager should understand the concept of financial leverage in order to
recognize that the volatility (the up-and-down movement) of earnings can be controlled by changing the amount of interest expense that the company must pay.

Financial leverage is used to measure a company's financial risk because financial leverage indicates the variability in the company's earnings after taxes. *Financial
risk* is the likelihood that a company's profit after taxes will differ from what investors expect. A company that uses debt financing has earnings that are more volatile
(that is, more changeable) than those of a company with no debt financing. A company with no debt has no financial risk.

Measuring Financial Leverage

An analyst measures financial leverage at a specific level of net operating profit using
the company's net operating profit and earnings before taxes. The measure of financial leverage is called the *degree of financial leverage,* and it relates the percent change
in earnings before taxes and in earnings after taxes to a 1 percent change in net
operating profit.[3] (Earnings before and after taxes change by the same percent because taxes are calculated as a percent of earnings before taxes.)

Specifically, a company's degree of financial leverage at a specific level of net
operating profit (noted by x) is net operating profit divided by earnings before taxes,[4]

$$\text{Degree of financial leverage}_x = \frac{\text{net operating profit}_x}{\text{earnings before taxes}_x}$$

Although interest expense does not appear in the equation used to calculate a
company's degree of financial leverage, interest expense directly influences it in the
following way: The difference between net operating profit and earnings before
taxes is interest expense. Consequently, the greater the amount of interest expense
is, the less earnings before taxes will be, and the greater the degree of financial
leverage will be.

---

[3] Financial leverage is often discussed by relating earnings before interest and taxes (EBIT) to earnings after taxes. The difference between net operating profit and earnings before interest and taxes
is explained by gains and losses on financial transactions (a company may lose or make profit on
selling securities) and on capital transactions (1231 gains and losses discussed in Chapter 21).
These gains and losses are usually not material (that is, they are small relative to total net operating
profit) so that the discussion of financial leverage may be in terms of either net operating profit or
earnings before interest and taxes.

[4] The degree of financial leverage (DFL) can be derived in a slightly more complicated way using the
contribution margin, output, total fixed costs, and dollar interest:

$$\text{DFL} = \frac{Q\,(P-V) - FC}{Q(P-V) - FC - I} = \frac{(TR-TVC) - FC}{(TR-TVC) - FC - I}$$

where I is dollar interest expense. Notice that the numerator in this equation is net operating profit
and the denominator is net operating profit less dollar interest, or earnings before taxes.

Example. The Harper Distributing Company has $888,000 net operating profit and $321,000 interest expense in 19x1 (see Table 12-2). Its earnings before taxes are $567,000. Harper Distributing's degree of financial leverage at $888,000 net operating profit is calculated as follows:

$$\text{Degree of financial leverage} = \frac{\$888,000}{\$321,000} = 2.77$$

Earnings before (and after) taxes will change by 2.77 × 0.01 = 0.0277 or 2.77 percent for each 1 percent change in net operating profit from $888,000 net operating profit.

Using the Degree of Financial Leverage. An analyst uses the degree of financial leverage to forecast expected levels of profit before and after taxes.[5] For example, if net operating profit is expected to increase by 12 percent during the next year, then a financial manager can multiply this percent change by the degree of financial leverage to find the expected percent change in profit after taxes.

Example. Harper Distributing Company's net operating profit is expected to increase in 19x2 by 12 percent from its $888,000 level in 19x1. Multiplying this percent change by its 2.77 degree of financial leverage at $888,000 net operating profit (NOP) gives us the expected percent change in earnings after taxes (EAT),

$$\%\Delta \text{ EAT } = \%\Delta \text{ NOP } \times \text{ DFL}$$

$$\begin{aligned}
\text{Percent change} \\
\text{in earnings after taxes } = 2.77 \times 0.12 \\
= 0.3324 \quad \text{or} \quad 33.24\%
\end{aligned}$$

Harper Distributing Company's financial manager expects 33.24 percent more earnings after taxes in 19x2 to use for dividends and reinvestment.

Other Measures of Financial Leverage

Sometimes an analyst wants to measure financial leverage in ways other than with the degree of financial leverage. That is the case if an analyst wants to measure the portions of debt and equity used by the company and the company's ability to pay interest expense from operations. The ratios that follow use an income statement and balance sheet to show creditors the margin of financial safety provided to the creditors by the stockholders.

The *debt ratio* measures the percent of total assets financed from debt. It tells an analyst the company's financial risk: The greater the debt ratio is, the greater the

---

[5] The percent change in profit after taxes is the same as the percent change in earnings per share if no preferred shares are outstanding and the number of common shares outstanding does not change. For this reason the degree of financial leverage is sometimes explained as the percent change in earnings per share associated with a percent change in net operating profit.

BOX 14-3
Corporate Acquisitions May Increase

Financial Leverage   Corporate acquisitions may increase a company's degree of financial leverage. A good example is the acquisition policy of Petro-Lewis Corporation whose stock trades on the American Stock Exchange. Petro-Lewis, which in 1981 and 1982 gobbled up oil and gas producing properties, was criticized by analysts about the wisdom of its strategy. In making large purchases, the company used borrowed money to buy participations in oil and gas producing properties. In other words, it leveraged itself on the assumption that oil and gas prices would rise, or at least remain steady. Some analysts and investors avoided recommending and buying Petro-Lewis stock because of concern about the company's growing debt burden. As one analyst commented, "Management has been a little too optimistic about the direction of oil prices and a little too willing to take on debt." In 1981, the company's long-term debt grew by 90 percent, to $518 million.

Large debts mean large interest payments. In good times, when oil and gas prices were high, Petro-Lewis could pay off the interest with revenue from oil and gas sales. Weak petroleum prices, however, not only reduce the cash available to service the company's debt, they also reduce the value of reserves still in the ground, reserves used for collateral on the loans. Oil priced at $38 per barrel is better for oil producers than is oil priced at $29 per barrel.

Years 1982 and 1983 were not good for Petro-Lewis. Higher interest expenses and higher operating and general administrative expenses are reasons the company cited for the fact that fiscal 1982 and 1983 earnings trailed earlier-year results. The company's stock price fell more than 40 percent in the six months following July 1, 1983. Jerome A. Lewis, the company's chief executive officer said, "The problems are a fairly normal business financing exercise: We've either got to refinance some debt or sell assets and pay the debt down. We obviously need to do something."

In early February, 1984, Petro-Lewis suspended sales operations. The company recorded a $54 million dollar loss for 1984, and its investors suffered losses of more than $1 billion. Mr. Lewis received a $163,091 bonus for the year and exercised an option to receive $1.1 million cash from the company. In January, 1985, Petro-Lewis traded at $3\frac{7}{8}$ ($3.875).

Source: The Wall Street Journal, January 22, 1985, p. 31.

company's financial risk will be. The debt ratio is measured by dividing total assets into total debt. For Harper Distributing Company (its balance sheet is Table 12-1) the debt ratio is 65.3 percent on December 31, 1981, measured as follows:

$$\text{Debt ratio} = \frac{\text{total debt}}{\text{total assets}}$$

$$\text{Debt ratio} = \frac{\$11,735,000}{\$17,983,000} = 0.653 \quad \text{or} \quad 65.3\%$$

BOX 14-4
Inflation, Interest Rates, and Financial
Statements   Interest rates rise and fall with inflation so that in periods of rapid inflation interest may gouge a gaping hole in corporate profit. Some experts have noted that the presentation format of accounting statements for financial reporting purposes can cause problems in periods of sustained high interest rates, periods when financing costs are important in determining profit. A conventional income statement places financing costs at the bottom of the statement, separate from cost of goods sold. Moving financing costs up and including them in cost of goods sold will give a more accurate picture of operating profit by showing it to be lower than it would be otherwise.

For example, conventional accounting might show a slow-moving product line producing an $8,000 gross operating profit for the year. However, inventory items must be financed, and $9,600 interest cost of carrying slow inventory may result in a $1,600 loss, which wouldn't be apparent from the traditional income statement constructed following generally accepted accounting principles.

Inflation and interest costs are often too large to be ignored in the day-to-day operating decisions or policies of a company. Financial and operating managers should make an adjustment like the one suggested here in order to measure accurately the results of their operating and financial decisions.

This ratio tells analysts that 65.3 percent of Harper Distributing Company's assets are financed from debt.

A ratio related to the debt ratio is the debt-equity ratio. The *debt-equity ratio* measures a company's financial risk by dividing a company's total debt by preferred and common shareholders' equity. A financial analyst measures the debt-equity ratio for Harper Distributing Company on December 31, 1981, as follows:

$$\text{Debt-equity ratio} = \frac{\text{total debt}}{\text{total equity}}$$

$$\frac{\$11,735,000}{\$6,248,000} = 1.89 \quad \text{or} \quad 189\%$$

This ratio tells analysts that Harper Distributing Company's total debt is 189 percent of the company's preferred and common shareholders' equity.

The *times-interest-earned* ratio (sometimes called coverage of interest expense ratio) indicates a company's financial risk because it shows the margin of safety with which interest expense is being earned from operations. It is used as a measure of risk by credit-rating agencies such as Moody's Investor Service and Standard & Poor's Corporation. The ratio is measured by dividing net operating profit by interest expense.

The times-interest-earned ratio for Harper Distributing Company for the period ending December 31, 19x1, is 5 calculated as follows:

$$\text{Times interest earned} = \frac{\text{net operating profit}}{\text{interest expense}}$$

$$= \frac{\$888,000}{\$321,000} = 2.77$$

This ratio tells analysts that net operating profit is covering interest expense 2.77 times.

The ratios presented here should be examined by comparing them with the ratios of other companies in the same industry and with past levels of the ratio. In this way management will get some idea of whether the ratio is too large or too small.

COMBINING OPERATING AND FINANCIAL LEVERAGE

An analyst can combine a company's degree of operating leverage and its degree of financial leverage to measure the percent change in profit after taxes associated with a change in output. The combined ratio is the *degree of combined leverage,* and it measures the percent change in profit after taxes resulting from a 1 percent change in output from a specific level of output (noted by x):

$$\begin{array}{c} \text{Degree of combined} \\ \text{leverage}_x \end{array} = \begin{array}{c} \text{degree of operating} \\ \text{leverage}_x \end{array} \times \begin{array}{c} \text{degree of financial} \\ \text{leverage}_x \end{array}$$

$$\frac{\text{Contribution margin}}{\text{earnings before taxes}} = \frac{\text{contribution margin}}{\text{net operating profit}} \times \frac{\text{net operating profit}}{\text{earnings before taxes}}$$

The degree of combined leverage measures a company's exposure to risk because it measures the variability in earnings when output changes: The greater the variability of earnings, the greater the likelihood will be that actual earnings will differ from expected earnings when output changes.

Practice. Bertho Corporation has no fixed operating costs and uses no debt. Its operating revenue is $360,000 and variable costs are $200,000. Calculate the company's degree of combined leverage. Answer: one. Show this answer to be correct by verifying that under these conditions the contribution margin is the same amount as net operating profit, and net operating profit is the same amount as profit before taxes.

In summary, operating and financial leverage combine to widen the swings in profit after taxes that result from any change in sales. Consequently, other things being equal, the more operating leverage a company has, the less financial leverage

---

BOX 14-5
Leverage and an Earnings Decline   Financial theory tells us that operating and financial leverage gang up to cause earnings per share to fall as activity declines. You can find many real-world examples of that happening, and the experience of International Paper Company offers us a typical one. International Paper, citing the continuing weak economy, reported that third-quarter 1982 earnings fell 40 percent and revenue fell 22 percent.

"The dismal condition of the economy has made the third quarter a most difficult period for the forest-products industry," said Edwin A. Gee, chairman and chief executive officer. Although shipments held up reasonably well during the quarter, Mr. Gee said, "very competitive pricing in all our product lines" reduced profit margins.

For the nine months, net earnings declined 53 percent to $133.6 million, or $2.30 a share, from $285.4 million, or $5.37 a share. Revenue for the nine months fell 24 percent to $3.02 billion from $3.96 billion in 1981.

Mr. Gee said International Paper expected results "to remain depressed until there is a meaningful improvement in the economic environment."

Source: Based on a report in *The Wall Street Journal,* October 13, 1982, p. 6.

---

it can afford. But other things are not necessarily equal. An important third consideration is the stability of output. The more stable output is, the higher degree of financial leverage a company can undertake for any degree of operating leverage. The mix of variable and fixed costs is largely determined by the industry in which a company operates so that management must usually accept operating leverage as a given factor. Thus, electric light and power companies have very great operating leverage because a huge proportion of their costs are fixed costs, but output is so stable that they also can afford to finance about two-thirds of their assets with bonds. By contrast, producers of specialty steels (a highly cyclical industry) have such unstable output and large operating leverage that it is doubtful whether they should issue bonds at all. Thus, sales stability is the link between operating leverage and the degree of financial leverage advisable.

FINANCIAL LEVERAGE AND PREFERRED STOCK: A NOTE

Preferred stock financing affects combined leverage in the same way as debt financing: A preferred stock's dividend is a fixed financial cost that increases a company's degree of combined leverage. A small proportion of corporations use preferred stock financing, so the measure of combined leverage in this chapter is correct for most companies. Preferred's stock's leverage effect is discussed in Chapter 17.

This chapter presented several measures that help a financial manager determine a company's financial liquidity and leverage. After determining the company's present position, a manager is prepared to make plans for the company by forecasting and preparing budgets. The next chapter presents a discussion of how a manager prepares budgets that require a forecast of future events, that include an accurate measurement of the impact of changing activity levels, and that provide for effective control of operations.

SUMMARY

The equations presented in this chapter are in Table 14-2. You should refer to them as you read this summary.

1. Static measures of liquidity are the current ratio, net working capital, and the quick ratio. They suggest how able a company is to meet its short-term obligations. Liquidity measures must be interpreted by referring to the stage of the business cycle. Failing to do so may be misleading because the amount of credit, the value of income-producing securities, and the credit-worthiness of customers change over the business cycle.

2. Operating leverage is the power of changes in output to change net operating profit more than proportionally. Operating leverage results from paying fixed operating costs, and is measured by the degree of operating leverage that tells an analyst the percent change in net operating profit associated with a 1 percent change in output. The degree of operating leverage suggests a company's business risk because the greater the degree of operating leverage, the greater will be the likelihood that actual net operating profit will differ from its expected amount. Three important characteristics of a degree of operating leverage are the following:

a. A degree of operating leverage may be negative, which means that it is being calculated at a point where net operating income is negative.

b. The closer that output is to the break-even level, the greater will be a calculated degree of operating leverage.

c. Calculating and using the degree of operating leverage requires inventory and prices to remain constant so that changes in operating revenue are directly related to changes in activity.

3. Break-even analysis illustrates the degree of operating leverage because the break-even figure relates fixed and variable operating costs to net operating profit. The break-even point may be calculated with a company's unit contribution margin or its contribution margin ratio.

4. Financial leverage is the power of changes in net operating profit to change profit after taxes more than proportionally. Financial leverage results from paying interest expense, and it is measured by the degree of financial leverage that tells an analyst the percent change in profit after taxes associated with a 1 percent change in net operating profit. The degree of financial leverage suggests a company's financial risk because the greater the degree of financial leverage is, the greater will be the likelihood that actual profit after taxes will differ from its expected amount. Three

TABLE 14-2 Liquidity and Leverage Measures

Name	Equation	Meaning
Liquidity		
Current ratio	Current assets/ current liabilities	Measures a company's ability to pay current liabilities from current assets
Net working capital	Current assets − current liabilities	Measures the amount of current assets financed from long-term sources
Quick (acid test) ratio	(Current assets − inventory)/current liabilities	Indicates a company's ability to pay current liabilities after removing least liquid of current assets
Leverage		
Contribution margin	Sales − total variable costs	Indicates the amount of total and per unit operating revenue remaining after paying variable costs to contribute toward paying fixed costs
Unit contribution margin	Price − unit variable cost	
Contribution margin ratio	Contribution margin/total revenue Unit contribution margin/ price	Percent of total revenue or price available to contribute to paying fixed costs and profit
Degree of operating leverage	Contribution margin/net operating profit	Measures business risk by measuring the percent change in net operating profit associated with a 1 percent change in output
Degree of financial leverage	Net operating profit/ earnings before taxes	Measures financial risk by measuring the percent change in earnings after taxes associated with a 1 percent change in net operating profit
Degree of combined leverage	DOL × DFL	Measures the percent change in earnings after taxes associated with a 1 percent change in output
Debt ratio	Total debt/total assets	Measures the amount of debt as a percent of total assets
Debt-equity ratio	Total debt/equity	Measures the amount of debt as a percent of total assets
Times interest earned	Net operating profit/ interest expense	Tells analysts the company's ability to pay interest from operating profit

additional measures of financial leverage are the debt ratio, the debt-equity ratio, and the times-interest-earned ratio.

  5. Operating leverage and financial leverage combine to relate changes in output to changes in profit after taxes. The degree of combined leverage measures the percent change in profit after taxes associated with a 1 percent change in output. The degree of combined leverage is a measure of a company's total risk.

KEY TERMS AND CONCEPTS

Current ratio	Degree of operating leverage
Net working capital	Debt-equity ratio
Quick ratio	Debt ratio
Operating leverage	Times-interest-earned ratio
Contribution margin	Degree of financial leverage
Unit contribution margin	Degree of combined leverage
Break-even point	

QUESTIONS

14-1. Registrant Process Company has a 2.6 current ratio and $600,000 net working capital. Explain what each of these measures tells a financial manager and state what additional information you would need to determine whether each is favorable or unfavorable.

14-2. Discuss some of the changes in the strength of liquidity ratios over the business cycle.

14-3. If a company has a high current ratio but a low quick ratio, you can conclude that
  a. the company has a large outstanding accounts receivable balance.
  b. the company has a large investment in inventory.
  c. the company has a large amount of current liabilities.
  d. operating leverage is extremely high.
  e. the two ratios must be recalculated because both conditions cannot occur simultaneously.
  Explain why the answers not selected are unacceptable.

14-4. Operating leverage
  a. is useful for determining the approximate mix of short-term and long-term debt financing.
  b. indicates the extent to which net operating profit changes in response to a given change in output.
  c. depends on the amount of debt in the capital structure.
  d. increases as variable costs rise, all other things being equal.
  e. none of the above.

14-5. A company's degree of operating leverage differs at each output level used in its calculation.
  a. Explain at what output level the degree of operating leverage should be calculated and its usefulness as a planning tool to managers.
  b. What is the smallest degree of operating leverage that a company can have?
  c. What is the meaning of the sign attached to a calculated degree of operating leverage?

14-6. Break-even analysis uses the distinction between fixed and variable costs to measure the level of output at which a company will break even on its operations.

a. Explain the difference between fixed and variable costs.

b. How does an increase in interest expense affect a company's break-even point?

c. Write the equation for the break-even point in dollars and units.

14-7. Financial leverage ratios show creditors

a. the liquidity of the corporation's accounts receivable.

b. the value that investors place on the corporation's stock.

c. how efficiently the corporation utilizes its assets.

d. the margin of safety provided to the creditors by the stockholders.

e. the profitability of the corporation's sales.

Explain your choice.

14-8. CMA Examination (modified). Financial leverage results from using a source of funds for which the firm

a. pays a fixed dollar amount.

b. pays a fixed percentage of revenue.

c. earns a higher rate of return from its use than its cost.

d. pays a variable return on each dollar amount raised.

e. assumes no additional risk.

Explain why you did not select the other choices.

14-9. A company's degree of financial leverage is a useful measure to a financial manager. Explain how a degree of financial leverage is calculated, show its equation, and discuss why it is a useful number.

14-10. A company's degree of operating leverage and degree of financial leverage combine to cause proportionally larger changes in earnings before taxes as activity changes. Show the equation for combined leverage and comment on the way that a company with a high degree of combined leverage has a great deal of business and financial risk.

PROBLEMS

14-1. Below are the projected pro forma income statements and balance sheets for Passman Enterprises and Stransteel Company. Answer the following questions by referring to these statements.

Projected Income Statements
For the Fiscal Year Ended June 30, 19x6
(000 omitted)

	Passman Enterprises	Stransteel Company
Net sales	$4,000	$1,100
Cost and expenses		
Cost of goods sold	1,400	250
Selling expenses	1,000	200
General & administrative expenses	800	50
Interest expense	20	16
Income tax expense	300	200
Total costs and expenses	$3,520	$ 716
Net income	$ 480	$ 384

Projected Balance Sheets
June 30, 19x6
(000 omitted)

	Passman Enterprises	Stransteel Company
Assets		
Current assets (20% is inventory)	$1,000	$ 500
Property, plant, and equipment (net)	3,500	800
Other tangible assets	400	130
Patent (net)	100	20
Total assets	$5,000	$1,450
Liabilities and owner's equity		
Current liabilities	$ 800	$ 200
Long-term debt	1,000	130
Total liabilities	$1,800	$ 330
Common stock	$2,250[a]	$ 700[b]
Retained earnings	950	420
Total owners' equity	$3,200	$1,120
Total liabilities and owner's equity	$5,000	$1,450

[a]Represented by 2,250,000 shares outstanding at $1 par value.
[b]No par value, no stated value, 250,000 shares outstanding.

a. Calculate the current ratio, net working capital, and quick ratio for each company and interpret each value.
b. Which company is more liquid? Support your choice and point out additional information that you would find useful.
c. Would the stage of the business cycle affect your interpretation of the ratios in (a) above? Explain your answer.

14-2. The following financial statements are for the Avery Firearms Company.

Avery Firearms
Income Statements for the 12-Month Period Ending December 31
(thousands of dollars)

	19x3		19x4	
Sales Revenues		$28,000		$35,000
Less Total Costs				
Variable	$ 3,000		$ 3,750	
Fixed	13,000	16,000	13,000	16,750
Net operating profit		$12,000		$18,250
Less: Interest ($6,000 @ 10%)		600		600
		$11,400		$17,650
Less: Taxes (40%)		4,560		7,060
Profit after taxes		$ 6,840		$10,590

a. Calculate and interpret the contribution margin ratio for Avery Firearms.
b. Calculate and interpret the following at $28 million sales revenue:
   (1) Degree of operating leverage
   (2) Degree of financial leverage
   (3) Degree of combined leverage
c. Calculate the percentage change over the year in total revenue, net operating profit, and in profit before and after taxes. Are these changes consistent with the measures calculated in (b) above?

14-3. CMA Examination (modified). Selected year-end data for the Bayer company are presented below:

Current liabilities	$600,000
Quick ratio	2.5
Current ratio	3.0
Cost of sales	$500,000

   Bayer Company's inventory turnover ratio based upon this year-end data is
a. 1.20
b. 2.40
c. 1.67
d. Some amount other than those given above.
e. Not determinable from the data given.
Explain your choice by showing calculations.

14-4. The following information applies to Griffith Telechron and Electronics:

Sales	19x1	19x2
Units	90,000	100,000
Revenues	$450,000	$500,000
Less		
Variable selling and production costs		
($4.50 each)	$405,000	$450,000
Fixed costs		
Selling and administrative	8,000	8,000
Depreciation	22,000	22,000
Net operating profit	$ 15,000	$ 20,000
Less interest	4,000	4,000
Profit before taxes	$ 11,000	$ 16,000
Less taxes (40%)	4,400	6,400
Profit after taxes	$ 6,600	$ 9,600

a. Calculate the contribution margin and contribution margin ratio for GTE.
b. Calculate the degrees of operating, financial, and combined leverage for GTE at sales levels in 19x1 and in 19x2.
c. Interpret your calculations in part (b). Why is the degree of operating leverage different at each sales and activity level?
d. Calculate and interpret the break-even point in dollars.

14-5. The Orestes Company has income statement and balance sheet amounts as follows:

Income Statement Variables (all in thousands)

Depreciation	$ 1,000
Cost of goods sold	4,000
Sales revenue	10,000
Interest expense	600
Selling and administrative expense	1,000
Taxes (40%)	—
Preferred dividend	500

Balance Sheet Variables (all in thousands)

Long-term debt	$ 4,000
Accounts receivable	3,000
Accounts payable	2,000
Total common shareholders' equity	8,000
Gross fixed assets	9,000
Inventory	4,000
Cash	1,000
Accumulated depreciation	3,000
Preferred shares (1.5 million shares with a $1 par value)	

a. Complete an income statement and balance sheet for Orestes Company. Label each component.

b. Calculate and interpret the following:
(1) Net operating profit margin
(2) Profit margin after taxes
(3) Return on assets
(4) Return on common equity

c. Orestes has 300,000 shares of common stock outstanding and paid dividends of $500,000 to preferred stockholders. The company paid a $540,000 dividend on common stock. Calculate the following:
(1) Earnings per share of common stock
(2) Dividends per share of common and preferred

d. What additional information would you need in order to comment on whether Orestes' ratios are good or bad?

14-6. P.R. Deltoid, Inc., a maker of oil drilling supplies, has experienced a steady growth in sales for the past five years. However, increased competition has led Pat Deltoid, the company's president, to believe that an aggressive advertising campaign will be necessary next year to maintain the company's present growth rate. To prepare for next year's advertising campaign the company's management accountant has prepared and presented the following budget for the current year, 19x7:

Variable Costs

Direct labor	$ 8.00 per pipe
Direct materials	3.25 per pipe
Variable overhead	2.50 per pipe
Total variable costs	$13.75

Fixed Costs

Manufacturing	$ 25,000
Selling and advertising	40,000
Depreciation	70,000

Total fixed costs $135,000

Selling price, per pipe	$25.00
Expected sales (19x7)	$500,000
Tax rate	40 percent

Mr. Deltoid has set the target sales for 19x8 at a level of $550,000 (or 22,000 pipes).
a. Calculate the projected net operating profit for 19x7.
b. What is the break-even point in units and dollars for 19x7?
c. What is the break-even point in dollars in 19x8 if the company plans to increase fixed costs by spending an additional $11,250 for advertising?

14-7. Using the income statement and balance-sheet amounts that you prepared in problem 5, calculate and explain the following ratios for the Orestes Company:
a. turnover of accounts receivable
b. average collection period
c. inventory turnover

14-8. Warford Corporation was formed five years ago through a public sale of common stock. Prissy Street, who owns 15 percent of the common stock, was one of the organizers of Warford and is its current president. The company has been successful, but currently is experiencing a cash shortage. On June 10, 19x2, Street approached the Bell National Bank, asking for a 24-month extension on two $30,000 notes, which are due on June 30, 19x2 and September 30, 19x2. Another note of $7,000 is due on December 31, 19x2, but she expects no difficulty in paying this note on its due date. Street explained that Warford's cash-flow problems are due primarily to the company's desire to finance a $300,000 plant expansion over the next two fiscal years through retaining earnings after taxes.

The Commercial Loan Officer of Bell National Bank requested financial reports for the two most recent fiscal years. These reports are reproduced below.

Warford Corporation
Income Statement
For the Fiscal Years Ended March 31

	19x1	19x2
Sales	$2,700,000	$3,000,000
Cost of goods sold	1,720,000	1,902,500
Gross margin	$ 980,000	1,097,500
Operating expenses	780,000	845,000
Net operating profit	$ 200,000	$ 252,500
Less interest expense	6,540	8,040
Earnings before taxes	$ 193,460	$ 244,460
Less taxes (46%)	88,992	112,452
Earnings after taxes	$ 104,468	$ 132,008

Warford Corporation
Balance Sheet
March 31

	19x1	19x2
Assets		
Cash	$ 12,500	$ 16,400
Notes receivable	104,000	112,000
Accounts receivable (net)	68,500	81,600
Inventories (at cost)	50,000	80,000
Plant and equipment (net of depreciation)	646,000	680,000
Total assets	$ 881,000	$ 970,000
Liabilities and owners' equity		
Accounts payable	$ 72,000	$ 69,000
Notes payable	54,500	67,000
Long-term liabilities	6,000	9,000
Common stock (60,000 shares, $10 par)	600,000	600,000
Retained earnings[a]	148,500	225,000
Total liabilities and owners' equity	$ 881,000	$ 970,000

[a]Cash dividends were paid at the rate of $1.00 per share in fiscal year 19x1 and $1.25 per share in fiscal year 19x2.

    a. Calculate the following items for Warford Corporation:
        (1) Current ratio for fiscal years 19x1 and 19x2.
        (2) Quick ratio for fiscal years 19x1 and 19x2.
        (3) Inventory turnover for fiscal year 19x2.
        (4) Return on assets for fiscal years 19x1 and 19x2.
    b. What additional information would you need in order to comment on Warford Corporation's financial performance based on the amounts that you calculated in part (a) above?
    c. Warford Corporation's cost accountant determines that fixed costs included in each year amounts are $460,000 in cost of goods sold and $160,000 in operating expenses. Use this information to calculate the degree of combined leverage at $3 million sales.

CHAPTER 15
Financial Planning and Control

PLANNING
Forecasting Financial Needs

SUITABILITY
Long- and Short-Term Needs · **Violating Suitability: The Dangers**

AVAILABILITY AND COST

CONTROL
Profit Centers and Responsibility · **Accountability** · **The Exception Principle**

TREASURER AND CONTROLLER FUNCTIONS

SUMMARY
Key Terms and Concepts · **Questions** · **Problems**

The previous chapters in this part of the book have explained the tasks of a financial manager and detailed the way that a manager uses financial reports to calculate a company's leverage, profitability, liquidity, and activity. Now, we turn our attention to the way that a manager makes decisions regarding a company's financial needs. Specifically, this chapter looks at the way a manager determines the amount of finance (debt and equity) the company needs and the appropriate source of finance to use.

The first part of this chapter discusses a method to forecast a company's financial needs. Called the percent-of-sales method, it relies on the forecast of a company's sales and automatic sources of finance to tell a financial manager the amount of external finance that a company will need. When you finish reading about the percent-of-sales method, you will be able to calculate a company's financial needs for a future period. The next part of the chapter deals with some of the items that a financial manager must consider when deciding on which sources of external finance to use. When you finish reading this part of the chapter you will be familiar with the principle of suitability and the dangers associated with violating the principle, and with the role that availability and cost of capital play in influencing the selection of external finance.

The final part of the chapter considers the need for financial control in a company. After reading about control, you will understand the way that control is implemented with profit centers and improved with the exception principle.

As Chapter 11 emphasized, modern business planning is *profit-planning*, and a profit plan always requires an accompanying financial plan. But plans are fruitless without effective controls to see that they are implemented. Thus planning and control are readily identified as major responsibilities of the financial manager.

Planning involves setting goals, identifying resource needs, forecasting events that lie beyond a company's control, and establishing a scheme of action that harmonizes both with these events and with the company's purposes.

Control involves the use of budgets to state a company's plan in detail. Results are then measured against budgeted objectives to see how performance has conformed with objectives. Finally, purposeful action is taken to correct deviations and deficiencies.

PLANNING

Necessarily, the financial manager is largely absorbed in day-to-day problems. But handling these problems will be orderly and effective only if there is an overall plan. This plan may be nebulous and inexact, suiting managers who prefer great flexibility, or concrete and specific, suiting those who emphasize detailed planning. But its main outlines and requirements should be clear to the manager working from day to day.

A plan begins with an objective and purpose. A business may set its 19x3 goal as a 20 percent sales gain and a 25 percent increase in after-tax profits. But however ambitious, one's objective must always be attainable. Judging the feasibility of an objective depends on a correct forecast of two factors: (1) the resources needed to reach the objective and (2) the business and other conditions that will prevail over the term of the plan.

Forecasting Financial Needs

Using sales to forecast financial needs is called the percent-of-sales forecasting method.[1] The percent-of-sales forecasting method is not intended to be precise or to be the only step in determining future financial needs. However, it has the distinct virtues of being (1) easily understood and communicated to operating managers and to a company's creditors and (2) quickly calculated. The method begins by relating sales to total assets; then total assets are related to financial needs. The final step in the forecasting procedure is to measure the need for external finance, debt and new common stock. It is important to forecast the amount of external finance needed because a company must usually make arrangements to acquire it far in advance of the time when it is actually needed.

The percent-of-sales forecasting method assumes that total assets will remain a constant percent of sales. A financial manager forecasts total assets by multiplying the forecast amount of sales by the historical ratio of total assets to sales. For exam-

---

[1] Some managers use regression analysis to forecast financial needs.

BOX 15-1
Slow Economic Growth and Increased
Competition Will Make Forecasting in the
1980s Difficult   Forecasting a company's sales, profit, and financial needs will probably be more difficult in the 1980s than in the 1960s and 1970s. The
reason that many financial managers feel this way is their anticipation that the
inflation-fighting resolve of the Federal Reserve and the Reagan Administration will
restrict growth in the money supply and in the economy. Any expansionary fiscal
policy (taxing and spending by the federal government) will be unable to overcome
the force of a restrictive monetary policy.

In the 1960s and 1970s "demand was in the air," said John Welch, chairman of
General Electric Company. "We needed managers to control growth, to direct it."
Productivity and economic growth began to falter in the late 1970s, but rising inflation hid this slowdown for a while as companies still found it easy to pay big wage
increases, to raise prices, and to show profits. In the 1980s many companies "won't
find growth" in their industries, Mr. Welch predicts. Instead, he says, successful
companies must "make growth happen—that's the only way out of a slow-growth
environment." Mr. Welch adopted a market share orientation for GE: He wants GE
sales to grow so that its products rank either first or second in market share in all 250
lines of its business.

Although the principles of successful management don't change much from
decade to decade, slower growth and a more competitive environment that many
executives foresee in the 1980s will make forecasting sales and financial needs more
difficult and more important. Increasingly, the qualities of entrepreneurial vision,
numbered-minded operational efficiency, and bold marketing necessary for success
aren't likely to be the interests or skills of any one person in a company. As corporate growth becomes more challenging, you can expect to see a greater emphasis on
team management.

Source: Based on Kenneth H. Bacon, "Managing the 1980s Won't Be Easy Task," *The Wall Street Journal,* September 20, 1982, p. 1.

---

ple, if total assets have been 70 percent of sales, then total assets are expected to be
$70,000 if sales are forecast to be $100,000. The method to calculate total assets is

$$\text{Forecast total assets} = \frac{\text{total assets}}{\text{sales}} \times \text{forecast sales}$$

We must exercise care in using the percent-of-sales method to forecast future
assets because changes may overturn formerly stable relationships: Better management control may reduce inventories as a percent of sales, or the average collection
period may change. Fixed assets may rise as a percent of sales because computers

are acquired to control inventories. In addition, fixed assets, like factory buildings or large machines, grow in lumps, increasing only after an increase in sales, but not falling when sales fall.

Example. An example will clarify this forecasting procedure. In 19x1 the Dalton Company had a profit margin after taxes of 2 percent (the ratio of earnings after taxes to sales). Sales were $200,000 and the Dalton Company directors pay a dividend equal to 30 percent of earnings. Management expects the 2 percent profit margin to persist during the coming year.

Table 15-1 shows the ratio of each asset to the year's 19x1 sales calculated by the financial manager. The percent-of-sales method to forecast assets requires that the financial manager note the following: For every $1 of sales, there are 37.5 cents of assets; for every $1 *change* in sales, assets will *change* by 37.5 cents; for every percent change in sales, assets must change by the same percent in order for the ratio of total assets to sales to remain constant.

Now, suppose that the marketing manager forecasts 19x2 sales to be $220,000, a 10 percent increase from 19x1's $200,000 sales. Dalton's total assets will also be expected to increase by 10 percent to $75,000 $\times$ 1.10 = $82,500, because a 10 percent increase in assets will leave the ratio of total assets to sales constant at $82,500/$220,000 = 0.375. Dalton Company needs new assets totaling $7,500:

Expected 19x2 total assets	$82,500
Less 19x1 total assets	75,000
Expected change in assets	$7,500

TABLE 15–1 Assets and Claims as a Percent of Total Sales

		Percent Of Sales
Assets		
Cash	$ 4,000	$ 4,000/$200,000 = 0.020
Securities	2,000	$ 2,000/$200,000 = 0.010
Accounts receivable	8,000	$ 8,000/$200,000 = 0.040
Inventory	11,000	$11,000/$200,000 = 0.055
Plant and equipment		
(net of depreciation)	50,000	$50,000/$200,000 = 0.250
Total	$75,000	$75,000/$200,000 = 0.375
Liabilities and Shareholders' Equity		
Accounts payable	$10,000	$10,000/$200,000 = 0.050
Taxes payable	4,000	$4,000/$200,000 = 0.020
Bonds	28,000	$28,000/$200,000 = 0.140
Shareholders' equity		
Common stock	14,000	$14,000/$200,000 = 0.070
Retained earnings	19,000	$19,000/$200,000 = 0.095
Total	$75,000	$75,000/$200,000 = 0.375

Once assets have been forecast, the next step is to forecast specific sources of finance. Some sources of finance are *automatic*—that is, they tend to increase by the same percent as sales. Automatic sources (sometimes called spontaneous sources) are accounts payable and taxes payable. Accounts payable are automatic because trade credit is usually granted automatically. And purchases are usually closely related with sales so that as sales rise, purchases increase and with them accounts payable. We consider taxes payable to be automatic because of the following assumptions: (1) the profit margin before taxes is constant, (2) the tax rate does not change, and (3) the company follows the same tax payment policy in the future that it has followed in the past. A financial manager calculates the expected level of automatic sources by using the percentage change in sales because automatic sources change by the same percent as sales.

The Dalton Company needs $7,500 in new financing by the end of 19x2, the same amount as the dollar change in total assets. Its two automatic sources (accounts payable and taxes payable) increase by the same percent as sales, 10 percent. If that is the case, accounts payable will increase to 1.10 × $10,000 = $11,000 and taxes payable will increase to 1.10 × $4,000 = $4,400. Table 15-2 and the calculations below show that these sources will provide $1,400 in finance:

Ending Expected Amounts
    Accounts Payable $11,000
    Taxes Payable   4,400
                                  $15,400

Less Beginning Amounts (See Table 15–1):
    Accounts payable $10,000
    Taxes payable   4,000
                                  14,000
    Supplied from automatic sources $ 1,400.

A financial manager must be alert to the possibility that these automatic sources may not continue to be a constant percent of sales. The only way that the ratio between automatic sources and sales (10 percent in the Dalton Company example) will remain constant is for the following items to remain unchanged: the tax rate, the ratio of cost of goods sold to sales, the average payment period, and the

TABLE 15–2 Automatic Financial Sources

(1) Source	(2) Percent of Sales	(2) × $20,000 = (3) Amount Provided
Accounts payable	0.05	$1,000
Taxes payable	0.02	400
Total	0.07	$1,400

method used to calculate taxable earnings. A change in any of these items will alter the ratio and overturn the forecast.

The difference between $7,500 total financial needs for the Dalton Company calculated above and the $1,400 supplied from automatic sources is $6,100. This amount must be provided by (1) the change in retained earnings (called internal equity) and (2) external sources. The dollar change in retained earnings is the company's earnings after taxes less the common-stock dividend. For the Dalton Company the expected earnings after taxes are 2 percent of the forecast $220,000 sales, or $4,400. The company's dividend of 30 percent of earnings after taxes is subtracted to leave the amount of finance provided from retained earnings:

Expected earnings after taxes (0.02 × $220,000)	$4,400
Less dividend (0.30 × $4,400)	1,320
Provided from the change in retained earnings (internal equity)	$3,080

Now, the financial manager calculates external finance needed in 19x2 by subtracting from total financial needs the financing furnished by automatic sources and by internal equity. For Dalton Company external finance must supply $3,020:

Total needs	$7,500
Less automatic sources	1,400
Remaining needs	$6,100
Less change in retained earnings	3,080
External needs	$3,020

Acquiring external finance typically requires a financial manager's preparation and time before it can be accomplished. For example, bonds, commercial paper, new common stock, and bank loans require knowledge, effort, costs, and time to acquire.

Table 15-3 is a worksheet for use in estimating the amount of external finance needed by a company. The procedure illustrated there consists of the following steps:

1. Estimate the expected percent change in sales for the forecast period. This change is calculated in step 1. The same percentage change will occur in total assets and in automatic sources of finance.
2. Use the percent change from step 1 to calculate the expected *dollar* change in total assets. Step 2 shows this calculation. This amount is the amount of new finance needed from debt and equity sources.
3. Use the percentage change in sales that you calculated in step 1 to measure the expected dollar change in the two automatic sources: accounts payable and taxes payable. Step 3 shows this measure.
4. Subtract the amount of automatic financing that you measured in step 3 from the amount of total financing needed calculated in step 2. This difference is the amount of needed finance remaining.
5. Estimate the change in retained earnings you expected over the period. The esti-

---

TABLE 15–3 Worksheet to Estimate External Finance Needed by the Dalton Company

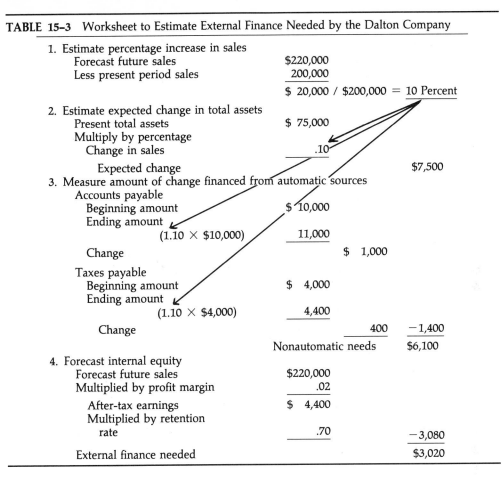

1. Estimate percentage increase in sales
   Forecast future sales $220,000
   Less present period sales   200,000
                                    $ 20,000 / $200,000 = 10 Percent

2. Estimate expected change in total assets
   Present total assets $ 75,000
   Multiply by percentage
     Change in sales   .10
       Expected change $7,500
3. Measure amount of change financed from automatic sources
   Accounts payable
     Beginning amount $ 10,000
     Ending amount
       (1.10 × $10,000)   11,000
     Change $ 1,000

   Taxes payable
     Beginning amount $ 4,000
     Ending amount
       (1.10 × $4,000)   4,400
     Change   400   − 1,400
                                    Nonautomatic needs $6,100
4. Forecast internal equity
   Forecast future sales $220,000
   Multiplied by profit margin   .02
     After-tax earnings $ 4,400
     Multiplied by retention
       rate   .70   − 3,080
       External finance needed $3,020

---

mated amount is the total level of forecast sales in step 1 multiplied by the after-tax profit margin and less any dividends. Step 4 of Table 15-3 makes this estimate.
6. Subtract the dollar amount of internal equity that you expect over the period (the change in retained earnings) estimated in step 5 from the amount of finance needed measured in step 4. The difference is the estimate of external finance needed over the period.

SUITABILITY

On what basis should the financial manager of Dalton Company decide the source of the $3,020? The most important yardstick is *suitability*. Suitability (sometimes called *financial matching*) means financing permanent asset requirements from long-term debt or equity sources and temporary asset needs from short-term sources. Suitability is a principle of symmetry, or time balancing, between sources and uses of funds. The consideration of suitability raises two issues. (1) What actually constitutes long- and short-term uses of funds? (2) What dangers do companies incur by violating suitability?

Long- and Short-Term Needs

Clearly, the growth of a company's fixed assets imposes a permanent financing need. These assets are long-lived, essential to operation of the enterprise, and illiquid. Therefore, they should be financed from long-term debt or equity sources so that no renewal problem will arise.

Fixed assets, however, do not represent a company's only requirement for permanent financing. Although current assets are short-lived and liquid, their level can never fall to zero. Even at the lowest point of the sales year or business cycle, some inventory and receivables are needed. Moreover, no company can afford to run completely out of cash. Thus, at the lowest point of a company's activity, an *irreducible minimum* of current assets must remain in the business. And since it must remain, it, like fixed assets, should be financed from long-term debt or equity sources.

On the other hand, a substantial part of a company's current-asset needs is temporary. Inventories and receivables have large bulges at seasonal peaks or during business booms. They shrink back again at seasonal low points or during recessions. This changing component of current-asset needs should not be financed from long-term sources. The need for funds is temporary, and the company will minimize the investment on which earnings are required if it raises these funds from sources that permit their retirement when the need is past.

Figure 15-1 illustrates the principle of suitability operating through time. It shows a firm's fixed assets growing by lumps, its permanent current-assets requirement rising steadily as the company itself grows. Both these types of assets should be financed from permanent sources. The wavy line in Figure 15-1 permanent cur-

FIGURE 15-1 Temporary and permanent uses and sources.

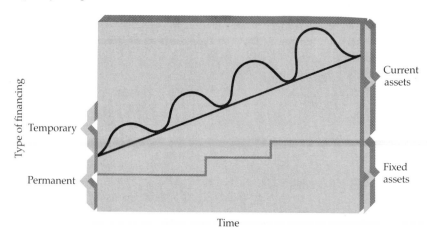

BOX 15-2
Some Companies Use a Worst-Case
Method in Their Planning

One method to avoid over-optimism in financial planning is to forecast a company's performance based on pessimistic forecasts of output. The key here is to think negative.

Here's the way that management may implement the worst-case method: After forecasting a pessimistic level of sales, we then estimate expenses for the planning period based on the company's variable-cost ratio, the ratio of variable costs per unit divided by the price of each unit of output. We assume that the variable cost ratio will remain constant and so reduce variable costs proportionally with the projected decrease in sales revenue: A 40 percent drop in sales is associated with a 40 percent drop in variable costs. We increase fixed operating costs to cover the increased current replacement costs of resources, then complete the worst-case method by subtracting total costs from the pessimistic sales level.

That may not be the extent of the bad news because a company should make enough profit to cover its interest expense and to please shareholders. To provide for these conditions, the worst-case method includes a reasonable profit figure by using some reasonable net operating return on equity (net operating profit divided by shareholders' equity) to calculate the company's minimally acceptable net operating profit.

Suppose that a company's management forecast a $500,000 negative net operating profit before considering the company's targeted profit level. If the company had $1.5 million shareholders' equity and a reasonable net operating return on equity is 20 percent, then its targeted net operating profit was $1,500,000 × 0.20 = $300,000. That meant a $500,000 + $300,000 = $800,000 total loss on targeted net operating profit. Management must cut costs, raise prices, or both to the extent of $500,000 in order to break even on its operations and to the extent of $800,000 to make its targeted net operating profit.

---

rent-assets requirements shows the firm's temporary needs for current assets. Because these needs occasionally fall to some minimum amount, they should be met from temporary sources.

Violating Suitability: The Dangers

Observing suitability helps the financial manager maintain two important goals: liquidity and profitability. Conversely, violations of suitability expose a company to illiquidity on one side and low profitability on the other. Let us now see what mistakes the financial manager must avoid in selecting external sources of finance.

Losing Liquidity. Suppose a company buys a piece of capital equipment, perhaps a turret lathe with a five-year life, and finances the purchase with a one-year note for $75,000 at the bank. The company's liquidity immediately suffers in two ways. First, its liquidity ratios (current, quick, and working capital) decline. Its borrowing power and credit-worthiness are thus undermined. Second, cash has been sunk in a fixed asset, yet the cash itself is due for repayment within one year.

With good luck, the company may get the bank to renew the loan, though the bank will be violating the key principle of sound banking by supplying its depositor with short-term funds for a long-term purpose. But suppose the bank is unwilling or unable to renew the loan. Then the borrower will be forced to pay it off. How? Where will it raise the money? If it cannot find another lender, and cannot raise cash from its other assets, it will be forced to default on the loan and likely to announce bankruptcy. This is often the penalty for those who "borrow short and invest long," as all too many companies did to their sorrow in 1981–1982.

Since the late 1970s violation of suitability has been the most common financial mistake made by American corporations. Hoping that trends toward costlier long-term funds would be reversed, too many financial managers have taken a chance. They have borrowed heavily at short term to finance fixed assets and permanent additions to net working capital. They have done this expecting that long-term rates would fall and thus enable them to do their long-term financing at lower cost. But they have guessed wrong. Through late 1984, the cost of equity and of long-term debt capital had fallen very little from peak levels. Meanwhile, an ever-growing volume of short-term borrowing had repeatedly driven short-term interest rates high, forcing bankers and other short-term lenders to ration loans. Many businesses have found themselves overextended, their credit standing destroyed. No longer able either to borrow long term or to get their short-term loans renewed, these businesses have been forced into bankruptcy. Adherence to suitability would have avoided much of this difficulty and loss.

Losing Profitability. An opposite mistake regarding suitability can impair a company's profitability. This mistake consists of financing temporary needs from permanent sources—for example, selling new stock or a 25-year bond to finance a seasonal rise in inventory. Such financing will improve a firm's liquidity because current assets (inventories) rise with no corresponding climb in short-term liabilities. But while current ratio and working capital both increase, profitability falls. It falls because, while the earning power of the newly acquired funds lasts only part of the year (the time when it is gainfully invested in inventories), the investment on which the company must earn a return is permanently enlarged. A look at the Du Pont model explained in Chapter 13 will show you that when new investment in a company can be made to earn a return only part of the year, the ROA is bound to fall.

Stated differently, once the peak inventory season passes, the funds will sit around as idle cash or as low-earning temporary investments. But interest payments on the bonds, or dividends on the stock, by which the funds were raised, will continue. By contrast, if the temporary rise in inventory had been met from short-term sources, the money could have been repaid to the lender when no longer needed. The company's assets would shrink with repayment.

One other consideration arises. A normal yield curve tells us that long-term loans ordinarily cost more than short-term loans. A six-month loan may cost 6 percent, but a 10-year one, 9 percent. Again, management should seek to avoid the more expensive long-term sources of funds if it is borrowing for a short-term purpose.

AVAILABILITY AND COST

In addition to suitability, availability and cost of finance play unavoidable parts in deciding what external financing sources to tap. If no long-term sources of finance are available, or the yield curve is inverted so that long-term rates are below short-term rates (suggesting that all future rates will be lower) management should violate the principle of suitability.

Planning—looking ahead—is the only way to protect a business from unavailable or prohibitively costly funds. If its managers foresee what the company's financial requirement will be, then they can often acquire the funds in advance of need, thereby ensuring their availability or acceptable cost.

Planning is based on a forecast of sales, and it combines the decision concerning what assets to acquire with the decision about how the assets will be financed. So constituted, it serves as a managerial framework to optimize choices and minimize the chance of a crisis. A well-planned financial program cannot guarantee the absence of crises—a shortage of cash may still develop from lost sales due to a wildcat strike, for example—but it does ensure that damage from such mishaps will be minimized.

CONTROL

A profit plan is a reasonably precise statement of the steps and resources by which a company's goals for present and future years will be achieved. But to keep operations and performance aligned with this plan, effective control is indispensable. Because the guiding framework of the plan—profit—is financial, the basis of control is also financial: the money yardstick (return on investment, or ROA) is the chief measure of managerial performance.

How is the ROA criterion applied? Chapter 13 suggests the answer: If return on investment is the product of profit margin times investment turnover, then the key to financial control lies in various relations centered in the Du Pont method. How adequate is the profit margin—the spread between price and cost? Are enough sales being generated for the investment? How effective is the utilization of various assets—cash, inventory, receivables, fixed assets—as measured by their turnover? Are manufacturing costs too high? Is the company getting too low a price for its product? Is sufficient order volume per sales call being generated? Is telephone expense too high in relation to business volume? This list of questions could be amplified almost endlessly, but each would relate in some way to one of four main criteria of the company's operating and financial performance: profitability, turnover, liquidity, and leverage.

Profit Centers and Responsibility

Modern methods of financial control typically reflect two features of company organization: (1) division of a company into profit centers and (2) pushing profit responsibility as far down into management ranks as possible.

A segment of a company is a profit center if it has authority to make decisions affecting the major determinants of profit, including the power to choose its own markets and sources of supply.

Example. A $20 million company might divide its investment into eight sections. It might allocate $3 million of its investment to the manager of Division C, requiring her to earn 12 percent after taxes ($360,000) in the coming year.

Managers with profit-center responsibility typically enjoy wide authority and discretion over the specific steps through which they attain their goals.

Pushing profit responsibility down into management ranks means that each higher manager delegates, as far as possible, a part of overall profit responsibility to subordinates.

Example. The manager of Division C may allocate to each of her three product managers $1 million of the $3 million investment for which she is responsible. Each product manager would then be held responsible for earning 12 percent ($120,000) on the investment committed to his charge. In this way, even subordinate managers receive direct responsibility for generating profit on the firm's investment: their compensation is likely to depend heavily on their ability to meet earnings targets.

Companies may employ either fixed or variable budgets. A *fixed budget* is rigidly based on a given sales forecast and makes no allowances for deviations beyond a manager's control. *Variable budgets,* by contrast, gear expected results to different levels of activity. If, for example, a company's sales volume was less than expected, the vice-president in charge of manufacturing would be allowed a higher cost per unit of output, since there would be fewer units to absorb plant overhead.

Operating managers commit themselves to profit goals through budgets, which are accounting-type blueprints of intended performance. The financial manager must then measure each manager's performance with respect to his own budget, and report the degree of success or failure to the manager and to superiors. A company's accounting system, if properly designed and administered, provides an immense range of information about each manager's performance. In preparing the reports, the financial manager's chief problem is to select those data that are (1) relevant to measuring a given manager's performance and (2) understandable to those for whom they are intended.

How can the financial manager make these reports relevant and effective? By following the two principles of *accountability* and *exception.*

Accountability

Reports going to a particular manager should generally include only those matters for which that manager is accountable. A district sales manager, for example, might be measured each month on such matters as unit sales volume, prices obtained, sales mix, sales salary expense, travel expense, telephone expense, average revenue per salesperson, average revenue per sales call, and so on. Performance on each criterion would be measured against planned operations for the period—against sales and expense budgets.

The Exception Principle

The exception principle is an instance of the familiar saying "The squeaky wheel should get the grease." The focus of reports organized on this principle is on deviations from set standards or from planned (budgeted) performance. Large variances from planned results are red-flagged to the lower-level manager directly responsible, and only these exceptions to satisfactory performance are brought to the attention of higher management. A manager's superior thus wastes no time reviewing those aspects of performance that are in line. The subordinate's remedial action or followup on red-flagged items is reported to, and checked by, the boss.

In the example above, the district sales manager might have met or surpassed all but two of her budgeted goals: salary expense was above, and average revenue per sales call below, budgeted levels. The division manager would ask her to explain why. The explanation might be that, because of promotion and retirements, the sales manager's district had several new sales representatives on the job who were not yet fully productive. This explanation might be entirely acceptable, but at least higher management would have investigated what could have been a symptom of more serious trouble.

TREASURER AND CONTROLLER FUNCTIONS

Who handles the functions of financial planning and control? In smaller companies it is usually one person, often the president or owner. The larger the company is, the more likely these functions will be divided between a treasurer and a controller.

Table 15-4 presents a detailed view of treasurer and controller functions. As you can see, the *controller function* is concerned primarily with selecting appropriate assets, measuring operations, and presenting results in a form meaningful and useful to management. To a great extent it is an internal function. The *treasurer function* is, broadly speaking, concerned with identifying the best sources of finance to utilize in the business and timing the acquisition of funds. Its focus is largely external.

Another way of looking at these functions is this: The controller function generally concentrates on the asset (debit) side of the balance sheet and the investment decision, while the treasurer function concentrates on the claims (credit) side and the financial decision.

SUMMARY

1. The percent-of-sales forecasting method is a way to forecast a company's need for external finance. It begins with a forecast of sales, then assumes that assets

TABLE 15-4 Controller and Treasurer Functions

Controller

Planning for control. To establish, coordinate, and administer a plan for the control of operations. The plan provides for profit-planning programs for capital expenditures and expense budgets.

Reporting and interpreting. To compare actual and expected operating plans and report and interpret the results to all levels of management and to the company's owners. To consult with management about the financial implications of its actions.

Tax administration. To establish and administer tax policies and procedures.

Government reporting. To supervise and coordinate the preparation of reports to government agencies.

Protection of assets. To assure protection of assets through a system of internal control and internal auditing.

Economic appraisal. To forecast and evaluate economic and social forces and government influences, and to interpret their impact on the company.

Treasurer

Providing finance. To establish and implement programs for providing the debt and equity the company needs, calculating its cost, acquiring it, and maintaining the necessary arrangements.

Investor relations. To establish and maintain a market for the company's securities and to maintain contact with investors.

Short-term financing. To maintain adequate sources for the company's short-term borrowing.

Banking and custody. To maintain banking arrangements. To receive and disburse the company's money and securities and manage its real estate transactions.

Credits and collections. To direct the granting of credit and the collection of amounts due the company.

Investments. To invest excess cash.

Insurance. To provide necessary insurance coverage.

and financial needs will increase at the same rate as sales. A financial manager assumes that automatic (or spontaneous) sources increase at the same rate as sales and assets. Automatic sources are taxes payable and accounts payable. The next step in the percent-of-sales method is to forecast the amount of internal financing that will be available. Internal financing is earnings after taxes less dividends, or the change in retained earnings. External financial needs are

Total needs		xxxxxxx
Less automatic and internal sources		
Automatic sources	xxxx	
Change in retained earnings	xxxx	
		xxxxx
External needs		
		xxx

2. A financial manager uses the principle of suitability to select external sources. Suitability (sometimes called financial matching) means a time symmetry between sources and uses of finance so that long-term uses are financed with long-term sources and short-term uses are financed with short-term sources. Violating the principle may cause the company to lose liquidity or profitability.

3. Availability and cost of capital are also important in determining the source of external finance. When costs are extremely high in one market (for example, the bond market) financial managers turn to sources other than those dictated by the principle of suitability. In addition, if an appropriate source of finance is not available, then a financial manager must turn to a source that may not be consistent with the principle of suitability.

4. Control is the way that a manager makes sure that a profit plan is implemented successfully, and if it is not, then a well-developed control system helps the manager to find the reasons. Control is implemented with profit centers so that each area of a company is responsible for generating an acceptable return on its assets. Managers examine deviations from budgeted profit only when the deviations are exceptional. This method of control is called management by exception.

KEY TERMS AND CONCEPTS

Profit planning
Sales forecast
Percent-of-sales method
Automatic sources
External financial needs
Treasurer and controller functions

Suitability
Permanent current assets
Profit center
Exception principle
Control

QUESTIONS

15-1. The percent-of-sales method helps a financial manager to estimate the company's external financial needs. Explain what *external needs* are and why it is important to forecast them.

15-2. Consider the following statement: "The percent-of-sale forecasting method assumes that sales, total assets, total sources, and automatic sources of finance change by the same dollar amount." Do you agree with this statement? Explain your answer.

15-3. CMA Examination (modified). Working-capital policy raises questions that relate both to a company's profitability and liquidity. Which one of the following statements would most accurately describe financial relationships if it were aggressively pursuing high profits?
a. The company would probably have a high ratio of current assets to total assets and a high ratio of long-term debt to total debt.
b. The company would probably have a low ratio of current assets to total assets and a low ratio of current liabilities to total debt.
c. It would probably have a low ratio of fixed assets to total assets and a low ratio of current liabilities to total debt.
d. The company would probably have a high ratio of fixed assets to total assets and a high ratio of current liabilities to total debt.

e. None of the above responses accurately describes the financial relationships of a company aggressively pursuing high profits.

Explain your choice.

15-4. Suppose a marketing manager forecasts a 12 percent increase in sales, but the actual increase is 18 percent. How would that affect the financial manager's ability to acquire the needed finance?

15-5. An important source of finance for a company is its automatic sources. Explain what the automatic sources are and why financial managers call them automatic.

15-6. Explain what the suitability principle is and discuss the implications of violating the principle by
  a. using long-term sources to finance short-term uses.
  b. using short-term sources to finance long-term uses.

15-7. Consider the following comment: "The principle of suitability should never be violated." Do you agree? Explain your answer.

15-8. A segment of a company is a profit center if it has
  a. authority to make decisions affecting the major determinants of profit, including the power to choose its markets and sources of supply.
  b. authority to make decisions affecting the major determinants of profit, including the power to choose its market and sources of supply and significant control over the amount of invested capital.
  c. authority to make decisions over the most significant costs of operations, including the power to choose the sources of supply.
  d. authority to provide specialized support to other units within the organization.
  e. responsibility for combining the raw materials, direct labor, and other factors of production into a final output.

15-9. Management implements a system of controls by determining profit centers and using the exception principle. Describe each of these parts of a successful control system.

15-10. Variable budgets provide a better planning and control system than fixed budgets provide.
  a. Explain the difference between a variable and a fixed budget.
  b. Do you agree with the comment? Explain your answer.

15-11. Place a T or a C in the space at the left of each comment if it applies to the treasurer (T) or the controller (C) function
  _____ Concern with cost and availability of finance
  _____ Determining ways to minimize the company's tax burden
  _____ Supervising trade credit and collections
  _____ Investment decision
  _____ Financial decision
  _____ Capital budgeting
  _____ Maintenance of working capital and investing cash
  _____ Managing the accounting division
  _____ Determining the proper level of cash

PROBLEMS

15-1. In 19x4 Abdullah Petroleum's sales were $800,000. Its statement of financial position looked like this at the end of 19x4:

Assets	Liabilities and Shareholders' Equity	
	Accounts payable	$ 200,000
	Taxes payable	100,000
	Bank loan (3 months)	300,000
	Shareholders' equity	400,000
$1,000,000		$1,000,000

The company's profit margin ratio after taxes is 5 percent and management expects this rate to prevail in 19x5. Management also expects sales to expand in 19x5 by 20 percent, and Abdullah has a 60 percent earnings payout rate. The tax rate is 40 percent. How much external finance will Abdullah Petroleum need during 19x5?

15-2. Consider the original position of Abdullah Petroleum in problem 1 above. Now assume that management expects sales to expand by 30 percent. The company's profit margin after taxes remains at 5 percent and the payout rate remains at 60 percent.
   a. How much external finance will be needed in 19x5?
   b. What should Abdullah's management consider in deciding which sources of finance to use?

15-3. Saxon-Muckett Company's latest financial statements appear below. The company's after-tax profit margin is expected to persist over the near future. Heather Prewitt, the company's marketing manager, anticipates a 30 percent sales increase. Saxon-Muckett subscribes to a 30 percent earnings payout rate.
   a. How much external finance is needed next year?
   b. Should the external finance be debt or equity?
   Explain your answer.

Financial Statements:
Statement of Financial Position
As of December 31, 19x8

Assets		Claims Against Assets	
		Liabilities	
Cash	$ 10,000	Accounts payable	$ 20,000
Marketable securities	20,000	Taxes payable	10,000
Accounts receivable (net)	30,000	Accrued pension contributions	
Inventories	40,000	payable	5,000
Plant and equipment (net)	100,000	Bonds payable	50,000
Trademarks, patents,			
and goodwill	10,000		
		Equity	
		Preferred stock	
		(100 shares)	10,000
		Common stock	
		(1000 shares)	100,000
		Retained earnings	15,000
	$210,000		$210,000

Income Statement

For Year Ending December 31, 19x8

Sales	$320,000
Less cost of goods sold	275,000
Gross profit	$ 45,000
Less operating expenses	9,500
Net operating income	$ 35,500
Less interest expense	4,700
Earnings before taxes	$ 30,800
Less taxes (40%)	12,320
Earnings after taxes	$ 18,480

15-4. Goodson and Tudman Machine Foundry (GTMF) is attempting to estimate its external finance needed during 19x5. Rod Blaine, the treasurer of the company, asks you to determine the amount of external financing needed, and he gives you the company's financial statements presented below. The corporate accountant prepares the statements for you and the marketing vice-president tells you that she expects sales to rise by 16 percent during 19x5.

a. Use amounts from 19x4 and the percent-of-sales method to calculate the amount of external finance needed by GTMF during 19x5. Show your calculations.

b. Write a memo to Mr. Blaine explaining the assumptions of this method.

c. What do you suggest GTMF do with the excess of internal finance over the amount needed?

Financial Statements

Goodson and Tudman Machine Foundry

Income Statements

(thousands of dollars)

	Year Ending December 31	
	19x3	*19x4*
Sales	$7,000	$8,000
Cost of goods sold	4,200	5,300
Gross profit	$2,800	$2,700
Selling and administrative expense	939	973
Net operating profit	$1,861	$1,727
Interest expense	101	87
Earnings before tax	$1,760	$1,640
Income tax (50%)	880	820
Net profit	$ 880	$ 820

Statement of Financial Position, December 31
(thousands of dollars)

	19x3	19x4
Assets		
Cash	$ 210	$ 280
Receivables (net of bad debt alalowance)	1,190	1,370
Inventory	1,400	1,650
Total current assets	$2,800	$3,300
Plant and equipment		
(net of depreciation)	2,000	2,200
Total assets	$4,800	$5,500
Liabilities and net worth		
Accounts payable	$ 500	$ 600
Taxes payable	700	700
Other current liabilities	200	200
Total current liabilities	$1,400	$1,500
Bonds payable (8%)	1,000	1,000
Common stock (500,000 shares, $1 par)	500	500
Retained earnings	1,900	2,500
Total liabilities and net worth	$4,800	$5,500

15-5. Ecological Sciences, Inc., is a major retailer of pollution control equipment. The chief executive officer (CEO) is concerned with the slow growth of both sales and net income, and the subsequent effect on the trading price of the common stock. Selected financial data for the past three years are below.

Ecological Sciences
(In millions of dollars)

	19x4	19x5	19x6
1. Sales	$187.0	$192.5	$200.0
2. Net income	5.6	5.8	6.0
3. Dividends declared and paid December 31 balances	2.5	2.5	2.5
4. Owners' equity	63.02	66.5	70.0
5. Debt	30.3	29.8	30.0
Selected year-end financial ratios			
After-tax profit margin	3.0%	3.0%	3.0%
Total asset turnover	2x	2x	2x
6. Return on equity	8.9%	8.7%	8.6%
7. Debt to total assets	32.4%	30.9%	30.0%

The CEO believes that the price of the stock has been adversely affected by the downward trend of the return on equity, the relatively low earnings payout ratio, and the lack of dividend increases. In order to improve the price of the stock, she wants to improve the return on equity and dividends. She believes the company should be able to meet these objectives by
    1. increasing sales and net income at an annual rate of 10 percent a year

2. establishing a new dividend policy that calls for a payout of 50 percent of earnings or $3 million, whichever is greater.

The 10 percent annual sales increase will be accomplished through a new promotional program. She believes the present after-tax profit margin of 3 percent will be unchanged by the cost of this new program and any interest paid on new debt. She expects that the company can accomplish this sales and income growth while maintaining the current relationship of total assets to sales. Any capital needed to maintain this relationship that is not generated internally (that is, by earnings retention) would be acquired through long-term debt financing. The CEO hopes that debt would not exceed 35 percent of total capital.

a. Using the CEO's program, prepare a schedule that shows the appropriate data for the years 19x7, 19x8 and 19x9 for the items numbered 1 through 7 on the schedule presented in the problem.

b. Calculate the percentage increase in the company's debt and equity from 19x8 to 19x9.

c. What items should the CEO consider in determining the sources of the company's needed external finance.

d. Can the CEO meet all her requirements if a 10 percent per year growth in income and sales is achieved? Explain your answer.

FIVE

FINANCING BUSINESS ACTIVITY

Part 4 introduced you to the ways that a financial manager plans and controls a company's operations in order to finance the company in the best way. Now, we turn our attention to the specific ways that a manager may finance the company. Chapter 16 deals with intermediate-term financing and leasing so that you may understand the importance of these financial sources and how a financial manager evaluates them. Chapter 17 turns our attention to financing with common and preferred stock so that you will recognize important features of each and the rights of individuals owning preferred and common shares. Chapter 18 addresses the characteristics of bond and note financing. After reading and studying Chapter 18, you will know how to calculate the cost of each source and the reasons for their widespread use. Chapter 19 concludes this part of the book by examining dividend policy. Here you will see that dividend policy is important to investors and managers because it determines the amount of finance in the company and the amount of cash distributed to owners.

CHAPTER 16

Intermediate-Term Financing and Leasing

TERM LOANS

Characteristics · Uses and Costs · Repayment

CONDITIONAL-SALES CONTRACT

LEASING

Types of Leases · Capital Lease · Operating Lease

ACCOUNTING FOR LEASES

LEASING VERSUS BORROWING AND BUYING

SUMMARY

Key Terms and Concepts · Questions · Problems

T his chapter is concerned with financing methods that are neither short nor long-term, but either of intermediate duration (1 to 10 years) or of the avoidance-financing sort. By *avoidance financing,* we mean some substitute for borrowing that still permits managers to obtain assets for their companies to use. One such device is leasing. A second is the conditional-sales contract under which the seller finances and maintains ownership of the asset until the loan is paid. The chief form of intermediate-term financing is the term loan, a loan for more than one year that the borrower pays off in periodic installments, usually from the earnings of the asset(s) the loan finances.

When you finish this chapter you will know the characteristics and uses of a term loan and how such a loan differs from a conditional sales contract and a lease. In addition, you will be able to decompose debt service payments into interest and principal and to calculate a loan's after-tax debt service payments. The final part of the chapter deals with leasing, and here you will learn some of the details of FASB *Statement 13* that spells out the way that leases must be presented in financial reports. In the last part of our discussion of leases you will learn how to calculate the interest cost on a lease so that you will be able to compare its cost with a loan equivalent to the lease.

TERM LOANS

The primary sources of term loans are commercial banks and insurance companies. Because loans from these two sources are similar in most respects, the following discussion will center on those from commercial banks.

Characteristics

Generally, the maturity of a term loan is three to five years, although New York banks occasionally have made them up to eight years. Term loans have three major characteristics. (1) The key to obtaining a term loan is *earning power*. The lender, in determining likelihood of repayment, looks to a company's future earnings, rather than to pledged property or to its current financial strength. (2) A term loan involves a *direct relationship* between borrower and lender. There is a formal loan agreement stipulating terms of repayment, to which both parties agree. Such face-to-face negotiation is in contrast to the stock and bond markets, where the company financed rarely contacts the supplier of money personally. (3) A term loan involves *repayment in periodic installments* beginning no more than one year after the loan is made. This arrangement signifies the lender's insistence that the borrower make regular provision for repayment. In 1983 the net increase in bank term loans to business corporations was about $10.5 billion.

Uses and Costs

Companies use term loans to acquire permanent assets, as a form of interim financing, and to repay other borrowings. Often the permanently added assets take the form of increases in working capital. As interim financing, a term loan will be used to finance early stages of market development for a new product. Then, when the market matures, the treasurer will *fund* the loan, shifting into a long-term financial source. Proceeds from term loans are used to pay off short-term bank loans and, on occasion, to retire a bond issue. The latter occurs when the bond issue matures, or when it carries a high interest rate that the company wants to escape.

Term loans usually command higher interest rates than short-term loans do. One reason is that they run longer, and bankers need to be compensated for their resulting loss of liquidity. Also, a term lender incurs larger costs of credit investigation and loan supervision, and it adds these to the borrower's cost. Another possible cost, though not explicit, is that a borrower may be required to provide security for the loan. The pledging of security impairs a company's further borrowing ability. A majority of term loans, however, do not require security.

Repayment

More often than not, term loans are repaid in equal monthly or quarterly installments over the life of the loan. The loan is *amortized*, meaning that some of its principal is repaid in each period. The final installment of principal is repaid with the last payment. Relatively few term loans involve a *balloon*—a final payment much larger than the previous payments. By avoiding a balloon, the bank forces a borrower to provide for repayment of the loan at regular intervals instead of relaxing unitl a large lump of money is due at maturity.

Suppose that a company borrows $5,000 for three years at 8 percent interest, repayable in three annual installments. We can use present-value calculations to determine how much each payment will be. If the firm were charged no interest, each payment would be $5,000 ÷ 3 = $1,666. But we know that each installment must be greater than $1,666, because the firm is paying 8 percent interest. Since the payments will form an annuity, their amount can be calculated through the method suggested in Chapter 2. The retirement constitutes an annuity, and since it is not a sinking fund (we are not building up a future pool of money), we must use the table incorporating annuity to present worth, Appendix B-4. We then have

$$PVA = A(PVIFA_{0.08,3})$$
$$\$5,000 = A(2.577)$$
$$A = \$1,940$$

The company will make three equal *debt-service payments* of $1,940. Each payment will pay interest and principal as follows:

(1) Year	(2) Debt Service Payment	(3) Interest (.08)	(2) − (3) = (4) Principal Amortized	(5) Balance
1	$1,940	$400	$1,540	$3,460
2	1,940	277	1,663	1,797
3	1,940	143	1,787	0
	$5,820	$820	$5,000	

In the first year the borrower pays $1,940: Interest is 0.08 × $5,000 = $400 and the rest ($1,540) amortizes principal. After reducing the principal, the balance remaining is $3,460, the amount that determines how much interest the firm will pay in the second year. Notice that the company will repay a total of $5,820 for the $5,000 borrowed, so that interest is the difference:

Total Repaid		
(3 × $1,940)	$5,820	
Less Principal	5,000	
Interest	$ 820	

The after-tax cost of borrowing is less than its before-tax cost because interest is a tax-deductible expense. The debt service payments in the schedule above require cash, but one dollar in interest payment reduces taxable earnings by one dollar so that the after-tax cash outlay is reduced. Specifically, a financial manager calculates the after-tax debt service in either of two ways with each one giving the same answer: (1) annual debt service less the saving in taxes associated with the interest payment or (2) principal repayment plus the after-tax cost of interest.

Example. If the loan portrayed above is repaid by a company in the 40 percent marginal tax bracket, after-tax debt service in the first year is calculated in either of the following ways:

Principal repayment	$1,540	Debt service	$1,940
Add after-tax interest		Less tax saving	
$400 − (0.40 × $400)	$ 240	(0.40 × $400)	$ 160
After-tax debt service	$1,780	After-tax debt service	$1,780

The after-tax debt service increases each year because as we have seen the portion of debt service to repay principal rises and to pay interest falls as maturity approaches.

Practice. Calculate for years 2 and 3 the after-tax debt service of the loan portrayed on the $5,000 loan above if the borrowing corporation is in the 40 percent marginal tax bracket. Show that the correct amounts are $1,829 for year 2 and $1,883 for year 3.

Because a term loan runs for an extended time, the bank protects itself by placing restrictions in the loan agreement. For example, the banker may stipulate that the borrower's current ratio must not fall below some specified level over the life of the loan. In addition, the bank may (1) restrict the borrowing company's right to pay dividends, (2) require the bank's consent for management changes within the borrowing company, and (3) subject future acquisition of fixed assets to prior bank approval (in order to keep cash from being sunk into fixed investments). These additional restrictions originate in the bargaining between borrower and lender. As you might imagine, they are usually more pronounced in term loans to small companies than to large companies.

CONDITIONAL-SALES CONTRACT

A *conditional-sales contract* is one in which the seller of an asset also finances it. The buyer does not receive title to the asset until the loan is completely paid off. The purchaser makes a down payment, then makes periodic payments of principal and interest to the seller. Contracts are of moderate duration, typically three years and rarely more than five. A good-sized down payment, often one-third the contract price, gives the buyer a substantial stake and discourages defaulting. Both asset and obligation will show up on the purchaser's balance sheet, and if the purchaser defaults on a payment, the seller-lender can easily repossess the asset. Conditional-sales contracts are widely used by manufacturers of machinery, dental and medical equipment, and some kinds of vehicles. Sellers have access to major sources of financing and so are able to finance their customers. This actually puts them in two businesses: manufacturing and equipment financing.

LEASING

Leasing involves the use of an asset without assuming, or intending to assume, ownership. A company, called the *lessee,* acquires use of the asset. It does so by agreeing to pay the owner of the asset, the *lessor,* a periodic money rental for that use.

Types of Leases

There are two major types of leases. A *capital lease* is a long-term financial arrangement. An *operating lease* is relatively short-term. Capital leases also may be described as *financial leases* and as *service leases.* Each type is examined below.

Capital Lease

A capital lease is a long-term lease meeting specific conditions. It must be capitalized on the balance sheet of a company whose financial statements are prepared by a CPA firm. Capitalization means that the future annual lease rentals are discounted to yield a long-term debt equivalent.

A lease meeting any one of the following conditions is a capital lease and will be included in both long-term assets and liabilities sections of the lessees' balance sheet:[1]

1. The lease transfers title to the asset to the lessee at the end of the lease term.
2. It contains an option for the lessee to purchase the property at a bargain price.
3. The lease term equals 75 percent or more of the economic life of the asset.
4. By the end of the lease the property's fair value will be less than 25 percent of its initial value.
5. The property is special-purpose.

Financial Lease. A *financial capital lease* is one in which a lessee agrees to make payments that in total exceed the purchase price of the asset and that are spread over a time period equal to the economic life of the asset. A financial lease is usually noncancellable by either lessor or lessee for some stated period of time. The lessee is responsible for all service and maintenance on the equipment.

A special type of financial lease is the *sale and leaseback.* Here, a company sells an asset to a second party, which, in turn, immediately leases the asset back to the company. The lessee obtains cash from the sale of the asset and still maintains the asset's use. Consider, for example, the needs of Stacy's Department Store. It owns a building built in 1934 for $10 million, now with a $60 million replacement value but

---

[1] How the capitalized values appear on the balance sheet is illustrated in the "Accounting for Leases" section of this chapter.

still depreciated on its low historical value. Stacy's wants (1) to cash in on the building's risen value, (2) to continue occupying the building, and (3) to enlarge its after-tax cash return from the building. It can accomplish all three objectives by entering into a sale-and-leaseback arrangement with, say, the state University Endowment Fund. The fund buys the building for $60 million cash, then leases it back to Stacy's at a $5,620,609 annual rental, with Stacy's to pay all upkeep and taxes. The annuity formed by these payments will yield the fund 8 percent per year and return its entire investment in the 25 years' time.[2] Stacy's gets $60 million in cash, continued use of its building, and a $5,620,609 tax deduction anually on its rental payments.

New uses for capital leases continue to be developed. Electric utilities, hard pressed for cash, plan to lease nuclear fuel. Lessors would be dummy corporations, organized by the utilities and financed with commercial paper backed by standby credit lines at commercial banks. And corporations in need of pollution-abatement facilities are often leasing such equipment from municipalities. The municipality sells tax-exempt bonds bearing a lower interest rate than the corporation could obtain, buys the antipollution equipment, and leases it to the corporation. The lessee's payments, based on the amount the municipality needs to pay interest and amortize principal on the bonds, are lower than the cost of ownership would be.

Service Lease. A *service lease* is one in which the lessor provides both financing and maintenance services. Frequently, this type of lease is not fully amortized, meaning that the lessor will not fully recover the assets' cost through lessee payments. The lessor hopes to recover the remaining value by selling or releasing the asset after the present lease expires. In addition, a service lease often includes a cancellation clause, permitting the lessee to cancel the contract and to return the asset at any time. Cancellations usually incur a cash penalty.

Operating Lease

A lease not meeting any of the five conditions of a capital lease is an operating lease. Operating leases are usually of shorter duration than capital leases. Operating leases need not be capitalized in the long-term liabilities and assets sections of a lessee's balance sheet. However, the present worth (or capitalized value) of the future lease payments must be disclosed somewhere on the balance sheet, typically in a footnote or in parentheses. In this way an operating lease is not included in balance-sheet totals. Table 16-1 shows a typical reference to lease totals.

ACCOUNTING FOR LEASES

The Financial Accounting Standards Board has ruled in *Statement 13* that audited financial reports must show the capitalized or present value of a lease on a compa-

---

[2] This becomes evident if you divide the $60 million by 10.675, the annuity-to-present-worth factor for 25 years at 8 percent, which is equivalent to converting $60 million into a 25-year annuity at 8 percent.

TABLE 16-1 United Industrial Corporation Footnote Discussion of Leases (Annual Report, 1983)

Note 13—Leases

Total rental expense for all operating leases amounted to $3,617,000 (1983), $3,712,000 (1982) and $2,864,000 (1981). Contingent rental payments were not significant.

The future minimum rental commitments as of December 31, 1983 for all non-cancellable leases are as follows:

	Capital Leases	Operating Leases
	(Thousands of dollars)	
1984	$ 203	$2,047
1985	205	999
1986	206	420
1987	206	255
1988	206	192
Thereafter	806	122
Total minimum lease payments	1,832	$4,035
Amounts representing interest	567	
Present value of net minimum lease payments	1,265	
Less amount due in one year	100	
Long-term capitalized lease obligations	$1,165	

---

ny's balance sheet if the lease is a capital lease. The rate at which the future lease payments are capitalized is either (1) the lessor's implicit interest rate (a lessor may divulge this information) or (2) the lessee's borrowing rate on a loan equivalent to the lease.

Example. Suppose that Allenton Manufacturing leases a sheet metal stamping machine. The lease calls for payments of $1,940 annually at the end of each of the lease's three-year life. Allenton's commercial bank informs Allenton's financial manager that the bank will lend the company money at 8 percent interest. The present value of the lease payments is

$$PVA = \$1,940 \ (PVIFA_{0.08,3})$$
$$PVA = \$1,940 \ (2.577)$$
$$PVA = \$5,000$$

At the beginning of year 1, Allenton Manufacturing's balance sheet will show the following long-term asset and liability:

Assets		Liabilities	
Leasehold improvements Stamping machine	$5,000	Capitalized lease obligations	$5,000

At the end of each year, the asset and liability will be amortized (written down) by the principal amounts on the schedule portrayed on page 335.[3] In other words, at the beginning of year 2, the balance sheet will show

Assets		Liabilities	
Leasehold improvements		Capitalized lease	
Stamping machine	$3,460	obligations	$3,460

The income statement will show the tax-deductible expense "Lease Payment." The tax-deductible expense will be the total lease payment made during each accounting period. For Allenton Manufacturing, taxable earnings depicted on its income statement will be reduced by $1,940 in each of the next three years. The tax deductibility of lease payments has encouraged many companies to use lease financing. Notice that the impact of the FASB's decision is to make explicit the fact that leasing is an alternative to borrowing and buying an asset.

Many leases include nonfinancial services and require that a lessee make payments at the beginning of each period rather than at the end. When that is the case, a financial manager must reduce each year's payment by the amount of the nonfinancial portion of the payment and adjust the pattern of payment. Then, only the net financial payments are capitalized on the balance sheet.

Example. A lease agreement includes maintenance and insurance. The amount of each payment that goes toward paying maintenance and insurance must be subtracted from each payment to leave the net financial payments.

When a company makes lease payments at the beginning of a year rather than at the end, the payments comprise an annuity due. An *annuity due* is a series of fixed annual payments at the *beginning* of each year. An initial payment (or receipt) occurs immediately and all subsequent payments occur at the beginning of a year. In this way an amount at the beginning of year 2 is at the end of year 1, an amount at the beginning of year 3 is at the end of year 2, and so on. Each payment or receipt has simply been moved toward the present by one year.

The necessary adjustment to the present value of an annuity equation is straightforward: Subtract the initial payment from the present value of the annuity on the left-hand side of the equation (because it is undiscounted) and also subtract one (always one) from the number of periods to become $N-1$ because there is one less period for discounting. The equation for solving an annuity-due problem is

$$PVAD - A = A(PVIFA_{i,N-1})$$

where

$PVAD$ = present value of an annuity due
A = amount of the annuity
$PVIFA$ = present value interest factor of an annuity from Appendix B-4

---

[3] In fact, the part of the lease due within one year will be a current liability.

Example. Suppose a company leases some equipment for five years that requires $22,817 annual lease payments at the beginning of each year. The lease agreement calls for the lessor to be responsible for maintenance and insurance. The lessee calls its commercial bank and finds out that the company could borrow money for five years at 12 percent, so this rate will be the rate the financial manager uses to capitalize the financial portion of the lease payments. A call to the lessor discloses that $3,000 of each lease payment is for maintenance and insurance, so that the financial component is $22,817 − $3,000 = $19,817.

The capitalized value of the lease is the present value of the financial part of the future lease payments found with the present value of an annuity-due equation above:

$$
\begin{aligned}
\text{PVAD} - \$19,817 &= \$19,817 \ (\text{PVIFA}_{0.12,4}) \\
&= \$19,817 \ (3.037) \\
&= \$60,183 \\
\text{PVAD} &= \$60,183 + \$19,817 \\
&= \$80,000
\end{aligned}
$$

Figure 16-1 illustrates the annuity due and shows the present value of the lease payments to be $80,000. This is the amount that the beginning balance sheet shows, and the amount of principal in each lease payment will reduce the balance each year in much the same way that we amortized the $5,000 three-year term loan above.

Practice. A five-year net financial lease (meaning there are no payments for such items as maintenance and insurance) has an $80,000 present value with $21,680 payments at the beginning of each year. What is the annual compound interest rate

FIGURE 16-1 Present value of a five-year $19,817 annuity due discounted at 12 percent annually. Note that present value annuity due amount (80,280) is within a rounding error of the $80,000 answer in the example.

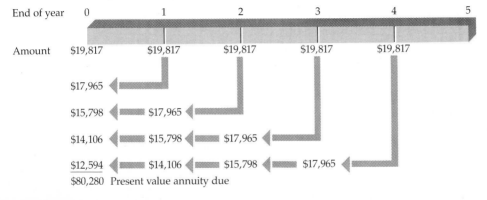

BOX 16-1
Leasing a Car Is Worthwhile only if
Payments Are Tax Deductible   You can look in the financial section of your daily
newspaper on almost any day and see advertisements
telling you to lease a car. In 1983 about 10 percent of all leased autos (or about 1.7
million cars) were leased by individuals. The rest were leased by commercial and
governmental fleets. Banks are trying to lure more individuals into leasing. Manufacturers Hanover Trust leases about 6,800 autos to individuals, an investment portfolio worth $100 million. First Pennsylvania has a portfolio of individual leases about
the same size.

There is no question that leasing looks attractive. There is no down payment
on a lease, and monthly charges on a $10,000 three-year lease are about $241 plus
$20 tax. That compares favorably with the $1,500 down payment plus $800 tax and
the $282 a month you would have to pay if you financed a $10,000 car by borrowing
from GMAC at 11.9 percent. And it is much better than a three-year bank loan at 16
percent, where the same deal would mean monthly payments of $300.

But leasing's advantages may be more apparent than real. Unless you are a
professional who can deduct lease fees as a business expense, you will wind up
paying more on an after-tax basis by leasing—$9,400 versus $7,432 if you financed
the purchase of that Buick through GMAC. That is because while most individuals
cannot deduct lease payments, they can deduct loan interest charges. Even if you
invested the equivalent of that $2,300 down payment and taxes in a money-market
fund paying 8 percent, you would still pay more by leasing. And, of course, by
borrowing the money you wind up owning a car that is still worth $4,200 after three
years. When you lease, the bank owns the car.

Source: Based on Jeff Blyskal, "The Car Leasing Dream," *Forbes,* March 14, 1983, p. 176.

in the lease? Answer: 18 percent. Make sure that you know how to find this answer
with the annuity-due equation before continuing to the next section.

LEASING VERSUS BORROWING AND BUYING

You may ask what the relative benefits of leasing and borrowing and buying are. In
general, a lease offers the advantages of tax deductibility of the lease payment, a
reduced initial cash outlay, and reduced risk to the lessee from the asset's obsolescence. On the other hand, borrowing and buying offer the advantages of tax deductibility of the interest portion of the loan and the asset's depreciation expense, lower
costs, and the opportunity of a large terminal cash flow at the time the contemplated
lease expires. This last point is especially important in real estate finance.

Most decisions to lease or borrow and buy an asset begin with calculating the implicit interest rate on the lease. The *implicit interest rate* is the rate of discount that equates the future net financial payments to the asset's purchase price. We can calculate the implicit interest rate and compare it with the interest rate on a loan to purchase the asset to help us decide if we should lease or borrow and buy the asset. Begin by setting the purchase price equal to the lease payments; then use the present value of an annuity-due equation to find the implicit interest rate, the discount rate equating the future net financial payments to the purchase price.

Example. Bland United is considering whether or not it should lease or borrow and buy a delivery truck that has a $42,000 purchase price. Lease America will buy the truck then lease it to Bland United with a four-year lease. Net financial payments will be $12,643 payable at the beginning of each year. Alternatively, First State Bank will loan the money to buy the truck at a 17 percent interest rate. Should Bland United lease or borrow and buy the truck based on the interest rate of each financial source?

The financial manager begins by using the present value of the annuity-due equation, the net financial lease payments, and the purchase price.

$$\$42,000 - \$12,643 = \$12,643 \ (\text{PVIFA}_{i,4-1=3})$$
$$\$29,357 = \$12,643 \ (\text{PVIFA}_{i,3})$$
$$2.322 = \text{PVIFA}_{i,3}$$

Appendix B-4 tells us that the interest rate associated with a PVIFA of 2.322 and three years is 14 percent. The implicit interest rate in the lease is 14 percent; therefore Bland United should lease the truck rather than borrow and buy it because the interest rate on the loan is 17 percent.

Leasing. Leasing conserves cash by avoiding a large immediate outlay for a down payment. This advantage especially benefits cash-starved companies and new businesses whose future cash needs may be difficult to predict. Offsetting this benefit is the usual condition of a lease that lease payments must be made at the beginning of a period rather than at the end of each period. Thus, the first payment is immediately due when the lease agreement is signed.

Second, where technological change is rapid, the lessee runs less risk of getting stuck with an obsolete asset. For example, a firm may lease a computer, then cancel the lease when a next-generation machine becomes available, thus gaining at the lessor's expense. Of course, this advantage exists only if the lessor underestimates the rate of technological change. If it forecasts the introduction of the next-generation computer correctly, it will factor the probable obsolescence of the old one into the payment schedule or stiffen the penalty for canceling the lease.

Borrowing and Buying. On the other hand, borrowing and buying an asset is usually less costly. Every benefit has a cost, and leasing's cost to the lessee is reflected in the lessor's profit margin.[4] The substantial profit of the leasing industry suggests that over an asset's life, borrowing and buying usually cost less than leasing. It should also be noted that the purchaser of an asset can take depreciation on it, thereby getting a tax-deductible cash flow from ownership.

Often, the greatest attraction of ownership lies in expecting a large terminal cash flow. This is especially true where the asset acquired is real estate. Land and a building may cost $1 million today, and thanks to inflation, be worth $3 million 25 years hence, after a generation of use. A company buying these assets would have enjoyed both their full use and a large capital gain. Best of all, it would be assured of continued possession at no added cost. By contrast, a company leasing the land and building for 25 years would wind up with nothing but a file of rent receipts. If at the end of 25 years it wished to renew the lease, it might easily find that rental payments have tripled.

It is often claimed that leasing is advantageous because lease payments are fully deductible for tax purposes. However, two annual charges associated with buying an asset are also tax-deductible: depreciation and interest on borrowed money. In most lease versus buy comparisons, these rival advantages about cancel out.

A full-scale lease versus borrow and buy analysis goes beyond comparing the implicit interest rate with the interest rate on the loan, but we shall not discuss models for the decision here. You may want to take an additional course in financial management to learn about the models or wait until you are in a position where you must make such a decision.

SUMMARY

1. Banks and insurance companies make term loans based on the borrowing company's earning power. A term loan involves a direct relationship between borrower and lender and involves the periodic repayment in installments beginning no more than one year after a lender makes the loan.

2. Debt-service payments are the principal and interest payments made on the loan over its life. A financial manager calculates the debt-service payments by using the present value of an annuity equation solved for the annuity A,

$$PVA = A(PVIFA_{i,N})$$

3. The after-tax debt-service payments reflect the fact that interest is a tax-deductible expense. After-tax debt service is the amount of principal repayment plus the after-tax dollar cost of interest.

[4] This observation recalls the frequent saying of economist Milton Friedman that "there's no such thing as a free lunch."

4. A conditional sales contract is one in which the seller also finances the equipment. The buyer does not receive title to the equipment until the loan is completely paid.

5. A capital lease is a long-term lease that must be capitalized on the lessee's statement of financial position. The interest rate that a financial manager uses to capitalize the future net financial lease payments is either the lessor's implicit interest rate (the rate that the lessor is charging for the money) or the interest rate on a loan to the lessee that is equivalent to the lease. An operating lease is one that does not meet the requirements of a capital lease and so need not be capitalized on the statement of financial position.

6. A company usually makes lease payments at the beginning of a year rather than at the end, so a financial manager must modify the present value of an annuity equation in order to be able to use the table in Appendix B-4. The equation for the present value of an annuity due is

$$\text{PVAD} - A = A(\text{PVIFA}_{i,N-1})$$

7. Leasing is an alternative to borrowing and buying an asset. Leasing offers the advantages of full tax deductibility of the lease payment, a reduced initial cash outlay, and less risk from the asset's obsolescence. Borrowing and buying offer the advantages of tax deductibility of the interest on a loan and of depreciation expense, lower costs, and the opportunity of a large terminal cash flow at the end of the project's life.

KEY TERMS AND CONCEPTS

Term loan

Debt service

Amortization

Conditional-sales contract

After-tax debt service

Annuity due

FASB *Statement 13*

Capital lease

Operating lease

Terminal cash flow

Sale and leaseback

QUESTIONS

16-1. "Leasing has disguised the fact that profitability in our economy is declining. If the truth were known, profitability is probably 20 percent below what a look at the financial statements indicate." Comment on this observation.

16-2. Some economists see a threat to economic liquidity in the policy of commercial banks to make term loans. Explain how such a policy may be a threat.

16-3. List and explain the three major characteristics of a term loan.

16-4. Your classmate in accounting says, "I see no difference between a lease and a conditional-sales contract." In what way are they similar? In what way do they differ?

16-5. "There are two types of leases, capital and financial." Do you agree? Explain your answer.

16-6. How do a corporation's shareholders benefit when a municipality sells a bond, acquires pollution abatement equipment, and leases this equipment to the corporation?

16-7. A financial lease is a form of intermediate- to long-term financing. Which of the following statements concerning financial leases is *false*?

    a. Restrictive covenants imposed under a loan agreement or bond indenture usually are not found in lease agreements.

    b. Leasing provides a convenient form of piecemeal financing.

    c. The financial cost of leasing is generally somewhat higher than borrowing and buying.

    d. Lease financing has no effect on a company's ability to make arrangements for other forms of debt.

    Explain your choice and comment on why the other choices are unacceptable.

16-8. Term loans differ from short-term loans in two significant areas: yield (or cost) and noninterest dimensions.

    a. List and briefly discuss three reasons that term loans typically have higher yield than short-term loans.

    b. List and briefly discuss four examples of noninterest dimensions of term loans.

16-9. CMA Examination (modified). Using a financial lease as a source of financial capital,

    a. is less expensive than using long-term debt.

    b. results in increased fixed charges for a company.

    c. increases a company's ability to issue long-term bonds.

    d. permits the company to change sources of capital freely if economic conditions change.

    e. allows the company to raise capital without affecting its borrowing capacity.

    Explain your choice and comment on why the other choices are unacceptable.

16-10. List and briefly discuss the benefits and costs of leasing versus borrowing and buying an asset.

PROBLEMS

16-1. Servico, Inc., borrows $12,000 from the United National Bank. The loan is for five years at 12 percent interest with payments at the end of each year. Servico is in the 40 percent marginal tax bracket.

    a. How much is annual debt service?

    b. Show a complete debt-service schedule for years 1 to 5.

    c. How much is after-tax debt service in year 1? In year 3?

    d. How much is annual debt service if payments are made at the beginning of each year?

16-2. Swift National Bank loans $730,000 to Bentham Broadcasting Group. The loan is for six years at 16 percent annual interest.

    a. Calculate annual debt-service payments if each payment is made at the *end* of each year. Show the first two years of interest and principal.

    b. Calculate annual debt service payments if each payment is made at the *beginning* of each year.

16-3. Calculate the present value of $20,000 annually for six years discounted at 12 percent under the following conditions:

    a. Payments occur at the *end* of each year.

    b. Payments occur at the *beginning* of each year.

16-4. Scott Financial Service borrows $720,000 from the Sanford State Bank of Commerce. The bank requires $247,083 annual debt service payments to service the four-year loan.

Bill Scott, chief financial officer of Scott Financial Services, is calculating the interest rate on the loan.

a. Calculate the interest rate if debt-service payments are made at the *end* of each year.

b. Calculate the interest rate if debt service payments are made at the *beginning* of each year.

c. Explain the reason(s) for the large increase in the interest rate in your calculations above. (No equation or calculation is called for.)

16-5. A 12-year lease agreement calls for $123,000 payments at the beginning of each year with the first payment due immediately. Maintenance and insurance are estimated to be $13,000 annually. The implicit interest rate in the lease is 18 percent.

a. What is the annual cash outlay associated with each lease payment? How much of this outlay is financial.

b. Calculate the capitalized value of the financial part of the lease under the following conditions:

(1) No interest rate (discount rate) is charged.

(2) The interest rate (discount rate) is 18 percent.

c. Show how the lessee's balance sheet looks after its second lease payment.

16-6. Firestone Enterprises is considering whether or not it should lease or borrow in order to acquire the use of drilling equipment. The equipment will have a $102,084 purchase price. Regal Leasing of Eugene, Oregon, offers to lease the equipment to Firestone under the following conditions:

> Term: 8 years
> Rental payments: $26,000 annually

Payments will be made at the end of each year and maintenance will be provided by the lessor. Firestone estimates maintenance to be $2,500 annually included in the lease.

a. Calculate the interest rate implicit in the lease by equating the net financial payments to the purchase price.

b. If rental payments are made at the beginning of each year, what is the interest rate?

16-7. The Marinay Company has selected a machine that will produce substantial cost savings over the next five years. The company can acquire the machine by outright purchase for $240,000. Marinay could obtain a five-year loan from a local bank to pay for the outright purchase. The bank would charge interest at a stated (and actual) annual rate of 10 percent. The principal would be paid in five equal installments. Each payment of principal and interest for the year would be due at the end of the year.

A local financier and investor heard of Marinay's need and offered it an unusual proposition. She would advance the company $240,000 to purchase the machine. The company would agree to pay her a lump sum of $545,450 at the end of five years. The manufacturer would offer the machine on a capital lease, with all tax benefits of ownership accruing to Marinay. The title would be transferred to Marinay at the end of the five years at no cost to Marinay. The manufacturer would be responsible for maintenance of the machine and has included $8,000 per year in the lease payment to cover the maintenance cost. Marinay will pay $70,175 at the beginning of each year for the five-year period.

a. Calculate the before-tax interest rate of each alternative.

b. Which method should Marinay use?

Explain your choice.

CHAPTER 17
Long-Term Financing with Corporate Stock

Whenever we think of corporate stock, we usually have in mind common stock. Common shareholders are a corporation's real owners. They are the last to participate in the earnings stream—receiving their return after employees, creditors, and the government—and last to receive anything if the corporation is forced into liquidation. Because of this low priority, common shareholders bear the greatest risk in a corporation's financial structure.

The first part of this chapter examines several different measures of value. The major emphasis of this examination is on the relationship between market value and intrinsic value and the way that these two values relate to each other. When you finish with this discussion, you will be able to explain several measures of value, to calculate the intrinsic value of a share of common stock, and to explain the way that market value converges (moves toward) an investor's intrinsic value. The discussion then turns to the rights of a common shareholder. In this discussion you will learn the various rights of a shareholder and how to measure the theoretical value of a right. The chapter concludes with a brief look at preferred stock so that you will be able to understand its relationship with a company's common equity.

COMMON STOCK: MEASURES OF WORTH

Common stock has several measures of worth. Among them are par value, book value, market value, intrinsic value, and liquidation value.

Par Value

Par value is the most clear-cut of the measures of common-stock worth because it is fixed on the firm's books. It is an arbitrary dollar amount selected by management for showing common stock on the balance sheet.[1] Companies usually select as low a par value as possible, because some states tax corporations that do business within their boundaries according to par value of their stock.[2]

Par value has only limited significance for the common shareholder. If stock is sold below par when it is issued, creditors in a bankruptcy proceeding can hold whoever *then* owns the stock liable for the difference between par and the lower original selling price (the discount).

Par value is one component of shareholders' equity. The number of shares issued and outstanding multiplied by par value per share governs the dollar amount entered on the balance sheet for common stock. In the balance sheet a few paragraphs further on, for example, Perkison Enterprises has outstanding 100,000 shares at a par value of $5 per share, so the amount in common stock is $500,000.

Book Value

Book value of common stock is the accounting net worth, or shareholders' equity, of a corporation. Since net worth equals total assets less total liabilities, book value represents the shareholders' net claim on total assets. Recall that shareholders' equity itself comprises three components: common stock, paid-in capital in excess of par, and retained earnings. The first two components, sometimes called *external equity*, represent the amount a corporation receives when it first issues its stock. Perkison sold its entire 100,000 shares for $7.50 per share, a total of $750,000. Consequently, it has entered 100,000 shares times $5 par value = $500,000 under common stock and the remainder ($750,000 − $500,000 = $250,000) under paid-in capital in excess of par.

Retained earnings, sometimes called *internal equity*, constitute that part of a company's past profits not paid out in dividends. It should be unnecessary to point out that retained earnings are not a cash fund but simply a *claim* that common shareholders have on a corporation's assets, a claim resulting from management's decision to plow earnings back rather than to pay them out in dividends.

Book value per share is total book value divided by number of shares outstanding. It can be figured either by subtracting total liabilities and preferred stock from total assets, and dividing this difference by the number of common shares, or by taking the sum of the common stock, paid-in capital in excess of par, and retained earnings. Perkison's book value per share is $5,000,000/100,000 shares = $50.

---

[1] See chapter 12 for an additional discussion of par value.

[2] Stock can be no-par, meaning that management has assigned no par value to its common. Where that is the case, many states levy the tax on an assumed $100 par value.

Perkison Enterprises

		Current liabilities	$ 3,000,000
	$10,000,000	Long-term debt	1,000,000
		Preferred stock	1,000,000
		Common stock (100,000 shares at par value of $5)	500,000
		Paid-in capital in excess of par	250,000
		Retained earnings	4,250,000
Total assets	$10,000,000	Total claims	$10,000,000

Market Value

Market value is the price at which the stock sells. It reflects the value a seller and buyer place on the stock. For a sale to occur, buyer and seller must ordinarily hold different expectations for future market value. The seller must expect the price to be lower in the future, the buyer, higher. (Of course, a seller might be forced to sell for other reasons—distress, more profitable use of funds, and so on.) If both parties held similar expectations, no exchange would occur because the owner would not release the shares. If a corporation's stock is listed on an exchange, then the most recent trade gives the approximate market value. Most daily newspapers list the market prices of stocks traded on the New York and American Stock exchanges. Table 17-1 shows a reference to common stock (and preferred stock) price behavior in a large corporation's annual report to shareholders.

What is the relation between book value and market value? Some stocks sell above book value, others below. To a great extent, the difference between the two values is this: book value measures the accountant's estimate of the original contribution by shareholders in the past, including sale of new issues and retention of earnings, whereas market value reflects investors' assessment of future cash flows. When a firm's shares are priced in the market below book value per share, the firm is said to be worth more dead than alive.

Remember that a financial manager wants to maximize the company's common-stock price by making investment and financial decisions that increase the future cash flows to the company's common shareholders or reduce the risk that they perceive. However, a financial manager cannot affect the company's stock price directly, but only indirectly through an investor's evaluation of the stock. An investor's evaluation of a common stock introduces us to the concept of intrinsic value, the topic of the next section.

Intrinsic Value

Intrinsic value is an estimate of a stock's worth, based on its apparent earning power, without regard to present market price. Financial theory teaches us that the present

TABLE 17-1 Gulf + Western, Inc. (Annual Report, 1983)
Quarterly Per Share Market Prices and Regular Cash Dividends[a]
(Stock prices from trading on the composite tape.)

Quarter Ended	High Sale Price	Low Sale Price	Dividends Paid Per Share	Quarter Ended	High Sale Price	Low Sale Price	Dividends Paid Per Share
Common Stock				**$5.75 Preferred**			
10-31-81	$ $19\frac{1}{8}$	$ $14\frac{3}{8}$	$ .1875	10-31-81	$ 58	$ 56	$1.4375
1-31-82	$17\frac{1}{2}$	$14\frac{7}{8}$	.1875	1-31-82	$56\frac{3}{4}$	54	1.4375
4-30-82	$16\frac{3}{4}$	14	.1875	4-30-82	$54\frac{1}{2}$	52	1.4375
7-31-82	$15\frac{1}{2}$	$11\frac{1}{2}$	.1875	7-31-82	$52\frac{1}{2}$	51	1.4375
			$ .75				$5.75
10-31-82	$ $17\frac{3}{4}$	$ $11\frac{1}{2}$	$ .1875	10-31-82	$ $51\frac{1}{2}$	$ $49\frac{1}{4}$	$1.4375
1-31-83	$18\frac{3}{4}$	15	.1875	1-31-83	$52\frac{3}{4}$	$50\frac{1}{2}$	1.4375
4-30-83	27	$17\frac{1}{8}$	.1875	4-30-83	$60\frac{1}{2}$	$51\frac{1}{2}$	1.4375
7-31-83	$30\frac{1}{8}$	$25\frac{3}{8}$	.1875	7-31-83	62	60	1.4375
			$ .75				$5.75

[a]Effective October 1, 1983, Gulf+Western increased the quarterly cash dividend to an indicated annual rate of $.90 per share.

value of a stock's future dividends and its expected selling price determine its intrinsic value. Unlike bonds and preferred stocks, a common stock pays a dividend that changes as the company's earnings change, increasing or decreasing each year so that intrinsic value becomes difficult to determine.

The equation for determining a common-stock's intrinsic value is future dividends and the expected selling price discounted at a rate that reflects the stock's risks:

$$V_c = \sum_{t=1}^{N} \frac{D_t}{(1 + R)^N} + \frac{P_t}{(1 + R)^N}$$

or

$$V_c = \sum_{t=1}^{N} D_t \, (PVIF_{i,N}) + P_t \, (PVIF_{i,N})$$

where

$V_c =$ intrinsic value of a share
$D_t =$ expected dividend at time t
$R =$ investor's required rate of return
$P_t =$ expected selling price at time t

Example. An investor expects Mason Pipeline, Inc., to pay a $2.80 per share dividend at the end of each of the next three years, at which time the stock will be selling for an expected $26 per share. If the investor is considering buying the stock now and then selling it in three years, what is the stock's intrinsic value with a 16 percent required rate of return?

The answer involves discounting at 16 percent both the three-year annuity of $2.80 and the $26 expected selling price. The calculations follow and Figure 17-1 illustrates the process:

FIGURE 17-1   Intrinsic value of Mason Pipeline, Inc. (discounted at 16 percent).

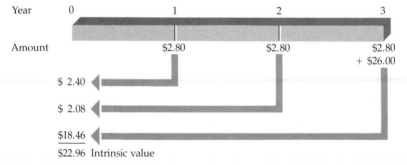

Present value of dividends
    PVA = $2.80(2.246) $ 6.29
Present value of expected selling price
    PV = $26(0.641)   16.67
                                                  $22.96

Practice. Before continuing, calculate the intrinsic value of Mason Pipeline common stock if all of the conditions remain the same, but the investor's required rate of return falls to 12 percent. Answer: $25.24. Make sure that you can find this answer before you continue.

Future dividends will probably not comprise an annuity as they did in the example above because a common-stock dividend depends on the company's ability and willingness to declare a dividend. (We shall examine dividend policy in Chapter 19.) When expected dividends differ each year an investor must discount each expected dividend—whatever its amount—with the required rate of return, then add this amount to the present value of the expected selling price.

Example. Marcia Staff is considering investing in Wisco Brake and Bearing Company's common stock. She expects the common-stock dividend to decline each year and to be the following amounts:

(1) End of Year	(2) Amount
1	$1.80
2	$1.40
3	$1.12
4	$1.00

She expects the selling price in four years to be $17.00 per share. What is her intrinsic value if she requires an 18 percent rate of return?

Marcia calculates the intrinsic value of the stock by finding the present value of the future dividends and adding to this amount the present value of the expected selling price. The process is exactly the same that we employed above, but we must make more calculations because each year's dividend is a different amount.

(1) End of Year	(2) Amount	(3) Interest Factor (R = 0.18)	(2) × (3) = (4) Product
1	$1.80	0.847	$1.52
2	$1.40	0.718	$1.00
3	$1.12	0.609	$0.68
4	$1.00	0.516	$0.52
		Present value of dividends	$3.72

BOX 17-1

"Do the Bosses Own the Stock?"   By many yardsticks John Templeton owns the best
25-year investment record among the world's mu-
tual-fund managers. He recommends investors ask the question above when they
are looking for a stock to buy.

The corporate form of business enterprise can result in almost total separation
of ownership from management. In most big name companies, top-level managers
and directors as a group own less than one-tenth of one percent of the stock. They
find their company attractive as a source of giant salaries, fat bonuses, stock options
(which they quickly cash), and golden parachutes (to give them big payoffs if new
owners of the company fire them). But they do not find the company they manage
good enough to invest their own money in.

That does seem to raise a question. You would not patronize a bar where the
bartenders refused to drink their own brew, would you?: So why isn't "bosses who
own the stock" the acid-test of a worthwhile investment?

Now, she calculates the present value of the expected selling price four years from
now,

$$PV = \$17(0.516) = \$8.77$$

Finally, she adds these two amounts to find Wisco Brake and Bearing's intrinsic
value,

Present value of dividends	$ 3.72
Add present value of selling price	8.77
Intrinsic value	$12.49

Because it is subjective, an intrinsic value set by a particular person may have
little relation to any of the other values. But it does affect market value. When an
estimate of intrinsic value exceeds market value, an investor will buy the share (if he
has the money) because the present value of the expected stream of future earnings
exceeds the present cost of obtaining that stream. If market value exceeds intrinsic
value, then investors will not buy the stock; indeed, they will sell it if they already
own it. The net result is that market value will be driven toward people's guess
about intrinsic value.

Liquidation Value

Liquidation value is the estimated amount shareholders would receive if all assets
were liquidated and all liabilities paid. This value reflects a stock's worth upon
dissolution of the corporation. Since assets rarely sell for their full book value,

liquidation value is usually below book value. In Perkison Enterprises, if assets in liquidation brought 50 cents on the dollar, claimants would receive $5 million. That would be enough to satisfy only the claims of the creditors and preferred stockholders, leaving nothing for common shareholders. In this instance, liquidation value is zero.

RIGHTS OF A COMMON SHAREHOLDER

Corporations have legal obligations to their owners, the shareholders. Unlike proprietorships and partnerships, ownership and management in corporations are often separated. Large corporations employ professional managers who use the funds of thousands of stockholders. A system of checks and balances has developed over the years to prevent abuses. The system concerns the rights of common shareholders—the right to share in earnings, the right to vote for directors, the right to maintain their ownership position, and other rights discussed below.

Right to Participate

The most important right of shareholders is their right to participate in the stream of earnings that is left after all expenses. This participation comes in two ways: dividend payments and the reinvestment of earnings. While stockholders individually have little recourse to force directors to declare dividends out of earnings, once dividends are declared, they become a liability and must be paid.

Voting Right

Another important right of shareholders is the voting right. Each share owned entitles that shareholder to one vote in corporate elections. Elections are held to elect directors and to vote on mergers, charter amendments, and other issues. However, voting control over management is often an empty formality. In large companies the stock is spread among so many shareholders that individual shareholders—sometimes even a large number of shareholders—have virtually no voice in policy decisions. A large group must unite in order to muster decisive voting power.

Management or anyone else can solicit the right to vote in a shareholder's place in any corporate election. The document in which the shareholder delegates the voting right to another is called a *proxy*. A group wanting to force management or directors to change a policy may seek the proxies of shareholders. Proxy voters vote for the shareholder but vote their own desires unless the shareholder directs that they vote a particular way.

Traditionally, shareholders have given management their proxies when they are satisfied with company performance—if they have been dissatisfied, they have sold their stock. However, in recent years a new militancy has arisen among those seeking to change management through proxy fights. An independent group, discouraged by current management performance, might solicit proxies to replace the incumbents. Although a proxy fight may be unsuccessful in the sense that the dissidents cannot muster enough votes to win, the fight itself may prompt management to change its policy. Some recent proxy battles between corporation managements and social groups seeking greater ecological concern from firms are an example of the residual success of a proxy fight. Though the outsiders failed to achieve their direct objectives, they often succeeded in influencing management decisions.

To maintain control, controlling stockholders have often established different *classes* of common stock with different voting rights. Often these classes are labeled A and B, with one group entitled to vote and the other excluded from voting or restricted to voting on a minority of directors. Such devices are often employed when new capital is needed but current owners wish to preserve control.

Preemptive Right

Another means by which existing shareholders maintain control is through preemptive rights. Bylaws have usually obliged corporations to offer present shareholders the opportunity to maintain their proportionate ownership of the firm. They can do so by exercising their preemptive right, which entitles them to buy new stock in proportion to their current holdings. This preemptive right also applies to securities convertible into common stock.

Example. Suppose that Global Corporation has one million shares of stock outstanding and Sidney Parsons owns 100,000 shares, 10 percent of the total shares. If Global decides to sell an additional 10,000 shares, then Parsons' preemptive right entitles her to buy 10 percent (1,000 shares) of the new issue before it is offered publicly.

Many corporations have amended their bylaws to eliminate this preemptive right because it limits their ability to buy other companies by issuing new stock to swap for the shares of the acquired company.

When preemptive rights exist, sale of a new stock issue is made through a special device called a *rights offering.* Each outstanding share of stock receives one right to maintain its pro rata share of ownership in the firm. These rights are options to buy the new stock at a specified price. A specific number of rights is needed to buy a new share, and this number is determined by dividing the number of shares outstanding by the number of new shares to be issued.

Suppose the Falcon Company wishes to raise $10,000 by selling additional common stock through a rights offering. The company decides to offer this new stock for $100 per share, called the *subscription price.* One hundred new shares must be issued, determined in the following way:

$$\text{Total new shares} = \frac{\text{Capital required}}{\text{Price of stock}} = \frac{\$10,000}{\$100} = 100 \text{ shares}$$

Falcon already has 1,000 shares outstanding at a market value of $150 per share. Consequently, the number of old shares, or rights, needed to buy one new share of stock is

$$\frac{\text{Old shares}}{\text{New shares}} = \frac{1,000}{100} = 10$$

In other words, since there are 1,000 rights and 100 new shares to be issued, 10 rights (old shares) are needed to buy one new share. Alternatively, since there are 1,000 old shares outstanding and 100 new ones to be issued, 10 old shares will command one new share.

Valuing a Right

If a corporation sells its shareholders new stock for less than the market value of the existing stock, then the privilege of buying this stock has a value. The market value of Falcon's existing stock is $150 times 1,000 shares, or $150,000 for all shares. The new subscription adds 100 shares at $100, bringing the market value for Falcon stock to $160,000 for the 1,100 shares. Theoretically, the average market value of each share after the new issue will be $145.45.[3] With 10 rights and $100, a share that is worth $145.45 may be purchased. The 10 rights are worth this difference in value, $45.45. Each right is worth $4.545. Here are the calculations:

Aggregate values

Before offering	1,000 shares @ $150 =	$150,000
New offering	100 shares @ $100 =	10,000
After offering	1,100 shares	= $160,000

To buy

$$\$100 + 10R = \$145.45$$
$$10R = \$145.45 - \$100 = \$45.45$$
$$1R = \$45.45/10 = \$4.545$$

The equation below shortcuts the reasoning process and calculates, directly, the theoretical value of a right,[4]

$$R = \frac{M_o - S}{n + 1}$$

---

[3] Rights usually remain exercisable only three or four weeks. Thereafter they are worthless.
[4] This equation gives the right's value when the stock is selling "rights on." After the rights come out of it and certificates evidencing the rights are issued, the market price of the stock will fall by the value of one right. The formula for the new market price after the flotation and without the right is $M_e = M_o - R$, where M_e is market price *ex rights*, or rights off, M_o is market price *cum rights*, or with rights, and R is the value of one right. The value of the right remains the same and is now equal to

$$R = \frac{M_e - S}{n} = \frac{\$145.45 - \$100}{10} = \$4.54$$

where

$R=$ value of one right
$M_o=$ market price of the stock selling with rights "on," or included
$S=$ subscription price
$n=$ number of rights needed to buy 1 share of new stock

For Falcon Company, the calculation for the theoretical value of a right is

$$R = \frac{\$150 - \$100}{10 + 1} = \frac{\$50}{11} = \$4.545$$

If a shareholder does not wish to maintain his pro rata share in the firm, he can sell the rights. If he owns 10 shares of stock, he has 10 rights to sell for $45.45. The person buying the rights would put $100 in cash with the 10 rights to buy one share of stock.

Did the holder of rights get something for nothing? At first it might seem so, because the shareholder appears to have paid $145.45 for $150 share. However, recall that *after* the flotation there are more shares outstanding than before, and theoretically the resulting market price is $145.45 per share. In principle, we neither gain nor lose whether we exercise rights or sell them. Only when we let them expire do we lose. In our example, had our shareholder with 10 existing shares failed to exercise or to sell his rights, his wealth would have fallen as follows:

Before issue: 10 shares @ $150.00 = $1,500.00
After issue: 10 shares @ $145.45 = $1,454.50
                                    Loss $45.50

Other Rights

Other rights granted shareholders include the right to be issued a certificate of ownership (stock certificate), to receive information on company operations through annual reports, to attend meetings, and to transfer ownership. The right to transfer unwanted stock is especially important because transfer is an effective way to liquidate an investment.

NEW FLOTATIONS

As corporations expand, they need new equity. Creditors demand an equity base before they will lend money, and the more ample the ownership stake in an enterprise is, the more readily creditors will furnish funds. Thus, equity forms the foundation for all financial expansion.

Apportioning Equity

Given that a company has an optimal, or least costly, debt-equity ratio, this ratio should be maintained over the years. This means that future long-term funds will

BOX 17-2
Costs Other than Financial May
Accompany an Initial Public Offering

An initial public offering can bring management and owners face-to-face with a new, uncomfortable development: Intrusion of outsiders into a formerly private domain and an instant change in wealth and lifestyle. Consider the example of Dynatrend, Inc. The company sold $1.9 million stock in December, 1981, making three Dynatrend owners near millionaires and increasing the company's equity base.

Dynatrend's founder and chief executive, Ronald J. Massa, says selling stock was the best way to get money for product development. However, he has mixed feelings about going public. "It has basically changed my whole world," says the 47-year-old executive. One thing it changed was his management style. Employees he used to be friendly with seldom speak to him now. The company is judged by Wall Street standards that he disagrees with, yet he bends operations to meet them. "I have a new boss," he says, "I don't work for myself anymore." There is a general uneasiness about being a public company at Dynatrend, Mr. Massa says. "We've all become circumspect and a little jittery." What used to be no one's business must be disclosed now "My wife," says Mr. Massa, "thinks it's terrible that everyone knows my salary," which is $98,800.

Massa is in the grip of outside forces that he does not believe are entirely good for the company. "Despite what people tell you, investors want to make money tomorrow. They aren't in this for the long run. They aren't willing to wait five years." Investors like to see earnings rise each quarter. That influences Massa's decisions, though he says bluntly: "This quarter-to-quarter pacing is manipulating the company, not managing it." Dynatrend's underwriter owns 16 percent of the stock. One of its partners is on Dynatrend's board of directors and reminds Mr. Massa of Wall Street's views.

Source: Based on an article in *The Wall Street Journal,* November 15, 1982, p. 31.

need to be raised in these optimal proportions. Suppose Scotch Adhesives Corporation wants to maintain a 1:3 ratio of long-term debt to equity. If the company raises $400,000 from long-term sources, three-fourths, or $300,000, must come from equity. Some of this equity probably will be supplied by retained earnings. The rest must come from new stock sales.[5]

---

[5] The amount of external equity needed is affected by dividend policy, an influence discussed in Chapter 19.

Timing

Once management decides to issue new common, it must pick the best time to do so. Unfortunately, financial managers often follow the principle of least resistance in financing expansion and in timing the acquisition of external finance: Convenience crowds out foresight. Treasurers raise funds, so long as possible, from commercial banks, because that is the easiest way. They ignore both the use to which funds will be put and the dangers of a loan renewal crisis. And they fail to consider future conditions in the equity markets. As a result, they undertake sale of new equity only after they have been forced to because finance from other sources has become unavailable. With no concern for timing their company's entry into the equity market, they are often obliged to obtain equity at the worst possible time, when the stock market is low or declining.

Three- to five-year forecasts of financial needs can help management time its future equity offerings advantageously. The treasurer then knows when it is necessary to sell new common stock. Armed with this knowledge, he can plan to enter the equity market at a favorable time, selling new common stock when prices are high, expectations buoyant, and the market outlook generally favorable.

How significant is timing? It determines how much dilution of earnings and control will occur. In the rights problem discussed above, Falcon needed $10,000. At a market price of $100 per share, it needed to sell 100 new shares, but at a price of $125, it would need to sell only 80 new shares. Fewer shares can be sold more easily than can a large issue. Fewer shares also involve less dilution of earnings—future earnings will be spread over a smaller number of shares and future earnings per share will be greater. Less dilution may also keep the stock's price-earnings multiple higher. Finally, selling fewer shares means that present owners run less risk of losing voting control of the firm.

PREFERRED STOCK

Preferred stock, like common stock, represents ownership in a corporation. The difference between these forms lies in the priority of their respective claims on the company's earning stream and its assets. Preferred stock receives a stated dividend that must be paid ahead of any common dividends. In the event of liquidation, preferred shareholders recoup their investment at par before any cash can be alloted to common shareholders. Preferred owners usually have no voting rights unless the firm fails to pay them dividends for some period. The preferred dividend is often *cumulative*, meaning that if it is missed for one or more periods, the arrearage must be paid, along with the current dividend, before any dividend can be declared on the common.

Debt or Equity?

Preferred stock is in many respects like debt. Table 17-2 lists the ways in which preferred stock is similar and dissimilar to bonds.

TABLE 17-2   Comparison of Preferred Stock with Corporate Bonds

Similar	Dissimilar
1. Fixed payment obligation	1. Little or no penalty for missing payment of charge
2. Claim superior to common equity	2. No principal repayment
3. Often convertible into common stock	3. Dividend payment not tax-deductible
4. Often used to acquire stock of a merger partner	4. Dividends received by corporation are 85 percent tax-free
5. Long-term source of finance	5. Preferred stock offers higher yield

Should we treat preferred as debt or equity? Legally, and in an accounting sense, preferred is equity. Most managers, however, consider preferred as debt because of its fixed charge and leverage effect on common-share earnings. Holders of common shares also think of preferred as debt, because of its superior claim, but bond holders consider it as equity because it supplies assets against their claims in case of liquidation. Generally, we believe it is more accurate to think of preferred as most corporation managers do, as debt.

Straight Debt Versus Preferred

The deductibility of bond interest reduces the cost of debt to a corporation. Thus it can be argued that bonds are a cheaper source of capital than preferred stock, on which (with a 50 percent tax rate) a company must earn $2 in taxable earnings for each $1 of dividend payments. This argument may be disputed, however, if the bond issue includes a sinking fund to retire the debt. For a 20-year sinking-fund debenture, 5 percent of the issue would be retired annually, so that 95 percent of the issue would be retired before maturity. Adding the sinking-fund payment to the yearly interest payments of debt will sometimes result in a larger cash outflow than would preferred dividends, even when the tax implications are considered.

Less cash in the company may impair future earnings. If the company earns 10 percent on assets, every $1 less in assets means 10 cents less in earnings. Thus, where bond investors would require sinking funds or other highly burdensome restrictions, management and shareholders alike may prefer to use preferred stock.

Recall that in Chapter 14 we examined the way a financial manager measures a company's financial leverage. There we saw that using debt increases a company's degree of financial leverage because debt requires a company to pay a fixed amount of interest. The impact of financial leverage is to cause percentage-wise greater changes in a company's earnings after taxes from changes in earnings before interest and taxes. Preferred stock dividends are a fixed financial cost and increase a company's degree of financial leverage so that a company with preferred stock outstanding has greater financial leverage than does a company without preferred stock outstanding. The increased financial leverage from preferred stock means that the company's earnings available to common shareholders and its earnings per share of common stock will change more percentage-wise than the company's earnings after taxes. We shall not discuss this relationship further, but encourage you (if you are interested) to take an additional course in managerial finance so that you may study preferred stock's role in increasing a company's financial leverage and its implications.

SUMMARY

1. A common stock has several measures of value. Par value, book value, market value, intrinsic value, and liquidation value are the major measures of value.

2. Market value is the price of stock in the market, and it reflects the intrinsic value that a buyer and seller place on the share. A financial manager wants to maximize the market value of the company's common stock.

3. Intrinsic value is subjective value. Financial theory teaches that intrinsic value is the present value of the future expected dividends and selling price discounted at a rate determined by the stock's risk. An equation for estimating intrinsic value is

$$V_c = D_t(\text{PVIF}) + P_t(\text{PVIF})$$

4. Common shareholders have the right to participate in dividends, to elect the company's directors, and to participate in a new offering of common stock. The theoretical value of a right is measured by the following equation:

$$R = \frac{M_o - S}{n + 1}$$

5. A company usually obtains long-term financing in an optimum or best ratio of debt and equity. As a result, management must sell new common stock in order to maintain an optimum debt-equity ratio whenever a company is growing rapidly. In addition, a company should acquire new equity from the financial market whenever stock prices are high and investors have high expectations of increasing earnings.

6. Preferred stock is like common stock because both represent ownership in the company. Preferred stock is also like debt because both have a fixed financial cost associated with them—the debt requires interest payments and the preferred stock requires dividends.

KEY TERMS AND CONCEPTS

Par value	"Rights on"
Book value	Principle of least resistance
Intrinsic value	Timing
Market value	Cumulative
Subscription price	Sinking fund

QUESTIONS

17-1. The chapter points out that value depends on expected cash receipts and required rate of return. Explain what is meant by the term *expected cash receipts* and *required return*.

17-2. Intrinsic and market values are closely related. Describe how they are related and explain what would happen to market value if a stock's intrinsic value is $12 and its market value is $13.50.

17-3. Two individuals are considering whether or not each should buy a share of Burroughs Corporation common stock. One person determines that the stock's intrinsic value is $46 per share. The other, a $32 per share intrinsic value.
  a. Explain how each person may have come up with an intrinsic value.
  b. What action would each person take if the market value of Burroughs Corporation were $36 per share.

17-4. Sometimes, in referring to a stock that is selling below its book value per share, an analyst will say, "The firm is worth more dead than alive." Explain this statement.

17-5. Relate book value to
  a. common shareholders equity.
  b. external equity.
  c. net worth.
  d. market value.
  Which value is most relevant to financial managers?

17-6. Par value of a common stock is
  a. the present value of the expected cash flows.
  b. the liquidation value of the stock.
  c. the book value of the stock.
  d. the legal nominal value assigned to the stock.
  e. the amount received by the corporation when the stock was originally sold.
  Explain your choice and state why each other alternative was not chosen.

17-7. Explain what happens to a stock's price under each of the following conditions. No calculations are necessary.
  a. A stock's dividend growth rate increases.
  b. The investor's required rate of return rises.
  c. An investor expects to receive the first dividend payment immediately rather than one year from now.
  d. The expected selling price in year-four rises.

17-8. A corporation's preemptive right
  a. gives holders of common stock first option to purchase additional common shares.
  b. gives bond holders first claim on assets in liquidation.
  c. gives preferred stockholders the right to vote at annual meetings.
  d. gives bankers the right to demand prepayment of the principal amount of a loan.
  Explain your choice and state why each other alternative was not chosen.

17-9. Many corporations issue new common stock by using a rights offering. Explain why a corporation would use this method and describe what happens to the value of a share of common stock when it begins to trade ex rights.

17-10. CMA Examination (modified). A firm issues new common-stock and uses the proceeds to retire a bond issue that has matured. Which one of the following statements will hold in all cases?

a. The firm has increased its financial leverage.

b. The firm has decreased its operating leverage.

c. The firm has increased its earnings per share.

d. The firm has decreased its earnings per share.

e. The firm has expanded its capital base.

Explain your choice.

17-11. A rights offering will probably fail

a. if the new issue is small compared to the total common outstanding.

b. if the issue has shown price stability over the past year.

c. if the stock is very widely held.

d. if the subscription price is close to the market price.

e. if the stock appears likely to increase in price.

Explain your choice and state why each other alternative was not chosen.

17-12. Preferred stock has features that may make it a more desirable form of financing than long-term debt. Which of the following statements concerning the advantages of preferred stock over long-term debt is generally *false*?

a. Preferred stock dividends are a weaker legal obligation than bond interest for the issuing corporation.

b. Preferred stock normally has no final maturity date.

c. Preferred stock adds to the corporation's equity base, which strengthens its financial condition.

d. Preferred stockholders cannot force a corporation into legal bankruptcy for unearned dividends.

e. Preferred stock is sold on a lower-yield basis than bonds.

Explain your choice and state why each other alternative was not selected.

17-13. Cousins Corporation is planning a large capital-expenditure program to add plant capacity and to modernize manufacturing equipment. Management's projections of cash flows reveal that internal equity will not be adequate to finance the capital-investment program. A preferred stock issue has been suggested because the capital requirement is long-term and Cousins has never had a preferred stock issue in its capital structure. Top management has asked the financial manager to investigate thoroughly the general attributes of preferred stock. Major points to consider that came immediately to management's mind included cost, financial risk, and capital structure flexibility. The financial manager plans to address these points as well as other important issues in his analysis.

a. Identify and explain the principal provisions or features usually associated with preferred stock.

b. From the viewpoint of a prospective issuer, explain the advantages and disadvantages of preferred stock with respect to the financing alternatives of common stock and long-term debt.

PROBLEMS

17-1. Jack's Metal Supply Corporation has the following balance sheet:

Assets		Claims	
		Current liabilities	$ 2,000
		Bonds	4,000
		Preferred	1,000
		Shareholders' equity	
		Common stock (500	
		shares @ $4)	2,000
		Paid-in capital in excess	
		of par	500
		Retained earnings	1,500
	$11,000		$11,000

a. Calculate book value and par value per share.
b. Jack's common sells for four times book value. What is the market price? Explain the difference between market and book values.
c. Calculate liquidation value if assets can be sold for (i) $10,000; (ii) $6,000; (iii) $2,000
d. How much external equity has Jack's raised? How much internal equity?
e. An analyst's estimate of the intrinsic value of Jack's common is $85. Will she bid for any stock? If the analyst's view is typical, what will subsequently happen to the relation between market and intrinsic values?

17-2. An investor expects General Telephox to pay a $3.60 dividend on its common stock at the end of each of the next four years and for the stock to trade at $46\frac{3}{4}$ at the end of the four-year period. Calculate the stock's intrinsic value if the investor requires a 20 percent rate of return. What will the investor do if the stock is now priced at $37\frac{1}{4}$?

17-3. An investor expects a company's common stock to pay a $4.20 per share dividend at the end of the year and expects the growth rate in dividends to be 8 percent annually over the foreseeable future. She intends to invest in the stock for five years and then sell it for an estimated $36.50.
a. Calculate this investor's intrinsic value if she requires a 14 percent rate of return.
b. Would she buy the stock if it were priced now at $27.75 per share? Explain your answer.
c. An important determinant of the intrinsic value is the investor's required rate of return. Explain how an investor should determine it.

17-4. Crabfern, Inc., needs to raise $30,000 in external equity. Management decides on a subscription price of $6, and the market price of each of the 5,000 shares outstanding is $8.
a. How many new shares will be issued?
b. How many rights will be required to buy one new share?
c. What is the value of one right? Explain your answer verbally.
d. What is the price of the stock ex rights (without rights) when the stock is finally issued? (Hint: Calculate the average price after the issue.)

17-5. CMA Examination (modified). Dixon, Inc., plans to issue 500,000 new shares common stock through a rights offering. Each common stockholder will be entitled to subscribe to one additional share of common stock at $60 a share for each four shares held. The 2 million shares of stock currently outstanding have a market price of $75. What is the theoretical value of one share of stock when it goes ex rights?

a. $75.00.

b. $63.00.

c. $71.25.

d. $72.00.

e. Some amount other than those given above.

Support your choice with calculations.

17-6. Triton Corporation has a share of common stock outstanding now trading for $16 per share. The company is issuing new common stock in a rights offering. The theoretical value of a right is $4.

a. What is the value of Triton Corporation's common stock ex rights.

b. A right will often trade at a premium above its theoretical value. Explain why such a condition may exist.

17-7. Jemco Enterprises is in need of new equity, and the company can sell new shares with a rights offering. The current market value of its stock is $65 per share and the subscription price will be $58. Book value per share is currently $20. Jemco Enterprises will sell 400,000 new shares, and the company currently has 1 million shares outstanding. The company now earns after taxes 18 percent return on equity measured in book value.

a. Calculate current earnings per share.

b. Determine the value of a right and the market value of a share ex rights.

c. Assume that the entire issue is sold to existing owners and that the *marginal* after-tax return is 15 percent on equity or book value. (That is, the return on the new equity is 15 percent.) Earnings per share after the issue are what amount?

d. Explain what happens to the wealth of a shareholder who

(1) exercises rights.

(2) sells rights for the theoretical value.

(3) lets rights expire.

Note: No calculations are required on part (d).

17-8. The Sandown Electronics Corporation needs $5 million to acquire new distribution facilities. The new facilities will provide an estimated after-tax return of 12 percent. A review of the company's financial position and current capital markets led corporate officials to decide on equity financing rather than debt financing. E. G. Morris, vice-president of finance, has obtained the following information to be used to compare a rights offering for common stock with a public offering for common stock through an investment banker:

Present after-tax earnings are $11,250,000 annually. The 4.5 million outstanding shares sell for $50 each in the market now. The price-earnings ratio is 20 and is expected to continue at this level.

The proposed rights offering would permit Sandown shareholders to subscribe at $40 for the one common share for each 36 shares of common stock held. An investment banking company consulting with Sandown believes that a public offering of stock at $45 would be successful.

The investment banker's commission and other costs for this offering to the general public would be 6 percent if this alternative is used.

a. Compute the earnings per share and market price of the common stock assuming:
   i. the rights offering proposal is carried out successfully.
   ii. the public offering of stock is carried out successfully.
b. Assume the company selected the rights proposal.
   i. Calculate the theoretical value of a right.
   ii. Calculate the market value of the stock when it trades ex rights.

CHAPTER 18
Long-Term Financing with Bonds and Notes

Large corporations use bonds and notes to finance their operations. This chapter examines these sources with emphasis on bonds. The first part of the chapter looks at the advantages and disadvantages to the corporate issuer of using bonds and how a financial manager may calculate interest rates on bonds. When you finish this discussion, you will be able to discuss the reasons for and limitations on bond use from a financial manager's perspective, to calculate the explicit cost of a bond, and to discuss the implicit cost of a bond. After this discussion, we turn our attention to bond types, the computation of interest coverage, and the way that bonds are rated by the rating agencies. You will become familiar with the various types of bonds, the way that a financial manager calculates interest coverage when there are several bonds outstanding, and the various ratings assigned by bond rating agencies.

The final part of the chapter addresses the related issues of retiring bonds and issuing bonds that are convertible or that have warrants attached. When you complete this final part you will know the financial implications of issuing convertible bonds or bonds with warrants. In addition, you will be able to calculate the theoretical value of a convertible bond and to determine the minimum price at which the bond will trade in the financial market. Finally, you will understand the way that retiring a convertible bond by calling it forces bond holders to become common shareholders.

BOND USE

Along with common and preferred stocks, bonds provide a company with permanent financing—that is, they help finance fixed assets and net working capital. Since bonds are debts owed to creditors, a company cannot, as a rule, market them unless its financial position is sound. Ordinarily, this means (1) that there is a sufficient "cushion" of equity to protect the bond holders' principal and (2) that profits provide a margin of protection for the bond interest.

On the other hand, the interest payable on bonds is both tax deductible and typically less than the rate of profit a company must earn on its common stock. Thus bonds outstanding offer a profitable company the advantage of financial leverage. It is in this framework that both the reasons for using bonds and the limitations on their use can be explored.

Reasons for Use

There are six main reasons why companies use bonds in their financial structures.

1. The growth rate of a company's sales and assets may be so rapid that it cannot be supported entirely from retained earnings. To acquire additional assets, management must go outside the firm for finance, and bond financing is often preferable to short-term debt, common or preferred stock, or other modes of financing.
2. An increase in debt may bring a desirable increase in ROE. So long as financial leverage works favorably, a company can use debt financing to increase the return accruing to its shareholders. Larger financial leverage means greater risk, but so long as the expected return rises faster than the risk premium applied by investors, the value of common shares should increase.

   Example. Expected earnings may now be $1 per share for infinity. Discounted at 10 percent, the intrinsic value is $1/.10 = $10. If financial leverage raises the average return to shareholders 20 percent to $1.20 and the discount rate from 10 to 11 percent, the theoretical value rises to $10.91.

3. Reduced fears of depression and long periods of easy money have made business people less fearful of downturns in economic activity. Monetary and fiscal policies are biased in an expansionary direction. This expansionary bias is interpreted by business managers to ensure that sales revenues will be high enough to meet interest expense and that leverage will be favorable. Hence, business people have turned increasingly to the use of debt, including bonds, rather than equity financing.
4. Interest expense on bonds is tax deductible. At a 50 percent income tax rate, only $1 before interest is needed to meet $1 of bond interest expense, versus $2 to pay $1 in preferred dividends or to provide $1 of earnings on common. That means that if

everything else is equal, then the financial manager chooses to use bond financing rather than preferred or new common stock.

5. A general decline in stock prices increases the cost of common-stock financing, and investors often refuse to buy the new shares of financially weak or low-profit companies at any price. Thus considerations both of economy and of necessity have driven many companies into bond financing.

6. Finally, inflation has encouraged companies to use more long-term debt, since repayment is likely to be made in cheaper dollars. So long as lenders do not tack on a large price-level premium to protect themselves from loss through inflation, borrowers gain at their expense.

Points 4 and 6—inflation and the tax deductibility of interest—may reduce the cost of interest payments appreciably. We can adjust the Fisher equation (see Chapter 3) for the tax deductibility of interest expense to find the real cost of interest on an after-tax basis:

$$i_R = \left(\frac{i_m - \Delta P}{1 + \Delta P} \right)(1 - T)$$

where

i_R = real or constant-dollar interest rate on an after-tax basis
i_M = money or current-dollar interest rate
ΔP = annual rate of change in the price level; in other words, it is the annual inflation rate
T = issuer's marginal tax-rate

Example. A company issues a bond with a 12 percent interest rate. If the company is in the 46 percent marginal tax bracket and inflation is 8 percent annually, then the real interest rate after taxes is 2 percent calculated as follows:

$$i_R = \left(\frac{0.12 - 0.08}{1 + 0.08} \right)(1 - 0.46) = 0.02 \quad \text{or} \quad 2\%$$

Practice. A company in the 40 percent marginal tax bracket issues a bond with a 14 percent interest rate during a period when inflation is 6 percent annually. What is the bond's real interest rate after taxes? Answer: 4.53 percent. Show how you found this answer before continuing to the next section.

Limitations on Use

There are four major limitations on a firm's use of bonds for long-term financing. First, conservatism in management can restrict the willingness to incur long-term debt. Some managers see all debt as risky and prefer to have as little of it as

BOX 18-1

Flexibility for a $1,000 Minimum   Managers of investment companies are a creative group. They seem always to come up with a new way to appeal to investors. Consider the development of a new type of bond investment program developed by Scudder, Stevens & Clark. The fund introduced its Target Fund in 1983, a fund that lets you buy shares in any of 10 different portfolios. Five of the portfolios are made up of U.S. government securities and five of corporate bonds and bank certificates of deposit that mature in 1984, 1985, 1986, 1987, or 1990.

For a minimum investment of $1,000 for shares in any one portfolio, you select a maturity date and yield. As you would expect, the further off the maturity date, the higher the yield. You collect monthly dividends while being invested. Then, when the fund matures, all the securities in the portfolio are liquidated and the cash distributed to the shareholders. The objective of each managed fund is to return a sum that at least equals the cost of your shares. Shares can be switched from one portfolio to another or redeemed at their existing net asset value (which may be more or less than you paid for them initially).

Source: **Based on** *Business Week,* April 4, 1983, p. 90.

possible. Second, inflation cuts two ways: it may encourage companies to go into debt, but it can also discourage the use of debt. If lenders expect inflation, they will adjust their interest-rate demands upward to compensate for the expected rate of increase in the price level. If they overestimate the inflation rate, their interest requirement may prove exorbitant. In such circumstances many would-be borrowers will shun bond issues. Third, creditors may make various noninterest demands that are financially burdensome or that restrict management's freedom. They may insist that working capital be maintained at a specified level or that the bond holders (acting through their trustees) have the right to veto some management decisions. In times of rapid inflation, creditors may demand an equity "kicker"—that is, a share of profits or gross receipts in addition to interest. Companies may be unwilling to accept these kinds of provisions, and so they avoid the use of debt by limiting the firm's growth to what can be financed out of internally generated funds, new common stock, and short-term borrowing. Fourth, credit stringencies resulting from a tight money market or a change in creditor attitudes may oblige companies to restrict long-term borrowing. Because demands for long-term funds frequently exceed supplies, creditors ration loans by limiting them to the best-known, most creditworthy borrowers. Companies with excessive debt-equity ratios or short, vague financial histories cannot borrow long-term at any price. In general, the longer inflation has gone on since the middle 1960s, and the faster it has accelerated, the more bond buyers' sense of risk seems to have increased, and the less willing they have become to buy the bonds of second-rate borrowers.

Role of Trustees

The bond market, unlike the bank loan market, is impersonal, in the sense that lenders and borrowers rarely meet in person. A person in St. Paul, Spokane, Miami, or New Dime Box, Texas, may buy the bonds of a corporation in Philadelphia without ever meeting that firm's management or employees. To protect the widely scattered creditors, a *trustee* is appointed. The trustee, usually a bank, must act at all times to protect the interests of bond holders. It has three primary responsibilities. (1) It certifies the bond issue by making sure that it conforms with legal requirements. (2) It makes sure that the corporation fulfills all responsibilities set forth in the *indenture*, the legal document specifying all phases of the agreement between the lender and borrower (property pledged, form of bond responsibilities of the corporation, and so on). (3) It takes suitable action in the bond holders' behalf if the corporation defaults on principal or interest or violates any of the restrictions. For example, the trustee will enforce the acceleration clause found in most indentures. An *acceleration clause* accelerates principal repayment by making an entire bond issue immediately due in the event the issuing company fails to pay interest or to repay principal. An acceleration clause forces the defaulting corporation into bankruptcy.

CALCULATING COST

There are explicit and implicit costs associated with bond and note financing. The explicit cost is the yield to maturity at which bonds are sold. The implicit costs are the restrictive covenants and conversion privileges set forth in the bond indenture.

Explicit Cost

The explicit cost of a bond issue is its true rate of interest. The *true rate of interest* is the rate of discount that equates the price and interest payments of the issue to its face value at maturity. A financial manager may estimate the true rate of interest with the yield to maturity. A bond's yield to maturity differs from its stated or coupon yield, which is the bond's annual dollar interest divided by its face value, usually $1,000. Yield to maturity is the return that a bond holder receives if the bond is held to maturity. This return consists of two amounts: annual interest and the change in the value of the bond toward its face value. If an investor buys a bond below face value, then some of the discount will be added to the price each year. If, on the other hand, an investor buys a bond above its face value, then some of the premium will be lost each year as the bond price moves down toward its face value. An approximate equation for yield to maturity is

$$Y_M = \frac{C + \dfrac{(\$1,0000 - P)}{N}}{\dfrac{P + \$1,000}{2}}$$

where

C = annual dollar coupon interest paid by the bond
P = bond's principal
N = number of years to maturity
Y_M = approximate yield to maturity

Example. A 10-year bond is paying $4\frac{3}{4}$ percent ($47.50 per year), and selling at 82 ($820).[1] Its approximate yield to maturity will be

$$Y_M = \frac{\$47.50 + \dfrac{\$1,000 - \$820}{10}}{\dfrac{\$820 + \$1,000}{2}} = \frac{\$47.50 + \$18}{\$910} = 0.072 \quad \text{or} \quad 7.2\%$$

If the bond is selling at a premium, that is, for more than $1,000, then the yield to maturity will be *less* than the coupon yield.[2]

Implicit Costs

Implicit interest costs are the costs of a bond (or any debt for that matter) that do not show up on the borrower's income statement. They are the noninterest burdens of borrowing. The first implicit cost is the increase in the cost of equity as a company's debt-equity ratio rises. The increase in the debt-equity ratio increases the company's financial risk because there is a greater likelihood of the borrower failing to make debt service payments (called *default risk*), the company becoming bankrupt, and the owners losing their investment. Shareholders' required rate of return rises to compensate them for the increased risk, and the increase in their required rate of return means that the company's cost of equity increases.

There are other implicit costs of a bond. A sinking fund attached to a bond issue to retire much of it before maturity will create great inflexibilities for the issuing company. This is so because, in addition to interest on the bonds, the company must also produce the retained earnings and cash to retire the issue. Although this does not actually increase the cost of bond issue, it adds to the company's obligations. A conversion privilege (the holder's right to convert a bond into common stock) also raises the cost of a bond issue through an eventual dilution of stockholders' equity. Lastly, bond indentures and other lending agreements often include burdensome restrictions on management's freedom to act. These restrictions are intended to safeguard creditor rights. Their cost can rarely be assessed in dollars-and-cents terms. But their cost is *felt* when a company is forced to maintain a specific current ratio, to limit or omit dividends, or to submit officer promotions to the trustee of a bond issue.

BOND TYPES

Several bond types exist, reflecting a variety of creditor and borrower positions and desires. The different types have evolved through bargaining and maneuvering in the new-issues market, as business people and investment bankers have innovated in order to reconcile companies' needs with those of bond investors.

[1] Bond prices are quoted in percentages and eighths of their par value, which is usually $1,000. A bond selling at $102\frac{1}{8}$ has a dollar price of $1,021.25.
[2] Bond yields are sometimes expressed in *basis points*. A basis is one one-hundredth of a percentage point, so when interest rates rise by one percentage point we usually say by 100 basis points.

The most important classes of bonds are mortgage bonds, debentures, and collateral-trust bonds. Of closely related character are equipment-trust certificates and corporate notes.

Mortgage Bonds

A mortgage bond is backed by a pledge of fixed assets. Such a pledge is called a mortgage. If the borrower defaults on repayment of principal and/or payment of interest, then the lender can claim the pledged property. To restrict a borrower from pledging the same asset for another loan, the lender may require that the issue be a *closed-end issue.* This means that no new claims can be issued against the pledged assets. The lender may also insist that any fixed assets acquired in the future be pledged as collateral for the loan. Such a requirement is called an *after-acquired property clause.*

Collateral-Trust Bonds

Collateral-trust bonds are similar to mortgage bonds but are secured by a list of securities (either stocks or bonds) deposited with a trustee rather than by fixed assets. They are used primarily when a company wishes to borrow on the pledge of securities it would find inconvenient or impossible to sell—for example, the common stock of its subsidiaries.

Equipment-Trust Certificates

In contrast to mortgage bonds, which are secured by fixed assets, equipment-trust certificates are secured by mobile equipment. They are issued chiefly by railroads and airlines to finance purchase of locomotives, cars, and aircraft. As with other bonds, equipment-trust certificates have a trustee to represent the holders. These certificates differ, however, in that they are issued with serial maturities. For example, in a $15 million railroad issue, $1 million worth of certificates may be dated to mature each year for 15 years.

The purchaser of equipment must make a substantial down payment, typically 20 to 25 percent, and the serial certificates are paid off at a faster rate than the equipment depreciates. This substantial equity in the equipment gives borrowers a strong financial incentive not to default, and they rarely do. If they should default, the equipment is highly mobile and easily resold to satisfy the debt.

Debentures

A debenture bond is a promise to pay backed only by the general credit of the issuer. Not backed by the pledge of any specific asset, it is simply an IOU of the issuing corporation. Usually, the credit of a firm selling debentures is so strong that investors are willing to forgo a pledge of assets.

A *subordinated debenture* has a claim to interest and principal after that of any claim to which it is specifically subordinated. In bankruptcy, claims of a senior and its subordinated issue are lumped together. In this way the subordinated creditors receive nothing until the senior claim is completely satisfied, and they usually come out worse than general creditors. All debt claims, including accounts payable, are classed as general creditors unless the indenture specifies a lien on property or

BOX 18-2
Bond Prices May Anticipate Economic
Conditions   Bond-price trends often are more accurate forecasters than the government's much-publicized index of leading indicators, economists find.
Geoffrey H. Moore, director of Columbia University's Center for International Business Cycle Research, says that the economy "would have held fewer surprises" for
forecasters in recent years if bond prices had been more widely monitored.

Among bond-market measures that have signaled early and reliable signs of
what is ahead, analysts say, is a Dow Jones index reflecting the average price level
for 20 highly rated bonds of industrial and public-utility companies. It began climb-
ing 13 months before the 1982 economic upturn began—five months sooner than the
leading-indicator index turned up. The bond index reached a post-recessionary high
of nearly 78 in May of 1983 and slipped to about 71.2. Most analysts viewed the
drop as a typical early-recovery retrenchment rather than a signal of a new slump.
But economic consultant David Bostian warns that unless the peak is topped in six
months or so, "I would start worrying about a new recession." In early 1985 the
index hovered around 73, prompting some economists to forecast a recession beginning in mid-1985.

Source: The Wall Street Journal, December 5, 1983, p. 1.

subordination. Without subordination, each creditor class would receive cash equal
to its percentage share in the firm's liabilities. Of course, any mortgage bond holders
(mortgages) receive the liquidated value of the mortgaged asset, and any of their
remaining claim is placed in the pool with general creditors.

How subordination works can be illustrated this way. Assume that a bankrupt
company has debentures specifically subordinated to a bank note and the balance
sheet shown under "Claims" and "Amounts" below. Assets are liquidated for $500.

(1)	(2)	(3)	$(3) \times \$500 =$ (4)	(5)	$(5) \div (2) = (6)$
		% of	Unsub- ordinated	Sub- ordinated	% Claim
Claims	Amount	Total	Allocation	Allocation	Satisfied
Note	$ 400	40	$200	$300	75
Subordinated debentures	200	20	100	0	0
Trade creditors	400	40	200	200	50
	$1,000	100	$500	$500	50

Note and subordinated-debenture holders constitute 60 percent and trade
creditors 40 percent of the claims. With $500 available, $300 goes to the first group,

$200 to the second. Note holders receive $300, the subordinated debentures zero, and trade creditors $200. If $800 were available, then note holders would receive $400, subordinated-debenture holders $80, and trade creditors $320.

Capital Notes

Rather than selling its bonds to the public at large, which involves time, expense, and registration, an issuer may choose to place its bonds privately.[3] Five or six large life-insurance companies (or bank trust departments) may buy an entire $50 million issue of these nonmarketable bonds, called *capital notes*. On such issues the purchasers negotiate terms (payment of principal, maturity, and so on) to meet their preferences. The issuer can obtain money quickly. Since the issue is not registered, it cannot be sold in the open market so purchasers are buying an illiquid asset. To compensate them for this illiquidity, the issuer pays a higher interest rate than on comparable marketable bonds. Issues of privately placed notes have, and need, no trustee, since purchasers are few and knowledgeable.

In addition, the issuer may make the interest a floating rate so that when market yields increase, the dollar interest it pays rises, too. By insisting on this provision, creditors can obtain a return that will vary, at least roughly, with the rate of inflation. If, for example, rising inflation moves the prime rate up one percentage point, the bond yield may do likewise. Although floating rates may be used in publicly issued bonds, they are more often found in privately placed capital notes.

Deep Discount Bonds

In 1981 a new type of bond made its public market debut. Martin Marietta Corporation issued a *deep discount bond* (DDB), a bond that pays interest below the current market rate and initially trades at a price discount from face value. Most deep discount bonds are privately placed notes.

Example. A 30-year, $100 million deep discount issue may carry a 7 percent coupon yield when the market rate is $14\frac{1}{2}$ percent. The bond would be priced to investors to yield $14\frac{1}{2}$ percent, so that its market value would be about $534 per bond.

An extreme form of deep discount bond is a zero coupon bond. A *zero coupon bond* has no coupon payment at all and is therefore sold at a very large discount from face value. Most zero coupon bonds are of intermediate-term maturity. J.C. Penney's 1981 zero coupon bond had an eight-year maturity and each $1,000 bond was priced at $332.50. The yield on such a bond is the discount rate equating the face amount to the market value. The face repayment is called a *balloon* or *bullet maturity*.

Example. The J.C. Penney zero coupon bond above has an interest rate calculated with the future value interest factor equation:

$$\$1,000 = \$332.50(\text{FVIF}_{i,8})$$
$$3 = (\text{FVIF}_{i,8})$$

[3] Private placement is discussed in detail in Chapter 25.

Appendix B-1 tells us that the interest rate on this bond is slightly less than 15 percent.

Deep discount bonds offer the corporate issuer several advantages. The discount on the bond is amortized annually on a straight-line basis and shown as an interest expense on the income statement. This tax-deductible expense is a noncash item called a *tax shelter* and so provides a tax saving to the issuer. The liability recorded on the balance sheet when the bond is sold is limited to the proceeds received, and the liability increases each year by the amoritization of the discount. The bond's indenture typically states that the issuer is liable in the event of bankruptcy for only the amount shown on the balance sheet at the time of bankruptcy. Corporate record keeping is easier and less expensive because semiannual interest payments are not mailed. Finally, zero coupon bonds usually have no sinking-fund requirement.

Deep discount bonds are not without drawbacks. From the issuer's perspective, the bonds are usually callable only at face value so that as a practical matter an issuer will not be able to substitute lower-cost financing if it becomes available. Also, placement costs are large because the corporation must sell more bonds than it would otherwise—it must issue twice as many deep discount bonds at $500 as coupon bonds at $1,000 to raise needed cash. Finally, the fact that the calculation of interest income reported on the investor's tax return is complicated makes these bonds unsuited for public offering. That explains why most are privately placed.

Other Types

There are many other bond types, and we shall mention only a few more. First, *income bonds* are promises to pay interest only if it is earned. If the firm does not earn enough revenue to cover expenses, then no interest is legally due. Whether the interest accumulates and so must be paid before any dividend is declared depends on the particular indenture. *Revenue bonds* are issued by states or governmental divisions and pay interest out of the revenue generated from the specific project financed by the bond. Turnpikes and municipal sports arenas are examples of assets financed with revenue bonds. *General-obligation bonds* are backed by the general taxing power of a state or municipality. Interest received on revenue and general-obligation bonds is exempt from federal taxation.

The interest yield on a tax-exempt bond is often computed as a taxable yield equivalent, which means the yield necessary for a taxable bond to provide the same after-tax yield as the tax-exempt bond. Taxable yield equivalents are easy to calculate. Let Y_m equal the interest yield on a tax exempt bond. Then the taxable yield equivalent TYE is given by the formula

$$\text{TYE} = \frac{Y_m}{(1 - T)}$$

where T is the bond purchaser's marginal tax bracket. For example, a municipal bond yielding 4 percent would be equivalent to a corporate bond yielding 10 percent for an investor in the 60 percent marginal tax bracket,

$$\text{TYE} = \frac{.04}{(1 - .60)} = 0.10 \text{ or } 10\%$$

COMPUTING INTEREST COVERAGE

In Chapter 14 we examined the ratio of earnings before interest and taxes (EBIT) to interest expense. This ratio measures the margin by which interest is covered and indicates a firm's risk of default. Where more than one debt issue is outstanding, the ratio must be adjusted to measure the coverage of the different issues. A junior issue is not as secure as a senior one, and to reflect this an analyst must use the cumulative method of computing interest coverage.

Assume that Kyklos Corporation has three bond issues outstanding, presented here:

First mortgage 7%, due 1990	$2,000,000
General mortgage[4] 8%, due 1997	1,000,000
Debentures 10%, due 1990	500,000
	$3,500,000

The analyst would expect the first mortgage bond to be covered more times than the general mortgage or debentures because the first mortgage holder has a superior claim. The *cumulative (or overall) method* of computing coverage of interest expense takes the interest requirement on a particular issue *plus the requirements on all issues senior to the one in question* and divides this sum into earnings before interest and taxes.

Suppose Kyklos Corporation had earnings before interest and taxes of $600,000. The interest coverage on the three above issues would be as follows:

1. First-mortgage bonds: $\dfrac{\$600,000}{\$140,000} = 4.29$ times

2. General-mortgage bonds: $\dfrac{\$600,000}{\$80,000 + \$140,000} = 2.73$ times

3. Debentures: $\dfrac{\$600,000}{\$50,000 + \$80,000 + \$140,000} = 2.22$ times

The cumulative method of calculating times interest earned shows what you intuitively expect: each issue shows better coverage and a stronger position than those inferior to it.

---

[4] A fancy name for a second (or third) mortgage.

BOND RATINGS

How do creditors judge the investment merit of a bond? The easiest way is to rely on the bond ratings provided by Standard & Poor's Corporation and Moody's Investor's Service, Inc., the two major rating services. These agencies examine an issuer's profitability, total size of its debt, cyclical and other risks of his business, "average year" and "worst year" interest coverage on the bonds in question, strength of the bond holder's indenture protection, and so forth and then assign letter ratings to indicate the bond's probable quality.

Moody's uses these symbols: Aaa, Aa, A, Baa, Ba, B, Caa, Ca, C.[5] The first three classes designate the least investment risk, the last three, the greatest. These two agencies do not rate all bonds but only those they are specifically requested to examine (sometimes the issuer will ask them to do so) or those they believe will receive widespread attention. Moody's covers over 15,000 issues.

Moody's and Standard & Poor's sometimes rate the same company differently. This happens—even though both undertake much the same analysis that we covered in Chapters 13 and 14, carry out on-site inspections, and hold interviews with management—because subjectivity and intuition inevitably creep into the evaluation.

Receiving a high bond rating is important to a company for two reasons. First, the higher the rating is, the lower the interest the issuer will pay.[6] Second, many institutional buyers are restricted to securities of investment grade only, which usually means the top three ratings. If an issue falls below these three, then it loses a large potential demand and its bonds will sell at a lower price (and have a higher yield).

BOND RETIREMENT

To reassure lenders that a company will be able to repay the debt, the borrower may be required to provide a *sinking fund*, a periodic payment of money into a fund for retirement of the bonds. Bonds are retired in three ways. First, sufficient funds may be accumulated in the sinking fund for retirement of the bonds when they mature. Second, the trustee-manager of the sinking fund may buy back bonds in the open market and then retire them. Third, if the bonds are redeemable (callable), particular bonds may be periodically selected by lot for call-in and retirement.

Where a sinking fund is provided, management can estimate through present-value calculations how much must be invested each year to ensure the issue's retirement at maturity.

---

[5] Standard & Poor's uses AAA, AA, A, BBB, BB, and so on. The first five ratings translate roughly as follows: Aaa or AAA: unusually thick protective margins, no possibility of impairment foreseen. Aa or AA: good margins, though not so thick as above, no likelihood of impairment foreseen. A: protective margins all right for now; future impairment possible, though unlikely. Baa or BBB: definitely in trouble in a major depression or industry setback. Ba or BB: definitely speculative and future interest highly uncertain.

[6] Recall that any return can be expressed as a minimum-risk return plus a risk premium. The higher the rating is, the lower the risk premiums, and vice versa.

Example. A company will retire a $10,000 issue in 10 years. Management wants to know what amount must be set aside at the end of each year in order to have $10,000 on hand at the end of 10 years. The amount depends on the rate at which annual deposits in the sinking fund are expected to earn interest. Assume this rate is 5 percent. Using the method suggested in Chapter 2 to accumulate a future value of $10,000 in 10 years, the required annual deposit is $795 calculated as follows:

$$FVA = A(FVIFA_{0.05,10})$$
$$\$10,000 = A(12.578)$$
$$A = \$795$$

The company can deposit $795 at the end of each year and, earning 5 percent on each deposit, accumulate $10,000 in 10 years.

As an alternative to contributing to a sinking fund, a corporation may issue *serial bonds.* Under this arrangement bonds are redeemed in order of their serial numbers. A specified portion of the issue matures each year and is paid off. The chief example of serial bonds is the equipment-trust certificate, which has already been described. Finally, we should note that bond issuers are often free to use cash to repurchase their bonds in the open market.

CONVERTIBLE ISSUES AND WARRANTS

A *convertible issue* is a security that may be converted into another issue at the option of the investor. Most convertible issues are bonds, but preferred stock is sometimes made convertible. A *warrant* is an option to purchase a share of common or preferred stock at a specific price called an *exercise price.* Corporations sometimes attach warrants to a bond or preferred stock issue. The following discussion concentrates on convertible bonds, although the concepts and terminology apply also to convertible preferred.

Convertibility and warrants are often called equity kickers and sweeteners. *Equity kicker* means that the issue has benefits of the underlying equity issue into which the bond may be converted or warrants exercised. *Sweetener* means that conversion and warrants sweeten or enhance the desirability of owning such an issue. During periods of credit stringency, corporations encourage purchase of their bonds by adding a sweetener to their issue to lower the effective interest rate a company must pay on its issue. These sweeteners lead eventually to an increase in the company's equity as warrant holders and convertible bond holders exercise their privilege.

Convertible Bonds

Convertible bonds are usually debentures rather than mortgage bonds. They are exchangeable (as spelled out in the indenture) for the preferred or common stock of the issuing corporation. Besides serving as a sweetener, convertibility is an indirect way for management to sell common or preferred stock: If when long-term finance is needed the market price of the stock is below what management considers its fair value, the company can issue convertible bonds and wait for a stock-price recovery to produce conversion.

To understand the benefits of convertible bonds, you must become comfortable with the following terms.

1. **Conversion Ratio.** Number of shares into which each bond can be converted. For example, a $1,000 par debenture may have a common-stock conversion ratio of 20:1. One debenture can be presented to the corporate treasurer who must give 20 shares of common stock in exchange.
2. **Conversion Price per Share.** Per share price at which the common stock is received in conversion. Since a $1,000 principal debenture is the equivalent of 20 shares of common stock, the conversion price is $1,000/20 = $50 per share. Given the conversion price you can find the conversion ratio and *vice versa.*
3. **Straight-Debt Value.** Value of a bond without its conversion privilege. This value can be approximated by the price of nonconvertible bonds issued with the same rating and maturity.
4. **Conversion Value.** Value of the bond in terms of its common stock. If the price of the stock is $60 per share, then the above convertible debenture's conversion value is conversion ratio times price per share, or 20 × $60 = $1,200. Conversion value per share is conversion value divided by the conversion ratio, or $1,200/20 = $60. Notice that conversion value per share is the common stock's market value per share.

Figure 18-1 depicts the relationship between the theoretical value of a convertible issue and the price of its common stock. It shows an important feature of a convertible bond: The *theoretical value,* is the *higher* of either straight-debt value or conversion value. Theoretical value is portrayed by the heavy line in Figure 18-1.

FIGURE 18-1   Valuation of a convertible bond.

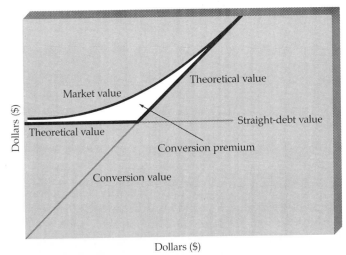

Above the straight-debt value, the convertible theoretical value rises and falls with the market value of the common stock.

Example. A bond's conversion ratio is 50. A $1 rise in per share market value of the common stock into which the bond can be converted is accompanied by a 50 × $1 = $50 rise of the conversion value of the bond. If conversion value is greater than straight-debt value, then the bond's theoretical value rises by $50.

As the market value of the underlying common stock (read along the horizontal axis in Figure 18-1) declines to zero, the conversion value declines to zero. But the theoretical value does not decline to zero because its level is halted by the horizontal line depicting straight-debt value. As your eye slides down the line depicting conversion value you will notice that the theoretical value of the convertible takes an abrupt turn at straight-debt value. Why doesn't theoretical value decline below its straight-debt value? Because investors can buy the bond and receive the interest associated with its straight-debt value.

Example. A $1,000 face value convertible bond with a 14 percent coupon yield and a 40 conversion ratio will have a $1,400 conversion value when the underlying common stock is $35 per share:

$$\$35 \times 40 = \$1,400$$

If nonconvertible bonds of equal risk have a 13 percent current yield, the bond's straight-debt value is $1,076.92, calculated as follows:

$$\text{Current yield} = \frac{I}{P}$$

where

I = annual dollar interest calculated by multiplying the coupon rate by the face value
P = price of the bond

$$\text{Current yield} = \frac{0.14 \times \$1,000}{P} = 0.13$$

$$P = \frac{\$140}{0.13} = \$1,076.92$$

In this example, the theoretical value of the bond is its conversion value because conversion value is above straight-debt value. If it sold for less than $1,400, investors would buy the bond and convert it into 20 shares of common stock then sell the stock for $1,400, a procedure called arbitrage. *Arbitrage* means to buy and sell simultaneously in two separate markets in order to make a profit. Arbitrage raises the theoretical value of the convertible to $1,400.

Example. Suppose that current yields on nonconvertible bonds of similar risk decline to 8 percent from 13 percent. The straight-debt value of the above bond becomes $1,750 calculated as follows:

$$\text{Current yield} = \frac{0.14 \times \$1,000}{P} = 0.08$$

$$P = \frac{\$140}{0.08} = \$1,750$$

The convertible bond would have a $1,750 theoretical value rather than the $1,400 conversion value (assuming the per share stock price remains at $35) because straight-debt value is above conversion value. To sell for less than $1,750 would mean that the convertible's yield is greater than 8 percent, a situation that would attract bond investors to the convertible and away from other bonds, driving up the price of the convertible (here, to its $1,750 theoretical value).

Conversion Premium. Figure 18-1 shows a shaded area above the theoretical value. This shaded area is a *conversion premium,* an amount between market value and theoretical value. This premium exists for the following reasons:

1. Investors like the downside risk protection of a convertible versus straight-debt bond. Convertibles trade at the higher of either straight-debt or convertible value.
2. Investors like the speculative appeal of participating in gains associated with the common stock.
3. Some financial institutions are restricted from buying common stock but can buy convertibles.
4. Lower transaction costs are on convertible bonds than on trading common stock. Common-stock investors often buy a convertible bond and immediately convert into common in order to avoid the higher brokerage fees on common stock. Buying the convertible bids up its price above the theoretical value measured by the dark line in Figure 18-1.

A company may want to increase its amount of equity by forcing convertible bond holders to convert their bonds into common stock. Management may encourage conversion in the following ways:

1. Increasing the dividend rate on the underlying common stock so that the greater return to the holder after conversion more than offsets the greater risk he assumes by becoming an owner rather than a creditor.
2. Giving attractive subscription rights or other privileges to common stockholders which can be obtained by bond holders only when they convert.

3. Making the debentures callable at the option of the company, then subsequently calling them. This contingency holds down the size of the conversion premium in Figure 18-1 at a high common-stock price because bond holders become fearful that the bond will be called and they may lose large potential profits.

Callability is a condition in which a security can be called and paid off before maturity by the issuing corporation. The price at which a security is called is its *call price*. Both convertible and nonconvertible bonds may be callable. By calling a convertible bond when the conversion value is higher than the call price, the corporation is assured that bond holders will present their bonds for shares rather than for cash. In this way management forces conversion on the bond holders. The result of conversion is a decline in debt and interest expense, an increase in common shareholders' equity, and a decrease in financial leverage and risk.

Example. Appleton Industries' bond has a 40 conversion ratio and a $1,100 call price. Call price per share is $1,100/40 = $27.50. If the bond is called when the price of the common stock is $35 per share, bond holders will present their bond for 40 shares valued at $35 × 40 = $1,400 rather than for the $1,100 call price.

Warrants

A warrant is the option to purchase a company's common stock at some specified price called its *exercise price*. Warrants may be detachable or nondetachable. *Detachable warrants* may be sold independently of the bond, and it is not uncommon for such warrants to be traded in securities markets. (The New York and American Stock Exchanges list several warrants.) *Nondetachable warrants* may not be separated from the bond and so cannot trade independently.

When a company issues the bond, the exercise price stipulated on the warrant is always above the current price of the common.

Example. An exercise price of $50 per share may be associated with a $30 market value. If the exercise price is below the market value when the bond is issued, bond holders may immediately acquire the common stock. In such a situation the company might just as well have sold common stock.

Like a conversion privilege, warrants (1) enable an issuer to market bonds at a higher price and lower interest rate and (2) add a speculative flavor to bond ownership. If the common stock to which the warrant applies rises well above the exercise price before warrants expire, warrant holders may make large profits.

Convertibles Versus Bonds with Warrants. When a conversion privilege is exercised, the debt-equity ratio falls. There is no change in a company's total assets. When warrants are exercised, the company's debt-equity ratio likewise falls, but its total assets increase because to exercise the option of obtaining common stock with a warrant, a bond holder must pay cash. Conversion may increase a company's earnings per share (but not its operating income) by eliminating interest expense, though the resulting increase in number of shares outstanding also tends to dilute ownership and control. On the other hand, the exercise of stock-purchase warrants brings new cash into the company and at least partially offsets the dilution effect of new shares. In general, bonds with warrants attached appear to be more beneficial to shareholders, present and future, than do convertible bonds.

Convertible Preferred: A Note

Like bonds, preferred stock may be convertible into common. The logic of conversion ratios, prices, and values for preferreds precisely parallels that of bonds and does not require further explanation here. Preferred stocks may also be subject to call prices and sinking funds. Again, these features closely resemble such features in bonds.

SUMMARY

1. Companies issue bonds for several reasons. The growth rate of the company may be so great that it must use debt financing, and long-term debt may be the suitable source. Debt increases financial leverage, and a company's management may want to take advantage of favorable financial leverage in order to increase the return to the common shareholder. In addition, reduced fears of recession and increased confidence in a Federal Reserve easy money policy have encouraged contemporary financial managers to rely more heavily on bonds than their earlier counterparts did. Interest expense is tax deductible, so this cash saving has encouraged many companies to choose bonds rather than equity financing, which has no such tax deductibility associated with it. Finally, inflation has encouraged corporations to issue bonds.

2. Many items limit a company's reliance on bonds. Issuing bonds increases a company's financial risk, thus many managers are reluctant to increase their company's use of bonds. Inflation encourages investors to add a price-level premium to the constant-dollar interest rate that they charge, so interest rates generally rise during inflationary periods and discourage companies from issuing bonds. In addition, creditors often add restrictions to the indenture, and these implicit costs serve to discourage companies. Tight money and capital markets from Federal Reserve policy discourage new bond issues.

3. The explicit cost of a bond is the true interest rate, the rate of discount that equates the bond price to the future cash (principal and interest payments) that the company must pay. The true interest rate may be estimated by the approximate equation for the yield to maturity. The implicit cost of a bond is the increase in the cost of equity as the issuing company's debt-equity ratio increases and other noninterest dimensions of the issue.

4. Important bond types are mortgage, collateral-trust, equipment-trust, debentures, and deep discount bonds. A debenture is often subordinated to another issue, which means that in the event of the issuing company's liquidation the debenture holders receive no cash until the senior issue is completely paid. A deep discount bond has a low coupon interest rate and so must trade at a discount from face value. A zero coupon bond is a type of deep discount bond. The interest rate on a zero coupon bond is the rate of discount that equates the future face value (that is, face value at maturity) to the bond's price.

5. The cumulative method to calculate a company's coverage of interest expense takes the interest requirement of a particular issue plus the requirements on all issues senior to the one in question and divides the sum into the company's earnings before interest and taxes. In this way a senior issue will have a greater coverage of interest expense than will a junior issue.

6. Moody's and Standard & Poor's rate bond issues based on the issuer's ability to pay interest and principal.

7. Bond's may be retired either before or at maturity. Often a company is required to make annual contributions to a sinking fund to provide for retirement at maturity.

8. Convertible bonds are a sweetener that helps a corporation to sell bonds at a higher price and lower yield than would be the case on a straight-debt issue. A convertible bond should trade at its theoretical value, the higher of either its straight-debt or conversion value. In fact, a convertible bond trades at a premium, a price slightly above its theoretical value. When a convertible bond is called by the issuing corporation, bond holders are forced to convert their bonds into common stock.

9. Bonds may be issued with warrants. A warrant permits an investor to buy a share of common stock at a predetermined price whenever the investor desires. Warrants, like the conversion privilege, are a bond sweetener.

KEY TERMS AND CONCEPTS

Trustee	Cumulative method
Real burden of interest	Investment-grade bonds
True rate of interest	Sinking fund
Yield to maturity	Serial bonds
Implicit costs of a bond	Exercise price
Bond types	Conversion value
Zero coupon bond	Straight-debt value
Taxable yield equivalent	Theoretical value
Call price	

QUESTIONS

18-1. List and discuss four reasons that corporations use bonds and four limitations on their use.

18-2. "To say that debtors benefit from inflation at the expense of creditors assumes that creditors underestimate the pace of inflation."
a. Do you agree?
b. What will creditors do to protect themselves?

18-3. The text suggests that inflation is a Catch-22: Its presence both encourages and discourages increase use of bond financing. Explain how inflation serves this dual function.

18-4. A financial instrument that promises to repay the principal at a specified date but will pay interest only when earned is called
  a. a nonparticipating preferred stock.
  b. a revenue bond.
  c. an income bond.
  d. a mortgage bond.
  e. a subordinated debenture.
  Explain your choice.

18-5. Bonds have both an explicit and an implicit cost. Explain the difference between these two costs and comment on which one you believe to be the most important to a corporate issuer.

18-6. CMA Examination (modified). The implicit cost(s) of debt financing is (are) the
  a. increase in the cost of debt as the debt-equity ratio increases.
  b. increases in the costs of debt and equity as the debt-equity ratio increases.
  c. decrease in the cost of equity as the debt-equity ratio increases.
  d. increase in the cost of equity as the debt-equity ratio increases.
  e. decrease in the cost of capital as the debt-equity ratio increases.
  Explain your choice.

18-7. Which type of security would you prefer to have: a senior issue or a junior issue? Explain your choice by defining each term and discussing the financial implications of each in the event that the issuer becomes bankrupt and is liquidated.

18-8. Which would be the stronger bonds, mortgage bonds or debentures? Assume first that they are bonds of the same company. Then, that they may be the bonds of different companies. Do the different assumptions produce a difference in your answers? Why?

18-9. Deep discount bonds are a useful financing tool for a corporation to use. State whether each of the following is true or false as it relates to a DDB and explain your choice.
  T F   Usually sold to the public.
  T F   Callability likely.
  T F   Amortized interest is a tax shelter.
  T F   Bullet maturity.
  T F   May have no coupon interest.
  T F   Liable for face value in bankruptcy.
  T F   Contains sinking fund.
  T F   Usually of intermediate term maturity.

18-10. Some corporations issue zero coupon bonds while others continue to issue conventional coupon bonds. List and briefly discuss three advantages and three disadvantages to the issuer of zero coupon bonds.

18-11. A company wishing to shift from debt to equity capital would most likely call a callable convertible bond issue prior to maturity when
  a. the yield-to-maturity exceeds the stated interest rate of the bond.
  b. the conversion value exceeds the call price.
  c. the market price of the common stock is less than the conversion price.
  d. the premium of market value over conversion is large.
  e. the market price of the bond is less than the call price.
  Discuss the acceptability of your choice.

18-12. CMA Examination (modified). The market value of a convertible bond is equal to or
   a. less than its conversion value.
   b. less than the value of a similar nonconvertible bond.
   c. less than either the smaller of its conversion value, or the value of a similar nonconvertible bond.
   d. less than either the larger of its conversion value, or the value of a similar nonconvertible bond.
   e. greater than either the larger of its conversion value or the value of a similar nonconvertible bond.

18-13. Examine Figure 18-1.
   a. Explain why the theoretical value of the convertible bond does not fall below the straight-debt value.
   b. Why is market value above the theoretical value?

18-14. The straight-debt (or pure bond) portion of a convertible bond is
   a. the same as the market price of the convertible bond.
   b. the difference between the market price and the call price of the convertible bond.
   c. the value of the stock into which the convertible bond can be converted.
   d. the value of the convertible bond if it did not have the conversion option.
   Explain your choice.

18-15. The following points refer to a company's reasons for using warrants in a debenture offering. Circle true or false and comment briefly on each choice.
   T F   **a.** A warrant lowers the cost of a bond issue.
   T F   **b.** It decreases the debt-equity ratio in the future.
   T F   **c.** A warrant makes a debenture more attractive to investors.
   T F   **d.** It permits management to retire the debenture before maturity.
   T F   **e.** A warrant increases the future cash available to the company.

18-16. An important difference between a convertible bond and a warrant is
   a. the company receives a cash inflow when a warrant is exercised but not when a bond is converted.
   b. a cash outflow is required from the company during the life of a warrant but not during the life of a convertible bond.
   c. as the life of a warrant decreases, its value increases whereas a shortening of the life of a convertible bond generally decreases its value.
   d. the investor generally pays extra for a convertible bond but not for a warrant.
   Explain why the other choices are unacceptable.

PROBLEMS

18-1. Lawrence, Inc., issues $50,000 in closed-end mortgage bonds with an after-acquired property clause. The bonds have a 15-year life. Management must, according to the indenture, contribute annually equal sums to a sinking fund. Deposits are made at the end of each year.
   a. If the sinking fund is held in idle cash, earning no interest, then how much must each deposit be?
   b. If the fund earns 4 percent, how much must each deposit be?
   c. If the fund earns 10 percent, how much must each deposit be?

18-2. Cole, Inc., has the following financial structure:

Bank loan	$ 3,000
Debenture	5,000
Subordinated debenture	4,000
Shareholders' equity	8,000
	$20,000

The subordinated debenture is junior to all debts of the firm.
a. Assets are liquidated for $10,000. How much does each claimant receive?
b. Assets are liquidated for $8,000. How much does each claimant receive?

18-3. The accompanying statement of financial position is that of the Helms Corporation on the date that it declared bankruptcy. The debentures are subordinated specifically to the long-term bonds. Calculate how much cash the debenture holders receive under the following circumstances. (Note: consider each liability equal in priority.)
a. Assets are liquidated for $400 million.
b. Assets are liquidated for $447 million.

HELMS CORPORATION
Statement of Financial Position
as of December 31
(000 omitted)

Assets	
Cash	$ 16,800
Accounts receivable	81,900
Inventories	119,700
U.S. Treasury bills	33,450
Total current assets	$251,850
Land	217,500
Plant & equipment (net of accumulated depreciation)	391,500
Patents (less accum. amortization)	28,500
Total assets	$889,350
Liabilities and Owners Equity	
Accounts payable	$136,500
Taxes payable	3,000
Interest payable	6,000
Notes payable	30,000
Total current liabilities	$175,500
Bank loan	11,400
Long-term bonds	150,000
Subordinated debenture	111,000
Total liabilities	$447,900
Common stock	360,000
Retained earnings	81,450
Total liabilities and owners' equity	$889,350

18-4. Calculate the taxable yield equivalent to a revenue bond that offers a 12 percent interest and the bond holder is in the
  a. 20 percent marginal tax bracket.
  b. 40 percent tax bracket.

18-5. Ron Alfred, treasurer of Dippel Amalgamated, asks you to calculate coverage of interest expense on the firm's bonds. Here are the issues:

First mortgage, 5% due 19x7	$10,000,000
Debenture, 6% due 19x1	4,000,000
Subordinated debenture, 8% due 19x0	6,000,000
	$20,000,000

The subordinated debenture is subordinated to the other two issues. Dippel Amalgamated's earnings *after* taxes are $2,100,000. The company's tax rate is 30 percent. Using the cumulative method, calculate the coverage of each issue.

18-6. Short Circuit Electric 6 percent coupon bonds due in 10 years are selling at a price of 82. What is the approximate yield to maturity?

18-7. Skinner Services, a conglomerate firm, has outstanding a subordinated convertible debenture. The conversion ratio is 25, par value, $1,000.
  a. What is the conversion price?
  b. If the stock is selling for $40, what is the bond's conversion value?
  c. Suppose that with the stock selling at $40, the bond is selling for $1,200. What is the conversion premium? Why does a convertible have a conversion premium?
  d. Now assume the bond is selling for its straight-debt value, $1,150, with its conversion value at $1,208. What would arbitragers do?
  e. If the bond is callable with an 8 percent call premium, what is the call price?

18-8. Claremont Beverages issues a zero coupon bond with a six-year maturity. The bonds will mature at $80 million face value. If the offering price is $40,526,800 what is the interest rate on this issue?

18-9. CMA Examination (modified). Darty Corporation needs to raise $2.6 million in order to finance a plant expansion and renovation project. One proposed financing alternative is a zero coupon bond issue. This bond issue would be sold with an original issue discount and would not bear interest. The other financing alternative is to issue 14 percent coupon bonds. The pertinent facts for each bond issue are as follows:

	Coupon Bond Issue	Zero Coupon Bond Issue
Face value	$1,000	$1,000
Annual interest (coupon) rate	14%	—
Selling price	$1,000	$ 260
Maturity	10 years	10 years

Darty Corporation is subject to a 40 percent corporate income tax rate.
  a. Determine for the coupon bond issue and the zero coupon bond issue:
    (1) the number of bonds that would be issued in order to raise the necessary capital, and the total face value of the debt issue in each case.
    (2) the before-tax percentage yield to the investors in each case.

    b. Discuss how the annual after-tax cash flows, exclusive of the flows at the date of issue and the date of payment, would differ between the coupon bond issue and the zero coupon bond issue.

    c. Discuss the advantages and disadvantages associated with a zero coupon bond issue from the viewpoint of a company using this type of debt instrument.

CHAPTER 19
Internal Financing and Dividend Policy

INTERNAL FINANCING

DIVIDEND DETERMINANTS

Shareholders' Income Needs, Risk Attitudes, and Tax Brackets · Growth and Reinvestment Opportunities · Company's Cash Position · Cyclicality of Earnings · Capital Structure · Legal Restrictions · Business Outlook · Rising Current Costs

FITTING DIVIDEND POLICY TO SHAREHOLDERS

TYPES OF DIVIDENDS

Cash Dividend · Stock Dividend · Stock Split · Other Dividends

STOCK REPURCHASE

SUMMARY

Key Terms and Concepts · Questions · Problems

T his chapter completes part of our study of the financial decision, the part dealing with intermediate and long-term sources of finance available to a company. Recall that the financial decision deals with the right-hand side of a balance sheet, and that it considers the short-term, intermediate-term, and long-term sources available to a company. (We shall examine the short-term sources when we consider working-capital management in Chapter 24.)

This chapter begins with a discussion of the relationship between retained earnings and divided policy to show how the decision to pay a dividend determines the amount of capital that a company may reinvest. After this discussion we shall turn our attention to the items that determine a company's dividend policy. Perhaps the most important determinants are shareholder variables, that is, what the shareholders want. After all, they own the company so that it is only right that the company's dividend policy conform with their demands. However, other items influence a company's dividend policy. These are company variables and economy-wide variables. When you finish this part of the chapter you should understand the items that any financial manager and corporate director must consider in establishing a company's dividend policy.

A company can pay different types of dividends, and we examine these types in the third part of this chapter. When you finish studying this part, you will recognize the different impacts of a cash and a stock dividend on the company's cash position and the impact of a stock split on the market value of the company's common stock. The chapter concludes with a brief discussion of share repurchase in order to familiarize you with a method some companies use to pay dividends.

INTERNAL FINANCING

By internal financing, we mean sources of funds available to the financial manager from year to year without raising them outside the company. For the short run, several internal sources of funds exist, as a review of the "Statement of Changes in Financial Position" in Chapter 12 will show. These sources include depreciation (and other capital-consumption allowances), funds from sale of fixed assets or investments,[1] and funds provided by retained earnings.

The first two of these sources represents funds only in a restricted sense. Consider depreciation flows first. Given a stable or rising sales level, depreciation recoveries cannot contribute in the long run to a firm's growth—they are destined eventually to replace the company's fixed assets.

This does not mean that depreciation dollars generated by a building, for example, cannot be used this year to buy a new machine—they can and will be. In the short run, depreciation is the most flexible source of discretionary spending money at the financial manager's disposal. However, depreciation is an *encumbered source* of internal financing. Suppose that a series of new machine investments is financed by depreciation flows from a building. Eventually, the building itself will need replacement. Unless some provision has been made to generate the necessary funds, the company will encounter financial trouble.

Sales of investments or fixed assets—the second internal source of funds—are relatively infrequent and certainly not reliable as regular sources, though a company with a large, liquid investment portfolio is in an enviably flexible position.

The remaining source of internal finance, retained earnings, is of major importance. From year to year, it stands second only to depreciation in volume of funds provided. Furthermore, except in eras of rapid inflation (when earnings must be retained to supplement deficient depreciation allowances), retained earnings usually represent an unencumbered source of funds, available to finance the firm's expansion or improvement.

The wide reliance of business managements on retained earnings for expansion is explained by their ready availability, not by their cost. Ordinarily, retained earning are a more expensive source of funds than bonds or preferred stock because they are supplied by the common shareholders, and common shareholders require a higher return on their capital than other suppliers do. Retained earnings accumulate in the firm when earnings are not paid out in dividends. If earnings after taxes are

---

[1] In the very short run, a firm can raise *cash* by running down its inventories and receivables, or by pledging or selling them, as we shall see in Chapter 23. We are using the word *funds* here in its customary sense of working (or net working) capital. For some applications, however, funds can be defined as cash with "sources and uses" tables drawn up on that basis.

not paid to shareholders, their retention is reflected in an increase in shareholders' equity on the *sources* side of the balance sheet, and in assets on the *uses* side.

Recall that retained earnings are not cash. They are simply a *claim* on a company's total assets, not matched by cash or any other particular asset. A firm can have large retained earnings (reflecting past profitability) but no cash (indicating present illiquidity).

The rest of this chapter will closely examine retained earnings, but from the other side of the what-to-do-with-profits coin—dividend policy. Because all earnings must be either retained or paid out in dividends, there is really only one decision involved. Earnings not paid out are automatically retained. We could deal with this decision under either heading but have chosen to treat it as a dividend decision.

DIVIDEND DETERMINANTS

Legally, all earnings belong to a corporation's shareholders. That is true whether earnings are paid out or retained. But in deciding how much to pay out and how much to retain, a corporation's directors often face a complex decision. Among the many issues typically weighed in this decision are the items listed on Table 19-1. To a considerable degree, these items overlap, but Table 19-1 classifies each determinant according to whether it is a shareholder, company, or economy-wide variable. The following sections discuss each determinant in turn.

Shareholders' Income Needs, Risk Attitudes, and Tax Brackets

Shareholders' income needs, risk attitude, and tax bracket fall under a general classification of dividend policy termed *clientele effect*. The clientele effect refers to the tendency for a company to attract a type of clientele, one that prefers the company's dividend policy to that of other companies. A change in dividend policy will lead to a change in the clientele of investors, and the company's stock price may as a result decline.

TABLE 19-1   Dividend Determinants

    Shareholder Variables
Need for immediate income
Risk attitude
Income tax bracket
    Company Variables
Growth and reinvestment opportunities
Cash position
Cyclicality of earnings
Capital structure
Legal restrictions
    Economy-wide Variables
Near-term business outlook
Rising current costs

Income Needs. Some people need cash immediately more than others do. Examples of such investors are retired persons, small investors, and others to whom current income is important. American Telephone, Exxon, and General Motors are conspicuous examples of companies with such shareholders. Recognizing this need in a majority of their shareholders, these companies' directors typically pay out a high percentage of their earnings in dividends. Their stocks are known as *widows and orphans stocks* because dividends are both generous and well maintained—features that are supposedly appealing to widows and orphans.

On the other hand, many companies have their shares held by individuals in the high-income years of their working lives to whom current income from common stocks is not important. Companies like Milton-Bradley, Rockwell International, and Hewlett-Packard are examples. A high payout rate is of no value to shareholders such as these, so that dividend policy may be irrelevant to them (for income purposes), or they may prefer shares in companies with low earnings payout rates.

Risk Attitudes. Although everyone may be classified as a risk averter, there are varying degrees of risk aversion because some individuals are less fearful of a loss than are others. We call individuals who are less fearful of a loss *risk seekers*. Risk averse shareholders (called *risk averters*) will prefer a company with a high payout rate, and risk seekers will gravitate to companies with a low payout rate because of the relationship between futurity and uncertainty: The farther into the future an event is expected to occur, the less certain we can be of its occurrence because too many intervening factors intrude between now and then.

Shareholder Tax Bracket. A shareholder's tax bracket influences corporate dividend policy because dividends received are taxed at the ordinary tax rate— irrespective of the source of corporate earnings and even though the corporation may have suffered a taxable loss. If a shareholder is in a low marginal tax bracket, the tax bite will be small so that she will be able to spend or save most of the money received in dividends. Conversely, if a shareholder is in a high tax bracket, cash dividends will bring little after-tax benefit. Mostly, they will wind up in the coffers of the Internal Revenue Service. Consequently, the income tax position of the most influential class of shareholders will strongly sway a corporation's directors toward a high or low earnings payout rate.

High-bracket shareholders benefit chiefly from long-term capital gains, on which maximum income tax rates are one-half of the ordinary rate not to exceed 20 percent. Capital gains come from a stock price that rises across time in step with growth of a company's earnings. While all shareholders benefit from earnings growth and a rising stock price, these benefits are especially important to well-to-do shareholders whose cash dividends would be largely taxed away. Consequently, companies dominated by wealthy shareholders typically reinvest most of their earnings to accelerate earnings growth and capital gains on their shares.

Clientele Effect Illustrated. Figure 19-1 summarizes the influence of a company's payout rate on its price-earnings multiple, the ratio of its common-stock price to after-tax earnings. An earnings payout rate (measured on the horizontal axis) is

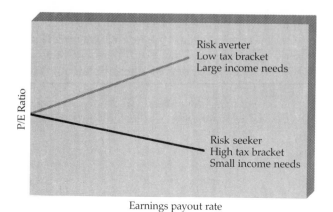

FIGURE 19-1   Clientele effect and price-earnings ratio.

linked to a price-earnings ratio (measured on the vertical axis) via the clientele effect. The two lines on Figure 19-1 represent two different clienteles:

Increasing P/E Ratio	*Decreasing P/E Ratio*
(Prefer Payout)	*(Prefer Retention)*
Risk averter	Risk seeker
Low tax bracket	High tax bracket
Large immediate income needs	Small immediate income needs

The figure tells us that by knowing its clientele—the individuals and institutions that invest in its stock—a corporation can establish a dividend policy that will maximize the common-stock price.

Example. Tensen Corporation has shareholders whose desires plot along the lower line or function of Figure 19-1. The financial manager knows that by increasing the payout rate Tensen's stock price will not be maximized because amounts on the vertical axis decline as the payout rate rises. If Tensen Corporation cuts back on its payout rate, its stock price-earnings ratio rises and the stock price is maximized.

Practice. Explain why a company with shareholders having a line like the top one in Figure 19-1 is making a mistake if it cuts its earnings payout rate from 80 to 30 percent.

Growth and Reinvestment Opportunities

The more profitably a company can reinvest its earnings, the more its stockholders will benefit in the long run from its earnings being retained. Suppose a company has an exceptional product, invention, or management that enables it to earn 25 or 30 percent annually on every reinvested dollar. Then unless the shareholder's need for immediate income is pressing, he can profit greatly by demanding little or nothing in cash dividends and leaving earnings in the company to compound at these above-average rates. If he receives dividends, he must pay income tax on them before reinvesting the funds in the company. By simply leaving earnings in the company, the shareholder avoids, for the time being, any loss to taxes and plows 100 cents out of every profit dollar back into future earning power.

As a matter of experience, companies in high-growth, high-profit industries typically pay out a much lower percentage of their earnings in dividends than do slower-growing, mature companies that earn only average profits. Partly, this difference reflects the opportunities discussed above, wherein shareholders in growth firms enjoy the double benefit of avoiding income taxes on dividends and of reinvesting their earnings at above-average rates. But rapidly growing companies also usually *need* to retain a much higher percentage of their profits to finance increasing requirements for fixed assets, working capital, and cash. This is especially the case with young companies that are growing rapidly but are still too small to tap the stock and bond markets with new issues of securities. They need additional equity capital badly to support bank loans and accounts payable, but their only source is retained earnings.

Company's Cash Position

Cash dividends require cash to pay them. Cash is not assured by high earnings because of the relation between high earnings, asset growth, and cash. High earnings are closely related to rapid growth, and rapid growth absorbs cash often as fast as cash comes into the company. Indeed, rapidly growing young companies almost never have the cash to pay dividends—even though their annual profits may run extremely high.

Substantial cash dividends normally come with a company's maturity. As growth slows and assets required to support rising sales increase at a less rapid rate, a company typically commences to pay a small cash dividend. Payment may start at a 10 or 20 percent payout rate, then increase as the rate of sales growth further declines. A mature company whose asset needs are largely limited to replacements and whose sales are stable over the business cycle may have an 80 percent payout rate.

Public utilities had a dividend-paying method available permitting them to preserve their cash, but give the shareholders a dividend. Some public utilities were permitted to establish a *dividend reinvestment plan* allowing individual shareholders to exclude from federal income taxes up to $750 per year ($1,500 on a joint return) of the dividends, if they chose to receive stock instead of the cash dividend. Stock purchased by the utility with the reinvested dividends had a zero cost basis for tax purposes. If the stock were held for more than one year, the amount realized upon sale was taxed at capital-gains rates. Dividend reinvestment plans were eliminated by Congress beginning with the 1986 tax year.

Example. You may choose to receive a utility's $200 dividend in the form of common stock. Two years later when you sell the shares you would pay a capital-gains tax on the entire selling price because the stock has a zero cost basis.

Cyclicality of Earnings

Companies whose earnings are relatively insensitive to the business cycle can usually afford high payout ratios. Electric, telephone, and gas utilities are in this category, as are many large, stable, well-established food and tobacco companies. Because earnings are steady and relatively predictable from year to year, directors of these kinds of companies are rarely forced to worry about holding back cash for unforeseen misfortunes.

Dividend policy is different for a steel company, a machine tool maker, or a railroad serving an industrialized region. The earnings of these companies swing widely between boom and recession periods. A year of high profits may be followed by one of deep losses. Directors of such companies recognize that part of the earnings from good years must be held back to pay dividends—and maybe even operating expenses—in the bad years that will come in due course. A heavy machinery manufacturer may pay out only 30 percent of its boom-year earnings, a sacrifice necessary to maintain its dividend intact in some future year of deficit.

Capital Structure

A company's capital structure influences its dividend policy in two ways: The amount of principal and interest payments affects the availability of cash and its capital structure changes as dividends are paid.

Repaying a loan requires cash. Companies with bonds that will soon mature must accumulate cash to meet these maturities. Companies with term loans outstanding need cash to make periodic debt service payments of interest and principal. Companies whose bonds have sinking-fund provisions attached must set aside cash to repurchase or retire their own bonds in the open market. Evidently, a company heavily encumbered with debt must restrain itself in declaring and paying dividends to shareholders. Conversely, debt-free companies or those with debt maturing in the distant future are often candidates for liberal dividend payments.

When a dividend is declared and paid, a company's equity declines. If the equity decline moves equity away from the company's best or optimum proportion in the capital structure, then management should not declare and pay a dividend because the company's cost of capital would rise and the value of the common stock would decline. Alternatively, if paying a dividend and reducing retained earnings move a company closer to its optimum capital structure, then a dividend is called for. We examine capital structure in detail in Chapter 20.

Legal Restrictions

There are three legal determinants of a company's dividend policy. First, a closely held corporation must avoid an excessive accumulation of earnings because the Internal Revenue Service interprets this action as an attempt by the company to help shareholders avoid taxation. The Internal Revenue Service will then impose an excessive accumulation tax, a tax discussed in Chapter 21. The company's board of directors may choose to declare and pay a dividend in order to avoid being hassled by the Internal Revenue Service.

Statutory constraints on capital impairment are the second legal determinant of dividend policy. Many states do not permit dividends to be paid from the common-stock account, although it may be perfectly alright to pay them from present earnings, retained earnings, and paid-in capital in excess of par. This constraint is imposed to make creditors confident that a company will not liquidate after raising debt, leaving creditors with no equity base to absorb an initial decline in the market value of assets.

The third legal determinant of dividend policy is contractual restrictions. A company's contract with its bond holders or preferred stockholders may include requirements that limit the board of directors' freedom to declare and pay a dividend. Called *protective covenants*, these requirements may state that dividends may be paid from only profit earned after the debt or preferred shares are issued or that the company must maintain some specified minimum level of net working capital. When preferred stock is *cumulative*, there can be no common-stock dividend until all present and accumulated preferred stock dividends have been paid. Figure 19-2 is an example of a dividend restriction on a company with about $5.5 billion total assets and $113 million after-tax earnings in 1983.

Business Outlook

All companies are in some degree affected by the business cycle, and all are greatly affected by a major depression. As a result, the business outlook for a planning period should be considered carefully by a corporation's directors, especially when at issue is committing the company to an increase in the regular dividend rate.

Example. A company's long-term economic forecast suggests that double-digit inflation, federal deficit spending, and increasingly bitter competition for world markets will turn the next recession into a major depression of the 1930s variety. Directors would consider an increase in the regular dividend to be untimely. Paying an extra dividend might be voted down on grounds that the company should conserve its cash against a coming recession.

Rising Current Costs

Table 19-1 indicates that the final dividend determinant is rising current costs of nonmonetary or real assets—inventory items and fixed assets. Rising current costs (often called *replacement values*) are associated with inflation. Earnings achieved during periods of rising current costs may not justify the high earnings payout rates acceptable with stable current costs because a greater portion of earnings must be retained to replace the deteriorating capital equipment. Depreciation calculated at historical costs is not sufficient to provide for replacement, so earnings or new stock offerings must rise.

Dividend policy must be based on a company's distributable income. *Distributable income* is current-cost income, the dividend that a company can pay without impairing its ability to maintain operating capacity. The following discussion presents a way that management determines distributable income by considering fixed assets, but you should recognize that the analysis applies equally for inventory items and cost of goods sold.

Example. Suppose a company experiences a 20 percent increase in the current cost of a depreciable asset. This increase means that the company needs 20 percent more finance—debt and equity—to replace the asset. The board of directors must reduce

Extract from 8.35% Senior Bank Term Loan Due August 1, 1985 Agreement

4.4 Restriction on Dividends, Stock Purchases and Retirement. The Company will not

A. declare or pay any dividends on any shares of any class of the capital stock of the Company (other than dividends payable solely in capital stock of the Company);

B. pay or deliver anything of value (other than shares of capital stock of the Company), or set apart for payment or apply any of its property or assets (other than shares of capital stock of the Company), for the purchase, redemption or retirement of any shares of any class of the capital stock of the Company, or

C. pay or deliver anything of value (other than shares of capital stock of the Company), in connection with the reduction of capital stock of the Company or make any other distribution (other than shares of capital stock of the Company) upon, or permit any Subsidiary to purchase, any shares of any class of the capital stock of the Company,

unless after giving effect to such action, the sum of

(a) the amounts declared and paid or payable as dividends (other than dividends paid or payable in shares of capital stock of the Company) on all shares of all classes of the capital stock of the Company or distributed in respect of such shares of capital stock subsequent to July 31, 1977 plus

(b) the excess of (1) the consideration (other than shares of capital stock of the Company) paid, or set apart for payment, for the purchase (including purchases by Subsidiaries), redemption or retirement of shares of all classes of the capital stock of the Company subsequent to July 31, 1977 over (2) the net cash proceeds received by the Company after July 31, 1977 from sales of shares of all classes of the capital stock of the Company (including the net cash proceeds of any convertible indebtedness issued after July 31, 1977 which has been converted into stock)

will not be in excess of (x) $75,000,000 plus (or minus if a deficit) (y) Consolidated Net Income of the Company and its Subsidiaries subsequent to July 31, 1977.

Anything in this Section 4.4 to the contrary notwithstanding, as to preferred stock of the Company in an Amount not in excess of $50,000,000 issued for cash to institutional investors subsequent to January 1, 1972, or issued for cash subsequent to January 1, 1972, through a public offering pursuant to a bona fide underwriting agreement, or issued in exchange for such shares so issued for cash, or issued subsequent to January 1, 1972 in connection with the acquisition by the Company of substantially all the property or the voting stock of any Person not an Affiliate (provided that the Amount of the preferred stock issued in connection with any such acquisition shall not exceed 150% of the book value of the property or stock so acquired) the Company (1) may pay regular cash dividends at the rate specified therein and (2) may purchase, redeem or retire such preferred stock to the extent required by mandatory sinking funds or other mandatory retirement provisions established at the date of issue, provided that any such dividend, purchase, redemption or retirement shall be included in any computation required by the foregoing provisions of this Section 4.4 with respect to other dividends, purchases, redemptions or retirements, and provided further that if shares of such preferred stock are outstanding at any time in an Amount in excess of $50,000,000, the provisions of this sentence shall be applicable only to those outstanding shares, taken in the order of initial issue or sale, which do not exceed $50,000,000 in aggregate Amount. The term "Amount", when used with respect to a share of preferred stock, means the par value, the stated value, the involuntary liquidating value or the initial sales price, whichever is greater, of such share.

TABLE 19-2 Income Statements, Historical And Current Costs

	Historical Cost	Current Cost	Difference
Sales	$ 800,000	$ 800,000	$ 0
Less cost of goods sold	260,000	260,000	0
Gross income	$ 540,000	$ 540,000	0
Less depreciation expense	200,000	240,000[a]	$ 40,000
Net operating income	$ 340,000	$ 300,000	($ 40,000)[b]
Less taxes	136,000	136,000	0
Earnings after taxes	$204,000	$164,000	($ 40,000)
Less dividend	122,400	122,400	0
Carried to retained earnings	$ 81,600	$41,600	($40,000)

[a]$200,000 × 1.20 = $240,000
[b]( ) means negative.

its dividend in order to be able to finance replacement without selling new, external equity.

Table 19-2 shows the impact of a 20 percent increase in current costs for a company with $200,000 historical depreciation. Current-cost depreciation rises at the same rate as the current cost of the underlying depreciable assets, so that depreciation becomes

$$\$200,000 + 0.20\ (\$200,000) = \$240,000$$

The impact of current costs on the income statement is striking. Notice in Table 19-2 that the $40,000 increase in depreciation expense does not affect the company's income tax because the Internal Revenue Service does not recognize current-cost accounting. As a result, the effective tax rate rises to $136,000/$300,000 = 45.3 percent. After-tax earnings and the amount of earnings retained in the company are less by $40,000. What about the earnings payout rate? From its 60 percent rate on a historical basis, the earnings payout rate rises to 74.6 percent:

Basis	Calculation (Dividend/Income)	Ratio (%)
Historical cost	$122,400/$204,000	60
Current cost	$122,400/$164,000	74.6

This company is going to be unable to sustain the 74.6 percent payout rate if its capital budget has been established by assuming a 60 percent payout rate. The dividend should in fact be $98,400 because that is 60 percent of distributable income:

$$\text{Dividend} = 0.60 \times \$164,000 = \$98,400$$

BOX 19-1

Exxon's Dividend Policy   Exxon Corporation took Wall Street by surprise in July of
1983, announcing a 6.6 percent boost in its quarterly dividend, to 80 cents a share from 75 cents, payable September 10 to stock of record August 15.

How surprised were investors? Well, the stock rose $\frac{3}{8}$ (37.5 cents) on the announcement day, or, expressed another way: "It was as recently as six months earlier that some were anticipating a dividend cut," noted Constantine Fliakos, a Merrill Lynch vice president.

"To me, it's a fairly significant move even though the increase is small," said Mark Gilman, a vice president at Lehman Brothers. "It's a real confidence builder." He explained that the uncertain days before March 1983—when OPEC cut the price of crude by $5 a barrell—are now behind Exxon, the world's largest petroleum company.

Exxon, which has been paying dividends since 1882, raised its dividend to 85 cents from 75 cents quarterly in 1984. In May 1981, it declared a 2-for-1 stock split. The latest dividend increase works out to an additional $3.56 million annually for the company's 890,899 shareholders.

Exxon's dividend payout ratio is high, analysts note, no matter what earnings figure you use. Taking a $6.93 per share estimate for 1985, the payout ratio is about $3.40/$6.93 = 49 percent. In 1982, Exxon earned $4.82 a share, and 1986 forecasts range from $7.40 to $8.20 a share.

Source: Based on Elizabeth Sanger, "Speaking of Dividends," *Barron's,* August 1, 1983, pp. 49–50, and *Value Line Investment Survey,* September 1984.

FITTING DIVIDEND POLICY TO SHAREHOLDERS

In small, closely held companies, where shareholders are also usually the managers, dividend policy is typically set by direct vote of the shareholders and in accordance with majority need. If most shareholders are in relatively low income tax brackets and need an amount beyond their salaries to live on, then a liberal dividend policy is probable. This will be true even if it keeps the firm from growing as fast as it might with more earnings being plowed back. Conversely, independently wealthy stockholder-managers are unlikely to desire dividends, preferring to see all earnings retained to accelerate their firm's growth.

With large companies traded on the nation's stock markets, dividend policy is usually set by the directors in keeping with their long-range plans for the company's future and the kind of financial image they want their company to project. They may want the company to have a large body of small shareholders to give it favorable public relations and strong political muscle. This will sway them toward a liberal dividend policy. Or they may prefer to have their firm known as a growth company, attractive to wealthy individuals and financial institutions. This will prompt the directors to retain most of the earnings to pave the way for rapid assets growth without the need to sell more common shares. Once these decisions are made, they are quickly reflected in a company's stock market image, and investors are guided accordingly. Widows, orphans, and retired people buy stocks of the liberal dividend payers. Well-to-do executives, growth-type mutual funds, and rich heiresses buy low-dividend growth stocks. Thus each type of shareholder gravitates to companies with dividend policies that fit a particular need for current income, long-term capital growth, or some combination of the two.

TYPES OF DIVIDENDS

Besides cash dividends, regular and extra, a corporation may declare other forms of dividends. The most common form is stock, but stock splits and distributions of other assets also may be used. Each form has its particular appeal to shareholders and can play a definite role in a firm's financial strategy. Each also has a distinctive impact on a company's balance sheet, which we now examine.

Cash Dividend

Part of the shareholder's claim consists of retained earnings, and these are legally available in their entirety for dividend payments. (Some state laws prohibit dividends that would reduce the common-stock account or paid-in capital in excess of par account.) However, as already noted, sufficient cash must also be available.

Suppose that management decides to pay a $100,000 dividend in cash. The effect on the company's balance sheet is illustrated below.

Before Dividend

Assets		Claims	
Cash	$500,000	Shareholders' equity	
		Common stock	
		(10,000 shares	
		outstanding at	
		$10 par)	$100,000
		Paid-in capital in	
		excess of par	50,000
		Retained earnings	350,000
	$500,000		$500,000

After-Cash Dividend

Assets		Claims	
Cash	$400,000	Shareholders' equity	
		Common stock	
		(10,000 shares	
		outstanding at	
		$10 par)	$100,000
		Paid-in capital in	
		excess of par	50,000
		Retained earnings	250,000
	$400,000		$400,000

The payment reduces both cash and retained earnings by $100,000. If the company had distributed any other kind of asset as a dividend, then *that asset* and retained earnings would have shown similar declines.

Stock Dividend

A stock dividend is simply a means of redistributing the amounts in the shareholders' equity section of the balance sheet. For that reason it is sometimes called a *recapitalization* (or permanent capitalization) *of earnings*. The asset side of the balance sheet is unaffected, retained earnings decline, and both common stock and paid-in capital in excess of par increase.

Suppose the firm represented by the balance sheet above chose to pay a 10 percent stock dividend rather than a cash dividend. A 10 percent stock dividend means the company will distribute .10 times 10,000, or 1,000, new shares—one additional share to each shareholder for every 10 formerly held.

Stock dividends are governed by a definite accounting rule. The paying company must transfer—from retained earnings to its permanent capital accounts—an amount equal to the full market value of the dividend paid. Suppose, in our example, that the stock is selling on the market at $25 per share. Then retained earnings will be lowered by 1,000 shares times the market price of $25, or $25,000. How much will be credited to common stock? Since par value is $10 per share, $10,000

After-Stock Dividend

Assets		Claims	
Cash	$500,000	Shareholders' equity	
		Common stock	
		(11,000 shares	
		outstanding at	
		$10 par)	$110,000
		Paid-in capital in	
		excess of par	65,000
		Retained earnings	325,000
	$500,000		$500,000

will be allocated to the common-stock component ($10 par times 1,000 shares). That leaves $15,000 ($25,000 dividend less $10,000 to common) that must be allocated to paid-in capital in excess of par.

Why declare a stock dividend? By so doing, management may have the best of all possible worlds: this can make the shareholders feel they are getting something of value, yet it keeps funds in the firm, where management can use them as it sees fit. But notice that the shareholders actually receive nothing they did not have before. Book value per share (shareholders' equity divided by number of shares outstanding) is approximately 10 percent less after the dividend than it was before ($45.45 versus $50), but each shareholder owns 10 percent more shares. However, many people *believe* a stock dividend has value. Thus management can satisfy both those shareholders wanting dividends and those wanting the capital gains that come from plowing back earnings. Management keeps the cash in the company and reinvests it.

Because there are more shares outstanding after the stock dividend, the market price per share declines. The total market value of the firm's shares before the dividend was $25 per share times 10,000 shares = $250,000. Since shareholders were given nothing they did not have before, the total value of their claim theoretically does not increase. Hence, theoretically the new market price of their shares would be $250,000 divided by the 11,000 shares now outstanding, or $22.72.

Occasionally, a stock dividend may be declared in order to lower the stock price into a more active trading range. Since more people will buy a low-priced stock, the resulting increase in demand may make the stock sell higher in relation to book value. In this way, a stock dividend *may* increase the wealth of existing shareholders, even though the dividend simply means that the same pie is cut into a larger number of smaller pieces. In the example above, the price may decline only to $23.50, rather than to the theoretical figure of $22.72, as demand for the stock rises.

Stock Split

Another way management can lower the price of its stock, and hence increase trading activity, is to declare a stock split. In a stock split no total dollar amount on either side of the balance sheet is affected. Only the two figures within the common-stock

Stock Split

Assets		Claims	
Cash	$500,000	Shareholders' equity	
		Common stock	
		(20,000 shares	
		outstanding at	
		$5 par)	$100,000
		Paid-in capital in	
		excess of par	50,000
		Retained earnings	350,000
	$500,000		$500,000

entry are changed—number of shares and par value. Suppose our firm declares a two-for-one stock split. Here, management is in effect calling in all outstanding stock and reissuing twice as many shares.[2] The balance sheet would appear as it does below. After the split there are 20,000 shares outstanding.

Since the total dollar amount in the common-stock component is unchanged, par value must be halved (on a three-for-one split, par would fall to one-third, on a four-for-one split, to one-fourth, and so on).

A stock split would probably increase trading activity in the stock. That could produce a windfall gain for existing shareholders, in the same way that a stock dividend does. It could also help the firm sell new issues of its common stock more easily. A more active resale market enhances the appeal of new shares.

Stock splits are usually welcomed by investors. Along with their enhancement of a stock's trading appeal, they are milestones in a company's progress and growth. Stocks reach and hold high prices because their earnings and dividends have risen, and it is the high prices that make splits both attractive and feasible. People who have held stocks like IBM and American Home Products over the past generation are likely to remember their road to riches as being paved with repeated splits of their favorite stock.

Other Dividends

In addition to cash and stock, management may declare other types of dividends. Any asset may be distributed so long as the distribution does not exceed the amount in retained earnings. The distribution of other assets can be in the form of stocks owned by the firm (called a *spinoff*) or products the firm produces. For example, liquor was a favorite dividend of liquor companies—and their shareholders—at the end of World War II. Such distributions are infrequent, however, compared with cash and stock dividends.

STOCK REPURCHASE

Instead of paying a dividend, directors may choose to repurchase some of the company's stock. Total assets will then decline by the cash needed to buy the stock, and shareholders' equity will decline equally. The shares repurchased become treasury stock, entitled to no share in earnings or voting power but available to the company for buying assets, acquiring other companies, and selling outright in the future. Any gain on the sale of treasury stock is tax free to the corporation.

Example. Glickman Corporation buys 100 shares of its own stock for $82 per share and resells it for $100 per share. The cash flow received by Glickman is $100 \times \$100 = \$10,000$ because the company pays no tax on the $18 per share gain. Of course, if it had sold the shares of another company (for example, shares of XYZ Corpora-

---

[2] A two-for-one stock split is similar to a 100 percent stock dividend in its impact on market price and book value per share.

BOX 19-2
An Unusual Cost of Going Private   You probably believe that when a company goes private by repurchasing its shares the company's need for a highly paid and prestigious board of directors declines. Not so in the case of Twentieth Century–Fox Film Corp., which Denver oil millionaire Marvin Davis bought in June 1981. Mr. Davis brought in former President Ford and former Secretary of State Henry A. Kissinger. According to the company's 1982 Form 10-K annual report, Fox paid each of the men $50,000 a year. Arthur B. Modell, president of the Cleveland Browns football team, got $20,000 a year for being a director.

Before the company went private, directors who were not officers of the company received annual fees of $15,000 each. But the company still attracted celebrities—including Princess Grace of Monaco, who was a director for many years before her death in 1983.

Source: Based on "Private Payments," *The Wall Street Journal,* April 30, 1982.

---

tion that it had been holding as an investment), then Glickman would pay tax on any gain.

Stock repurchase is a financial decision with mixed merits. It may help management support the stock's price by bidding for it in the market, and the company may be able to resell the stock in the future at a premium, thus raising more capital. If the stock is selling below book value, then repurchases will increase the book value per share for the remaining shareholders. On the other hand, repurchase reduces cash and a company's equity-to-debt ratio and amounts to liquidating some of the corporation. Obviously, such a practice can only be followed within careful limits.

SUMMARY

1. A company's internal sources of finance are its retained earnings and its depreciation reserves. Depreciation, however, is an encumbered source of finance destined to replace assets that wear out in producing earnings. The retained earnings are the difference between a company's after-tax earnings and its dividends: Earnings that are not paid out as a dividend are reinvested and become a part of retained earnings.

2. Shareholder variables are important determinants of a company's dividend policy. If shareholders need immediate income, are averse to risk, and are in low tax brackets, they will prefer a high earnings payout rate to a low payout rate. Conversely, if shareholders do not need immediate income, are risk seekers, and are in high tax brackets, they will prefer a low earnings payout rate. In this way the shareholders' wishes strongly influence a company's dividend policy.

3. Company variables also influence the company's dividend policy. A company with a high growth rate in sales and with opportunities to reinvest earnings to yield a high rate of return will have a low earnings payout rate. Also, companies with little cash and cyclical earnings will have a low payout rate in order to reduce the likelihood of financial failure. Companies with a high debt-equity ratio will have a low earnings payout rate because a large amount of debt requires cash payments that cannot be used to pay a dividend, and earnings must be retained in the company to build up the equity base. Legal restrictions cause a company to reduce its earnings payout rate when a lender insists on restrictions to protect the lender from default.

4. A pessimistic near-term business outlook causes a company to reduce its earnings payout rate because the company will want to increase its cash position to help it meet the downturn in sales and earnings. Finally, rising current costs cause a company to reduce its earnings payout rate because the amount of earnings shielded from taxation by depreciation expense is not enough to finance replacement of deteriorating assets.

5. A cash dividend reduces the company's cash and shareholders' equity. A stock dividend does not affect a company's assets but merely redistributes amounts within shareholders' equity: Retained earnings decline by an amount equal to the number of shares multiplied by market value per share, and the common-stock account increases by an amount equal to the number of shares multiplied by par value per share. A stock split affects only the par value per share and the market value of the company's common stock.

6. Some companies repurchase their common stock rather than paying a dividend. The company's total assets and shareholders' equity decline by the amount of the purchase. Any gain on the subsequent sale of the stock by the company is exempt from taxes.

KEY TERMS AND CONCEPTS

Encumbered source	Current costs
Widows and orphans stocks	Distributable income
Clientele effect	Cash dividend
Risk seekers and averters	Stock dividend
Dividend reinvestment plan	Stock split
Cyclical earnings	Stock repurchase
Protective covenants	Spinoff

QUESTIONS

19-1. Which of the following factors does not affect dividend policy?
   a. The rate of asset expansion.
   b. The restrictions in debt covenants.
   c. The par value of the common stock.
   d. The stability of earnings.
   e. The cash position of the company.
   Explain your choice.

19-2. On November 11 of last year, the Yatsabishi Cycle Company declared its fourth-quarter dividend. Rather than its usual $2 per share, the dividend was $1.20. Within three trading days, Yatsabishi's stock price declined from $28 to $18 per share. Explain why market price would decline in this way.

19-3. Which of the following factors is least likely to influence a publicly held corporation's dividend policy?
  a. The internal investment needs of the corporation.
  b. The tax position of the corporation's shareholders.
  c. The tax position of the corporation.
  d. Legal rules on dividends as established by state statutes and court decisions.
  e. Desire to maintain a relatively stable dividend payment.
  Explain why the other choices were not selected.

19-4. Table 19-1 lists several dividend determinants. Explain briefly each of these determinants and comment on which group captures the clientele effect.

19-5. When current costs are rising, a company's distributable income differs from its statement income. Explain why these amounts differ.

19-6. The declaration of a 10 percent stock dividend should be accounted for by the issuing corporation by
  a. capitalizing retained earnings equal to the par or stated value of the stock.
  b. capitalizing retained earnings equal to the fair market value of the stock.
  c. capitalizing retained earnings per share equal to the total paid-in capital per share for the stock on which it is based.
  d. making only a memorandum entry in the capital accounts.
  e. capitalizing whatever amount of retained earnings the board of directors deem appropriate.
  Explain your choice.

19-7. A stock dividend
  a. increases the debt-equity ratio of the corporation.
  b. decreases earnings per share.
  c. decreases the size of the corporation.
  d. increases shareholders' wealth.
  e. increases the size of the corporation.
  Explain your choice.

19-8. The purchase of treasury stock
  a. increases a company's assets.
  b. increases a company's financial leverage.
  c. increases a company's equity.
  d. increases a company's interest coverage ratio.
  e. dilutes a company's earnings per share.
  Explain your choice.

19-9. Share repurchase offers advantages and disadvantages to a company. Summarize these advantages and disadvantages and comment on whether share repurchase is a financial decision or an investment decision.

19-10. Corporations occasionally repurchase their shares (treasury stock). A financial justification for share repurchase is
  a. to raise the debt-equity ratio by reducing shareholder's equity.
  b. to increase the corporation's total assets.
  c. to reduce the idle cash and increase marketable securities.
  d. to give large gains to nonselling stockholders.
  e. to raise the market price of the stock by stimulating demand.
  Explain why you did not select the other choices.

PROBLEMS

19-1. At the beginning of 19x8, Railwick Corporation had a deficit of $275,000 in its accumulated earnings and profits. The 19x8 taxable income of Railwick was $250,000, including a long-term capital gain of $50,000. During 19x8 Railwick distributed two cash dividends to its shareholders: $35,000 on March 31, 19x8, and $45,000 on September 29, 19x8. Calculate the amount that shareholders of Railwick will report as

a. ordinary income.

b. nontaxable return of capital.

c. long-term capital gain.

19-2. Ward, Inc., has an abbreviated balance sheet that looks like the following:

Assets		Claims	
Cash	$ 200	Shareholders' equity	
Other	1,800	Common stock	
		(100 shares	
		outstanding, $5	
		par)	$ 500
		Paid-in capital in	
		excess of par	500
		Retained earnings	1,000
	$2,000		$2,000

Ward's stock sells for $40 per share. Show the balance sheet after each transaction. Each transaction is independent.

a. A $2 per share cash dividend is declared and paid.

b. A 10 percent stock dividend is declared and paid.

c. A five-for-one stock split occurs.

d. A one-for-five reverse stock split occurs.

19-3. Curran, Inc., has an abbreviated balance sheet that looks like this (in thousands of current dollars):

Assets		Claims	
Cash	$1,200	Current liabilities	$ 80
Other	800	Long-term liabilities	600
		Shareholders equity	
		Common stock	
		(1,000 shares	
		outstanding, $50	
		par)	50
		Paid-in capital in	
		excess of par	70
		Retained earnings	1,200
	$2,000		$2,000

Curran's common stock has a $60 per share market price on the day of each transaction below. Assume that an event is independent of each preceding event. Show the balance sheet after each event.

a. A $1 per share cash dividend is declared and paid.

b. A 2 percent stock dividend is declared and paid.

c. A four-for-one stock split occurs.

d. A one-for-four reverse stock split occurs.

19-4. Wolski Compressor and Valve, Inc., has depreciable assets totaling $3.6 million in historical costs. Depreciation based on this amount was $640,000 in 19x3. The rate of increase in current cost of these assets averaged during 19x3 12 percent.

    a. Calculate depreciation expense based on replacement value (current cost).

    b. Discuss briefly how this adjustment affects the dollar amount of taxes paid by Wolski Compressor and Valve.

    c. Are there any implications for dividend policy from this adjustment?

19-5. Wascomb Enterprises has an income statement for 19x8 like that presented below. A search of corporate records indicates that the average age of depreciable assets is eight years and that current cost of depreciable assets during 19x8 increased an average of 16 percent.

Wascomb Enterprises
Income Statement for the 12 Months
Ending December 31, 19x8

Sales	$260,000
Less costs	120,000
Gross margin	$140,000
Less depreciation	80,000
Net operating profit	$ 60,000
Less interest expense	36,000
Earnings before taxes	$ 24,000
Less taxes (16.5%)	3,960
After-tax earnings	$20,040
Less dividend (40%)	8,016
To retained earnings	$12,024

    a. Calculate distributable income.

    b. Calculate the following on both historical and current-cost bases:

      1. Tax rate.

      2. Earnings payout rate.

      3. Amount of earnings carried to retained earnings.

    c. Which measure of income seems more appropriate for Wascomb Enterprises? Explain your answer.

19-6. Bazaar Corporation purchased 20,000 shares of its $10 par value common stock in the open market for $540,000 in February 19x3. This stock was originally issued in 19x0 at $18 per share. In October 19x6 Bazaar sold 10,000 of these treasury shares for $31 per share. As a result of these transactions, Bazaar recognizes for tax purposes:

    a. No gain or loss.

    b. A $180,000 long-term capital gain and $40,000 short-term capital gain.

    c. $220,000 ordinary income.

    d. $40,000 long-term capital gain.

    e. Some amount other than those shown above.

Show all necessary calculations to receive credit for this problem.

SIX

CAPITAL BUDGETING

An important task of any manager is to decide in which long-term income-producing assets to invest. This part of the book shows you several ways that such a task is carried out successfully. Chapter 20 introduces you to the cost of capital—its definition, its calculation, and its use. You will learn that it provides a manager with a minimum acceptable rate of return on a prospective capital project. Chapter 21 addresses the way that a manager measures the cash flow from a project. The discussion places special emphasis on the impact that ordinary and capital-gains taxes have on cash flow so that you will be comfortable with some of the important taxes affecting business decisions and the often complicated calculations taxes introduce to the decision. Chapter 22 shows you several methods that financial managers use to rank and select proposed capital projects. In addition to examining the decision in a certain environment in which a manager knows the timing and amount of future cash flows, the chapter shows you a straightforward way to adjust the decision to reflect uncertainty.

CHAPTER 20
Cost of Capital

SOURCES OF FINANCING CLASSIFIED

RECENT SOURCES OF FUNDS

THE COST OF CAPITAL
Debt · Preferred Stock · Common-Stock Equity

COST OF COMMON EQUITY: METHODS OF ESTIMATION
Earnings-Price Ratio · Present Return on Common Equity · Capital-Asset Pricing
Model · Constant Growth

WEIGHTED COST OF CAPITAL: AN EXAMPLE

MINIMIZING COST OF CAPITAL

SUMMARY
Key Terms and Concepts · Questions · Problems

Begin your study of this short but precise chapter by understanding fully the difference between a corporation's internal and external sources of funds. Make sure you can name the major sources from which internal and external funds are drawn and that you can explain why the sources listed in Table 20-1 have behaved as shown in recent years.

In familiarizing yourself with the cost of capital, begin by noting two points. (1) The cost of capital is a *composite*, a weighted average, of the different kinds of capital a company uses; no one class of capital has a meaningful cost viewed in isolation from the others. (2) *Present* market prices and yields, not historical ones, are the plausible basis for setting costs on capital being acquired and invested today.

Equations for the cost of senior capital (debt and preferred stock) are easy to learn and use. The only real challenge in this chapter is the cost of common equity, and we review and demonstrate four measures currently employed. Be sure you can explain the logic behind each measure and how the measure is found (usually by an equation). The methods are (1) the earnings-to-price ratio of the common stock, (2) the return currently being earned on the common equity, (3) the capital asset pricing model, and (4) the discounted cash-flow method. Once you have mastered these items, you will find calculating a company's overall cost of capital easy. That cost is simply a weighted average of the costs of the three kinds of capital a corporation uses—debt, preferred stock, and common equity.

A brief final look at minimizing a company's overall cost of capital by adopting an optimum capital structure—maintaining a proper balance among the three capital sources—concludes this brief, meaningful chapter.

Having forecast financial requirements and gauged the suitability of different sources, management must act to procure the financing. Major considerations here are (1) cost, (2) availability, and (3) timing. In approaching the financing decision, however, we should first note how sources are classified and the extent to which corporate business has been using each class.

SOURCES OF FINANCING CLASSIFIED

Companies finance themselves from both internal and external sources. *Internal sources* are chiefly depreciation and retained earnings. *External sources* divide into long- and short-term financing. Long-term funds arise from the sale of new securities (stocks and bonds), mortgage loans, term loans from commercial banks, and leases. Short-term credit is provided principally by bank loans, loans from nonbank lenders (finance companies, factors, commercial-paper sales, and the like) and from increased trade credit (accounts payable).

Internal sources derive from company operations. They comprise what is called *cash flow*, the sum of capital-consumption allowances (usually depreciation) and after-tax profits. To some extent cash flow is automatic, although depreciation involves a choice of method, and retained earnings depend on decisions about dividend payments. External sources, however, must be selected. Management must decide whether the financing sought should be debt or equity—and if debt, whether short- or long-term.

RECENT SOURCES OF FUNDS

Table 20-1 shows the sources of long-term funds for U.S. nonfinancial corporations over the five years 1980–1984. Each entry is the net amount raised in the year shown and does not represent the total outstanding. Table 20-1 suggests four significant points. First, internal sources greatly predominate, with depreciation being by far the largest single source. Second, the proportion of net new stock issues is extremely unstable, reflecting such capricious influences as companies' heavy repurchasing of their own stock (1981); a strong stock market, making new share sales attractive (1983), or recession, reducing companies' need for funds and depressing stock prices (1981–1982). Third, five- to ten-year term loans from banks have become a significant financing source for companies too small to sell publicly offered bond issues. Fourth, financing at the taxpayers' expense through tax-exempt industrial bond issues has become a popular item with corporate borrowers.

THE COST OF CAPITAL

Capital funds, like labor or materials, have a cost to the business. Unless the return from using these funds covers their cost, the business cannot prosper and will ulti-

TABLE 20–1   Long-Term Sources of Funds—Business Corporations (billions of current dollars)

	1980	1981	1982	1983	1984
Internal Sources					
Undistributed profit (retained earnings)	87.4	78.5	40.0	44.0	62.0
Depreciation	153.1	177.1	205.0	246.0	275.0
Total internal sources	240.5	255.6	245.0	290.0	337.0
External Sources					
Net new bond issues	26.7	22.1	18.8	16.2	14.6
Net net stock issues	12.9	2.5	11.4	26.8	17.5
Total net new issues	39.6	24.6	30.2	43.0	32.1
Mortgages	2.0	−1.5	−0.2	2.0	2.5
Term bank loans	12.5	17.5	19.5	−2.5	10.5
Industrial tax exempt bonds	4.4	6.9	10.1	8.7	7.5
Total	58.5	47.5	59.6	51.2	56.6

SOURCE: *Bankers Trust Company of New York*, Credit and Capital Markets, 1984, T26.

mately fail. To invest capital wisely, therefore, a company must know its approximate cost. Only then can it tell whether the projects, products, and assets in which the capital is invested are really paying their way. They will be paying their way only if they earn at least what the capital committed to them is costing the company.

A company's capital—the long-term elements on the right-hand side of its balance sheet—is actually a composite whole. True, it consists of different kinds of debt and equity, but the portions in which these are joined together are very important. In particular, the debt-equity mix and the relative shares of long- and short-term financing must be acceptable to the investors who put up the funds. In a sense, therefore, to speak of a company's cost of *debt* capital or *common-stock* capital, as if either were totally separate from the other, creates an artificial and misleading picture. As we shall see, a company's capital actually consists of composite slices made up of debt and equity in some fairly constant proportion. Thus, attempts to attach costs to particular *ingredients* of capital structure are not only artificial but also likely to involve a famous fallacy in logic, the *fallacy of division.*[1]

Nevertheless, we must learn how to compute the costs of different kinds of funds. The cost of each slice of a company's capital can only be figured as a weighted average of the costs of the different kinds of securities composing it, and the cost of each kind of security—bonds, preferred stock, common stock equity—is arrived at in a different way.

Before illustrating these calculations, one other point is important. Logically, the cost of capital is figured not on the basis of what it cost to sell securities at the time they were issued but on what it would cost the company to sell these securities today. *Present* market prices and yields measure what the money raised by securities

[1] Division is the fallacy of asserting of things separately what is only true of them taken collectively.

BOX 20-1
How Do Companies Choose to Grow—By
Building New Assets or by Acquisitions?
The "Q Ratio" Could Give the
Answer   According to 1981 Nobel laureate James Tobin, the stock market's major
effect on investment comes not from a company's ability to sell new issues,
but from how stock prices influence the investment decisions that never go near
Wall Street. When stock prices are high, Tobin argues, companies find it profitable
to expand by building new plant and equipment. But when stocks are low, companies grow by buying other companies through purchases of their stock.

Tobin explains this effect through what he calls the Q ratio. That ratio, which
helped the Yale University economist win his Nobel prize, measures the value that
the financial markets place on the economy's real assets. It is a corporation's market
value—the total price of its stock and debt securities—divided by the current cost of
its assets. A Q greater than one means that the market values a company's assets at
more than their current cost; a Q less than one, *vice versa*. A Q ratio rises and falls
depending on how investors view a company's profit prospects—and bid the price of
its stock up or down accordingly.

Changing Q ratios are signals to company management. A rising Q ratio tells
managers that investors see rising profits ahead for their company; that encourages
them to add to plant and equipment to cash in on the prospects. Conversely, a falling
Q inclines a management to restrict its internal investment. George Von Fursten-
berg, an economist at the International Monetary Fund, recently calculated Q ratios
for various industries. He found that utilities, basic steel, and textiles all have Qs of
about 0.5. This helps confirm the widespread opinion that growth prospects for these
companies are anything but bright.

Source: Based on "Wall Street's Big Gift to the Recovery," *Business Week,* May 9, 1983, p. 127.

is worth now—what interest, dividends, or other returns these securities must pay to
be acceptable to *present* investors. Money being invested today, whether in stocks
and bonds or in plant and equipment, should be appraised at today's cost.

Debt

The cost of debt capital is determined by three factors, two clearly measurable, the
third usually less so. These three factors are (1) the yield to maturity at which a
company's bonds are now selling, (2) the cost-reducing influence of income tax, and
(3) the noninterest dimensions of cost (such as restrictive covenants in the indenture). Each of these influences was discussed in Chapter 18. A satisfactory measure
of the after-tax cost is simply the prevailing yield to maturity reduced by the tax
saving. The equation would be

$$K_d = Y_m(1 - T) \qquad (20\text{--}1)$$

where

$$K_d = \text{after-tax yield}$$
$$T = \text{company's marginal income tax rate}$$
$$Y_M = \text{yield to maturity}$$

Since costs of equity capital are always expressed in after-tax dollars, debt costs are usually reduced to this basis so that all costs of financial capital can be compared directly.

Example. A company in the 40 percent tax bracket paying a 12 percent rate of interest would have an after-tax cost of debt of 7.2 percent—$(1 - 0.40)$ times 12 percent.

Practice. Dempsey Corporation is in the 35 percent income tax bracket with bonds that yield 16 percent. Show by calculation that the Corporation's after-tax cost of debt is 10.4 percent.

Preferred Stock

The cost of preferred stock is simply the dividend rate the company must pay on its preferred shares. In the absence of sinking funds, convertibility, or other special features, it is simply

$$K_p = \frac{D}{P} \qquad (20\text{--}2)$$

where

$$K_p = \text{cost of preferred}$$
$$D = \text{annual dividend in dollars}$$
$$P = \text{current market price per share in dollars}$$

The ratio D/P tells a company what yield will attract investors to its preferred shares. Note that P is *current* market price, and not the price at which shares may originally have been issued.

Example. Brownell Power & Light $4.50 preferred was originally sold at $100 per share. The present price, however, is $40. The present cost to the company of new preferred stock is $4.50/$40, or $11\frac{1}{4}$ percent.

Practice. Two years ago Lubell, Inc., sold $9 dividend preferred stock at $50 per share. Today, these shares are selling at $65. What is the company's cost of new preferred equity? Your answer should be 13.85 percent.

Common-Stock Equity

The cost of common equity is generally taken to mean the rate of return required by the company's common shareholders. In practical terms this equates to the return that must be earned to keep the common stock at its current price.

What common-stock equity costs a corporation is a complicated issue on which experts disagree. Reasons for this disagreement are clear. Unlike bonds or preferred stock, common stock does not promise a contractual return to its holder. The prospective buyer of a stock can only estimate what that stock may earn in the future and what dividends it can be expected to pay in years ahead. Different investors may hold radically different expectations about future returns from the same stock. It is true that a given stock at any instant will have a definite market price. But what future returns this market price implies in the mind of the marginal investor who pays that price can only be estimated from past earnings or dividend payments or from forecasts and guesses about what earnings and dividends will be in the future.

COST OF COMMON EQUITY: METHODS OF ESTIMATION

While all methods of estimating a company's cost of common equity thus involve considerable guesswork, such estimates nevertheless need to be made. Each method has its strengths and weaknesses, and each may prove more useful in some situations than in others. Four methods, each of which has its advocates, are described below. These are (1) earnings-to-price ratio, or *earnings yield,* (2) present return on common equity, (3) capital-asset pricing model, and (4) constant-growth or Gordon model.

Earnings-Price Ratio

Common sense suggests that one measure of the cost of common equity might be the ratio of net earnings per common share to stock price. Earnings are what the stockholder gets from the company, and the stock price shows what the stockholder pays for these earnings. This ratio, written E/P, is the earnings-to-price ratio of the stock, also called the *earnings yield.*

If a company's stock is selling below book value, then this is a logical measure of its cost of common equity.

Example. Suppose Eczema Corporation has a book value of $100 per common share, a return on equity of 5 percent (meaning earnings per share of $5), and a market price per share of $35. What would Eczema have to earn on each new share to keep average earnings per share at $5? The answer is $5. If $5 must be earned on each $35 raised, then the return required on this equity is $5/$35, or 14.3 percent. That is Eczema's cost of common-stock equity, E/P.

Present Return on Common Equity

The E/P ratio, however, is not always a plausible measure of the return investors are requiring to buy a company's stock. This is obviously true if a company is earning a very high return on its common equity, with the result that its stock is selling far above book value. In these circumstances the current return on book equity, rather than the E/P ratio, would plausibly measure the company's cost of common equity.

Example. This point can be illustrated with reference to the stock of Fantasticomputer Corporation, which has a book value of $20 per share and current annual earnings of $6 per share and sells in the stock market at $100 per share. The high market price—five times its book value per share—is explained by the fact that the company is earning 30 percent per year on its common equity; this permits the stockholders' wealth to compound very rapidly, making Fantasticomputer a highly esteemed growth stock.

Using the E/P ratio to measure this company's cost of common equity involves a contradiction. The E/P ratio is $6/$100, and its use to measure cost of equity implies that the company needs earn only 6 percent on new commitments of equity to maintain its stock at the $100 market price. In actuality, however, the stock sells for $100 at least partly because the company earns a dazzling 30 percent on its common equity. This analysis suggests that Fantasticomputer's managers can measure the company's cost of equity with its return on equity, here 30 percent.

Is 30 percent Fantasticomputer's true cost of common equity? Almost certainly not. It is the average rate of return now being earned on common equity, but it is not a marginal or cutoff rate—not the hurdle rate needed to justify an investor in committing new equity to the company. That marginal rate may well be lower than the average rate, which is likely to include the effects of some extremely profitable projects. However, the present rate of return on common equity cannot be totally dismissed as a measure of equity cost, because two things are true: First, if the company insists that new investments return at least 30 percent, it is more likely to maintain a 30 percent average return than if it sets its sights on a lower figure. Second, it is undeniable that the 30 percent return provides strong support for the stock's $100 price and that a lower rate of return may cause the stock's price to fall.

Capital-Asset Pricing Model

This third measure of the cost of equity is based on the familiar principle that an investor's required return is the sum of two elements: the time value of money plus an allowance for risk. The equation for the model runs,

$$K_{cap} = R_F + \beta(R_m - R_F) \tag{20-3}$$

where

K_{cap} = return investors require from a particular stock
R_F = return from some low-risk investment, such as a U.S. Treasury security
R_m = average return that stocks in general have produced over some past period
β = beta, a measure of the particular stock's tendency to change with stocks in general. (A stock with beta of 1 has average volatility. A beta less than one

signifies less than average volatility; a beta more than one denotes above average volatility. For example, a beta of 1.4 would mean that if the market rose 20 percent, the given stock would rise 1.4 times 20 percent, or 28 percent. If the market fell 30 percent, the given stock would fall 42 percent.)

A look at Equation 20-3 indicates that the allowance for risk is simply beta times the difference between the return on the average stock and the return on some low-risk investment.

Example. Texaco, Inc., has a beta of 1.40. U.S. Treasury securities yield 10 percent, and Standard & Poor's 500-stock index has returned 13 percent over the past five years. Texaco's estimated cost of common equity would be 13.2 percent calculated as

$$K_{cap} = .09 + 1.40(.13 - .10)$$
$$= .09 + .042 = 0.132 \quad \text{or} \quad 13.2\%$$

Practice. Distilleries, Inc., has a beta of 1.50. Long-term Treasury bonds are yielding 14 percent, and the *Value Line* common stock index has given investors a 16 percent return over the last seven years. Show that according to the CAPM Distilleries' cost of common equity is 17 percent. (Use the *Value Line* return as R_M.)

While this procedure looks exact and scientific, it contains serious weaknesses. First, beta confuses risk with volatility. They are not the same thing. A stock may swing widely in price but rise strongly over the years, while another fluctuates very little but steadily declines.[2] Second, the return from stocks in general is a past return, not necessarily the return investors are now expecting. Third, endless arguments usually develop over what interest rate to use as the measure of a low-risk return. Should it be the rate on Treasury bills, commercial paper, government bonds, AAA-rated corporate bonds, or something else? For these reasons the capital-asset pricing model may not be a satisfactory one for measuring a company's cost of equity.[3]

Constant Growth

What price a company can obtain for its stock depends on the return investors expect to obtain from it. An investor's return from a stock comes in two separate streams: a dividend stream and a capital-gains stream. The dividend stream consists of the future dividends the shareholder expects to be paid. The capital-gains stream is the increase in market price which the investor expects to realize while holding the

---

[2] Beta measures only a stock's tendency to change with the general market. If the stock collapses while the market is rising, beta does not register the loss. A stock that fluctuated widely around a price of 40 would have a higher beta than one that dropped from 40 to 10 and stayed there.
[3] The capital-asset pricing model is really a device for gauging a stock's rise in an investor's portfolio, not for measuring a company's cost of capital. See the Instructions for using *The Value Line Investment Survey. Value Line* estimates that beta measures only 30 percent of the risk of the average stock. For a proposed (and promising) improvement on the capital-asset pricing model, consider the arbitrage pricing theory model described in Box 20-2.

BOX 20-2
A New and Improved CAPM   For financial writers and others who have disparaged
                                      the capital asset pricing model (CAPM), better days
could loom ahead. Since the day of Adam Smith most financial analysts have agreed
that the cost of common equity can plausibly be estimated as the sum of a safe
interest rate plus an add-on for risk. What they have not liked is the way the CAPM
equates *all* risk with unstable stock market prices. Well, they are now greeting a new
and improved version of the CAPM. It is called the arbitrage pricing theory (APT)
model.

   What this model does is to break down the total risk stocks confront into the
several kinds that smart investment analysts have long recognized. Besides the market risk recognized in the CAPM, most financial writers will agree that there are
business and financial risks unique to each company. Even this list of risks is too
short to be meaningful. Financial risk can be broken down into default risk and
interest-rate risk, while business risk subdivides into recession risk, regulatory risk,
risk of technological change, competitive risks, foreign exchange risk, and several
other kinds of risk.

   In principle, the APT model is simply a common sense adding up of the
percentage points of return investors need to equalize the attraction of a given stock
with that of stocks in general. (That is where the notion of arbitrage or tradeoff
comes in.) Let us say, for example, that U.S. Treasury bills yield 10 percent. Then if
Brownell Electric Light and Power needs 2 percentage points of return to offset the
risk of inflation, 3 percentage points to offset the risk of adverse regulation, and 1
percentage to offset default risk, then its cost of common equity would come to a
total of 16 percent.

   Sounds logical doesn't it? The APT model is another example of how you can
often get a better grip on the factors in a problem by breaking them down into their
component parts, as APT does with the overall notion of risk.

---

stock. If we make the simplifying assumption that the stock's price, earnings, and
dividends per share will all grow across time at the same rate, we can write an
equation for the shareholder's expected rate of return:

$$K_e = \frac{D_1}{P_0} + g \qquad\qquad (20\text{--}4)$$

where

$$K_e = \text{cost of equity}$$
$$D_1 = \text{dividend (in dollars) expected over coming}$$
$$\text{year}$$
$$P_0 = \text{present market price per share}$$
$$g = \text{annual growth rate of earnings and dividend}$$

Equation 20-4 is a market-derived estimate of the cost of equity. It is often referred to as the Gordon model, after Myron Gordon, a finance professor who did much to develop it.

If management is shrewd or fortunate, it will be investing in assets that yield a very high return so that earnings and dividends may be growing rapidly.

Example. Fantasticomputer Corporation is paying an annual dividend of $2 per share and retaining the other $4 of annual earnings. Since the $4 of retained earnings will increase the $20 book value by 20 percent, it will permit book value, earnings, and dividends—all three—to grow at a 20 percent annual rate. Under these circumstances, a stockholder's expected rate of return and the company's cost of equity is

$$K_e = \frac{D_1}{P_0} + g = \frac{\$2}{\$100} + .20 = 22\%$$

Note that this 22 percent return is substantially below the $6/$20 = 30 percent return on equity actually being earned.

Practice. Fallnell Power & Light common stock trades for $20 per share, pays a $2.28 dividend, and is expected to pay a $2.40 dividend over the coming year. Earnings and dividends per share have increased at a 5 percent annual rate over the past five years. Show by the Gordon model that the company's cost of common equity is an estimated 17 percent.

Although the Gordon model method raises a number of problems,[4] it is generally considered the most plausible and reliable method of assessing a company's cost of common equity. It would appear to be the method most widely used in the real world by major companies and professional investors.

WEIGHTED COST OF CAPITAL: AN EXAMPLE

Now we can pull all the costs together and figure what average return the providers of capital as a whole require. In the following example, we compute a *weighted* average cost of capital. In such an average, the cost of each kind of capital is weighted according to its percentage share in the firm's capital structure. Weights can be based on either the book values or the market values of the different classes of securities, but should be market values whenever they are available. We use book values to keep our example simple.

---

[4] For example, how do you measure the growth rate investors anticipate in paying the price they are paying for the stock? The usual method is to see what past growth rates have been and plug these into the equation as the g factor. This practice, however, assumes that the future will be like the past, a specially dangerous assumption when interest rates, inflation rates, accounting methods, and stock prices have been changing widely and erratically.

Global Corporation, a company in the 50 percent tax bracket, has the following capital structure:

Assets	Claims	
	Bonds (7% coupon)	$200,000
	Preferred (10%)	50,000
	Equity	150,000
$400,000		$400,000

On the market, the bonds yield 6.5 percent to maturity. This tells us what the money they represent would cost today. But since interest is tax deductible, the net cost is reduced by the company's tax rate. Using Equation 20-1, K_d = 6.5 percent × $(1 - .50)$ = 3.25 percent. Similarly, if the 10 percent preferred sells at par, Equation 20-2 tells us that the cost—dividend divided by market price—is 10 percent. Let us assume finally that the cost of common equity, estimated by one of the methods discussed, is 20 percent. We can then construct the following table.

(1) Type	(2) Amount	(3) Cost (Rounded)	(4) % Total	(3)×(4)=(5) Weighted Share
Bonds	$200,000	.032	.50	.016
Preferred	50,000	.10	.12	.012
Equity	150,000	.20	.38	.076
	$400,000		1.00	K_A = .104

Column 4 is simply the proportion of total capital each component constitutes. Bonds are $200,000/$400,000, or 50 percent; common-stock equity is $150,000/$400,000, or 38 percent; and preferred stock is $50,000/$400,000, or 12 percent. We now multiply column 3 by column 4 to obtain the weighted cost of each component in the capital structure. Finally, we total these figures to obtain K_A, the weighted average cost of capital, 10.4 percent.

This 10.4 percent, then, represents the cost of each slice of capital consisting of 50 percent debt, 12 percent preferred stock, and 38 percent common-stock equity. You should now see why one commits a fallacy of division by speaking of separate costs for the different kinds of capital—clearly, these separate costs depend on the proportions in which the different kinds of capital are brought together. If, for example, the percentage of debt rose to 60 percent, it is unlikely that the bond yield would remain as low as 6.5 percent. Bond buyers would claim that the company was over-leveraged, they would pay less for its bonds, and its cost of debt capital would rise. Likewise, the cost of equity would increase. Management would have to select in-vestments yielding a higher return to reward shareholders for incurring the in-creased financial risk associated with greater financial leverage. Otherwise, share-holders would probably sell their common and acquire a stock more suited to their risk attitude.

Practice. Fallwell Power & Light Company's capital structure consists of $100 million of debt at an average cost of 10 percent, $30 million in 11 percent preferred stock, and $70 million of common equity at an estimated cost of 17 percent. Assuming the company pays income tax at a 50 percent rate, show that its cost of capital is 10.1 percent.

MINIMIZING COST OF CAPITAL

As already noted, companies aim at maintaining through time a capital structure acceptable to investors. By so doing, they can minimize their cost of capital. Figure 20-1 illustrates how changes in a firm's debt-equity ratio affect its cost of capital. As you can see, K_A, the cost of capital, is saucer-shaped and minimal over a large range, indicating that investors find a *range* of leverage acceptable for the company. Outside this range the cost of capital increases on either side. Too much leverage makes bonds more costly to issue. Too little leverage makes the stock unattractive and unduly lowers its price.[5]

Figure 20-1 also suggests a theoretical reason why management will want to minimize its cost of capital. The market value of the firm is theoretically equal to the present value of the firm's future earnings, just as the value of any asset is equal to the present value of its future receipts. For the value of the firm, earnings are discounted at the firm's cost of capital. We can say that

FIGURE 20-1   Leverage and cost of capital.

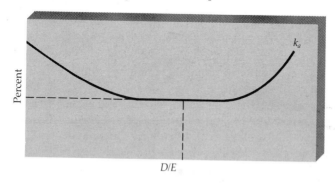

[5] But what governs the right amount of leverage? (Remember, we are dealing here with *financial* leverage.) It depends on the relation between two other factors: (1) the stability of sales revenue and (2) the degree of operating leverage involved in producing a company's service or product. The more stable sales are, and the lower the degree of operating leverage, the more debt a company can safely carry. The electric utilities have high degrees of operating leverage, but their revenues are so stable and well assured that they can typically support debt ratios of 50 percent, then obtain another 15 percent of their capital from preferred stock. A specialty steel maker, on the other hand, has high operating leverage plus a boom-and-bust sales pattern. It would be best off with no bonds at all outstanding.

$$V = \frac{E}{K_A}$$

where

V = market value of the company
E = future earnings of the company
K_A = average cost of capital

BOX 20-3
Some Questions and Answers about the
Cost of Capital

Calculating a company's cost of capital is no easy task, as most financial managers do not hesitate to tell you. The mechanics of calculating are easy, but deciding what goes into the equations you use poses some vexing questions. Here are a few of those questions (together with our answers):

1. Should we consider debt at its historical cost or replacement cost? It should be the replacement cost because we are calculating the cost of new financing for new capital projects.
2. How should we treat a deferred charge? Is this a free source? Deferred charges and depreciation reserve have a cost equal to a company's overall cost of capital, so usually their individual costs are omitted from the cost of capital calculation.
3. Should we base the cost of equity on conditions in present markets? We must use present markets and currently required returns because present shareholders and investors active in the market are the ones that will buy the company's new offering of securities.
4. Does stock ownership by institutions change the way we calculate the cost of equity? No, but it may change the resulting cost because institutions may require a rate of return that differs from that of individual shareholders.
5. How does a proprietorship or partnership determine its cost of equity? This is an easy question to answer. A proprietorship's cost of equity is whatever the owner says the minimum acceptable return is. A partnership's cost of equity is a weighted average of each partner's minimum acceptable return, the weights determined by a partner's percentage of ownership.
6. How can we determine the cost of capital for a privately held corporation or one without a market for its securities? Here, a financial manager will be forced to base an estimate on a similar publicly held and traded corporation or an industry average published by some source like Standard & Poor's Corporation. We should add a risk premium to the publicly held and traded company's cost of capital to reflect the decreased marketability of a privately held corporation.

Source: Based on Allen H. Seed, III, "Structuring Capital Spending Hurdle Rates," *Financial Executive,* February 1982, p. 22

As with any other present value computation, the lower the discount (or capitalization) rate applied, the higher will be the present value of the foreseen earnings stream. Minimizing the cost of capital will maximize V, the value of the firm. If a company can enlarge its V by changing the debt-equity ratio, the ratio should be changed.

Not all financial analysts believe that the cost of capital changes with capital structure in the way shown in Figure 20-1. Two famous professors, Franco Modigliani and Merton Miller, have long contended that, aside from the income tax saving that results from use of bonds and default risk, a company's total value and cost of capital cannot be changed by altering its capital structure.

They say that a company's total value depends on its net operating profit. All that changes in capital structure do is to split net operating profit in different ways between stockholders and bond holders. It is like dividing 10 pounds of potatoes between two sacks. However you bag them up, they still weigh 10 pounds.

The mathematical arguments the two professors use are too complicated for this book, and most financial managers do not accept them anyway. But we wanted to let you know of M & M's dissent to the usual view of cost of capital to keep you from being taken by surprise if someone who has taken more advanced courses in finance happens to mention it.

SUMMARY

1. Corporate businesses raise long-term capital from internal sources (depreciation, biggest of all single sources, and retained earnings) and externally from sales of stocks, bonds, and mortgages and from term loans made by banks and insurance companies.

2. A corporation's cost of capital is simply a weighted average of the three kinds of capital it uses—debt, preferred stock, and common equity. Costs of these three components should reflect current costs, not historical ones.

3. A company's cost of debt is the average interest rate paid on that debt multiplied by the factor $1 - T$, where T is the company's marginal income tax rate. The $1 - T$ adjustment is needed to allow for the tax-deductibility of debt and to express the cost of debt in after-tax terms.

4. The cost of preferred stock is simply the annual preferred dividend divided by the price per share.

5. The cost of common equity is both less certain and more debatable. Four popular measures of this cost are now in use. The *earnings-to-price* ratio on a company's stock is self-explanatory. So is the *return currently earned on a company's common equity.* More sophisticated is the *capital asset pricing model,* based on the volatility of a company's stock as the measure of its risk and viewing cost of common equity as a function of that risk. Finally, the *constant-growth* approach treats the cost of common equity as the sum of the stock's dividend yield and the growth rate investors expect for the dividend in years ahead. (A new and still untested measure of common equity cost is the *arbitrage pricing theory model,* reviewed in Box 20-2.)

6. In theory, a company maximizes its value (really the value per share of its stock) by minimizing its cost of capital—the weighted average referred to above. It does so by adjusting its financial leverage—the percentage of debt in its capital structure—to harmonize with the stability of its sales revenue and with the degree of operating leverage involved in producing its product or service.

KEY TERMS AND CONCEPTS

Internal sources	Capital asset pricing model
External sources	Gordon model
Cost of capital	Constant-growth model
Earnings-price ratio	Modigliani and Miller

QUESTIONS

20-1. What explains the increase in term loans to business during recent years?

20-2. The Economic Recovery Tax Act passed by Congress in 1981 provided much shorter depreciable lives for most forms of business plant and equipment. What effect would this have on the share of business financing provided by depreciation? Why?

20-3. Are internal or external sources of long-term funds larger? Why?

20-4. CMA Examination (modified). The critical assumption in any weighting system for the determination of the cost of capital for a company is that
   a. bonds always are less risky than stocks.
   b. it will raise capital in the proportions specified by the weights of the individual capital sources.
   c. its current capital proportions are optimal.
   d. taxes are immaterial in the computations.
   e. the cost of bonds is always less than the cost of preferred stocks on a before-tax basis.
   Explain your choice.

20-5. Do costs of the different sources of external capital—bonds, preferred stock, and common stock—exist independently of each other? Why or why not? Explain.

20-6. Why is it customary to reduce the yield to maturity on a company's debt securities by the factor "one minus the income tax rate"? Suppose you failed to do this for debt. What kind of cost of capital would you be calculating? What would you have to do then to get a correct reading on the costs of preferred and common equity?

20-7. CMA Examination (modified). The two bond-rating agencies, Moody's and Standard & Poor's, lowered the ratings on Appleton Industries' bonds from triple-A to double-A in response to operating trends revealed by the financial reports of recent years. The change in the ratings is of considerable concern to the Appleton management, because the company plans to seek a significant amount of external financing within the next two years.
   a. Identify several events or circumstances that could have occurred in the operations of Appleton Industries which could have influenced the factors the bond-rating agencies use to evaluate the firm and, as a result, caused the bond rating agencies to lower Appleton's bond-rating.
   b. If Appleton Industries maintains its present capital structure, what effect will the lower bond ratings have on the company's weighted average cost of capital? Explain your answer.

c. If Appleton Industries' capital structure was at an optimum level before the rating of its bonds was changed, explain what effect the lower bond ratings will have on the company's optimal capital structure.

20-8. Name four methods to calculate a company's cost of common equity. Tell—by equation if you like—how each approach is carried out.

20-9. Describe a situation in which the earnings-to-price ratio would not be a suitable measure of a company's cost of common equity.

20-10. Explain what is theoretically necessary for a company to minimize its cost of capital.

PROBLEMS

20-1. Examine the equation for the net cost of interest expense, K_d.
  a. The interest rate is 8 percent. What is the net cost if the tax rate is 30 percent? 70 percent?
  b. Does this mean that business people prefer a higher tax rate so that they can minimize the net burden of their debt? Explain.

20-2. Jefferson Products, Inc., has a capital structure like this:

Bonds (6 @ 6%)	$6,000
Preferred (5% $100 par)	2,000
Shareholders' equity	2,000

Bonds, though originally issued at par, are now selling for $600 each and have 10 years remaining to maturity. Preferred is quoted in the *Wall Street Journal* at $50 a share. Jefferson Products last year earned 12 percent on equity. Corporate tax rate is 40 percent. Assume a before-tax interest cost on the bonds of 10 percent. What is the cost of capital for Jefferson Products?

20-3. Guaranty Trust Limited has earnings of $4 per share. The current market price of the stock is $80.
  a. What is Guaranty's P/E multiple?
  b. What is the firm's earnings yield?
  c. What do you think would happen to the price of its common if Guaranty's management used the earnings yield as its cost of equity instead of its ROE of 20 percent? (Hint: Be sure to include in your answer how the cost of equity—and capital—is used by management.) This question does not call for a precise answer.

20-4. Fallmeadows Corp. earns 8 percent on a book common equity of $40 and its stock sells at 60 percent of book value. What is the cost of common equity measured by the earnings-to-price ratio?

20-5. U.S. Treasury bonds yield 8 percent. Standard & Poor's 500 stock index has averaged a 14 percent return over the past five years. Great Eastern common stock has a beta of 1.70. What is Great Eastern's cost of common equity according to the capital-asset pricing model?

20-6. Great Western's stock sells for 38, its book value per share is $15, its earnings per share are $3.45, and it pays an 80 cent annual dividend. Calculate what you consider the best estimate of its cost of common equity and defend your choice.

20-7. Amalgamated Caps, Inc., presents the following financial data. Market price of stock $30, book value per share of stock $20, rate of return earned on common equity 18 percent, payout percentage 40 percent, and growth rate 10.8 percent. Using these data calculate the company's cost of common equity by the constant-growth or Gordon model.

20-8. Rust Steamship Co. has a beta of 1.5. If the Dow-Jones Industrial Average (a measure of the overall stock market) goes from 800 to 1100, to what price should Rust stock move from 30?

20-9. If Ball Drug's dividend has risen from $1.00 per share in 1975 to $2.60 per share in 1985, what is the value of g in the constant-growth equation?

20-10. CMA Examination (modified). James Thompson, vice-president of finance at Walker Company, is preparing for the company's annual capital-investments meeting. The purpose of the meeting is to determine which projects the company is going to adopt and the amount of the financial commitments for the coming year. Thompson is responsible for presenting an investment analysis for each of the potential projects. Walker Company includes the discounted cash-flow technique in its evaluation of investment projects. Consequently, Thompson must calculate the firm's cost of capital before he can complete the analyses.

Walker Company's board of directors has indicated that the firm's present 70 percent owners' equity and 30 percent long-term debt structure should be maintained. The company's projected earnings, accompanied by periodic common-stock sales, will permit it to maintain the present 70 percent owners' equity structure. After consultation with the firm's investment banker, Thompson has determined that the debt could be sold to yield 9 percent. The common stock is currently selling for $42 on the market. The company is currently paying a dividend of $2 per share, and the dividends are expected to grow at an annual rate of 6 percent. The firm's effective income tax rate is 40 percent.

a. Using the data supplied, calculate the cost of capital for Walker Company.

b. Why would the board of directors want to maintain a capital structure comprised of 30 percent long-term debt and 70 percent equity?

CHAPTER 21
Corporate Taxation and Cash Flow

An important task of a financial manager is to manage the company's taxes—providing payments when they are due, being knowledgeable about tax laws, and seeking ways to minimize the company's tax bill. Tax management is also important because it affects the company's cash flow and the price of the common stock. Fewer dollars paid in taxes mean that more cash remains in the company to invest in profitable assets or to pay out as dividends to shareholders.

This chapter considers the legal forms of business and then examines corporate taxation. Corporate rather than personal taxes are emphasized in this book because corporations are economically the most important legal form of business and are the type of company that you will probably work for when you graduate.

When you finish this chapter, you will be able to determine a corporation's tax liability and to recognize the benefit of the loss carry-back and carry-forward tax provision available to a company experiencing a taxable loss. The accelerated cost-recovery system determines a company's depreciation amounts for tax purposes, and much of this chapter discusses the system. As a part of the discussion of depreciation, you shall see the role that depreciation plays in a company's cash flow. This discussion will be of special importance when we turn our attention to capital budgeting in Chapter 22.

The benefit resulting from the investment tax credit is an important calculation for a financial manager to perform, and you will learn to calculate it in this chapter. We conclude our discussion of corporate taxes with a brief examination of gains and losses on disposal of depreciable assets and a brief look at dividends and interest.

LEGAL FORMS OF BUSINESS

Businesses exist in various sizes, shapes, and forms. Although sizes and shapes are countless, the important forms number only three: proprietorship, partnership, and corporation. Each form is distinct so far as legal and tax status are concerned, but their financial management has much in common.

A proprietorship is a business owned by an individual. Although size is not the sole factor, a proprietorship is usually a small company managed by the owner. A partnership is owned by two or more individuals who have entered into an agreement. No legal documentation of the agreement is necessary, although formal partnership agreements are strongly advised. A corporation, on the other hand, is formed by an agreement between the state and the several persons forming the business, and legal documentation of the agreement is needed.

The *1984 Statistical Abstract of the United States* reports that in 1980 (the latest year for which complete data are available), there were about 14 million proprietorships and partnerships generating $798 billion in receipts and $63 billion in earnings. In the same year there were about 2.7 million corporations generating $6,360 billion in receipts and $239 billion in earnings. Consequently, though much fewer in numbers than proprietorships and partnerships, the corporation has the dominant economic impact on U.S. society.

These figures suggest that when you graduate from college the chances are high that you will work for a corporation. For that reason and because corporations play an important role in our society, we shall turn our attention to tax management in the corporation.

In the twentieth century the corporate form has dominated business enterprise. Although corporations are numerically a minority (about 2.7 million), by all other measures they prevail. Much of the reason lies in the area of finance—corporations are efficient at tapping large amounts of money to finance growth.

A corporation is a taxable entity that pays its own taxes at a rate that may be less than that applied to owners of a proprietorship or partnership. A corporation may as a result enjoy larger after-tax earnings and cash flow that can be reinvested in productive assets.

TAX MANAGEMENT IN THE CORPORATION

Tax management is the responsibility of the financial manager, but it is usually implemented by a tax accountant or an attorney with specialized knowledge of tax laws and regulations. Here, we can only scratch the surface of a technical area to

BOX 21-1
Transition from Small Business to
Professionally Managed Corporation
Offers Management Benefits   An examination of American business history suggests
that companies evolve from entrepreneurial ventures in
the form of partnerships and proprietorships into professionally managed corporations. The characteristics of small-business decision making are

> Highly centralized decision making
> Overdependence for the company's survival on one or two key individuals
> Inadequate reportory of management skills and training
> Paternalistic atmosphere

The transition to a decentralized, professionally managed corporation occurs usually
over a number of years, and the act of incorporating is merely legal recognition of
previously made management changes. Professionally managed corporations have
the following characteristics, which are listed so that you may contrast them with
those of a small business above:

> Permits delegation of authority
> Uses formal information analysis and an intracompany consultation process to
>   make decisions
> Frees company from dependence on a few key individuals
> Displays interchangeability among components

The change is often painful to those who are old (but not of retirement age) and
those who have been with the company since its inception. One of those that may
have to step down is the entrepreneur, the original proprietor. When the time comes
for the company to become a professionally managed corporation, the entrepreneur
must be willing to examine objectively the benefits of being merely an owner rather
than an owner-manager.

make you comfortable with terms and calculations that are used most often in
corporate-tax management. For more specialized information you should take a tax
accounting course offered by your university's accounting department.

Taxes constitute a large part of business costs, and alert companies manage
their affairs in ways that minimize—legitimately—the bite of taxes out of earnings.
Major areas of tax management are:

1. Planning.
2. Complying with tax laws and regulation.
3. Measuring the effectiveness of company tax strategies.

Planning calls for keeping in mind the tax consequences of all business decisions
and evaluating different courses of action on an after-tax basis. Compliance often

requires specialized knowledge of tax laws and regulations and typically involves the use of outside experts. A company's cash flow and stock price are increased whenever the company pays the lowest total tax and delays payment as long as legally allowable.

Corporate Tax Rates

A corporation is a separate entity from its owners, and so must pay federal income taxes, state taxes, and capital-gains taxes. All ordinary earnings are taxed at the federal income tax rates presented in Table 21-1. In addition, most states impose their own taxes.

Example. In 19x4 a corporation has $60,000 taxable earnings. Its 19x4 federal tax liability is $11,250 found by using the graduated rates on Table 21-1:

$$0.15 \times \$25,000 = \$\ 3,750$$
$$0.18 \times \$25,000 = \$\ 4,500$$
$$0.30 \times \$10,000 = \underline{\$\ 3,000}$$
$$\$60,000 \qquad \$11,250$$

This corporation is in the 30 percent *marginal* tax bracket because that is the highest rate applied to its earnings. Its *average* tax rate is the amount of taxes divided by the amount of taxable earnings, $11,250/$60,000 = 0.187 or 18.7 percent. The marginal tax rate is the one that we shall use in making financial decisions because it is the rate that affects a company's marginal cash flows.

Practice. Before continuing to the next paragraph, use Table 21-1 to calculate the tax liability of a corporation with $80,000 taxable earnings. Verify that the marginal tax rate is 40 percent and the average tax rate is 22.2 percent.

Corporations experience operating losses. Like individual taxpayers, corporations may carry a loss back three years and forward 15 years with the loss applied to the most recent year. Management applies the unused portion of the loss to the previous year, then the preceding year, and finally to the third year back. Any loss still remaining is then carried forward for up to 15 years into the future to be applied against operating earnings. A company may elect to forgo the carry-back provision and simply carry forward for 15 years an operating loss.

TABLE 21–1 Corporate Tax Rates, 1985

Taxable Earnings	Marginal Rate (%)
0–$25,000	15
$25,001–$50,000	18
$50,001–$75,000	30
$75,001–$100,000	40
More than $100,000	46

BOX 21-2

Who Gets the Benefit . . .   . . . of a loss carry-back–carry-forward? The answer to that question might seem to be easy—the shareholders. But that was not the complete answer with the automobile industry in 1984. The managers got a large part of the benefit through performance bonuses.

Consider as an example Chrysler Corporation, which paid its president, Lee Iacocca, $1.2 million in 1984 ($2.58 million over the period 1981–1983) based on the company's $701 million profit after taxes. Chrysler's bonus fund is a percentage of its after-tax accounting profit, and the company's 1980–1981 loss carry-forward enlarged its after-tax accounting profit for 1984 by reducing the company's taxes. The bonus fund in 1984 totaled $52 million, but if you remove the tax saving from the loss carry-forward (the company paid less taxes on its 1984 earnings because of the carry-forward), then the fund should be more like $30 million. Iacocca and the other Chrysler managers were compensated for the 1980–1981 losses.

Perhaps Chrysler should give a bonus to Lynn Townsend, its president during the 1960s when Chrysler bought European companies that took cash from the parent company, helping to create the losses that caused the tax savings that made the enlarged 1984 bonuses possible.

Source: Based on Donald Woutat, "Grilled on Bonuses, Auto Chiefs Weave," *The Wall Street Journal,* May 23, 1984, p. 27, and "Executive Pay: The Top Earners," *Business Week,* May 7, 1984, pp. 90–91.

Any tax refund claimed because of the loss carry-back provision should be shown on the company's financial reports as a reduction in the loss for the year in which the actual loss occurs.

Example. Truco Corporation has a $40,000 loss in 19x6 that it applies against $70,000 taxable earnings in 19x5. Taxable 19x5 earnings become an adjusted $70,000 − $40,000 = $30,000. Truco was in the 30 percent marginal tax bracket, but its adjusted earnings place it in the 18 percent marginal bracket. Its refund is $9,600 calculated using the rates on Table 21-1:

Actual Taxes Paid
$0.15 \times \$25,000 = \$ 3,750$
$0.18 \times \$25,000 = \$ 4,500$
$0.30 \times \$20,000 = \$ 6,000$
$\qquad \$70,000$ $14,250

Less Adjusted Taxes
$0.15 \times \$25,000 = \$ 3,750$
$0.18 \times \$ 5,000 = \$\quad 900$
$\qquad \$30,000$ $ 4,650

Refund Claimed $ 9,600

Truco Corporation's 19x6 reported loss is less by the $9,600 refund:

Actual loss	$40,000
Less refund claimed	$ 9,600
Reported loss	$30,400

The Internal Revenue Service allows corporations with 35 shareholders or less to forgo paying any income tax as a corporation. A corporation may become an S corporation in which shareholders report their share of corporate earnings (whether distributed as dividends or not) as their own for tax purposes. This provision benefits shareholders with marginal tax rates less than corporate tax rates and enables shareholders to apply a business loss against their personal income from other sources.

Other Taxes

Corporations are subject to state taxes. Some states impose an incorporation tax when the charter is granted based on the amount of common stock authorized in the corporation's charter. In addition, states often levy an annual franchise tax. Finally, the U.S. Treasury can impose an excessive-accumulation tax on privately held corporations that it believes to be helping shareholders avoid taxes by accumulating earnings rather than paying them out as dividends. When dividends are paid, the recipient must pay ordinary income taxes on the amount received, but if the company pays no dividend it deprives the U.S. Treasury of tax revenues. The tax regulations state that $250,000 or less of a corporation's retained earnings are automatically exempt from an excessive-accumulation tax. Retained earnings of small corporations above $250,000 are subject to the tax (which averages about 35 percent), if the U.S. Treasury can prove that the accumulation is undertaken with the intent to help shareholders avoid personal taxation.[1]

TAXES AND DEPRECIATION EXPENSE

A *depreciable asset* is property with a useful life greater than one year that is used by the company to generate its output. Buildings, machinery, and office equipment are examples of depreciable property. Depreciable property is used up over time so that a company calculates depreciation expense. We examined depreciation expense in the discussion of expenses on a company's income statement (in Chapter 12). You may recall that depreciation expense is the allowance made each year for loss of value in long-lived assets used in production. A company may use any of several methods to calculate and show its depreciation for financial reporting purposes, but the Internal Revenue Service requires that companies calculate their depreciation

---

[1] The Ninth Circuit Appeals Court ruled in 1978 that the excessive-accumulation tax does not apply to publicly held corporations. Congress never intended that, the court said. When the tax rate was enacted, the House of Representatives explicitly excluded widely held companies, but the Senate dropped that provision because it was considered to be obvious and therefore unnecessary.

using specific guidelines called the accelerated cost-recovery system. We shall concentrate only on this system of depreciation because it affects the company's taxes, cash position, and value.

Accelerated Cost-Recovery System (Depreciation)

The Economic Recovery Tax Act of 1981 spelled out an accelerated cost-recovery system (ACRS) for depreciable property. The system employs standard recovery percentages based on accelerated methods of cost recovery over predetermined periods. Table 21-2 shows the recovery percentages or depreciation rates in 1985 for equipment or capital assets placed in service after 1980. The rates apply equally to both new and used equipment. In addition to these accelerated rates, a taxpayer may use straight-line depreciation. Straight-line depreciation is the allocation of equal annual percentages of the asset's cost over the tax life.

Example. If you buy a car for $16,000 and it has a four-year tax life, then you can depreciate each year $16,000/4 = $4,000, which is 25 percent annually. If straight-line depreciation is used, the taxpayer (1) may use either the estimated life of the asset or the optional recovery period and (2) must include an estimated salvage value that is not depreciated.

Assigning Cost-Recovery Periods

Capital equipment is depreciated on a 5–3 system in which a company recovers the cost of the equipment over a five-year or three-year period. Capital is assigned cost-recovery periods based on the following classes:

> **Three-year Property.**   Autos, light-duty trucks, research and development equipment, and other property with a maximum estimated life of four years or less.

> **Five-year Property.**   All other equipment except long-lived public utility property and special real estate investments.

TABLE 21–2   Depreciation Rates in 1985 for Property Placed in Service after 1981

		Class of Investment		
Year	3–Year (%)	5–Year (%)	10–Year (%)	15–Year Utility Property (%)
1	25	15	8	5
2	38	22	14	10
3	37	21	12	9
4		21	10	8
5		21	10	7
6			10	7
7–10			9	6
11–15				6
	100	100	100	100

The 1981 tax act also designates some property to be 10-year and 15-year property, and Table 21-2 shows their depreciation rates. Special equipment like railroad tank cars, manufactured homes, and theme park structures (like Disney World) are 10-year property. Specialized public-utility assets are 15-year property. Few businesses will use the 10 and 15 year schedules.

Each year's depreciation is the depreciable basis multiplied by the depreciation rate in Table 21-2. *Depreciable basis* is the amount to be depreciated. The calculated depreciation is a tax-deductible expense.

Example. Betancourt Contracting, Inc., acquires a light truck to use in handling equipment between construction sites. The outlay for the truck is $42,000 and sales taxes are .05 × $42,000 = $2,100 so that the cash outlay is $42,000 + 2,100 = $44,100. Estimated salvage value is $4,100 and the estimated life is four years.

Eric Betancourt, the company's accountant, may use for tax purposes either the accelerated cost-recovery system in Table 21-2 or straight-line depreciation. If straight-line depreciation is used, the depreciable basis (the amount to be depreciated) is total investment less salvage value, or $44,100 − $4,100 = $40,000. If the company uses the accelerated cost-recovery system, the entire cash outlay is the depreciable basis. The following calculations show each depreciation method:

Year	Accelerated Cost-Recovery System	Straight Line Estimated Life	Accelerated Period
1	.25 × $44,100 = $11,025	$40,000/4 = $10,000	$40,000/3 = $13,333
2	.38 × $44,100 = $16,758	$40,000/4 = $10,000	$40,000/3 = $13,333
3	.37 × $44,100 = $16,317	$40,000/4 = $10,000	$40,000/3 = $13,333
4		$40,000/4 = $10,000	
Totals	$44,100	$40,000	$40,000

There are two calculations for the straight-line method because a taxpayer may use either the appropriate accelerated period (three years) or the estimated four-year life. Notice, too, that using straight-line depreciation means that estimated salvage value is not depreciable so that the company recovers $40,000 of the capital outlay rather than the entire $44,100 permitted under the accelerated cost-recovery system.

Depreciation and Operating Cash Flow

Depreciation increases a company's operating cash flow because it reduces the amount of taxes that a company must pay. *Operating cash flow* is the change in a company's cash or checking account during a period of time as a result of its operations. Depreciation expense is a *tax shelter* because it is a noncash, tax-deductible expense whose cash impact is the amount of taxes that it saves the company. Looking at depreciation expense as a tax shelter tells us that the way we can measure its impact on operating cash flow is to multiply the depreciation expense by the company's marginal tax rate. The product is the tax saving associated with depreciation:

$$\text{Tax saving} = \text{depreciation expense} \times \text{marginal tax rate}$$

A company with depreciation expense will have greater operating cash flow than one without depreciation expense, and the difference is the difference in the two companies' tax bills.

Example. Prev Corporation has $20,000 operating revenues and $6,000 salary expense during a budget period. The company's depreciation expense for financial reporting purposes is $8,300 and for tax purposes $8,000. How does depreciation expense affect Prev Corporation's operating cash flow if the company is in the 15 percent marginal tax bracket?

Depreciation expense is a tax shelter, so we should expect Prev Corporation's cash flow to be greater with depreciation than without depreciation by the marginal tax rate multiplied by the amount of depreciation expense for tax purposes:

$$\text{Tax saving} = \$8,000 \times 0.15 = \$1,200$$

We can see this difference if we calculate Prev Corporation's taxes with and without depreciation, then calculate operating cash flow under each condition. First, let us calculate taxes:

	No Depreciation		Depreciation	
Revenues		$20,000		$20,000
Less expenses				
Salary	$6,000		$6,000	
Depreciation	0		8,000	
		6,000		14,000
Taxable earnings		$14,000		$ 6,000
Less taxes (15%)		2,100		900
Net operating profit after taxes		$11,900		$5,100

Now, we can calculate operating cash flow under each condition to see how depreciation expense affects Prev Corporation's cash account:

	No Depreciation		Depreciation	
Cash inflow		$20,000		$20,000
Less cash outflows				
Salary	$6,000		$6,000	
Taxes	2,100		900	
		8,100		6,900
Operating cash flow		$11,900		$13,100

The difference in operating cash flow is $13,100 − $11,900 = $1,200, and this amount is the difference in taxes under the two conditions. The example should

BOX 21-3
Financial Depreciation Affects Earnings,
But Not Taxes and Economic Value   Many companies change their depreciation amounts for financial reporting purposes in order to change reported earnings. These changes have no economic value to the company or its shareholders because they do not affect the company's cash flow. The cash flow is affected by the depreciation reported on the company's tax return.

Changing depreciation can contribute to a large change in reported earnings, as the table below shows. Inland Steel changed to the units of production depreciation method so that the 1982–1983 recession brought about reduced output and depreciation expense. Inland Steel reduced 1983 losses by $43 million or $1.20 per share.

Denny Beresford, partner in charge of accounting standards for Ernst and Whinney, expects that more companies will follow the lead of Inland Steel by switching to units-of-production depreciation. Beresford raises a related issue: quality of earnings. "Some people would view a company that uses accelerated depreciation as being more conservative in its financial reporting and thus having a higher quality of earnings," he comments. IBM, for example, is still using for financial reporting purposes the sum-of-the-years method, which raises depreciation charges dramatically in the early years of an asset's life and then slows down as time passes. As Beresford states, "A company changing away from accelerated to straight line might be viewed by some people as reporting at that time lower quality earnings."

For tax purposes, companies must use the accelerated cost-recovery system, which classifies assets as either three-year or five-year property for tax purposes. Changing depreciation on a financial statement does not affect the company's tax bill. What about companies that use straight-line for financial reporting purposes and the accelerated cost-recovery system for tax purposes? The only method that has any economic value is the one for tax purposes because it affects the company's cash flow. Depreciation for financial reporting purposes is merely an accounting artifact.

Company	Change	Year	Addition to Earnings (per share)
Asarco	Straight line to units of production	1980	$0.38
Bell & Howell	Accelerated to straight line	1981	0.04
Burlington	Accelerated to straight line	1981	0.15
Chrysler	Accelerated to straight line	1981	0.52
Cone Mills	Accelerated to straight line	1981	0.10
Harsco	Accelerated to straight line	1981	0.08
Inland Steel	Straight line to units of production	1982	1.20
McGraw-Edison	Accelerated to straight line	1981	0.13
JP Stevens	Accelerated to straight line	1980	0.06

Source: Jill Andresky, "Double Standard," *Dun's Business Month*, March 1983, p. 127.

convince you that depreciation's cash impact is to reduce taxes and that its cash flow impact is the depreciation amount multiplied by the company's marginal tax rate:

$$\text{Tax saving} = \$8,000 \times 0.15 = \$1,200$$

Practice. Calculate the Prev Corporation's operating cash flow above, but assume that depreciation expense for tax purposes is $12,000 rather than $8,000. Answer: $13,700. Show how you calculate this amount and verify that the cash inflow is $20,000 and the cash outflows are $6,300.

Some financial managers calculate the amount of operating cash flow by adding depreciation expense to net operating profit after taxes. This short-cut method works well if depreciation expense is the only noncash operating expense, and you should convince yourself of its accuracy by going back to the examples above and recalculating operating cash flow under each condition.

INVESTMENT TAX CREDIT

The investment tax credit (ITC) allows a taxpayer to take a direct tax credit for investments in capital equipment. The credit applies against the ordinary tax liability. Table 21-3 summarizes the major changes in tax provisions affecting capital investment with the investment tax credit at the bottom. You will notice that the present provisions were enacted as part of the Tax Equity and Fiscal Responsibility Act of 1982 (TEFRA).

An asset's depreciable life for tax purposes determines the amount of the credit. The investment tax credit is 6 percent of the investment amount (including cash outlays to put the equipment in place) for three-year property and 10 percent for five-year property. The tax laws limit how much credit you can take for the year to the year's tax liability or—when the liability is more than $25,000—to $25,000 plus 85 percent of the difference between the year's tax liability and $25,000. In an equation (using TL for the year's tax liability) the year's maximum is as follows:

$$\text{Year's Maximum} = \$25,000 + [0.85(TL - \$25,000)]$$

Note that any credit unused in a year may be carried back 3 years and forward 15 years. Thus you will still receive the entire tax credit even though the restriction may prevent your taking it in a specific year.

Example. Malch Company's qualified five-year investments are $826,000, and its 19x8 tax liability is $80,000. Malch Company's investment tax credit is $0.10 \times$ $826,000 = $82,600 but the amount used in 19x8 is $71,750 calculated as follows:

$$\text{Year's Maximum} = \$25,000 + [0.85 \times (\$80,000 - \$25,000)] = \$71,750$$

The company will pay $80,000 − $71,750 taxes in 19x8. The $82,600 − $71,750 = $10,850 tax credit Malch Company cannot use during tax year 19x8 may be carried back and forward. Malch Company will receive the entire available tax credit.

Example. Suppose that in the example above the Malch Company's tax liability had been $20,000. Then its investment tax credit is still $82,600 but the company is able to use only $20,000 of it. In this case the company would have a $62,600 credit to carry back three years and forward 15 years:

Investment tax credit	$82,600
Less taxes	20,000
Credit remaining	$62,600

Table 21-4 shows the investment tax credit rates and indicates that an additional adjustment is needed: Management must reduce the depreciable basis by 50 percent of the total amount of the investment tax credit (ignoring the 85 percent limit), or reduce the investment tax credit itself by two percentage points. The choice is the taxpayer's.

Example. Friedhoffer Restaurants invests $420,000 in new kitchen equipment. The equipment has a five-year estimated life for tax purposes and the company's tax liability is $60,000.

Choice 1: The investment tax credit is $42,000 if Friedhoffer's management chooses to use the entire 10 percent credit and reduce the depreciable basis by one-half of the investment tax credit amount:

$$ITC = 0.10 \times \$420,000 = \$42,000$$

We must remember that the year's credit is limited to a maximum of $25,000 plus 85 percent of the tax liability greater than $25,000:

$$\$25,000 + [0.85(\$60,000 - \$25,000)] = \$54,750$$

The company may use the entire credit this year. Taking the entire 10 percent credit requires Friedhoffer's management to reduce the depreciable basis by one-half of the investment tax credit, so that the accelerated cost-recovery system rates (on Table 21-2) apply to $399,000:

$$\text{Depreciable basis} = \$420,000 - [0.50(\$42,000)] = \$399,000$$

Choice 2: Alternatively, Friedhoffer's management could take a 10 percent − 2 percent = 8 percent investment tax credit and depreciate the entire $420,000. The investment tax credit would be $33,600:

$$ITC = 0.08 \times \$420,000 = \$33,600$$

TABLE 21-3   Major Changes in Tax Provisions Affecting Capital Investments[a]

Depreciation method	Pre-1954: Regulations fairly strict. Though not mandated, in practice asset costs were amortized primarily by the "straight-line" method.	1954: Permitted the use of declining balance method for new property; permitted "double-declining balance" and "sum of digits" methods.	
Depreciable lives	1931–1962: Suggested useful lives of over 5,000 separate items published by IRS.	1962: Simplified classification scheme and assigned guideline lives to much broader classes of assets. A reserve ratio test permitted depreciation allowances to be geared more directly to the actual lives of assets. Abandoned in 1971.	1969 Tax Reform Act: permits five-year straight-line depreciation of assets having "high social priority."
Investment tax credit (ITC)	1962: ITC is not applicable to structures, only equipment. Initially, 7% of the amount of new investments with service lives of 8 years or more. Credit deducted from the cost of the asset before computing depreciation.	1964: Requirement of deducting credit from cost of asset before computing depreciation considered too complicated a procedure and is eliminated.	1975: ITC temporarily increased to 10% from 7% until 1981.

TABLE 21-3   Continued

	Economic Recovery Tax Act of 1981: Cost recovery (depreciation) schedules reflect 150% declining balance method. Schedules accelerate in 1985 and 1986.	Tax Equity and Fiscal Responsibility Act of 1982: Repealed 1985 and 1986 accelerations of cost recovery (depreciation) schedules. Schedules for 1982 remain in effect.
1971: Congress authorized the use of an asset depreciation range (ADR) of service lives 20% above or below the 1962 IRS guidelines.	Economic Recovery Tax Act of 1981: Replaces highly complex ADR system with 4 basic classes of assets: 3 years (autos) 5 years (equipment); 10 years and 15 years (real property)	
1978: Tax Revenue Act: 10% rate extended indefinitely. Amount of ITC which could be used to reduce tax liability is $25,000 plus 90% of any tax liability above $25,000.	Economic Recovery Tax Act of 1981: 7 year carryover provision extended to 15 years. ITC extended to cover rehabilitation of qualified buildings.	Tax Equity and Fiscal Responsibility Act of 1982: Depreciation basis reduced $\frac{1}{2}$ of ITC amount or 2 percentage point reductions: 10% ITC reduced to 8% and 6% ITC reduced to 4%. The 90% limitation imposed in 1978 is reduced to 85%.

[a] Congress was considering in 1985 several provisions to change each of these items. Specific changes had not been made when this book was published.

TABLE 21-4 Investment Tax Credit and Impact on Depreciable Basis[a]

Asset Life	Investment Tax Credit (ITC)	How Applied
3-Year property	6%	Depreciable basis reduced by 50% of ITC, or ITC reduced to 4%.
5-Year property	10%	Depreciable basis reduced by 50% of ITC, or ITC reduced to 8%.

[a] Limitation: Maximum year's credit is $25,000 plus 85 percent of the amount above $25,000.

which is still less than the year's $54,750 maximum. The depreciable basis is the entire $420,000.

Companies usually choose to take the entire investment tax credit and reduce the depreciable basis by 50 percent of its dollar amount because this choice results in delaying the company's tax payment. The benefit to the company results from the fact that it can use the cash savings to earn a return. Friedhoffer Restaurants in the example above will choose to receive now a $42,000 investment tax credit and report depreciation for tax purposes using the $399,000 depreciable basis.

Example. Friedhoffer Restaurants buys for $16,000 a light delivery truck with a three-year taxable life. Its investment tax credit is $960, calculated as follows:

$$\text{ITC} = 0.06 \times \$16,000 = \$960$$

Friedhoffer's tax liability is immediately reduced by $960. Management reduces the depreciable basis by 50 percent of the investment tax credit, so that it becomes $15,520 calculated as follows:

Purchase price (historical value)	$16,000
Less 50 percent of investment tax credit (0.50 × $960)	480
Depreciable basis	$15,520

The study of the investment tax credit completes our examination of the major influences on a corporation's taxes. However, there are several other items that are important because of their impact on management's decisions. We shall summarize these other items in a brief section.

OTHER TAX ITEMS

Other tax items affect management's decisions, and we should briefly examine some of the important ones. Corporations sell depreciable equipment and must pay a tax on any gain and may recognize a tax saving on any loss, so the first part of the following discussion considers gains and losses on disposal of depreciable assets.

Interest expense is tax deductible, and dividends and interest income are taxable. Exceptions to these conditions will become apparent as you read the following information.

Gains and Losses on Disposal of Depreciable Property

A company may make a taxable gain or loss on disposal of depreciable property, and we shall consider each in this part of the chapter. A gain occurs when the company sells an asset for more than its taxable book value. *Book value* is an asset's depreciable basis for tax purposes (usually historical value) less accumulated depreciation. Accumulated depreciation is the total depreciation that management calculates using the accelerated cost-recovery system. Any gain that occurs on property held longer than 12 months is taxed at either the ordinary tax rate or at an alternative 28 percent, depending on the type of gain. Any loss is tax deductible at the ordinary tax rate.

1. Gain through accumulated depreciation is *depreciation recapture* and is taxed at the ordinary tax rate.
2. Gain that is greater than depreciation recapture is *1231 gain* and is taxed at the ordinary tax rate or a 28 percent alternative rate at the tax payer's option. If the corporation has taxable earnings less than $50,000 it is in the 18 percent marginal tax bracket, and management will choose to have 1231 gain taxed at the lower ordinary rate.
3. Loss on disposal of a depreciable asset is tax deductible at the ordinary tax rate because the company has been understating depreciation on its tax returns. A loss is measured by the difference between selling price and book value.

The only way that a company will pay a 1231 tax is if it sells the asset for more than its historical value. In this case depreciation recapture is the difference between historical value and book value.

Example. Suppose that Strand Corporation sells for $70,000 a depreciable asset originally acquired two years ago for $60,000. Book value is $30,000 and the company is in the 46 percent marginal ordinary tax bracket.

In this example the company sells an asset for more than its historical value, so we know that there is a 1231 gain. And if there is a 1231 gain, there must be depreciation recapture. A 1231 gain is quickly calculated (selling price less historical value) and depreciation recapture is exactly accumulated depreciation:

1231 Taxes	
Selling price	$70,000
Less historical value	$60,000
1231 Gain	$10,000
Multiplied by tax rate	× 0.28
	$ 2,800
Add ordinary taxes [($60,000 − $30,000) × 0.46]	$13,800
Taxes	$16,600

Practice: Before continuing to the next section, calculate the net cash flow for the Strand Corporation from this transaction. Answer: The Strand Corporation has a $53,400 net cash flow calculated as follows:

Cash inflow (selling price)	$70,000
Less cash outflow (taxes)	$16,600
Net cash flow	$53,400

What would be the net cash flow if Strand Corporation sold the asset for $26,000? The company would have a tax-deductible loss measured by the difference between book value and selling price. The loss is a tax shelter because it is a noncash tax-deductible expense. First, consider the tax reduction from the loss:

Selling price	$26,000
Less book value	30,000
Loss	$ 4,000
Multiplied by tax rate	× 0.46
Tax reduction	$ 1,840

Notice that the tax rate is the company's ordinary rate. Now, we can calculate the cash flow from this transaction:

Cash inflow (selling price)	$26,000
Add tax saving	1,840
Cash flow from disposal	$27,840

Dividends

Common and preferred stock dividends *paid* by a corporation are not tax deductible. But dividends *received* by a corporation are either 85 percent or 100 percent tax exempt. A corporation receiving a dividend from an unaffiliated corporation pays tax on only 15 percent of the gross amount. On $100 worth of dividends, a corporation in the 46 percent marginal tax bracket would pay 0.46 × ($100 − $85) = $6.90. However, dividends received by members of an affiliated group from other members are completely tax exempt. An *affiliated group* consists of a parent company and one or more other corporation in which the parent owns stock with at least 80 percent of the total voting power.

The low tax rate on dividends received from other corporations explains why some corporations often buy preferred stock instead of bonds as long- or short-term investments. Although price fluctuations and other risks on preferreds may be greater, after-tax income is larger, just as the capital asset pricing model tells us.

Interest

Interest *paid* by a corporation is tax deductible. Interest *received* from federal government and private securities is fully taxable. However, interest received from munici-

---

BOX 21-4
The Burden of Tax Calculation May Give
Way to a Flat Tax   Corporate taxation, like all taxation, is not merely a source of revenue for the government, but also a tool of public policy. Congress often taxes corporations to encourage activities considered by Congress to be desirable or to discourage activities considered undesirable. Do we really want to lead companies to do what is otherwise not in their best interest by holding up the tax carrot or threatening with the tax stick when both are cumbersome and when the basic tax level is so high that it dominates some corporate decision making?

The entire corporate income tax was set forth in five pages of the first graduated income tax law, enacted in 1913. Today's tax code fills several thousand pages and is incomprehensible in total to even tax specialists. Our tax laws consist of a maze of trivialities, pitfalls, and complexities. It may be time to wipe the slate clean and start over with a fresh approach.

The fresh approach may be a flat tax offered to Congress in 1985 in which each person and business pays a tax rate based on total income with few deductions. As a result, tax calculation would be simplified and special-interest groups lobbying for favorable tax treatment would become things of the past.

---

pal securities (those issued by municipal governments and their subdivisions) is exempt from federal taxation. This means that a corporation or an individual can buy a municipal bond with a lower yield than a corporate bond, but receive an equally attractive after-tax yield. You may want to look back at the discussion in Box 7-3 to remind yourself of the method to calculate a taxable yield equivalent to a tax-exempt yield.

Example. A municipal bond yielding 7 percent interest has an equivalent taxable 10 percent yield for an investor in the 32 percent marginal tax bracket:

$$Y_T = \frac{0.07}{1-0.32} = 0.10$$

If the bonds have equal risk, then this investor will invest in the municipal bond when the taxable bond is yielding less than 10 percent and in the taxable bond when it is yielding more than 10 percent.

Now, we can work through an example that illustrates the tax implications of dividends and interest for a hypothetical corporation.

Example. Corvi Corporation has $76,000 in taxable earnings before the following receipts: A $12,000 dividend on the preferred stock of an unaffiliated corporation, $28,000 interest from a U.S. Treasury bill, and $14,000 interest from an independent school district bond. Corvi's earnings after taxes are $91,382 calculated by recognizing the $12,000 dividend reduced by the tax-exempt portion, recognizing the entire amount of interest on the U.S. Treasury bill as income, and ignoring all of the interest on the school district bond for tax purposes.

Initial taxable earnings		$ 76,000
Add taxable portion of financial receipts:		
Dividends (0.15 × $12,000)	$ 1,800	
U.S. Treasury bill interest	28,000	
		29,800
Taxable earnings		$105,000
Less taxes:		
0.15 × $25,000 = $ 3,750		
0.18 × $25,000 = 4,500		
0.30 × $25,000 = 7,500		
0.40 × $25,000 = 10,000		
0.46 × $ 5,800 = 2,668		
		28,418
Earnings after taxes and before tax-exempt item		$ 77,382
Add municipal bond interest		14,000
Earnings after taxes		$ 91,382

Practice. How much would Corvi Corporation's earnings after taxes be if all of the amounts above remain the same, but the company pays an $18,000 dividend? Answer: Earnings after taxes would be the same $91,382 because dividends are deducted from earnings after taxes.

SUMMARY

1. Corporate marginal tax rates range from 15 percent to 46 percent of ordinary earnings. Losses may be carried back three years and forward 15 years.

2. Congress has established an accelerated cost-recovery system that determines the depreciation rates on property. Property is either three-year or five-year.

3. The investment tax credit is 10 percent for five-year assets and 6 percent for three-year assets. Either the investment tax credit must be reduced by two percentage points or the depreciable basis of the asset must be reduced by 50 percent of the investment tax credit at the taxpayer's option.

4. A corporation pays either a 1231 or ordinary tax on disposal of a depreciable asset held for more than 12 months. A 1231 tax is paid on the amount of selling price above historical cost. Ordinary tax is paid on any gain that is depreciation recapture. A loss on disposal of depreciable property occurs when selling price is below book value. A loss is tax deductible at the ordinary rate.

5. Dividends *paid* by a corporation are not tax deductible. Dividends *received* by a corporation are 100 percent tax exempt if received from an affiliated corporation; otherwise, they are 85 percent tax exempt.

6. Interest expense that a corporation pays is tax deductible. Interest income from federal and private bonds is taxable. Interest income from municipal bonds is exempt from federal taxation.

KEY TERMS AND CONCEPTS

Accelerated cost-recovery system

S corporation

Excessive accumulation tax

Average tax rate

Marginal tax rate

Investment tax credit

Loss Carry-back–carry-forward

1231 Gain

Municipal Bond

QUESTIONS

21-1. The Internal Revenue Code permits a corporation to be taxed as an S corporation. Explain what an S corporation is and its advantage to shareholders.

21-2. The loss carry-back–carry-forward provision of the Internal Revenue Code permits losses to be carried back 3 years and forward 15 years. Explain why this provision suggests that a new business suffering a loss should be a proprietorship rather than a corporation. Does the right to be taxed as an S corporation affect this choice? Explain your answer.

21-3. The financing component that would be affected directly in determining after-tax costs of capital if the corporate tax rates were changed is

a. long-term debt.

b. new preferred stock.

c. retained earnings.

d. new common stock.

e. treasury stock.

Explain your choice.

21-4. The accelerated cost-recovery system permits companies to expense a capital outlay over a specified period of time.

a. Explain the different time periods associated with the accelerated cost-recovery system.

b. How does the investment tax credit affect the depreciable basis and the time period in the accelerated cost-recovery system?

c. Must a company use the accelerated cost-recovery system for financial reporting purposes? If not, which method is relevant for financial decision making?

21-5. Table 21-4 presents the investment tax credit rates. Explain the usefulness of the investment tax credit (a) for society and (b) for an individual company.

21-6. Explain the different tax treatment for a company that receives a dividend from an affiliated corporation and from an unaffiliated corporation.

21-7. Some companies and individuals like to invest in municipal bonds rather than in corporate bonds. Explain the tax advantage of investing in a municipal bond rather than in a corporate bond. Refer to Box 7-3 to guide your answer.

21-8. The investment tax credit has an 85 percent limit rule. Explain this rule and comment on how the limit affects acquired equipment's depreciable basis.

PROBLEMS

21-1. Calculate the corporate taxes for a company with $183,000 ordinary taxable earnings.

a. Show this company's marginal tax rate.

b. Show this company's average tax rate.

c. If the company has $28,000 in depreciation expense for tax purposes, what is the tax saving associated with depreciation?

21-2. Len Cormier is trying to decide which depreciation method to use for his company's $260,000 equipment. Estimated life of the equipment is eight years, and it has a $30,000 estimated salvage value. In addition, the company's estimated taxes are $26,000.

a. Calculate the amount of the investment tax credit. What is this year's maximum credit? How much is the depreciable basis if the entire ITC is used?

b. Calculate annual depreciation using
(1) the accelerated cost-recovery system.
(2) straight-line depreciation using the equipment's estimated life.
(3) straight-line depreciation using the equipment's accelerated life.

c. Comment on which method you believe Cormier should select.

21-3. Treton Company, a manufacturing company that transacts business exclusively in this country, was formed five years ago and has had profitable operations every year except the current one. In the current year Treton incurred a $1 million net operating loss.

a. How much of the loss remains to carry forward if the taxable earnings in each of the previous four years were $200,000? Support your answer with a calculation.

b. What loss amount will Treton show on its current income statement? (Use the tax rates on Table 21-1.)

21-4. Thomasan Corporation purchases equipment for $160,000 that has a five-year esti-mated life for tax purposes.

a. Use the accelerated cost-recovery system to calculate the annual depreciation. As-sume that the company uses the entire 10 percent investment tax credit and must reduce the depreciable basis by one-half of the credit amount.

b. Thomasan Corporation uses units-of-production depreciation for financial reporting purposes. Which method—accelerated cost-recovery system on the tax return or units-of-production on the financial statements—is relevant for calculating the com-pany's tax shelter? Explain your answer.

21-5. Merrill Enterprises, Inc., is disposing of production equipment it has had for three years. The equipment was acquired for $160,000. Accumulated depreciation is $92,800 and the company has $247,000 in taxable earnings (excluding this transaction). Use the current corporate tax rates to calculate Merrill Enterprises's net cash flow from the following transactions:

a. Selling the asset for $180,000.
b. Selling the asset for $120,000.
c. Selling the asset for $67,200.
d. Selling the asset for $40,000.

e. Comment on the following statement, which occurs in the Annual Report To Share-holders of Merrill Enterprises, Inc., (no calculations are called for): "Your company's treasurer is aware of the tax benefits of incurring a tax-deductible loss. Manage-ment's judgment indicated that your interests would be best served if the company incurred tax losses. For this reason, we accepted a $40,000 purchase price for the asset discussed above."

21-6. Fremont Company has an asset with a $70,000 book value for tax purposes. The asset was originally acquired for $120,000 several years ago. Use the actual corporate income tax rates and 1231 tax treatment to calculate net cash flow under the following conditions. Assume Fremont Company has $72,000 ordinary income before taxes.

a. Selling the asset for $280,000.
b. Selling the asset for $90,000.
c. Selling the asset for $30,000.

21-7. Letter Corporation's income before taxes is $350,000 for the calendar year 19x3. In addition, the corporation has $60,000 of 1231 gains.

a. What is Letter Corporation's total tax liability for 19x3? Use the actual corporate rates.
b. What is the company's average tax rate?

21-8. Truco Company was organized in 19x2 and was profitable through 19x5, reporting $40,000 income before taxes in each of the four years. However, in 19x6 Truco suffered a loss before taxes of $120,000 due to a lack of demand and increased competition.

a. How much tax refund will Truco Company receive in 19x6? Assume that the current tax rates prevailed over the entire period.
b. How should this be reflected on the Truco Company 19x6 financial statements?
   (1) The refund claimed, due to the loss carry-back provision, should be shown as a prior period adjustment.
   (2) The refund claimed should be shown as a deferred charge and amortized over the next five years.
   (3) The refund claimed, due to the loss carry-back provision, should be reflected as revenue from operations for 19x6.
   (4) The refund claimed, due to the loss carry-back provision, should be shown as a reduction from the loss of $120,000 to determine the net loss for 19x6. Explain your choice.

21-9. The Brass company has $276,000 in taxable earnings before the following transactions:
   The company receives a $20,000 common-stock dividend from an affiliated company and a $12,000 preferred stock dividend from an unaffiliated company.
   The company receives $10,000 interest from a U.S. Treasury bond, $5,000 interest from a corporate bond, and $15,800 interest from a local school board bond.
   The Brass Company pays a $42,000 dividend to its common shareholders.

a. List each of the above transactions and explain briefly its tax treatment.
b. Calculate Brass Company's after-tax earnings using the actual corporate tax rates.
c. Show the company's average tax rate.

CHAPTER 22
Ranking and Selecting Capital Projects

A CAPITAL-BUDGETING OVERVIEW

RANKING AND SELECTING PROJECTS
Net Investment Cash Outflow · Cash Inflows · Example

UNDISCOUNTED METHOD: PAYBACK PERIOD

DISCOUNTED CASH-FLOW METHODS
Net Present Value · Net Present-Value Index · Internal Rate of Return · Relation
Between Discounted Cash-Flow Methods

DISCOUNTED CASH-FLOW METHODS: THE UNCERTAINTY CASE

SUMMARY
Key Terms and Concepts · Questions · Problems

This chapter completes our discussion of
the capital budgeting process that began in Chapter 20. The first part of the chapter
presents the overall capital-budgeting process in order to show how its various parts
relate to each other. After discussing the process, we turn our attention to measuring
cash flows from a capital-budgeting proposal. This part of the chapter teaches you
the correct method to calculate a proposed project's net investment cash outflow and
its total annual cash inflows.

The second part of the chapter examines several ranking-selection methods
that can be classified into two groups: (1) an undiscounted method called the payback period calculation and (2) discounted cash flow methods, which include the
internal rate of return, net present value, and net present-value index. You will be
able to calculate each of these measures and to discuss each one's strengths and
weaknesses when you finish this part of the chapter. Capital budgeting takes place in
a world in which risk is present so that a manager examining a proposed capital
project does not know the timing and amounts of future cash flows. Consequently,
the chapter concludes with a discussion of a way to adjust the capital-budgeting
process for risk. When you complete this material you will be able to calculate a
project's risk-adjusted net present value using the capital-asset pricing model.

454

A CAPITAL-BUDGETING OVERVIEW

Capital budgeting is the process of ranking, selecting, and controlling an investment in assets with an expected life in excess of one year. Capital projects are property, plant and equipment, and other activities such as exploration, major research, and new-product development. Outlays for long-term projects are in large degree irrevocable and, therefore, they require management to organize the capital-budgeting procedure so that decisions are systematic and documented with economic and financial analysis. Figure 22-1 presents as an illustration a capital-budgeting appropriation form used by a medium-size truck rental company. As you will note, it is detailed and requires a project sponsor (the person requesting that the project be accepted) to complete an analysis of a project's profitability.

FIGURE 22-1 Capital-budgeting appropriation form.

Division:	Date:	COST OF PROJECT	
		Fixed Assets—Purchased	_____
		Fixed Assets—Leased	_____
	Sponsor:	Net Working Capital	_____
		TOTAL	$_____

Proposal:

APPROPRIATION GROUP	No.	ECONOMIC LIFE	PAYBACK PERIOD	NET PRESENT VALUE	DATE OF FIRST COMMITMENT
Growth Projects	1				
Replacement Machinery	2				
Replacement Automobiles	3	INTERNAL RATE OF RETURN		REQUEST BUDGET INCREASE	COMPLETION DATE
Automobile Additions	4				
Miscellaneous Projects	5				

Priority: Justification:

A. Absolutely Essential ____.
B. Necessary ____.
C. Economically Desirable ____.
D. General Improvement ____.

COMPANY APPROVALS	DATE	
Immediate Supervisor:		
Division Head:		
Controller:		

Figure 22-2 presents a simplified conceptual framework of a capital-budgeting system, a framework that combines investment and financial decisions:

1. The investment decision (often called economic analysis) determines the cash flows associated with an investment, calculates expected profitability, and ranks projects in order of expected profitability. Chapter 21 dealt with the way that a financial manager calculates cash flows, and this chapter addresses the way that he calculates expected profitability and ranks projects.
2. The financial decision determines a company's optimum capital structure, calculates the cost of capital, and selects the best method to finance individual projects.[1] Chap-

FIGURE 22-2 Overview of the capital-budgeting process.

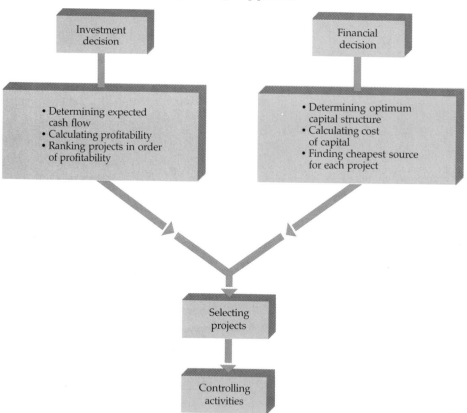

[1] Separation of investment from financial decisions is needed to prevent the investment process from becoming chaotic. For example, if you made investment decisions based on earnings after taxes (and after financing costs), you would get different measures of profit depending on how a project is financed: All equity would yield the greatest return (because no interest would be deducted) and all debt would yield the lowest return. Hence, your level of profitability would vary over a range. Which level would be correct? There would be (and is) no theoretical basis for determining which one would be correct, so your answer would be intuitive and perhaps even capricious. Separating investment and financial decisions avoids this ambiguity and confusion.

ter 20 addressed the way that a financial manager calculates the cost of capital, and Chapters 16 to 19 dealt with the individual sources of capital available to a company.

3. Management combines investment and financial decisions to select projects. This chapter deals with the way that a financial manager selects projects.

4. Management then monitors and controls projects in order to measure the accuracy of the decision-making process by comparing actual profitability with budgeted or expected profitability.

The following sections discuss the way that a financial manager calculates the profitability of proposed projects in a world of perfect certainty, that is, where the timing and amounts of future cash flow are known without doubt. At the end of this chapter we shall touch briefly on capital budgeting in a world of uncertainty, but more discussion of this topic must await your study in advanced accounting, finance, and economics courses.

RANKING AND SELECTING PROJECTS

What properties should a capital-budgeting system ideally possess? There are three: First, a capital-budgeting system should consider cash flows over a project's entire life. That is important because it will prevent us from selecting a project based on only a short and perhaps unrepresentative history. Second, a capital-budgeting system should recognize the time value of money by preferring an early receipt to a later one and a delayed outlay to an immediate one. Finally, it should incorporate a project's required rate of return so that management will be able to evaluate the profit prospects based on each proposed project's risk.

Management begins the capital-budgeting process by calculating a project's cash flows. *Cash flow* is a project's cash inflows and outflows. Table 22-1 summarizes the cash inflows and cash outflows associated with acquiring capital equipment.

A financial manager examines operations and estimates their impact on cash. A cash inflow either immediately or subsequently increases cash and a cash outflow either immediately or subsequently reduces cash.

Example. Buying raw material for cash (an immediate cash outlay) or on 90-day credit (a subsequent cash outlay) is a cash outflow. Selling merchandise for cash (an immediate cash receipt) or on 60-day credit (a subsequent cash receipt) is a cash inflow.

The cash flows that management considers are those that economists call marginal cash flows. *Marginal cash flows* are the changes in total cash flows associated with a project. It makes no difference whether the cash flow is a fixed or a variable amount, so long as it is a *new* cash flow. The rule to follow in deciding if we must consider a specific cash flow is to ask if the cash inflow or outflow is associated with the project. If it is, then we must consider it in the analysis. If it is not, then we must ignore it.

Example. A company may make its own capital equipment to produce a new line of cosmetics. If the workers used to make the capital equipment were on the payroll,

---

TABLE 22–1 Capital Budgeting Cash Inflows and Outflows

Net Investment Cash Outflow
Cash outflow for equipment
  Purchase price
  Sales taxes
  Delivery
Less investment tax credit
Net working capital
Cash Inflows
Operating cash flow
Liquidation (terminal) cash inflow
  After-tax disposal of capital equipment
  After-tax disposal of net working capital

---

but not presently productively employed, then management must not consider their wages in the analysis because they would be paid anyway. But on the other hand, if the workers were taken from some productive use so that new employees must be hired to replace them, then management must consider the cost of the new employees in the analysis because their wages are marginal cash outflows.

Practice. Explain which of the following is part of a capital-budgeting project analysis: Overhead allocated to a project that does not require the company to make a cash outflow; overhead allocated that reflects a new cash outflow for equipment and supplies required to control the project.

Net Investment Cash Outflow

A look at Table 22-1 shows you that the first cash items that management must measure are the amounts surrounding the net investment cash outflow. These outflows consist of

1. Purchase price of the equipment adjusted for sales taxes, shipping, and installation costs.
2. Less the investment tax credit.
3. Add any needed investment in net working capital.

The investment tax credit reduces the cash needed to invest in a project because it reduces, dollar for dollar, the company's tax bill. Management considers an increase in net working capital to be a part of the investment because net working capital is an increase in cash, receivables, and inventory financed with long-term debt and equity. Management could have used this finance to invest in other long-term projects, so it is only right that we consider it a part of the investment in this project.

Cash Inflows

Management estimates the cash inflows from a project by calculating the expected operating cash flow and disposal (or terminal) cash inflows from the capital equipment and net working capital.

Table 22-1 shows that operating cash flows are an important part of the total cash inflow from an investment. *Operating cash flow* (OCF) is the after-tax increase in operating cash plus the tax saving from depreciation.[2] We saw it calculated in Chapter 21, and you may want to turn back to the discussion on page 440 to remind yourself of it.

Example. Powell Company is estimating the annual operating cash flow for a prospective project under the following conditions: Annual depreciation for tax purposes is $40,000 and the cost-accounting and marketing departments provide the following annual revenue and cost estimates:

Unit Selling Price		$5.00
Unit production costs		
Materials	$1.80	
Labor	$1.65	
		$3.45
Unit Contribution Margin		$1.55
Estimated unit volume		40,000
Total contribution margin		$62,000
Annual incremental fixed costs		
Supervision	$16,000	
Maintenance	3,000	
		$19,000

The first thing that we must do is calculate the taxes by constructing a small income statement:

---

[2] There are several accounting methods to measure operating cash flow. We will summarize them for you here rather than later in the chapter. (1) OCF = (EBIT + depreciation)(1 − T) + T(depreciation). This method is similar to the one used in the chapter and is consistent with the definition of operating cash flow—the after-tax increase in cash from operations plus the tax saving from depreciation. It unfortunately does not distinguish between incremental and sunk costs. Rearranging terms yields a second measure. (2) OCF = (EBIT)(1 − T) + depreciation. This measure gives the same amount, but erroneously suggests that depreciation is a source of cash. Another method starts with earnings after taxes (EAT). (3) OCF = EAT + depreciation + (1 − T)(DINT), where DINT is the dollar interest expense. This measure gives the same amount as the two measures above, but it suggests that interest expense influences operating cash flow—which it does not. By the way, some texts suggest adding after-tax earnings to depreciation expense to get operating cash flow. That measure is correct only for a project financed from all equity—which means that it mixes the investment and financial decisions and, therefore, violates the separation principle.

Contribution margin		$62,000
Less		
Incremental fixed costs	$19,000	
Depreciation	40,000	
		59,000
Net operating profit before taxes		$ 3,000
Less taxes (0.40 × $3,000)		1,200
Net operating profit after taxes		$ 1,800

Now we are ready to calculate operating cash flow by netting from operating cash inflows the amount of operating and tax cash outflows:

Cash inflows (40,000 units × $5.00)		$200,000
Less cash outflows		
Variables costs (40,000 units × $3.45)	$138,000	
Incremental fixed costs	19,000	
Taxes	1,200	
		158,200
Operating Cash Flow		$41,800

Notice that we considered only incremental or additional cash flows in the calculation. Sunk costs, costs incurred whether or not a specific project is accepted, must be ignored. And we ignore financial costs such as interest expense, lease payments, and dividends because they are part of the financial decision and considered when we calculated the cost of capital.

Management must consider the cash inflows that occur at the end of a project's expected life, inflows consisting of the after-tax disposal cash flows from selling equipment and net working capital remaining. By considering these cash flows we assume that the cash from liquidating the equipment and net working capital is distributed to those who contributed capital to finance the project—the long-term creditors, preferred stockholders, and common shareholders receive the cash from the project.

Now that we have seen the cash flows that a manager must consider in evaluating a project, let us look at an example that illustrates the various methods available to rank and select projects.

Example

Suppose that a five-year project requires a net investment cash outflow like that in Table 22-2: $120,000 net invested in equipment and $70,000 in net working capital—cash, receivables, and inventory financed from long-term sources. This investment occurs at the beginning of year 1, or at time zero. The company's allowable tax credit is the full 0.10 × $120,000 = $12,000 because it will reduce the depreciable basis by one-half of the investment tax credit amount. Table 22-2 shows the net investment cash outflow and the annual depreciation expense for tax purposes using the accel-

---

TABLE 22-2   Net Investment Cash Outflow and Depreciation
(Beginning of Year 1)

Purchase Equipment	$120,000
Less 10% investment tax credit	(12,000)
Add net working capital	70,000
Total	$178,000

Depreciation Schedule Using the Accelerated Cost Recovery System:

Depreciable basis: $120,000 - [0.50 \times $12,000] = $114,000

Year	Depreciable Basis	Rate	Depreciation
1	$114,000	.15	$ 17,100
2	$114,000	.22	$ 25,080
3	$114,000	.21	$ 23,940
4	$114,000	.21	$ 23,940
5	$114,000	.21	$ 23,940
		1.00	$114,000

---

erated cost-recovery system. Recall that a company may choose to use a different depreciation method for financial reporting purposes, but the tax method is the one that affects cash flow and the company's value to its shareholders.

The financial manager calculates operating cash flow and disposal cash inflow for a proposed project from cost-accounting and marketing departments' estimates presented in Table 22-3: The unit contribution margin is $0.50 and sales are forecast to vary in the pattern presented in the table. There are no incremental fixed costs.

Table 22-4 uses the cost and sales information to calculate an operating statement and below it a cash-flow statement for each year. We combine each year's operating cash flow with the liquidated net working capital and equipment at the end of the project's life.

Example. Recall that you can use a shortcut method to calculate operating cash flow when depreciation expense is the only noncash expense: Add depreciation expense

---

TABLE 22-3   Marketing and Cost Estimates for a Proposed Project

Contribution Margin		
Unit selling price		$5.00
Unit production costs		
Labor and material	$3.00	
Variable overhead	$1.50	
		$4.50
Unit contribution margin		$0.50

Estimated Unit Sales

Year 1	Year 2	Year 3	Year 4	Year 5
90,000	100,000	110,000	110,000	70,000

TABLE 22-4   Expected Earnings and Cash Flows from a Proposed Project

	Year 1	Year 2	Year 3	Year 4	Year 5
Earnings					
Sales	90,000	100,000	110,000	110,000	70,000
	× $5	× $5	× $5	× $5	× $5
Sales revenue	$450,000	$500,000	$550,000	$550,000	$350,000
Less costs					
Variable costs	405,000	450,000	495,000	495,000	315,000
Depreciation	17,100	25,080	23,940	23,940	23,940
Net operating profit					
Before taxes	$27,900	$25,000	$31,060	$31,060	$11,060
Less taxes (46%)	12,834	11,500	14,288	14,288	5,088
Net operating profit					
after taxes	$15,066	$13,500	$16,772	$16,772	$5,972
Cash Flows					
Cash inflow	$450,000	$500,000	$550,000	$550,000	$350,000
Less cash outflows					
Variable costs	405,000	450,000	495,000	495,000	315,000
Taxes	12,834	11,500	14,288	14,288	5,088
Operating cash flow	$ 32,166	$ 38,500	$ 40,712	$ 40,712	$ 29,912
Add after-tax disposal					
Net working capital					70,000
Equipment					19,440
Total cash flow	$32,166	$38,500	$40,712	$40,712	$119,352

to net operating profit after taxes. For year 1 the shortcut method gives us $15,066 + $17,100 = $32,166, which is the same answer that we have at the bottom of Table 22-4.

Notice on Table 22-4 that year five's cash flow consists of operating cash flow and the after-tax disposal value of the equipment and net working capital. We assume that the company disposes of its net working capital at book value so there is no tax calculation. However, in this example, management expects to dispose of the equipment for $36,000 so that the cash flow from disposal must recognize the tax on the gain. Book value for tax purposes is zero (remember that the accelerated cost-recovery system uses a zero ending book value), so the entire selling price is gain. This gain is depreciation recapture taxed at the ordinary rate so that the cash flow from disposal is $19,440 calculated as follows:

Cash inflow (selling price)	$36,000
Less cash outflow: taxes ($36,000 × 0.46)	16,560
	$19,440

The above estimates of cash flows and the following calculations assume that the $178,000 net investment cash outflow occurs at the beginning of year 1 (that is, at time zero) and that cash inflows occur at the end of each year. This assumption leads to an understatement of profitability in the discounted cash-flow methods because in actual situations, cash flows would occur throughout each year as the company makes sales and pays its bills. Cash flows may occur at any time and in any period, and management can change the calculations to reflect these differences.[3]

The discussion that follows goes through the following steps: First, we shall examine an undiscounted cash-flow measure, the payback period. This method is an undiscounted method because it fails to recognize the time value of money. Second, we shall examine three discounted cash-flow (DCF) methods: the net present value, net present-value index, and internal rate of return methods. These three methods are discounted cash-flow methods because each recognizes the time value of money in its calculation.

UNDISCOUNTED METHOD: PAYBACK PERIOD

The simple payback period calculates the time required to recapture through cash flows a project's net investment cash outflow. In the example in Tables 22-2 and 22-4, the payback period is about four years and $2\frac{2}{3}$ months calculated by adding each year's cash flow until the total equals the net investment cash outflow.

	Year 1	Year 2	Year 3	Year 4	Year 5
Cash flow	$32,166	$38,500	$ 40,712	$ 40,712	$ 25,910
Sum of cash flow	$32,166	$70,666	$111,378	$152,090	$178,000
Sum of years	1	2	3	4	

$$\$25,910/\$119,352 = 0.22$$
$$4+0.22 = 4.22 \text{ years}$$

The company must recapture the entire $178,000 cash outflow for investment. The first four years' cash flows total $152,090, and the fifth year must supply $25,910 from its $119,352 cash inflow, which is $25,910/$119,352 = 22 percent of the year. Twenty-two percent of a year is 0.22 × 12 months = $2\frac{2}{3}$ months so that the project has a four-year and $2\frac{2}{3}$ months payback period.

How does management use payback to rank and select projects? The ranking step occurs when management lists investment proposals according to payback periods, beginning with the shortest. Management then selects projects with an acceptable payback period. Suppose that the management evaluating the project above used a three-year maximum acceptable payback period. Then management will reject this project. If the acceptable maximum had been five years, then management will accept the project.

Theoretically, payback is unsound because it possesses none of the three ideal

[3] A major timing difference in real-world capital budgeting involves net working capital. Usually, net working capital increases gradually over time as sales rise, so that the investment in net working capital increases in several steps. Each period's change should then be capitalized, and this value used as a part of the net investment cash outflow in Table 22-1.

properties: (1) It does not consider the time value of money because it treats all cash flows as time equivalents. (2) It does not consider cash flows over a project's entire life because once payback occurs the method ignores additional cash flows. (3) It ignores a project's required rate of return.

The point, of course, is that payback is not a measure of profitability at all. Payback measures speed of capital recovery, a return *of* capital rather than return *on* capital. Yet, in practice, payback is a popular capital-budgeting method. It appeals especially to companies short of cash and to companies operating in the face of large uncertainties: If a company must recover its cash quickly to avoid either going broke or suffering financial strain, a short payback standard is sensible.

DISCOUNTED CASH-FLOW METHODS

The three discounted cash-flow (DCF) methods—internal rate of return, net present value, and profitability index—are related in their recognition of the time value of money. The following discussion considers the merits and weaknesses of each method, beginning with the most widely used one, the net present value.

Net Present Value

A project's net present value is the dollar change in shareholders' wealth if management accepts a proposed project. We measure it by the difference between the net investment cash outflow and the present value of cash inflows. Management accepts a proposed project if its net present value is positive and rejects it if the net present value is negative.

Example. A project has $6,477 net present value. Management should accept the project because shareholders' wealth will rise by $6,477 if the project is accepted. Alternatively, management should reject a project with a *negative* $17,247 net present value because if it were accepted, then shareholder's wealth would *fall* by $17,247.

The net present-value method uses the following equation:

$$NPV = \sum_{t=1}^{n} \frac{CF_t}{(1 + R)^t} - I_0$$

where

$$NPV = \text{net present value}$$
$$CF_t = \text{annual total cash flow}$$
$$R = \text{project's required rate of return (equal to the risk-free rate of return where there is no uncertainty)}$$
$$I_0 = \text{net investment cash outflow at time zero}$$

The net present-value equation tells us that the net present value is the sum of annual total cash inflows discounted at the project's required rate of return less the net investment cash outflow necessary to acquire the project.

Table 22-5 and Figure 22-3 illustrate the necessary calculations for determining the net present value of the five-year $178,000 project presented in Tables 22-2 and 22-4. Discounting the cash flows at the 8 percent risk-free rate of return (remember there is no uncertainty in the decision) gives us the project's $21,894 net present value:

Present value of cash inflows	$206,308
Less net investment cash outflow	$178,000
Net present value	$28,308

This project's $28,308 net present value is the increase in shareholders' wealth resulting from accepting the project. Here is an additional way to interpret a net present value: Given a choice between investing $178,000 in this project and investing $178,000 in a project yielding the required rate of return (the risk-free 8 percent in this example) shareholders will be $28,308 (the amount of the net present value) wealthier if management accepts this project.

Practice. Before continuing, interpret a $21,600 net present value for a $65,000 project if the project's required rate of return is 10 percent.

Ranking and Selecting Projects. Management implements the net present value in the following way: Projects are laddered in order of each one's net present value and, in the absence of capital rationing, management accepts each project with a positive net present value. *Capital rationing* is a condition in which a company

FIGURE 22-3 Calculating net present value (RF = 8 percent).

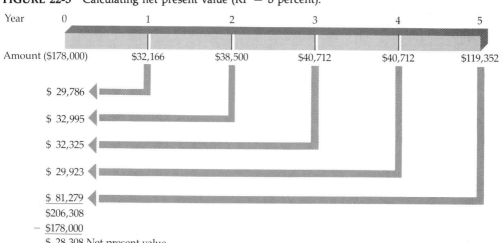

Year	0	1	2	3	4	5
Amount ($178,000)		$32,166	$38,500	$40,712	$40,712	$119,352

$ 29,786
$ 32,995
$ 32,325
$ 29,923
$ 81,279
$206,308
− $178,000
$ 28,308 Net present value

TABLE 22-5   Net Present-Value Solution Table

(1) Year (n)	(2) Annual Total Cash Flow	(3) Interest Factor (RF = 8%)	(2) × (3) = (4) Product
1	$ 32,166	.926	$ 29,786
2	38,500	.857	32,995
3	40,712	.794	32,325
4	40,712	.735	29,923
5	119,352	.681	81,279
			$206,308

Calculation:
Present value of cash inflows	$206,308
Less net investment cash outflow	178,000
Net present value	$ 28,308

cannot finance all acceptable projects. When capital rationing exists, management selects from the acceptable projects those which will maximize the sum of the net present values.

The net present value conforms with all criteria that an ideal ranking and selection process should have: The net present value recognizes the time value of money, considers all cash flows over a project's life, and incorporates the project's required rate of return.

Net Present-Value Index

The net present value is sometimes modified into a ratio to become a net present-value index, often called a net profitability index. It is the percentage change in shareholders' wealth associated with accepting the proposed project. This index shows us the dollars of net present value per dollar invested, and is the project's net present value divided by its net investment cash outflow. Management calculates the index with the following equation:

$$\text{Net present-value index} = \frac{\text{NPV}}{I_0}$$

where all items are defined in the net present-value equation.

Consider the calculation of the net present-value index for the $178,000 project presented in Tables 22-2 and 22-4 in which the required rate of return is the risk-free 8 percent. Table 22-5 illustrates the necessary calculations. The net present-value index is 16 percent calculated as follows:

$$\text{Net present-value index} = \frac{\$28,308}{\$178,000} = 0.16 \quad \text{or} \quad 16\%$$

BOX 22-1
Some Critical Comments about
Discounted Cash Flow
Some critics have pointed out that discounted cash-flow methods may have contributed to America's competitive decline and that managers using discounted cash flow have systematically rejected investments important to the livelihood of many U.S. industries.

These critics note that discounted cash flow is a sound conceptual model for valuing a company because it focuses on cash rather than accounting profits. It also properly emphasizes the opportunity cost of the cash invested by recognizing that the cash you get out should be greater than the cash you put in plus the interest you could have earned by investing the money elsewhere.

Here are a few of the problems. One problem is in identifying the relevant cash flows. Far from being an exact science, this step requires imprecise assumptions about market growth, price levels, and, perhaps above all, the likely actions of competitors.

Too often managers neglect to ask, "What will happen if we *don't* make this investment?" GM failed to invest in response to Toyota's challenge because small cars looked less profitable than its then-current mix. As a result, Toyota was able to expand and eventually challenge GM's business. Many American companies that thought global expansion would be too risky find today their worldwide competitive positions eroding. They did not evaluate carefully enough the results of not building a worldwide position.

Some critics point out that discounted cash flow is more easily applied to the gains from simple cost-reducing investments like the acquisition of labor-saving equipment. Yet other companies are making cost-saving investments as well. Thus, if prices reflect the changing cost structure of a competitive industry, actual earnings and cash flows may be lower than anticipated. This result may explain why actual earnings and cash flows may be lower than anticipated and why many companies' returns fall short of their hurdle rates for investment.

A 16 percent net present-value index means this: Given the choice between a $178,000 opportunity (for example, investing in a U.S. Treasury bill) yielding exactly the required rate of return (8 percent in this example) and this $178,000 project, shareholders are 16 percent wealthier by accepting this project. A zero net present-value index means that a project returns only its required rate of return and leaves shareholders' wealth unchanged.

Internal Rate of Return
The internal rate of return (IRR) is the discount rate that equates the present value of a project's total cash inflows with its net investment cash outflow. Another way to explain the internal rate of return is to say that it is the discount rate that makes a

project's net present value zero. The method is in practice an iterative or trial-and-error method: A manager tries several discount rates until finding the one that makes the cash inflows equal the net investment cash outflow. Mathematically, the internal rate of return solves the following equation for IRR:

$$I_0 = \sum_{t=1}^{n} \frac{CF_t}{(1 + IRR)^t}$$

where

$$I_0 = \text{net investment cash outflow}$$
$$CF = \text{annual total cash flow}$$
$$IRR = \text{solved-for internal rate of return}$$
$$t = \text{time (annual) subscript}$$
$$n = \text{proposed project's estimated life in years}$$

Management compares the internal rate of return with the required rate of return to see if the project should be accepted. In a world of certainty, the decision rules are

1. Management should accept the project if the internal rate of return is *greater than* the risk-free rate of return.
2. Management should reject the project if the internal rate of return is *less than* the risk-free rate of return.

What should management do with a project with an internal rate of return *equal to* the required rate of return? To be correct, management would be indifferent in the sense that it would not care if it accepted or rejected the project because shareholders' wealth would not change under either condition. As a practical matter, management would go back and examine its estimates and calculations to make sure that they reflect its view of reality.

In the example in Tables 22-2 and 22-4, a manager might find the internal rate of return by first trying a discount rate of 20 percent. He would then solve the equation by substituting 0.20 for IRR:

$$I_0 = \frac{\$32,166}{(1 + IRR)^1} + \frac{\$38,500}{(1 + IRR)^2} + \frac{\$40,712}{(1 + IRR)^3}$$
$$+ \frac{\$40,712}{(1 + IRR)^4} + \frac{\$119,352}{(1 + IRR)^5}$$

Rather than using the equation, a manager might use a solution table like that in Table 22-6. Here, IRR is a guess of what the internal rate of return is. The product column is each year's after-tax cash flow multiplied by the interest factor for 20 percent from Appendix B-2. When the summed products equal the present value of the net investment cash outflow, we have the internal rate of return.

TABLE 22-6 Solution Iteration, IRR = 20%

(1)	(2)	(3) Interest Factor (Trying 20%)	(2) × (3) = (4) Product
Year	Cash Flow		
1	$ 32,166	.833	$ 26,794
2	38,500	.694	26,719
3	40,712	.578	23,532
4	40,712	.482	19,623
5	119,352	.402	47,980
			$144,648 < $178,000

Because, as Table 22-6 demonstrates, the present value of the cash inflows does not equal the net investment cash outflow ($178,000 > $144,648), the manager knows that the internal rate of return is not 20 percent and to try another rate. Should the other rate be greater or less than 20 percent? It should be less because at 20 percent the present value of cash inflows was too low, and a look back at the internal rate of return equation suggests that a smaller discount rate will increase the present value by lowering IRR in the denominator.

Table 22-7 shows the solution for a 12 percent discount rate. Notice that the present value of the future cash flows is now above the net investment cash outlay, so we know that the internal rate of return lies between 20 percent and 12 percent. We may want to try 14 percent.

Practice. Estimate the internal rate of return by trying a 14 percent discount rate. You will find that the present value of the annual cash flows is $171,413.

The present value of annual cash flows capitalized at 12 percent is $181,982 and at 14 percent $171,413. Our analysis has sandwiched the internal rate of return between 12 percent and 14 percent.

A more precise answer can be found by interpolating, a mathematical proce-

TABLE 22-7 Solution Iteration, IRR = 12%

(1)	(2)	(3) Interest Factor (Trying 12%)	(2) × (3) = (4) Product
Year	Cash Flow		
1	$ 32,166	.893	$ 28,724
2	38,500	.797	30,685
3	40,712	.712	28,987
4	40,712	.636	25,893
5	119,352	.567	67,673
			$181,962
			<
			$178,000

dure examined in Box 2-4. The interpolated internal rate of return is 12.73 percent. However, interpolating may be unnecessary and perhaps misleading because it suggests accuracy in a process that at many points is based on approximation and even guesswork. Managers use a bracketed internal rate of return most of the time.

Ranking and Selecting Projects. A manager ranks proposals according to internal rates of return and accepts all of those that exceed the project's required rate of return—the risk-free (RF) rate of return in a certain environment. Suppose that the risk-free rate of return is 8 percent. In the example calculation a manager accepts the project because the bracketed internal rate of return is greater than the required rate of return.

$$IRR > RF$$
$$14\% \text{ to } 12\% > 8\%$$

Management cannot accept all projects with returns greater than the required return when capital is rationed. Management then ladders all projects in order of internal rates of return and selects those that are acceptable until all capital is invested.

Companies operating in stable business environments or priding themselves on precision in evaluating capital-spending proposals use the internal rate of return. It satisfies all theoretical criteria. Clearly, it recognizes money's time value and incorporates a project's required rate of return and cash flows over the project's life. However, there are two issues that make this method less useful than it might otherwise appear to be. First, a manager using the internal rate of return method to evaluate a proposed project may correctly find more than one internal rate of return for a single project. The number of solutions depends on the number of changes from net cash inflows to net cash outflows. When a project has more than one change between cash outflows and inflows, as many correct IRRs occur as there are changes: If six changes occur, there will be six returns; if seven occur, there will be seven returns, and so on. There is no systematic way to determine which of several returns is the true one because each is correct. The example we dealt with above had only one change, thus there is only one internal rate of return.

The second issue is this: The internal rate of return method assumes that cash flows can as they occur be reinvested at the internal rate of return. As a result, each project has its own unique reinvestment rate. On the other hand the net present value assumes that each project's cash flows can be reinvested at the discount rate used to find the present value of the future cash flows. There are several implications associated with the reinvestment assumption, but we shall leave their discussion to your future study of capital budgeting.

Now that we have examined three discounted cash-flow methods to rank and select proposed capital projects, you may find it useful to see how they relate to each other. That is the topic of the next section of this chapter.

BOX 22-2
How Rational Are Investment
Decisions?   John Maynard Keynes, a famous economist, was skeptical about how sci-
entific or rational business decisions are. To hear him tell it, business
decisions are no more rational than those made by many investors in common stock.
Here's what Keynes wrote:

> Enterprise only pretends to itself to be mainly actuated by the statements in its
> own prospectus, however candid and sincere. Only a little more than an expedi-
> tion to the South Pole, is it based on an exact calculation of benefits to come.
> Thus if the animal spirits are dimmed and the spontaneous optimism falters,
> leaving us to depend on nothing but a mathematical expectation, enterprise will
> fade and die—though fears of loss may have a basis no more reasonable than
> hopes of profit had before.*

* John Maynard Keynes, *The General Theory of Employment, Interest and Money*, Harcourt, Brace, &
World, Inc., Harbinger Edition, 1964, pp. 161–162.

Relation Between Discounted Cash-Flow Methods

The three discounted cash-flow methods this chapter discusses are closely related
because any project acceptable using one method is always acceptable using another,
and any project unacceptable using one method is always unacceptable using another. Table 22-8 summarizes the decision similarities: Acceptance and rejection
swing above and below the indifference level, the level where the net present value
is zero, the internal rate of return equals the required rate of return, and the net
present-value index is zero. Management would be indifferent to such a project
because either accepting or rejecting it will not change shareholders' wealth. In
practice, the nearer a project is to the indifference level, the more desirable it becomes to review estimates of inputs because there will be little room for error in
such cases. Here is a summary of the way the methods relate to each other:

1. A project with a positive net present value means the project's internal rate of return
   exceeds its required rate of return, the net present-value index is greater than zero,
   and shareholders' wealth rises if management accepts the project.
2. A project with a negative net present value means its internal rate of return is less
   than the project's required rate of return, the net present-value index is less than
   zero, and shareholders' wealth declines if management accepts the project.

There are technical distinctions between the internal rate of return, the net
present value, and net present-value index methods that go beyond the scope of this
book, and you may want to take an advanced financial management course to learn
about them. However, most experts agree that the net present value is probably the
best one to use. It is easy to calculate because the discount rate is given and need not

TABLE 22-8 Relation Between DCF Capital-Budgeting Methods and Shareholders' Wealth

Net Present-Value Method	Internal Rate of Return Method	Net Present-Value Index	Change in Shareholders' Wealth if Project Accepted
NPV > 0	IRR > R	NPVI > 0	Increase
NPV = 0	IRR = R	NPVI = 0	No change
NPV < 0	IRR < R	NPVI < 0	Decrease

be sought with several iterations. In addition, the net present-value method emphasizes a dollar return, the change in shareholders' wealth if the proposed project is
accepted. The dollar return is more meaningful than the internal rate of return or net
present-value index's percentage because we spend and consume out of dollars, not
rates. For example, we can consume more with a 10 percent return on $1 million
than we can with a 50 percent return on $10 because $100,000 is greater than $5, but
the internal rate of return fails to recognize this fact.

DISCOUNTED CASH-FLOW METHODS: THE UNCERTAINTY CASE

Proposed capital-budgeting projects have different amounts of uncertainty or risk
because each project has a different likelihood of causing a financial loss. *Risk* is the
difference between an actual value and an expected value, although in a financial
sense it is the chance or likelihood of incurring a financial loss. Risk in capital
budgeting means that management does not know the amount and the timing of a
proposed project's future cash flows. Each project has its own unique risk because
each has its own cash flow pattern so that each one must be evaluated with its own
required rate of return consisting of a risk-free rate of return and a risk premium.

Management uses the capital-asset pricing model to evaluate projects in an
uncertain environment. Recall from our discussion in Chapters 13 and 20 that the
capital-asset pricing model is an equation that determines an investor's return when
investing in a capital asset. The model is written

$$R^* = RF + \beta \, (RM - RF)$$

where

R^* = risk adjusted required rate of return
β = risk index, usually called a beta, for a proposed project
RF = risk-free rate of return, usually measured by the annual return on
      a U.S. government security like a Treasury bill
RM = return on a market collection of investments available to all investors

---

BOX 22-3

Risk **Is a Four-Letter Word**   *Risk* is one of those words that people often use without
having a clear-cut meaning for it. And it is not uncom-
mon to see someone try to get away with its definition by telling us how it is
measured.

Large amounts of money and time are spent to measure and reduce risk because risk is always present in a decision. We can sound sophisticated in the class-
room or in a textbook if we substitute the work *risk* for ignorance, stupidity, negli-
gence, forgetfulness, blunder, mistake, error, or act of God.

Here is how several experts defined risk when each was asked to define the
term:

FINANCIAL MANAGER: Variation about an expected return.
ACCOUNTANT: Errors and irregularities.
PRODUCTION MANAGER: Making decisions in the face of unknown conditions.
QUANTITATIVE TYPE: Decision making in which at least one decision variable is
random.
ECONOMIST: Uncertainty about the outcome.
LAWYER: Not a legal concept.

Source: Based on Daniel L. Schneid, "Risk—Just Another Four-Letter Word," *Financial Executive,*
January 1984, pp. 16–17.

The company's financial manager calculates the risk index for a proposed project
and the return on the market collection of investments (called the market portfolio),
then uses this information along with the risk-free rate of return to find the project's
required rate of return. The following list presents the way that a project's risk-
adjusted required rate of return R^* relates to the market's return RM:

Project's Risk	Project's Risk Index	Required Rate of Return
Greater than the market	Greater than 1	Greater than RM
Same as the market	Equal to 1	RM
Less than the market	Less than 1	Less than RM
No risk	Zero	RF

Practice. Use the capital-asset pricing model to determine the required rate of return
on a project with a 1.3 risk index when the risk-free rate of return is 12 percent and
the return on the market portfolio is 16 percent. Answer: 17.2 percent. Make sure
that you can find this answer before continuing.

Figure 22-4 illustrates the way that a project's required rate of return relates to the return on the market. Notice that as the risk index measured on the horizontal axis falls to zero, the required rate of return declines to the risk-free rate. The risk index of the market portfolio is 1, and it is located on the horizontal axis. The market portfolio's return is noted on the vertical axis. A proposed project's required return will be above and below the market portfolio's return as the project's risk is above and below the market portfolio's risk. You should pause now and trace through these relationships before you leave this discussion.

Now we can apply the capital-asset pricing model to the proposed $178,000 project that we have been examining in this chapter. Suppose that the company's financial manager has estimated the market portfolio's return to be 15.5 percent. The risk-free rate is 8 percent. After considering all factors, management decides to use a 1.20 risk index for the project. The capital asset pricing model tells us that the required return is 17 percent,

$$R^* = 0.08 + 1.20(0.155 - 0.08) = 0.17 \quad \text{or} \quad 17\%$$

Management uses this risk-adjusted discount or hurdle rate to find the risk-adjusted net present value. The *risk-adjusted net present value* is the change in shareholders' wealth on a risk-adjusted basis if management accepts the proposed project. We implement it in the same way as the net present value in a risk-free environment, except that the discount rate is the required return calculated with the capital-asset pricing model.

Example. The $178,000 proposed project has a $20,800 negative net present value capitalized at 17 percent using interest factors from Appendix B-2 and illustrated in Figure 22-5.

FIGURE 22-4 Project's risk and required rate of return.

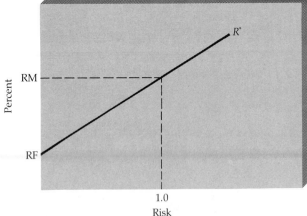

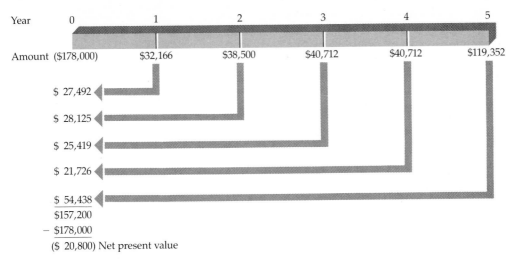

FIGURE 22-5   Calculating net present value $R^* = 0.08 + 1.2(0.155 - 0.08) = 0.17$.

Practice. Should management accept the project illustrated in Figure 22-5? Explain your answer.

If all projects with a risk-adjusted net present value greater than zero cannot be accepted, then management selects projects offering the greatest total risk-adjusted net present value.

SUMMARY

Table 22-9 presents a summary of the equations used in capital budgeting. Refer to it as you read this summary, answer questions, and solve problems.

    1. An ideal ranking and selection procedure should (1) consider cash flows over a project's entire life, (2) recognize the time value of money, and (3) incorporate a project's required rate of return.

    2. The investment in a project consists of the cash price of the equipment adjusted for sales taxes and for the investment tax credit and the increase in net working capital. Cash inflows consist of operating cash flow, liquidated net working capital, and the capital equipment's after-tax disposal value.

    3. Simple payback measures the length of time required to recapture through cash inflows a project's net cash outflow. It is a measure of a project's return *of* capital rather than return *on* capital. It fails to fulfill the properties of an ideal capital-budgeting method.

    4. The net present-value method measures the expected change in shareholders' wealth associated with project acceptance. A variation of the net present-value

TABLE 22-9 Summary of Capital-Budgeting Equations

Equation	Meaning
OCF = (Cash inflows–cash Outflows) $(1 - T) + T$ (Depr)	After-tax increase in cash from operations plus the tax saving from depreciation.
$NPV = \sum_{t=1}^{n} \dfrac{CF_t}{(1+R)^t} - I_0$	Cash flows capitalized at the required rate of return and outflow subtracted to give the dollar change in shareholders' wealth.
$NPVI = \dfrac{NPV}{I_0}$	Net present value of cash flows divided by net investment cash outflow to yield the amount of net present value per dollar of investment.
$I_0 = \sum_{t=1}^{n} \dfrac{CF_t}{(1+IRR)^t}$	Rate of discount that equates present value of cash flows to a project's net investment cash outflow.
$R^* = RF + \beta (RM - RF)$	Risk-adjusted required return on a project using the capital asset pricing model.

method is the net present-value index. Management calculates the net present value by discounting future annual total cash inflows at the project's required rate of return (the risk-free rate where there is no uncertainty) and subtracting the net investment cash outflow. Management ranks projects in order of net present value, and all projects with a positive net present value are accepted. If capital rationing exists, projects maximizing the sum of net present values are selected.

5. The internal rate of return is a rate of discount that equates the present value of a project's cash inflows with its net investment cash outflow. Management ranks projects in order of internal rate of return and accepts projects having internal rates of return greater than their required rate of return. This method implicitly assumes that incremental cash flows over a project's life are reinvested at the calculated internal rate of return. The method also may yield multiple solutions if there is more than one reversal of cash flows.

6. Any project acceptable when evaluated with the net present-value method is acceptable with the net present-value index and internal rate of return methods. Most experts consider the net present value to be the best method to use for evaluating projects because it is easiest to calculate and measures the dollar change in shareholders' wealth if management accepts the proposed project.

7. Management calculates a risk-adjusted net present value by using a discount rate estimated with the capital-asset pricing model. The capital-asset pricing model is an equation that relates a project's required rate of return to the risk-free rate plus a risk premium. For capital-budgeting purposes, the risk premium is a project's risk index multiplied by the difference between the return on a market collection of investments and the risk-free return:

$$R^* = RF + \beta (RM - RF)$$

Management estimates the risk-adjusted net present value by discounting the expected cash flows with the risk-adjusted required rate of return.

KEY TERMS AND CONCEPTS

Operating cash flows
Net investment cash outflow
Payback period
Discounted cash-flow methods
Iterative process

Multiple solutions
Reinvestment assumption
Net present-value index
Risk-adjusted discount rate

QUESTIONS

22-1. Classify each of the following as either a cash inflow or a cash outflow in a capital-budgeting decision:
   a. An increase in sales revenue.
   b. Depreciation deduction.
   c. Taxes.
   d. Decline in labor expenses.
   e. Increase in raw material prices.
   f. Liquidation of net working capital.
   g. Equipment acquired on trade credit.
   h. Investment tax credit.
   i. Price per unit declines.
   j. Variable costs per unit decline.

22-2. Operating cash flow is an important amount associated with a capital-budgeting decision. Define operating cash flow and explain how it is measured. How does an $86,000 increase in interest expense affect operating cash flow?

22-3. Explain why we do not classify the payback period as a discounted cash-flow capital-budgeting method.

22-4. If a company invests in projects in which the required rate of return exceeds the internal rate of return, the market value of the company's stock over the long run
   a. will rise due to the historic upward bias of all stocks.
   b. will suffer due to this divergence between the cost of capital and rate of return.
   c. will not be affected because of the lack of dissemination of such information to the securities markets.
   d. will rise because investors are not sophisticated enough to evaluate the effect of such differences between the cost of capital and rate of return.
   e. will not be affected because stock prices move on a random basis.
   Explain why the choices that you did not select were unacceptable.

22-5. An important part of the net investment cash outflow in capital budgeting is the necessary increase in net working capital.
   a. How is net working capital measured? How is it defined?
   b. How is the liquidated net working capital at the end of a project's life considered in capital-budgeting analysis?

22-6. A financial manager of Rayson, Inc., has prepared an analysis of a proposed capital project using discounted cash-flow techniques. One manager has questioned the accuracy of the results because the calculations employed in the analysis have assumed that cash flows occurred at the end of the year, when the cash flows actually occurred uniformly throughout each year. The net present value calculated by the financial manager

    a. will not be in error.

    b. will be slightly overstated.

    c. will be unusable for actual decision making.

    d. will be slightly understated but usable.

    e. will produce an error the direction of which is undeterminable.

22-7. Explain why the internal rate of return method for ranking and selecting investment proposals is referred to as an "iterative method."

22-8. Contrast the role of a project's required rate of return in the internal rate of return method with its role in the net present-value method.

22-9. Explain how acceptance and rejection decisions using the three discounted cash-flow methods presented in this chapter are consistent in their impact on shareholders' wealth. Refer to Table 22-8 to guide your answer.

22-10. Ecomcon, Inc, has a small capital budget. When faced with indivisible projects each of which is estimated to generate a return greater than its required rate of return, the company should select the combination of projects that will fully utilize the budget and

    a. maximize the sum of the net present values.

    b. maximize the sum of the internal rates of return.

    c. minimize the sum of the payback periods.

    d. have the highest net present-value indexes.

    e. are ranked the highest by their net present values.

    Explain your choice.

22-11. Magnum Optics is considering the following projects:

Project	Investment	IRR	NPV
A	$70,000	28%	$18,000
B	12,000	16%	12,000
C	18,000	12%	16,000
D	6,000	8%	(2,000)
E	26,000	7%	(6,000)

    a. The required rate of return on each of these projects is nearest

      (1) 18%

      (2) 15%

      (3) 13%

      (4) 10%

      (5) 8%

      (6) 5%

    b. The present value of project C's future cash flows discounted or capitalized at the project's required rate of return used to answer (a) is

      (1) $12,000

      (2) $19,000

      (3) $22,000

      (4) $26,000

      (5) $34,000

      (6) cannot be calculated with this information.

    c. If projects are not mutually exclusive and there is no capital rationing, the size of the capital budget is nearest

(1) $32,000
(2) $70,000
(3) $92,000
(4) $100,000
(5) $106,000
(6) $132,000

d. Project A has an $18,000 NPV. Interpret this amount.

e. Explain which project should be selected (B or C) if capital rationing prevents management from accepting both.

22-12. One method to include risk in the capital-budgeting decision is to use the capital-asset pricing model. Define capital-asset pricing model and explain how it is useful in capital budgeting.

PROBLEMS

22-1. Ella Cochran has come up with an idea for a labor-saving device. If the device is accepted, its only impact will be to reduce wages by $216,000 annually in each of the next six years. Her employer, Tustin Products, is in the 46 percent marginal tax bracket.

a. Show the equation for calculating operating cash flow.

b. Calculate the dollar impact on operating cash flow if Ms. Cochran's suggestion is accepted by Tustin Products.

22-2. Pinky Randall is the controller for Collingswood Crosstiks, a publishing company that publishes and distributes crossword puzzles. His immediate task is to calculate the cash flows associated with an investment project. His boss places before him the following financial numbers associated with the proposed project:

Selling price per unit		$14.60
Costs per unit		
Variable labor	$2.60	
Variable materials	$4.20	
Variable selling and Administrative	$3.80	
Total		$10.60
Fixed cost: Depreciation (annual) for tax purposes		$400,000
Fixed cost: selling and administrative (annual)		$53,000

According to the marketing department, the five-year project will result annually in 200,000 units of sales. A check with Collingswood Crosstiks' tax attorney reveals to Pinky that the company is in the 46 percent marginal tax bracket. According to the accounting department, the selling and administrative fixed costs will be incurred whether or not this project is accepted.

a. Explain why you should ignore the fixed selling and administrative costs in evaluating this project's profitability.

b. Calculate annual expected operating cash flow associated with this proposed investment project.

22-3. Tretorn USA is considering investing in a project with the following characteristics:

Expected annual sales (units)	28,000
Price per unit	$4.00
Variable production, administrative, and	
selling costs per unit	$2.60
Annual allocated overhead (from home office)	$15,000
Depreciation annually (for tax purposes)	$18,000
Interest expense	$ 7,000
Tax rate	40%

a. Calculate operating cash flow for this project. Explain why management correctly ignores interest expense and annual allocated overhead in the calculation.

b. Suppose that the allocated overhead is an incremental cash amount rather than an allocation of existing overhead. What is the amount of operating cash flow under this condition?

22-4. An immediate $770 net investment cash outflow has the following after-tax cash returns:

Year	Return
1	$500
2	$125
3	$250

a. Find the internal rate of return.

b. Explain what is meant by the IRR's reinvestment assumption. Is it the same as the assumption for the net present value?

c. How will management decide whether or not to accept the project?

22-5. The Goodman Corporation has been presented with an investment opportunity that will yield 10 years of increased operating cash flow presented below. The net investment cash outflow is $174,000 and the project requires a 10 percent rate of return.

a. Calculate the payback period. What information must you have to determine whether or not the project is acceptable using the payback method to evaluate it?

b. What is the net present value of the investment? Ignore the investment tax credit in your calculation.

c. What is the net present value if Goodman Corporation takes the investment tax credit (adjusted by two percentage points)? Do not recalculate cash inflows to solve this part of the problem, but adjust the net investment cash outflow. (Ignore the 85 percent ITC limitation for the year.)

End of Year(s)	Cash Inflow
1	$80,000
2–9	$25,000
10	$30,000

22-6. A project sponsor presents the capital-budgeting committee of Helstrom Fish and Hatchery a project that will expand capacity at its Lake Como plant by 30 percent. The initial outlay is $500,000 for plant and equipment and $60,000 for net working capital. The project's required rate of return is 12 percent. Sales revenues in each of the project's three years is $420,000 and cash operating costs are $200,000 annually. The project will be liquidated at the end of the third year with net working capital sold for $60,000 and plant and equipment for $42,000. The company is in the 46 percent marginal tax bracket and the alternative rate is 28 percent. Ignore the 85 percent limitation on the investment tax credit.

a. Calculate the net investment cash outflow assuming that the company takes the full 6 percent investment tax credit and adjusts the depreciable basis by the appropriate amount.

b. Calculate each year's cash flow for the project. Remember that the accelerated cost-recovery system results in a zero ending book value and that the company adjusts the depreciable basis by one-half of the investment tax credit.

c. Calculate the payback period for this project and interpret your answer.

d. Calculate the net present value of the project and interpret your answer.

e. Calculate the internal rate of return on this project. Should it be accepted? Explain your answer.

22-7. Pelham Airlines is considering acquiring a concession stand at the international airport. Sales of concession units and the costs will be as follows for the next five years:

	1	2	3	4	5
Sales					
Units	90,000	100,000	110,000	110,000	70,000
Revenues	$450,000	$500,000	$550,000	$550,000	$350,000
Less Costs					
Variable					
Labor	$170,000	$200,000	$230,000	$230,000	$110,000
Material	67,500	75,000	82,500	82,500	52,500
Overhead	67,500	75,000	82,500	82,500	52,500
Fixed					
(Incremental)	100,000	100,000	100,000	100,000	100,000
Depreciation					
(straight-line)	22,000	22,000	22,000	22,000	22,000
EBT	$ 23,000	$28,000	$33,000	$33,000	$13,000

The total investment will be $110,000 in equipment and $8,000 in net working capital. Pelham is in the 40 percent marginal tax bracket. The project's required rate of return is 20 percent and a 10 percent investment tax credit is available on the equipment. (Ignore the 85 percent limit on the year.) Assume that the investment is made at the beginning of year 1 and subsequent cash flows occur at the end of the year. No cash flows occur from liquidating the investment.

a. Pelham Airlines' accountant points out that the concession stand will be charged at a rate of 20 percent of variable costs each year for support services from the central administration. These budgeted costs are not included in the above calculations. Explain under which of the following conditions the costs are correctly considered in measuring the profitability of the concession stand.

  (1) No new outlays are required at central administration because there is sufficient excess capacity (labor, equipment, storage area, and so on) to service the concession stand.

  (2) Central administration must hire new employees, add computer hardware and software, and expand its storage facilities to service the concession stand. These costs are estimated to be equal to 20 percent of the project's variable costs.

b. What is the net investment for capital budgeting assuming that Pelham Airlines reduced the ITC by two percentage points and that there are no cash flows other than those on the schedule above. The company has enough tax liability so that it may use the entire amount of the investment tax credit.

c. Calculate and interpret each of the following under the assumption that after-tax cash flows are $28,000 in each of the first four years and $36,000 in year 5.

(1) Payback period (2½ years or less is acceptable).

(2) Net present value.

(3) Net present-value index.

22-8. CMA Examination (modified). Hazman Company plans to replace an old piece of equipment which is obsolete and is expected to be unreliable under the stress of daily operations. The equipment is fully depreciated, and no salvage value can be realized upon its disposal. One piece of equipment being considered would provide $7,000 annual operating cash before income taxes and depreciation. The equipment would cost $18,000 and have an estimated useful life of five years. Hazman's management will take a 10 percent investment tax credit adjusted by two percentage points. (Ignore the 85 percent limit on the amount for the year.)

Hazman uses the straight-line depreciation method on all equipment for book purposes and the accelerated cost-recovery system for tax purposes. The company is subject to a 40 percent tax rate, and the project's required rate of return is 14 percent. Assume all operating revenues and expenses occur at the end of the year.

a. Use the capital-asset pricing model to explain how management determined the project's 14 percent required return.

b. Calculate and interpret each of the following measures for Hazman Company's proposed investment in new equipment:

(1) Payback period.

(2) Net present value.

(3) Net present-value index.

(4) Internal rate of return.

c. Identify and discuss the issues Hazman Company should consider when deciding which of the decision models identified in (b) above it should employ to compare and evaluate alternative capital investment projects.

22-9. Fredonia Manganese and Calcite (FMC) is considering investing in a project with the following characteristics:

Project's risk index (beta)	1.2
Annual operating operating cash flows	$26,000
Life	5 years
Total investment	$72,000
Disposal value after taxes	$ 7,000

The yield on U.S. Treasury bills is 9 percent and the return on the market is 14 percent.

a. Is this project riskier than the market portfolio? Explain your answer.

b. Calculate the risk-adjusted net present value of this project. Show your work and interpret your answer.

22-10. Joslin Industries is considering capital projects for the coming year. Management is evaluating two prospective projects. Project A has a 1.76 beta and project B has a 0.66 beta. The company's beta is 1.1 and the return on the market portfolio is 12 percent. The risk-free return is 9 percent.

   a. Calculate the risk-adjusted required rate of return for each project.
   b. Sketch a figure like Figure 22-4 to illustrate the risk and return of each project. Be
      sure to label each axis.

22-11. Alan Feyt, assistant controller for Belleview Tectronics, is considering two prospective
       projects. Project A has a 1.32 beta and project B has a 1.10 beta. The company's beta is
       0.80, the annualized yield on a risk-free investment is 6 percent, and the return on a
       portfolio of assets is 12 percent.
   a. Which project has more risk? Explain your answer.
   b. Calculate the hurdle rate for each project.
   c. Sketch the relation between each project's beta and its hurdle rate.

22-12. Singletary Corporation is considering adding a new stapler to one of its product lines.
       More equipment will be needed to produce the new item. One method to obtain the
       equipment is for the company to construct it. The estimated departmental costs for the
       construction of the special-purpose equipment are as follows:

Materials and parts	$ 75,000
Direct labor	60,000
Variable overhead	
(50% of DL$)	30,000
Fixed overhead (allocated)	15,000
Total	$180,000

       The entire $180,000 (after adjustment for the investment tax credit) will be de-
       preciated using the accelerated cost-recovery system for five-year equipment. The
       company will take the entire investment tax credit and make the appropriate adjust-
       ment to the depreciable basis. (Ignore the 85 percent limit on the year's amount.) The
       company's financial manager recognizes that the fixed overhead must not be consid-
       ered as part of the net investment cash outflow for capital-budgeting purposes because
       the fixed overhead is not a cash outlay. The estimated disposal value of the equipment
       at the end of five years is $30,000.
       Engineering and management studies suggest that the following revenue and
       costs will occur in each of the next five years:

Unit selling price	$5.00
Unit production costs	
Materials	$1.70
Labor costs	1.40
Total unit production costs	$3.10
Unit contribution margin	$1.90
Estimated unit volume	40,000
Estimated total contribution margin	$76,000
Incremental fixed costs (annual)	
Supervision	$18,000
Insurance	5,000
Maintenance	2,000
Total	$25,000

The Singletary Corporation is in the 46 percent marginal tax bracket, the alternative (1231) tax rate is 28 percent, and the return on a market portfolio is 14 percent. The risk-free return is 10 percent.

a. Calculate the net investment cash outflow.

b. Calculate the operating cash flow of this equipment.

c. Calculate the cash flow associated with disposal of the equipment at the end of five years.

d. Should this equipment be acquired if its risk measure β is
   (1) 1.6 and
   (2) 0.8? Support your answers by calculating the risk-adjusted net present value under each condition and interpreting your answer. (Notice that you cannot use the interest factor appendices at the end of this book in your calculations because the discount rates are not even numbers. You must use an equation like that on page 468.)

SEVEN

WORKING-CAPITAL MANAGEMENT

The previous part of this book examined the area of long-term decision making. Now, we enter the important area of short-term decision making. Chapter 23 presents several features of a company's system to manage its current assets. The emphasis here is on cash and receivables management because these two assets play an important role in the company's liquidity and, ultimately, in its ability to survive and prosper. Chapter 24 looks at the other side of the balance sheet from current assets: current liabilities. Chapter 24 emphasizes trade credit and bank borrowing because these are the two most widely used sources of short-term financing.

CHAPTER 23
Managing Current Assets

CASH

The Cash Budget · A Cash-Budget Illustration · Speeding Inflows–Slowing Payments · Excess Cash

ACCOUNTS RECEIVABLE AND CREDIT POLICY
Cost of Trade Credit

MEASURING THE EFFECTIVENESS OF TRADE CREDIT
Investing in Receivables · Collection Practices

INVENTORY

SUMMARY
Key Terms and Concepts · Questions · Problems

Managing current assets is the financial manager's most time-consuming job because, with its short turnover, current assets are continually absorbing and releasing cash. To minimize the company's investment, the financial manager should keep current assets at the lowest level consistent with profitability and safety. In so doing, he will enable the company to increase its asset turnover and produce a higher rate of return on assets.

The first part of this chapter considers cash management with emphasis on how to construct a cash budget. Here, the discussion concentrates on the systematic preparation of a document that specifies the inflow and outflow of cash from operations and financing. When you finish studying this discussion you will be able to prepare a simple cash budget for a company. The second and largest part of the chapter deals with accounts receivable and credit policy. You will learn how to calculate the cost of trade credit so that you can compare it with the costs of other short-term sources of finance. After this important calculation you will read about the items management must consider when it extends trade credit to customers. The decision depends upon the net cash flow resulting from granting trade credit—only when the cash inflow is greater than the cash outflow should we grant someone trade credit. After completing study of this chapter you will be able to compute the cash flows associated with extending trade credit.

Current assets consist of cash, accounts receivable, and inventory. Each of these assets presents unique managerial problems, and for each, accepted methods of management have been developed.

CASH

Holding cash is a necessary evil. Cash earns no return, so having it on hand lowers the average return the company earns on total assets. Why, then, hold cash? We examined the primary reasons in Chapter 4, but they merit reiterating. They are transactions, precautionary, and speculative motives.

A firm needs a pool of cash because its receipts and expenditures are not perfectly synchronized—a company usually pays its bills before it receives cash from its own sales. This pool of cash is known as a *transaction balance*. The most advantageous size of this balance is calculated by using a cash budget, a managerial tool we shall look at shortly.

Management cannot forecast the future infallibly. Unexpected losses or emergencies may occur. To guard against these, a company needs a rainy-day fund of cash, a *precautionary balance*. Through this reserve, it can prevent a *linkage of disasters* wherein failure to meet one cash obligation, however small, can bring other debts due and so lead to collapse of the firm. For example, failure to pay a $3,000 advertising bill could arouse the fears of other creditors, causing them to press for payment.

A business must also keep cash on hand to take advantage of unexpected opportunities. Cash cannot always be borrowed when needed, and exceptional opportunities are most likely to arise when almost no one has, or can procure, cash. How large this *speculative cash balance* needs be depends on a company's holdings of liquid, marketable securities, on its lines of credit at commercial banks, and on its ability to squeeze cash out of its operations by delaying payables, running down inventories, and so on. But some reserve of money itself is always advisable.[1]

The Cash Budget

The prudent financial manager forecasts the cash that will be needed on a monthly, weekly, sometimes even daily basis. The tool for this forecast is the cash budget.[2]

The cash budget is a detailed forecast of expected cash flows stretching several periods ahead. It summarizes in a single view the factors expected to affect cash inflows and outflows. It serves not only to forecast expected levels of cash but also to indicate when management should take steps to deal with an impending shortage or excess.

---

[1] In 1932 Gulf Oil Company missed the chance to buy much of the great East Texas oil field at a bargain price for lack of ready cash. Management never forgot the lesson. As depression gave way to recovery and, later, to war boom, the company piled up cash and marketable securities and awaited another opportunity. It came in 1946. Gulf was able to buy a half-interest in the fabulous Kuwait oil concession at a distress price from the nearly bankrupt Anglo-Iranian Oil Company.

[2] First encountered through the eyes of Ms. Luferac in Chapter 11.

BOX 23-1
Boston Takes Steps to Accelerate Cash
Flow   Companies and people like you and me are not the only ones with cash-flow
problems. Governments have them, too. Cities sometimes have unwieldy receivables problems because tickets that are written generate accounts receivable which
some people refuse to pay.

Consider the example of Boston. Boston was like many cities. Drivers there
trashed more parking tickets than they sent to the municipal courts. Parking-fine
collections dropped from $8.5 million in fiscal year 1979 to $4.1 million in fiscal
1981. By then, only 10 percent of parking tickets were being paid. "I'll be honest.
Our whole ticketing process was something of a joke, and deservedly so," said a
traffic and parking commissioner.

A cash-flow turnaround began in 1981 when Boston paid $3.2 million to Data-
com Systems Corp. of New York for a computerized parking-ticket system similar to
those the company operates in Detroit, Philadelphia, and Washington, D.C. The
system is tied to the Massachusetts Registry of Motor Vehicles. No one with an
unpaid ticket can get a driver's license or vehicle registration renewed.

In addition to computerizing the system, Boston replaced its 6,000 parking
meters with sturdier models and added 4,000 more. Drivers who get parking cita-
tions now receive an official letter a few days later urging them to pay promptly. "It's
to let them know we know they've been ticketed," an official says.

Finally, there has been a big, and conspicuous, increase in use of the "Denver
boot," a viselike device used by many university police. The boot clamps onto a car's
wheel, immobilzing the vehicle. Five or more tickets unpaid in Boston for more than
21 days gets a car booted, and Boston police have been clamping on more than 100
a day. It costs $56, plus all the unpaid fines to get the boot removed. Boston officials
recognize the power of public ridicule. For visual impact and to let passersby know
the city is serious about violations, it prints parking tickets on shocking orange paper
and paints boots fluorescent yellow.

Is all of this effort worthwhile? It seems to be when we consider the cash flow.
Parking-meter collections doubled in 1982 to $4 million from $2 million annually. In
one year revenue from fines and other parking enforcement rose to $22.1 million
from $4 million. The deputy mayor estimated the take at about $30 million in 1983.
"It was easy pickings," he says.

Source: Based on *The Wall Street Journal,* June 14, 1983, p. 31.

A Cash-Budget Illustration

Gladstone Company has already forecast next year's total sales. But to set up a cash
budget, it must forecast sales on a monthly basis. Suppose that the bulk of sales
comes in early spring and—because of an elaborate sales compaign—in late winter.
Gladstone extends trade credit to its customers. A 1 percent discount can be taken if

the customer pays within 30 days. Historically, 30 percent of sales is paid for during the month the goods are sold, and the remaining 70 percent within the second month.

Purchased materials and parts amount to 80 percent of sales. Materials and parts are purchased during the month preceding the sales, to provide for assembling, and paid for in the month in which sales are made. Wages and taxes are the other variable outlays—variable in the sense that they are geared to sales. However, another outlay looms on the horizon: Gladstone must repay $15,000 in bonds during June. Finally, the financial manager has decided that, to ensure minimum liquidity, Gladstone's cash level should not fall below $3,000.

Table 23-1 presents a worksheet of expected cash flows for Gladstone Company over the coming year. It shows clearly when anticipated sales will be collected and when contemplated purchases will be paid for. Since cash receipts flow into the company during the month sales are made and the following month, the worksheet has two entries for receipts. For example, March sales of $22,000 generate receipts in March of $6,600 (30 percent of sales) and in April of $15,400 (70 percent of sales). Gladstone must pay for its purchases during the month following purchase, and this timing accounts for bottom-line entries. March purchases of $19,200 (80 percent of anticipated April sales) are paid for in April.

Combining the purchases-payments and sales-receipts data with other cash outlays and receipts and entering the desired cash level complete the budget. Table 23-2 shows Gladstone's cash budget in final form. The receipts and payments rows of figures have been transferred directly from the worksheet (Table 23-1). Wages and salaries, taxes, and the bond retirement of $15,000 have next been entered. Payments for these outlays have then been deducted from receipts to give the cash gain or loss from the month's transactions. Adding a net cash gain to, or subtracting a net cash loss from, the beginning cash balance gives the ending cash balance for each month. To complete the budget, each month's anticipated ending cash balance is compared with the desired balance to see how available cash compares with requirements.

The bottom line in Table 23-2 highlights the relation between actual and desired cash. Each month's entry is a cumulative total measuring cash shortages (and so borrowings) or excesses (and so near-cash investments). Each month's dollar amount is the total borrowings (if shortage) or investments (if excess) outstanding at that time. You will notice that the *changes* in the final line of Table 23-2 equal the cash gain (loss) during a month. The reason is that any cash excess is used to discharge debt, and any shortage is covered by borrowing.

During February, Gladstone can expect a $6,200 excess of cash that it can temporarily invest, but in March, outlays will exceed receipts by $8,900. This net outlay would pull the cash balance down to $9,200 minus $8,900, or $300—$2,700 below the desired level. The treasurer will borrow $2,700 to meet the company's target cash level. In April cash receipts exceed outlays by $1,900. Adding this amount to March's $300 ending balance (assuming no adjusting), the treasurer sees that the company will end April with an unadjusted balance of $2,200. Comparing this amount with the amount desired, the treasurer sees that the company must

TABLE 23-1 Gladstone Company, Cash-Flow Worksheet for 19x1

	Jan.	Feb.	Mar.	Apr.	May	June	July	Aug.	Sept.	Oct.	Nov.	Dec.
Sales (net)	$10,000	8,000	22,000	24,000	9,000	5,000	5,000	10,000	12,000	12,000	30,000	33,000
Receipts												
1st mo., 30%	3,000	2,400	6,600	7,200	2,700	1,500	1,500	3,000	3,600	3,600	9,000	9,900
2nd mo., 70%		7,000	5,600	15,400	16,800	6,300	3,500	3,500	7,000	8,400	8,400	21,000
Total	3,000	9,400	12,200	22,600	19,500	7,800	5,000	6,500	10,600	12,000	17,400	30,900
Purchases (80% of next month's sales)	6,400	17,600	19,200	7,200	4,000	4,000	8,000	9,600	9,600	24,000	26,400	6,400
Payments (total from preceding month)		6,400	17,600	19,200	7,200	4,000	4,000	8,000	9,600	9,600	24,000	26,400

TABLE 23-2 Gladstone Company, Cash Budget for 19x1

	Jan.	Feb.	Mar.	Apr.	May	June	July	Aug.	Sep.	Oct.	Nov.	Dec.
Receipts[a]	$3,000	9,400	12,200	22,600	19,500	7,800	5,000	6,500	10,600	12,000	17,400	30,900
Outlays												
Payments[a]		6,400	17,600	19,200	7,200	4,000	4,000	8,000	9,600	9,600	24,000	26,400
Wages and salaries	800	800	1,500	1,500	850	800	800	900	1,000	1,000	2,000	2,500
Other payments												
Taxes			2,000			2,200			2,000			3,000
Bond												
Repayment						15,000						
Total payments	800	7,200	21,100	20,700	8,050	22,000	4,800	8,900	12,600	10,600	26,000	31,900
Cash gain (loss)	2,200	2,200	(8,900)	1,900	11,450	(14,200)	200	(2,400)	(2,000)	1,400	(8,600)	(1,000)
Beginning cash	4,800	7,000	9,200	300	2,200	13,650	(550)	(350)	(2,750)	(4,750)	(3,350)	(11,950)
Ending cash (assuming no adjusting)	7,000	$9,200	300	2,200	13,650	(550)	(350)	(2,750)	(4,750)	(3,350)	(11,950)	(12,950)
Cash level desired	3,000	3,000	3,000	3,000	3,000	3,000	3,000	3,000	3,000	3,000	3,000	3,000
Cumulative cash excess (or shortage)	4,000	6,200	(2,700)	(800)	10,650	(3,550)	(3,350)	(5,750)	(7,750)	(6,350)	(14,950)	(15,950)

[a]From 23-1.

borrow $800 in April. This will pay down the $2,700 loan taken out in March. How much will the loan be reduced and where do the funds come from? It will be reduced by $1,900 with funds from operations—the excess of receipts over expenditures.

Relations among the rows and figures are easily traced, and you should pause now to work through some of them to make sure you understand their sequence and meaning.

Example. The $11,450 cash gain in May will be used to pay off the $800 loan outstanding, leaving a net excess of $11,450 − $800 = $10,650. The $14,200 cash deficit in June minus the $10,650 cumulative excess means that $3,550 must be borrowed to bring July's beginning cash balance to the $3,000 desired level.

Here is another perspective on Table 23-2. The cash gain or loss in any month can be found by looking at the changes in the "cumulative cash excess or shortage" row. Take, for example, May:

May cumulative cash excess	$10,650
Add: April cumulative shortage	800
May cash gain	$11,450

Since Gladstone begins May with $800 in borrowing outstanding (to have its desired $3,000 opening balance) and ends May with a $10,650 excess, it obviously gains $11,450 cash from operating receipts and outlays in May.

A cash budget forces management to be explicit in its cash planning. Management must forecast all factors that influence cash flows in the planning period. Then, the manager plans action to cope with a cash gain or loss, investing or repaying a loan with a gain and borrowing or liquidating investments to cover a shortage. Aware that such forecasts cannot be accurate, the treasurer must build flexibility into both worksheet and cash budget. This can be done through the use of variable budgets, which recognize that some expenditures will vary at different levels of sales—for example, wages and taxes.

Speeding Inflows–Slowing Payments

Shrewd cash management boils down to getting maximum mileage out of every dollar. To do this, a company will speed its cash inflows and slow down its payments to the maximum degree permissible.

One method of speeding inflows is the *lockbox*, a post office box rented by a company and serviced by a local bank where the company keeps its account. Its primary purpose is to reduce mail float. For instance, if a company based in New York has many West Coast customers, it can trim its payment-receiving time by directing them to send their remittances to a lockbox in, say, Los Angeles instead of to the company's New York headquarters. The bank picks up the checks, credits the company's account, and keeps the company informed. The company does not even see the checks.

How does the business gain? It obtains cash two or three days earlier than it would otherwise, and it can use the cash for investment or for repayment of debt.

How does a company plan its lockbox system? It does so by selecting the banks that give it the best service and the locations that are reached the fastest by mail. One study shows that more mail gets to St. Louis faster from more places than to any other city in the country. For this reason, St. Louis banks are often used as lockbox banks by companies in other parts of the nation.

Companies also use various strategies to slow down their payments. One obvious way is to take trade discounts on accounts payable at the last possible moment—that is, paying a 2/10, net bill on the tenth day instead of on the first. Another way is to mail out dividend checks and other checks to different parts of the country and allow time for the checks to come back for collection before transferring funds to pay the checks into the checking account.[3] Meanwhile, the funds earn another two days or so of interest in Treasury bills or commercial paper.

Excess Cash

What should a firm do with its excess cash? The answer depends on the economic outlook in general and on management's particular degree of conservatism. The safest short-term investments for cash are Treasury bills, short-term obligations of federal agencies, commercial paper, short-term tax-exempt obligations of state and local governments, and certificates of deposit. If the cash is permanently in excess—that is, will not be needed in the predictable future—management probably should use it to acquire fixed assets, retire debt, or enlarge dividends.

ACCOUNTS RECEIVABLE AND CREDIT POLICY

The level of accounts receivable that a company has reflects the volume of the company's sales on account and the company's credit policy. Credit policy consists of determining the following points:

1. Maximum risk group to which credit is extended.
2. Length of time for which credit is extended.
3. Length of the discount period.
4. Size of the prompt payment (or cash) discount offered.

The following discussion presents two complementary methods to help a manager determine an appropriate credit policy. The first emphasizes the need to com-

---

[3] One very large company has worked out a detailed probability distribution showing how many dividend checks per day will come back to its New York bank. The treasurer sells only enough money-market instruments each day to provide the bank with cash for that day's expected payments.

BOX 23-2
Are Hot Ice and Business Ethics
Oxymorons?   An oxymoron is a figure of speech using an apparent contradiction in
                    terms. Jumbo shrimp is an example. Practices of some managers suggest
that managers have a low ethical threshold. For example, a company delaying payment to suppliers beyond the past-due date, then taking the cash discount clearly
smacks of unethical behavior.

Business students have become more concerned with the ethics of their chosen
profession. "There's a perceived relevance to ethics, and less resistance to the subject
than five years ago," says a Stanford University professor. "Business and Legal
Ethics," a course at the University of California, Berkeley, attracted about 100 students in 1983, up from 65 previously. Business ethics courses are "a growth industry," said a Harvard Business School professor.

Ethics students at the University of Washington, Seattle, study corporate whis-
tle-blowers and sexual harrassment of workers. Yale University students study
whether Citicorp evaded taxes in Europe by switching funds between countries—an
issue raised by the Securities and Exchange Commission (which dropped the matter). Manville Corporation's filing for bankruptcy to protect itself from asbestos-
related lawsuits raises questions in classes at Illinois Institute of Technology.

A Bentley College survey in 1982 turned up 317 schools with business-ethics
courses, about five times as many as in 1973.

Source: Based on Jeffrey A. Tannenbaum, "Is Business Ethics, Like Jumbo Shrimp, An Oxymoron?" *The Wall Street Journal,* May 5, 1983, p. 1.

---

pare the cost of trade credit with costs of alternative financial sources available to
customers. The second uses benefit-cost analysis to estimate the impact of a change
in credit terms.

Cost of Trade Credit

Two of the points listed above that determine a company's credit policy are the
length of the discount period and the size of the prompt payment (or cash) discount
that a company offers its customers. A financial manager calculates the cost of trade
credit resulting from these two items, compares the cost with other financial sources
available to customers, and determines credit policy. If the cost of trade credit is less
than the cost of other financial sources, a credit-granting company must change its
credit terms or be prepared to see its average collection period lengthen and its
receivables turnover decline.

Example. Suppose that a company offers credit terms of 1/10, *n*40 days: These terms
mean that a customer may take a 1 percent discount from the invoice amount if the
account is paid in 10 days. The entire amount is payable in 40 days. The creditor is
extending credit for $40 - 10 = 30$ days at a 1 percent yield if the customer pays 40

days after receipt of the invoice. Figure 23-1 portrays the interest payment for terms of 1/10, *n*40 days. The first 10 days of trade credit are free, but a 1 percent payment is made for the remaining 40 − 10 = 30 days.

The annual percentage rate of trade credit is measured by calculating the yield for the period credit is used (the credit period) and then annualizing this yield. The annual percentage rate (APR) for estimating the cost of trade credit is measured with the following equation:

$$APR = \frac{D \times (360/N)}{1 - D}$$

where

$$D = \text{discount rate as a decimal and}$$
$$N = \text{number of days in the credit period.}$$

In this calculation it is conventional to use 360 days in a year.

Example. Calculate the annual percentage rate of trade credit if a company grants terms of 1/10, *n*40 and receives payment on the fortieth day:

$$APR = \frac{0.01 \times (360/30)}{1 - 0.01} = 0.1212 = 12.12\%$$

Here are the steps required in the calculation:

1. Estimate the credit period by subtracting discount date from final payment date: 40 − 10 = 30 days.
2. Calculate the number of credit periods in a year using 360 days for convenience: There are 360/30 = 12 such periods.
3. Calculate the approximate annual percentage rate by multiplying the number of periods times the discount rate:

$$12 \times .01 = 0.12$$

4. Adjust the annualized yield for the amount of discount by dividing it by 1 minus the discount rate:

FIGURE 23-1   Interest payment for trade credit of 1/10, net 40 days.

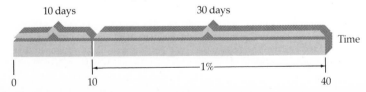

$$\frac{0.12}{1 - 0.01} = 0.1212$$

This final adjustment is necessary because the creditor company is in fact lending 99 percent of the invoiced amount.[4] Table 23-3 presents annualized rates of interest for various trade credit terms. Each calculation follows the four steps presented above.

Management must monitor its credit terms and compare them with alternative credit sources available to its customers. When the cost of trade credit lags behind (that is, rises more slowly than) the costs of other sources, customers begin to rely more heavily on the trade credit. If a company's customers can borrow from commercial banks at the prime lending rate, a company will want to consider changing the length of the discount period and prompt payment discount as the prime rate changes.

Example. Table 23-3 shows that a company selling merchandise on terms of 1/10, $n40$ days is granting trade credit at a 12.12 annual percentage rate. If alternative rates rise much beyond 12.12 percent, the company's customers will rely increasingly on trade credit. To combat this condition, the creditor company should consider changing its credit terms to a higher annual percentage rate (for example, to 3/10, $n40$ days) or increasing the selling price of goods, either of which requires diplomacy to avoid alienating customers.

The following section looks at receivables management from a different perspective. You will see that the decision to grant or change credit policy depends on a critical examination of the cash flows resulting from the change.

MEASURING THE EFFECTIVENESS OF TRADE CREDIT

Trade credit to customers is justified only to the extent that profits are improved by selling on terms rather than for cash only. This means that the marginal return from granting trade credit must exceed its marginal cost.

The marginal return from trade credit is simply the contribution margin that a company makes on the additional sales. Trade credit involves three marginal costs: (1) cost of cash tied up in trade receivables, (2) credit losses, and (3) handling expense. Bearing these costs in mind, a credit manager will classify customers according to (1) how long they take to pay (which shows the cost of money for each class), (2) probability of nonpayment (which measures expected loss on each class), and (3) allocable processing and collection cost.

---

[4] An example will help to clarify this relation. If the purchasing company were to pay a $10,000 invoice in 10 days, the creditor company will receive $10,000 − (.01)($10,000) = $9,900. Receiving the entire amount at the end of the period means that the company receives $10,000 of which $100 is interest. The cost expressed as a rate is therefore ($100/$9,900) × 12 = 0.1212 or 12.12 percent.

TABLE 23–3 Annual Percentage Rate of Trade Credit Terms

Credit Terms	1/10, *n*40	3/10, *n*40	3/10, *n*50	3/20, *n*60
Periods in a year	$360/30 = 12$	$360/30 = 12$	$360/40 = 9$	$360/40 = 9$
Approximate APR	$0.12/(1-.01)=$ 0.1212	$0.36/(1-.03)=$ 0.3711	$0.27/(1-.03)=$ 0.2783	$0.27/(1-03)=$ 0.2783

Investing in Receivables

An important amount in helping us to decide on appropriate credit terms is the cash invested in accounts receivable. If we do not extend trade credit, then we collect cash at the moment we make a sale so that the cash is not tied up in receivables. Here you must note that the investment in accounts receivable is not the total amount of accounts receivable (estimated net of bad debts), but the cash invested measured by accounts receivable multiplied by the complement of the contribution margin ratio. This complement is called the *variable-cost ratio* (VCR) and measures the variable cash outlays associated with sales.

Example. A company with $80,000 sales and $20,000 contribution margin will have a 25 percent contribution margin ratio and a $1 - 0.25 = 75$ percent variable-cost ratio:

Sales on credit	$80,000
Less variable costs	60,000
Contribution margin	$20,000
Contribution margin ratio:	$20,000/$80,000 = 0.25
Variable cost ratio:	$60,000/$80,000 = 0.75

In this example the company has $0.75 \times \$80,000 = \$60,000$ cash invested in accounts receivable.

You may wonder why we do not use the entire amount of accounts receivable to determine the investment. The cash invested in receivables is in fact the cash for variable costs that we used to produce an item for inventory, and this item is then sold on credit to someone to generate the receivable. This cash could have been used in other ways (invest in CDs, buy U.S. Treasury bills, pay a dividend, and so on), so we will consider this amount as the cash invested in receivables to generate a cash inflow measured by the contribution margin. The total receivable reflects not only the cost of the item but also the profit margin.

The cost of the investment in accounts receivable is an opportunity cost: It is the rate of return from an alternative use of cash in an investment of equal risk. In other words, if management did not extend trade credit but sold merchandise on a cash basis, then the company could invest the cash and receive a return. Thus, it is appropriate that we consider this rejected alternative return in the analysis.

Example. Lifesco Company's contribution margin ratio from credit sales is 10 percent. The company's financial manager has determined that the company can invest cash to yield 12 percent annually. Rob Cleese, the company's credit manager, is deciding whether or not to continue to extend trade credit to its customers. Table 23-4 shows the customer classes, the average collection period (days' sales in accounts receivable), and bad debts and collection expenses as a percent of sales to each class.

Rob will make the decision regarding trade credit by measuring the cash benefits and costs associated with each customer class based on the amount of annual sales to each group. We shall use $50,000 annual sales in this example.

The first step is to calculate the amount of accounts receivable in each customer class by using daily sales and the average collection period, then to measure the amount of the investment in receivables by using the variable-cost ratio and amount of receivables. Table 23-5 shows the necessary calculations for each group. We multiply the average collection period in column 2 by Lifesco Company's daily sales ($50,000/360 = $138.90) to each customer class to give the amount of accounts receivable in column 4. Accounts receivable multiplied by the company's $1 - 0.10 = 90$ percent variable-cost ratio gives us in column 6 the investment in accounts receivable for each class.

Practice. A company has $160,000 in annual credit sales and its average collection period is 40 days. If the company's contribution margin ratio is 16 percent, what is the investment in accounts receivable? Answer: $14,933. Make sure that you know how to find this answer before continuing and verify that daily sales are $444.44.

The next step in the analysis is to find the opportunity cost of cash tied up in receivables by multiplying the investment by the opportunity cost, expressed as an annual rate. Then add this cost to bad debts and collection expense. That total will be the company's total cost of trade credit. In this example Rob will construct a table like Table 23-6. Column 2 is the product of the investment in receivables and the 0.14 opportunity cost.[5] The amounts of bad debts and of collection expense are added to the cost of the investment to give the amount of total cost in column 5.

TABLE 23–4   Customer Classes and Expenses

Customer Class	Average Collection Period (Days)	Percent Uncollectible (Bad Debts)[a]	Collection Expense[a]
A	10	0	0
B	30	1	2
C	60	2	3
D	90	5	3

[a] As a percent of sales to each class.

[5] If sales were stated on an other than annual basis, then the opportunity cost would need to be restated on the same basis. For example, if we were here dealing with quarterly sales, then the rate would be restated to $0.14 \times (90/360) = 0.04$ or 4 percent.

TABLE 23–5 Investment in Accounts Receivable

(1) Customer Class	(2) Average Collection Period	(3) Daily Sales	(2) × (3)=(4) Accounts Receivable	(5) Variable-Cost Ratio	(4) × (5)=(6) Investment
A	10	$138.90	$ 1,389	0.90	$ 1,250
B	30	$138.90	$ 4,167	0.90	$ 3,750
C	60	$138.90	$ 8,334	0.90	$ 7,500
D	90	$138.90	$12,501	0.90	$11,251

The final step in the analysis of trade credit is for management to compare the contribution margin with the total costs. Only if the contribution margin is greater than total marginal costs should the company continue its credit policy because only then is the policy profitable. Table 23-7 shows us the profitability for each of Life-sco's customer classes. The analysis suggests that Rob should change the credit terms for class D customers, perhaps insisting on partial payment with each sale, the remaining payment in 30 days, and no credit to any company going beyond a 60-day collection period.

Collection Practices

Sound customer classification must be accompanied by effective collection practices. Credit sales must be collected approximately within the allowed payment period. Effective collections treatment of overdue accounts is always an exercise in diplomacy as well as firmness. Many accounts with "slow pay" reputations are nonetheless sound, and their business much too valuable to lose by abrupt or insulting efforts to collect money a few days sooner than they genuinely intend to pay.

Most collection procedures are based on a series of periodic and gradually stronger reminders to customers that payment is due. Notices, letters, and telephone calls from management officials are the usual sequence. Collection treatment begins

TABLE 23–6 Total Costs

(1) Customer Class	(2) Cost of Cash in Receivables	(3) Bad Debts	(4) Collection Expense	(5) Total Cost
A	$ 1,250×0.14 = $175	0	0	$ 175
B	$ 3,750 × 0.14 = $525	0.01 × $50,000 = $500	0.02 × $50,000 = $1,000	$2,025
C	$ 7,500 × 0.14 = $1,050	0.02 × $50,000 = $1,000	0.03 × $50,000 = $1,500	$3,550
D	$11,251 × 0.14 = $1,575	0.05 × $50,000 = $2,500	0.03 × $50,000 = $1,500	$5,575

TABLE 23-7   Measuring Profit of Trade Credit Policy

(1) Customer Class	(2) Contribution Margin	(3) Total Costs	(2)−(3)=(4) Profit
A	0.10 × $50,000 = $5,000	$ 175	$4,825
B	0.10 × $50,000 = $5,000	$2,025	$4,225
C	0.10 × $50,000 = $5,000	$3,550	$2,450
D	0.10 × $50,000 = $5,000	$5,575	($ 575)

sooner and quickly becomes more insistent, of course, for customers in lower credit classes than for those in higher ones. In our example, class D customers approved for credit might receive a reminder notice even before bills are past due, a phone call from the credit manager the day payment is due, and a letter five days later threatening suit.

In addition to close followups on individual accounts that are slow-paying or delinquent, a company must watch the *general trend* of its collections. Management should be continually aware of how many days' credit sales are currently tied up in uncollected accounts, and whether this figure is trending up or down. A general lengthening-out of payment periods is usually one of the first signs that business conditions are deteriorating and that credit policy, therefore, should be guided with

BOX 23-3

Cutting Float to Increase Return   High interest rates available on money-market securities make financial managers aware of the need to minimize their companies' investment in collections and receivables because cash freed from these areas can be used to invest in money-market securities.

An efficient collection system minimizes a company's investment in float, which consists primarily of (1) dollars in transit from the customer (mail float) and (2) deposited checks which have not yet become available for company use (check clearing float).

Periodically, the financial manager should evaluate the company's collection system. Changes may have occurred in the customer base, the location of customers, the banks used by customers, or in the volume of business done with a particular customer. Additionally, both the mail and the check clearing time will change periodically. A fine-tuned collection system can potentially save a company several days in collection time, which may translate into six- to seven-figure dollar amounts. These savings are especially significant in periods of high interest rates and lead to an increased cash flow with no increase in risk. The net result should be an increase in the price of the company's common stock.

Source: Based on Daniel M. Ferguson, "Optimize Your Firm's Lockbox Selection System," *Financial Executive,* April 1983, p. 8.

BOX 23-4

Inventory Controls Increase Earnings   Rules of thumb can be misleading because some thumbs are bigger than others, but financial managers often use them (rules, not thumbs) to help make decisions. One such rule involves inventory costs. A member of President Reagan's Commission on Industrial Competitiveness says that each $1 of inventory costs $0.25 a year to carry—half of that for interest and the rest for storage, insurance, deterioration, and handling.

A well-reasoned inventory control system has allowed Westinghouse Electric with $2 billion invested in inventory to cut its inventory-to-sales ratio. Dow Chemical Corporation's inventory declined to 89 days of sales in 1984 from 110 days in 1981. The effects of these efficiencies made the companies more profitable.

Source: Based on *Forbes,* April 9, 1984, p. 33.

---

a firmer hand. A company should frequently *age* its receivables. This means classifying the number of accounts and dollar receivables outstanding according to the length of time they have been outstanding. Accounts that are 60, 90, or 120 days overdue obviously demand special attention.

INVENTORY

The objective of inventory management, like accounts-receivable management, is to minimize the company's investment while maximizing the company's return from holding the asset.

Companies hold inventories to be sure no sales are lost from orders that cannot be filled and to give flexibility between production and sales. A company may experience a strike by production employees, shortages of raw material, or delays in delivery of equipment, all of which will delay production. Thus, precautionary stocks of raw materials and goods in process, as well as finished goods, are advisable. On the other hand unforeseen surges of demand for the firm's product must be satisfied or sales may be lost permanently. By holding inventory, then, management reduces uncertainties surrounding both production and sales.

Many sophisticated approaches to inventory control exist, and most of them lend themselves to computer simulation and linear programming. Because inventory control is an area within the domain of the production manager, we leave discussion of these topics to other courses.

SUMMARY

1. Companies maintain a cash balance for transaction, precautionary, and speculative purposes.

2. A cash budget helps a manager to forecast a company's need for cash. The budget shows cash inflows and outflows for a future period, and tells a manager whether or not the company will have its desired cash level.

3. A company can use a lockbox system to accelerate cash inflows to the company. It can slow down the cash outflow by paying bills on the final due date and by transferring cash at the last moment into its account to cover checks.

4. Credit policy consists of determining the maximum risk group to which a company wishes to extend credit, the length of time for which credit is extended, length of the prompt-payment discount period, and the size of the prompt-payment discount.

5. The length of the discount period and the size of the discount determine the cost of trade credit. If a company is granting trade credit that is cheaper than other sources, then the credit granting company will experience an increase in the average size of its receivables and in its average collection period. The annual percentage rate of trade credit is measured by the equation

$$\text{APR} = \frac{D \times (360/N)}{1 - D}$$

6. A financial manager measures the effectiveness of a company's trade credit policy by examining the net profit associated with sales made on trade credit. The steps required to measure trade credit's profitability are

   a. Determine the size of the accounts receivable by combining the daily credit sales and the average collection period.

   b. Multiply the size of the accounts receivable by the variable-cost ratio to find the company's investment in receivables. Then, multiply the investment in receivables by the opportunity cost (alternative return) to find the cost of the investment in receivables.

   c. Add the cost of the investment in receivables to the bad debts and collection expense to find the total cost of the company's trade credit policy.

   d. Subtract the total cost from the company's contribution margin to find the profitability.

7. Management implements a company's collection practices with a series of periodic and gradually stronger reminders to customers that payment is due.

8. The objective of inventory management is to minimize the company's investment while at the same time trying to maximize its return from holding the asset.

KEY TERMS AND CONCEPTS

Cash holding motives	**Variable-cost ratio**
Cash budget	**Investment in receivables**
Cumulative cash excess (shortage)	**Total cost of receivables**
Lockbox	**Collection practices**
Cost of trade credit	

QUESTIONS

23-1. "Cash is a nonearning asset, and the less of it we have around the better." Do you agree with this businessman's assertion? Why?

23-2. Cure Corporation's cash budget shows the following entries for cumulative cash excess or shortage: September $8,000, October $2,000, November ($3,000), December ($4,000). What cash gain or loss from its operations did Cure have in October, November, and December?

23-3. "A deterioration of customer quality impacts on the accounts-receivable turnover." Do you agree? Why or why not?

23-4. An important item management considers in the evaluation of trade credit is the investment in receivables. Is this amount equal to total accounts receivable? Explain your answer.

23-5. CMA Examination (modified). Of the following, which one is *not* a major variable in establishing credit policy?
   a. Credit standards.
   b. Credit period.
   c. Discounts for early payment.
   d. Collection policy
   e. The lender's sales volume.
   Explain your choice.

23-6. Someone has suggested that the level of accounts receivable reflects both the volume of a company's sales on account and its credit policy. Which one of the following items is *not* considered as a part of a company's credit policy?
   a. The length of time for which credit is extended.
   b. The length of the discount period.
   c. The size of the discount that will be offered.
   d. The extent (in terms of money) to which a company will go to collect an account.
   Explain the meaning of each choice.

23-7. Opportunity cost is an important item in determining a company's trade credit policy. Define the term *opportunity cost* and explain its role in trade credit policy.

PROBLEMS

23-1. Albert Seberg, controller for Carload Toys, Inc., is asked to prepare a four-month cash budget. He calls on you to help him do so. The company is faced with the following situation: Sales in each of the next five months are expected to be, respectively, $10,000, $15,000, $30,000, $30,000, and $10,000. The company desires to have a $4,000 minimum cash balance. The company's beginning cash balance is $6,000, and it has a $6,000 loan from State Bank of California. Sales revenue is collected 60 percent in the month of the sale and 40 percent in the succeeding month. Purchases amount to 90 percent of a subsequent month's sales and are paid for in the month after the purchases are made (which is the month in which the sales occur). Carload Toys, Inc., has additional collections during the first month of $8,000 and payments of $13,000. In the second month the company must repay a $2,600 loan to State Bank of California.
   a. Collections are $8,000 during the first month. What were sales in the preceding month?
   b. Complete a cash budget for the initial four months.

23-2. Slitz Brewing Company has the following situation. Sales will be $20,000 in January, $15,000 in February, $30,000 each in March and April, and $20,000 in May. The treasurer insists on a $5,000 minimum cash balance. On January 1, Slitz has a $10,000 loan from its bank. The company has a $8,000 beginning cash balance. All sales revenue is collected in the month after sales are made. Wages and purchases of merchandise are paid for in the month preceding a given month's sales. Merchandise purchases and wages are 90 percent of the subsequent month's sales.

a. Prepare a cash budget covering the four months beginning in January. Assume that collections in January are $22,000.

b. What is the largest loan Slitz needs to cover cash shortages? In what month is that loan made?

23-3. Karla Mouritsen is preparing her company's cash budget for the month of May. The following information is available concerning its accounts receivable:

Estimated credit sales for May	$200,000
Actual credit sales for April	$150,000
Estimated collections in May for credit sales in May	20%
Estimated collections in May for credit sales in April	70%
Estimated collections in May for credit sales prior to April	$ 12,000

What are the estimated cash receipts from accounts-receivable collections in May?

23-4. Mr. Sparks, the owner of School Supplies, Inc., is interested in keeping control over accounts receivable. He understands that accounts-receivable turnover will give an indication of how well receivables are being managed. School Supplies, Inc. does 70 percent of its business during June, July, and August. The terms of sale are 2/10, $n/60$.

Net sales for the year ended December 31, 19x1, and receivables balances are given below.

Net sales on credit	$1,500,000
Receivables, less allowance for doubtful accounts of $8,000 at January 1, 19x1.	72,000
Receivables, less allowance for doubtful accounts of $10,000 at December 31, 19x1.	60,000

a. Calculate the average accounts-receivable turnover from the data above. (Remember to use an average of receivables.)

b. Is the accounts-receivable turnover computed here representative of the entire year? Explain your answer.

c. What is the company's average collection period? Is the company doing an effective job of managing its trade credit? (Hint: Compare your answer with the terms granted by the company.)

23-5. The high cost of short-term financing has recently caused Freemont Company to reevaluate the terms of credit it extends to its customers. The current policy is 1/10, $n30$. If Freemont customers can borrow at the prime rate, at what prime rate must Freemont change its terms of credit to avoid an undesirable extension in its collection of receivables?

a. 12.5 percent.

b. 16.0 percent.

c. 14.5 percent.

d. 10.0 percent.

e. 19.0 percent.

23-6. Chico Cabinet Makers is trying to determine whether or not to grant trade credit to its customers. If trade credit is granted, net accounts receivable will rise to an estimated $26,000 and the company's annual sales will rise by $140,000. The contribution margin will be $14,000. The company will have $3,500 bad debts and $4,200 collection expense annually. The opportunity cost on cash invested in accounts receivable is 16 percent.

a. Calculate the contribution margin and variable-cost ratios.

b. Should Chico begin to extend trade credit? Support your answer with calculations.

23-7. Chutney, Inc., has four classes of customers with the payment patterns presented below. The company has a 15 percent contribution margin on the $10,000 sales that the company makes to each class. The opportunity cost on the cash invested in receivables is 20 percent.

Class	Average Collection Period	Bad Debts (%)	Collection Expense (%)
1	15 days	1	1
2	28 days	3	4
3	36 days	5	7
4	58 days	10	15

a. Explain the term *Bad Debts*.

b. To which customer classes should Chutney continue to sell on existing terms? Support your answer by constructing a table like Table 23-7. (Use a 360-day year in your calculations.)

23-8. The marketing vice-president of Zeta Services complains that the company's credit policy is unrealistic because it is too restrictive. The company's chief financial officer is concerned that the policy may be too liberal and therefore may not be in the best interest of shareholders. After a heated argument between the two executives, the chief financial officer retires to her office and examines data to help make the decision. Presently, collection expense is 3 percent and bad debts are 4 percent of sales. Additional information follows:

Credit sales	$300,000
Contribution margin ratio	8%
Tax rate	40%
Average collection period	38 days
Accounts receivable	_____

There is a 14 percent rate of return available on investments with risk comparable to an investment in accounts receivable.

a. How much is accounts receivable?

b. Calculate the variable-cost ratio and use it to estimate Zeta Company's investment in receivables.

c. Calculate the marginal profit from the trade credit policy. Which executive was correct? Explain your choice.

CHAPTER 24
Short-Term Liabilities: Sources and Costs

B egin your study of this chapter by recognizing that companies can obtain short-term credit by increasing their liabilities and obtain cash by liquidating other current assets. In this framework of understanding, the short-term financing sources dealt with here should be easy to remember and describe.

In viewing trade credit, master at the outset how to calculate its annualized cost. (Remember that interest rates are always quoted on an annual basis—even where they involve one-day loans.) Fix in your mind also why trade credit is popular and why it varies from industry to industry and customer to customer.

On bank loans, it is important for you to grasp the several ways a bank can increase its *effective* rate of interest over the *nominal* rate it quotes to its borrower. Be sure you can calculate the effective rate produced by the different ways a bank can set charges on a loan. Also be clear on what a bank line of credit is and how the standby fee is applied.

Next be able to describe commercial paper, tell who issues it, and explain why it is popular with companies that use it. Remember, too, that paper is non-interest-bearing and thus purchased by investors at a discount from its face value.

The closing section on raising cash by selling other assets should prove straightforward and easy for you to remember. The main points here will involve understanding the difference between *pledging* and *factoring* a company's accounts receivable and how *field warehousing* and *public warehousing* permit a company to raise cash from its inventories.

Applied to a business, short-term financing means liabilities that must be paid off within one year or less. The major sources of short-term business finance are trade credit, commercial banks, and commercial paper. Firms also can *raise cash* by reducing other assets. If a company holds marketable securities, they can be sold. Financial managers can usually obtain cash—for short periods, at least—from accounts receivable and inventories. In unusual instances fixed assets may be liquidated.

SOURCES: INCREASING LIABILITIES

Companies receive finance from an array of short-term creditors. The major sources are trade creditors, commercial banks, and commercial paper.

TRADE CREDIT

Trade (or "book") credit arises when a company receives goods from a supplier without the requirement of immediate cash payment. A wholesaler may give a retailer-customer 30 days after receipt to pay for 100 dozen Titleist golf balls. Over the 30 days, the supplier is financing the customer; not, to be sure, lending the customer cash, but providing goods which the buyer can use for some time without paying for them.

For each party, trade credit shows up differently on the books. The grantor's credit takes the form of an account receivable from the customer. The recipient's books will show the same amount as an account payable.

Trade credit is described by three elements: (1) the amount of a cash discount from the invoice price, (2) the period within which the gross bill can be discounted, and (3) the time when the gross amount of the bill must be paid. For example, a company might receive an invoice for material of $10,000, with terms of 2/10, *n*30 (read as "two-ten, net thirty"). This means that the company receives a 2 percent discount from the $10,000 gross amount if the invoice is paid within 10 days, a $200 saving. However, should it not meet the 10-day deadline, it must pay the full $10,000 within another 20 days, or 30 days from receipt of the invoice.

Trade credit stands second only to bank credit as a source of short-term finance for business. It is the chief standby of small- and medium-size firms. Three reasons explain trade credit's popularity.

1. Trade credit is automatic. Sellers usually grant it because their competitors do.
2. Trade credit is convenient. A firm need not go through the time-consuming, and perhaps embarrassing, procedure of applying for a loan. The firm can simply defer paying cash for its purchases.

3. Trade credit appears to be inexpensive. To many users, trade credit has no apparent cost. The only cost may seem to be the price of the goods purchased. However, the firm granting the credit incurs a cost by tying up its money in an account receivable, and it must cover this cost to stay in business. Since it is not charging interest on the trade credit, the firm granting it must recoup the cost by charging more for its products. A business that pays cash for its purchases without demanding a discount may be paying for something it is not receiving.[1]

Cost

The cost of trade credit, as you saw in Chapter 23, is usually concealed in the supplier's price. What if, in the $10,000 example above, the purchaser waits 30 days after the invoice and then pays the full $10,000? In so doing, it is paying 2 percent ($200/$10,000) to use money an additional 20 days, the difference between the discount date and date of payment.[2] Just how expensive this $10,000 is can be disclosed by *annualizing* the interest rate involved. To annualize a rate is to state it on an annual basis rather than as a portion of a year. This enables us to compare the cost of trade credit with other sources. To do so, we set up the equation for the annual percentage rate

$$APR = \frac{D \times (360/N)}{1 - D}$$

Recall that N is the time interval for which the purchaser gets the use of the credit by forgoing the discount, and it is customary to use a 360-day year for ease of calculation. Substituting the figures above, we have

$$APR = \frac{0.02 \times (360/20)}{1 - 0.02} = 0.3673 \text{ or } 36.73\%$$

Solving for APR, we find that the annual cost of failure to take the discount is 36 percent. With trade credit so costly, a company should obviously make every effort to take the cash discounts offered. If necessary, it should borrow money from a bank to do this because the cost of bank credit is usually much less then 36.73 percent.

Practice: Pound Corp. bought goods on terms of 3/20, n50. Show that the company, paying on the 50th day, was paying for trade credit at an annual rate of 37.1 percent.

If a buyer misses the discount date, should it pay as promptly as possible? Certainly not. A purchaser's effective rate of interest declines the longer it defers

---

[1] In effect, the cash customer is subsidizing the credit customer. By paying cash, this customer induces the supplier to keep its prices lower than would otherwise be the case. The lower price is enjoyed not only by the cash customer but also by the credit customer. Hence, the latter receives credit at a lower rate than he would otherwise have to pay, thanks to the cash customer. The same reasoning applies to the subsidy of credit-card customers by those who prefer to pay cash.

[2] Technically, the debtor is paying $200 for $9,800, so the precise rate is $200 \div $9,800 = .0204$ for 20 days.

BOX 24-1
**The Giant Jockeys (Or, All About Trade
Credit When Money Gets Tight)** Jockeys who ride horses at the race track are always little. But there's another (and more expensive) kind of racing in which giant jockeys take the lead. It comes about when the race is on to use the other fellow's money at times when interest rates go sky high and bankers want your left eyeball in hock for a loan.

At such times all companies have an understandable aversion to borrowing more money than they must. So what's the alternative? Well, as this chapter teaches you, trade payables (accounts payable) are also a source of short-—and not necessarily all that short—term financing.

So in recent periods of tight money, big companies have formed the habit of making small suppliers who depend on their business finance them. That way they avoid the sky-high rates banks charge for loans. Giganticus Corporation may order parts from Small-Fry Manufacturing on terms of 2/10, net 30, then stall payment for three or four months. If Small-Fry complains, its credit manager gets short shrift. "Do you want our business, or don't you? Then quit your *#*&# complaining!"

Guess who winds up borrowing from Last National at 22 percent?

And guess who enjoys an exhilarating race to continued profit, riding, as they put it, their small-supplier payables.

And, oh yes. When Giganticus pays on the 121st day, guess what else it may do? You're right. Take the discount for prompt payment.

---

payment. Suppose, for example, that a company pays 40 days from invoice date—getting 30 days' use of the seller's funds. (Remember that the first 10 days were free.) Cost, expressed as a rate on terms of 2/10, n30 becomes based on the use of trade credit for 30 days.

$$\text{APR} = \frac{0.02 \times (360/30)}{1 - 0.02} = 0.245 \text{ or } 24.5\%$$

Thus, companies often try to avoid paying their accounts as long as possible, a practice known as "riding" credit. Of course, if they are habitually slow to pay their bills, they run the risk of impairing their credit rating. And if the supplier becomes too impatient for its cash, a company exceeding its credit period may be sued.

Practice: Slowpay, Inc., buys goods on terms of 3/10, n30 and pays on the 50th day. What is the annual percentage rate for trade credit? You should get 27.84 percent.

Determinants
The terms on which a company grants trade credit are determined by the interplay of several forces. First, *competition* is a relevant factor. A new company entering an

industry will be forced to grant terms at least equal to those granted by its competitors. To do otherwise would limit its sales. Second, the *nature of the product* affects trade credit. Products with very high turnover are sold on short credit terms. That is why, for example, the dairy industry has shorter credit terms than the steel industry. Third, *financial position* is important. A financially strong buyer will ordinarily receive liberal terms because the seller need not fear a default. If the buyer is financially weak, the seller runs a greater risk of default and will probably restrict both the amount and the terms.

Widespread reliance on trade credit, despite its high cost, reflects the conflict between cost and availability of finance. Companies use trade credit because it is available, a factor often completely dominating cost. If businesses are unable to obtain finance elsewhere, they rely on suppliers to finance them. For many struggling firms trade credit is the only source of external finance available and must be relied upon regardless of its cost.

COMMERCIAL BANKS

Commercial banks are typically the largest source of short-term credit to business corporations. To small- and medium-size companies, banks play a primary role in financing business growth because these companies do not have easy access to the capital markets.

The bank loan market is a personal market in which borrower and lender meet face to face. Consequently, there is room for personal persuasion on the borrower's part. For this reason, a potential borrower is well advised to cultivate a strong relationship with a banker.

In addition to being a source of finance, a commercial bank can give a business other valuable help. It may supply credit information on customers. A knowledgeable banker will be familiar with developments in a particular industry or region and know much about business conditions in general. Often bankers are able to make cool, rational assessments of profit potentials in a new undertaking—an ability frequently lacking in business people, who may be too close to the trees to see the forest. Clear, objective advice from a good banker-adviser can be a major advantage to one in business.[3]

Cost

Bank loans to business are made at quoted rates of interest consisting of a base rate, which only the biggest, most credit-worthy company can qualify for, plus a percentage-point add-on based on the credit standing of the particular borrower. Over most years since the late 1930s, the base rate has been a *prime rate* set by a more-or-less

---

[3] You might keep this in mind, should you decide to become a banker. You can enhance your worth to both your bank and your clients by becoming as broadly informed as possible on both general business conditions and the economics of one or more particular industries. One of the authors had a friend who went from trainee to full vice-president of one of the nation's largest banks in three years by so mastering the background of the motor freight industry that his advice to truckers became indispensable, and they flocked to do business with his bank.

informal agreement among the country's leading banks. The prime rate has varied over time, sometimes following market rates of interest up and down with close timing, sometimes with appreciable lags. Among large, strongly financed business borrowers, prime-rate loans receive sharp competition from typically cheaper borrowing in the commercial-paper market. During 1982–1984, a number of large banks were suspected of lending to major companies at rates well below the quoted prime. At least one large bank was successfully sued by a prime-rate borrower that paid the prime rate while other companies borrowed from the bank at less than prime.

The cost of a bank loan is computed using the relation between proceeds, dollar interest, and maturity. *Proceeds* are the funds that the borrower actually receives from the loan. The general equation is

$$C = \frac{D}{P}$$

where

D = dollar cost of interest
P = proceeds
C = cost, or effective interest rate

If a company borrows $10,000 for 12 months and repays $10,600 at maturity, then D is $600 and P is $10,000. This would be a loan at simple interest with a cost of 6 percent. If the same loan had matured in 8 months, then it would be necessary to annualize the rate. Here the annualized rate is

$$C = \frac{6\%}{8 \text{ months}} = \frac{x\%}{12 \text{ months}} = 9\%$$

Increasing Interest Rates

Banks can increase the interest rate to a level above the nominal or stated rate by discounting interest, requiring a compensating balance, and making the loan on an installment basis. We examine each of these.

Discounting Interest. When a bank discounts the interest on a loan it deducts the interest in advance from the stated amount of the loan rather than letting the borrower wait until the end of the period to pay it. If the bank discounted the interest from the above $10,000 loan, then the proceeds would be $10,000 − $600 = $9,400. The annual percentage rate (APR) for the 12-month loan would be

$$APR = \frac{D}{P} = \frac{\$600}{\$9,400} = 6.38\%$$

The annual percentage rate has moved up as a result of making the loan on a discount basis.

BOX 24-2
The "Annual Clean-up" of a Bank
Loan   It is a tradition of sound banking (also of sound business borrowing) that goes
back to Adam Smith, who wrote as follows in *The Wealth of Nations.*

> The bank . . . in dealing with such customers, ought to observe with great atten-
> tion, whether in the course of some short period (of four, five, six, or eight
> months, for example) the sum of the repayments it commonly received from
> them, is, or is not, fully equal to that of the advances which it commonly makes
> to them.

In other words, sound banks are in the business of making temporary loans, not of
supplying companies with permanent capital. (That, you should remember from
Chapter 8, is because a bank lends out money which its depositors are entitled to
withdraw on demand or on relatively short notice.) In principle, a business borrower
proves that its need for money is short-term by paying its way out of debt to the
bank for at least a few weeks every year. That is known in the trade as the *annual
clean-up* of a company's bank loans.

Alas! This has become a principle, as Shakespeare put it, "more honored in the
breach than in the observance." Today, and for many years past, thousands of good
sized companies have been permanently in hock to the banks, making banks their
suppliers of permanent capital.

If the bank regulators accuse Bank A of being a long-term lender to Weak
Corporation, what do you think happens? Weak pays its way out of debt to Bank A.
How? Why, by borrowing from Bank B for the next few weeks.

It is well known that there are tricks in any trade. But this is one of the tricks
that has helped put more and more risk in the U.S. banking industry in recent years,
as bank failures have grown steadily bigger and more numerous from one business
cycle to the next.

Source: Adam Smith, *The Wealth of Nations,* Book II, Chapter II, Modern Library Edition, New
York, p 289.

Practice: Squeeze Corp. borrowed $50,000 at 16 percent on a discount basis. Show
that the annual percentage rate paid was approximately 19.05 percent.

Compensating Balance. A bank may require a borrowing company to maintain a compensating balance. A *compensating balance* is an amount that must be left
on deposit with the commercial bank at all times. It is supposed to compensate the
bank for the reserves it must hold against the loan. If a borrower is required to
maintain a 20 percent compensating balance, its cost of borrowing will be increased
25 percent. In the 6 percent simple-interest loan above, 20 percent compensating
balance would mean that the bank would retain $2,000. Only $8,000 would be
available to the borrower, and the effective cost of the loan would be

$$\text{APR} = \frac{D}{P} = \frac{\$600}{\$8,000} = 7.5\%$$

Had the loan also been discounted, the proceeds would have been $10,000 − $600 − .20($10,000) = $7,400. The effective cost would have been

$$\text{APR} = \frac{D}{P} = \frac{\$600}{\$7,400} = 8.1\%$$

Practice: Queasy Brothers, Inc., borrows $100,000 at 12 percent and is required to maintain a 15 percent compensating balance. Show that its annual percentage rate of borrowing is approximately 14.12 percent.

Practice: Suppose further the loan is made on a discount basis. Demonstrate that the annual percentage rate would then be approximately 16.44 percent.

   Monthly Repayment. Finally, the bank may require its client to repay the loan in monthly installments rather than repaying in full at maturity. This arrangement almost doubles the quoted rate on the loan, since the borrower has, on average, the use of only about half the funds ostensibly lent. On a $10,000 loan repayable in 12 monthly installments, the borrower would have the full $10,000 only for the first month. In the twelfth month, it would have the use of only $10,000/12, or $833.33. On average it would have the use of ($10,000 + $833.33)/2 = $5,416.66. If the loan was neither discounted nor subject to a compensating balance requirement, the effective rate of interest would be

$$\text{APR} = \frac{D}{P} = \frac{\$600}{\$5,416.66} = 11.08\%$$

Practice: Hardesty & Sons borrowed $50,000 at 16 percent to be repaid in 12 monthly installments. Show that the borrower's effective rate of interest is approximately $29\frac{1}{2}$ percent.

Line of Credit

In lieu of continuous borrowing, a financial manager may try to obtain a *line of credit*. In this case the bank agrees to lend up to a certain amount of money any time the company requests it during some fixed future period. The interest on the amount borrowed is usually stated as *prime plus*, meaning that the borrower must pay the prime, or basic, lending rate plus some extra percentage whenever it draws on the credit line. In addition, the borrower must pay the bank a *standby fee*, usually one-half of one percent, on the unused amount of the line.

Example. A firm may have a $200,000 line stated at prime plus 2 percent, and the borrower is to pay one-half of one percent on the unused portion. If the firm borrows $100,000 when the prime rate is 6 percent, then it would pay 8 percent on $100,000 and one-half of one percent on $100,000.

BOX 24-3

Bridge Financing   You might think from its wording that bridge financing refers to borrowings made to finance the structures that span rivers, ravines, gullies, and the like; but that is not what is involved. It all goes back to some points you studied long ago in Chapter 3.

Bridge financing means using a short-term loan to get through (or bridge over) a period of tight money and very high interest rates to avoid getting hooked on a long-term loan at a high rate. It is a favorite device of the Herculeses of the business world who sell commercial paper or bully the banks into lending them money while they wait for the next recession to pull long-term rates back down to reasonable numbers.

Of course, the demand for bridge loans swells the demand for short-term loans in periods of boom and tight money. And since the bridgers are not looking to sell bonds yet, that takes some heat off the long-term debt markets. All in all, bridge financing is a major reason why, when a business expansion is on its last legs, you will usually see short-term interest rates poking above long-term ones: one sign of a coming recession.

Trade Credit and Bank Loans

A company may decide to borrow money from a commercial bank to pay its overdue accounts. For example, suppose that Aphax Products has $1,173,913 credit purchases annually and presently has $150,000 payables, and its average payment period (number of days purchases in accounts payable) is 46 days.

To become current on its payables, Aphax must borrow a sufficient amount to make its average payment period 30 days, a reduction of $46 - 30 = 16$ days. Daily purchases are $\$1,173,913/360 = \$3,261$. Aphax must borrow $16 \times \$3,261 = \$52,176$. Payables will decline to

Payables before decision	$150,000
Less: Payments	52,176
Payables after decision	$ 97,824

In this example the payables reduction is matched by an increase in bank loans, so that liabilities will not change. The company may decide to fund the bank loan. *Funding* means to shift from a short-term source of finance to a long-term source. For example, the bank loan may be paid with proceeds from a bond issue or common-stock issue or from operations.

COMMERCIAL PAPER

Commercial paper is the unsecured promissory note of a large business of high credit standing, usually maturing in four to six months. Maturities longer than 270

BOX 24-4
Acquisitions Through Leveraged
Buyouts   Bank loans became widely used in 1984 to finance leveraged buyouts in
          which a group of investors (often the company's management) acquires the
stock of a company with borrowed money. Ultimately, the debt is paid with money
generated by the acquired company's operations or the sale of its assets. In May of
1984 the largest leveraged buyout in history took place: A group led by Boston
Ventures, Ltd., acquired Metromedia for $1.3 billion.

     Leveraged buyouts became less popular after the 1984 peak because banks
became worried that the loans may not be repaid. Some bankers feared that the
buyouts would form the next round of loan problems for the banks—along the lines
of the real estate investment trusts in the mid-1970s and the woes related to energy
loans and Third World debts in the early 1980s.

     The major risk in leveraged buyouts comes from the fact that banks usually
make them with a floating interest rate. If interest rates rise, buyout borrowers may
not be able to pay the higher rates. A few buyout arrangements capped interest-rate
exposure at predetermined levels to reduce the risk of default when rates rise. When
the interest rate reaches a specified level, banks, for a fee, provide credit to pay
current interest, adding the extra amount to the principal on the loan. Purex Industries, Inc., a Lakewood, California, bleach maker that went private in a leveraged
buyout in 1982, had a line of credit of $25 million that it could use if interest rates
topped 16 percent.

days (nine months) do not exist, because beyond this time period the issue must be
registered with the Securities and Exchange Commission. Registration is an expensive and time-consuming process that would remove commercial paper's flexibility.
The paper is issued in denominations of $50,000 and more.

Use

Larger companies use commercial paper primarily as a substitute for bank borrowing. The interest rate on commercial paper is generally about one percentage point
below the banks' prime rate. Since the effective rate on bank borrowings exceeds the
nominal rate—because of compensating balances—commercial paper stands as an
attractively cheap source of finance.

     Ordinarily, commercial paper is used to meet temporary needs: seasonal or
cyclical bulges in asset requirements. But a company also uses it to meet unforeseen
expenses and as temporary financing for long-term outlays. Later, when the company moves into the capital markets and sells stock or bonds to pay off the commercial paper, it is shifting from a short-term source of funds to a long-term source, a
process already identified as *funding*.

     To be marketable, commercial paper ordinarily must be backed, dollar for
dollar, by a line of credit which the issuer maintains at a large bank or group of
banks. Brokers and dealers require this backing to assure their customers who buy

the paper that it will be paid off at maturity. During 1982s recession, the financial condition of many companies deteriorated to the point where it was impossible for them to roll over their maturing commercial paper by selling a new issue to replace it. When this happened, the standby bank line provided funds to pay the paper off.[4]

Market and Cost

Commercial paper is bought by banks, other financial institutions, and nonfinancial corporations. They use it for liquid, interest-earning storage of short-term surplus funds. Since commercial paper *pays* no interest, it is bought at a discount from face (maturity) value.

Example. The treasurer of Teasley Publishing may buy a $200,000, 90-day House-hold Finance Company note for $197,000. At maturity, the buyer will collect $200,000. Its interest cost is

$$\text{APR} = \frac{\$3,000}{\$197,000} \times \frac{360}{90} = 6.09\%$$

The short maturity of commercial paper makes it impractical for purchasers to make a prolonged analysis of the borrower's credit-worthiness, and its unsecured status involves obvious risk. Issuers are limited to companies whose paper is favorably rated by Standard & Poor's and Moody's, the chief bond-rating agencies, which also rate commercial paper.

CASH SOURCES: DECREASING ASSETS

Management can obtain cash to pay currently maturing debt by liquidating its current assets: inventory, accounts receivable, and securities. If it does so, both current assets and current liabilities decrease when it pays off the short-term debt. The result will be an increase in the company's current ratio[5] and no change in its working capital. Unless, however, a company has been carrying excessive amounts of inventory or extending credit to customers too liberally—the financial relief from these moves is at best temporary. Smaller inventories and a failure to provide competitive credit terms will mean reduced sales, and sales are a company's life-blood.

Accounts Receivable

A company that is against the wall, moneywise, can use its accounts receivable to generate cash immediately. Rather than waiting for the receivables to be paid off, management can either pledge or factor the accounts.

---

[4] Of course, this left the bank on the hook with the weak borrower. In 1972–1973, banks had not always shown good judgment in extending standby credit lines to companies issuing commercial paper.

[5] Improvement of the current ratio depends on its being greater than 1:1 initially. If the ratio is exactly 1:1, then decreasing current assets and current liabilities by the same dollar amount will not change the ratio. And if the ratio is less than 1:1, then the current ratio will actually deteriorate. In each instance, working capital is constant.

Pledging consists of borrowing money by putting up the accounts receivable as collateral. If a firm has $200,000 in accounts receivable, it may borrow perhaps $180,000 from a bank or finance company. The lender then has a *lien,* or legal claim, on the receivables and recourse against the borrower. *Recourse* means that if the receivables go bad, the borrower remains liable to the lender for any balance due on the loan. Risk of default on the receivables thus remains with the borrower.

Factoring involves the sale of accounts receivable without recourse. The purchaser of the accounts, called the factor, bears the risk of default; if customers do not pay, the factor absorbs the loss. To protect itself, a factor usually insists on giving prior approval to all credit sales made by a client company. In other words, the factor assumes the credit function of the client. Thus, when the company receives an order, it must ask the factor for approval to make the sale on credit. If the factor says no, the company will refuse credit, making the customer pay cash. If the factor approves the credit of the purchaser, the firm will make the sale on credit, then discount that account with the factor. The factor will advance a client 85 or 90 cents on the dollar, enabling the business to recycle cash back into inventory at once. The factor will collect the credit invoice at maturity, settling at that time any remaining amount due the client.

The cost of factoring receivables falls into two parts. First, the factor charges the customer from 1 to 2 percent of the amount of each invoice as a basic factoring fee. Second, a factor charges its client interest for the number of days in which the factor's own funds are tied up in the receivable. In addition, the factor deducts any amounts that the receivers of merchandise dispute as representing unsatisfactory, damaged, or wrong items, and the like. After all charges are known, the factor will refund whatever is left owing to a client.

Although factor financing has the reputation of being high-cost financing, there is no overwhelming case that this is so. Interest charges made by factors are generally in line with those of other lenders. By factoring its receivables, a firm dispenses with both the worry and cost of a credit-and-collections department. Furthermore, factored accounts are much less likely to default on or delay payments, since factors work together and share information about companies with poor payment histories.

Inventory

Rather than waiting for inventory to flow through accounts receivable and into cash, management may be able—at a cost—to obtain cash immediately. It does this by pledging the inventory as collateral for a loan. One way is through *field warehousing,* where the inventory is kept on the borrowing firm's property, but in a walled or roped-off area. The lender will employ a third party to control the flow of goods into and out of inventory. Only the third party can permit the removal of any inventory. In *public warehousing,* the inventory is placed in a public warehouse as it is produced. There, it is controlled by an independent third party. Through warehousing, the lender has assurance that the collateral actually exists and is in the condition specified in the loan agreement. Costs of warehousing are charged against the borrower, making this sort of accommodation quite expensive unless very large amounts of inventory are involved.

Securities and Unpaid Withholdings

A company fortunate enough to hold marketable securities can, of course, raise cash by selling them. For government securities, the financial manager can find a ready market by calling his banker. For listed securities—that is, those traded on a stock exchange—the financial manager will call the company's broker.

Finally, employers can make the federal government their unwilling lender by withholding money deducted from employees' wages for income tax or social security payments. However, unless a company is already at death's door, penalties and interest charges from the IRS set definite discourgements to this source of financing.

SUMMARY

1. Businesses obtain short-term credit by increasing their liabilities; their chief sources are trade (supplier) credit, bank loans, and for the strongly-financed "biggies" commercial paper. Cash can be raised by selling marketable securities, and, for short periods at least, by liquidating or borrowing against other assets, notably inventories and receivables.

2. Although convenient and widely used, trade credit is far from free. You impute its annual percentage rate by dividing the discount offered for prompt payment multiplied by 360 days over the discount period by one minus the discount. Trade credit terms depend on a buyer's credit standing, the nature of commodity purchased, and the customs of the industry.

3. Bank loans, the largest source of short-term business credit, are made at stated rates of interest, which may differ widely from the rate borrowers actually pay. Bankers increase their rates in three main ways: through discounting the loan interest, requiring that a compensating balance be left in the borrower's account, and by calling for repayment in monthly or quarterly installments. Large, strong borrowers receive a bank's *prime* (or lowest business) rate. Lesser business lights borrow on a prime-plus basis. Banks also provide business clients with lines of credit for which clients pay an annual standby fee for the bank's guarantee that a loan will be available if the customer requests it.

4. Only firms with high credit ratings are privileged to sell commercial paper, which comes in denominations of $50,000 or more, matures in 270 days or less, and is bought by investors at a discount from its maturity value. It yields a little more than Treasury bills and is a popular short-term financing vehicle in industries where money needs are seasonal or intermittent.

5. Companies also can raise cash by *pledging* or *factoring* their accounts receivable. Cash can often be obtained from inventories on loans secured by field warehouses or by public warehousing.

6. For short periods, at least, a company can effectively retain credit already in hand by delaying payment on its accounts payable, taxes payable, and other matured obligations, although this course, pursued too zealously, can wreck the perpetrator's credit and even, where federal taxes are involved, land its managers in jail.

KEY TERMS AND CONCEPTS

Annualized cost
Riding trade credit
Effective versus nominal interest
Compensating balance
Line of credit

Prime plus
Commercial paper
Factoring
Field warehousing
Public warehousing

QUESTIONS

24-1. CMA Examination (modified). Short-term debt financing generally has the following three characteristics from the viewpoint of the borrower when compared with long-term debt financing:
 a. Greater flexibility, lower total cost, and greater risk.
 b. Greater flexibility, higher total cost, and greater risk.
 c. Greater flexibility, higher total cost, and lower risk.
 d. Less flexibility, lower total cost, and lower risk.
 e. Less flexibility, lower total cost, and greater risk.
 Explain your choice.

24-2. State three factors that explain the popularity of trade credit. What kind of firms principally rely on it?

24-3. State the equation by which we calculate the cost of trade credit as an annual percentage rate.

24-4. Anita Renfer, the 73-year-old treasurer of Griffins Distributing Company, says to you, "We don't want to borrow from a bank to pay our bills within the cash discount period because a bank charges 8 percent. Trade credit is free." How would you explain to her that it is not free, and that the company might benefit from borrowing even though interest on the bank loan would show up on the income statement?

24-5. What major factors govern the amount and length of the trade credit a buyer-business may receive from its supplier?

24-6. Why is the cost of factoring accounts receivable usually overstated in comparison with pledging or with bank borrowing?

24-7. Explain how a compensating balance compensates a bank.

24-8. Why is borrowing against inventory typically expensive?

24-9. What sources of short-term funds might be available to a business without resort to any kind of borrowing?

24-10. Explain these terms: prime rate, line of credit, prime plus, standby fee.

24-11. Summarize the ways in which a bank lending at a stated nominal rate of interest can increase the effective rate.

24-12. Why is commercial paper a popular short-term financing vehicle with large, strong companies? How do we calculate its cost?

PROBLEMS

24-1. What is the annual percentage rate of trade credit to a firm buying on terms of 1/20, n60 and paying on the 60th day?

24-2. Bilkum Brothers bought on terms of 2/10, n30 and paid on the 70th day. What was its annual percentage rate of trade credit?

24-3. Weak Corp. received terms of 3/10, *n*40, and paid 12 days after receiving the invoice. What was the annual percentage rate of missing the discount?

24-4. Addendum Corp. bought $10,000 worth of merchandise from Giganticus, Inc., on terms of 3/10, *n*40. On the tenth day after billing Addendum borrowed $9,700 at 14 percent from the Hart State Bank and paid Giganticus. The loan from Hart was repaid in 30 days. How much did Addendum save or lose by borrowing from the bank to take the discount?

24-5. Calculate the annual percentage rate of interest on a bank loan of $1,000 for 6 months.
    a. At 10 percent simple interest.
    b. At 10 percent on a discount basis.

24-6. What is the annual percentage rate of interest on a bank loan for 12 months at 12 percent where the borrower must pay principal and interest in monthly installments?

24-7. A company borrows $1,000 for 18 months at 14 percent and must maintain a 20 percent compensating balance. What is the annual percentage rate of interest?

24-8. Schoen Machinery Company has an agreement with its bank allowing the company to borrow up to a total of $300,000 at any time. This line of credit costs Schoen Machinery $1\frac{1}{2}$ percent for the unused line, and prime plus 4 percent for any used. The prime rate is 5 percent. Schoen is using $80,000 of the line. How much does it pay in interest if the condition persists for 12 months?

EIGHT

SPECIAL TOPICS

This final part of the book presents special topics, so called because they are more specialized than are the other 24 chapters. Chapter 25 examines the new-issues market, the market in which a company sells its debt and equity for the first time. Chapter 26 turns our attention to the international arena and presents several characteristics of the multinational corporation. In addition, this chapter shows you many of the unique problems that a company contemplating buying and selling in foreign markets confronts. Chapter 27 concludes the book with a look at several indicators that a canny manager uses to time investment and financial decisions.

CHAPTER 25

Marketing
New Security Issues

LEGAL RESTRICTIONS
Securities Act of 1933 · Securities Exchange Act of 1934 · Blue-Sky Laws

MARKETING A NEW ISSUE
Investment-Banking Functions · Originating · Underwriting · Syndication ·
Distribution · Payment · Floatation Costs · Selecting an Investment Banker ·
For Elephants Only? · Private Placement · Shelf Registration

LISTING SECURITIES

SUMMARY
Key Terms and Concepts · Questions

There is little in this short chapter to tax either your memory or your understanding—only a few points about how companies raise capital by selling new stocks and bonds will call for emphasis, and these are easily pointed out. There are the laws that govern new securities issues, the five main tasks that investment bankers perform for issuers, and a scattering of follow-up details. These complete the chapter.

Understand clearly the difference between the federal securities acts passed by Congress in 1933 and 1934 and the fact that all 50 states have antifraud statutes governing securities issues—the aptly named blue-sky laws. Memorize the names and principal features of the five investment banking functions: (1) originating securities issues, (2) underwriting them, (3) forming syndicates, (4) distributing the new securities, and, often, (5) maintaining an after-market by acting as a dealer.

Other points to fix in your mind include how the total payment received for underwriting is split among participating securities firms, the range of floatation costs and what decides their size, the difference between competitive bidding and negotiated offerings, and three final definitions: private placements, shelf offerings, and listing.

All in all, a quick, easy chapter to bring you useful new knowledge.

A firm trying to raise money by floating stock or bonds faces both marketing and legal problems. It wants to get the best price for its issue, and it must conform to the laws and regulations that govern new issues.

LEGAL RESTRICTIONS

Restrictions placed on new issues—debt or equity—stem largely from the 1929 stock market crash. The preceding bull-market years (1927–1929) had brought massive corporate security floatations. Congressional investigations after the crash revealed that many abuses and no few frauds had occurred in the new-issues market. To prevent such abuses in the future, Congress enacted regulatory legislation. Financial managers must be familiar with the resulting federal rules and requirements before their companies market a new security issue.

Securities Act of 1933

The Securities Act of 1933, which applies to the primary, or new, issues market, is a full-disclosure act. It requires issuers of all securities, except those specifically exempted, (1) to file a registration statement (called an S-1) with the Securities and Exchange Commission (SEC)[1] and (2) deliver a prospectus (actually, a condensed S-1) to any prospective security buyer before he purchases the security. Exempt securities include intrastate issues (new issues sold in one state only), governmental securities, securities of companies regulated by some federal commissions (such as railroad securities, which are regulated by the Interstate Commerce Commission), issues of nonprofit organizations, and issues below $1.5 million or those sold to a limited number of financially informed buyers.[2]

An S-1 is a detailed statement of information about a company—its management, directors, divisions, finances, accounting, history, operations, earnings, and so on—that might have a bearing on the value of the security being offered. The SEC is not concerned with the profit potential of the company, the price at which its security is being offered, or even the legality of its operations. It *is* concerned that such information be made available to prospective purchasers. However, although the SEC can order the seller to send buyers prospectuses, no way has been found to make buyers read them. Probably, 90 percent do not.

Securities Exchange Act of 1934

The Securities Exchange Act of 1934 applies to the *secondary*, or existing issues, market. It regulates the securities exchanges and their trading practices, provides for control over corporate insiders (by requiring them to file reports of their stock transactions), and empowers the Federal Reserve to set margin requirements for security purchases. Margin is the amount of cash a buyer must put up to purchase a security on credit from a broker, bank, or other lender. The security serves as collateral for the loan.

Blue-Sky Laws

In addition to federal regulation of new securities issues, all 50 states have regulations restricting new securities issues within their borders. The state regulations are

---

[1] Before passage of the Securities Exchange Act of 1934, which established the SEC, the Federal Trade Commission was responsible for registering new issues.

[2] How many? The SEC judges each case on the sophistication of the buyers. Half a dozen "little old widow ladies" might be too many. A hundred professional portfolio managers might qualify.

BOX 25-1
Do Prospectuses Protect Investors?   Hardly. Maybe if investors read and understand
the prospectuses, there is some protection, but
the mere fact that the SEC approves a security issue does not mean it is worth the
money or even that it is guaranteed to be around this time next year.

The SEC (and some state securities commissions) operates on the basis of
what's called the *disclosure* standard.* That simply means the law requires an issuer
to tell the truth and the whole truth about the securities it is selling. So long as the
registration statement and prospectus do not lie or hide material facts, issuers are
free to offer their securities and price them as they please. Using a disclosure standard appears based on the presumption that if people are smart enough to pick the
presidents and governors that manage their political destinies, they are smart
enough to know what to do with their money if they are given the facts.

Considering how technical many investment judgments are, that is probably
stretching things. Besides, it is likely that 95 percent of all prospectuses mailed to
securities buyers wind up in wastebaskets unread. However, these documents do
find their way into the hands of securities analysts and brokers in reputable brokerage firms, who read and ponder them. Even if you do not (or cannot) read a prospectus, your broker can and usually will. So maybe prospectuses do give investors
protection—in a second-hand way.

* In contrast, there is the *permissive* standard. Under it, the securities commission decides whether
new securities are worth a proposed offering price. An adverse decision means the company
cannot offer them in the state in question. A few states take this approach.

---

called *blue-sky laws*. Kansas passed the first such act in 1911. A state legislator at the
time commented that the laws should prevent unscrupulous stock salesmen from
promising the blue sky to unsuspecting citizens. Issues must comply with these
regulations before securities can be offered in particular states.

MARKETING A NEW ISSUE

Once management has decided to raise money in the capital, or long-term financial,
market, it faces the task of marketing its security. Though it is possible for companies to sell new securities directly to investors, the usual route is through investment
bankers.

Investment-Banking Functions
Investment banking is probably a misleading term. An investment banker does not
make loans or accept deposits. It is a financial intermediary that links suppliers of
long-term funds with firms needing them. In doing this, it will perform one or more
of four main functions: (1) originating a new issue of securities, (2) underwriting, (3)
syndicating, and (4) distributing. (A fifth function, not uncommon, is to make an

after-market in underwritten securities by acting as a dealer. The securities dealer's role is outlined in Chapter 10.)

Originating

Originating an issue means planning for it through negotiations between investment banker and issuing company. Originating occurs only on negotiated issues. For those, the investment banker is present in the planning stage to advise on questions such as debt versus equity, premium versus discount pricing, what indenture provisions to make, timing, and so on. On competitively bid issues, a company must usually decide what features its security will have, then put its "design" out for bids.

In a negotiated issue, the investment banker helps the issuer get its financial position in order before the securities are offered by arranging for an audit and legal services. An accounting firm audits the corporate records and prepares financial reports. Attorneys prepare registration papers for the SEC. The investment banker obtains a printer familiar with the exacting forms in which the prospectus and other documents must be set.

In originating issues, an investment banker protects his reputation carefully. He makes certain that all required information is included in the registration data, and assures himself that the offering is sound. If buyers trust his financial judgment, they will be inclined to view favorably any issue he offers.

To price issues the investment bankers consider how the market is performing and what prices similar issues are commanding. They bring their expertise to bear in a disagreement with management over pricing an issue. Managers sometimes have inflated ideas of the worth of their company's shares or bonds and want a higher price than investment bankers would deem advisable. Bankers must reconcile the issuers' demands with those of their other clients, the security buyers. Buyers are happiest if the price of a new issue increases after they buy it. Thus, the banker tries to price an issue somewhat below the absolute maximum the issue could command so that its price will move up in subsequent trading.

Timing an issue depends on the length of time needed to prepare the issue and conform with registration requirements, and on conditions in the capital markets. The average time lapse after first contact between originator and issuer is six months. But new issues are often delayed because of market conditions—a jammed new-issues calendar,[3] a badly declining market, or an investment banker's advice to wait for a better opportunity can effectively stall an issue. Contrariwise, issues can be accelerated if conditions seem unusually favorable.

Underwriting

Underwriting means the outright purchase of an entire new issue of securities, by an investment banker or group of investment bankers, for resale to clients. Through this device, an issuer frees itself of the risks and uncertainties ordinarily present

---

[3] A new-issues calendar gives a preview of announced floatations. Issuers select their dates in advance after conference with their underwriters and try to pick vacant dates that do not conflict with other issues already announced.

while an issue is being sold to investors. The instant an underwriting agreement is signed, whether the transaction was negotiated or bid competitively, the issuer is home free. It has obtained a firm price for its securities, and risks of future market fluctuations—or a completely unsalable issue—now fall on the underwriter.

Naturally, underwriters bid a lower price for the securities than the price at which they expect to resell them. But competition among underwriters has usually kept this gross spread, or total compensation, relatively small. Thus, underwriting is at best a hazardous business, calling for supremely accurate judgment. In the past decade, gross spreads on large-company flotations have typically ranged from 1 percent on negotiated bond offerings to 6 percent on industrial equity offerings. In the volatile stock and bond markets since 1965, investment banking firms have often run large and prolonged losses on both competitively bid and negotiated underwritings.

Underwriting hazards are magnified by the fact that underwriters operate largely on borrowed capital. This heavy use of financial leverage multiplies the chance of loss when an issue fails. If an investment banker borrows $9 for every $1 of his own capital going into a new issue, then a 1 percent loss on the gross price of the issue will cost it 10 percent of its own capital.

This perilous degree of leverage often induces investment bankers to curtail the volume of new issues during periods of monetary restraint, thereby restricting the supply of new capital for business firms. An investment banker is loath to buy a $300 million, 30-year debt issue if it expects interest rates to increase during the floatation period. The capital loss on such an issue might jeopardize its solvency. If the issue is a competitively bid one, the investment banker may choose not to bid. If it is a negotiated issue, the banker will probably advise its client to wait until the market "cools off."

How narrow spreads may become in competitive bidding is illustrated by one large issue in 1973. On $100 million of $7\frac{1}{2}$ percent bonds, due in 1999, sold by Philadelphia Electric Company, the total underwriter's spread was only $3.84 per $1,000 bond—less than four-tenths of one percent.

Syndication

Several investment banking firms usually band together on a given issue to spread the risks and pool their capital. Such a temporary combination is called a *syndicate*. It exists only for a single issue, though on Wall Street the same firms are found together in syndicates time after time. The firm that organizes the syndicate—the one that has got the business on a negotiated underwriting—is the manager. The manager assigns syndicate shares, usually on a reciprocity basis, that is, "You included me in your last syndicate, so here's a piece of mine."

Syndication enables an investment banker to spread the firm's capital among several underwritings instead of gambling it all on the outcome of one floatation.

Where does an underwriting syndicate get the funds to buy, say, a $300 million bond issue? Perhaps $20 million will come from the syndicate members' own capital. The rest will be borrowed on a short-term basis from some of the very large New York City banks.

BOX 25-2

Who Are the Investment Bankers?   Some of their names are household words, like Merrill Lynch, Pierce, Fenner & Smith, Inc., because, along with underwriting securities for big corporate customers, they also do a brokerage business with the general public. Others, such as Salomon Brothers and Goldman Sachs, are known as institutional houses. Like Merrill Lynch, they do a brokerage business, but only to serve institutional clients—pension funds, the trust departments of major banks, insurance companies, foundations, mutual funds, and the like.

The people who run the investment-banking departments of big securities firms must be experts, men and women of seldom failing judgment, especially in judging what the securities markets will do. A look at Table 25-1 will remind you how slim underwriting profit margins are. To make money on an offering, underwriters must make an accurate guess about (1) what price the selling corporation will accept and (2) what investors will pay for the new issue. That is especially true on competitive bidding for the big bond issues that utility companies bring to market. If an underwriter bids too low a price, then it fails to get the business. If it bids too much, then it cannot break even on the reoffering to investors. The issue becomes, in the jargon of Wall Street, a "sales turkey." The underwriters must cut price and absorb the loss.

Maybe you believe that you are good at guessing odds, having been successful already in the stock market or at the race track. If that is the case, then a career in investment banking could be for you.

A syndicate continues until either the issue is sold out at its offering price or it becomes evident that sale at this price is impossible. In the latter case, the syndicate breaks up, each member taking its share of the unsold securities[4] and selling this residue at the best obtainable price.

In addition to regular underwriting, there are agency marketings (sometimes called "best efforts" deals) and standby underwritings. In *agency marketings,* the investment banker does not take title to the new issue but acts simply as the issuer's agent, tries to sell as much as possible, and earns a commission on each bond or share sold. Beyond an outlay of time and sales personnel, the banker makes no investment and assumes no risk in the floatation. A *standby underwriting* is one in which a syndicate agrees to buy a forthcoming issue at a predetermined price (usually considerably below the expected one) if the issuer is unsuccessful in selling the new securities. This arrangement is typically used to guarantee an issuer of rights that all rights will be exercised. The underwriters agree, for a stated fee, to take up

---

[4] How unsold securities are allocated among syndicate members is spelled out in advance by the syndicate agreement.

all unexercised rights, exercise them, and resell the new securities at whatever price they can get.

Distribution

Distribution means selling a new issue to investors, be they individuals or financial institutions. Syndicate members enlist other firms to help distribute or sell the issue. These distributors (called the *selling group*) are merely agents, functional middlemen, who do not take title to the securities they sell but merely collect a salesman's commission. Underwriters, in contrast, are merchant middlemen who actually take title.

Payment

No fixed formula exists for apportioning the spread (between resale price and price paid for a new issue) among manager, underwriters, and selling group members. Generally, 20 percent of the spread goes to the manager, 30 percent to the underwriters, and 50 percent to the distributors. Why do selling group members get so large a share when they assume no risk? They do because the manager and underwriters know that the best way to get inventory off their hands quickly is to have salespeople out beating the bushes. The bigger the commission is, the harder salespeople will beat the bushes. Of course, the manager also serves as underwriter and distributor, so if he can sell some of the securities, then he stands to make the entire spread on the securities he sells.

Suppose, for example, that a syndicate managed by Goldman Sachs successfully underwrites a $300 million AT&T issue on which the spread is $6.97 per bond. Then the underwriting proceeds might be distributed as in Table 25-1. On each bond Goldman sells, it will make $6.97; on each bond it underwrites but sells through a selling group member, $3.48; on each bond underwritten and sold by other firms, $1.39 as manager.

Floatation Costs

The cost of floating a new issue varies with its size and type. Cost falls as a percentage of issue price as issues become larger. There are two reasons for this. First, fixed expenses—underwriting investigation, registration, legal fees, and so on—are spread over more units. Second, smaller underwritings involve less well-known companies and so require greater sales effort. By type of issue, cost is highest for common stock,

TABLE 25-1 Hypothetical Distribution of Gross Spread per $1,000 Bond on $300 Million AT&T Debenture Issue

	Amount	Percent
Manager (Goldman Sachs)	$1.39	20
Underwriters	2.09	30
Distributors	3.49	50
	$6.97	100

BOX 25-3
Talking About "Divided Loyalties"   If you are an investment banker, you've got 'em.
And that means you walk a chalk line. On one
side, there is your issuer, who wants to sell its securities at the best possible price.
On the other side are your investor-customers. They want to buy bargains. Caught
in the middle, you have the task of setting—or recommending—a price fair to both
parties.

To stay in business, an investment-banking firm must win respect both for its
judgment and its integrity. It will not last long if it consistently overprices new
offerings so that corporate issuers rub their hands over the money they take in while
investors lick deep, nasty gashes in their bank accounts. But unless issuers think an
investment banker will get them a good price, it will not get their business.

However, there is a saving grace in the investment banker's picture. On most
new issues, there is some degree of underpricing. What it comes down to is that
when an underwriter has a lot of bonds or shares of stock to sell in a hurry, it offers
them at prices slightly below what similar securities already in the public's hands are
selling for.

The way it typically works out is that since the new securities come to market
at a volume discount, their price ordinarily enjoys a little bounce after they are all
sold and people who did not buy on the offering begin bidding for the securities in
the resale market. This means that for a few days at least those who bought from the
underwriters have a profit to point to. That gives them a good feeling about the
securities—and, most importantly from the underwriter's standpoint—about the underwriter.

next for preferred, and lowest for bonds. Common stock is the most expensive
because price and market risks are larger, because stock issues are typically smaller
than bond issues and so must bear a larger share of fixed cost per unit, and because
stocks are typically resold in small lots to individual investors—a time-consuming
process. Equity-offering costs, as a percent of gross-market value, are shown in
Table 25-2. For large issues, they average around 5 percent. By contrast, large bond
issues are often floated for less than 1 percent of market price.

Selecting an Investment Banker

How do companies select their investment bankers? The law requires railroad companies and utilities doing interstate business to select investment bankers on the
basis of competitive bidding—the banker who bids the highest price (or lowest
yield) wins the issue. Industrial firms typically select their investment bankers
through private negotiations with one or more candidates.

Competitive bidding is usually required of regulated companies on the ground
that it makes for lower floatation costs. But there is no real evidence that this is true.
Indeed, in falling markets, competitive bids often turn out to be more expensive. If
new issue prices are falling badly, a negotiated issue can often be postponed or

TABLE 25–2   Equity Flotation Costs as a Percent of Issue

Size	Cost (%)
Less than $500,000	27
$500,000–less than $ 1,000,000	22
$1,000,000–less than $ 2,000,000	14
$2,000,000–less than $ 5,000,000	10
$5,000,000–less than $10,000,000	6
$10,000,000–less than $20,000,000	6
$20,000,000–less than $50,000,000	5

SOURCE: Securities and Exchange Commission.

renegotiated, but competitive bids are irrevocable. Consequently, in bad markets, competitive bidders will either (1) try to bid a low enough price (and get a large enough spread) to protect themselves against any possible adversities or (2) simply refuse to bid at all, leaving the issuer out in the cold. For example, late in 1974, several major security offerings by financially strained electric utility companies failed to attract a single underwriting bid. In these instances, the SEC was obliged to waive its competitive bidding requirement and reluctantly allow the issuers to negotiate their underwritings.

For Elephants Only?

As the 1980s began, fewer and fewer companies were able to sell new securities through the nation's investment bankers. Because inflation had greatly enlarged the capital needs of almost all companies, future capital requirements were projected to exceed future capital supplies by very wide margins. This suggested that investment bankers would be forced to turn away many fund-seeking enterprises in future years. Even in the early 1970s, regional underwriting firms were rarely willing to handle new issues of less than $5 million. In early 1975, despite recession and a considerable drop in high-grade bond yields, lower-rated borrowers of any size found it virtually impossible to get new bonds underwritten. Triple-B-rated utilities were limited to selling bonds with five- and six-year maturities[5] at yields four percentage points higher than those lenders charged to high-rated utilities. Credit alarms on utility debt issues subsided with the business upswing of the later 1970s, to return again in 1983–1984 as power companies with troubled nuclear construction programs swayed on the brink of bankruptcy. And by the early 1980s it had become clear that bond issues amounting to less than $50 million were becoming hard to place.[6]

[5] Lenders insisted that maturities be short because they saw great dangers in lending for more than five or six years to companies that might go broke or be nationalized.

[6] Why? Mainly because of a change in habits on the part of institutional investors—big pension funds, foundations, and others. Formerly content to hold bonds to maturity for secure income, these investors were now heavily engaged in trading bonds for profit: playing the swings in interest rates for capital gains, selling one bond and buying another with the same rating and maturity if they could pick up a few hundredths of a percentage point of yield. To provide a market that would accommodate institutional bond trades in units of 500 or 1,000 bonds, a bond issue needed at least 50,000 bonds ($50 million worth) outstanding.

Private Placement

If a company chooses to sell new securities itself, by *direct placement*, then it makes no use of underwriting service, though an investment banker may still serve as its adviser or negotiator. Ordinarily, direct placements take the form of *private placements* in which issuers sell securities to one or more financial institutions. The issuer does not offer the securities to the general public. Private placements are exempt from registration under the Securities Exchange Act of 1933, since purchasers are few and presumably sophisticated enough to protect their own interest.

For the corporate borrower, a private placement holds advantages as well as disadvantages in comparison with a public offering. Major advantages include (1) a lower issuing cost (both SEC registration and underwriting expense are avoided), (2) greater speed, (3) privacy of information (by avoiding registration disclosures), and (4) a provision for taking down funds as they are needed, thus saving interest costs. The major disadvantages are (1) a higher rate (typically about one-half percentage point), (2) more restrictive legal covenants to protect the lender, (3) lack of market for the issue, and (4) no advertising of the corporate name.

Although the purchaser of a private placement gets a higher yield that it would obtain on marketable bonds of the same quality, the risk is greater if the loan begins to go bad. Since the corporate notes it holds have not been registered with the SEC, they cannot be sold.[7] This lack of marketability explains both the higher yields and the more restrictive terms of private placements.

How widespread are private placements? They have comprised nearly half of all long-term corporate debt financing since World War II. They have been used primarily by smaller companies, and their percentage has been highest in periods of relatively slack business. At such times, the volume of new marketable bonds is not sufficient to absorb the funds piling up in insurance companies, pension funds, and other financial institutions, so these lenders then aggressively solicit private placements. This happened during business slowdowns in 1971–1972 and again in 1976–1977. By contrast, boom years offer big lenders their "fill"—and more—of marketable bonds, so private placements decline.

Shelf Registration

Under the Securities and Exchange Commission's Rule 415, in effect since 1982, corporations may shelf register debt or equity offerings in advance, then sell the securities "off the shelf" anytime during the next two years, in one sale or several. By using shelf registration, issuers are spared the expense and bother of filing several registrations, and they gain flexibility in timing their sales to take advantage of favorable market conditions.

This procedure has been popular with large issuers, and a 1983 study by the SEC staff indicated that companies using it in 1982 saved an average of 29 percent on underwriting fees. On the other hand, smaller regional underwriters oppose shelf registration because it limits their chance to participate in new offerings. Some inves-

---

[7] They could be sold, of course, if they were put through registration. But that requires telling the truth about the issue, a requirement that may be noxious.

tor groups also have voiced opposition on the ground that a registration statement
filed as long as two years previously may omit new information that investors need
in order to make an informed decision about the securities.

LISTING SECURITIES

Marketing stocks (and sometimes bonds) is easier if they are listed on a national
securities exchange and therefore widely known to investors.[8] Listing entails additional expense plus the need to comply with the requirements of the exchange
whereon a security is traded. Listing requirements typically include such items as
full disclosure of financial information, maintaining independent facilities for transferring shares and registering ownership, and a minimum number and value of
outstanding shares. Whenever any of these requirements are violated, a stock will be
suspended from trading.

SUMMARY

    1. Corporations raising new capital through stock and bond issues must com-
ply with federal laws and with the "blue-sky" (antifraud) statutes of the 50 states.
The federal Securities Act of 1933 requires a corporate issuer to file detailed information about itself and the new issue with the Securities and Exchange Commission
(a *registration statement*) and to deliver a summary of this information to the buyer of
its new securities (a *prospectus*).

    2. Another major federal securities law, the Securities Exchange Act of 1934,
regulates trading in securities once they have been issued. It also empowers the
Federal Reserve Board to set margin requirements.

    3. Most new issues are handled by financial intermediaries called investment
bankers, which serve five principal functions: (1) originating (helping to plan the
issue and ready it for market), (2) underwriting, (3) syndication, (4) distribution, and
(5) providing an after-market. Investment banking firms also serve corporate issuers
through agency marketings and standby underwritings.

    4. Costs of floating new securities fall as a percentage of the issue price as
issues become larger; they are higher for stocks than for bonds. Laws usually require
railroads and utilities to select their underwriters through *competitive bidding* for the
securities to be offered; unregulated companies, enjoying a free choice of underwriters, make *negotiated offerings*. In either case, small issues of securities have become
increasingly hard to market. $50 million has become about the lower limit for under-
written bond issues.

    5. Companies can often save money through *private placements*, the sale of an

---

[8] This advantage is disappearing rapidly as the unlisted market becomes fully automated and as the
government pushes for a single, central securities market, wherein all securities would be traded
and quoted.

entire issue of securities to a small number of sophisticated financial institutions, a tactic which avoids the costs of registration and underwriting. A new device for marketing securities is *shelf registration*, which permits a company to register securities for sale anytime over the next two years.

6. The listing of securities means obtaining the right to trade on a national securities exchange; the added publicity and disclosure may help make further issues of the same or similar securities more acceptable to investors.

KEY TERMS AND CONCEPTS

Securities Act of 1933	Agency marketing
Securities Exchange Act of 1934	Competitive bidding
Investment-banking functions	Negotiated underwriting
Underwriting hazards	Private placement
Syndicate	Listed security
Standby underwriting	Shelf registration

QUESTIONS

25-1. Can an investment banker make money buying a bond from an issuer at a yield of 9.45 percent and selling at a yield of 9.51 percent? Does the banker make .06 percent? Explain your answer.

25-2. Distinguish between the Federal Securities Acts of 1933 and 1934. Which applies to the primary market for securities? Is the New York Stock Exchange a primary market? Explain your answer.

25-3. A $100 million 12 percent coupon bond issue is acquired by a syndicate at par ($1,000). It is retailed at 11.8 percent current yield (dollar interest divided by market price).
   a. At what price was the bond retailed?
   b. What is the dollar spread per bond? Show a plausible dollar breakdown on the spread among the manager, underwriter, and distributor.
   c. Should the issuer privately place the issue and save the spread? Why?

25-4. Describe the two methods used by corporations to select an investment banker. Is one method required by law for particular classes of corporations? What classes?

25-5. List and briefly describe the four functions of an investment banker. What additional function can it serve if it is also a brokerage house?

25-6. What factors affect the percentage of corporate securities that is privately placed (as opposed to being offered publicly) during a given year?

25-7. Which have the larger underwriting spreads—bonds or common stocks? Why? Why do underwriting spreads decline with size of issue?

25-8. Why should yields be more generous on privately placed bonds than on publicly offered ones? Use the capital asset pricing model in answering.

25-9. Explain how the investment banker's use of financial leverage increases financial hazard during a flotation. How does syndication reduce this hazard?

25-10. What is shelf registration? Why has it proved popular with large companies? Might it entail risks for investors? Explain your answer.

CHAPTER 26
Financing International Business Activity

FOREIGN EXCHANGE MARKETS

Foreign Exchange Rates · Reading Foreign Exchange Rates · Financial Instruments

RISKS IN FOREIGN BUSINESS

Foreign Exchange Risk · Economic and Transaction Risk · Translation Risk

CAPITAL BUDGETING BY A MULTINATIONAL CORPORATION

SUMMARY

Key Terms and Concepts · Questions · Problems

Most companies do not halt business operations at the U.S. borders, and managers and students should not limit their thinking only to U.S. activities and opportunities. We live to a great extent in a global community in which actions of one country are felt by companies and individuals of another country. In addition, profitable opportunities often exist in international business transactions. This chapter looks at the international financial setting by introducing you to two international areas:

1. **International Finance.** The environment of international markets and institutions, foreign exchange rates (foreign-money costs), and the documents used in international trade and finance.
2. **International Financial Management.** The area of decision making by a financial manager.

As you might guess, international finance has grown in response to the expansion of trade between individuals and governments of different countries. Financial management and models have become refined to assist financial managers in their decisions.

The first part of this chapter examines international finance. When you finish this part you will understand the usefulness of a forward-exchange market, the way that foreign exchange rates (or prices) change, and how to read and interpret foreign exchange quotations. In addition, you will know what function two international financial documents perform for a financial manager. These two documents are a draft or bill of exchange and eurocurrency. The remainder of the chapter concentrates on international financial management. In this section you will learn the distinction between the types of financial exposures faced by a company transacting international business—economic, transaction, and translation risk. After this distinction you will examine methods to reduce these exposures in order to minimize the risk of transacting international business. A student of business should have some understanding of the accounting disclosures required of a company with international operations, so a discussion to acquaint you with FASB *Statement 52* completes the study of translation risk. This chapter concludes with a brief discussion of capital budgeting designed to show the similarity between capital budgeting in a domestic and international setting.

FOREIGN EXCHANGE MARKETS

Foreign exchange is foreign money. A U.S. corporation buys and sells foreign exchange in order to pay foreigners for merchandise or to make investments abroad. It may buy or sell foreign exchange for dollars if the company is to receive or make payment for merchandise.

Example. If you travel to Italy next summer, you will buy lira to spend while you are there. When you return you will sell your lira and buy dollars. If you subscribe to a British magazine, you may have to pay with the British pound sterling.

Financial managers and other people buy and sell foreign exchange at a stated rate, or price in a spot, forward, or futures market.

1. **Spot Market.** Market in foreign exchange for delivery within two business days after the dealing date. Often called the cash market.
2. **Forward Market.** Telephone market dealing in contracts to buy and sell foreign exchange for future delivery.
3. **Futures Market.** A place that specializes in dealing in options to buy and sell foreign exchange for future delivery.

Spot and forward markets consist of a network of commercial banks that buy and sell foreign exchange (usually bank deposits). The futures market consists of a listed market and an over-the-counter market for buying and selling options at a predetermined price. Table 26-1 briefly discusses the distinction between organized futures and forward markets.

Anyone may buy and sell options and forward contracts. To buy an option or forward contract means to agree to accept for a specified price foreign exchange delivered on a future date. To sell an option or forward contract means to agree to deliver on a future date foreign exchange for a specified price.

BOX 26-1
Currency Options and Forward Contracts:
Financial Managers Have a Choice   A financial manager may use currency options or
forward contracts to buy and sell a fixed amount
of currency at a prearranged price within a set time from a few days to several years.
The buyer or seller chooses the exchange rate and the length of the contract.

An *option* buyer or seller may choose to take advantage of the agreed-upon
exchange rate at any time within the contract period. But if the option is not exercised, then the option buyer or seller is out only the contract premium, or cost of the
contract. That is not the case with a *forward contract* in which the buyer or seller
must buy or sell the currency at the prearranged price.

Financial institutions such as Citibank, Marine Midland Trust, and Merrill
Lynch are now writing over-the-counter options for large corporate customers because the volume on the organized futures market (discussed on Table 26-1) is too
small to handle the activity. The fee income from writing options for corporate
customers offers a big incentive to write them: On a $5 million yen contract the fee
may be $100,000 or greater.

How can you or anyone else choose between using options (futures) and forward contracts? Economics usually dictates the choice: You should select whichever
market has the lowest transactions costs. If the standardized commission in the
organized futures market is less than the negotiated commission in the forward
market, a financial manager will want to use options. Of course, there may be
circumstances when the forward contracts will be used instead of options even
though the futures market's cost may be less. For example, a forward contract with

TABLE 26-1 Comparison of Organized Futures Market and Forward Market

Feature	Forward	Future
Contract size	Tailored to meet individual needs	Standardized options
Delivery date	Tailored to meet individual needs	Standardized options
Commissions	Set by spread between bank's buy and sell	Standardized (about $60 per transaction)
Marketplace	Telephone	Central exchange floor
Regulation	Self-regulating	Commodity Future's Trading Commission
Frequency of delivery	Greater than 90% settled by actual delivery	Less than 1% settled by delivery
Speculation	Not encouraged	Encouraged
Price fluctuations	No daily limit	Daily limit imposed by the exchange

a bank may bring with it the banker's advice on political and economic developments in a foreign country.

Foreign Exchange Rates

A *foreign exchange rate* is the price of foreign exchange. The rate is set in the foreign
exchange markets as individuals, companies, commercial banks, and central banks
like our Federal Reserve System buy and sell foreign exchange.

Figure 26-1 illustrates the adjustment of a foreign exchange rate to an increase
in demand for foreign exchange. Suppose that the foreign exchange in Figure 26-1 is
the Japanese yen, although any would serve equally well. An increase in demand for
the yen occurs when U.S. imports of Japanese products increase, U.S. citizens travel
to Japan, and U.S. corporations invest in Japan. The increased demand for yen from
D_1 to D_2 is in this figure associated with an increase in the quantity of yen supplied,
and the price of the Japanese yen has increased. An increase in the price of foreign
exchange means that it appreciates, and a decrease in the price of foreign exchange
means that it depreciates.[1] The yen has appreciated and the U.S. dollar has depreciated in Figure 26-1.

Example. Suppose that you order a microcomputer direct from a Japanese manufacturer. The manufacturer wants to be paid in yen. Buying the necessary yen increases
the demand for yen from D_1 to D_2 in Figure 26-1 and drives up its price relative to
the U.S. dollar.

FIGURE 26-1   Adjustments under fluctuating exchange rates.

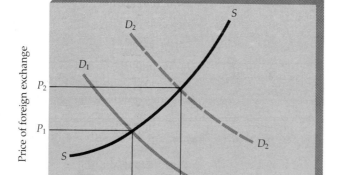

Quantity of foreign exchange

[1] A currency depreciates when its price falls as a result of market forces. This term must be distinguished from *devaluation,* which is the formal act of a government in reducing the stated or par
value at which it agrees to buy and sell its currency. *Revaluation* is the counterpart of appreciation.

In a later period the supply of yen may increase (for example, as Japanese imports of U.S. equipment soar), causing the yen to depreciate and the U.S. dollar to appreciate.

Reading Foreign Exchange Rates

Foreign exchange rates can be quite sensitive and may change rapidly when people are busy getting out of one currency and into another. Because of their volatility, exchange rates are closely watched by bankers and multinational financial managers. Figure 26-2 presents foreign exchange rates from *The Wall Street Journal*. The quotations are in terms of the dollar cost of foreign exchange (columns 1 and 2) and the foreign exchange cost of U.S. dollars (columns 2 and 3). In other words column 3 is the reciprocal of column 1, and column 4 is the reciprocal of column 2. For example, on Friday, May 11, 1984, the Chinese yuan cost $0.46 and a dollar could buy $1/0.46 = 2.1737$ yuan.

Practice. Figure 26-2 tells us that the spot Swiss franc (F_{SW}) traded at 2.289 per dollar (written F_{SW} 2.289/U.S.$) on Friday. How much was each Swiss franc? Answer: $0.4369. Make sure that you can calculate this amount before continuing to the next section.

Spot and Forward Rates. Foreign exchange bought in the spot market is bought at the spot rate. The price of foreign exchange for future delivery in either the forward or the futures market is called the *forward rate*. The forward rate ordinarily leads or moves ahead of the spot rate. Thus, where a forward rate stands in relation to its spot rate has forecasting significance with respect to a currency's eventual spot price. A forward rate below its spot rate (called a *forward discount*) suggests that market participants anticipate weakness in the spot rate. A forward discount prevails mainly for two reasons:

1. Merchants who are to receive a weak currency in the next few weeks or months sell it in the forward market to avoid still larger losses if an exchange rate topples.
2. Speculators sell a weak currency in the futures market, hoping that it will collapse before their options mature (in which case, they can buy the currency at a new spot price below the option price and profit from the difference).

By similar reasoning, a forward rate above its spot rate (called a *forward premium*) suggests that market participants anticipate an increase in the future spot price.

Practice. Before continuing to the next section, examine the relation between the spot and 180-day forward rate for the British pound (£) and the French franc (F_F) on Figure 26-2. Which currency did market participants expect to appreciate and which to depreciate? Explain your answer.

Financial Instruments

American companies can buy and sell goods and services from foreign companies on either a cash or a credit basis. When credit is used, it is often associated with a

The New York foreign exchange selling rates below apply to trading among banks in amounts of $1 million and more, as quoted at 3 p.m. Eastern time by Bankers Trust Co. Retail transactions provide fewer units of foreign currency per dollar.

Country	U.S. $ equiv.		Currency per U.S. $	
	Fri	Thurs	Fri	Thurs
Argentina (Peso)	.02683	.02683	37.274	37.274
Australia (Dollar)	.9014	.9037	1.1094	1.1066
Austria (Schilling)	.05144	.05105	19.44	19.59
Belgium (Franc)				
Commercial rate	.01774	.01763	56.365	56.715
Financial rate	.01745	.01736	57.320	57.600
Brazil (Cruzeiro)	.0006809	.0006898	1468.50	1449.50
Britain (Pound)	1.3850	1.3840	.7220	.7225
30-Day Forward	1.3880	1.3868	.7205	.7211
90-Day Forward	1.3940	1.3928	.7174	.7180
180-Day Forward	1.4031	1.4023	.7127	.7131
Canada (Dollar)	.7732	.7711	1.2934	1.2969
30-Day Forward	.7733	.7712	1.2931	1.2966
90-Day Forward	.7733	.7712	1.2931	1.2966
180-Day Forward	.7733	.7712	1.2931	1.2966
Chile (Official rate)	.01117	.01117	89.50	89.50
China (Yuan)	.4600	.4600	2.1737	2.1737
Colombia (Peso)	.01037	.01037	96.45	96.45
Denmark (Krone)	.09872	.09824	10.1300	10.1795
Ecuador (Sucre)				
Official rate	.01656	.01656	60.40	60.40
Floating rate	.01129	.01129	88.55	88.55
Finland (Markka)	.1713	.1706	5.8375	5.8600
France (Franc)	.1174	.1172	8.5180	8.5300
30-Day Forward	.1174	.1172	8.5210	8.5350
90-Day Forward	.1172	.1170	8.5310	8.5475
180-Day Forward	.1168	.1166	8.5605	8.5750
Greece (Drachma)	.009212	.009158	108.55	109.20
Hong Kong (Dollar)	.1279	.1279	7.8180	7.8175
India (Rupee)	.0905	.0905	11.0497	11.0497
Indonesia (Rupiah)	.000993	.000993	1007.00	1007.00
Ireland (Punt)	1.1105	1.1055	.9005	.9046
Israel (Shekel)	.005274	.005369	189.60	186.25
Italy (Lira)	.0005857	.0005858	1707.25	1707.00
Japan (Yen)	.004344	.004363	230.20	229.20
30-Day Forward	.004364	.004383	229.17	228.17
90-Day Forward	.004405	.004424	227.03	226.06
180-Day Forward	.004472	.004492	223.62	222.63
Lebanon (Pound)	.1770	.1770	5.65	5.65
Malaysia (Ringgit)	.4348	.4357	2.2998	2.2950
Mexico (Peso)				
Floating rate	.005208	.005291	192.00	189.00
Netherlands (Guilder)	.3212	.3202	3.1130	3.1235
New Zealand (Dollar)	.6474	.6480	1.5446	1.5432
Norway (Krone)	.1276	.1270	7.8375	7.8745
Pakistan (Rupee)	.07326	.07326	13.65	13.65
Peru (Sol)	.0003437	.0003437	2909.22	2909.22
Philippines (Peso)	.07133	.07133	14.02	14.02
Portugal (Escudo)	.007148	.007117	139.90	140.50
Saudi Arabia (Riyal)	.2840	.2840	3.5210	3.5210
Singapore (Dollar)	.4760	.4769	2.1008	2.0970
South Africa (Rand)	.7765	.7765	1.2878	1.2878
South Korea (Won)	.001251	.001251	799.40	799.40
Spain (Peseta)	.006459	.006435	154.83	155.40
Sweden (Krona)	.1231	.1227	8.1250	8.1480
Switzerland (Franc)	.4369	.4371	2.2890	2.2880
30-Day Forward	.4397	.4400	2.2741	2.2727
90-Day Forward	.4459	.4459	2.2427	2.2426
180-Day Forward	.4546	.4546	2.1995	2.1997
Taiwan (Dollar)	.02524	.02524	39.62	39.62
Thailand (Baht)	.04351	.04351	22.985	22.985
Uruguay (New Peso)				
Financial	.01909	.01909	52.38	52.38
Venezuela (Bolivar)				
Official rate	.1333	.1333	7.50	7.50
Floating rate	.07052	.07052	14.18	14.18
W. Germany (Mark)	.3606	.3598	2.7730	2.7795
30-Day Forward	.3624	.3615	2.7596	2.7663
90-Day Forward	.3659	.3650	2.7332	2.7396
180-Day Forward	.3713	.3705	2.6930	2.6990
SDR	1.03866	1.03715	.962778	.964178

Special Drawing Rights are based on exchange rates for the U.S., West German, British, French and Japanese currencies. Source: International Monetary Fund.
z-Not quoted.

FIGURE 26-2 Spot and forward rates of foreign exchange, Friday, May 11, 1984. [Reprinted by permission of the Wall Street Journal © Dow Jones & Company, Inc. (1984). All right reserved.]

draft or bill of exchange. A supplement to the financial manager's domestic sources of finance is the eurocurrency market where eurodollars and eurobonds trade.

Draft. A *draft* is an order written by an exporter or seller requesting an importer or buyer to pay an amount of money on a specific date. If the importer honors the draft (that is, agrees to pay it), the draft is a trade draft. If the draft is honored by the importer's bank, it is a bank draft. Drafts conforming to specific terms become negotiable because they may be transferred by signature. Trade and bank drafts are either of two types:

1. Sight draft, payable upon presentation.
2. Time draft, which allows a delay in payment. When a bank honors a time draft, it becomes a *banker's acceptance*.[2] Interest rates on banker's acceptances are quoted daily in financial publications like *The Wall Street Journal*.

Eurodollars and Eurobonds. A company may choose to raise capital from the eurodollar and eurobond markets. Eurocurrency and eurobonds (spelled without a capital letter), are usually defined in a way that covers Asia, Latin America, and anywhere else in the world:

1. **Eurocurrency.**   Any currency or bank deposit denominated in a foreign currency. One estimate placed the eurocurrency market at $2,000 billion at the end of 1984.
2. **Eurobond.**   Securities issued outside of the borrower's country beyond the regulatory domain of any nation and denominated in one of a variety of currencies. In early 1984 there was an estimated $210 billion outstanding.

Examples: A deposit in an Argentinian bank denominated in Japanese yen is a euroyen. A deposit in England denominated in U.S. dollars is called a eurodollar. A bond denominated in dollars issued by General Electric in West Germany is a eurobond.

The eurobond market has grown because it remains largely unregulated and untaxed. As a result, big borrowers like Texaco (it issued $1.5 billion of eurobonds in 1983–1984) can raise money more cheaply and quickly than they can in the U.S. capital markets. The bonds are issued in bearer form without the owner's name either on the bond or listed elsewhere. Thus, the bonds if stolen can vanish without a trace. And as unregistered securities eurobonds facilitate tax evasion.

Almost any medium-size and large corporation can acquire a eurocurrency loan by negotiating with a foreign bank. However, eurobond financing is available to only the largest and most prestigious corporations. *The Wall Street Journal* quotes daily eurocurrency interest rates.

---

[2] The actual process is more complicated. For a description, see First Boston, *Handbook Of Securities Of The U.S. Government And Federal Agencies*, 31st ed., New York, 1984, pp. 187–190.

RISKS IN FOREIGN BUSINESS

Any company or person transacting business across national boundaries faces several types of risk. Recall that risk includes a difference between an expected and an actual amount or value. Foreign transactions open the door to differences between expected and actual values for three reasons.

1. Laws, languages, and business customs differ widely from one country to another.[3] This risk is often referred to as *social risk.*
2. Each nation is a sovereign power with the right under international law to repudiate contracts with citizens of other countries, confiscate their property, or subject them to punitive or discriminatory regulations. This risk is usually referred to as *sovereign risk.*
3. Each country has its own currency whose value may change suddenly and unpredictably in relation to the world's other currencies. This risk is usually referred to as *foreign exchange risk.*

The following discussion concentrates on foreign exchange risk, but we should not forget that the other two may at times be more important. A look at Box 26-2 will show you the plight of one American who misjudged the role of social and sovereign risks.

Foreign Exchange Risk

Foreign exchange risk is the likelihood that an actual value will differ from that expected as a result of changes in foreign exchange rates. A financial manager wants to measure foreign exchange risk and to manage it in such a way that it is minimized.

There are three main types of foreign exchange risk. A company with operations in a foreign country (a *multinational corporation*) confronts the first two, translation (or accounting) and economic risks. The third type of risk is transaction risk, and it is faced by anyone—a person or business—who buys or sells foreign items.

1. Translation risk arises when foreign-currency denominated operations must be translated into U.S. dollars. To translate means to restate a set of values denominated in one currency into another. Balance sheets and income statements prepared in a foreign currency must be restated in terms of the dollar in consolidated financial statements. Figure 26-3 shows us that translation risk is backward looking because it reflects a change in exchange rates that has already occurred. Translation risk is an accounting phenomenon affecting accounting income rather than cash flows.

2. Economic risk is the change in cash flows of foreign operations as a result of an unexpected change in an exchange rate. (An expected change in foreign exchange rates is not important because managers and investors include expected exchange rates in their evaluation of operating results and market value.) Economic risk is

---

[3] Congress passed in 1977 the Foreign Corrupt Practices Act making it illegal for American companies to bribe foreign officials or politicians. Grease or facilitating payments are excluded from the act. Grease or a facilitating payment goes to someone other than a foreign politician or official.

BOX 26-2

An Expensive Lesson Learned in the

Mideast   The importance of social and sovereign risks is illustrated in the plight of an
American transacting business in Saudi Arabia. Donald Fox of Larkspur,
California, found himself trapped in Saudi Arabia because of a dispute with his
Saudi partner in a janitorial-supply venture there. The partner, Sackher Abou Sackher, sponsored Fox's entry into Saudi Arabia early in 1982, but refused to sponsor
the American's leaving unless he paid $100,000 the Saudi claimed the American
owed.

Here is what Fox forgot to consider before the Saudi joint venture: Under
Saudi regulations, a foreigner cannot leave the country without the endorsement of
the person who sponsored his entry! Fox settled the dispute by paying Sackher
$55,000. "It was the only way I could get out," he said by telephone from his
California home. Fox might have avoided the mess that cost him his freedom for a
time, according to trade experts, if he had insisted on a written agreement with the
Saudi.

Source: Based on an article in *The Wall Street Journal,* May 3, 1982, p. 27.

---

more important for the long-run performance of a multinational corporation than
translation risk because economic risk arises from future, long-run cash flows over
several periods. Figure 26-3 shows us that economic exposure is forward looking and
occurs after the unexpected change in foreign exchange rates.

3. Transaction risk refers to gains and losses that arise from settling transactions with payment stated in a foreign currency. Transactions include buying and
selling or borrowing and lending. Figure 26-3 shows us that an unexpected change in
foreign exchange rates before payment occurs subjects us to transaction risk.

Example. If exchange rates change after we buy or sell an asset and before payment
is made, we face transaction risk because actual payment will differ from what we
expected.

FIGURE 26-3   Relationship between types of risk in international business.

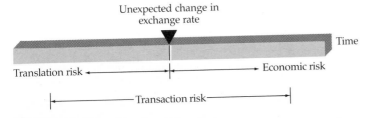

The following discussion addresses the three types of foreign exchange risk in detail so that you may have a feel for how a company can reduce their influence. We will begin with economic and transaction risks because they are financially more important than translation risk.

Economic and Transaction Risks

Let us look at the distinction between economic and transaction risks. Economic risks exist without the need to convert foreign exchange into U.S. dollars, but transaction risk requires conversion. To *convert* a foreign currency means physically to exchange one currency for another. Suppose that you plan to go to England when you graduate. You must *convert* dollars into pounds upon entering England, but before you go you may follow in the newspaper the relationship between the U.S. dollar and English pound and *translate* dollars into pounds.

Example. Unexpected depreciation of the Italian lira will result not only in the receipt by a U.S. exporter to Italy of less dollars in settlement of lira-denominated receivables (transaction risk), but also in the loss of future sales to Italy and of future cash flow (economic risk) because the U.S. product will cost more than before the lira depreciation, and that encourages Italian customers to place orders with Italian suppliers.

Coping with Economic Risk. Economic risk is usually a long-term problem. A corporate manager reduces economic risk by making long-run adjustments to the company's production and marketing strategies. A manager that expects a long-term depreciation in the currency of its foreign customers can react in the following ways:

1. Locate a new plant in the foreign country.
2. Increase advertising for its products to increase sales.
3. Market products that are targeted toward higher-income, less price-sensitive customers.

Example. Following the substantial dollar devaluation of 1971, Volkswagon was forced to revise its product line for the U.S. market and sell Rabbits and Audis rather than the previously successful low-priced Bug. Datsun and Toyota have done the same because the Japanese yen appreciated in the late 1970s. In addition, Volkswagon, Honda, and Sony have opened manufacturing plants in the United States.

Coping with Transaction Risk. Transaction risk is usually a short-term problem. It is incurred by only one participant in a foreign transaction—the participant with settlement stated in foreign exchange.

Example. Trade between Italian and German companies presents the German company with transaction risk if payment is stated in Italian lira, and the Italian company if payment is stated in German marks. It makes no difference which one is to receive or pay—only the currency denomination is important.

A U.S. company avoids transaction risk in five ways. First, the company may require all payment in U.S. dollars. Then whenever foreign exchange appreciates or depreciates the U.S. dollar price does not change. A requirement such as this may not be financially wise because a U.S. company may not be able to force foreigners to make or receive payment in dollars. Attempting to force them to do so may drive business away. Second, the American company may pay or receive cash when merchandise is ordered. Paying in advance avoids the risk of any subsequent exchange rate changes. Third, the American company may use options and forward contracts to lock-in a forward rate. Fourth, the company may adjust credit, collection, and payment policies by speeding collections in a weak currency and slowing them in a strong currency, and by speeding payments in a strong currency and slowing them in a weak currency. Fifth, an American company may price products to preserve contribution margin.

The specific action taken to minimize transaction risk depends on whether the foreign currency is expected to depreciate or to appreciate. Each of the final three methods mentioned above requires elaboration.

A financial manager may use options or forward contracts to hedge foreign transactions and reduce transaction risk. *To hedge* means to take a position in the forward market equal to and opposite an existing or developing position in the spot or cash market.[4]

Example. U.S. Grain and Wheat sells grain to a French customer with F$_F$ 5 million payment required in 90 days. The U.S. company's financial manager may sell French francs 90-days forward against the dollar in order to eliminate transaction risk. If the franc for 90-day delivery costs $0.1172, then the U.S. exporter is assured of collecting $586,000 in 90 days:

$$\$0.1172 \times 5,000,000 = \$586,000$$

No matter what happens to the franc's value between now and settlement date, the company receives $586,000 for the francs that it delivers when it collects the receivables. Actual cash flow will equal expected cash flow.

In one respect this example is oversimplified. In an actual case of depreciation jitters, the forward franc would be below the spot. Such a situation is illustrated in Table 26-1 where the franc is trading at a forward discount ($0.1174 and $0.1172).

A company may use its credit, collection, and payment policies to reduce transaction risk. Exporters use credit and collection strategies when settlement is stated in foreign exchange. Importers use payment strategies when settlement is stated in foreign exchange:

---

[4] The tax rate applied to gains and losses presents a problem associated with hedging by using options or forward contracts. The U.S. Tax Courts are deciding cases that will determine whether or not a gain or loss is an ordinary or a long-term capital transaction for tax purposes.

1. **Credit Policy.** Grant liberal credit terms to customers whose currencies are expected to appreciate. Grant strict credit—or insist on cash payment—to customers whose currencies are expected to depreciate.
2. **Collection Policy.** Accelerate collections from customers whose currencies are expected to depreciate. Delay collections from customers whose currencies are expected to appreciate.
3. **Payment Policy.** Accelerate payment to suppliers whose currencies are expected to appreciate. Consider paying cash. Delay payment to suppliers whose currencies are expected to depreciate.

Example. Suppose that Intec Gypsum, Inc., purchases £80,000 of merchandise from its British supplier with payment in pounds sterling. If Intec Gypsum expects the British pound to appreciate, the company may choose to accelerate payment or pay cash.

In the example above, the American importer may want to pay cash in advance for its imports. When the spot pound is $1.385, Intec Gypsum pays

$$\$1.385 \times 80,000 = \$110,800$$

If management delays paying until after the pound sterling appreciates, then the U.S. dollar cost of the merchandise would be greater. For example, a pound appreciation to $1.4031 means that Intec Gypsum would pay $112,248 calculated as follows:

$$\$1.4031 \times 80,000 = \$112,248$$

A method mentioned above for a company to reduce its transaction risk is to use product pricing that reflects the change in foreign exchange. It is not uncommon for a company to include estimated foreign exchange appreciation and depreciation in its pricing policy so that if expected appreciation or depreciation occurs, the contribution margin ratio is unchanged.[5] Suppose that Intec Gypsum budgets a 20 percent contribution margin ratio (dollar contribution margin divided by sales). If its management anticipates a 5.55 percent appreciation in the pound during the year, then Intec Gypsum will now raise selling prices 5.55 percent. Table 26-2 illustrates that by marking up U.S. prices by the anticipated appreciation rate, the contribution margin ratio is preserved if the expected appreciation actually occurs.

Translation Risk

Translation risk is associated with reporting in U.S. dollars a company's operations located in a foreign country. Translation risk is measured by any difference between foreign-currency denominated amounts that must be reported at current exchange

---

[5] Elasticity of demand enters the picture. The analysis here assumes an inelastic demand so that increased costs can be passed on to the customers. Such a condition may not in fact be the case.

TABLE 26–2   Pricing Policy to Preserve Contribution Margin Ratio

Price at Present Exchange Rate

Sales	100
Less: Variable costs	80
Contribution margin	20

Contribution margin ratio = (100 − 80)/100 = 20%

Price Reflecting 5.55% Appreciation

Sales (1.055 × 100)	105.55
Less: Variable costs (1.055 × 80)	84.44
Contribution margin	21.11

Contribution margin ratio = (105.5 − 84.44)/105.55 = 20%

---

rates. A *current exchange rate* is one prevailing on the statement date and differs from an *historical exchange rate,* the rate on the date when an asset or liability is created or a transaction occurs. A *net exposed position* is an excess of either assets or liabilities that must be reported at current exchange rates. A company with a net exposed position faces translation risk.

Example. Boulder Affiliates, Inc., has F_{SW}760,000 (Swiss franc) assets and F_{SW}426,000 liabilities that must be reported at current exchange rates. Boulder Affiliates' net exposed position is

Swiss franc assets	F_{sw} 760,000
Less Swiss franc liabilities	F_{sw} 426,000
Net exposed position	F_{sw} 334,000

Practice: Calculate Boulder Affiliates' net exposed position if it has 312,000 Peruvian sol assets and 246,000 Peruvian sol liabilities that must be reported at current exchange rates. Answer: 66,000 Peruvian sol. Show how this answer is calculated and comment on how your answer would differ if these assets and liabilities must be reported at historical exchange rates.

Table 26-3 summarizes the impact of changing exchange rates on balance-sheet items. Here is what Table 26-3 is telling you:

1. When foreign exchange appreciates, foreign-currency denominated assets rise in dollar amounts and yield a translation gain, but foreign-currency denominated liabilities also rise and yield a translation loss.
2. When foreign exchange depreciates, foreign-currency denominated assets fall in dollar amounts and yield a translation loss, but foreign-currency denominated liabilities also fall and yield a translation gain.

Changing exchange rates also subject a company's foreign-currency denominated income statement to translation exposure. Further analysis of the income

TABLE 26-3   Impact of Exchange Rate Fluctuations on Foreign Currency Denominated Assets and Liabilities

Balance Sheet Item	Foreign Currency	
	Appreciates	Depreciates
Asset	Translation gain	Translation loss
Liability	Translation loss	Translation gain

statement is left for you to study in accounting classes and to examine in a course in international finance.

A financial manager can eliminate the balance-sheet part of translation risk either by reporting all assets and liabilities at historical rates or by hedging. This use of hedging is here different from that above involving options and forward contracts. *Hedging* here means setting exposed assets equal to exposed liabilities so that a translation gain on one is exactly offset by an equal translation loss on the other. The following examples will clarify both the concept and the process.

Net Exposed Position Example. Consider an illustration of the way that a U.S. multinational corporation must report a loss as a result of a net exposed position. The Indian affiliate of U.S. Enterprises has 600,000 rupees in accounts receivable and no offsetting liability that must be reported at the current exchange rate. If the rupee stays at its present $0.0905, then the receivables are translated to be $54,300:

$$\$0.0905 \times 600,000 = \$54,300$$

However, if the rupee depreciates to $0.09 on the next statement date, then these receivables will be translated

$$\$0.09 \times 600,000 = 54,000$$

Only the foreign exchange rate has changed, but U.S. Enterprises has a $300 translation loss measured by the depreciation of the rupee:

Receivables at $0.0905	$54,300
Less Receivables at $0.09	54,000
Translation loss	$ 300

Of course, if the rupee were to appreciate, then U.S. Enterprises would experience a translation gain measured by the rupee's appreciation.

Hedged Position Example. U.S. Enterprises may hedge in order to eliminate its R600,000 net exposed position. Management hedges the R600,000 receivables by creating an offsetting R600,000 liability reported at current rates. Suppose that U.S. Enterprises' affiliate borrows R600,000 from an Indian commercial bank. Now, changes in the dollar price of rupees will not lead to a net translation gain or loss because (as Table 26-3 shows):

1. Rupee appreciates. Gain on receivables equals a loss on the bank loan.
2. Rupee depreciates. Loss on receivables equals a gain on the bank loan.

Consider the situation above in which the rupee depreciates from $0.0905 to $0.09. If U.S. Enterprises is hedged, then it has a zero net exposed position and the loss on the asset equals dollar for dollar (or rupee for rupee) the gain on the liability.

> Translation Loss on Receivables
>   Original exchange rate:
> $0.0905 × 600,000 $54,300
>   Less current rate:
> $0.09 × 600,000 =   54,000
>   Translation loss $ 300
> Translation Gain on Bank Loan
>   Original exchange rate:
> $0.0905 × 600,000 = $54,300
>   Less current rate:
> $0.09 × 600,000 =   54,000
>   Translation gain $ 300
>   Net translation gain (loss)   0

Financial Disclosure. Financial Accounting Standards Board *Statement 52,* "Foreign Currency Translation," requires foreign exchange adjustments to both an income statement and balance sheet. A detailed analysis of *Statement 52* goes beyond the scope of our study, but you should be aware of the fact that it requires most multinationals to use the *current rate method* in which all assets and all liabilities are translated at the current exchange rate, and all income statement items are translated at the average exchange rate for the reporting period. In this way a multinational's net exposed position is the amount of its foreign-currency denominated net worth. Translation gains and losses from the balance sheet do not affect earnings because gains and losses are carried to a reserve account in the shareholders equity component of the balance sheet.[6]

---

[6] FASB *Statement 52* requires management to select the functional currency of the foreign entity. *Functional currency* is the currency of the primary economic environment in which an entity (affiliate, division, and so on) operates and in which it is expected to generate net cash flows. Generally, if operations are relatively self-contained and integrated within a foreign country, the functional currency would be the currency of that country. On the other hand, the U.S. dollar would be the functional currency for foreign operations that are a direct extension of the U.S. parent's operations. The relationship between the functional currency and the translation method is summarized in the following way: (1) Functional Currency U.S. Dollar. Monetary assets and liabilities are translated at the exchange rate in effect on the balance sheet date. Nonmonetary assets at the historical rate, the rate in effect when the asset was put in place. Gains and losses are presented on the income statement. (2) Functional Currency Foreign Currency. Translation is done using the current-rate method so that all assets and liabilities of a foreign entity are translated using the exchange rate in effect on the balance sheet date. Most multinationals fall into this category and the discussion in the chapter concentrates on the current-rate method.

BOX 26-3

Americanization of Foreign Countries May

Prove Embarrassing   International problems may be created because brand names, slogans, and copy used in advertising and personal selling in this country come out differently and often bizarre when translated into another language.

Consider these examples:

Chevrolet's Nova was a good name here but translated into Spanish it meant "doesn't go." American Motors had to change its Dart to Matador in Spanish speaking countries because Dart was translated into Spanish to mean lacking but seeking sexual vigor.

"Coke adds life" translated into Chinese to mean Coke brings ancestors back to life.

General Motor's "Body by Fisher" in Japanese translated to "Corpse by Fisher."

Enco was rejected by Exxon as a worldwide brand name because in Japanese it meant "stalled car."

An airline advertised its lounge section to be a rendezvous section which translated in Spanish to be an area for affairs.

Pepsi-Cola's "come alive" translated in a number of languages as "Come out of the grave."

Example. Tipton International has an affiliate in Mexico with P17,000,000 assets (P is peso) and P8,000,000 total liabilities so that its peso-denominated net worth is P9,000,000. If the peso depreciates from $0.005208 to $0.0042, then Tipton International experiences a $9,720 translation loss calculated as follows:

```
Loss on Assets
   Value before depreciation:
      $0.00528 × 17,000,000          $89,760
   Less value after depreciation:
      $0.0042 × 17,000,000            71,400
                                                    $18,360
Less Gain on Liabilities
   Value before depreciation:
      $0.00528 × 8,000,000           $42,240
   Less value after depreciation:
      $0.0042 × 8,000,000             33,600
                                                     8,640
                                                   $ 9,720
```

BOX 26-4
A Comment on the Economic and Market
Effects of FASB *Statement 52*   A brief comment is needed about the economic or
market impact of translation risk and translation gains
and losses before we leave this topic. In an efficient market security prices impound
or reflect all publicly available information so that accounting information like that
prepared according to FASB *Statement 52* is valueless because this information will
already be processed by market participants, included in their expectations, and
reflected in security prices. The financial statements reflect events that have already
happened. By their knowledge of foreign exchange rates, international developments, and operations of the affected corporation, investors have already acted to
buy and sell the company's common stock. In other words, some investors have
much the same information as that used by the auditor to prepare translation adjustments, and these investors have used the information in making their investment
decisions.

The result of research into the impact of FASB *Statement 52* has a very clear
message to companies transacting business internationally: Management should
manage its foreign exchange risk by (1) emphasizing measurement and control of
economic and transaction risks and (2) reducing its emphasis on translation risk.

Multinational corporations have operations abroad with assets greater than liabilities, so that their reserves for foreign-currency gains and losses rise as foreign currency appreciates and the U.S. dollar depreciates and fall when the opposite occurs.
Table 26-4 shows you the way that a corporation presents translation gain and loss
information in the footnotes to its financial statements.

CAPITAL BUDGETING BY A MULTINATIONAL CORPORATION

A multinational corporation completes a capital-budgeting analysis before investing
in a foreign country. Capital budgeting for a foreign project is conceptually similar
to that for a domestic project: Management calculates the net present value of future

---

TABLE 26-4   Footnote Disclosure of Foreign Currency Translation, Associates Corporation of
North America, 1983 Annual Report

Note 2. Financial statements denominated in foreign currencies are translated into
U.S. currency based on the current rate of exchange. Effective August 1, 1981, Associates adopted the Statement of Financial Accounting Standards No. 52, "Foreign Currency Translation." Financial statements for periods prior to August 1, 1981, have not
been restated. Total assets of subsidiaries denominated in foreign currencies were
$314,626,000 and $361,363,000 at July 31, 1983 and 1982, respectively.

cash flow with the company's risk-adjusted cost of capital. Most experts agree that a financial manager should measure the cash flows of the foreign operations from the subsidiary's viewpoint exactly as though it were a separate corporation. The perspective then shifts to that of the parent corporation because management must estimate the amount, timing, and form of the cash flows transferred to the U.S. parent. Management estimates the cash flow from the foreign subsidiary to the parent and uses the appropriate expected exchange rate to forecast the dollar receipts.

Do not let the above description fool you because there are many controversial and unresolved issues in the process. And probably no two companies or textbooks use the same method. However, conceptually, the process is straightforward as presented here, only the implementation varies. Let us wait until another course (or until you are on the job) to examine in greater detail capital budgeting for a multinational corporation.

SUMMARY

1. Foreign exchange markets respond to demand and supply conditions. There are two foreign markets: A spot market for immediate delivery and a forward market for future delivery.

2. Movements of spot and forward rates contain information about the expectations of market participants. A forward rate above its spot counterpart suggests that participants anticipate a strengthening of the foreign currency. The opposite condition suggests an anticipated weakening.

3. Important financial instruments used in international transactions are drafts, eurobonds, and eurocurrency. A time draft presented to and honored by a U.S. commercial bank is called a banker's acceptance. Eurocurrency and eurobonds are financial assets denominated in a foreign currency.

4. There are three types of foreign exchange risk:
   a. Translation risk results from translating foreign-currency denominated income statements and balance sheets into U.S. dollars.
   b. Economic risk results from unexpected changes in foreign exchange rates that affect expected cash flows and values.
   c. Transaction risk results from changes in exchange rates between the time that a transaction occurs and payment made.

5. Management can eliminate transaction risk by requiring payment in dollars. When that is not possible, management may reduce risk by paying when the company orders merchandise, by using options or forward contracts, by adjusting credit, collection, and payment practices, and by pricing items to preserve the company's contribution margin ratio.

6. A net exposed position for most multinationals is the difference between foreign-currency denominated assets and liabilities, or the amount of equity. Management reduces translation risk by reporting all items at historical exchange rates or by hedging.

7. Capital budgeting by a multinational corporation is complicated because the procedure must include adjustments for political risk, economic risk, and accounting risk. A project is evaluated from the subsidiary's perspective, and then future cash flows are forecast using the expected exchange rate prevailing when the cash is transferred to the U.S. parent.

KEY TERMS AND CONCEPTS

Banker's acceptance
Forward and futures markets
Forward discount and premium
Draft
Option

Eurocurrency market
Sovereign and societal risks
Foreign exchange risks
FASB *Statement 52*
Hedging

QUESTIONS

26-1. Match the item in column A with its closest counterpart from column B.

A	B
_____ Spot market	1. Fixed commission
_____ Conversion	2. Increase in price
_____ Translation	3. Restate foreign values
_____ Futures market	4. Cash market
_____ Forward market	5. Physically exchange
_____ Appreciate	6. Negotiated contract
_____ Depreciate	7. Decrease in price

26-2. Does the relation between a currency's spot and forward rates contain information? Explain your answer.

26-3. Explain how an American importer and a German exporter create a near-money in the form of a banker's acceptance. Be sure to include in your explanation what the term *acceptance* means.

26-4. "In a foreign transaction, only one participant incurs transaction risk." Do you agree? Explain your answer.

26-5. Examine the exchange rates on Figure 26-2 and comment on which one(s) is (are) selling at a forward discount and forward premium.

26-6. A U.S. importer will expect to pay more (in U.S. dollars) for its imports when
  a. speculators are selling dollars for other currencies or for gold.
  b. there is a big increase in the net inflow of foreign capital into the United States.
  c. there is an increase in the foreign demand for American products.
  d. foreign countries raise tariffs on imports from the United States.
  e. the U.S. economy slows down to the level of a recession brought about by tight fiscal and monetary policies.
  Explain your answer and refer to Figure 26-1 in your explanation.

26-7. Does the Foreign Corrupt Practices Act apply to bribery of any foreigner? Explain your answer by referring to Footnote 3 in this chapter.

26-8. Explain how an account payable in foreign currency is hedged by buying the foreign currency in the forward market.

26-9. How can a company use pricing policy to offset the increased costs of imports resulting from foreign exchange appreciation?

26-10. If the U.S. dollar is expected to appreciate against foreign currencies, and if a company pays for its imported raw materials with foreign currencies and sells its exported finished goods for U.S. dollars, which one of the following policies should the company undertake?

a. Place orders immediately to increase its inventory of raw materials.

b. Accelerate the collection of accounts receivable and stretch payment to its trade creditors.

c. Expedite the payments of accounts payable and reduce its average collection period for accounts receivable.

d. Increase its holding of foreign exchange.

e. Decrease its holding of foreign exchange.

Explain your choice.

26-11. The following choices should be judged true or false. Circle your choice in each case. Eurodollars are

T F   dollar balances held outside the United States by Europeans and others.

T F   dollar balances held in the United States by Europeans.

T F   dollar balances held in the United States by the oil producing countries through their European bankers.

T F   currency issued by the European Common Market.

T F   currency issued by the European central banks through the International Monetary Fund in order to operate in the foreign exchange markets.

26-12. This chapter discussed three types of risk faced by a company or person transacting business internationally—social, sovereign, and foreign exchange risks. Define each of these risks and state which one you believe to be the most important.

26-13. There are three types of foreign exchange risk—translation (TL), economic (EC), and transaction (TR). Place the appropriate abbreviation for each before the following statements:

_____ **a.** Reflects past changes in foreign exchange rates.

_____ **b.** Exists between purchase and payment date.

_____ **c.** Long-run cash flows.

_____ **d.** Best hedged in the forward market.

_____ **e.** Best hedged by reducing net exposed position on the balance sheet.

_____ **f.** Virtually impossible to hedge because it is long-run.

_____ **g.** Faced by individuals buying foreign merchandise.

_____ **h.** Faced by multinationals. (Select two.)

_____ **i.** Has little if any impact on price of a multinational's common stock.

_____ **j.** Associated with unexpected changes in foreign exchange rates. (Select two.)

26-14. A company with a net exposed position may incur a translation loss or gain, but a hedged company will not. Explain what is meant by the term *net exposed position* and how hedging eliminates the possibility of a translation loss and gain.

26-15. The Amerigo Airframe Company, a U.S. multinational, has an affiliate in Malaysia. The Malaysian ringgit appreciates during an operating period. Explain whether the U.S. parent company has a translation gain or loss under the following circumstances:

a. The Malaysian entity's net exposed position has assets greater than liabilities.

b. The Malaysian entity's net exposed position has liabilities greater than assets.

c. The Malaysian entity is hedged.

PROBLEMS

26-1. Destructo Racket Distributing orders $4,200 of Danish graphite tennis rackets. The krone costs $0.098. Shipment will be made in 30 days, with payment due 30 days thereafter. The krone costs $0.08 on the 60-day forward market, and the transaction is fixed in krones.

   a. The equivalent krone price of the orders in the forward market is

      (1) K1,260

      (2) K1,092

      (3) K14,000

      (4) K16,154

      (5) K18,222

      (6) none of these.

   b. Destructo Racket can hedge the transaction by

      (1) buying krone in the spot market.

      (2) buying krone in the forward market.

      (3) selling krone in the spot market.

      (4) selling krone in the forward market.

   c. T F: The relation between the krone's cash and forward value suggests that the krone will depreciate over the ensuing 60 days.

   d. Destructo insists on a 40 percent contribution margin ratio on its rackets. To reflect the expected change in its cost (as an alternative to hedging) management can price the rackets to reflect a change in the expected cost of the krone. Assuming that management expects the krone to change at the rate indicated by the spot-forward relation, a price change of what percentage should be incorporated to preserve its 40 percent contribution margin?

      (1) 15.3 percent increase

      (2) 15.3 percent decrease

      (3) 40 percent increase

      (4) 40 percent decrease

      (5) 18.37 percent increase

      (6) 18.37 percent decrease

26-2. Volvo Motor Works sells Volvos in Sweden for K97,492. The Swedish krona is presently trading at the rate stated for Friday on Figure 26-2. The krona is expected to depreciate by 5 percent within six months.

   a. Calculate the spot dollar price of a Volvo.

   b. What is the dollar price of a Volvo in terms of the future (six-month) krona?

   c. Cite three items that might cause the Swedish krona to depreciate against the U.S. dollar.

26-3. Switzerland is one of the leading financial centers of the world. Consequently, many foreign banks buy securities sold by the Swiss government. Suppose that a U.S. bank wishes to buy a six-month F_{SW} 100,000 security sold by the Swiss government. The security pays 12 percent annual interest and is purchased at par.

   a. What is the franc amount of interest paid by this security? Use a 360-day year in your calculation.

   b. How many U.S. dollars are invested? Use the spot Friday rate in Figure 26-2.

   c. How many U.S. dollars are expected to be received when the Swiss francs (including interest) are converted to U.S. dollars? Use the 180-day forward rate in Figure 26-2.

   d. Explain how this transaction can be hedged with options.

26-4. Staja, Inc., imports and sells Moto Guzzi and Kagiva motorcycles from Italy. The com-

pany's financial manager expects the price of the Italian lira to appreciate by 12 percent during the coming year. Presently, Staja's contribution margin ratio is 15 percent and its marginal tax rate is 40 percent. Anticipated sales, ignoring the appreciation, are $70,000.
  a. What is the expected price of the lira after its appreciation if the present lira is $0.0007?
  b. What must be the percentage increase in price to preserve Staja's after-tax contribution? Support your answer with calculations showing the after-tax contribution margin ratio.
    (1) before the appreciation.
    (2) after the appreciation.
  c. Does Staja, Inc., have transaction or translation risk? Explain your answer.

26-5. Lando Marketing orders YU173,913 worth of merchandise from China. The yuan (YU) is presently trading at $0.46. Invoices are stated in yuan. Alf Lando, president and financial manager of Lando Marketing, expects an 8 percent appreciation in the yuan in the next 30 days.
  a. What is the dollar cost of the merchandise after the appreciation?
  b. The 30-day forward exchange rate of the yuan is $0.50.
    (1) What is the dollar cost of the merchandise based on the forward exchange rate?
    (2) Should Lando hedge this transaction? Explain your answer.
  c. What are some items that Alf should consider to help him decide between
    (1) paying for the merchandise in advance.
    (2) using options.
    (3) using forward contracts.

26-6. Barnes Food Processors has an affiliate in Saudi Arabia that packages and distributes food items in that country. At present, the Saudi riyal costs $0.284 and the 90-day forward riyal costs $0.33. Barnes Food Processors has an R72,400 net exposed position calculated as follows:

Exposed assets	R393,000
Less exposed liabilities	R320,600
Net Exposed Position	R 72,400

Stacey Barnes, the company's financial manager, is concerned about the stability of the riyal and wants to protect her company against unexpected foreign exchange fluctuations.
  a. Does the relationship between the spot and 90-day forward riyal suggest that the riyal will appreciate or depreciate? Explain your answer.
  b. If the net exposed position does not change and the actual riyal becomes $0.33, will Barnes Food Processors show a translation gain or loss on its consolidated statements? Support your answer with calculations.
  c. Explain how Stacey can hedge the translation risk of the Saudi affiliate.
  d. Explain what is meant by economic risk and comment on whether or not the affiliate may have an economic risk.

26-7. Bellwood Corporation has an affiliate in Madrid, Spain. At the beginning of 19x4 the balance sheet stated in pesetas appeared as follows (in thousands):

Current assets	P 800,000	Total liabilities	P1,000,000
Other assets	P 600,000	Net worth	P 400,000
Total	P1,400,000	Total	P1,400,000

The peseta at the beginning of 19x4 was $0.009 and presently is $0.0065.

a. Calculate the affiliate's net exposed position at the beginning of 19x4 using the current-rate method.

b. Translate total assets and liabilities at the beginning exchange rate and at the present peseta exchange rate.

c. Calculate the net translation gain (loss) over the period.

d. Explain how translation gains and losses might affect the price of Bellwood Corporation's common stock if the security market is efficient.

26-8. The British pound sterling depreciates by 15 percent. Your company has a British subsidiary with £80,000 assets and £60,000 liabilities over the period.

a. How much is the net exposed position?

b. The parent company incurs a translation gain or (loss) of
   (1) $12,000
   (2) $9,000
   (3) $3,000
   (4) ($12,000)
   (5) ($9,000)
   (6) ($3,000)

26-9. Plock Corporation is a manufacturing company with several overseas subsidiaries. Chantille, S.A., Plock Corporation's principal French subsidiary, operates entirely within France and submits financial statements translated into U.S. dollars to corporate headquarters on a regular basis. The projected year-end balance sheet as of December 31, 19x6, and the projected income statement for December 19x6, for Chantille, S.A., had been submitted to corporate headquarters in November. The statements appearing below were prepared when the exchange rate was 8.5 francs to the dollar.

During December, the French franc depreciated 10 percent against the U.S. dollar, dropping its cost to 0.90 × $0.1176 = $0.1058 at the end of December. Plock Corporation instructs the management of its foreign subsidiaries to use current exchange rates when translating the financial statements.

a. Calculate the translation gain or loss experienced by Chantille, S.A., on its projected balance-sheet accounts as of December 31, 19x6, due to the depreciation of the French franc. Use the current-rate method to determine the amount.

b. Briefly describe two ways that an anticipated depreciation can be hedged.

c. Is the Plock Corporation incurring translation or economic risk? Explain your answer.

Chantille, S.A.
Projected Balance Sheets
December 31, 19x6
(French Franc — $0.1176)

Assets

Cash	$ 100,000
Receivables	500,000
Prepaid expenses	50,000
Inventory	1,200,000
Plant & equipment (net)	2,000,000
Goodwill	100,000
Deferred charges	50,000
Total assets	$4,000,000

Claims

Accounts payable	$1,200,000
Other current liabilities	600,000
Long-term debt	1,000,000
Deferred income	200,000
Stockholders equity	1,000,000
Total claims	$4,000,000

Chantille, S.A.
Projected Income Statement
For the Month of December 19x6
(French Franc = $0.1176)

Sales	
Costs and expenses:	$400,000
Cost of sales	$307,000
Depreciation	9,700
Other operating expenses	36,000
Amortization of goodwill	300
Interest	8,000
Total costs and expenses	$360,000
Net income before income taxes	$ 40,000
Income taxes	16,000
Net income	$ 24,000

CHAPTER 27
Financial Indicators for Business Timing

There is a lot to learn and remember in this closing chapter, which deals fundamentally with that most important of all considerations, business timing. Essentially, four topics are discussed: (1) the business cycle, (2) the tactics financial managers should employ over the cycle, (3) three financial signals that do most to tell you where the economy is heading, and (4) the widely followed system of business indicators used by the U.S. Department of Commerce.

Your key to an easy grasp of all that follows is a thorough understanding of what happens in each of a business cycle's four stages. Be sure you can describe each stage in detail: the upswing, the upper turning zone, the downswing, and the lower turning zone. It will help you to make a list of main events in each stage, then memorize it.

Having gained a clear idea of what happens in each stage of the business cycle, you will have no problem understanding or remembering the tactics a financial manager should follow as the cycle proceeds. It is a simple matter of preparing financially in each stage for the stage that is coming next.

Next financial barometers of the business weather will be examined. As Chapter 1 emphasized, the financial system is really a subsystem of the economic one, and the subsystem that reacts most quickly to developing trends in the economy. In this chapter you will see why the future course of business can be read in three basic signals: (1) interest rates, (2) stock prices, and (3) the condition of business balance sheets. Ease or strain in these three indicators foreshadow coming changes in the direction of the nation's business. All managers, not just financial managers, profit by observing these indicators and being able to interpret them.

Finally, you will get a nodding acquaintance with the U.S. Department of Commerce system of business indicators: statistical series that lead, move with, or lag the cycle. As you study them, see if you can explain to your own satisfaction why each indicator moves as it does in relation to the economy.

A final test of how well you understand this chapter: Can you explain how an indicator that lags can nevertheless provide a forecast?

Whatever the business, timing is a crucial factor in management. Operations may be highly efficient. Asset-acquiring decisions may be sound. Financing choices may be correct. But if timing is based on misconception or ignorance, the firm may suffer disappointment, loss, even failure. The company, for example, that enters a recession with swollen inventories, poorly screened receivables, and excess productive capacity is clearly in line for trouble.

On what does effective business timing depend? The key requirement is accurate forecasting. If a manager knows what is going to happen next, most decisions will be clear and easy. If you are certain a recession is coming, you do not have to be a genius to understand what is called for. You scale down your inventories, confine credit to sure-pay customers, cancel any plant expansion still on the drawing board, and get your assets liquid as possible. The trick in this case—as in most situations in business—is not knowing *what* to do, but *when* to do it. And that depends on accurate forecasting.

Financial statistics are among the most useful forecasting devices available to business managers. That is another reason why the study of finance offered in this book should help you in your career. Only a minority of business people are directly responsible for financial management. But all managers must forecast. They must forecast their work volume, personnel requirements, operating expenses, and often much more. In this endeavor, financial trends and events often provide them with the clearest insights into what they should expect. The ability to interpret these financial signals correctly, however, depends on an understanding of business cycles and what happens in their successive phases.

THE BUSINESS CYCLE

For at least two centuries, alternate expansions and contractions have marked the course of the business system. We call this phenomenon the business cycle, even though the term *cycle* implies a regularity of timing and amplitude seldom present in business fluctuations.

The business cycle typically consists of an interlude of prosperity rising into boom, peaking out, sliding into recession, recovering, and launching into a new phase of prosperity. Although the length and breadth of its phases have differed widely from one cycle to another, this general pattern has repeated itself with little variation. The business cycle is accompanied by wide swings in the main economic and financial variables—incomes, output, employment, business profits, interest rates, and stock prices.

The cycle is a major factor in business and financial decisions. Its massive changes lie far beyond control of the individual business manager, indeed largely beyond the control of government. Since he is powerless to alter these fluctuations, the manager must accommodate himself and his enterprise to their swings. A good motto to remember in thinking about the business cycle would run: "Swing with business cycles, not against them."

CYCLE PHASES

Although each business cycle is unique, all cycles contain characteristics that are sufficiently similar for us to generalize about them. A typical cycle has four phases: (1) upswing, (2) upper turning zone, (3) downswing, and (4) lower turning zone.

The Upswing

We begin with the economy emerging from recession. Conditions for business expansion are highly favorable. A prolonged spell of subnormal business has depleted inventories of both merchants and manufacturers. Shelves and warehouses must finally be restocked. Factories also need repairs—and in many instances replacement—of buildings and machinery. Interest rates are low. The demand for money has been light and money is readily available for borrowing. Consumers, long fearful of losing jobs or suffering reduced incomes, must finally replace worn-out goods—the old shoes, bed sheets, car, and so forth bought before the recession have now reached their limit of usefulness.

Business revival begins slowly at first, then gains momentum. Merchants order to restock their shelves. This stimulates manufacturers' activity. The recalling of laid-off workers to their jobs adds to payrolls, wages, and spending power. New incomes, flowing into the hands of consumers, bring a rise in retail sales, increasing merchants' orders for still more inventory. Business activity rises in a kind of push-pull interplay between consumer demand, manufacturing activity, and increasing incomes. As idle capacity comes into use, fixed costs per unit of output tumble, and profit margins and profits soar. Early in recovery, profits outstrip all other economic series in percentage rate of climb.

Gradually, business returns to normal, then becomes unusually good. Demand begins to press on existing manufacturing capacity. Managers foresee a need for more plant and equipment to handle the rising tide of orders, and soon capital investment committees are busy placing orders for new buildings and new machines. In spite of a continual increase in manufacturing output, consumer buying absorbs inventory as fast as merchants can stock it.

Other evidences of prosperity become noticeable. The cost of money begins to rise. Merchants commence to borrow heavily at banks to finance larger inventories and receivables, and consumers enlarge their borrowings to acquire more houses, automobiles, and appliances. The upsurge in plant and equipment expenditures by businesses brings a flood of new bonds to market, and bond yields begin to rise.

A spirit of optimism takes over as incomes increase faster than the supply of goods and services. Prices begin to rise. Wages also rise, and the government begins to show concern over symptoms of inflation.

At this point the rise in business becomes self-reinforcing. To the extent that economic resources are employed to create new plant and equipment, they are not available to enlarge the supply of consumer goods. However, the investment in new plant and equipment generates large additions to people's incomes. Since their resulting expenditures meet a limited supply of goods, this pushes prices up at an accelerating rate. Much of the accelerated price rise is due to the speculative buying of goods—merchants order inventory in excess of needs because they expect to make a speculative profit on the continuing rise in prices. The ready availability of credit strengthens this speculative buying, and merchants and manufacturers gladly pay the rising interest rates charged on loans.

Speculation now flows over into the securities and commodities markets. The stock market, which typically rises ahead of business anyway, leaps into a real boom. Speculators buy stocks not only in anticipation of better business earnings, which will lead to higher dividends, but also in the hope of selling to other speculators at inflated prices. Similar speculative price rises grip the commodity and real estate markets.

The general rise in prices strengthens the collateral value of all sorts of pledgable items, reinforces the confidence of both lenders and borrowers, and increases the availability of credit while lowering credit standards.

The Upper Turning Zone

What forces end the upswing? Basically, the fact that a business boom cannot sustain itself indefinitely. The boom develops because businesses are adding to their productive capacity and building inventory at an abnormally rapid rate. But at some point, all the capacity that can profitably be used will have been created, and inventories will have become large enough to meet all foreseeable needs. Indeed, much new plant and equipment creation and inventory enlargement will have been prompted by speculation rather than by the economy's real needs. Thus, it is quite probable that the expansion of both new capacity and inventories will have been badly overdone. When this discovery is made, a rush may develop to cancel projects and orders already under way. This rush will not only precipitate a downturn in business but also give the downturn much momentum.

Price-level and monetary factors also play large parts in reversing a business boom. The central bank reacts to inflation by slowing down the growth of the money

---

BOX 27-1
**Business Cycle Theories, Including "Sun
Spots"**   A business cycle theory must explain why the cycle is self-generating, that is,
why it keeps repeating itself despite people's effort to control it. Most cycle
theories emphasize what are *endogenous factors,* forces within the business system
itself. Prominent among these forces are the recurring overproduction of long-lived
capital goods (overinvestment theories), the tendency of credit to overexpand (credit
theories), the alternating overoptimism and overpessimism of managers (psychological theories), and the effect of leveraged costs on business profits (profit margin
theories).

   Probably the most unique business cycle theory ever to be taken seriously
emphasized an *exogenous influence,* one originating outside of the business system—
and in this case, beyond the planet Earth. This was the famous sun-spot theory,
advanced late in the nineteenth century by the English economist- astronomer William Stanley Jevons. Jevons, a Renaissance man in his day (mathematician, logician,
and public servant along with other interests), thought he had established a periodic
connection between sun spots and depressions. The connection he visualized ran
from the influence of sun spots on weather conditions, to crop yields, to the cost of
food, and on to the economy's regularly recurring ups and downs.

   Modern investigators have long since rejected Jevons theory. In fact, most
modern work on business cycles does not put undue weight on any of the endogenous factors mentioned above but sees them all working together and, in most
cycles, reinforcing each other. This approach is *eclectic,* a term derived from two
Greek words, *ek,* meaning out, and *legein,* meaning to choose. An eclectic believes
that good thinking, like gold, is where you find it.

---

supply. Money begins to get tight, and interest rates rise. As money becomes expensive and hard to borrow, many people—merchants, manufacturers, home builders,
and home buyers—begin to think twice about borrowing. As interest rates soar to
ration an inadequate supply of funds, mortgage borrowers begin to be priced out of
the market.[1] With markets for corporate bonds congested, many companies heed the
advice of their investment bankers and postpone their issues.

   Meanwhile, the Treasury and federal government may also restrain the boom
by increasing income taxes (personal and business) and by cutting expenditures.
Since a Treasury surplus withdraws funds from the economy, it can aid powerfully
in putting brakes on the boom.

   Presently, the stock market and business profits begin to suffer. Stocks have

---

[1] This happens because residential mortgage yields do not rise sufficiently to meet the competition
of yields on either corporate bonds or commercial and industrial mortgages. However, the development of "mortgage-based securities," a kind of bond backed by mortgages and having an active
trading market, is tending to eliminate this problem. See the discussion at the end of Chapter 9.

already climbed a long way before the business boom begins. For a while during the boom they move higher. But rising interest rates and tight money make margin accounts more difficult to finance, and falling bond prices and rising bond yields make bonds an increasingly attractive alternative to stock investment. Finally, far-sighted investors and speculators perceive that the rate of gain in profits for many companies is slowing down and preparing to reverse itself. They begin to sell their stocks, and soon stock prices are falling. Falling stock prices discourage speculators who hold stocks on margin, and their selling soon becomes contagious, leading to a real break in the stock market.

At the same time, the rate of gain in business profits starts to slow down. The capital goods ordered at the start of the boom become available. The economy's ability to produce consumer goods now expands. Supply begins to overtake demand, and manufacturers, goaded by unused capacity, compete vigorously against each other for consumer markets. Price rises become harder and harder to achieve in the face of intensifying competition and tightening money. Meanwhile, the economy has reached the limit of its labor supply. Workers are difficult to hire. Labor discipline becomes difficult—if workers are fired for loafing on one job, then another job is easy to find. Employers compete vigorously against one another for a limited labor supply, driving wages up sharply at a time when price increases are difficult to come by. This puts profit margins under great pressure, and profits generally begin to fall. The boom ends in a great flurry of "profitless prosperity," with rising labor costs devouring the gains companies had hoped to make.

The boom has now reached its peak and begins to fade rapidly. Businesses cancel their orders for plant expansion and new inventory. Some companies, hit with declining profits and even losses, cut their dividends. Reports of reduced earnings, falling dividends, some business failures, and the still-prevailing reign of tight money all drive the stock market down at an accelerated rate. Confidence oozes out of business people, speculators, and consumers alike. Everyone now expects the worst to happen, and the swing of expectations from overoptimism to pessimism now drives business into a rapid decline. Sales fall, workers are laid off, and many people reduce their spending to conserve cash for a "rainy day."

The Downswing

Once the downswing in business is under way, reinforcing influences accelerate its decline. Businesses liquidate inventories and do not replace them. Some inventory may have to be sold to pay pressing debts. Dumping it on the market depresses prices. Having liquidated inventory, and fearing further declines in both prices and sales, merchants buy only on a "hand-to-mouth," or as-needed, basis. Weak inventory ordering backs up on the factories. Manufacturers cut production runs. Employees lose overtime, get short-timed, or get laid off. As people lose jobs and go on unemployment compensation, their incomes and buying power fall, further reducing economic demand and business activity.

Business profits fall along with sales. Since most companies are affected by both operating and financial leverage, the percentage decline in profits is typically a multiple of the percentage decline in sales. Some businesses meet the fall in profits by reducing their dividends. Some may experience such large losses that they are unable to meet bond or bank interest or to pay other fixed charges. They go into receivership or bankruptcy.

Pessimistic expectations darken the outlook for both businesses and consumers. The demand for borrowed funds dries up. Speculation in the stock market comes to an end, and the volume of stocks bought and sold falls to a trickle. Liquidity preference is high—everyone would rather own cash than stocks or inventories. Real estate and commodity prices fall along with stock prices, and the lower level of collateral values makes borrowers less credit-worthy. Lenders become highly selective and only "preferred risks" can borrow money.

One bright spot shows up even as the downturn is under way. Interest rates begin to ease. Alarmed by signs of recession, the central bank reverses its tight-money policy and begins an aggressive program to lower interest rates and increase the availability of lendable funds. Meanwhile, borrowers at banks and other financial institutions hasten to pay off their loans and get out of debt. As spending by businesses and consumers slows down, money begins to pile up in the banks in idle pools. Conditions gradually become superliquid, and interest rates fall to low levels.

Meanwhile, of course, the government also uses fiscal policy to fight the recession. Taxes for individuals and corporations are cut, government spending for unemployment relief and public works is increased, and a large government deficit is fueled by massive Treasury borrowings at the banks. The proceeds of the deficit are promptly spent by the government in an effort to provide jobs and to prevent an excessive slowdown in the economy.

The Lower Turning Zone

Even without intervention by the central bank and government, the downswing must eventually end. There are three primary self-limiting factors, and several lesser ones come into play.

1. The end of inventory liquidation and the fall of inventories to an irreducible minimum oblige merchants to place new orders for goods. Even though ordering begins on a "hand-to-mouth" basis, this replenishment in inventories brings a step-up in factory activity.
2. Time, wear, and obsolescence oblige manufacturers to begin replacing plant and equipment. Autos, appliances, and other consumer durables also wear out and require replacement. The resulting orders for new durable goods are a powerful spontaneous force in bringing about revival.
3. People's consumption does not fall as much as their income does. As incomes decline, families cut back on their savings and spend a higher fraction of their income to maintain accustomed living standards. Thus, the fall in wages, salaries, dividends, and profits is matched by a less-than-proportionate fall in demand. This helps keep the economy going even in the darkest days.

Other factors take a favorable turn. The liquidity of the system improves, and the stream of business failures gradually subsides. With increased output, labor productivity increases. Businesses increase output without resorting to hiring, and capacity utilization rates rise. And even during recession, the stock market begins to rise as traders and investors start to "look over the valley" toward the next business upswing.

All these factors work together to end the decline and produce a gradual upturn. Invisible at first and recognized by only a few, this upturn gradually gathers strength as new orders, new hirings, new incomes, and new sales begin to spread in ever-widening circles.

FINANCING TACTICS OVER THE CYCLE

To the financial manager, the business cycle is a fact of life. He must accept it because he cannot change it. Since he cannot control its action, he must therefore adjust his own actions to it. How does he do this?

The financial manager's main strategy is simply to move with the cycle, taking advantage of his knowledge of what the next stage will be. Clearly, he does not want his company to complete an expensive new plant or saddle itself with a huge inventory just as a recession is beginning. On the other hand, he does not want his company to enter a period of good business without ample manufacturing capacity, or without the ability to finance an increasing volume of inventory and receivables. Decisions to expand the company's scale of operations are not made by the financial manager alone, but his voice can powerfully influence the votes and decisions of the firm's other officers.

What is good financial strategy over the typical business cycle? As the downturn ends and the company is very liquid, it is a good time to begin thinking about lines of banking credit and possible future bond issues. The company does not need to add to its idle funds right now. But better business lies ahead and should be planned for.

As business revival begins, inventories and receivables start to increase. This brings a rise in the company's need for new working capital. Before long, too, demand may be pressing on factory capacity. Operating executives may be thinking about adding to plant and equipment. Each of these projects is likely to call for outside financing. Where should this financing come from? Most of the new financing need is likely to be permanent. Plant and equipment, being long-lived assets, must be financed from permanent sources. Most of the increased need for new working capital will probably prove permanent, for the business will grow over the next few years and it is doubtful whether the next recession will carry new working capital needs back down to their present level. Thus, the bulk of the new financing will be permanent. At this stage of the cycle, it should be done through a bond issue. Bond yields are still low and rising only slowly. The bond market is broad and uncongested. Investment bankers are eager for business and will give an issue better attention. It is a good time to sell bonds.

As the stream of recovery widens into prosperity, it may be well to market one or more additional issues of bonds before bond yields go out of sight (as they

---

BOX 27-2

When Problem Loans Are Made   Why study business cycles and become familiar with their habits? Because if you are in business, it can save you big trouble, that is why.

One fellow who seems to understand this is John G. Medlin, Jr., the president and chief executive of Wachovia Bank & Trust Company in Wiston-Salem, North Carolina. Eighteen months into a vigorous business expansion, *The Wall Street Journal* for May 1, 1984, quotes Mr. Medlin as saying, "This is the part of the cycle when the problem loans of the next recession are made."

Why not? Things look trouble-free at that stage of a business rise. As May 1984 began, output had just jumped at an 8.3 percent annual rate in the year's first quarter, unemployment had taken its biggest percentage tumble ever over the preceding year, and for back-to-back years consumer prices had climbed at a less than 4 percent annual rate. Sunny skies, indeed. Few clouds, it seemed, even on the far horizon.

What managers must understand is that these are just the sort of good times that beguile them into costly mistakes. Take bank loan officers, for example. There is an inevitable tendency to look at a would-be borrower's present sales and profits, not at the financial staying power the company would have if business turned down—as it is bound to do eventually, given cycles as a fact of business life. At such times, practically all loan applicants look safe for now, and a banker is naturally anxious to grab the borrower's business before it goes to some other bank.

A little forethought, though, should slow that banker down. Maybe the applicant's latest income statement does look all right. But what about its balance sheet? Does it show the low debt ratio and strong working-capital position that would enable it to weather a real financial storm? After all, go back two years from May 1984, and the economy was locked in one of its worst recessions of the past 50 years. Weak companies were toppling like pins in a busy bowling alley. Come May 1987, the same thing could be happening again.

Question for the banker: Will the loan you just made still look good when that day rolls around?

---

typically do at the peak of a boom). By now the need to finance rising levels of inventory and receivables has grown to large dimensions. The economy and, probably, your business have begun to operate above balanced levels. Now if a drop were to come, your inventories and receivables would face a sharp contraction. It makes no sense to use permanent financing for needs that may evaporate with a change in the cycle. From this point on, circulating capital needs should be met from temporary sources, preferably bank loans or factoring agreements.

Now prosperity climbs into boom. The stock market approaches a peak. This is the time for the astute financial manager to sell new common shares for two or three times the price he could have gotten during the recession, using some of the proceeds to retire debt. Bond financing has become very costly with tight money, high interest rates, long periods of nonrefundability, and stringent indenture restrictions on borrowers. It is a good time to stay out of the bond market, and astute financial managers will have timed financing at this point to consist of common stocks.

Common-stock financing at the peak of a boom is not only cheap, it also provides an equity base for debt financing during the next recovery. By entering the recession period with a comfortable equity-to-debt ratio, the company not only minimizes its financial risk but also impresses future lenders with a large "cushion" of equity to protect their loans.

Bank loans —

Temporary Source of capital

Now the boom peaks out and recession is under way. The stock issues sold at the boom's peak, plus ample lines of bank credit, make the company comfortably liquid despite the downturn. As the recession gathers headway and sales begin to drop, the company's need to finance inventories and receivables declines. This decline is met by retiring bank loans—the temporary source of circulating capital. Liquidity is maintained, but excess liquidity is avoided as the company slips down into the nadir of recession.

From here the financing cycle will begin again.

MIRROR OF THE ECONOMY

What stage is the business cycle in now? What can I expect to happen next? For alert, vigilant managers, these must be unrelenting questions. Where can the answers be read? They can be read earliest and most reliably in the economy's financial indicators.

Why? Because, as Chapter 1 pointed out, nothing takes place in the economy without an accompanying flow of money (or of its stand-in, credit). Money flows cast clear reflections on the economy's screen, telltale traces of which way business is heading. These signs, visible in the financial statistics, show the rate at which people are stepping up or slowing down their buying and selling, producing and consuming, spending and saving, borrowing and lending. Collectively, they signify the direction and strength of the economy.

Students familiar with systems analysis will see at once why this should be so. The economy is a system. The financial sector is one of its most important subsystems. What happens in the system (the economy) is bound to be reflected in the subsystem (the financial sector). The financial system is, in fact, a faithful mirror of major trends in the economy.

Which financial indicators are most significant and, at the same time, easiest for the average business manager to understand and follow (say, by reading the *Wall Street Journal, Business Week,* or some other good business periodical)? We have selected three to highlight in this concluding chapter, and several others to mention briefly. The three deserving attention are (1) interest rates, (2) stock prices, and (3) the state of business balance sheets.

INTEREST RATES AS AN INDICATOR

Of all business indicators, interest rates are probably the most significant. The economy is never vulnerable to a downturn until interest rates have risen strongly, and, conversely, a business recovery out of recession never commences until interest rates have turned downward. Furthermore, the stage which the business cycle has reached, and a glimpse of what lies ahead, are clearly readable in the term structure of interest rates, already studied in Chapter 3.

Behavior of Interest-Rate Levels

Interest rates typically reach their low point some months after business activity has passed its trough. Businesses are cash-rich after having liquidated their boom-time levels of inventories and receivables, and business, although expanding, is still not putting any pressure on either long- or short-term loans. Interest rates reach their peak near, or shortly after, the peak of a boom, when strains on available credit supplies are maximal and when the Federal Reserve is keeping credit very tight.

Peaks for short-term rates and bond yields, however, may be separated by some months, as they were in 1974–1975 and to some extent in 1981. Some long-term financing is always postponable, especially for big companies with enough financial muscle to sell commercial paper, or to make the banks grant them short-term loans, for what is called bridge financing—that is, bridging over a period of shortage or unavailability for long-term loans. After the credit crunch is past, these big borrowers may flock into the bond market and actually pay higher yields on their bonds than prevailed at the time short-term rates peaked.[2]

Reading the Term Structure

The term structure of interest rates (yield versus maturity curve) will be steeply upsloping when credit conditions are easy and higher interest rates are expected in months ahead as business picks up steam. The more sharply pressures on credit supplies intensify, the more level the yield curve becomes. Finally when credit becomes very tight, and when many lenders and borrowers expect a recession and lower interest rates ahead, the yield curve typically becomes level—or even inverted, with short-term rates above long-term ones. Figure 3-3 in Chapter 3 portrays these relations.

A sound rule for managers to follow would seem to run as follows: When the

---

[2] Why should they *be willing* to pay more? Because they are no longer scared. At the worst of tight money, they may fear the economy is going over the precipice into another 1932. As money eases, it becomes clear this will not happen. The banks start to complain, so the big companies sell bonds to pay them off.

rate on three-month Treasury bills reaches 90 percent of the yield on 20-year Treasury bonds, begin pulling in your horns.

2. STOCK PRICES AS A BUSINESS BAROMETER

Over the past century, industrial stock prices have been the most accurate *leading indicator of business cycles*.[3] Although its record is far from infallible, the stock market has characteristically made timely announcements of coming changes in the business weather; stocks have usually commenced to decline before a business boom has ended, and they have started to rise before the end of a recession. While variable, the market's lead over business has averaged about six months' time.

Why should stock prices be ranked among our most dependable business barometers? There are at least eight reasons why the curve of stock prices should lead the curve of business.

1. **Speculation and Expectations** Profits in trading stocks come from foreseeing future business conditions "ahead of the crowd"—buying in a recession before other investors see the upturn coming, selling out in a boom before others perceive its shakiness. The largest profits are made by those who see farthest ahead with the greatest accuracy, and the collective effort of traders as a group to buy and sell on the basis of expectations and forecasts causes the market to discount business conditions "as far ahead as the clearest eye in Wall Street can foresee." Clever speculators govern their tactics less by following reversals in trends than by watching the acceleration or deceleration of trends.[4]

2. **Operation of Interest Rates** Interest rates begin rising strongly as business expansions mature; they fall sharply as a recession heads toward its trough. These changes affect the decisions of both businesses and investors. For businesses, rising interest rates increase borrowing costs and put pressure on reported profits—something stock prices are very sensitive to. For investors, rising interest rates make stocks less attractive because competing fixed-income securities offer improved yields. This is true of yields on bonds, which compete with stocks as long-term investments, and of yields on Treasury bills, negotiable CDs, and commercial paper, which begin offering high returns with minimal risk of loss. As the stock market begins to look shaky, many investors head for the safety of money-market instruments, and their selling

---

[3] A finding by the National Bureau of Economic Research. See Geoffrey H. Moore, ed., *Business Cycle Indicators*, 2 vols. (Princeton, N.J.: Princeton University Press, 1961; a study by the National Bureau of Economic Research). See also Geoffrey H. Moore and Julius Shiskin, *Indicators of Business Expansion and Contraction* (New York: National Bureau of Economic Research, distributed by Columbia University Press, 1967); and Geoffrey H. Moore, *Business Cycles, Inflation, and Forecasting*, 2nd ed., published for the National Bureau of Economic Research by Ballinger Publishing Company, Cambridge, Mass., 1983.

[4] If you have studied differential calculus, you will remember that in spotting the start of a change in the trend of a graph or function, the crucial thing to identify is the inflection point. Successful speculators are apparently adept at identifying inflection points in the rise or fall of stocks and of the stock market.

out of stocks helps turn the stock market down. Rising interest rates also make stocks more expensive to carry on margin and thus lessen their attractiveness to speculators.

3. **"Spare" or Unavailable Business Cash**   As recessions close in, businesses gradually liquidate their inventories and collect their receivables. At the low levels of business encountered during recessions and early in periods of recovery, businesses rarely need to employ all their capital in financing sales. Often the owners of businesses will use their "spare" money to trade in stocks. When sales begin to boom again, this capital will be needed back in the business, and many business proprietors must begin selling off their stocks. Finally, if money becomes very tight, as it typically does near the peak of a boom, many businesses may be unable to obtain loans. To raise money, they sell off stocks in which they have invested their reserve funds.

4. **Monetary Policy and Credit Availability**   Monetary policy typically provides an excess of credit during recessions. Money is easy to borrow, and a good deal of borrowed money clearly finds its way into the stock market. Margin requirements are low, and stocks, depressed below their long-run values, may offer more attractive investment opportunities than investments in inventory or plant and equipment. By contrast, when a boom is near its peak, the Fed is "leaning against the wind." Credit is tight and margin requirements are high. There may not be enough credit available to meet the legitimate needs of business borrowers, and banks and other lenders may refuse to provide credit to stock speculators.

5. **Changing Volume of New Stock Issues**   As a boom nears its peak, corporations typically sell large volumes of new stock to finance plant expansion and enlarged working-capital needs. Often the inability of investors to buy all the new shares offered weakens the price structure of stocks in general and helps turn the market down. By contrast, in a recession, new stock issues are rare; the market in existing shares has no competition from new issues, and this helps push stock prices up strongly if investors foresee the recession ending and rush to buy stocks.

6. **Effect on Cost of Corporate Equity**   Stock-market trends also act to help turn the business cycle around. When stock prices begin to fall in the later stages of a business boom, this means the cost of new equity capital for corporations rises. (As was noted in Chapter 20, one widely used measure of a company's cost of common equity is the ratio of earnings per share to price per share; and if a stock's price falls while its earnings hold constant, the company's cost of capital clearly increases.) The increased cost of equity discourages some business investment, and this decline in business spending on new plant and equipment helps bring on the downturn. Conversely, the rise in stock prices as the recession starts to bottom out lowers the cost of equity capital and encourages new business commitments. This adds to the stream of spending and helps the economy to begin expanding again.

7. **Wealth Effects**   People, both individuals and managers of corporations, feel optimistic when stocks are going up, making them and their companies richer. They spend more freely because they feel wealthier. By the same token, declining stock prices make them feel poorer and discourage them from spending. These "wealth effects" of changing stock prices are very noticeable, in their impact not only on

individuals' willingness to spend but on corporations' willingness to undertake new investments, or even to replace worn-out facilities.

8. **Role of Normal Values** The enduring value of a stock is based on its earning power and ability to pay dividends. Such a value measures the intrinsic value of the stock to a long-term holder.[5] But over the business cycle, speculators and short-term traders also operate in the stock market. Almost invariably, a boom in business generates speculative enthusiasm that drives stock prices in general far above their sustainable, long-run values. The artificially high prices last only until there is some check to confidence, or until enough investors recognize that prices are unsustainably high. Then a rush to unload overpriced stocks drives the market down. On the other hand, investor pessimism and precautionary selling at the beginning of a recession drive stock prices well below levels warranted by their long-run earnings and dividend-paying power. When this undervaluation is recognized, the market rebounds, even though a recession may still be under way.

 STATE OF BUSINESS BALANCE SHEETS

The balance sheets of businesses reflect their financial position. How readily the nation's manufacturers and retailers can raise spendable funds, meet their debts as they come due, and finance more inventories, receivables, or plant and equipment is clearly discernible through the ratio analysis you reviewed in Chapters 12 through 14. This is as true of companies taken collectively as of companies considered individually.

Various agencies, public and private, publish periodic figures on the collective state of corporate finances. Of special value are reports issued by the Department of Commerce, the Securities and Exchange Commission, the Federal Reserve Board, and several publications of the McGraw-Hill Company.

How one analyzes the collective balance sheet of American business closely follows the pattern used in analyzing an individual company. Measures of liquidity, financial leverage, profitability, and asset turnover are applied to determine whether overall financial strength is improving or deteriorating.

A few measures are important enough to justify special emphasis: As booms intensify, the ratio of short-term debt to long-term debt may rise dangerously.[6] The composition of current assets typically weakens—that is, the ratio of inventories and receivables to cash and government securities increases, signifying sharply reduced

---

[5] Investors try to calculate the "normal" or "intrinsic" values of stocks by capitalizing their expected future earnings and/or dividends at rates which reflect the time value of money plus an allowance for business risks, price-level inflation, and other hazards. In principle, the theoretical value of any investment is the present value of its future returns thus capitalized.

[6] One of the key points this book has sought to emphasize has been that short-term debt is inherently more dangerous to a firm than long-term debt. As a friend of ours remarked long years ago, "It's not the debt that's due twenty years from now that kills you; it's what's due next week." Long-term debt, by definition, carries only the obligation to pay, over the year ahead, interest and perhaps a sinking fund. On short-term debt, interest plus *principal* fall due within the year.

liquidity in the nation's corporate sector.[7] As booms become top-heavy, a pile-up of inventories (the least liquid of current assets) signifies problems ahead for many companies.[8] A significant increase in the debt-to-equity ratio for corporations in general suggests that a boom financed through rapidly rising indebtedness must soon prove unsustainable. Reverse trends in the forgoing financial measures would obviously suggest that the financial strength of the nation's corporate sector was increasing.

Other Financial Indicators

Professional forecasters and business leaders watch many other financial indicators, a list too long to enumerate. These include the growth rate of the money supply or the monetary base, the rise or fall in credit (both total credit and particular kinds, such as mortgage credit, consumer credit, and business credit), the financial condition of banks and other lenders, and the size and tendency of the federal deficit. Each of these has a particular significance to the specialist or experienced observer.

Price inflation is, of course, a highly important financial indicator. Falling as a recession ends, it typically begins accelerating a year or so into recovery. As it becomes disturbingly rapid, the Federal Reserve is likely to begin tightening money and permitting interest rates to rise sharply. This hoists a warning that a business boom is in its late stages. Conversely, a decline in the inflation rate late in recession is the usual forerunner of a business pickup.

NONFINANCIAL INDICATORS

Obviously, financial indicators are not the only business barometers a manager can, or should, watch. Much useful information may come from salespeople, who report customers' willingness to place new orders; from suppliers' representatives, who offer lengthening or shrinking delivery periods (thus indicating a tightening or easing in supplies of raw materials, components, or finished goods); and from a company's own analysis of trends in its sales, profits, and profit margins. These indicators

---

[7] The liquidity of the corporate sector as a whole depends on the cash it holds plus claims, such as Treasury bills, which it can enforce against other sectors of the economy. Commercial paper held by corporations does not add to the liquidity of the corporate sector because it is the obligation of other corporations. The same is true of negotiable CDs, which are the obligations of banking corporations, also part of the corporate sector.

[8] Of all factors in the business cycle, changes in the rate of inventory accumulation have the largest swings between prosperity and recession. They move from an annual rate that is positive by tens of billions of dollars to one that is often negative by tens of billions of dollars. It is almost axiomatic in business-cycle forecasting that the more overdone inventory accumulation gets, the worse the ensuing recession will be, since the longer it takes a business to "sweat off" its excess inventories, the farther output and employment are likely to fall.

BOX 27-3
The Alarm Bells That Didn't Ring   As the closing pages of this chapter state, the government publishes a regular list of business indicators, including 12 leading ones that are supposed to warn business people, investors, and others of coming changes in the economy's direction. These barometers of business conditions seem to work reliably so long as the economy maintains a fairly constant pattern of cycle-to-cycle behavior. When major shifts occur in the economy's structure or operation, the indicators can go awry and fail to give the timely warnings they are intended to sound.

The classic case of failure came in 1974, when the economy was in a recession for almost a year before the government indicators showed it (and before most forecasters were aware of it). Actually, the recession got under way in November 1973, when the OPEC oil embargo began to snarl up the economy, but the downturn did not show up in the indicators. Why not? Because the indicators, based on the economy's behavior during the 1960s when prices were relatively stable, were expressed in current dollars, that is, dollars of the given year. But by late 1973, inflation was trotting fast, and in 1974 (with some generous help from OPEC), it was really galloping. The rise in prices drowned out, as it were, the dip in business activity, so the indicators kept on rising even though business and employment were starting to fall out of bed. "Water in the barometers," as the weather forecasters would say.

That is why the government's whole system of economic indicators underwent its biggest overhaul ever in the Spring of 1975. The aim was to inflation-proof the measures of economic activity on which the indicators depended. That is also why, as you look at many of the indicators today, you will see that they are in 1972 constant dollars, or simply, 1972 dollars. It is to keep the water of inflation from messing up the barometers that provide our economy with its early-warning system.

reveal trends and changes that immediately affect the business. They are the most important indicators of all, but they usually provide much less advanced warning than do the financial indicators reviewed in this chapter and other broad indicators now to be discussed.

All business managers should be familiar with the widely followed list of business indicators developed since about 1960 by the joint study of the National Bureau of Economic Research and the United States Department of Commerce.[9] These indicators, published monthly in *Business Conditions Digest* (U.S. Department of Commerce), fall into three groups. Since April 1975 they have consisted, with minor changes, of the following.

[9] These indicators were developed and came into use as a consequence of the two-volume study by the National Bureau, cited in Footnote 3.

Leading Indicators. As the title suggests, these indicators typically move in advance of the business cycle, rising in recessions before business turns up and falling in booms before the downturn begins.

1. Average workweek in manufacturing.
2. Average weekly claims for state unemployment insurance (inverted).
3. New orders for consumer goods expressed in 1972 dollars.
4. Percentage of companies or suppliers reporting slower deliveries.
5. Net new business formations.
6. New orders for plant and equipment (in 1972 dollars).
7. New building permits.
8. Change in business inventories (on hand or on order, in 1972 dollars).
9. Percentage change in a price index of sensitive raw materials.
10. Common-stock prices.
11. Nation's money supply (M_2 in 1972 dollars).
12. Change in business and consumer borrowing.

Coincident Indicators. These indicators move approximately in step (coincide) with business. Their acceleration or slowdown, upturn or downturn, thus confirm or contradict what business people have previously concluded by watching the leading indicators. The four coincident indicators most commonly used are:

1. Nonagricultural employment.
2. Personal income in 1972 dollars.
3. Industrial production.
4. Manufacturing and trade sales in 1972 dollars.

Lagging Indicators. You might think that a lagging indicator would be useless, since by definition it changes direction after business does. However, lagging indicators become *leading* indicators when read in reverse; that is, business rarely starts up until the lagging indicators turn down, and business rarely turns down until the lagging indicators start up. The reasons for this should be apparent. Lagging indicators do one of two things. Either they restrain the economy, as do rising interest rates or larger business and consumer indebtedness (which become increasingly burdensome to carry). Or they indicate an acceleration in the rate at which business is slowing down: for example, inventory pile-up or lengthening of the average period of unemployment. Six widely followed lagging indicators are:

1. Average duration of unemployment.
2. Ratio of manufacturing and trade inventories to sales (in 1972 dollars).
3. Labor cost per unit of output in manufacturing.
4. The prime rate of interest.
5. Commercial and industrial loans outstanding.
6. The ratio of consumer installment credit to personal income.

Composite Indicators. Like other business forecasting devices, the NBER/Department of Commerce system of indicators is far from perfect. During 1979, for example, it was often quipped that the leading indicators had "predicted nine of the last four recessions." This suggests that no single set of forecasting tools should be relied on alone, and that the more readings managers can get on the business outlook, the better assessment they are likely to arrive at.

One further type of indicator has been suggested in recent years: a composite indicator consisting of the ratio of one kind of indicator to another. Studies have suggested, for example, that a ratio of coincident indicators to lagging indicators may give earlier warning of changes in the business climate than the leading indicators do. The underlying premise is plausible: so long as this ratio is increasing, measures that coincide with business expansion are increasing faster than those that restrain business expansion. When the ratio turns down, it means that influences that brake or choke off business expansion have begun to increase faster than those that accompany it.

An ingenious manager can readily devise, and experiment with, a variety of other composite indicators fashioned from among the business barometers discussed in this chapter. In this endeavor, the understanding of financial principles and the financial system that this book has attempted to impart should prove especially helpful.

SUMMARY

1. Whatever your role in business, timing is a crucial factor. The greatest challenges to effective timing arise from the recurring swings of the business cycle. No firm, however large, can measurably affect the cycle. Managers cannot oppose the cycle. They can only adjust their operations to the changes it brings.

2. A business cycle consists of four distinct stages. (1) An *upswing* brings increasing prosperity and an expanding employment of economic resources. (2) An *upper turning zone* is marked by growing slowdown, financial and other forms of strain, and an eventual downturn into recession. (3) In the *downswing,* recessionary forces make the economy "pay" for excesses of the preceding boom through falling sales, employment, and profits. (4) In the *lower turning zone,* recessionary influences exhaust their force, and the economy bottoms out and turns up again. The process is automatic and reflects the play of accelerating influences during the economy's rise and fall, and of self-limiting forces at the two extremes.

3. Like other business specialists, financial managers must anticipate the cycle's stages as they come, preparing in each stage for the one coming next. There are optimal times in which to secure credit lines, float bonds, obtain bank loans, sell new stock, and pay off bank loans. Each of these moves identifies with a particular point in a firm's cycle of expanding and contracting business.

4. Because people place their money-bets as far ahead as they can foresee business developments, financial indicators give the earliest and most reliable warnings of coming changes in the direction of business cycles. Three such indicators usually combine to flash a green or red light for the economy. (1) Interest rates (and especially the term structure) indicate the liquidity that precedes a business upturn or the illiquidity that heralds a downturn. (2) Stock prices, with few exceptions, begin bull markets before recessions end and topple into bear markets late in periods of prosperity. (3) Business balance sheets, like interest rates, indicate ease or strain in the financial resources available to support a business rise, specifically in the financial resources available to business firms.

5. Among other indicators, those published monthly by the U. S. Department of Commerce have the widest following. The three types—leading, coincident, and lagging—each serve a special purpose. Leading indicators actually move in advance of business. Lagging indicators consist of influences that put brakes on a rising economy; hence, they are read in reverse. Coincident indicators, moving along with business, work to confirm whatever trend is actually under way.

KEY TERMS AND CONCEPTS

Business cycle	Interest rates
Cycle phases	State of business balance sheets
Mirror of economy	Leading indicators
Moving with the cycle	Coincident indicators
Business indicators	Lagging indicators
Stock prices	Composite indicators

QUESTIONS

27-1. Is it correct to call recurring business fluctuations "cycles"? Explain your answer.

27-2. What happens to a company's financial condition during a business expansion?

27-3. Does a company's liquidity improve or deteriorate during a recession? Explain.

27-4. Describe a typical business upswing. Why does it not continue indefinitely? What part do financial factors play in limiting it?

27-5. Describe the downswing of the cycle. Would it go on forever if there were no Federal Reserve? Why or why not?

27-6. Describe in detail the financial manager's proper tactics over the business cycle.

27-7. Why should the financial system be called a "mirror" of the economy?

27-8. How does the term structure of interest rates look
   a. when money is very easy?
   b. when money is very tight
   Why that appearance in each case?

27-9. Cite at least six reasons why stock prices should lead business trends.

27-10. If you were analyzing the collective balance sheet of all U. S. manufacturing corporations for the purpose of gauging their ability to maintain a business expansion, what three ratios would you emphasize most? Defend your choices.

27-11. Recalling from Chapter 7 the five "Cs" of credit, what would you, as a business manager, look at to assess credit "conditions."

27-12. Name five leading indicators of the business cycle and tell why each of them typically moves ahead of business.

27-13. If lagging indicators change direction after business has already reversed its trend, how can they be useful?

27-14. Briefly explain how you would interpret a ratio of lagging to coincident indicators.

APPENDICES

Appendix A
Glossary

Definitions of terms not included in the glossary may be found by consulting the index for text references.

Accounting rate of return.   Rate of return on an investment computed as accounting profit divided by some measure of investment; e.g., average profit per year divided by average investment.

Acid-test ratio.   See *quick ratio.*

Activity ratio.   Financial ratio that indicates how efficiently a company uses its assets; inventory turnover, average collection period, fixed-asset turnover, and total asset turnover are examples.

After-acquired property clause.   Provision in a bond indenture providing that all property acquired by a company in the future will also serve as collateral for the bonds.

Agency issue.   See *best-efforts issue.*

Amortize.   To pay off a debt by installments. An amortized loan is repaid in regular installments, each payment consisting of some principal and some interest.

Annuity.   Series of equal periodic payments or receipts.

Arbitrage.   Simultaneously buying and selling the same or equivalent securities in different markets to profit from a divergence in their prices.

Balance sheet.   See *statement of financial position.*

Bankers' acceptance.   Company's short-term promise to pay which has been guaranteed for payment (accepted) by its bank. It is used largely in foreign trade to substitute a bank's known credit for the unknown credit of an individual or company.

Bankruptcy. Condition in which a company is unable to pay its debts, and its assets are consequently surrendered to a court for administration.

Best-efforts issue. Issuing securities without underwriting. Securities are sold on a commission basis by an investment banker with no guarantee of the total amount that will be sold.

Beta. Measure of slope in a regression equation. Also used to designate risk index and systematic risk. See *capital-asset pricing model.*

Bill. Short-term, non-interest-bearing promise to pay, issued by a business or government to borrow money. Sold at a discount, the holder obtains interest when the bill matures at face value.

Bond. Promise to pay issued by a corporation or government to borrow money for five years or longer. It pays a stated rate of interest to a registered owner at regular intervals, usually six months, and repays its face amount (ordinarily $1,000) at maturity.

Budget. Plan or schedule that adjusts spending over a coming period to expected income or available funds. A blueprint of intended financial activity.

Business risk. Risk arising from the uncertainty of future operating revenues and expenses (not including debt interest). Riskiness of a company's net operating income is often quantified by the variance of net operating income.

CD (certificate of deposit). Interest-bearing time deposit in a commercial bank, usually maturing in one to six months, and typically negotiable when made in large amounts. Often used by businesses for temporary investment of surplus cash.

Call premium. Difference between the call price and the face value of the bond.

Call price. Price a company must pay per bond to bond holders if the bonds are called (repurchased by the firm directly from bond holders).

Call provision. Stipulation in a bond or preferred stock agreement that a company has the right to repurchase (call) the outstanding bonds or preferred stock at a given price from the security holder.

Capital asset. Any income-producing asset.

Capital-asset pricing model. Specification of a risk-adjusted rate of return relating an asset's return to its risk, $R_j = R_F + \beta(R_M - R_F)$ where β is a risk index theoretically measured by the covariance of returns ($r_{j,M} \, \sigma_j \, \sigma_M$) divided by the variance of the independent variable's return σ_M^2. Thus, the model may be written

$$R_j = R_F + \frac{r_{j,M}\sigma_j\sigma_M}{\sigma_M^2}(R_M - R_F) = R_F + r_{j,M}(R_M - R_F)\frac{\sigma_j}{\sigma_M}$$

See also *security market line.*

Capital budget. Company plan of expenditures on assets whose returns are expected to extend beyond one year.

Capital gains (losses). Difference between the original historical cost of an asset and its selling price. May be 1231 gain and depreciation recapture.

Capital note.   Interest-bearing, long-term promise to pay issued by a corporation to borrow money. Differs from a bond in that a note has no trustee to represent creditors (note holders).

Capitalize.   To calculate the present or future value of expected future cash flows using a cap rate.

Central bank.   Government-owned or government-controlled bank that holds the reserves of commercial banks, issues currency, and regulates a country's supply of money and credit. The Federal Reserve System is the U.S. central bank.

Certainty equivalent.   Amount to be received for certain at a particular point in time which is equal in desirability to a risky cash flow occurring at the same point in time.

Clientele effect.   Attraction of investors who purchase a company's stock because they prefer the company's policies, such as the company's earnings payout rate.

Collateral.   Property pledged by a borrower as security on a loan.

Commercial finance company.   Nonbank lender to companies. Chiefly, it makes short-term loans secured by inventory or receivables and raises cash by selling its own securities in the open market.

Commercial paper.   Promissory notes, usually maturing within six months, used by major corporations to raise short-term money. Non-interest-bearing, they are sold at a discount to investors as liquid investments.

Compensating balance.   Minimum deposit at a bank to compensate the bank for services; may be a requirement of a loan.

Conglomerate.   Group of corporations in different lines of business controlled by a single corporation.

Contribution margin.   Dollar amount from operations available to contribute toward paying fixed operating costs after meeting variable operating costs. Measured by operating revenues less variable operating costs.

Contribution margin ratio.   Contribution margin divided by operating revenues.

Conversion price.   Price in terms of dollars of par or principal of a security paid per share of common stock acquired through conversion.

Conversion ratio.   Number of common shares received for converting the convertible security. Principal divided by conversion price.

Conversion value.   Market value of the common stock into which the convertible security can be converted.

Convertible bond.   Bond that can be converted at the option of the bond holder into common stock of a corporation.

Cost of financial capital.   Minimum acceptable rate of return on an investment undertaken by a company; often measured as an average of the rates on the individual securities issued by the company. Part of the financial decision.

Cover.   To buy or sell a futures contract in the forward market to protect against a loss that may occur as a result of exchange rate changes.

Cumulative voting.   System of electing directors under which a significant minority of the shares is able to elect at least one director.

Debenture.   Long-term debt instrument issued by a corporation that is not secured by specific property but instead by the general credit of the corporation.

Depreciation.   Deduction of part of the cost of an asset from income in each year of the asset's life. Congress established an accelerated cost-recovery system for depreciation on tax returns.

Dilution.   Reduction in earnings per share due to an increase in the number of shares outstanding as a result of new shares issued.

Direct issue.   Securities sold without using an investment banker directly to investors by the issuing company.

Disintermediation.   Withdrawal of money from financial intermediaries in order to reinvest it in the securities issued by corporation's and governmental units.

Dividend.   Distribution to stockholders of part of their claim to a corporation's net worth, usually from profits and typically in cash.

Efficient market.   Market for securities in which information about the securities is readily available to investors.

Equity.   Ownership interest in a business. In a corporation, equity consists of the sum of stockholder's claims. A synonym for stock.

Eurodollars.   Dollar-denominated deposits in a foreign bank.

External equity.   Common stock and paid-in capital in excess of par components of shareholders' equity.

External investment.   Expansion by acquiring another firm (contrast with *internal investment*).

Factor.   Lender to businesses that supplies short-term loans by buying their accounts receivable.

Financial asset.   Claim to a present or future payment of dollars, e.g., cash or a corporate bond that is a claim to future interest and principal payments by a corporation. Compare with *monetary asset.*

Financial leverage.   Use of debt or preferred stock financing.

Financial risk.   Uncertainty about future returns to a company's owners resulting from the use of debt or preferred stock. Often measured by the standard deviation of earnings available to common shareholders.

Fiscal policy.   Government's effort to regulate the economy through federal spending, taxation, and public debt management.

Fundamental analysis.   Analysis of a company's stock based on the company's business performance and financial position (compare with *technical analysis*).

Funding.   Converting short-term debt to long-term, usually by selling new long-term securities to replace maturing short-term ones.

Funds.   Net working capital. The amounts of current assets financed from long-term sources. Occasionally used to mean money and credit.

Funds statement.   See *statement of changes in financial position.*

Horizontal combination.   Union of companies that are in similar lines of business; e.g., two electronics manufacturers.

Illiquidity.   Condition in which a company or individual has inadequate cash to meet obligations.

Inflation.   Increase in the general or average price level and decrease in the purchasing power of money.

Insolvency.   Condition in which a company or individual's liabilities exceed assets and net worth is negative.

Internal equity.   Financing with earnings retained in a company. Compare with *external equity*.

Internal investment.   Company's investment in the direct acquisition of productive assets rather than the acquisition of another company or the productive assets of another company. Compare with *external investment*.

Internal rate of return.   Term introduced by Kenneth Boulding to indicate the rate of discount that equates the present value of cash outlays to the present value of cash inflows. Called marginal efficiency of capital by John Maynard Keynes and rate of return over cost by Irving Fisher. See *yield to maturity*.

Investment banker.   Financial intermediary that helps corporations sell new securities.

Investment tax credit.   Income tax credit available to companies and individuals for investing in plant and equipment.

Leverage.   Using operating and financing items that entail fixed cash outlays.

Leveraged lease.   Third-party lease in which the lessor borrows to cover part or all of the purchase price of the asset.

Liquidity.   Ease of conversion into cash with little chance of loss.

Margin.   Amount paid by an investor in acquiring a security, usually expressed as a percentage of the security's purchase price. The Federal Reserve sets minimum margin requirements of securities traded on the organized securities exchanges.

Marginal.   Economist's term meaning "one more." Marginal cost is the cost of producing one more unit; marginal revenue, the revenue derived by selling one more unit.

Matching principle.   See *suitability*.

Merger.   Combination of two or more companies.

Monetary asset.   Asset whose value is fixed in money terms. Examples are cash and receivables. Holders of monetary assets incur a purchasing power loss during inflation.

Monetary liability.   Liability whose value is fixed in money terms. Examples are payables, bank loans, and bonds. Holders of monetary liabilities incur purchasing power gains during inflation.

Monetary policy.   Central bank's effort to regulate the economy by varying the cost and availability of money and credit.

Multinational company.   Company that has direct investments in more than one country.

Mutually exclusive alternatives.   Alternatives or options of which only one can be adopted (adopting one eliminates the chance of adopting any of the others).

Negotiable.   Transferrable with or without signature.

Net present value.   Change in shareholders' wealth if an investment proposal is adopted. Measured by the present value of future cash inflows less that of future cash outlays.

Net working capital.   See *funds*.

Note.   IOU used to evidence a loan. May be long- or short-term.

Operating leverage.   Existence of fixed operating costs in a company's cost structure.

Over-the-counter market.   Market for securities made up of securities dealers who may or may not be members of an organized exchange.

Par value.   Stated value of a security.

Payback period.   Amount of time required for an asset to generate enough cash flow to cover the initial outlay for that asset.

Pooling of interests.   Method of accounting for a business combination which carries the assets of an acquired company on the post-merger books at the same value that they were carried by the selling company. Compare with *purchase method.*

Preemptive right.   Stockholder's right to purchase additional stock of the company before it is offered for sale to outsiders.

Price-earnings ratio.   Price per share of stock divided by the earnings per share over either the past or the next 12 months.

Primary market.   Market in which securities are originally issued.

Prime rate.   Interest rate charged by banks on short-term loans to large, low-risk businesses.

Principal.   Amount on which interest is paid by a borrower or the amount on which interest is received by a lender.

Private placement.   Selling new securities to a few large buyers rather than to the general public.

Prospectus.   Brief summary of a company's registration statement, which is sent to prospective buyers of new securities.

Proxy.   Document in which a stockholder yields voting power to someone else.

Purchase method.   Accounting for a business combination which carries assets of the acquired company on the merged company's books at the price paid for them in the merger acquisition. Compare with *pooling of interests.*

Quick ratio (or acid-test ratio).   Measure of a company's liquidity equal to the quantity current assets less inventory divided by current liabilities.

Refunding.   Selling a new bond issue to replace a maturing one.

Registration.   Process by which an issuer of new securities is required to file descriptive information with some government authority and obtain its approval before securities can be publicly offered.

Residual dividend policy.   Dividend policy under which all equity investment is financed first with retained earnings and then, if earnings are inadequate, by selling additional equity securities such as common stock and warrants. Earnings remaining after equity investment is made are paid out as a dividend.

Riding the yield curve.   Strategy of purchasing securities with maturities longer than the planned holding period and selling them prior to maturity.

Right.   Privilege offered to common stockholders to buy a specified number of additional shares of a corporation's stock before the stock is offered to outsiders. A stockholder has one right per share of stock already owned.

Risk.   Calculable chance of incurring a loss. Usually used in finance to mean the possibility that expected (or *ex ante*) returns will differ from actual (or *ex post*) returns. Risk of an asset in isolation is measured by its variance of expected returns. Risk of an asset in a portfolio context is measured by the covariance of its expected returns and those of a portfolio. See *capital-asset pricing model* and *standard deviation.*

Sale and leaseback.   Financial arrangement under which a user of an asset sells the asset and then leases it back from the purchaser.

Salvage value.   Price a company assumes it can receive for an asset after it has used it for an extended period of time. Used for depreciation calculation.

Secondary market.   Market in which previously issued financial assets are traded.

Security market line.   Relationship between risk and return on securities bought and sold in the financial markets. Return is portrayed on the vertical axis and beta (β) on the horizontal axis. See *capital-asset pricing model.*

Separation theorem.   Separation of investment and financial decisions in business finance. Investment decision determines expected return and financial decision determines required return.

Serial bonds.   Bonds issued at the same time but which mature at different times in the future.

Short sale.   Any sale of a security that is consummated by delivering to the buyer a borrowed certificate. Usually made in hope of profiting from expected decline in a security's price, which will enable the seller to replace the borrowed security at a lower price.

Short-term.   Maturing in less than one year.

Sinking fund.   Periodic payment by a debtor corporation to a bond-issue trustee, usually used to buy bonds or call them by lot for retirement. A means of retiring the bulk of a bond issue before maturity, and so strengthening the bonds that remain outstanding.

Spot rate.   Current cash rate of exchange between two currencies or commodities.

Standard deviation.   Measure of the degree of dispersion of a distribution. Standard deviation is the square root of the *variance.* To adjust for scale in making risk comparisons between projects, we use the project cash flow's coefficient of variation, which is the cash flow's standard deviation divided by the expected cash flow. See *risk.*

Statement of changes in financial position.   Financial statement detailing changes in net working capital (or cash) by showing the changes in long-term (or noncash) items on a balance sheet.

Statement of financial position.   Financial statement showing assets and claims against assets (debt and equity) at a specific date. Often referred to as a balance sheet.

Stock.   Equity or ownership interest in a corporation, represented by certificates for transferable shares. Divided into preferred stock, which has limited rights to earnings and assets ahead of common stock, and common stock, which represents the residual interest in earnings and assets after all other claimants have been satisfied.

Subordination.   Relegation to a lower priority position in receiving interest and principal; if an issue of debentures is subordinated to other debt, the latter debt is paid the amount due before the subordinated debentures receive anything. Subordinated issues are often referred to as junior issues.

Suitability. Financial principle of time symmetry between sources and uses of finance. Often referred to as matching.

Syndicate. Group of investment banking companies formed to underwrite a large security issue.

Synergy. Benefits from joining two or more economic units; e.g., the benefits from merging two companies if the merger lowers the per unit cost of output. Often summarized by statement that the total is greater than the sum of its parts.

Technical analysis. Analysis of a corporation's stock based on historical trends in the stock's market price (contrast with *fundamental analysis*). Associated with charting.

Term loan. Bank or insurance company loan to a company for several years, which is repaid in periodic installments.

Trade credit. Credit on goods purchased by a company from a supplier.

Trade discount. A reduction, ordinarily of 1 or 2 percent, in the billed price of goods which a supplier offers business customer.

Treasury bill. Short-term, non-interest-bearing promissory note sold to investors at a discount by the U.S. government to finance its deficit.

Treasury stock. Shares repurchased from a stockholder by the issuing company.

Underwriting. Purchase of an entire issue of new securities by investment banking companies for reoffer to investors at a markup in price.

Variable cost. Cost that changes as output changes.

Variance. See *standard deviation.*

Venture capital. Money invested in a small or new business as an investment by persons not directly managing the business.

Vertical combination. Combination of companies engaged in different stages of production of the same type of product.

Working capital. Current assets and current liabilities. Contrast with *funds.*

Yield curve. Schedule that indicates the *yield to maturity* for a debt security of a given type.

Yield to maturity. Rate of return earned on a bond if it is purchased at a specific price and held to maturity. The internal rate of return from owning a bond until it matures.

Appendix B Tables

APPENDIX B-1

Interest Factors to Find the Compound Sum of $1 at the End of N Years[a]

Year N	1%	2%	3%	4%	5%	6%	7%
1	1.010	1.020	1.030	1.040	1.050	1.060	1.070
2	1.020	1.040	1.061	1.082	1.102	1.124	1.145
3	1.030	1.061	1.093	1.125	1.158	1.191	1.225
4	1.041	1.082	1.126	1.170	1.216	1.262	1.311
5	1.051	1.104	1.159	1.217	1.276	1.338	1.403
6	1.062	1.126	1.194	1.265	1.340	1.419	1.501
7	1.072	1.149	1.230	1.316	1.407	1.504	1.606
8	1.083	1.172	1.267	1.369	1.477	1.594	1.718
9	1.094	1.195	1.305	1.423	1.551	1.689	1.838
10	1.105	1.219	1.344	1.480	1.629	1.791	1.967
11	1.116	1.243	1.384	1.539	1.710	1.898	2.105
12	1.127	1.268	1.426	1.601	1.796	2.012	2.252
13	1.138	1.294	1.469	1.665	1.886	2.133	2.410
14	1.149	1.319	1.513	1.732	1.980	2.261	2.579
15	1.161	1.346	1.558	1.801	2.079	2.397	2.759
16	1.173	1.373	1.605	1.873	2.183	2.540	2.952
17	1.184	1.400	1.653	1.948	2.292	2.693	3.159
18	1.196	1.428	1.702	2.026	2.407	2.854	3.380
19	1.208	1.457	1.754	2.107	2.527	3.026	3.617
20	1.220	1.486	1.806	2.191	2.653	3.207	3.870
25	1.282	1.641	2.094	2.666	3.386	4.292	5.427

Appendix B-1 *(Continued)*

Year N	8%	9%	10%	12%	14%	15%	16%
1	1.080	1.090	1.100	1.120	1.140	1.150	1.160
2	1.166	1.188	1.210	1.254	1.300	1.322	1.346
3	1.260	1.295	1.331	1.405	1.482	1.521	1.561
4	1.360	1.412	1.464	1.574	1.689	1.749	1.811
5	1.469	1.539	1.611	1.762	1.925	2.011	2.100
6	1.587	1.677	1.772	1.974	2.195	2.313	2.436
7	1.714	1.828	1.949	2.211	2.502	2.660	2.826
8	1.851	1.993	2.144	2.476	2.853	3.059	3.278
9	1.999	2.172	2.358	2.773	3.252	3.518	3.803
10	2.159	2.367	2.594	3.106	3.707	4.046	4.411
11	2.332	2.580	2.853	3.479	4.226	4.652	5.117
12	2.518	2.813	3.138	3.896	4.818	5.350	5.936
13	2.720	3.066	3.452	4.363	5.492	6.153	6.886
14	2.937	3.342	3.797	4.887	6.261	7.076	7.988
15	3.172	3.642	4.177	5.474	7.138	8.137	9.266
16	3.426	3.970	4.595	6.130	8.137	9.358	10.748
17	3.700	4.328	5.054	6.866	9.276	10.761	12.468
18	3.996	4.717	5.560	7.690	10.575	12.375	14.463
19	4.316	5.142	6.116	8.613	12.056	14.232	16.777
20	4.661	5.604	6.728	9.646	13.743	16.367	19.461
25	6.848	8.623	10.835	17.000	26.462	32.919	40.874

Year N	18%	20%	24%	28%	32%	36%	40%
1	1.180	1.200	1.240	1.280	1.320	1.360	1.400
2	1.392	1.440	1.538	1.638	1.742	1.850	1.960
3	1.643	1.728	1.907	2.067	2.300	2.515	2.744
4	1.939	2.074	2.364	2.684	3.036	3.421	3.842
5	2.288	2.488	2.932	3.436	4.007	4.653	5.378
6	2.700	2.986	3.635	4.398	5.290	6.328	7.530
7	3.185	3.583	4.508	5.629	6.983	8.605	10.541
8	3.759	4.300	5.590	7.206	9.217	11.703	14.758
9	4.435	5.160	6.931	9.223	12.166	15.917	20.661
10	5.234	6.192	8.594	11.806	16.060	21.647	28.925
11	6.176	7.430	10.657	15.112	21.199	29.439	40.496
12	7.288	8.916	13.215	19.343	27.983	40.037	56.694
13	8.599	10.699	16.386	24.759	36.937	54.451	79.372
14	10.147	12.839	20.319	31.691	48.757	74.053	111.120
15	11.974	15.407	25.196	40.565	64.359	100.712	155.568
16	14.129	18.488	31.243	51.923	84.954	136.97	217.795
17	16.672	22.186	38.741	66.461	112.12	186.28	304.914
18	19.673	26.623	48.039	85.071	148.02	253.34	426.879
19	23.214	31.948	59.568	108.89	195.39	344.54	597.630
20	27.393	38.338	73.864	139.38	257.92	468.57	836.683
25	62.669	95.396	216.542	478.90	1033.6	2180.1	4499.880

[a]Compounding: $S_N = P_0 (1 + i)^N$; $FV = PV (FVIF_{i,N})$.

Appendix B-2

Interest Factors to Find the Present Value of $1 at the End of N Years[a]

Year N	1%	2%	3%	4%	5%	6%	7%	8%	9%	10%	12%
1	.990	.980	.971	.962	.952	.943	.935	.926	.917	.909	.893
2	.980	.961	.943	.925	.907	.890	.873	.857	.842	.826	.797
3	.971	.942	.915	.889	.864	.840	.816	.794	.772	.751	.712
4	.961	.924	.889	.855	.823	.792	.763	.735	.708	.683	.636
5	.951	.906	.863	.822	.784	.747	.713	.681	.650	.621	.567
6	.942	.888	.838	.790	.746	.705	.666	.630	.596	.564	.507
7	.933	.871	.813	.760	.711	.665	.623	.583	.547	.513	.452
8	.923	.853	.789	.731	.677	.627	.582	.540	.502	.467	.404
9	.914	.837	.766	.703	.645	.592	.544	.500	.460	.424	.361
10	.905	.820	.744	.676	.614	.558	.508	.463	.422	.386	.322
11	.896	.804	.722	.650	.585	.527	.475	.429	.388	.350	.287
12	.887	.788	.701	.625	.557	.497	.444	.397	.356	.319	.257
13	.879	.773	.681	.601	.530	.469	.415	.368	.326	.290	.229
14	.870	.758	.661	.577	.505	.442	.388	.340	.299	.263	.205
15	.861	.743	.642	.555	.481	.417	.362	.315	.275	.239	.183
16	.853	.728	.623	.534	.458	.394	.339	.292	.252	.218	.163
17	.844	.714	.605	.513	.436	.371	.317	.270	.231	.198	.146
18	.836	.700	.587	.494	.416	.350	.296	.250	.212	.180	.130
19	.828	.686	.570	.475	.396	.331	.276	.232	.194	.164	.116
20	.820	.673	.554	.456	.377	.319	.258	.215	.178	.149	.104
25	.780	.610	.478	.375	.295	.233	.184	.146	.116	.092	.059

Appendix B-2 *(Continued)*

Year N	14%	15%	16%	18%	20%	24%	28%	32%	36%	40%
1	.877	.870	.862	.847	.833	.806	.781	.758	.735	.714
2	.769	.756	.743	.718	.694	.650	.610	.574	.541	.510
3	.675	.658	.641	.609	.579	.524	.477	.435	.398	.364
4	.592	.572	.552	.516	.482	.423	.373	.329	.292	.260
5	.519	.497	.476	.437	.402	.341	.291	.250	.215	.186
6	.456	.432	.410	.370	.335	.275	.227	.189	.158	.133
7	.400	.376	.354	.314	.279	.222	.178	.143	.116	.095
8	.351	.327	.305	.266	.233	.179	.139	.108	.085	.068
9	.308	.284	.263	.226	.194	.144	.108	.082	.063	.048
10	.270	.247	.227	.191	.162	.116	.085	.062	.046	.035
11	.237	.215	.195	.162	.135	.094	.066	.047	.034	.025
12	.208	.187	.168	.137	.112	.076	.052	.036	.025	.018
13	.182	.163	.145	.116	.093	.061	.040	.027	.018	.013
14	.160	.141	.125	.099	.078	.049	.032	.021	.014	.009
15	.140	.123	.108	.084	.065	.040	.025	.016	.010	.006
16	.123	.107	.093	.071	.054	.032	.019	.012	.007	.005
17	.108	.093	.080	.060	.045	.026	.015	.009	.005	.003
18	.095	.081	.069	.051	.038	.021	.012	.007	.004	.002
19	.083	.070	.060	.043	.031	.017	.009	.005	.003	.002
20	.073	.061	.051	.037	.026	.014	.007	.004	.002	.001
25	.038	.030	.024	.016	.010	.005	.002	.001	.000	.000

[a] Discounting: $P_0 = S_N/(1+i)^N$; PV = FV $(PVIF_{i,N})$.

APPENDIX B-3
Interest Factors to Find the Compound Sum of a $1 Annuity[a]

Year N	1%	2%	3%	4%	5%	6%	7%
1	1.000	1.000	1.000	1.000	1.000	1.000	1.000
2	2.010	2.020	2.030	2.040	2.050	2.060	2.070
3	3.030	3.060	3.091	3.122	3.152	3.184	3.215
4	4.060	4.122	4.184	4.246	4.310	4.375	4.440
5	5.101	5.204	5.309	5.416	5.526	5.637	5.751
6	6.152	6.308	6.468	6.633	6.802	6.975	7.153
7	7.214	7.434	7.662	7.898	8.142	8.394	8.654
8	8.286	8.583	8.892	9.214	9.549	9.897	10.260
9	9.369	9.755	10.159	10.583	11.027	11.491	11.978
10	10.462	10.950	11.464	12.006	12.578	13.181	13.816
11	11.567	12.169	12.808	13.486	14.207	14.972	15.784
12	12.683	13.412	14.192	15.026	15.917	16.870	17.888
13	13.809	14.680	15.618	16.627	17.713	18.882	20.141
14	14.947	15.974	17.086	18.292	19.599	21.051	22.550
15	16.097	17.293	18.599	20.024	21.579	23.276	25.129
16	17.258	18.639	20.157	21.825	23.657	25.673	27.888
17	18.430	20.012	21.762	23.698	25.840	28.213	30.840
18	19.615	21.412	23.414	25.645	28.132	30.906	33.999
19	20.811	22.841	25.117	27.671	30.539	33.760	37.379
20	22.019	24.297	26.870	29.778	33.066	36.786	40.995
25	28.243	32.030	36.459	41.646	47.727	54.865	63.249

Appendix B-3 *(Continued)*

Year N	8%	9%	10%	12%	14%	16%	18%
1	1.000	1.000	1.000	1.000	1.000	1.000	1.000
2	2.080	2.090	2.100	2.120	2.140	2.160	2.180
3	3.246	3.278	3.310	3.374	3.440	3.506	3.572
4	4.506	4.573	4.641	4.770	4.921	5.066	5.215
5	5.867	5.985	6.105	6.353	6.610	6.877	7.154
6	7.336	7.523	7.716	8.115	8.536	8.977	9.442
7	8.923	9.200	9.487	10.089	10.730	11.414	12.142
8	10.637	11.028	11.436	12.300	13.233	14.240	15.327
9	12.488	13.021	13.579	14.776	16.085	17.518	19.086
10	14.487	15.193	15.937	17.549	19.337	21.321	23.521
11	16.645	17.560	18.531	20.655	23.044	25.733	28.755
12	18.977	20.141	21.384	24.133	27.271	30.850	34.931
13	21.495	22.953	24.523	28.029	32.089	36.786	42.219
14	24.215	26.019	27.975	32.393	37.581	43.672	50.818
15	27.152	29.361	31.772	37.280	43.842	51.660	60.965
16	30.324	33.003	35.950	42.753	50.980	60.925	72.939
17	33.750	36.974	40.545	48.884	59.118	71.673	87.068
18	37.450	41.301	45.599	55.750	68.394	84.141	103.740
19	41.446	46.018	51.159	63.440	78.969	98.603	123.414
20	45.762	51.160	57.275	72.052	91.025	115.380	146.628
25	73.106	84.701	98.347	133.334	181.871	249.214	342.603

[a]Compounding: $S_{i,N} = A \dfrac{(1 + i)^N - 1}{i}$; FVA $= A$ (FVIFA$_{i,N}$).

Appendix B-4

Interest Factors to Find the Present Value of a $1 Annuity[a]

Year N	1%	2%	3%	4%	5%	6%	7%	8%	9%	10%
1	0.990	0.980	0.971	0.962	0.952	0.943	0.935	0.926	0.917	0.909
2	1.970	1.942	1.913	1.886	1.859	1.833	1.808	1.783	1.759	1.736
3	2.941	2.884	2.829	2.775	2.723	2.673	2.624	2.577	2.531	2.487
4	3.902	3.808	3.717	3.630	3.546	3.465	3.387	3.312	3.240	3.170
5	4.853	4.713	4.580	4.452	4.329	4.212	4.100	3.993	3.890	3.791
6	5.795	5.601	5.417	5.242	5.076	4.917	4.767	4.623	4.486	4.355
7	6.728	6.472	6.230	6.002	5.786	5.582	5.389	5.206	5.033	4.868
8	7.652	7.325	7.020	6.733	6.463	6.210	5.971	5.747	5.535	5.335
9	8.566	8.162	7.786	7.435	7.108	6.802	6.515	6.247	5.985	5.759
10	9.471	8.893	8.530	8.111	7.722	7.360	7.024	6.710	6.418	6.145
11	10.368	9.787	9.253	8.760	8.306	7.887	7.499	7.139	6.805	6.495
12	11.255	10.575	9.954	9.385	8.863	8.384	7.943	7.536	7.161	6.814
13	12.134	11.348	10.635	9.986	9.394	8.853	8.358	7.904	7.487	7.103
14	13.004	12.106	11.296	10.563	9.899	9.295	8.745	8.244	7.786	7.367
15	13.865	12.849	11.938	11.118	10.380	9.712	9.108	8.559	8.060	7.606
16	14.718	13.578	12.561	11.652	10.838	10.106	9.447	8.851	8.312	7.824
17	15.562	14.292	13.166	12.166	11.274	10.477	9.763	9.122	8.544	8.022
18	16.398	14.992	13.754	12.659	11.690	10.828	10.059	9.372	8.756	8.201
19	17.226	15.678	14.324	13.134	12.085	11.158	10.336	9.604	8.950	8.365
20	18.046	16.351	14.877	13.590	12.462	11.470	10.594	9.818	9.128	8.514
25	22.023	19.523	17.413	15.622	14.094	12.783	11.654	10.675	9.823	9.077

Appendix B-4 *(Continued)*

Year N	12%	14%	16%	18%	20%	24%	28%	32%	36%
1	0.893	0.877	0.862	0.847	0.833	0.806	0.781	0.758	0.735
2	1.690	1.647	1.605	1.566	1.528	1.457	1.392	1.332	1.276
3	2.402	2.322	2.246	2.174	2.106	1.981	1.868	1.766	1.674
4	3.037	2.914	2.798	2.690	2.589	2.404	2.241	2.096	1.966
5	3.605	3.433	3.274	3.127	2.991	2.745	2.532	2.345	2.181
6	4.111	3.889	3.685	3.498	3.326	3.020	2.759	2.534	2.339
7	4.564	4.288	4.039	3.812	3.605	3.242	2.937	2.678	2.455
8	4.968	4.639	4.344	4.078	3.837	3.421	3.076	2.786	2.540
9	5.328	4.946	4.607	4.303	4.031	3.566	3.184	2.868	2.603
10	5.650	5.216	4.833	4.494	4.193	3.682	3.269	2.930	2.650
11	5.988	5.453	5.029	4.656	4.327	3.776	3.335	2.978	2.683
12	6.194	5.660	5.197	4.793	4.439	3.851	3.387	3.013	2.708
13	6.424	5.852	5.342	4.910	4.533	3.912	3.427	3.040	2.727
14	6.628	6.002	5.468	5.008	4.611	3.962	3.459	3.061	2.740
15	6.811	6.142	5.575	5.092	4.675	4.001	3.483	3.076	2.750
16	6.974	6.265	5.669	5.162	4.730	4.033	3.503	3.088	2.758
17	7.120	6.373	5.749	5.222	4.775	4.059	3.518	3.097	2.763
18	7.250	6.467	5.818	5.273	4.812	4.080	3.529	3.104	2.767
19	7.366	6.550	5.877	5.316	4.844	4.097	3.539	3.109	2.770
20	7.469	6.623	5.929	5.353	4.870	4.110	3.546	3.113	2.772
25	7.843	6.873	6.097	5.467	4.948	4.147	3.564	3.122	2.776

[a] Discounting: $P_{i,N} = A \left[\dfrac{1 - \dfrac{1}{(1+i)^N}}{i} \right]$; $PVA = A\,(PVIFA_{i,N})$.

APPENDIX C
Solutions to Odd-Numbered Problems

Chapter 1

1-1. 40.48 failures
1-3. $8,000
1-5. $200,000
1-7. 96 cents
1-9. 9.6 percent

Chapter 2

2-1. $1,184.29
2-3. a. $1,050.40 > $1,000   **b.** $1,050.40 > $977.60
      c. $24,308 > $20,000   **d.** $24,308 > $22,018
      e. $1,574 and $1,605.
2-5. $15,120 and $19,044
2-7. About 24 percent
2-9. $33,860
2-11. $2 \times N = 20$ years, $N = 10$ years
2-13. $2,980.63 and $29,806.30 − $20,000 = $9,806.30
2-15. a. $1,077.32   **b.** $1,162.66

Chapter 3

3-1. Approximately 4.36 percent = (0.075 − 0.03)/1.03.
3-3. 8.4 percent
3-5. $500 = $40/0.08
3-7. On bond, 50 percent; on bill, approximately 1 percent. Invest in quick-maturing securities if you expect interest rates to rise.

Chapter 4

4-1. $50. (Discount would rise from $100 to $150.)
4-3. a
4-5. 50 percent rise.
4-7. 16 percent decline.
4-9. 18.6 percent.
4-11. 43.4 percent (rounded).

Chapter 5

5-1. $3,361.60
5-3. **a.**

Government Securities + $500 million	Member Bank Reserves + $500 million

b.

Discounts − $5 million	Member Bank Reserves − $5 million

c.

	Currency − $500 million Member Bank Reserves + $500 million

5-5. **a.** $200 million.
b. $180 million.
c. Zero.
5-7. $0.2 billion.
5-9. Find the additional reserves required.
Demand deposits require $2.8 million.
Time deposits required $0.8 million.
Difference and fall in lending power $2 million.

Chapter 6

No problems.

Chapter 7

7-1. **a.** Tax-exempt equivalent is 0.084, so prefer municipal.
b. Shifts decision toward taxable security.
c. Yes, municipal has greater risk so it should offer a higher after-tax return.

Chapter 8

8-1. 15 percent (75 cents on the $5 of capital for each $100 of assets).
8-3. $80,000 (Excess reserves rise by $80,000).

Chapter 9

No problems.

Chapter 10

10-1. $66\frac{2}{3}$ percent

10-3. 50 percent because bought at 40 and sold at 60 (order is irrelevant).

Chapter 11

No problems.

Chapter 12

12-1. Total current assets $2,980,000. Land $300,000. Accrued wages $400,000. Common stock $700,000. Retained earnings $2,440,000.

12-3. Beginning $1,746,000 + ($456,000 − $70,000) = $2,132,000.

12-5. a. $10 million on 1/1/x7 and $9 million on 1/1/x8

    b. Sources $4 + $2 = 6

        Uses   3 + 4 = 7

Chapter 13

13-1. a. 616,667   **b.** $1.46 × 6 = $8.76

13-3. 0.06/(1 − 0.40) = 10 percent

13-5. a. 0.39   **b.** 0.148   **c.** 0.035   **d.** 0.133

13-7. a. 0.04 = NOP/$2,000,000 and NOP = $80,000

    b. $666,667

    c. ($80,000 − $16,000) (1 − 0.40) = $38,400

Chapter 14

14-1. a. CR   1.25 and 2.5

       NWC $200,000 and $300,000

       QR   1.0 and 2.0

14-3. CA = 3.0 × $600,000 = $1,800,000

    CGS/INV = $500,000/$300,000 = 1.67 times

14-5. a. NOP = $4,000,000 and EAT = $2,040,000

       TA   = $14,000,000

    b. (1) 40 percent (2) 20.4 percent (3) 29 percent (4) 24 percent

    c. (1) $5.133 (2) $1.80 and $0.033

14-7. a. 3.33   **b.** 108.1 days   **c.** 1.0

Chapter 15

15-1. $120,800

15-3. $37,183.20

15-5. a.

Sales	$220	$242	$266.2
Net income	$6.6	$7.26	$7.99
Dividend	$3.3	$3.63	$4.0
SHE	$73.3	$76.93	$80.93
Debt	$36.7	$44.07	$52.07
ROE	0.09	0.094	0.099
D/TA	0.33	0.36	0.39

    b. 0.052 and 0.182

Chapter 16

16-1. a. $3,329
  c. Year 1 = $2,753
    Year 2 = $2,944
  d. $2,973
16-3. $92,100
16-5. a. $123,000 − $13,000 = $110,000
  b. (1) $1,320,000
    (2) $ 622,160
  c. Assets   = $506,149
    Current liabilities = $ 18,893
    Long-term lease = $487,256
16-7. Bank loan is 10 percent; financier is between 20 and 24 percent; lease is between 14 and 16 percent.

Chapter 17

17-1. a. $8 and $4
  b. $32
  c. (1) $6 (2) ($1) (3) ($10)
  d. External $1,500 and internal $2,500
17-3. $35.51
17-5. $R = \$3$; $V_x = \$72$
17-7. a. EPS = $3.60
  b. $R = \$2$; $V_x = \$63$
  c. EPS = $7,080,000/(1,000,000 + 400,000) = $5.057
  d. (1) No change (2) No change (3) Decline

Chapter 18

18-1. a. $50,000/15 = $3,333
  b. $2,497
  c. $1,574
18-3. a. Subordinated = $233,087,742 − $150,000,000 = $83,087,742
  b. Subordinated = $260,475,552 − $150,000,000 = $110,475,552
18-5. 8.44, 5.70, 3.46
18-7. a. $40
  b. $1,000
  c. $1,200 − $1,000 = $200
  d. $1,080
18-9. a. (1) 2,600 bonds and $2.6 million face value; 10,000 bonds and $10 million face value.
    (2) Coupon is 14 percent; zero is between 14 and 15 percent.
  b. Coupon has interest after-tax cash outflow of $140 × (1 − 0.40) = $84 per bond. Zero provides a cash saving because the amortized bond discount is a tax shelter.

Chapter 19

19-1. a. $35,000 + $45,000 = $80,000
  b. 0
  c. 0

19-3. a. Retained earnings decline by $1 × 1,000 = $1,000
Cash declines by $1 × 1,000 = $1,000
b. Stock dividend is 0.02 × 1,000 shares = 20 shares, and amount is 20 shares × $60
= $1,200:

Retained earnings decline by	$1,200	
Common stock rises by 20 × $50 =		$1,000
Paid-in capital in excess of par rises		$ 200

c. Number of shares rises to (4/1) × 1,000 = 4,000
Par value declines to (1/4) × $50 = $12.50 per share
d. Number of shares declines to (1/4) × 1,000 = 250
Par value rises to (4/1) × $50 = $200 per share
19-5. a. Depreciation becomes 1.16 × $80,000 = $92,800 and
Distributable income is $7,240
b. (1) 0.165 and 0.354
(2) 0.40 and 1.107
(3) $12,024 and ($776)

Chapter 20

20-1. a. 5.6 percent and 2.4 percent.
b. No, business would prefer no tax. But tax deductibility of interest does make debt
advantageous and encourages its use.
20-3. a. 20 times.
b. 5 percent.
c. Market value of common stock would decline because Guaranty would accept projects with too low a return.
20-5. 18.2 percent.
20-7. 16.1 percent.
20-9. 10 percent.

Chapter 21

21-1. a. $63,930
b. 0.349
c. 0.46 × $28,000 = $12,880
21-3. a. Carry-back $600,000 and remaining $400,000
b. Refund $71,750 and current loss becomes $928,250
21-5. a. 1231 gain is $20,000 and depreciation recapture is $92,800. Therefore taxes are
$48,288:

Cash in		$180,000
Less taxes		48,288
Cash flow		$131,712

b.

Cash in	$120,000
Less taxes	24,288
Cash flow	$ 95,712

c.

Cash in	$67,200
Cash out	0
Cash flow	$67,200

d. Cash inflows:

Selling price	$40,000
Tax saving	12,512
Cash out	0
Cash flow	$52,512

e. Sell the equipment for the maximum—$180,000

21-7. a. Ordinary tax on operations $140,750
       Add 1231 taxes   16,800
       Total taxes $157,550
  b. 0.384

21-9. b. Ordinary tax on operations $106,710
       Add nonoperating taxes   8,700
                                            $115,410
       Earnings after taxes = \$338,800 − \$115,410 = \$223,390
  c. 0.34

Chapter 22

22-1. a. OCF = (NOP + Depr) $(1 - T) + T$(Depr)
    b. \$216,000$(1 - 0.46)$ = \$116,640 increase.

22-3. a. Cash in $112,000
    Less cash out
        Costs $72,800
        Taxes   8,480
                                                        81,280
    Operating cash flow $ 30,720
    b. Cash in $112,000
    Less cash out
        Incremental cash costs $87,800
        Taxes   2,480
                                                        90,280
    Operating cash flow $21,720

22-5. a. 4.76 years or 4 years and 9 months
    b. NPV = \$205,538 − \$174,000 = \$31,538
    c. NPV = \$205,538 − [\$174,000 − $(0.08 \times \$174,000)$] = \$45,458

22-7. a. Charge the project under condition (2)
    b. NICO = \$110,000 − $(0.08 \times \$110,000)$ = \$101,200
    c. (1) 3.93 years
        (2) NPV = \$86,936 − \$101,200 = (\$14,264)
        (3) NPVI = (\$14,264)/\$101,200 = (0.14)

22-9. a. Yes, because its risk index is greater than one.
    b. 0.15

22-11. a. Project A.
     b. Project A, 0.1392 and project B, 0.126.

Chapter 23

23-1. a. \$20,000
    b. Excess (shortage):

Month 1	Month 2	Month 3	Month 4
\$2,500	(\$600)	(\$3,600)	(\$7,200)

23-3. \$145,000 + \$12,000 = \$157,000

23-5. e

23-7. b

Class	Contribution Margin	Costs	Return
1	\$1,500	\$ 270.80	\$1,229.20
2	\$1,500	\$ 832.20	\$ 667.80
3	\$1,500	\$1,370.00	\$ 130.00
4	\$1,500	\$2,774.00	(\$1,274.00)

Chapter 24

24-1. 9.09 percent

24-3. In principle, 540 percent. Three percent for two days' use of money (the first 10 days are free in any case) equates to a 556.7 percent annual rate.

24-5. a. 10 percent,   **b.** 10.53 percent.

24-7. $17\frac{1}{2}$ percent.

Chapter 25

No problems.

Chapter 26

26-1. a. K52,500

   b. 4

   c. T

   d. Krone declines to $0.08/$0.098 = 81.63 percent of its previous value, so it declines by 1 − 0.8163 = 18.37 percent.

26-3. a. $0.12 \times (180/360) \times$ F100,000 = F6,000

   b. F100,000 $\times$ 0.1174 = $11,740

   c. F106,000 $\times$ 0.1168 = $12,380.80

26-5. a. 173,913 $\times$ $0.46 $\times$ 1.08 = $86,400

   b. (1) 173,913 $\times$ $0.50 = $86,956.50

26-7. a. Net exposed assets = P400,000

   b. Assets = $12,600 and $9,100; liabilities = $9,000 and $6,500

   c. Translation loss = $3,500 − $2,500 = $1,000

26-9. a Translation loss = $402,800 − $302,100 = $100,700

Chapter 27

No problems.

Index of Names

Index of Subjects